CORRECTIONS
PRACTICE AND POLICY

Charles R. Swanson, Jr.
University of Georgia
Advisory Editor

CORRECTIONS
PRACTICE AND POLICY

David E. Duffee

School of Criminal Justice
University at Albany
State University of New York

RANDOM HOUSE
New York

To my parents
F. Eugene Duffee, Jr.
and
Dorothy C. Duffee
with gratitude

First Edition
98765432
Copyright © 1989 by Random House Inc.

Library of Congress Cataloging-in-Publication Data

Duffee, David.
    Corrections : practice and policy / David E. Duffee.
        p. cm.
    Bibliography: p.
    Includes index.
    ISBN 0-394-34714-5
    1. Corrections—United States. I. Title.
  HV9471.D83 1989
  364.6'0973—dc19
                                            88-7831
                                             CIP

Cover Art: Marjory Dressler

Cover Design: Nadja Furlan Lorbek

Text Design: Susan Phillips

Manufactured in the United States of America

PREFACE

Corrections: Practice and Policy is an introduction to the practice of criminal punishment and the operation of correctional systems. Punishment and corrections are related but not identical ideas: Criminal punishment is a legal and philosophical concept. Punishments are meted out after a finding of guilt for the breaking of the criminal law and are carried out by correctional agencies. The rationales and limitations on criminal punishment are important to understanding how convicted offenders are handled and why correctional agencies work as they do. But in modern industrialized societies, understanding why and how we punish is not a complete picture of correctional agencies. While this text covers criminal punishment, it also covers the many correctional activities that are not punishments.

What aspects of punishment and corrections will we cover? Should we be concerned primarily with facts? With a review of the types of punishments that are available and their frequency of use? For the student just entering this field, a descriptive account of who does what to whom, how often, and under what conditions is important. But we believe an introductory text in this field also should help a student raise questions, challenge assumptions, and test alternatives to current practice. So, while much of this book is descriptive, we also hope to improve the student's ability to test the veracity of the description and to challenge the soundness of the political and philosophical positions under which punishment and corrections are now practiced.

While all introductory texts must cover much of the same material, they each differ to some extent in their orientation. Here are some characteristics of our approach.

APPLIED SOCIAL SCIENCE

This book stresses the study of punishment and corrections as applied social science. To be sure, punishment and corrections are much more than that. They involve philosophy, law, politics, and a good deal of myth, ceremony, and raw emotion. However, since the time of the President's Commission on Law Enforcement and Administration of Justice, if not before, social science has played an increasingly important role in shaping and reshaping correctional practice and in explaining and predicting the consequences of that practice. In the years since the commission's report in 1967, a large number of research projects have cast doubt upon the assumptions that underlay the recommendations of the commission. Indeed, one of the most powerful current influences on punishment and corrections is that many of the claims made by our correctional agencies about their activities have become empirically testable.

We have tried in three ways to take advantage of and be guided by the explosion of research that has occurred in the field. First, it has been our editorial policy to select for review in this volume empirical studies rather than unsubstantiated claims, whenever possible. Second, we have given more attention to those studies that have used the most rigorous methods. Third, while this is a text, not a literature review, the bibliography is complete and current. Each chapter was organized after a thorough literature review, and we have attempted to include opposing viewpoints and contradictory research findings.

HISTORY

The old adage of being doomed to repeat an unstudied history appears to be an accurate prediction of correctional practice. Few philosophies of punishment are new; almost all current practices have been resurrected rather than developed. An appreciation of history is essential to an understanding of what is happening now. Therefore, we have incorporated the history of corrections into individual chapters. In each chapter, the historical development of policies and practices has been used to demonstrate how current positions emerged. More often than not, these comparisons of past and present indicate that currently controversial issues have always been points of contention. We have not learned from history so often as we have replicated it.

THE DEATH PENALTY

Some prepublication reviewers of the manuscript questioned making the death penalty the subject of a separate chapter. But just as prisons have much more influence over the entire field of corrections than would be assumed from the proportion of offenders punished in prisons, we think the death penalty is more important than the proportion of offenders sentenced to death. The death penalty raises in its purest form the issue of the use of the coercive power of the state and illustrates the conflicts that arise in the attempts to protect human rights both from and with the use of that coercive power.

RACE AND ETHNICITY

In corrections, racial and ethnic differences and disparity have become more visible and more important over time. In some states, black and Hispanic citizens comprise a majority of the prison population and a minority of the general population. In every chapter where these racial and ethnic differences are important, they receive attention. The most extended discussions of race and ethnicity in relation to the selection of punishments or the distribution of penal resources can be found in Chapter 6 (Sentencing), Chapter 15 (Life in Prison), and Chapter 16 (The Correctional Officer: Working in Prison).

COMPLEX ORGANIZATION

Students of corrections often complain that professors teach only "theory." Practitioners often say there is no substitute for experience, or that textbooks, whether theoretical or not, are only academic. Without entering the debate about theory and its uses, we feel that one valid complaint behind such observations is that academic materials often ignore implementation. One major reason for the differences between theory and action is that correctional action is actually a network of complex organizations. The dynamics and limits of organizations as instruments of social policy need more attention than they are sometimes given. In this book we stress the fact that punishment and corrections are formally organized social activities, with all the benefits and all the problems that social form entails. The organizational issues receive particular attention in Chapter 5 (Correctional Process and Correctional Systems) and Chapter 18 (Correctional Organization and Management), but they appear in all chapters.

INTERNATIONAL/CROSS-CULTURAL COMPARISONS

Our review of programs and of research has crossed many national borders. The most extended coverage of punishment in other countries occurs in Chapter 2. However, we have relied upon the literature from Canada, England and Wales, and Australia in many chapters, and discussions of correctional programs elsewhere in the world appear throughout the text.

SPECIAL FEATURES

In order to aid the study of corrections, the text incorporates a number of special features.

Orienting Questions. Each chapter begins with a series of questions that should help the student anticipate and rank the main topics in each chapter.

Inserts. Throughout the book, boxed inserts provide a synopsis of important research studies, significant court cases, or interesting policy positions. Although these inserts are brief, they provide more concentrated coverage of a particular point than we could justify incorporating in the text itself. These sections will give the student a flavor of important findings or positions that have either influenced corrections systems or may alter them in the future.

Numbered Summary. Each chapter has a numbered summary that reiterates the key points in the chapter in the order in which they appeared.

Projects and Questions. The end of each chapter contains a series of discussion questions and class projects. Some of these issue-focused problems may require interviews with correctional officials or panel discussions involving outsiders, and therefore need preparation. They have been posed in such a way that the relevant resources for conducting the project can be readily adapted to the correctional system near any particular campus.

Additional Reading. An annotated list of additional reading follows each projects and questions section. In most cases the books should be widely available. We have included an occasional journal article that is crucial to development in the field, or that raises points not readily available in book form.

Glossary. Within the text, glossary terms appear in bold type at their first extended use. Key words and their definitions are listed at the end of each chapter. A complete glossary appears at the end of the book, along with the chapter in which the major discussion of the term occurs.

Bibliography. We have used the APA reference style in this text, with references appearing in parenthesis directly in the text. A full bibliography appears at the end of the book.

Illustrations and Tables. Photographs illustrate facilities, issues, and practices described in the text. Descriptive statistics, decision processes, and conceptual summaries are presented in the form of tables and figures.

Cases. Finally, a feature of this book that we think is unique among correctional texts is the inclusion of cases. Each chapter begins with a case, and occasionally a major section within a chapter will open with one. These cases are accounts of events, discussions, and other correctional experiences that have actually taken place in one or another correctional system. These are not the typical clinical cases, which describe offenders and decisions about them, but vignettes that represent the actions, motivations, and feelings of a wide range of different correctional actors. These stories provide the student with a richer sense of corrections in action than could be provided in the text itself. While each of the stories presented is based on actual events, locations and identities of characters have been disguised or "fictionalized." Each story is set in the mythical state of Jefferson and involves a set of characters playing out roles similar to those found in any correctional system.

Punishment and corrections are the activities of human beings, sometimes causing pain, sometimes relieving pain, but never very far from the hard fact that punishment is the imposition of pain upon persons legally deemed to deserve it. Some of the roles played in correctional organizations are taken on involuntarily; others are accepted as duties or careers. We think such roles are difficult and therefore better portrayed at times by human beings than by discussions about them. So, we put some people in the book—in the cases, inserts, photos, and in the text itself. This book is above all a story of people and the various roles they play in the corrections process.

ACKNOWLEDGMENTS

A number of people have contributed to various parts of this book. Jeff Senese, Mary Egner, Cynthia Avery, and Kim Koscinski, all graduate students at Michigan State University, assisted with the research for chapters 10 and 12. Randy Sarju did the library search for Chapter 19. Shelley L. Kath did the research for Chapters 1, 2, 3, 4, 6, 7, 8, 9, and 13 and parts of other chapters. Lyn Markham stepped in to find additional references when I needed them quickly. As has been the case with so much of my work since 1969, this book would not have been completed without the editorial, secretarial, and just general all-round assistance of Jo Anne DeSilva. I am indebted to The University at Albany for the sabbatical that enabled me to finish this work.

Photographs were obtained from a number of sources and are credited individually. However, I would like especially to thank officials in three departments who helped me to obtain most of the photographs that were used. I am indebted to the New York Department of Correctional Services, and to two of its public information staff: Elaine Spear and Kelly Lather. I would like to thank the Pennsylvania Department of Corrections, and especially Press Secretary Kenneth Robinson for helping to select pictures from that system. Finally, I send appreciation to all the staff of the Albany County Probation Department for kindly allowing me to take pictures during their busy schedules. Special thanks are due to Bob Burns, deputy director, and Dan Fitzsimmons.

Lastly, I would like to recognize the extremely important services provided to the nation by the Bureau of Justice Statistics in the United States Department of Justice. While a book such as this would be possible without BJS, it couldn't possibly provide the same scope or depth of coverage.

CONTENTS

CORRECTIONS
PRACTICE AND POLICY

QUESTIONS

1. How is criminal punishment distinguished from other formal social controls?

2. How is criminal punishment defined?

3. What are the four common justifications for punishment?

4. To what extent are these different justifications compatible?

5. Are all the interactions between convicted persons and correctional staff part of the punishment process?

6. How have correctional organizations influenced the use of punishment?

THE DISAPPEARING MAN

Phil had just completed his first year of graduate school and now worked for the Jefferson Department of Correction in the staff development section. Actually, he worked for Professor Masters at the university, through whom the Department had gotten the federal grant to pay Phil's salary. It was Phil's summer job to interview all the top managers in the Department, as well as some staff and inmates, as preparation for a training conference.

Phil became anxious as he drew near the prison. New road signs appeared: "Prison Property: Absolutely No Parking." There was virtually no traffic on the road, and to

the left he saw a dozen men clad in T-shirts and gray trousers working with hoes while another man in khaki uniform watched them from the shade of the single tree. On the crest of the next hill he saw a complex of red brick buildings that looked like a high school. The green and white sign at the bottom of the drive said: S.C.F. Dunmore. Official Business Only. So *this* is a prison, thought Phil; doesn't look so bad to me.

The only entrance to the buildings from the outside was a series of glass panel doors opening into a tiled lobby. The doors were open wide, apparently to let in the mild June breeze. There was no one inside except for a small, skinny man with a mop, cleaning the already very clean tile floor. This man also wore a T-shirt and gray trousers. He paid no attention to Phil. "Where do I find Superintendent Smythe?" said Phil. The words were just out of his mouth when Phil realized that his words were directed at an inmate. This is really strange, he thought; there's no one around but an inmate with a mop, and the doors are wide open.

The inmate gave Phil a blank stare and merely pointed at a small sign. Phil reddened slightly and entered the hallway below the Superintendent sign. Smythe's appearance caught Phil totally off guard. He had been expecting some Cagneyesque character. Instead, Smythe was cheery and relaxed, his feet propped on the desk.

Smythe asked Phil what he could do to help. Questionnaires to inmates turned out to be the biggest problem. What bothered Smythe was how to get inmates to fill out questionnaires. This puzzled Phil. This man has these people locked up, but he can't just *ask* them to respond to a questionnaire? Smythe proposed that the most effective way to get cooperation was to ask the inmate editor of the inmate paper to run a story explaining the purpose of the study.

Smythe got up and led Phil down a long hallway, talking as he went. "Johnston will be over in a few minutes and you can explain the study to him and what you're asking the inmates to do. Then he'll write it up." The superintendent excused himself, and Phil had a few minutes to get his bearings. This area looked much more like a prison: There were two uniformed men in a small, glassed-in booth across the hall. One was busy with several phones and a clipboard on which he constantly checked off responses to incoming calls. The other officer kept pushing keys through a metal tray like those at a drive-in banking window. Guards would pick up the keys and walk off, then return later and push the keys back through the window. Phil realized that the administration building was unsecured because, with the exception of the inmate with the mop, no inmates could get through to the lobby. Virtually no one passed down that long hallway without documenting his destination to the two men in the glass booth.

Suddenly, a small, elderly gentleman was standing in front of Phil. He had silver hair and wire-rimmed spectacles that made him look like an elderly professor, except that he too was dressed in the white cotton T-shirt and gray pants. Johnston bowed his head as if Phil were royalty. "Yessir," he said in a subservient tone. "Good morning, sir. How can I help you?"

"Well . . ." Phil went through the project again, just as he had for the superintendent, although this time he stressed the need for accurate, objective responses about certain prison operations.

"That's a really refreshing idea," said Johnston. "An organizational development project in a prison system. My company did an O.D. project about ten years ago—or maybe fifteen. It's hard to remember. But the Superintendent is right to be concerned," he said. "Most of these inmates are so passive about their situation that getting valid answers won't be easy. I'll do the best I can."

Johnston was elaborating his own prison philosphy to Phil. Johnston sounded like a textbook on the modern prison, although he was more articulate than most textbook writers. "Most of these men need rehabilitation desperately," he was saying, "but how to get a distrustful person to participate in his own remaking. . . . " All this sounded good, or at least familiar to Phil, but none of it was consistent with the behavior of the man in front of him. Phil kept asking himself: Why is this man talking about rehabilitation? He obviously can read and write. And unless he's really pulling my leg, he worked in a major corporation. And he doesn't seem any more distrustful of the superintendent than I am.

Johnston was coming to the end of his speech. "This prison can't help me. If I ever get out, I'll be too old to have retained any of the skills I came here with. No, I'm just here because I deserve it." He smiled forlornly and prepared to return to the courtyard. "It's been a pleasure meeting you, doctor." Phil had just been promoted from graduate school to professor. Johnston turned back with a final thought: "You know, I never regretted this debt I'm paying, but when I first entered the prison, it never occurred to me what that payment would really mean." He looked at Phil for understanding, but Phil really had none to offer. "I mean, every day I serve is another day I disappear just a little bit more. The real hurt, when I think about it, is the fear that I'll be entirely gone before I die." He nodded again and shuffled away. When Phil returned to the superintendent's office, he had difficulty hiding his indignation. Just what was the prison system all about, anyway? That old man doesn't need education or counseling. He could have been a staff member if he were dressed in the other uniform. And he can't be any danger to anyone. What purpose is served by locking him up?

Smythe seemed to sense the difficulty Phil was having. "Has a master's degree from State," the Superintendent was saying. "Vice President of the Chief Rifle Company. Made all the papers when he did it. Actually pretty famous case. Caught his wife and her lover when he came home early one day. Shot them both dead. Two clean shots. The defense tried to argue for manslaughter rather than murder two. But when the judge heard that Johnston was an expert shot, he wouldn't go for it. He decided that any expert marksman knows just what he's doing when he pulls the trigger, angry or not."

Phil was still flustered. "But just what good will it do him to be here the rest of his life? I mean what good will it do anybody?"

"Well, said Smythe, "he killed two people."

PUNISHMENT AND SOCIAL CONTROL

In everyday discussions, we refer to many different actions as punishment. After two full days of interviewing, Phil might think of his drive back to the university as "punishing." At the end of the next semester, he might take a "punishing" exam. When his grade on this exam is well above average, other students in the class may "punish" him for doing well. The next time he visits his parents' home, he might once again hear his father recall the time Phil was punished for coloring in his father's books when Phil was 4 years old.

In these and similar examples, the concept of punishment is fairly fuzzy. None of these examples represents what is meant by criminal punishment. The three-hour ride home is "punishing" because Phil is exhausted. The ride might be painful because it taxes his endurance, but he has committed no wrong. No one has determined to punish him. The exam is an action by a professor, but Phil has not been subjected to the test in response to misbehavior. Phil and his classmates were given the test to assess their achievement. When Phil suffers negative social responses for doing too well on the test, is he being punished? If so, why did another classmate, who did very poorly on the test, receive similar treatment? What about his father's act of "punishment"? According to Phil's father, 4-year-old Phil was attempting to emulate his father's practice of making marginal notes in books.

Criminal punishment is one form of a broader category of activity referred to as **social control**. In the last thirty years, social control has come to mean those social actions taken to preserve the social order of a people. Social controls preserve group identification by preventing or limiting unusual behavior and maintaining or rein-forcing common or "normal" behavior (Wilkins, 1965). One of the earliest social control writers, E. A. Ross (1914), indicated that social controls were sanctions used to steer persons toward some behaviors and away from others. Ross suggested that sanctions could be negative or positive, but that modern societies tended to emphasize neg-ative sanctions for undesired behavior rather than positive sanctions for desired behavior.

The law is one form of social control. Donald Black (1976) and Leslie Wilkins (1965) hypoth-esized that as informal social controls, such as social approval, become weaker, formal social controls, such as commitments to mental hospi-tals and penal institutions, become more fre-quent. The law is a **formal control** because it relies on written, codified rules adopted by a decision-making body for a social group. Its adoption and implementation relies upon social actors performing official roles. It may seem easy enough to distinguish between this formal social control and informal controls, but how do we differentiate one formal control from another?

PUNISHMENT DISTINGUISHED FROM OTHER FORMAL CONTROLS

One common distinction among formal controls is the dichotomy between the criminal law and the civil law. The criminal law proscribes certain conduct and assigns particular penalties called punishments for violation of the proscriptions. Other forms of law also control behavior and often use similar means, such as assigning sanctions.

One part of civil law, called tort law, allows one party to sue in court for damages against another party. Indeed, one act can result in both criminal punishment and a tort action. For ex-ample, Phil can punch another classmate in the nose after he is teased about his grade on the test. If he does, he can be arrested, convicted, and punished for breaking the criminal law pro-hibiting assault and battery. But his victim can also sue Phil in civil court because Phil has committed a tort. What is the difference?

LeFave and Scott (1980:73) hold that the law of torts is used by one party against another to obtain compensation for harm that has been suf-fered, whereas criminal law is used by the state itself to protect the social order rather than com-pensate the victim. A. L. Covington observes that instances of "parallel suits" arising from the same actions are not considered a violation of the con-stitutional prohibition against double jeopardy, because the criminal sanctions are intended as punishment and the civil sanctions for remedia-tion (1980:190). But recent trends in civil suits indicate that remediation of damage is not always the sole outcome in civil suits. With increasing frequency, civil courts have awarded "punitive" as well as compensatory damages to claimants in civil actions. D. G. Owen argues that the criminal law is the principal legal mechanism with which to deal with serious misbehavior, but that in a rapidly changing society, some actions may be seen as reprehensible even though not proscribed by the criminal law. He suggested (1982:103) that civil punitive damages may be appropriate when the assignment of criminal responsibility for an act is either inappropriate or too great a condem-nation. Moreover, criminal punishments at times provide for compensation, such as when a judge orders a convicted person to pay restitution to the victim.

Some people have argued that the criminal law prohibits more serious misbehavior than the civil law and also involves more serious conse-quences. For a long time, this seriousness di-mension was interpreted to mean that the civil law could be applied with less stringent controls than is true in criminal cases. But the Supreme Court of the United States has rejected the idea that civil law interventions are always less serious than criminal law punishments. Many civil pen-alties in tort cases may be more severe than criminal punishments. Juvenile delinquency in-carcerations or mental health commitments, while civil, may be more serious interventions than many criminal punishments. The public goals protected by civil law may be just as important as those preserved by the criminal law (R. F. Wright, 1984). So the seriousness of the behavior or of the legal result is not always a good guide.

H. M. Hart (1958:56–57) proposed that the primary distinction between criminal and civil rested in the notion of public condemnation. Both civil and criminal law may seek the prevention of injury and use fairly similar procedures, but only in the criminal law is there a "community condemnation which accompanies and justifies its imposition." The major difference may be that the criminal punishment represents a social decision about the moral blameworthiness of the lawbreaker, a decision that is lacking or specifically excluded from controls available in the civil law.

The element of moral condemnation appeared to have particular weight for the Supreme Court in its leading case, *Bell* v. *Wolfish* (1979), concerning pretrial detention. The petitioners in this case were detained in the Metropolitan Correctional Center in Manhattan, a federal facility used to detain persons prior to trial if they could not make bail, and to incarcerate convicted federal prisoners serving short terms. The petitioners argued that they were being subjected to unconstitutional punishment because they were incarcerated under the same conditions as the convicted prisoners but had not yet been convicted. The Supreme Court agreed that the Fifth Amendment of the Constitution prohibited punishment prior to adjudication of guilt. However, the Court disagreed that the detainees were being punished. The opinion of the Court relied upon a **punitive intent standard** to determine whether the conditions of detention, no matter how similar to those experienced by convicted prisoners,

The moral condemnation of criminal punishment is evident in the nineteenth-century community use of the whipping post. (North Wind Picture Archives)

amounted to punishment. According to this standard, the practice of pretrial detention is not punitive if another valid governmental purpose can be demonstrated and the practice is not seen to be excessive in relation to that other purpose (see *Bell* v. *Wolfish*, 1979; and Gill, 1981:473). The Court decided that the stated purpose of secure jail administration was a valid one and that the restrictions to which the petitioners objected were reasonably related to achieving that security (for more detail on this case, see Insert 1.1).

Another legal process that results in conditions which may appear punitive but presumably are justified by another valid governmental purpose is pretrial preventive detention. In 1981, the Federal Appellate Court of the District of Columbia heard a challenge to the D.C. preventive detention statute. Under this statute, certain defendants can be detained pending trial, rather than released on bail, if the federal prosecutor meets certain statutory criteria which are used to predict that the defendant is dangerous and would commit additional crimes if released. The appellate court upheld this practice. The Court approved the purpose of preventing the repetition of dangerous acts and decided that incarceration for this purpose was constitutional because the behavior to be prevented was "reasonably predictable conduct" [*United States* v. *Edwards*, 1981].

Another area of civil law with severe consequences but lacking punitive intent is the civil commitment of the mentally ill. Norval Morris (1982:30) points out that both the powers of the state under the criminal law and the mental health law can separate a person from family, friends, and community. However, the prerequisite for imprisonment under the criminal law is that a person "has been convicted of a crime and that imprisonment is both deserved and socially desirable." In contrast, the prerequisite for involuntary commitment of the mentally ill is that a person "is mentally ill or retarded and that he is a danger to others or to himself or is incapable of caring for himself." Mental commitment is jus-

tified on evidence of the presence of a mental *condition* which is predicted to lead to dangerous consequences if not controlled. Criminal punishment follows not a prediction but a finding of *guilt* for the commission of a crime.

Hart (1958:60) has pointed out that while criminal punishment is the only form of law which symbolizes the moral condemnation of the person, criminal law also restricts the occasions for this condemnation. A criminal is punished for the act committed, not for his or her condition or character. It is on this basis that the United States Supreme Court distinguished the improper punishment for drug addiction in *Robinson* v. *California* (1962) from the proper punishment for public drunkenness in *Powell* v. *Texas* (1968). The California drug addiction statute, said the Court, was unconstitutional because it punished a condition. Addiction, said the Court, was not an act but a sickness, like the common cold, and as such was not deserving of condemnation. On the other hand, Mr. Powell was convicted of an act, public drunkenness, and could be punished despite the fact that the act might be traced to a condition, alcoholism, which would not itself be punishable.

DEFINING CRIMINAL PUNISHMENT

K. Greenwalt (1983:343–344) provided a typical definition of **criminal punishment:**

> . . . persons who possess authority impose designedly unpleasant consequences upon, and express their condemnation of, other persons who are capable of choice and who have breached established standards of behavior.

The definition has five important elements: (1) The person being punished must be *responsible* for the behavior. Those who are too immature or mentally incompetent to understand what they are doing may be controlled by other formal social controls, but they cannot be punished. (2) The punishment is intended to be *painful* in some

Insert 1.1 *BELL* V. *WOLFISH*—THE PUNITIVE INTENT STANDARD

This Supreme Court case concerns challenges made to certain conditions and practices of confinement at the Metropolitan Correctional Center (MCC), a federal short-term facility in New York City. Although MCC was designed primarily to house pretrial detainees, between 40 and 60 percent of the MCC population consisted of inmates convicted and awaiting sentencing or inmates serving short sentences. This inmate population rose above its planned capacity shortly after construction in 1975, resulting in frequent "double-bunking" (housing two inmates in a cell designed for one). In addition to the "double-bunking" problem, challenges were raised in this case against the practices of prohibiting receipt of hardcover books not mailed directly from publishers, bookclubs, or bookstores; prohibiting detainees from observing inspections of their rooms; and requiring inmates to submit to visual searches of body cavities after every contact visit.

At issue in this case was the constitutionality of practices and conditions for detainees that went beyond the restrictions inherent in incarceration. The Court of Appeals for the Second Circuit had ruled that any restriction not serving as a compelling necessity in managing a facility is in violation of the Due Process clause of the Fifth Amendment, which protects defendants from being punished before trial. The Supreme Court,

however, rejected that standard, arguing that the case should turn only on whether the practice in question violated detainees' right to be free from punishment—not whether government interests in promoting security outweighed the detainees' interests in being as unrestricted as possible. The Court relied on two factors from an earlier case (*Kennedy* v. *Mendoza-Martinez*, 372 U.S. 144, 1963) to determine whether the individual restrictions at MCC were punitive or merely regulatory restraints; whether the practice is reasonably related to a legitimate goal other than punishment, and whether it appears to be "excessive" in relation to that alternative purpose. The Court emphasized that the inmate bears the burden of proof to show that corrections officials' responses to security concerns were exaggerated and that judges should not become involved in the "minutiae of prison operations." Using this line of analysis, the Supreme Court reversed the Court of Appeals decision and ruled that none of the challenged restrictions violated detainees' rights under the Due Process clause of the Fifth Amendment. The Supreme Court, referring to earlier cases, made clear that while detainees retain *at least* those rights enjoyed by convicted prisoners, their rights are subject to restrictions and limitations for purposes of institutional security.

---

sense; it is a negative sanction that most rational persons would wish to avoid. (3) The pain inflicted is preceded by a judgment of *condemnation;* the person being punished is explicitly blamed for the act. (There are a few punishments that do not appear to include condemnation, such as those for traffic violations.) (4) Punishment is imposed only by those who have the legal *authority* over the responsible actor and for the implementation of the law or standard in question. Criminal punishment cannot be imposed informally, even by persons who feel directly injured. It can be imposed only by those who hold

formal office and are charged with determining guilt and imposing punishment. (5) Punishment follows a "legally demonstrated breach of *established rules of behavior* . . ." (1983:345). This means that the behavior to be punished, as well as the punishment that attaches to that behavior, must be specified in advance.

JUSTIFICATIONS FOR PUNISHMENT

What purposes are served by a formal system of blaming responsible actors for violating standards of conduct and providing painful consequences for proven violations? Greenwalt stated that the justifications for the actual implementation of punishment are inseparable from justifications of the criminal law itself. Since the criminal law is a series of threats, carrying out the threats is necessary if the law is to be taken seriously (1983:347). What does it mean to take the law seriously? Is the implementation of punishment to have some empirically verifiable results? Would the criminal law continue to be taken seriously if it were demonstrated that those results did not occur? Or is it sufficient to provide punishment in accordance with the law, regardless of consequences? In the various discussions of punishment, we will find both positions taken. **Utilitarian justifications of punishment** rely upon the demonstration of useful purposes achieved. Utilitarian justifications include deterrence, incapacitation, and rehabilitation. **Retributive justifications** rely upon nonempirical, ethical arguments.

RETRIBUTION

According to M. Davis (1983:727) a retributive justification for punishment has three elements: (1) Punishment is acceptable only against persons who have committed crimes. (2) The degree of punishment must match the severity of the crime. (3) The degree of punishment specified is independent of the actual or predicted consequences of the punitive act (see also van den Haag, 1975:11; and Greenwalt, 1983:384–385). Retribution generally has two strands. One stresses the moral guilt of the law violators and argues that punishment is the duty of society as a means of upholding the moral nature of the person who commits a crime. The other strand stresses that fairness to others who have obeyed the law demands punishment of those who have not.

Either version of retribution leaves the individual victim of crime in the background. Whether retribution is seen as an attempt to bring the offender back to the moral order by punishing his violations or reaffirming the moral order in the face of deviance, retribution would appear to stress the importance of the moral order of a group rather than righting specific harms.

> . . . the criminal's (act-related) "wickedness" varies with the value of the unfair advantage he takes from those who obeyed the law (even though they are tempted to do otherwise). They are the society he wrongs by his crime. (Davis, 1983:744)

> If a man profits from his own wrongdoing, from his disobedience, this is unfair or unjust, not merely to his victim, but to all of those who have been obedient . . . . (Murphy, 1979)

According to retributive theory, offenders are brought to justice by the state, acting as caretaker for society, for the violation of societal rules. Whether the victim is compensated in this process does not matter.

If we return to the definition of punishment, we should see that there is little in the retributive justification that is not present in the definition itself, except that a retributive justification asserts no other purpose or benefit is necessary. Indeed, a strict retributivist would claim that attaching other purposes to the act of punishment may dilute its value by implying that upholding the moral order and the moral nature of man is not sufficient.

Is there a way to test whether retribution works? Retributivists do not claim that retribution will provide a safer society or fewer offenders. They do not claim that it will reform offenders or frighten them. In fact, retributivists would continue to claim that punishment was justified even if the consistent practice of punishment was followed by a massive increase in crime. The preservation of a *moral* order is not necessarily the preservation of *public* order. Retributivists admit that many social control mechanisms might be more effective in the pursuit of public order. From a retributivist position, many of these possibly more effective strategies, such as preventive detention of the dangerous, would not be fair: They are not punishments for crime. According to retribution, punishment "works" if its practice is consistent with the tenets of retributivism, and if those tenets are logical and consistent.

DETERRENCE

Deterrence is usually divided into two types, general and specific. "General deterrence . . . is defined as the effect which threats of punishment . . . have in deterring non-offenders from becoming offenders" (van den Haag, 1982a:770). Tittle defined deterrence as "responsiveness to sanction threats" and suggested that it can be measured by whether those who perceive more threat in a sanction, independent of other factors, are those least likely to offend (Tittle, 1980:318). Specific deterrence, in contrast, refers to the effect that one punishment may have on the likelihood of reducing new offenses by the person who has been punished. Nigel Walker objected to the notion of "specific deterrence." He claimed that we cannot distinguish punished persons who have been "specifically deterred" from those who have been rehabilitated (1971:91). Following Walker, we will also reserve the term deterrence in this book to refer to general deterrence, or the impact of sanction threat upon the general population.

Van den Haag proposed that deterrence yields the greatest advantage of criminal punishment because using punishment for deterrence is the only way to lower the crime rate. Manipulating the severity and frequency of punishment can lower the net comparative advantage expected from crime by increasing the costs of committing crime (1982a:770–771). However, van den Haag's evidence for a deterrent effect is weak. He merely pointed to the "obvious" effect of incentives in general on behavior (1982a:770–771). He also accepted as evidence of deterrence the observation that most people do not commit crime (1975:115). A major review of the empirical literature on deterrence, however, is far more cautious (Tittle, 1980).

Part of the doubt about a deterrent effect of punishment is caused by the ambiguity of the term, and another part by the difficulty in measuring its effects, even if we can define it. Both informal and formal social controls may have deterrent effects. Both formal and informal controls tend to operate simultaneously, in most situations and for most people. Isolating the deterrent effect of the legal threat by holding constant such other deterrents as fear of peer reaction or loss of social status can be very difficult. It is not clear, however, whether the deterrence justification should be narrowly interpreted as direct threats or whether deterrence implies a much broader type of controlling action. For example, Johannes Andeneas (1974) distinguished three different "general-preventative" effects of punishment:

. . . it may have a deterrent effect, it may strengthen moral inhibitions (a moralizing effect), and it may stimulate habitual law-abiding conduct.

Andeneas tried to separate the direct threat of punishment from the other social dynamics the criminal law may influence, such as codifying and reinforcing existing norms and influencing persons to obey both norms and laws habitually (because they and others simply do it) without temptation controlled by threat. Van den Haag (1982a:774) and Herbert Packer (1968), among others, included these broader socializing effects of the law within their definitions of deterrence. By doing so, they seemed to justify deterrent punishments with the observation that most of us obey the norms of the social groups in which we live. This broadening of the definition makes deterrence very difficult to measure, and therefore a utilitarian argument which cannot be proven. The broader the concept becomes, the more it resembles protection of the existing moral order rather than response to threats. This broad definition of deterrence sounds like the retributive justification of punishment.

INCAPACITATION

The second utilitarian justification for punishment has probably been around as long as the others, but has become increasingly popular as a justification for punishment in the 1980s. **Inca-**

pacitation, in general, "refers to the crimes averted in the general society by isolation of the identified offenders during periods of incarceration" (Blumstein, 1983:93). Clear and Barry pointed out that this definition is actually too narrow, since it assumes isolation through imprisonment to be an essential element in incapacitation. Other incapacitation techniques are possible, including prefrontal lobotomies, chemical behavior control, electric monitoring of behavior, and intensive probation or parole surveillance (1983:530–540). Incapacitation makes a somewhat simpler claim than the other justifications: It focuses entirely on the offender being punished and is concerned only with the period of punishment itself. It makes no claims that its effects last beyond the period in which the offender is under control and incapacitated (Clear and Barry, 1983:529; Blackmore and Welsh, 1983:506). Incapacitation operates on the assumption that punishment can take "a slice out of an individual criminal career" (Blumstein, 1983:94).

Because incapacitation is based on predictions of future behavior, it is subject to a number of problems. The best known of these is error in prediction. If we are to punish on the basis of preventing future crimes, two types of prediction error need to be avoided: (1) "false positive" predictions, or the erroneous prediction that a person will commit another crime when in fact he or she would not; and (2) "false negative" predictions, or the mistaken prediction that a person will not commit another crime when in fact he or she will (Blackmore and Welsh, 1983:518). Unfortunately, these two types of prediction errors are inversely related. The more false negatives we try to avoid by increasing the frequency of punishment, the more false positives we will produce. Thus incapacitation, like other prediction tasks, becomes a balancing act with important ethical implications. Do we punish

A frequently mentioned advantage of maximum security prisons is their ability to incapacitate offenders, or to keep them from committing new crimes in the community during the sentence. (Pennsylvania Department of Corrections)

fewer persons in order to avoid the unnecessary punishment of those who would not recidivate, or do we punish more persons to avoid letting go those who will commit crimes in the future?

The incapacitation justification must wrestle with some other problems as well. The prediction problems will occur, even if no change takes place in offenders while they are being punished. But it is possible that some changes will occur. Blumstein (1983:95–96) identified two punishment effects that may reduce the overall utility of incapacitation. Some offenders may be rehabilitated, so that the original prediction of future behavior is no longer accurate and the cost of a portion of the incapacitive sentence turns out to be wasted. On the other hand, punishment may have a criminalization effect, so that even if incapacitation is effective, the released person commits more crimes upon release than he or she would have without the punishment. Perhaps more detrimental than these drawbacks is the possibility of a "replacement effect," the possibility that the crimes which would have been committed by the incapacitated offender are committed by someone else in the community who would not have had the opportunity to commit an offense if the punished person were free. If replacement does occur, then the net effect on the crime rate would be minimal (Blumstein, 1983:94).

In the early 1980s the general incapacitation justification received a new twist with the publication of two reports by the RAND Corporation (Forst, 1983:14). This new twist is the concept of "selective incapacitation," reserving scarce prison and jail space for those who are predictably the most dangerous and criminally active (Forst, 1983:10). Proposed originally by Peter Greenwood of RAND, selective incapacitation grew out of findings that within a given offense type, many of the crimes are committed by a very few "high-rate offenders." Greenwood argued it made sense to target selectively for incapacitation those most active offenders (Blackmore and Welsh, 1983:504). These assumptions have re-

cently been challenged by Gottfredson and Hirschi (1987).

Selective incapacitation makes most sense when prisons are overcrowded and rising public pressure for more crime control leads to a search for more efficient use of the scarce available space (Blumstein, 1983:87–90). Forst argued that a policy of selective incapacitation could actually reduce prison populations as long as alternative punishments were found for those who were not high-rate offenders (Forst, 1983:21).

REHABILITATION

The third utilitarian justification for punishment is **rehabilitation.** In the last ten years, it has been the most criticized justification, if not the most controversial. Rehabilitation, like incapacitation, focuses on the person being punished, rather than on the behavior of others. However, like incapacitation, it is doubtful that rehabilitation is proposed because of, or solely because of, benefits to the person being punished. As a justification for punishment, rehabilitation is a claim that certain things can be done to or with the person being punished so that after the punishment the person will not want to commit another offense—or at least will commit fewer offenses.

One of the major controversies surrounding rehabilitation is whether rehabilitative activities themselves should be considered punishment, or whether they are conducted along with but separate from punishment. Van den Haag, a vocal critic of rehabilitation, provided a definition that exemplifies this doubt (1982a:1022):

> [Rehabilitation] . . . attempts to produce law-abiding (or more law-abiding) behavior of convicts, usually by non-punitive means.

It is not obvious what nonpunitive connotes in this context. While rehabilitation frequently occurs in nonpunitive settings and with persons who are not convicts, van den Haag was clearly not referring to these activities. But if the rehabilitation is to eliminate criminal behavior and is pursued as a consequence of conviction, what makes it nonpunitive? The absence of pain? Many rehabilitative techniques may be painful. Moreover, the type of pain required of punishment is only that it be the kind of consequence most people would wish to avoid. If rehabilitation is coerced as a consequence of conviction, it may be painful in that sense, if not in others.

Part of the battle over rehabilitation as a justification for punishment has been waged precisely over the issue of coercion. The American Friends Service Committee in its 1971 report *Struggle for Justice* offered the first major attack on the viability of coercing rehabilitation as a consequence of convction. This attack was followed by Norval Morris's influential book, *The Future of Imprisonment* (1974), in which Morris contended that rehabilitation can be effective, but rehabilitation as a punishment cannot be. Morris proposed that all convicts, like other citizens, had a right to programs and resources that might result in self-betterment, but that the officials of the state could not set the type or length of punishment on the basis of rehabilitative potential.

The debate over coerced therapy is itself far from settled. Seymour Halleck (1971), a psychiatrist, has argued that the line between coerced and noncoerced treatments is extremely hard to draw, even in nonpunitive situations. Many therapists, particularly of the behavior modification school, have suggested that coerced therapy, while not the ideal mode, can be justified and effective in a number of situations (Gendreau and Ross, 1984; and see Trice and Beyer, 1984, for examples of coerced therapy for alcoholics in work settings).

The biggest blow to rehabilitation came from a research project begun as part of Governor Nelson Rockefeller's Special Committee on Criminal Offenders, a blue ribbon committee charged with examining corrections in the State of New York. This committee commissioned a review of existing research on the effectiveness of correctional treatment. Reviewing 231 studies of reha-

bilitation programs in corrections, the researchers concluded that the available research on rehabilitation in correctional agencies was generally poorly conducted, and that the more rigorous evaluations of rehabilitation programs were the least likely to uncover positive effects (Lipton, Martinson, and Wilks, 1975). The report did indicate that some programs had positive effects with some offenders, but it demonstrated that the confident claims made in the 1960s for rehabilitation as a means of crime reduction were unwarranted and inflated. Perhaps even more influential than the full report was an earlier article by one of its authors entitled "What Works: Questions and Answers About Prison Reform" (Martinson, 1974). Although forcefully criticized later, this article proclaimed that correctional rehabilitation was simply ineffective and rehabilitation bankrupt as a justification for punishment.

Following this controversial report, the National Academy of Sciences appointed a Panel on Research and Rehabilitation Techniques in 1977 to review and reassess what was known about rehabilitation. This panel defined rehabilitation as follows:

> . . . the result of any planned intervention that reduces an offender's further criminal activity, whether that reduction is mediated by personality, behavior, abilities, attitudes, values, or other factors. The effects of maturation and the effects associated with "fear" or "intimidation" are excluded, the result of the latter having traditionally been labeled as "specific deterrence." (Sechrest et al., 1980:20–21)

The panel identified three aspects it considered important in any definition of rehabilitation: (1) the desired outcome, (2) the intervening variables assumed to be the target of treatment, and (3) the intervention itself, or the specific steps taken to alter the variables assumed to cause the criminal behavior (Martin, Sechrest, and Redner, 1981:8). The panel's conclusions generally supported those of Martinson, but were more cautious and tended to stress how little we actually know about rehabilitation.

THE COMPATIBILITY OF GOALS

While many critiques of the purposes of punishment have aimed to establish the supremacy of one justification over the others, as a practical matter the various justifications all operate at the same time. Therefore, an important issue is whether the separate justifications operating together interfere with each other or are complementary.

RETRIBUTION AND DETERRENCE

Ernest van den Haag has argued that retribution by itself cannot match crimes and punishments, even though that match is an essential ingredient in retributivist theory, because there is no objective basis for determining such a match (1982b:782). He proposed that we can decide the severity of punishments by using the deterrent calculus of what disincentive will deter a particular crime (1982b:783). When he compared retributivist and deterrent penalties for the same crimes, he found considerable similarity. He suggested that retributivists have borrowed a utilitarian, deterrent ranking of severity in order to determine what penalty is deserved. Van den Haag concluded that there is a close relationship between deterrence and retribution because our notion of how much punishment will deter becomes our idea of how severe a penalty must be to maintain the moral order.

Some retributivists object to this similarity and insist that the retributive scale of punishments is constructed directly from the idea of fairness, or restoring the balance of advantage which the criminal has disturbed. They might admit that the retributive penalty would rarely be *greater* than the deterrent penalty, but they would enumerate many occasions where it would be less severe. Increasing the severity of punishments for certain crimes might provide a greater deterrent effect, but some severe punishments would violate retributive principles if they were greater than warranted by the severity of the crime. There may be instances when deterrence and retribution may be in conflict, because the principles for weighting punishments are not identical. However, there would appear to be room in actual practice for considerable compatibility.

RETRIBUTION AND INCAPACITATION

There is more conflict between retribution and incapacitation. The central policy question relating to incapacitation is the question of whether it is legitimate to punish someone for future crimes (Blumstein, 1983:102). Blackmore and Welsh contend that even if incapacitative predictions were perfect (which they would never be), punishment based on prediction would violate the principles that punishment be commensurate with the crime committed and that all citizens (including the dangerous) should have equal standing before the criminal law (1983:513).

Morris (1974) and Clear and O'Leary (1983) have argued that there may be sufficient play in the allowable range of retributive punishments for any one crime that incapacitative concerns could operate within those retributive limits. Retributivist Andrew von Hirsch has rejected this compromise. Retribution, like incapacitation, might allow more severe penalties for offenders with lengthy histories of prior convictions. But retribution would never use the other elements of criminal history which are vital to incapacitative predictions. Predictive sentencing uses information about an offender that has nothing to do with moral blameworthiness, but only offense and criminal history are valid on retributive grounds (von Hirsch, 1984:180–182). Thus incapacitation and selective incapacitation are severely constrained by the principles of retribution.

RETRIBUTION AND REHABILITATION

Perhaps the most visible conflict in the current debate about the justifications of punishment is the one between rehabilitation and retribution. Van den Haag (1982a:1035) has urged the abolition of parole, indeterminant sentences, and any other programs that have a rehabilitative intent because such elements detract from "doing justice," or providing retribution. Practices such as work release, halfway houses, and other forms of community supervision, which either replace or reduce incarceration, detract from the punitive value of the sentence and thus do not uphold the moral values protected by retribution (van den Haag, 1982a:1033).

The sentiments expressed by van den Haag were common in the mid-1980s, but they may obscure rather than illuminate the conflict. First, we have no way of knowing whether the community sentences to which van den Haag objects are rehabilitative in the first place. The *location* of punishment does not tell us anything about its intent, and there is no reason to assume that a noninstitutional sentence cannot "do justice" to the crime committed (Clear and O'Leary, 1983:13–20). A number of recent sentencing code revisions include probation as a punishment of sufficient severity for a number of less serious offenses. Second, rehabilitation and retribution may be compatible, if the rehabilitative process focuses on moral change rather than upon expert ministrations to psychological or physical conditions (Kidder, 1975). Van den Haag does admit that some rehabilitative programs may be interpreted in this way (1982a:1033).

So it would appear that the major dimension of conflict between rehabilitation and retribution is still the nature of retribution as a coerced, painful experience, coupled with the doubt that rehabilitation can be effective under these circumstances. We need more data about rehabilitation than we currently have to determine if these conflicts are insurmountable.

INCAPACITATION AND DETERRENCE

Although both incapacitation and deterrence focus on the protection of society, there may be difficulty in meshing an incapacitative sentencing scheme with the needs of deterrence. Selective incapacitation is not the most effective strategy for all crimes or all offenders, and would work best on serious, high-rate, violent offenders. But

if we reserve prison use for this category of offenders, punishment as a deterrent to other crimes might suffer (Forst, 1983:20). The problem might be resolved if nonincarcerative punishment were sufficiently threatening to provide deterrence.

DETERRENCE AND REHABILITATION

One argument against rehabilitation is that rehabilitative means detract from the deterrent effects of punishment:

> . . . if the interpretation by the public is that the individual is being excused from punishment and not held responsible, then it is reasonable to assume some loss in the general deterrent effect. (Miller, 1980:89)

Note that this conflict involves the public's *perception* of rehabilitative punishments. If people perceive punishment to be lenient, it will not have a proper deterrent effect. Legally, there is no such thing as a punishment, rehabilitative or otherwise, that treats the individual as not responsible. Punishment is an official act of placing blame on those perceived to be responsible. Many therapeutic interventions are designed precisely to make individuals accept personal responsibility for their actions. Thus, it is possible, once again, that the source of conflict resides in misconceptions of or misinformation about both punishment and rehabilitation, rather than in the justifications themselves.

Another objection to rehabilitation was raised by van den Haag (1982a:1023–1024), who argued that rehabilitation, even if completely effective, would have no significant effect on the crime rate because it cannot touch those who are not yet convicted. In contrast, deterrent penalties are designed to influence the behavior of the unconvicted. This objection, it should be noted, also applies to incapacitation, since incapacitation also influences only those who have been caught and punished. The real question here is whether the manner of punishing the person before the court is or can be incompatible with the intended influence of that punishment on persons who have not been caught but may be aware of the punishment that is taking place.

INCAPACITATION AND REHABILITATION

There may be some conflict in the simultaneous use of rehabilitation and selective incapacitation. The conflict arises from the requirement of incarceration for incapacitation, when incarceration may make persons more criminal and therefore detract from rehabilitation (Forst, 1983:20). But an incapacitative sentence may provide selective deterrence for an individual. If so, even if prisons are "schools for crime," the released inmate who has been educated in crime may be too fearful of punishment to proceed on a criminal career.

Other observers see a different sort of conflict between incapacitation and rehabilitation. If prisons actually succeed in making a positive change in a person during a prison stay (rather than a negative one), incapacitative sentencing would not accommodate this positive change (Blackmore and Welsh, 1983:520). If rehabilitation occurred, incapacitation beyond the period of rehabilitation would be wasteful.

Both the proposed negative and positive changes during prison sentences that may make rehabilitation and incapacitation incompatible are better understood as hypotheses than demonstrated relationships. There is not a great deal of evidence to substantiate prisons as schools of crime; nor do we have evidence that rehabilitation is undone by continued incarceration (Hawkins, 1976).

THE MERGING OF PURPOSES

Despite the continuing debates about incompatible goals, there is some greater optimism now than in the 1960s. Although some retributivists would object to attempts to merge any utilitarian goals with retribution (G. Newman, 1983), most of the participants in the justification debate tend to see some hope. The most common position

seems to be that punishment should have utilitarian aims, but that the pursuit of those aims must be constrained by the notions of fair procedure and commensurate desert as promulgated by retributivists (van den Haag, 1982a:1034; Greenwalt, 1983:354; Packer, 1968). The greatest congruence would appear to be between deterrence and retribution. Greater difficulties appear to emerge when justifications such as incapacitation or rehabilitation enter the picture. These two justifications focus on actions taken with specific, sentenced offenders, whereas deterrence and retribution focus on the influence of punishment upon persons not being punished.

Part of the difficulty would appear to be related to the specificity with which the different justifications address the notion of incarceration. Retribution and deterrence are relatively silent on what should happen during an incarcerative sentence, as long as the sentence is appropriate to the crime. Incapacitation does not say much more about the nature of incarceration, although it would specify the length of time on the basis of continuing danger rather than past offense.

Rehabilitation is much more specific about what happens during the sentence. Retribution and deterrence advocates seem to become most exercised whenever a description of a punishment sounds as if it is reducing the length of punishment. There appears to be some sensitivity as well, however, to rehabilitative descriptions that entail staff-inmate interactions, or prison climates and facilities that modify the painfulness of the experience, regardless of length. There are limitations on the cruelty of prison sentences, even if rehabilitation is absent. Therefore, part of the conflict among justifications may be inherent in the difference between asking "Why do we punish this person?" and "What do we do with the person during the sentence?"

One recent assessment of decision-making in criminal justice asserted that, regardless of ideological debates about purposes, in practice there may be a trend toward harmony of outcomes. Michael and Don Gottfredson (1980) observed that recent developments in correctional decision-making tend to focus on serious, violent offenders, whether the justification is retribution, deterrence, incapacitation, or rehabilitation. They indicated that the most recent statement of all four justifications reserves prison for persons who have committed violent street crimes. These are the offenders whose crimes we wish to punish most severely for both retributive and deterrent reasons. These are also the offenders we wish most to incapacitate or rehabilitate. But whether this empirical trend is accidental or the result of actual goal congruence will continue to be debated.

TYPES OF PUNISHMENTS

If visitors from another planet listened to a lecture on justifications of punishment, they might guess that there was a wide array of different punishments in order to implement the various goals. There is in fact an emergent trend to increase the variety of punishments. But perhaps surprisingly, the basic options remain few in number.

When a legislature specifies certain behavior as criminal, the statute also specifies the penalty or penalties to which a person can be subjected upon conviction. The most common penalties are a period of incarceration, a monetary fine, or both. In most states, the punishment can be suspended and the convicted person placed on probation. Finer distinctions can be made in terms of the place and length of incarceration and the amount and terms of the fine. Traditionally, probation has entailed a period of supervision by a probation officer. In recent years, other requirements have been added to the probation supervision period, such as payment of restitution to the victim or a period of community service. In some states, judges may have the option simply to suspend a sentence altogether, rather than to require supervised probation. This simple suspension may still be considered punishment, under the rationale that the conviction itself carries with it the moral condemnation of the community and, in many instances, certain collateral consequences. Finally, for a limited number of crimes, the death penalty is available in 37 states.

INCARCERATION

In most advanced countries, punishment has become nearly synonymous with **incarceration.** There is a deeply ingrained belief that unless a convicted person is confined, he or she has avoided punishment (Sherman and Hawkins, 1981:76–89). As we will see in Chapter 2, there are many more persons serving criminal sentences in noninstitutional than in institutional settings, and most of these are on some form of probation. Nevertheless, equating punishment with confinement is firmly rooted in the minds of many people, and this widespread perception may limit the legitimacy of other kinds of punishment.

In Anglo-Saxon legal tradition, there are two types of incarceration, distinguished by the seriousness of the crime: (1) A **felony** is commonly defined as a crime punishable by incarceration for a year or more in a state prison. (2) A **misdemeanor** is a crime punishable by confinement in a jail for less than a year. When a judge sentences a felon to incarceration, he or she sentences the person to the custody of a corrections department, which in turn determines the actual place and conditions of confinement. Most corrections departments have more than one prison. There is frequently a wide variety of conditions under which a convicted felon may serve a sentence of incarceration. In many systems, the period of incarceration will involve several transfers from one facility to another. In most states, the most common exit route from incarceration is through parole, a period of supervision in a noninstitutional setting while the sentence continues. If the person so released is determined to have broken the rules of parole supervision or to have committed a new crime, he or she may be revoked to serve the remainder of the original sentence in confinement.

Jails are typically reserved for the confinement of those convicted of less serious offenses or misdemeanors. Except in six states that have

In most states, prisons house felons, or inmates sentenced to serve one year or more. (David E. Duffee)

no counties, jails are usually run by local (often county) governments. In some jurisdictions, jails may be administered by a local corrections department or a local department of court services. However, jail sentences are usually served in one facility, and release prior to expiration of term has been rare until recently.

FINES

In the United States, most criminal offenses may be punished by a fine, either alone or in combination with another penalty. Violations against local laws, called ordinances, are punishable only by fines. Some statutes may indicate the specific amount of a fine, but most permit a judge some discretion in setting the amount, up to a statutory maximum.

Some years ago, it was not uncommon for a person to be fined for commission of a crime, and to be jailed immediately for failure to pay the fine. This situation was particularly common for poor defendants who could not afford to pay a lump sum. These indirect sentences to incarceration have now been limited by court decisions. An argument has been made that a poor convict must have equal opportunity to pay a fine rather than be incarcerated because of poverty (*Bearden* v. *Georgia*, 1983). On the other hand, the Supreme Court of the United States has argued that all defendants who may be incarcerated as punishment must have the right to be defended by counsel. Under this decision, ordering an uncounseled defendant to incarceration for failure to pay a fine can be construed as avoidance of the right to counsel (*Argersinger* v. *Hamlin*, 1972). As a consequence, it has become more common to set up installment plans for the payment of fines.

PROBATION

In all but three states, **probation** is not defined as a punishment, but as a suspension of punishment conditional on good behavior. Two types of suspension are possible: In some cases, the judge may pronounce the sentence, but suspend its execution and place the offender on probation. In these situations, if the offender violates the rules of probation, upon revocation the initially pronounced sentence is imposed. In other cases the judge may suspend the imposition of punishment, in which case no sentence is determined unless the probation is revoked. The supposed advantage of suspended execution is that the defendant knows while on probation what the punishment will be if he or she does not meet probation supervision standards. Presumably this acts as a deterrent. The supposed advantage for suspended imposition is that the judge may take into consideration at the later sentencing new information about the offender that has become available during the probationary period. In this case, the offender does not know what the precise penalty will be if probation is revoked, but he or she does know that the judge may consider the commission of a new crime or the violation of probation rules when determining the sentence.

As we will see in Chapter 8, although probation is legally a suspended sentence in most states, it is in practice considered a type of punishment. Since probation may involve serious impositions and restrictions on freedom, this perception is understandable. However, the legal status of probation has not yet changed to reflect this view. And with increasing frequency, probation includes more than a period of supervision by an officer of the probation department. These additions, it would appear, have emerged as a means of making probation appear harsher and therefore a more legitimate substitute for prison or jail. Three of the most common additions are an order of restitution, an order of community service, and a short jail term.

Restitution. Restitution is not a new requirement. It is not uncommon to find restitution ordered in addition to a prison sentence or as a condition of parole. However, because probation does not usually remove the offender from the community, it is typically easier for restitution to be paid from probation status (Harland, 1982).

Restitution means restoration, or the act of giving back or making whole again. Thus restitution typically involves the guilty party repaying or helping to repay the victim for damages done. This may often be a financial payment, but could also consist of services to the victim. Restitution is sometimes confused with retribution, but the two concepts should be kept separate.

Community Service. Community service sentences have also become more common in the last ten years. Often community service is ordered when the crime committed has no clear individual victim, as in vandalism of public property. Some judges have become fairly innovative in designing community service orders that may match the offense more appropriately than other punishments. For example, a police court judge in one upstate New York county sentenced a person found guilty of public urination to seven days of cleaning cages at the local animal pound. Vandals have often been sentenced to clean-up details.

Some people consider community service a type of restitution. There is a difference, however, between work orders not related to remediating damage suffered by a victim and restitution. The leading expert on community service considers it a retributive sentence (Pease, 1985).

Split Sentences. The addition of jail terms to probation sounds like a contradiction in terms, but is perhaps the best example of judges and prosecutors responding to the perceived demand to "get tough." A very common sentence, particularly for misdemeanants, is to order a short jail term, followed by a period of probation. This is often called a **split sentence.** Some argue that this allows judges to limit the use of incarceration while retaining deterrence and retribution goals in sentencing. One famous variation on the split sentence is known as **shock probation,** which is available only in some states. Where legislation allows, a judge may sentence an offender to a long jail or prison term, and then, before the expiration of the specified period, adjust the incarceration to a much shorter period to be followed by probation. The supposed shock in this split sentence is that of hearing a long confinement term pronounced at sentencing, followed by a period in which the inmate does not know if the term will be shortened.

These are the primary measures at the disposal of the state for the implementation of punishment, with the exception of the death penalty, which we discuss in Chapter 7. The limited range of punitive measures may restrict the types of offenders, and the types of crimes, that can be handled through the criminal law. The criminal justice system is aimed at the punishment of "street crimes" such as rape, robbery, and larceny. These traditional crimes have an individual transgressor and an individual victim (D. Newman, 1978). A second characteristic is that most common punishments require complex organizations, such as prisons, to carry them out. It is often problems with implementation of punishment, rather than its justifications, that makes punishment controversial.

ORGANIZATIONAL DYNAMICS AND THE NATURE OF PUNISHMENT

Crimes may occur rather quickly, but most punishments take time. During the time that an offender is subject to punishment, is everything that happens to him or her justified in the name of punishment? Obviously not. Offenders retain some freedoms during punishment, and correctional administrators have some responsibilities for continuing to treat the punished as citizens. The right to adequate medical treatment during imprisonment is a good example of the difficulties facing complex organizations charged with punishing. *Estelle* v. *Gamble* (1976) requires states to provide for serious medical needs during incarceration. While punishment is to be painful, it is not to include the pain of illness or disease. Thus the correctional system, which is responsible for punishing, also indirectly assumes re-

sponsibilities of a nonpunitive nature, such as providing medical care. Offenders are not punished in order to obtain medical care, but because punishment will endure for some time, other relationships between the punished and the punishers will occur. (A detailed examination of the legal limits on punishment can be found in Chapter 13.)

A large number of the interactions among the officials of punitive systems and the persons being punished are not considered part of punishment, but are essential parts of the correctional systems that deliver punishments. When the term "corrections" was adopted, it symbolized the rise of the rehabilitative justification and the assumption that punishment could correct either the causes of crime or its perpetrators. With the current trend toward retribution, deterrence, and incapacitation, "corrections" may be less appropriate. Nevertheless, it is probably useful to have a term other than punishment to refer to the work of the organizations that provide punishment. One would be just as inaccurate to refer to a "department of punishment" as to refer to a "department of corrections." Since **corrections** is now the traditional term by which to refer to prison systems, probation, and parole, we retain it.

We will use it to symbolize not the rehabilitative intent of such agencies, but rather to indicate that these agencies do much more than punish people. Some of those additional activities are necessitated by the basic limits on punishment; others arise out of the nature of complex organizations as behavioral systems that tend to take on a life and goals of their own, regardless of original purposes.

Perhaps the best known of all correctional organizations is the prison. In many cultures, imprisonment has become synonymous with punishment. But E. A. Fattah (1982) criticized imprisonment as a retributive sanction. He argued that because so much of what happens during a prison experience is uncontrollable and because individuals experience prison so differently, it is not possible to control the amount of pain experienced in prison. So incarceration is a faulty means of retribution, since we cannot match the severity of the crime with the amount of suffering the punished person experiences. (For a more elaborate argument along the same lines, and a controversial solution, see Insert 1.2.)

Prisons are built to punish people, but since punishment is limited, prison administrators are responsible for a host of other activities. Among the more obvious nonpunitive assignments are provisions for housing, food, and clothing. Beyond this is the problem of dealing with idleness. Should punishment mean restriction to a cell 24 hours a day? As we will see in Chapter 11, one early American prison system, which relied on solitary confinement for the duration of the sentence, was quickly abandoned. Among its other problems, the solitary system led to high rates of insanity.

But if inmates are let out of their cells and allowed to congregate with no planned activities to engage them, the incidence of violence increases. Prison administrators have the responsibility to protect inmates from attack by other inmates. Thus most prison inmates are engaged in a number of work activities as well as education and perhaps "treatment." These activities arise partially as a response to the demand to limit punishment and make it humane, even without rehabilitation as the justification. Indeed, Morris (1974) and Fogel (1975), both of whom attacked rehabilitation as a punitive purpose, insisted that inmates must have access to treatment and self-improvement resources. For these and other reasons, prison activities expand beyond punishment. In Donald Clemmer's words, the prison becomes a community (1940; and see Sykes, 1958).

Agencies responsible for nonincarcerative sanctions face similar problems, although to a lesser extent. No matter how probation and parole are defined, it may be impossible for offenders and officers to limit their interaction to the punitive aspect. Indeed, it is probably impossible for either the officer or the offender to determine what part of the interaction is punitive and what part is not (Studt, 1972). The dilemma faced by probation and parole officers who consider providing their clients with service or assistance illustrates the confusion. It is an objective of probation and parole to provide sufficient supervision and restriction that new crimes are not committed by the persons being supervised. But what should an officer do if a client is out of work? Does he say: "You must not steal in order to survive, so you must get work or I will seek a warrant for your revocation?" Or does he say: "I know an employer over on Third Street who could use a person with your skills." While the officer who provides assistance may have done more than enforce the conditions of supervision, which officer has done more to protect the public or to ensure that the sentence is served? The same difficulty may occur in prison. One guard may stand back and observe inmates, waiting to punish infractions. Another may intervene before arguments become infractions (Cressey, 1958). Which officer has performed better the task of ensuring that punishments are served quietly and without violence?

Once punishment has begun, offenders and staff will interact in a lot of ways. Some of these interactions are clearly part of the punitive process, and some are irrelevant to punishment. In between will be a large number of interactions that fall in a gray area—not clearly punitive and not altogether irrelevant. While correctional organizations expand internally beyond the interactions required by punitive purposes, these organizations also face their environments as systems seeking to survive. Correctional organizations, like any other organizations, seek to maintain a sufficient supply of resources in order to maintain their internal operations. Correctional agencies seek an adequate money supply, and they also seek to maintain a positive political image, or legitimacy, in order to obtain financial resources. Therefore, these organizations directly or indirectly enter the political debate about how public resources would be used.

Correctional organizations attempt to convince appropriate outside groups, such as legislatures, that they are necessary to the public

Insert 1.2 GRAEME NEWMAN'S PROPOSAL FOR CORPORAL PUNISHMENT

Graeme Newman's *Just and Painful: The Case for the Corporal Punishment of Criminals* (1983) met with immediate controversy. Newman put forward a strict retributivist argument for punishment, but unlike many other retributivists, attacked the use of imprisonment. He proposed instead a system of corporal punishments through the use of electroshock—which, he argued, would be more effective in achieving a match between offense and punishment.

Newman criticized other retributivists (such as von Hirsch, 1976) for equating punishment with imprisonment. The usual criticism of corporal punishments is that they are uncontrollable and inhumane. Newman countered that prisons are often at least as uncontrollable. Prisons are so heinous an option, in Newman's opinion, that they should be reserved for persons who are seen as really evil and therefore whose minds as well as bodies must be punished for long periods of time. But for most offenders, Newman asserts, society is not justified in punishing beyond the amount necessary for the particular conviction.

Since prisons inevitably entail more suffering than is related to the crime, we should seek another means to achieve retribution. A more ac-ceptable method, claimed Newman, is quick, severe, but controllable physical pain. Modern technology allows us to control the administration of physical pain more precisely than society can control its complex organizations.

Newman admitted that there would be strong objections to the use of corporal punishment as a violation of the Eighth Amendment ban on cruel and unusual punishment. But he pointed out that the Supreme Court is reluctant to classify any punishment as cruel and unusual. Additionally, he viewed the Court's objection to corporal punishment (which is by no means absolute) as illogical. If the Court were to prefer prisons to corporal punishment, Newman conjectured, it would seemingly

> ... affirm the infliction of harsh conditions, especially violence, upon the inmates largely because they are by-products of prison itself, whereas if we specifically chose to apply a violent or harsh punishment on a criminal, then this would be unconstitutional because it would be an act of "barbarous punishment."

Newman responds that the barbarism of neglect is just as barbaric as "brutality with a purpose."

welfare and could do a more effective job with an even greater share of public resources. The resource-seeking dynamic may vary from organization to organization and from state to state, but most correctional organizations are unlikely to leave their survival entirely up to outsiders. Consequently, the justifications for punishment are not always chosen by representatives elected to determine the public interest; often they are chosen by those protecting vested interests.

The trend in the United States from rehabilitation to retribution has often been perceived as the work of reformers who studied the failure of correctional organizations and demanded a change in their use. However, for correctional organizations, the discovery of rehabilitative failure was a rather large success. Since the ideological shift in the mid-seventies, these organizations have grown quickly both in perceived legitimacy and in the amount of resources appropriated. Even if the initial change in punitive philosophies did not originate with correctional organizations (and this would be difficult to rule out), these organizations succeeded in capitalizing on the new attitudes rather quickly.

A new force in the correctional political arena is associations that represent correctional personnel. Historically considered weaklings both as internal organizational forces and as political forces, associations of correctional administrators, probation and parole associations, and especially prison guard unions have gained new influence over the size of correctional appropriations and how those resources will be used. In addition, as we will see in Chapter 4, correctional staffs have expanded their domain, filling offices and carrying out responsibilities in preconviction agencies (Nelson, Ohmart, and Harlow, 1984:403–404).

As a consequence of these organized forces, correctional functions and correctional agencies have expanded. Ironically, this expansion has occurred during a period in which many groups have attempted to limit the frequency and costs of punishment. Liberal forces have sought to reduce the scope of punishment and the number of persons under correctional supervision by arguing for deinstitutionalization, diversion, and community rather than institutional programs. But a

number of reviews of these programs in practice have discovered that the organizations charged with the implementation of these reductions have actually used the new resources to increase both kinds of persons under supervision and the number of staff necessary to carry out programs (Lerman, 1975; Austin and Krisberg, 1981). Conservative forces have favored policy shifts that would reduce expenditures and limit the rehabilitative promise made by correctional agencies. However, conservatives have often been forced to increase allocations to accommodate soaring prison populations, and to support their own demands for crime control. In the next chapter, we examine how frequently the various punitive options are used, study the dramatic increase in use of punishment since 1975, and compare punishment in the United States and in other countries.

SUMMARY

1. Criminal punishment is one form of social control. Social control takes a variety of forms, some informal and some formal. Some theorists contend that as societies become more industrialized and urbanized, reliance on informal control decreases and reliance on formal control increases.
2. Criminal punishment is one form of formal social control. It relies on actions of complex organizations of officials with specific roles and responsibilities for different aspects of criminal punishment.
3. Punishment continues to be justified in a number of ways. The broadest distinction is between retributive and utilitarian justifications. The most common utilitarian justifications are deterrence, prevention of crime by the punished through incapacitation, and prevention of crime by the punished through rehabilitation. Retribution is the maintenance of the moral order, regardless of behavioral outcomes.
4. The measures used to punish have not changed a great deal since the early nineteenth century, when imprisonment became the dominant form of punishment. Incarceration of felons is accomplished in

state prisons, while misdemeanants are usually imprisoned in local jails. Fines are the most frequent form of punishment, but are usually reserved for minor offenses. Probation is the most common alternative to incarceration for more serious offenses. Probation has increasingly been coupled with additional sanctions, such as orders of restitution or community service, or a short jail term preceding the probationary period.
5. Both courts and administrators of correctional agencies have generally stressed that convict status does not justify unlimited cruelty or neglect. If one can be punished only for a wrongdoing duly proved in court, and only to the degree warranted by the seriousness of the offense, then the agencies which punish are under significant constraints to maintain order humanely. Therefore, correctional agencies have many responsibilities beyond punishment itself. The dynamics of correctional organizations seeking to sustain themselves, as well as the interaction of correctional staffs and offenders, make the tasks of corrections far more complex than the tasks of punishment.

KEY WORDS

COMMUNITY SERVICE. A punishment which requires an offender to work a specified number of hours, usually in a public or nonprofit organization.

CRIMINAL PUNISHMENT. "Persons who possess authority impose designedly unpleasant consequences upon, and express their condemnation of, other persons who are capable of choice and who have breached established standards of behavior" (Greenwalt, 1983:343–344).

DETERRENCE. Justification of punishment that seeks to use punishment to dissuade others from committing similar crimes.

FELONY. A crime punishable by incarceration in a state or federal prison for at least a year.

FORMAL CONTROL A social control which is governed by written rules and usually employing formal organizations for implementation.

INCAPACITATION. Justification of punishment that seeks to reduce crime in society by preventing a convicted offender from committing new crimes.

INCARCERATION. Confinement in a prison or jail as punishment for a crime.

MISDEMEANOR. A crime punishable by incarceration for less than a year, usually in a local jail.

PROBATION. Freedom granted by a judge to an offender under conditions supervised by an officer. In most states, legally defined as a suspension of sentence.

PUNITIVE INTENT STANDARD. A standard that distinguishes incarceration from other forms of confinement, such as detention, on the grounds of a demonstrable alternative purpose for the confinement, and reasonable relationships between the confinement practice and the alternate purpose.

REHABILITATION. A justification for punishment that seeks to reduce new crimes by a convicted offender by changing attitudes, values, beliefs, or behavior.

RESTITUTION Action by an offender to restore a victim to his or her condition prior to a crime.

RETRIBUTION. Justification for punishment on the grounds that it is a moral duty for society to punish wrongdoers in order to maintain the moral order. Usually includes the notion of just desert—that the seriousness of punishment be commensurate with the seriousness of the offense.

SHOCK PROBATION. Judicial resentencing to probation after an initially imposed incarcerative sentence has begun.

SOCIAL CONTROL. Any behaviors, formal or informal, that identify and attempt to control deviant behavior.

SPLIT SENTENCE. Any sentence that includes an incarcerative term preceding a period of probation.

UTILITARIAN JUSTIFICATIONS OF PUNISHMENT. Justifications which promise an empirical benefit from punishment, such as deterrence, incapacitation, and rehabilitation.

PROJECTS AND QUESTIONS

1. Greenwalt (1983) raises the following question about the fairness involved in retribution:

> If someone has achieved a comparative advantage over another by an unjust act, does fairness to the person suffering a comparative disadvantage require stripping the offender of his advantaage, even when that would do nothing to improve the position of the disadvantaged person?

Does this question indicate a weakness in retributive theory, or does Greenwalt misunderstand the nature of the advantages and disadvantages discussed in retributive theory? Should retribution ad-

dress the suffering of the victim? If so, how, if at all, does the use of imprisonment aid the victim?

2. Charles Tittle's examination of deterrence includes the finding that informal sanctions are more effective when the threat of their impact appears quite certain, while formal sanctions are more effective when the threat of their impact appears quite severe (1980:322–323). Does such a finding suggest that persons who have few attachments to friends, family, or other informal sanctioners can be controlled only by severe criminal punishments? Would this policy imply that middle-class persons who commit crimes should be punished less severely than per-

sons without stable families and occupations? Or would it mean that middle-class persons who have committed crimes despite presumably strong informal controls should be more severely punished? Or would it suggest that policy should aim to improve the informal controls on all persons, rather than to invest in punishments at all?

3. Do you agree that complex societies have reduced avenues of informal control and have become increasingly reliant on formal control systems? If so, why?

4. What do you think about the proposition that coerced treatments are ineffective? If treatment works only with those who seek treatment voluntarily, does this mean that they work only with those who have less severe problems? Is it fair to limit treatment to those who are well enough to understand that they need help?

ADDITIONAL READING

American Friends Service Committee. *Struggle for Justice* (New York: Hill and Wang, 1971). This is the landmark tract against the rehabilitative ideal as a justification for punishment. It is significant not only as a major policy statement concerning the evil consequences of good intentions, but is historically significant because the Quakers were influential in arguing for the use of the earliest American penitentiaries as humane and reformative punitive measures.

Norval Morris. *The Future of Imprisonment* (Chicago: University of Chicago Press, 1974). One of the more influential books in altering punishment policy. Morris asserts that prisoners deserve access to rehabilitative programs, but not in the context of setting the length of incarceration. He argues for reserving prisons for the more seriously violent offenders and concludes with a model prison program which the Federal Bureau of Prisons attempted to implement at its Butner, North Carolina, facility.

Joan Petersilia, Susan Turner, James Kahan, and Joyce Peterson. *Granting Felons Probation: Public Risks and Alternatives* (Santa Monica, CA: RAND Corporation, 1985). This report indicates that despite the get-tough movement in American corrections, more and more felons are being placed on probation because prisons are already overcrowded. An influential research project, particularly for those concerned about protection rather than retribution.

Andrew von Hirsch. *Doing Justice: The Choice of Punishments* (New York: Hill and Wang, 1976). One of the earlier determinant sentencing schemes founded upon retributive justifications for punishment. A good example of both the difficulties in attempting to match punishments and offenses, and an example of the fact that retributive punishments need not be more severe than those based on rehabilitative concerns.

2 THE USE OF CRIMINAL SANCTIONS

QUESTIONS

1. How frequently are different criminal sanctions used?

2. In the United States, has the frequency of punishment changed over time? In what direction?

3. What factors control the size of prison populations?

4. Can we explain changes in incarceration rate by examining social and economic factors? By studying policy changes?

5. Is the use of punishment similar in different states? In different countries?

THE OLD BARN AND THE NEW CEMENT BLOCKS

Phil was supervising the correctional internships at the university. Today he was off to the southern border of the state, to the Chauncey County Penitentiary. Phil remembered one journal entry from Joe Kulick, the student intern there:

2/12. Today I got the chance to see the old Chauncey jail. It's basically an old barn on a back street near the courthouse. I was told by the sheriff that the old jail was condemned five years ago and the county really had to scramble to find the money to build a new one. There is such a difference between the old building and the new one. I don't know how they used to operate out of the old facility. I asked the sheriff, but he said that in the old place they didn't have too many inmates. So not too many problems came up. Now they have sixty inmates most of the time, because the judges don't feel too bad sending someone there.

Somehow the county justice system had operated for years without incarcerating many people. But now there was a spanking new facility, with automatic doors and electronic cell surveillance. All of a sudden, the judges were discovering all sorts of evildoers who needed a taste of the new bars.

Phil found the new facility without trouble. It stood 4 miles east of town, next to

This chapter was written by Shelley L. Kath.

the county garage. The sheriff was proud of his new building. Phil was shown the new control center, which appeared to have fancier equipment than the one in the state prison at Dunmore. He saw the combination cafeteria/recreation room, a special cellblock for intensive monitoring (to help reduce suicides, said the sheriff), and a separate wing set aside for work release (inmates could come and go to work through a separate entrance, so there would be no contact with the regular inmates and less contraband).

Winding up the tour, the sheriff grinned. "You know the only problem? Well, we built this place based on population projections off the old facility. But we're already full up. Should have made it twice as big."

When he returned to the university the next day, he bumped into Jackson Green at the coffee pot. Phil had to tell someone about this situation.

Jackson stood quietly, sipping hot coffee, and listening patiently while Phil sputtered through a long-winded account of the situation at Chaunceyville. "And, you know," said Phil finally, "the guy doesn't show the least bit of discomfort. Why I bet he and the judges had to fill the place up just because it was there. I mean you can't spend five million bucks and leave it half empty, can you?"

Jackson smiled and opened on a skeptical note. "Are you sure, though, that they are actually locking up more people now than before?"

Phil was disappointed. "I said they had

Drastic increases in prison populations have been followed by massive prison construction campaigns in many states. (New York State Department of Correctional Services)

THE USE OF CRIMINAL SANCTIONS **29**

an average population of twenty a day and now they have sixty. Doesn't that say enough?"

Jackson frowned. "I'd say you're going a bit fast. I mean I certainly wouldn't be surprised if the new building caused some pressure to fill it up, sure. But don't you have to ask where the inmates came from?"

"What do you mean, Jackson?"

"I'm no expert on this criminal justice stuff, but don't you think it's possible that the judges are putting more people in the jail now that last year they might have shipped off to the state prison? Maybe the jail hasn't increased incarceration at all, just changed where it occurs."

"I hadn't thought of that," said Phil. "But I bet most of those inmates would have been on probation."

Jackson shrugged. "Maybe so. But you can't tell without the data. Well, it makes a better story your way. I gotta go."

Maybe he's right, thought Phil. But think of all the data you'd have to collect. We'd have to control for changes in the county population; we'd have to get complete data on characteristics for inmates in the old system, and the same data for inmates in the new system; and compare jail and prison commitments before and after the new jail was constructed. Phil walked off, shaking his head. Next time he'd be more careful about drawing conclusions.

PRISON AND JAIL POPULATIONS

Prison populations have been increasing since before 1925, except for temporary declines in the late 1930s and 1940s (World War II) and in the 1960s (Vietnam era). As Figure 2.1 suggests, some of this increase is attributable to increases in the general population. But, the prison population varies substantially over time, and is ob-

viously influenced by factors other than growth of the civilian population. In this chapter, we will examine recent trends in the use of prison, jail, and probation. Then we will consider some of the explanations for the large and swift increase in incarceration during the 1970s. We will review the evidence on whether prison populations expand to fill the available space (as Phil seemed to believe), or whether less visible factors are at work.

THE OVERCROWDING CRISIS

The number of persons in state and federal prisons at year-end 1984 was 445,381. This figure is nearly 2.3 times the number at year-end 1970 (See Table 2.2). The state and federal prison population only slightly more than doubled during the 44 years prior to 1970 (McGarrell and Flanagan, 1985:647). After the decline during the Vietnam era, the prison population began to rise rapidly. From 1972 to 1978, a 50 percent increase occurred nationwide (1985:647). State-level growth during this period was severe in several states. Florida, New York, and Delaware experienced increases of 100 percent, 75 percent, and 260 percent, respectively (Mullen, 1980:15). In 1983, Delaware Corrections Commissioner John Sullivan predicted that if his state's prison population continued to increase at the same rate, the entire state population would be locked up within 20 years (Gettinger, 1983:5).

With the exception of a slight abatement in growth from 1978 to 1980, prison populations have continued to rise sharply since the early 1970s and they are now at record levels. The annual growth rate has recently slowed; the annual increase of 6.1 percent between 1983 and 1984 is substantially lower than the peak rates of 12.2 percent and 11.9 percent in 1980–81 and 1981–82 (Bureau of Justice Statistics, hereafter BJS, April 1985:1). But to put this slowdown in persepctive, the annual growth rate prior to the peak was only 2.3 percent.

FIGURE 2.1   Sentenced Prisoners in State and Federal Institutions on Dec. 31 and Estimated Resident Population on July 1, United States, 1925–1978

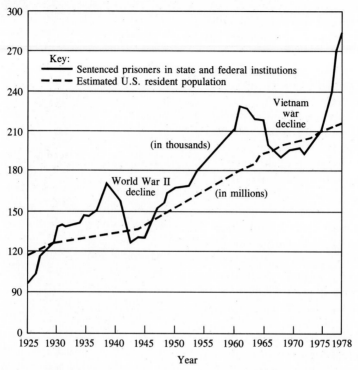

NOTE: Prison population data were compiled by a yearend census of prisoners held in custody in State and Federal institutions. Prior to Dec. 31, 1971, a "sentenced prisoner" was counted as any adult felon serving a sentence in a State or Federal correctional institution. Beginning on Dec. 31, 1971, respondents were asked to disregard the difference between felons and misdemeanants and to count as a "sentenced prisoner" those inmates who had been sentenced as adults or youthful offenders to a maximum term of at least 1 year and 1 day. Comparability of the data is affected by the various reporting differences.

Beginning on Dec. 31, 1978, a distinction was made between prisoners "in custody" and prisoners "under jurisdiction." As defined in the 1978 report (U.S. Department of Justice, Law Enforcement Assistance Administration, *Prisoners in State and Federal Institutions on December 31, 1978*, National Prisoner Statistics Bulletin SD-NPS-PSF-6 [Washington, D.C.: U.S. Government Printing Office, 1980]), "in custody" refers to the direct physical control and responsibility for the body of a confined person. "Under jurisdiction" is defined as follows: A State or Federal prison system has jurisdiction over a person if it retains the legal power to incarcerate the person in one of its own prisons. Jurisdiction is not determined by an inmate's physical location; jurisdiction is determined by the legal authority controlling the inmate. Examples of prisoners under the jurisdiction of a given system, but not in its custody, are those housed in local jails, in other States, or in hospitals (including mental health facilities) outside the correctional system; inmates out on work release, furlough, or bail; and State prisoners held in Federal prisons or vice versa.

Custody figures for 1977 may differ from those published in *Prisoners in State and Federal Institutions on December 31, 1977*, U.S. Department of Justice, Law Enforcement Assistance Administration National Prisoner Statistics Bulletin SD-NPS-PSF-5, because some States have refined their definitions of custody in light of the guidelines provided for the 1978 report.

The U.S. resident population is compiled by the U.S. Bureau of the Census. Estimates are presented for July 1. Excluded from the resident population are all armed forces abroad, as well as Alaska and Hawaii prior to 1940. Population estimates for 1925 to 1969 were taken from U.S. Department of Commerce, Bureau of the Census, *Statistical Abstract of the United States, 1976* (Washington, D.C.: U.S. Government Printing Office, 1976), p. 5, No. 2. Population estimates for 1970 to 1978 were taken from U.S. Department of Commerce, Bureau of the Census, *Current Population Reports* (Washington, D.C.: U.S. Government Printing Office, 1980), Series P-25, No. 880.

SOURCE: Michael Hindelang, Michael R. Gottfredson, and Timothy Flanagan, *Sourcebook on Criminal Justice Statistics—1980.* Washington, DC: Bureau of Justice Statistics, 1981, p. 491.

Since resources have failed to keep pace with demand for prison and jail space, institutions are overcrowded. In 1984, state prisons were estimated to be operating at approximately 10 percent over capacity. Federal prisons were estimated to average 24 percent over capacity (BJS, 1985:5). This level of overcrowding has existed for several years, but the number of prisoners as a percentage of capacity has not changed since 1978 (BJS, 1985:5). From 1972 to 1977, construction or remodeling increased reported prison capacity by about 23,000 beds. But the population increase for the same period was 81,000 (Mullen, 1980:12).

A study of prisons and jails in the United States, conducted for the U.S. Congress by Abt Associates, examined the extent of overcrowding in prisons, jails, and community prerelease centers in the late 1970s (Mullen, 1980). The study revealed that in 1978, 44 percent of state prisoners and 46 percent of federal prisoners lived in "crowded" conditions. Abt defined crowded as conditions in which inmates had less than 60 square feet of floor space and lived in a cell occupied by more than one person (Mullen, 1980:61–63). Figure 2.2 displays the overcrowding situation in 1978 by state. The data reveal huge variations across the nation in severity of crowding. Of the 4 percent of state and federal prisoners living in prerelease centers in 1978, 55 percent lived in facilities having less than 60 square feet per resident. Overcrowding in jails was just as severe, with over 50 percent of all jail inmates living in crowded conditions (1980:75).

Part of the jail crowding problem in 1978 stemmed from the fact that 45 percent of all jail inmates in the country were housed in only 4 percent of the jails (1980:73). Another factor was the increasing number of prisoners held in local jails due to crowding in state facilities. Table 2.1 shows that the number of such prisoners assigned to local jails from 1981 to 1984 increased from 6,900 to 11,555, with the most dramatic increase occurring in 1984. During that year, 2.8 percent

of the state prison population was held in local jails, and 17,365 early releases occurred due to overcrowding (BJS, April 1985:7). Again, great variation across the states existed. In 1983, 22 states and the District of Columbia reported no prisoners held in jails due to overcrowding (McGarrell and Flanagan, 1985:643). Four states—Alabama, Louisiana, Mississippi, and New Jersey—had almost two-thirds of all the state prisoners held in local jails at the end of 1982 (BJS, October 1983:20)

Although the nation's jail population is currently on the rise, the increase is fairly recent. According to the Abt study, the jail population nationwide actually decreased by 2 percent from 1970 to 1978 (Mullen, 1980:20). As emphasized in that report, jail populations are very unstable because of rapid turnover of inmates. So population figures must be interpreted cautiously. One reason for such rapid turnover in jail bedspace is that jails house many types of inmates for various purposes. Of those housed in 1978, for example, about half were awaiting trial and less than a third were serving sentences (1980:72). Jail populations underwent a sudden increase of 41 percent from 1978 to 1983, according to the most recent jail census (BJS, 1984:2).

A decrease in the number of jails has taken place since 1970, when 4,037 jails were reported in the census for that year (Mullen, 1980:1). During the huge growth in population from 1978 to 1983, the number of jails decreased by 4 percent. The decrease may not be a serious factor in the overcrowding crisis, however, because many municipal and county jails simply merged into joint complexes. Thus, although there were fewer jails, some now had larger capacities (BJS, November 1985:5). In contrast to the jail trend, the number of state and federal facilities increased by nearly 37 percent from 1970 to 1978 (Mullen, 1980:156). Although the number of prisons has been rising since before 1900, the growth rate has been exceptionally high since 1970. In the 1960s, in fact, some correctional facilities were empty and closing.

FIGURE 2.2 Percentage of Inmates Held in Crowded Confinement Units in State and Federal Correctional Facilities by State, March 1978

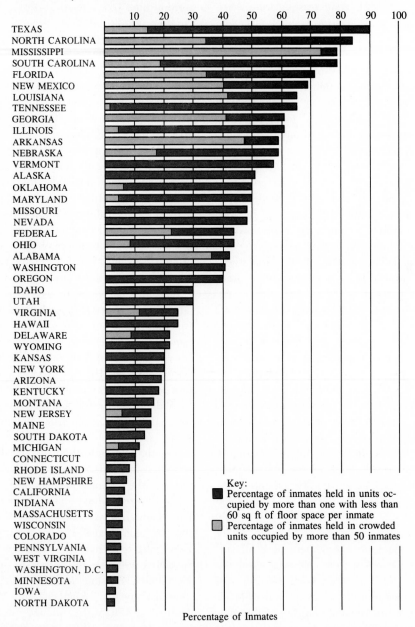

NOTE: A "crowded" confinement unit is a cell or dormitory with two or more inmates and less than 60 square feet of floor space per inmate.

SOURCE: Joan Mullen, *American Prisons and Jails*, Vol. 1. Washington, DC: National Institute of Justice, 1980.

TABLE 2.1   Number of Prisoners held in Local
Jails because of Overcrowding, 1981–1984

YEAR END	NUMBER OF PRISONERS
1981	6,900
1982	8,689
1983	8,078
1984	11,555

SOURCE: Data for 1981–1983 from *Sourcebook of Criminal Justice Statistics—1984*, Edmund McGarrell and Timothy Flanagan (eds)., 1985:643. Data for 1984 from *Prisoners in 1984*, BJS, April 1985:5.

INCARCERATION RATES

In order to examine trends in the use of prison and jail over time, it is necessary to consider more than just changes in confined populations. The rate of those in prisons and jails per 100,000 civilian residents provides a more accurate measure of correctional trends. Through an examination of yearly rates, for example, we can surmise whether changes in the incarcerated population can be accounted for by changes in the general population, or should be attributed to other factors.

The term **prison incarceration rate** will be used to refer to the number of state and federal prisoners serving sentences of more than one year, per 100,000 civilian population. The term **jail confinement rate** will refer to the number of persons occupying local jails, per 100,000 population. Both sentenced and unsentenced prisoners are counted in jail confinement rates, with the sentenced inmates usually serving one year or less (BJS, November 1984:1).

Prison incarceration rates from 1970 to 1984 and jail confinement rates for the years 1970, 1972, 1978, and 1983 are presented in Table 2.2. The incarceration rate declined slightly in the early 1970s, continuing a trend begun about 1962. The rate began to rise in 1972, and by 1984 it had increased by over 100 percent. Not until 1980, when the rate reached 138 per 100,000, did the prision incarceration rate surpass an earlier record high of 137 reached in

1939 (BJS, December 1982:1). The prison incarceration rate of 188 reported in 1984 is the highest ever recorded.

Incarceration rates appear more severe when presented as age- and sex-specific rates. In 1982, when the total prison rate was 183, the rate for males was 360 (females 15) and the rate for blacks was 716 (whites 114). The rate for black males was 1,445 compared to the white male rate of 225 (McGarrell and Flanagan, 1985:654). More will be said about race and sex differences later in the text (see especially Chapter 6).

The jail confinement rate, as Table 2.2 shows, seems to follow a pattern similar to the prison rate, dropping from 80 in 1970 to 69 in 1972, and then rising to a record level of 98 in 1984. Still, marked differences exist in the growth and decline of the two rates during specific periods. The jail rate appeared to drop much more sharply than the prison rate from 1970 to 1972 and then increased at a much slower pace from 1972 to 1978. From 1978 to 1983, the jail rate increased almost 30 percent, coming nearer to the prison rate increase of 36 percent for that period.

The reasons for slower growth in jail populations and confinement rates, in comparison to prison populations and incarceration rates, are not well understood (BJS, October 1983:82). It may be that one-day counts of population made during each jail census are inaccurate due to rapid turnover of jail inmates. It has been suggested that the true rate of change in jails since 1972 has been underestimated (BJS, October 1983:82). Problems in jail data considered, we can see from Table 2.2 that in 1970 approximately 176 out of every 100,000 people in the United States was incarcerated. In 1978, this figure reached 208, and in 1983 a record 277 per 100,000 were inmates in the United States.

THE USE OF PROBATION

The largest group of offenders in the criminal justice system are on probation. Figure 2.3 shows that probationers made up 63 percent of all those

TABLE 2.2   Prison and Jail Populations and Incarceration Rates for Selected Years, 1970–1984

YEAR	TOTAL INCARCERATED[f]	RATE OF TOTAL INCARCERATED	TOTAL STATE AND FEDERAL SENTENCED PRISONERS[a]	RATE OF SENTENCED PRISONERS PER 100,000 POPULATION	TOTAL INMATES IN LOCAL JAILS	RATE OF JAILED INMATES PER 100,000 POPULATION
1970	357,292	176	196,429	96	160,863[b]	80
1971	—	—	198,061	95	—	—
1972	337,680	162	196,092	93	141,588[c]	69
1973	—	—	204,211	96	—	—
1974	—	—	218,466	102	—	—
1975	—	—	240,593	111	—	—
1976	—	—	262,833	120	—	—
1977	—	—	278,141	126	—	—
1978	452,790	208	294,396	132	158,394[d]	76
1979	—	—	301,470	133	—	—
1980	—	—	315,974	138	—	—
1981	—	—	353,167	153	—	—
1982	—	—	394,374	170	—	—
1983	643,371	277	419,820	179	223,551[e]	98
1984	—	—	445,381	188	—	—

[a] Figures are for prisoners sentenced for more than one year in state or federal facilities who were present on December 31 of the year. Also 1970–1977 figures are for those "in custody." Beginning in 1978, prisoners were counted according to those "under jurisdiction" (BJS, December 1982: 3–4).
[b] All jail inmates present on March 15, 1970.
[c] Jail inmates present on June 30, 1972.
[d] Jail inmates present on June 30, 1978.
[e] Jail inmates present on June 30, 1983.
[f] The "total incarcerated" population and rate columns are rough approximations only, due to differences in the dates on which prisoner and jail populations were counted. Furthermore, this "total incarcerated" does not include those under state and federal jurisdiction who were unsentenced or sentenced to one year or less (such as inmates in federal or state-administered jails who are serving one year or less). Finally, the figures shown may be slightly inflated due to the fact that jail inmates who are under jurisdiction of state or federal authorities *and* who are sentenced to more than one year are included in both the jail and the prison data.

SOURCE: Columns 3 and 4 from *Sourcebook of Criminal Justice Statistics 1984*, Edmund McGarrell and Timothy Flanagan (eds). U.S. Department of Justice, Bureau of Justice Statistics. Washington, DC: U.S. Government Printing Office, 1985: 647,648. Data for 1984 in those columns is from *Prisoners in 1984*, Bureau of Justice Statistics Bulletin, April 1985: 2. Columns 5 and 6 are from *The 1983 Jail Census*, Bureau of Justice Statistics Bulletin, November 1984: 1, 2, 10.

under some form of correctional supervision, while prisoners represented 18 percent, jail inmates 9 percent, and parolees 10 percent. Examination of trends in probation is difficult because of the lack of yearly statistical reports for the nation prior to 1981. Furthermore, a number of problems concerning variation in reporting practices among states before 1981 makes the earlier data less reliable than those of more recent years. The statistics on probationers provided by BJS in its annual reports since 1981 are limited to adult probationers who have been placed under supervision of a probation agency as a consequence of a court order. It excludes certain probationers who are not receiving supervision (BJS, September 1984:1).

Between 1975 and 1983, the probation population increased by about 63 percent from a starting population of about 580,000 (Petersilia et al., 1985:1). The prison population grew at the lower rate of 48 percent. Figure 2.4 illustrates the approximate changes in prison, parole, and

FIGURE 2.3   Persons under Correctional Supervision, by Type of Supervision, on December 31, 1983

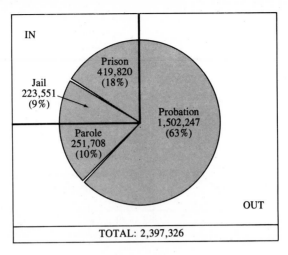

TOTAL: 2,397,326

NOTE: Excludes Indiana. Jail figure represents persons in jail on June 30, 1983.

SOURCE: Probation, parole, and prison data are from *Probation and Parole, 1983*, Bulletin NCJ-94776, Bureau of Justice Statistics, September 1984, p. 2. Jail figure is from *The 1983 Jail Census*, Bulletin NCJ-95536, Bureau of Justice Statistics, November 1984, p. 1.

probation populations during that decade. Since 1979, the number of probationers has increased by more than 38 percent, about the same level of increase as in the prison population during that period (BJS, September 1984:1). As of 1983, the probation population exceeded 1.5 million (September 1984:1). The rate of probationers per 100,000 population has increased by about 31 percent since 1980. In 1983, 897 of every 100,000 adults in the United States were probationers (September 1984:5). The rates have far exceeded prison and jail rates over the years. Data for 1979 show that the probation rate equaled, approximately, the violent crime rate, a pattern consistent across regions (National Council on Crime and Delinquency, 1981:13). Figure 2.5 depicts the trends by region.

It has been suggested that one major factor behind the increasing use of probation is the rise of probation for felons as prison space has become increasingly scarce. Petersilia (1985:4) comments: "Prison crowding has become so critical that the courts have increasingly used probation

to catch the overflow." She found that over one-third of the adult probationers were felons rather than misdemeanants. However, an earlier study reported that the felony-misdemeanor ratio for probation has been relatively constant since 1979, with probation being granted almost equally to misdemeanants and felons (National Council on Crime and Delinquency, 1981:9).

BJS reported that in 1983 the largest probation population (14.5 percent of the national total) belonged to Texas (September 1984:1). The increase in the Texas probation population occurred simultaneously with the first prison population reduction (− 2.5 percent) in that state since 1974 (September 1984:1). In 1983, 41 states, the District of Columbia, and the federal system all saw increases in probation population, although as with incarceration rates, a great amount of variation was reported (September 1984:1).

In 1979, the North Central and Southern regions were virtually identical in their proportions of prison, jail, probation, and conditional release populations. In these two regions, probation pop-

FIGURE 2.4   Change in U.S. Parole, Probation, and Prison Populations, 1974–1983

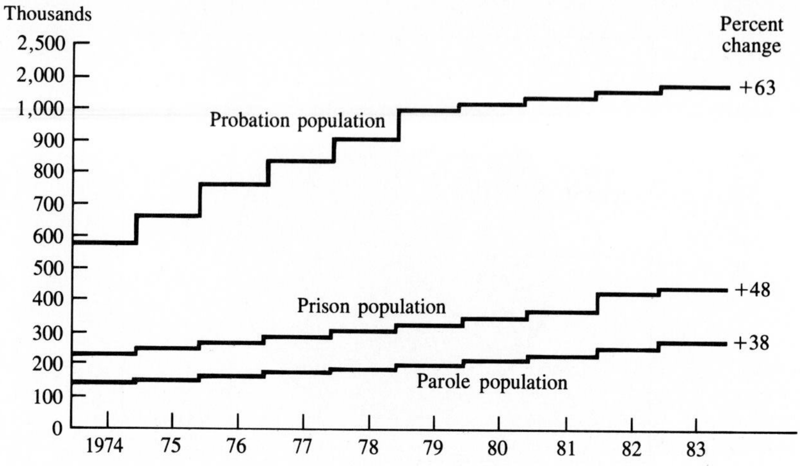

SOURCE: *Federal Probation* 49 (2), June 1985, p. 4.

ulations were lower and prison populations higher than the national averages (National Council on Crime and Delinquency, 1981:14–15). Proportions of sanctioned populations for the Northeast and West were also very similar, with the relative proportion of probationers being higher than the national level (1981: 14–15). Despite variations across states and regions, probation has grown in all regions, and one recent prediction stated that probation "will continue to grow in the forseeable future" (Nelson, Ohmart, and Harlow, 1984:404).

Sentences that combine probation with limited periods of incarceration represent a special type of "hybrid sentence" (Parisi, 1984:72), which is on the rise. Shock probation and split sentences are the most common alternatives of this type. The growth of hybrid sentences may be due in part to judicial avoidance of the new restrictions on traditional sentences (1984:72). The number of split sentences for federal prisoners increased from 1,168 in 1963 to 3,538 in 1983 (Brown, Flanagan, and McLeod, 1984:504–505). In 1983, 3 of the 16 states reporting data on mixed sentences (Maine, Michigan, and North Dakota) reported that 30 percent or more of their

probationers had also served some time in jail or prison (BJS, September 1984:3). In the federal system, 4,334 (18 percent of total entries) to federal probation involved split sentences in 1983 (September 1984:4).

DIRECT DETERMINANTS OF PRISON POPULATION

The size of a prison population over any given period of time is basically determined by the numbers of prisoners admitted and the length of time they actually serve in prison before release (Mullen, 1980:11). Because many of the decisions affecting inflow and outflow are made by sentencing and parole authorities, prisons have relatively little control over the inputs and the outputs (Gottfredson and Taylor, 1984:194). Inputs are regulated primarily by the decision of whether or not to incarcerate and by the rate of new admissions to prisons. Outputs are heavily affected by the decision to release on parole, which is still a major factor affecting time served in most states.

FIGURE 2.5 Violent Crimes, Jail Population, Prison Population, Conditional Release Population, and Probation Population per 100,000 Population, 1979

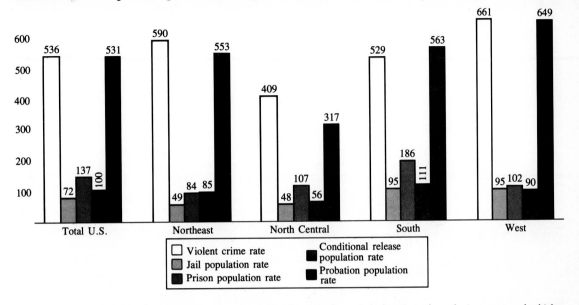

The Northeast and the West have violent crime rates higher than the national rate; in both regions, the probation rates are also higher than the national rate and somewhat lower than their crime rates. All other rates (jail, prison, conditional release) in these two regions, except the jail rate in the West, are lower than the national rates.

The North Central has a crime rate considerably lower than the nation's; its sanction rates all are considerably lower as well. The North Central's probation rate falls far behind its crime rate (22 percent lower).

The South's crime rate is slightly below the nation's; all its sanction rates, however, are higher than the nation's. The South is the only region with a probation rate higher than its crime rate.

SOURCE: National Council on Crime and Delinquency Research Center, West, *Probation in the United States*, 1979. San Francisco: National Council on Crime and Delinquency, 1981. Reprinted by permission.

INPUTS TO THE PRISONS

The lack of a national reporting system for sentencing renders in/out data "one of the more elusive figures in criminal justice . . . " (Parisi, 1984:65). Parisi reports that estimates of granting probation, the most frequent "out" sentence in serious crimes, range from 50 to 80 percent (1984:65).

Trend data for the in/out decision are available only for federal defendants (McGarrell and Flanagan, 1985:572–573). The number of defendants given sentences of imprisonment (jail or prison) as a percentage of the total sentenced has stayed relatively stable since about 1970, with the average being 46.6 percent. Although the percentage of inmates given in rather than out sentences rose slightly from 1981 to 1983, the figure of 50 percent for 1983 was no higher than the percentage in 1973 (1985:572–573). It does not appear that judges in federal district courts are sentencing offenders to prison rather than nonincarcerative options much more frequently now than in the past. But data from the federal system may not be representative of the trends among the states (see Chapter 11 for some important differences between the federal and state systems). BJS statistics, for example, reported that the record prison population growth (state and federal combined) in 1981 and 1982 resulted partly from a greater chance of being sentenced to prison during that time (September 1984:3).

In 1983, the chance of receiving a prison sentence lessened slightly due to the increased use of probation. This may have contributed to a less drastic prison population growth rate in that year.

Although systematic in/out data are basically unavailable for the states, some information about inputs to state prisons is available in prison admission data. Except in 1978, new commitments to state prisons have increased every year since 1974. The most drastic increases occurred in 1979 and 1982, when new admissions rose an average of 15,413, and from 1974 to 1975, when new admissions numbered 23,560. New court commitments to federal institutions have followed a somewhat different pattern: A gradual increase occurred from 1970 to about 1977, followed by a slight decline until 1982, when new admissions ballooned (McGarrell and Flanagan, 1985:572–573).

Although the number of new admissions to prison has exceeded the number of prison releases since 1981, a significant decline in the amount of serious crime has occurred. The ratio of prison admissions to serious crimes has increased significantly. By year-end 1983, the ratio for state prisons was 4.0, the highest since 1965 (BJS, April 1985:4). More will be said shortly on the relationship between crime rates and incarceration rate.

OUTPUTS FROM PRISONS

Correctional populations are regulated by outputs from the system as well as inputs. The actual time served by inmates affects the frequency with which prisoners leave the prison. Short sentences and brief periods of time served in areas such as Scandinavia may be one of the strongest factors limiting rapid growth of prison populations in those countries (Downes, 1982; Fitzmaurice and Peace, 1982).

In the United States, it is likely that time served, at least in state facilities, has been on the rise due to many recent changes in some of the mechanisms that control time served (BJS, August 1983:1). Determinate sentencing and mandatory prison terms for certain offenses,

among other things, may have resulted in longer time served than would have occurred under indeterminate sentencing. In states with determinate sentencing, those sentenced to prison received fixed sentences that must be served in full, sometimes with time off for good behavior (good time). As of 1983, only 9 states had determinate sentencing systems (BJS, August 1983:3). Almost all states now have mandatory prison terms for certain offenses (violent crimes, narcotic/drug law violations), and many have mandatory terms for repeat offenders. Although determinate sentencing could only have affected time served in less than one-fifth of the states, the adoption of more mandatory prison terms could be expected to raise time served in many states. National data on time served are generally not available, but data from 12 states indicate that the average prison stay is currently between 1.5 and 2.5 years for felony offenders. Table 2.3 gives the average time served for specific offenses.

In addition to the influence of new sentencing practices, relatively recent changes in parole release policies may have contributed to increases in time served. From 1979 to 1983, the parole population grew only 15 percent, with most of the growth (12 percent) occurring in 1983 (BJS, September 1984:1). The slow growth rate from 1979 to 1982 was due in part to the fact that an increasing number of states were restricting or abolishing discretionary release by parole boards and relying more on mandatory release options (September 1984:1). This tends to result in delayed release for many prisoners, and hence longer time served. It was a lessened chance of release on parole that may have contributed to the record prison growth in 1981 and 1982 (September 1983:3).

ARE PUNISHMENTS REALLY INCREASING?

Are we experiencing increases in the punishments of probation, jail, and prison? Although the data strongly suggest that the overall trend

TABLE 2.3   Average (Mean) Time Served for Specific Offenses, in Months

STATE AND RELEASE PERIOD	CRIMINAL HOMICIDE[a]	RAPE	ROBBERY	AGGRA- VATED ASSAULT	BURG- LARY	LARCENY	AUTO THEFT	ARSON	DRUG OF- FENSES[b]
Delaware, 1980–82[c]	74.3	25.5	39.3	18.6	15.7	6.5	12.8	9.4	15.0
Illinois, 1978–82[d]	52.1	46.0	29.1	18.7	20.7	14.1	*	*	*
Iowa, 1979–83[c]	72.4	47.1	51.7	33.1	30.5	22.7	15.5	29.9	24.0
Maryland, 1982[c]	63.1	63.7	61.5	30.0	29.2	14.2	20.9	35.6	15.9
North Carolina, 1977–81[c,e]	51.3	*	40.8	19.7	22.2	*	19.4	*	15.7
Ohio, 1980–81	78.6	50.0	34.9	26.6	27.0	15.4	24.9	22.5	17.3
Oklahoma, 1982	39.3	35.6	29.7	17.4	13.8	11.8	15.1	16.4	11.4
Oregon, 1979–82	41.2	36.0	25.2	23.1	15.3	11.3	11.9	25.5	10.4
Pennsylvania, 1981–82[c]	57.4	47.7	33.5	25.4	22.6	16.8	14.8	28.2	18.9
Washington, 7/81–6/82	63.2	36.3	38.8	37.0	*	*	*	*	17.8
Wisconsin, 1/80–5/83	41.8	33.5	42.3	30.7	26.5	22.6	20.6	24.7	22.3
Wyoming, 7/80–6/83[c]	59.5	51.5	29.5	29.4	22.5	15.8	18.2	25.8	15.2

[a] Includes murder and nonnegligent manslaughter.
[b] Includes sale and possession.
[c] Includes credited jail time.
[d] See footnote d, table 1.
[e] Derived from data in Clarke, Stevens H. et al, *North Carolina's Determinate Sentencing Legislation: An Evaluation of the First Year's Experience*, Institute of Government, University of North Carolina at Chapel Hill, October 1983.
* Data not available.
SOURCE: Bureau of Justice Services Special Report, *Time Served in Prison*, June 1984: 3.

since about 1930 has been upward, not all researchers agree that a real increase in punishment has taken place. Alfred Blumstein and associates have argued for a **stability of punishment hypothesis** which states that the proportion of people who are punished in a given society should remain stable over time, with minor variation (Blumstein and Cohen, 1979). Restating and illuminating the stability of punishment hypothesis, Blumstein and Moitra (1979:376) argued that if the amount of criminal activity in a society increased, "a society could find itself unable or unwilling either economically or politically to cope with that volume" and might decriminalize certain behaviors or reduce penalties. Conversely, if criminal activity declined, some noncriminal acts could be considered criminal. Blumstein and Moitra contend that variations in the level of punishment around a stable level occur because it takes several years for reactive shifts to take place (1979:376).

Blumstein and colleagues found evidence to support this hypothesis in a series of studies (Blumstein and Cohen, 1973; Blumstein, Cohen and Nagin, 1977; Blumstein and Moitra, 1979). Later, criticizing a study that found a fluctuating but increasing rate in incarceration from 1880 to 1970 (Cahalan, 1979), Blumstein and Moitra stated a major caveat to their hypothesis: Even the stable rate around which fluctuations occur could change (1980:42). Specifically, they said that from 1880 to 1970 there were two different stable rates of incarceration and that the second higher level had emerged after major social changes in the post-World War I era (1980:92–93).

One problem with the hypothesis appears to be that the difference between a period of time with multiple stable rates and one with significant increases may be only the language used to describe the trends. Several authors have criticized Blumstein's work on empirical as well as theoretical grounds. Richard Berk et al. tested the hypothesis using data from California for 1851–1970 and found no support for it (1981:805). They concluded that rates of punishment are not stable at all and that they respond primarily to major wars, economic depressions, and major demographic trends (1981:825).

Several other important reports on trends in punishment have also identified specific periods of growth and decline in prison populations and incarceration rates in conjunction with wars and the Great Depression of the 1930s (Cahalan, 1979; Mullen, 1980, BJS, December 1982). The general view held by these authors is that the long-range trend is upward, with the short periods of decline operating as interruptions in that general trend.

EXPLAINING THE TRENDS

In order to obtain the type of information about trends that could be relevant to policymakers and theorists, we need to look beyond the direct determinants of correctional populations to the causes underlying major shifts in punishment types and levels. As might be expected, however, many possible factors may influence the size of probation, jail, and prison populations. In this section, we will explore some of the many explanations that have been given for the trends in prison populations. Since few studies have focused specifically on recent trends in the United States, it is necessary to consider results from studies of other time periods and other countries to see if any general explanations exist.

Warren Young classifies these explanations into two groups: deterministic and policy choice and attitudes (1985:4). Deterministic explanations, according to Young, involve factors largely out of the control of criminal justice organizations. Such factors include the crime rate, the unemployment rate, and changes in the general population. Policy choice and attitude variables usually involve influences stemming from the criminal justice system itself. For purposes of

this discussion, to Young's types we will add a third. We will cover factors external to corrections, changes in correctional philosophy, and changes in sentencing and correctional policies.

CHANGES IN EXTERNAL FACTORS

Crime Rate and Incarceration. One of the most obvious, commonsense answers to the question of imprisonment rate increases is crime rate increases. The findings from empirical studies, unfortunately, neither confirm nor refute the existence of a relationship. Instead, the results vary widely, depending on the country studied and the methods used.

David Biles (1983) found a strong relationship between high crime rates and high prison rates in both Canada and Australia when he used data from a single year, but he found the opposite relationship when using data from a period of years. When Biles (1983) applied a longitudinal method to England and Wales, a strong relationship between high crime and high imprisonment rates surfaced again. Comparing Britain and Wales to Australia, Biles reported that although the crime rates for all three countries rose about the same amount (180 percent) during the 1960s and 1970s, the imprisonment rate increased in Britain and Wales but decreased in Australia (1983:166)

Several early studies from the United States reported no consistent relationship between crime and incarceration rates, regardless of method used (Nagel, 1977; Mullen, 1980; Bowker, 1981). A more recent longitudinal study, however, found that the nature of the relationship appeared to depend on the way in which they interacted over time (McGuire and Sheehan, 1983). The study revealed that during the years from 1960 to 1979, high crime rates tended to precede high incarceration rates, which in turn were followed by lower crime rates (1983:80). Another recent study reported that the violent crime rates in the 1970s were related to the rates of admission to prison in 49 states, although an even stronger relationship was found between region and incarceration rates (Carroll and Doubet, 1983). While these later studies seem to be more indicative of some relationship between crime rate and incarceration rate, the evidence is still inconclusive.

Crime and incarceration rates do not appear to have a simple relationship. Although prison incarceration rates have been rising rather steadily, victimization rates for violent crimes (the crimes most likely to be punished by imprisonment) remained fairly stable from 1973 to 1981 and then began to drop (BJS, October 1983:89; June 1984:2). Figures 2.6 and 2.7 illustrate the trends in victimizations. Since the victimization survey reflects unreported as well as reported crime, it may be more useful to compare incarceration rates to rates of reported crime in the *Uniform Crime Reports*. Only reported crime could result in imprisonment.

UCR data display an increase in index crimes (homicide, robbery, aggravated assault, rape, grand larceny, and auto theft) during the 1970s, but show a decrease beginning in 1980 (BJS,

FIGURE 2.7   Trends in Victimization Rates for Selected Crimes, 1973–1983

Rate per 1,000 persons of households

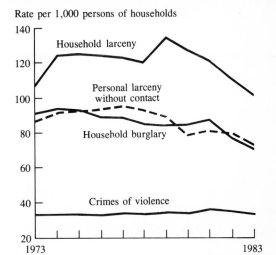

SOURCE: Bureau of Justice Statistics Bulletin: Trends in Victimization Rates 1973–1983. Washington, DC: Bureau of Justice Statistics, June 1984, p. 2.

October 1983:9). Looking at the arrest rate for all crimes, we see that it rose gradually until about 1982, when it began to decline (McGarrell and Flanagan, 1985:512). BJS reported that despite a significant decline in the number of serious crimes since 1981, the number of new prison admissions for every 100 serious crimes rose from 2.6 in 1980 to 4.0 in 1983 (April 1985:6). So data since 1970 seem to suggest that high incarceration rates have been followed by low crime rates, but that incarceration rates have continued to rise subsequent to the decline in crime rates.

Prison Capacity. A second explanation posited for increases in prison population concerns the capacity of incarcerative facilities. The essence of the argument is that increased prison capacity leads to greater use of imprisonment, regardless of whether a policy intended to achieve that effect. Perhaps the best-known empirical study supporting this position is contained in the Abt report, *American Prisons and Jails* (Mullen,

FIGURE 2.6   Trends in Victimization Rates for Violent Crimes, 1973–1983

Rate per 1,000 persons age 12 and older

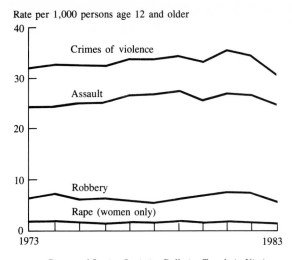

SOURCE: Bureau of Justice Statistics Bulletin: Trends in Victimization Rates 1973–1983. Washington, DC: Bureau of Justice Statistics, June 1984, p. 1.

1980). The conclusion reached in that study was that from 1955 to 1976, ". . . where a new space has been added, it has on average been followed two years later by population increases nearly equal in size" (Mullen, 1980:25). The Abt researchers conceded that their findings do not prove increased capacity drives population, but they suggested that increased capacity may "diminish reliance on non-custodial dispositions" (1980: 25).

A reexamination of the Abt study by Blumstein, Cohen, and Gooding (1983), however, revealed several problems with the data and the methodology. A reanalysis of the data led to the conclusion that capacity is not an important determinant of prison populations. Figure 2.8 illustrates the lack of relationship between prison population increases and capacity increases. The critique also emphasized that despite the existence of spare capacity in the 1960s, populations declined. The capacity hypothesis is also weakened by the fact that in many overcrowded jurisdictions limited capacity has not limited the growth of prison populations (Young, 1985:9).

Unemployment Rate. A third factor outside the control of correctional agencies is unemployment. It is often assumed that the idleness and lack of legitimate income that often accompany unemployment foster crime, which in turn increases the use of imprisonment. A review of studies on crime and unemployment led one author to conclude that the evidence linking the two was inconsistent (Freeman, 1983). But research on the relationship between unemployment and incarceration, holding crime rate constant, has generally produced positive results (e.g. Janhovic, 1977; Yeager, 1979; Greenberg, 1977).

One possible explanation for this direct connection between high unemployment and high incarceration rates is that the unemployed offender may be ineligible for punishments that involve financial payments (Young, 1985:7). It has been suggested that judges may rely more heavily on incarcerative sentences during times of high unemployment because they believe that unemployed offenders will be more likely to engage in crime (Box and Hale, 1983). Additionally, upon finding unemployment to be a strong

FIGURE 2.8   Total Population of State Prisons and Increases in Capacity by Year

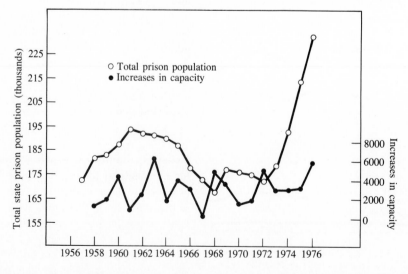

predictor of imprisonment, Yeager concluded: "It appears that imprisonment functions at least in part to contain and regulate the marginal or secondary labor force composed of the unemployed and the subemployed" (1979:588).

It cannot yet be concluded that unemployment is the most important factor influencing prison populations or rates. The Abt study found no evidence of a relationship between unemployment and imprisonment in the United States, and a very recent study of statewide trends from 1976 to 1981 reports no consistent relationship (Galster and Scaturo, 1985). Finally, Rutherford observes that in countries such as England, Japan, and The Netherlands, the use of imprisonment has at times been lower during periods of high unemployment.

Other Types of Institutionalization. The fourth explanation for prison population increases (or decreases) is that use of imprisonment is inversely related to use of hospitalization in psychiatric facilities. While research in other areas of the world has reported evidence of such a relationship (Penrose, 1939), more recent studies in the United States cast doubt on the prison-hospitalization link. After studying imprisonment and hospitalization rates from 1930 to 1970, Grabosky (1980) concluded that imprisonment and hospitalization rates are unrelated across jurisdictions and over time. Steadman et al (1984) confirmed the presence of an inverse relationship between the two types of populations, but found no evidence that prison increases resulted from a shift of former psychiatric patients to prisons.

Age Composition. The last external factor is the **age composition** of the population (the proportion of people of certain ages at a given place and time). As the persons born during the post-World War II baby boom reached their twenties, a relatively larger proportion of the population than before was at the age when imprisonment is most likely for those convicted. This age effect was cited by state departments of correction as an important reason for the rapid growth in prison population during the 1970s and 1980s (BJS,

October 1983:81). Additionally, younger criminals are more likely than older ones to have committed violent crimes, and this tends to enhance the possibility of imprisonment (Chaiken and Chaiken, 1982:209). Although the age structure explanation seems to have some merit, it is not clear how strong and direct the effect is or how it interacts with other factors that have been identifed.

Of the factors described above, none operated as the sole source of prison population increases in the past fifteen years. Instead, it is likely that the increase was influenced by some combination of those factors, all of which are basically outside the control of corrections agencies.

CHANGES IN CORRECTIONAL PHILOSOPHY

In 1973, the National Advisory Commission on Criminal Justice Standards and Goals (hereafter NAC) argued for reintegration as "a major purpose of corrections" (NAC, 1973:3) and for the increased use of probation and other noninstitutional punishments (1973:311). Although reintegration was proposed as an alternative to in-prison rehabilitation programs, it still represented commitment to reducing criminal tendencies by offenders—a commitment that had been in force for many years. The NAC made its view on the appropriateness of rehabilitation plain in this statement: "A rehabilitative purpose is or ought to be implicit in every sentence of an offender unless ordered otherwise by the sentencing court" (NAC, 1973:43).

Despite the NAC position, rehabilitation as a correctional goal began losing favor rapidly shortly thereafter. Norval Morris, writing only one year later, presented this view (1974:14):

Rehabilitation, whatever it means and whatever the programs that allegedly give it meaning, must cease to be a purpose of the prison sanction. This does *not* mean that the various developed treatment programs within prisons need to be abandoned; quite the contrary, they need expansion. But it does mean that they must not be seen as *purposive* in the sense that criminals are to be sent to prison *for treatment*. There is a sharp distinction between the purposes of incarceration and the opportunities for the training and assistance of prisoners that may be pursued within those purposes.

Basically, Morris argued that rehabilitation can succeed only if undertaken voluntarily and that linking the parole decision to program participation, a common occurrence in many prisons, violated this principle (1974:15,26,35). While Morris's view demonstrates one change in the thinking about rehabilitation, others in the field were more adamant in the rejection of that goal as the primary focus of corrections. Ernest van den Haag strongly contested that uncoerced treatment alone could ever work because, unless a criminal was punished for the offensive behavior, he would have no desire to undertake change and would be unresponsive to rehabilitation. Van den Haag stated: "Rehabilitative efforts make sense only if offenses are made unrewarding, self-defeating, irrational, and ultimately painful. Only punishment can achieve this. Hence, rehabilitation can follow, but it cannot take the place of punishment" (1975:991).

The rejection of rehabilitation is often associated with a comprehensive review and analysis of rehabilitation conducted by Robert Martinson and colleagues in the late 1960s. The essence of the findings is that nothing in the way of rehabilitative techniques works well toward preventing recidivism and that instances of success ". . . have been isolated, producing no clear pattern to indicate the efficacy of any particular method of treatment" (1974:49). Although this study became the subject of severe criticism by others (Cullen and Gilbert, 1982; Gottfredson, 1970c), and its findings were later reconsidered by Martinson (1979), its initial impact on the field of corrections was great. It strongly facilitated the shift away from rehabilitation to other goals for corrections (see Insert 2.1 for a brief summary of Martinson's 1974 article.)

The demise of rehabilitation led to the creation—or, more accurately—the resurrection of other objectives that could serve as replacements.

One of the more prominent replacements has been the "just deserts" or "justice model" approach in which the goal of corrections is to mete out punishment according to what is deserved in the interest of maintaining a moral code. A look at attitudes toward retribution since the turn of the century reveals that its popularity is relatively recent. In 1906, Roscoe Pound wrote: "Revenge and the modern expression, punishment, belong to the past of legal history" (1906:67). The opinion that retribution was uncivilized and undesirable was still strong in 1968, when Herbert Packer argued against the idea that retribution accomplished positive things such as strengthening the moral fiber of the individual. Packer stated: "Punishment is not a virtue, only a necessity" (1968:67). He viewed the urge to punish as morally unacceptable and claimed: "that fact that punishment involves suffering is moral embarrassment" (1968:59).

Only seven years later, van den Haag spoke strongly in support of retribution as a goal for corrections. But while this view has many adherents, others viewed the proper replacement for rehabilitation as the goal of protecting the public from dangerous persons. The thrust of this approach is that if we cannot rehabilitate and if punishment has little deterrent effect, than at least we can incapacitate those who have proved themselves to be dangerous by isolating them from free society.

CHANGES IN SENTENCING AND CORRECTIONAL POLICIES

As rehabilitation faded into the background and retribution and incapacitation gained momentum, certain policy changes in sentencing and corrections have emerged which have the potential of influencing the use of imprisonment.

Selective Incapacitation. One of the most controversial proposals is selective incapacitation. This policy would be expected to reduce prison populations if low-rate offenders, who are more numerous than high-rate offenders, were given

Insert 2.1 MARTINSON: "WHAT WORKS?"

In his 1974 article, Martinson reports a review of 231 empirical studies of correctional rehabilitation. To be eligible for review, the research design and execution had to meet the conventional standards of social science research. The review focused specifically on studies that used some measure of recidivism to gauge the effectiveness of rehabilitative techniques. Although the 231 studies still varied widely with respect to types of offenders, the measurement of recidivism, and other factors, Martinson concluded: "With few and isolated exceptions, the rehabilitative efforts that have been reported so far have had no appreciable effect on recidivism" (1974:25).

Martinson and his colleagues reviewed educational and vocational training, individual counseling (psychotherapy, counseling and casework), group counseling, milieu therapy, medical treatment (drugs and surgery), sentence length and security level, special programs administered outside the prison, individual and group psychotherapy in community settings, probation and parole, and intensive supervision for youthful probationers and adult parolees. None was reported to have had consistently positive results, and most techniques showed a mixture of successes and failures.

On an optimistic note, Martinson posited that even if many rehabilitation programs don't work, they do not usually make the offender worse. In particular, community rehabilitation programs may be cheaper to administer and sometimes may be less onerous to the offender than nonrehabilitative methods (1974:48). Thus, he states: "If we can't do more for (and to) offenders, at least we can safely do less" (1974:48). The major problem he sees in this course of action is that some of these programs may increase the offender population on the street and result in an increase in crime levels (1974:47).

Martinson offers some possible responses to this dilemma. First, much of the research evaluated was poorly conducted and may have masked the fact that some treatment programs were working (1974:49). It is also possible that the programs were not fully implemented (1974:49). Yet another possibility is that some programs administered in prison may not have been flawed themselves, but were not able to overcome the general effects of imprisonment (1974:28). Finally, it is possible that a rehabilitative approach is not suitable to the crime problem. Martinson closed by suggesting that crime prevention through deterrence may be the only sensible answer.

sentences other than imprisonment (Forst, 1983:21). Problems with implementing this strategy include poor ability to identify high-rate offenders (30 percent false positives) (Chaiken and Chaiken, 1982:220), and the historically unlikely chance that the low-rate offenders would actually be given alternate sanctions (Austin and Krisberg, 1981).

Career Criminal Programs. Closely related to selective incapacitation is the "career criminal" program. Such programs attempt to target resources on career criminals (Wolfgang, 1980:83). Although the primary objectives of career crimi-

nal programs do not explicitly include influencing prison populations (Greenwood, 1982:85), it would seem that increases or decreases could occur, depending on whether those who were not career criminals ended up in prison less often. Due to the many problems associated with career criminal programs, it seems unlikely that they will significantly affect prison use (Rhodes, 1980; Forst et al., 1983; Blumstein and Moitra, 1980).

Determinate Sentencing. Perhaps the most conspicuous policy change is the gradual move away from the indeterminate sentences of the rehabilitative era toward greater determinacy in sentencing (see Chapter 6 for more detail on de-terminate sentencing). This trend could, theoret-ically, either increase or decrease prison popu-lation. The nature of its influence on prisons would depend on the definition of desert used in retributive sentencing schemes.

The Federal Omnibus Crime Package. The new retributive approach has fostered attempts at implementation among individual correctional systems. An example of one adaptation is the Omnibus Crime Package, a "sweeping overhaul of the federal criminal law" that became law on October 12, 1985 (Bergman, 1985:1). While this package applies to the federal system and the District of Columbia, it may be seen as reflecting the kinds of changes occurring in other jurisdic-tions as well.

A number of the package provisions appear to involve changes that would be more likely to increase than reduce jail and prison populations. Examples of such provisions include (Bergman, 1985:1,12):

- The practice of detaining suspects before trial on the basis of predicted dangerous-ness
- The creation of sentencing guidelines that would drastically eliminate judicial discre-tion
- The creation of new federal crimes and in-creases in penalties for offenses
- Increased prison capacity
- Abolition of parole
- Reduction of good time

Whether these changes will bring increased fairness in the federal system is yet to be seen. The actual effects of changes on prison use will not be known until some time after the package has been implemented.

Impact of Court Orders. Another type of change that may be seen as having roots in the aim of the just deserts philosophy involves changes in prisons through court intervention.

BJS reported that federal and state courts have responded to overcrowding with court orders and consent decrees in an effort to alleviate these prison conditions (April 1983:4). Prison popula-tions grew at a combined rate of 9.2 percent from 1983 to 1984 in those states without court orders imposed and at a rate of only 2.9 percent in those states operating under court orders (April 1983:4). Whether or not court intervention was the sole cause of such variation among states has not been determined. The data do suggest, how-ever, that court-induced policy changes may have at least temporary effects in the use of impris-onment.

Does Policy Have an Effect? While it may seem from the situations presented above that changes in sentencing and correctional policy should have affected the use of imprisonment, there is no consensus among researchers and practitioners. Some believe that policy factors can work, alone or in conjunction with other factors, to affect prison use. State departments of correc-tion attribute recent population growth to a num-ber of factors, including changes in sentencing practices (BJS, October 1983:81). The Abt report on prisons and jails concluded that " . . . state and local policy decisions determine the size and composition of prison populations" (Mullen, 1980:100). Sherman and Hawkins state assuredly that sentencing policy influences construction policy and that together both affect the size of prison populations (1981, 100; for more detail on Sherman and Hawkins, see Insert 2.2). These authors demonstrated how changes in decision-making appeared to correlate with changes in imprisonment rates in both the United States and the United Kingdom (1981:48–75).

Others maintain that intended policy inter-ventions can have no significant or lasting effect on prison use because of the strength of shifts in societal factors. Even Mullen, who urges the view that policy can make a difference, observes some of the difficulties with that view: "The decisions to put people in and take people out of prisons and jails involve scores of discretionary transac-

Insert 2.2 SHERMAN AND HAWKINS' PROPOSAL FOR PRISON USE

Amid the extreme solutions commonly offered in the debate on prison construction is the moderate and modest proposal presented by Michael Sherman and Gordon Hawkins in *Imprisonment in America* (1981). Their summary of the proposal is as follows (1981:101).

(1) On sentencing, the dominant justifying aim at incarceration in a prison should be incapacitation. Imprisonment should be the punishment of choice, not for all offenses as it is under current practice but primarily where it seems necessary to meet the threat of physical violence. (2) On construction, new prison space should be built primarily to replace existing facilities or to bring them up to humane and constitutional standards. In most states, the effect on construction programs, indeed the condition of funding them, should be that they do not increase current capacity. (3) On programs, we recommend that administrators maintain those existing services and begin new ones that can be truly voluntary and facilitative. While there are dangers here, the alternatives are worse.

The author's rationale for incapacitation is that the only thing prison can do that other punishments cannot is isolate people from free society (1981:100). Thus, the prediction of future dangerousness is seen as central to sentencing policy. Exceptions would be allowed in the case of very serious offenses not likely to be committed again, but deserving of strong punishment. The concept of *desert*, seen as too subjective to do the full duty of sentencing, is used as a "limiting principle to ensure the humane and just treatment of those who are incapacitated." The construction component may involve putting a ceiling on prison resources in some areas, but each jurisdiction would remain ultimately responsible for such decisions. Concerning the use of programs, Sherman and Hawkins posit that the risk of false positives inherent in the incapacitative approach enhances the burden on prison officials to provide prisoners with sufficient human service programs for those who would seek help on a voluntary basis. While conceding that the plan is no panacea, they suggest that a substantial part of its strength lies in its binding together of liberal and conservative concerns.

Sherman and Hawkins base their proposal on an analysis of the causes for overuse of imprisonment. Of critical importance is the lack of mid-range punishments in corrections today. They state: ". . . the lack of punishments that are not incarcerative but are still frankly punitive perpetuates by default the dominance of the prison" (1981:100). Community corrections and other alternatives tend not to be considered punishments by either the public or policymakers. Rather than create a new brand of punishment that would be nonincarcerative and considered to be sufficiently retributive (a difficult task), the authors advocate the injection of the guiding principles contained in their proposal into the existing sanction of imprisonment. The primary objective is to limit prison use by restricting the punishment of prison primarily to violent or excessively harmful offenders.

tions among actors with independent goals, following policies which may or may not be uniformly defined and implemented" (1980:225). Although Young cites several optimistic examples of policies that appear to have affected prison use, he cautions that other examples demonstrate how policy effects may be inhibited by "countervailing pressures" from inside and outside the criminal justice system and/or may result in unintended consequences (1985:11). Finally, Berk et al. found changes in corrections policy to have no explanatory value with respect to growth rates of imprisonment in the United States (1981:825). They warned against expecting sentencing reforms to have significant impacts upon growth rates because the effect of the reforms would be swamped by the impact of social forces of greater magnitude (1981:826).

VARIATIONS IN THE USE OF PUNISHMENTS

VARIATIONS AMONG THE STATES

One of the more basic ways to examine variation in prison use in the United States is to make comparisons of incarceration rates among states and regions. Prison incarceration rates for every state and the federal system in 1983 are displayed in Figure 2.9. The highest rate for the states was Nevada, where 354 persons per 100,000 were imprisoned. Although the two states with the lowest rates were located in the North Central region (North Dakota with 51 and Minnesota with 52), the lowest regional average was in the Northeast. The rate in that region was 127, while the rates in the North Central, West, and South were 135, 152, and 225, respectively. Another indication of the great variability in imprisonment is that although 12 states had prison rates of less than 99, 18 states had rates exceeding 175.

FIGURE 2.9 Persons Under Correctional Supervision—Rate (per 100,000 Resident Population) of Sentenced Prisoners in State and Federal Institutions, by Jurisdiction, December 31, 1983

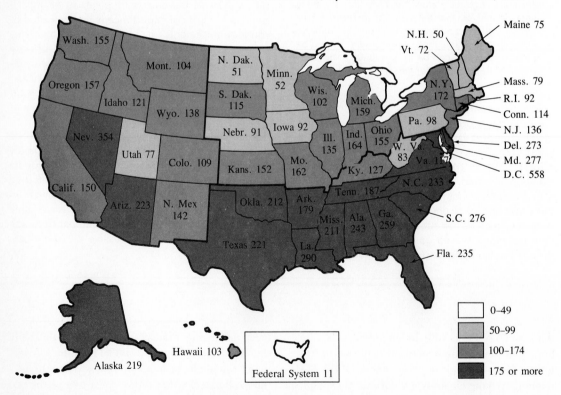

NOTE: Unpublished U.S. Bureau of the Census estimates for the resident population were used to calculate rates of incarceration. Sentenced prisoners are defined as those serving sentences of more than one year.

SOURCE: Edmund McGarrell and Timothy Flanagan (eds.), *Sourcebook of Criminal Justice Statistics—1984*. Washington, DC: Bureau of Justice Statistics, 1985, p. 649.

When rates of jailed inmates are examined, variation among the states is quite evident. Table 2.4 includes jail confinement rates for all states and the District of Columbia in 1983. The pattern of differences in jail confinement rates is somewhat different than for prison incarceration rates. For example, the lowest rate among the states having separate jail and prison systems was 29 in Iowa. The highest rate among the states belonged to Louisiana (192), but the District of Columbia had a rate of 456. Despite the South's lead in prison incarceration rates, it was the West that ranked highest in jail confinement in 1983 (129 per 100,000). The North Central, Northeast, and South had rates of 67, 82, and 113, respectively.

Another way in which states differ is the frequency with which they use one form of incarceration rather than another. In many states, the prison rate is substantially greater than the jail confinement rate. At the extreme of this situation is Iowa, with a prison rate of 92 and a jail confinement rate of only 29. Other states show a much smaller difference between jail and prison rates. In New Hampshire the two rates are equal, and in Minnesota the jail rate of 47 approximates the prison rate of 52.

The wide degree of variability stems from differing social and demographic conditions among the states, as well as differing punishment policies followed by the state criminal justice system (Mullen, 1980:16). Because of the many differences among the states, it is certainly difficult to speak of a single "national rate." Reference to a "national rate" can be very misleading because it can mask important differences among the states. High rates in some states will cancel out low rates in others. Examination of statewide rather than national data becomes critical when such data must serve as the basis for policy in a particular jurisdiction. Nonetheless, national rates of prison incarceration, jail confinement, and probation are generally used in the study of trends over time in the United States. National data are also necessary for comparing rates in the United States with those in other countries.

VARIATIONS AMONG COUNTRIES

The United States ranks near the top in the frequency and severity of its punishments for criminals when compared with other nations (NAC, 1973:151; Doleschal, 1977). This may seem surprising when one thinks of accounts of people being "locked away forever" in some foreign country. Based on the knowledge that public opinion polls have consistently shown the American public does not think the police and courts are tough enough with criminals, Doleschal predicted (1977:51):

> If asked, most Americans would undoubtedly express the belief that the United States is one of the most lenient nations in the world in dealing with the offender, thus demonstrating the triumph of folklore over fact.

Doleschal reported that on January 1, 1976, the United States had the highest rate of imprisonment in the world (1977:51).

In order to portray a sense of the magnitude of differences in imprisonment rates between the United States and other countries, Doleschal made comparisons with the Netherlands. He estimated that Florida alone imprisoned 16 times as many people as Holland in 1976, while it had only half of the total Dutch population (1977:56). Just as the United States is often cited as possessing one of the highest imprisonment rates in the world, the Netherlands has often been cited as representing the other extreme.

The Netherlands did not always enjoy this position, however. In 1951, the imprisonment rate was about 64 in England and Wales, and about 82 in Holland. By 1975, the situation was reversed, with England and Wales at 105 and Holland down to 26 (Downes, 1982). As we can see from the Council of Europe data presented in Table 2.5, the Netherlands, with an imprisonment rate of 28, still ranked the lowest of all European nations as of 1983.

Although the Netherlands is often used as a point of comparison for the United States in cross-cultural analysis, it may be more informative to

TABLE 2.4 Number of Jails, Number of Jail Inmates, and Rate of Inmates per 100,000 Population, by Sex, Legal Status, Region, and State, June 30, 1983

REGION AND STATE	JAILS	JAIL INMATES									RATE OF INMATES PER 100,000 POPULATION
		TOTAL			ADULTS			JUVENILES			
		TOTAL	MALE	FEMALE	TOTAL	MALE	FEMALE	TOTAL	MALE	FEMALE	
United States	3,338	223,551	207,782	15,769	221,815	206,163	15,652	1,736	1,619	117	98
Northeast	223	36,634	34,615	2,019	36,315	34,309	2,006	319	306	13	82
Maine	14	560	547	13	542	529	13	18	18	0	49
Massachusetts	17	3,304	3,301	3	3,304	3,301	3	0	0	0	57
New Hampshire	11	475	451	24	469	445	24	6	6	0	50
New Jersey	32	5,971	5,596	375	5,956	5,581	375	15	15	0	80
New York	72	16,154	15,100	1,054	15,877	14,836	1,041	277	264	13	91
Pennsylvania	77	10,170	9,620	550	10,167	9,617	550	3	3	0	85
North Central	972	39,538	37,000	2,538	39,200	36,689	2,511	338	311	27	67
Illinois	98	8,849	8,468	381	8,819	8,440	379	30	28	2	77
Indiana	93	3,599	3,359	240	3,466	3,235	231	133	124	9	66
Iowa	90	839	798	41	828	787	41	11	11	0	29
Kansas	86	1,328	1,244	84	1,305	1,222	83	23	22	1	55
Michigan	87	7,637	7,064	573	7,627	7,054	573	10	10	0	84
Minnesota	67	1,954	1,849	105	1,941	1,836	105	13	13	0	47
Missouri	129	3,783	3,523	260	3,761	3,503	258	22	20	2	76
Nebraska	67	844	796	48	817	773	44	27	23	4	53
North Dakota	31	243	222	21	236	215	21	7	7	0	36
Ohio	121	7,116	6,549	567	7,087	6,526	561	29	23	6	66
South Dakota	31	316	289	27	310	283	27	6	6	0	0
Wisconsin	72	3,030	2,839	191	3,003	2,815	188	27	24	3	64
South	1,607	89,479	83,696	5,783	88,639	82,916	5,723	840	780	60	113
Alabama	108	4,464	4,216	248	4,452	4,205	247	12	11	1	113
Arkansas	89	1,602	1,508	94	1,540	1,449	91	62	59	3	69
District of Columbia	2	2,843	2,570	273	2,820	2,547	273	23	23	0	456
Florida	103	14,668	13,489	1,179	14,313	13,157	1,156	355	332	23	137

consider the rates of a wider range of countries. Data in Tables 2.5 and 2.6 show the tremendous variation across both European and Asian countries for which data are available. Austria, the Federal Republic of Germany, and England and Wales had the three highest imprisonment rates on February 1, 1983. Austria's rate of 114 is still substantially lower than the prison incarceration rate of 179 in the United States (see Table 2.2). Although the rate tends to rise as populations increase, exceptions are evident (e.g., Luxembourg).

A number of countries have lower rates than Sweden and Denmark, countries which, along with the Netherlands, have been described as having "possibly the most advanced and most humane criminal justice systems in the world" (Doleschal, 1977:51). The data for countries in the Pacific in Table 2.6 show somewhat greater variation than the European data. Fiji, a small island with a population of only 619,000 in 1981, had a rate of 200.3 per 100,000, while the Philippines and Indonesia had much lower rates of 29.4 and 27.5, respectively. Australia and Japan were also among the lowest users of imprisonment reported for 1980 and 1981.

The prison incarceration rate of the United States in 1981 was 153, lower than those in Fiji

TABLE 2.4 *(Continued)*

| REGION AND STATE | JAILS | JAIL INMATES | | | | | | | | | RATE OF INMATES PER 100,000 POPULATION |
| | | TOTAL | | | ADULTS | | | JUVENILES | | | |
		TOTAL	MALE	FEMALE	TOTAL	MALE	FEMALE	TOTAL	MALE	FEMALE	
Georgia	203	10,214	9,659	555	10,213	9,658	555	1	1	0	178
Kentucky	96	3,711	3,471	240	3,652	3,423	229	59	48	11	100
Louisiana	94	8,507	8,046	461	8,501	8,040	461	6	6	0	192
Maryland	30	4,608	4,343	265	4,572	4,310	262	36	33	3	107
Mississippi	91	2,498	2,374	124	2,482	2,358	124	16	16	0	97
North Carolina	99	3,496	3,305	191	3,474	3,286	188	22	19	3	57
Oklahoma	104	2,215	2,034	181	2,164	1,986	178	51	48	3	67
South Carolina	58	2,690	2,572	118	2,674	2,556	118	16	16	0	82
Tennessee	108	6,005	5,614	391	5,975	5,588	387	30	26	4	128
Texas	273	15,224	14,215	1,009	15,176	14,173	1,003	48	42	6	97
Virginia	95	5,719	5,317	402	5,616	5,217	0	103	100	3	103
West Virginia	54	1,015	963	52	1,015	963	52	0	0	0	52
West	536	57,900	52,471	5,429	57,661	52,249	5,412	239	222	17	129
Alaska	5	37	32	5	34	29	5	3	3	0	8
Arizona	31	2,940	2,756	184	2,906	2,722	184	34	34	0	99
California	142	41,720	37,312	4,408	41,656	37,252	4,404	64	60	4	166
Colorado	60	2,747	2,591	156	2,739	2,584	155	8	7	1	88
Idaho	36	604	563	41	566	532	34	38	31	7	61
Montana	50	405	369	36	394	359	35	11	10	1	50
Nevada	26	341	313	28	309	282	27	32	31	1	66
New Mexico	23	940	847	93	928	835	93	12	12	0	105
Oregon	35	1,346	1,273	73	1,324	1,254	70	22	19	3	96
Utah	39	2,304	2,163	141	2,304	2,163	141	0	0	0	87
Washington	24	906	862	44	906	862	44	0	0	0	56
Wyoming	65	3,610	3,390	220	3,595	3,375	220	15	15	0	84

SOURCE: Edmund McGarrell and Timothy Flanagan, *Sourcebook of Criminal Justice Statistics—1984*. Washington, DC: Bureau of Justice Statistics, 1985:638.

and Thailand, but still higher than most of the countries in Table 2.6. Canada's 1981 rate of 40.1 appears to be very low, but the figure probably underestimates Canada's imprisonment rate substantially, since it includes only federal prisoners. Other countries reported to have imprisonment rates exceeding that of the United States are East Germany, Poland, and the USSR (Kaiser, 1984:184). East Germany's rate was estimated at 274 per 100,000 in 1977. Poland's rate was estimated at 305 in 1980; and estimates for the 1977 rate in the Soviet Union range between 350 and 660 (1984:184).

Several points must be emphasized regarding interpretation of incarceration rate data from other countries. As is the case with the data presented by Kaiser (1984), it is not often clear exactly what categories of offenders are included. For example, Kaiser's data appear to include jail and juvenile inmates as well as prisoners, since the figure he presents for the United States in 1978 is 247 (1984:182). The estimated rate of 208, based on prisoners and jail inmates, is presented in Table 2.2. It is likely that differences in methods used for compiling and computing statistics are often responsible for the discrepancies in figures reported by different authors for the same country.

TABLE 2.5 Prison Incarceration Rates per 100,000 Population for Selected Countries in Europe, February 1, 1983

COUNTRY	TOTAL PRISON POPULATION	RATE OF INCARCERATION PER 100,000 INHABITANTS
Austria	8,748	114.0
Federal Republic of Germany (West Germany)[a]	61,778	100.3
England and Wales	43,368	87.0
Luxembourg	287	72.0
France	37,649	67.8
Sweden	5,461	65.0
Italy	36,515	64.6
Denmark	3,236	63.0
Spain	22,720	59.8
Norway	2,051	51.5
Ireland	1,281	37.0
Greece	3,300	35.0
Malta	101	29.0
Netherlands	3,900	28.0

[a] Figures for Federal Republic of Germany refer to the situation on July 31, 1983.

SOURCE: Table constructed from data presented in Council of Europe, *Prison Information Bulletin No. 2.*, Strasbourg, France: Council of Europe, 1983: 17, 25, 28.

TABLE 2.6 Prison Incarceration Rates per 100,000 Population for Canada and Selected Countries in Asia and the Pacific, January 1, 1981

COUNTRY	POPULATION OF COUNTRY	TOTAL PRISON POPULATION	RATE OF INCARCERATION PER 100,000 INHABITANTS
Canada[a]	23,810,000	9,549	40.1
Fiji	619,000	1,240	200.3
Thailand	46,000,000	76,287	165.8
Singapore	2,410,000	2,410	116.1
New Zealand	3,149,000	2,800	88.9
Sri Lanka	14,500,000	11,073	76.4
Australia[b]	14,716,000	9,542	64.8
Japan	116,133,000	50,706	43.7
Philippines	50,000,000	14,705	29.4
Indonesia	130,000,000	35,723	27.5

[a] Figures for Canada include federal prisoners only.
[b] Figures for Australia are based on the daily average number of prisoners for the month of December 1980.

SOURCE: Australian Institute of Criminology, *Prison Statistics for Asia and the Pacific*, Quarterly Summary No. 5. Canberra, Australia: Australia Institute of Criminology, 1981.

The Netherlands has one of the lowest incarceration rates in the world and one of the most humane prison systems. At left is a new prison in Amsterdam. (Keystone/The Image Works)

All figures must be considered rough approximations because of the differences among countries in the definition of terms such as "prisoners." Some countries may consider only those who have been sentenced as prisoners, despite large numbers of pretrial detainees (Kaiser, 1984:182). In other countries, such as those presented in Table 2.5, unsentenced prisoners are included in the data. For Italy and France, unsentenced prisoners constitute 76 percent and 51.6 percent of the total prison population (Council of Europe, 1983:17).

Different countries often handle offenders differently as they pass through the criminal justice apparatus. While guilt or innocence is determined by the adversarial system in the United States, other countries such as Australia and many European nations employ an inquisitorial system in which guilt is more a matter of degree than clear right or wrong.

It is difficult to compare any pair of countries on any single characteristic, such as incarceration rate, because of enormous differences in geographical, historical, economic, political, and sociodemographic qualities. Just as variation occurs among individual states in the United States, it also exists among states or provinces of other countries. For example, rates per 100,000 population in Canada range from 454 in the North West Territories to 44 in Newfoundland (Waller and Chan, 1974).

Simple comparisons of imprisonment rates provide only a limited picture of how progressively or regressively countries handle offenders. Other indicators include the severity and constitutionality of punishments, the scope of prisoners' rights, the quality of programs and services, and the degree of humanization (Kaiser, 1984:179). To the question of how some countries are able to maintain lower imprisonment rates than others, Kaiser (1984:182) answers:

> Apparently these countries have adopted a mixed strategy of imposing relatively short prison terms and granting frequent conditional release, pre-term release, pardons, and other types of punishment reductions.

The regimen in Japanese prisons is strict. There is no talking during work. Prisoners work five and one-half days a week. (Neal Ulevich/AP New Features)

Another factor that may have curbed imprisonment in some European nations is their adoption of the Minimum Rules for the Treatment of Prisoners established by the European Human Rights Convention (Kaiser, 1984:164–166). These rules provide effective limitations on state interference with prisoner's personal rights and emphasize the importance of humane conditions.

PUNISHMENT TRENDS IN THREE COUNTRIES

ENGLAND: EXPANSION AND CONTRACTION BY DESIGN AND CRISIS

The use of imprisonment in England has come full circle, from expansion to reduction, to standstill, to expansion again. Rutherford (1984:172) summarized the changes as follows:

> Notions of general deterrence gave way to those of rehabilitation which, in turn, have been superseded

by the language of selective incapacitation and individual deterrence. The new expansionist phase in England leans heavily upon two justifications: the incapacitation of serious offenders and individual deterrence for minor offenders.

But other purposive and accidental forces also exerted a powerful influence on the English prison system. After an initial period of expansion, a combination of government policy and social dynamics worked together to effect a substantial reduction, despite rising crime levels. From 1908 to 1920, the size of the prison population was reduced by half, and the imprisonment rate fell from 62 to 30 (Rutherford, 1984:123). Remission and good time allowances were introduced around 1910, largely as a means of clearing the prisons of the many offenders, such as fine defaulters, who were serving short terms for petty offenses. Additionally, sentencing practices shifted to allow more time for payment of fines and fewer commitments for public intoxication, among other things (1984:130–136). The period of reduction, which continued until 1938, was followed by a phase of "relentless expansion" that continues today (Rutherford, 1984:147).

The expansionist trend gained momentum in 1945, and by 1970 the incarceration rate had increased to 80 per 100,000. The upward spiral appeared partly caused by a high level of tolerance for overcrowding. Several crises in the 1960s and 1970s encouraged the general trend. There was a "security crisis" in the 1960s, after the successful escape of several infamous criminals (1984:76–79). The Mountbatten Report, an important document of the time, recommended concentration of all high-risk prisoners ("A" level) in one isolated prison. The government, however, opted for the dispersal of dangerous offenders among several prisons in order to effect a kind of "divide and conquer" strategy. Once dispersal became the policy, a continual demand for more dispersal prisons emerged. Today, all "B" level prisoners are in dispersal prisons as well.

The second crisis involved the prisoners' rights movement, which in England peaked in 1972. During that year, 130 demonstrations occurred in over 40 institutions. In addition to heightening concern about prison security, the riots and actions around the issues of prisoners' rights generated a militant mood among the prison guards (1984:81–82). This militancy led to a third crisis, when the Prison Officers Association all but usurped control of the prisons from the managers during the latter half of the 1970s.

Prison officers were angry that the wardens and other supervisory staff had not responded to their demands for quelling prison riots. The result of these two crises was a recommendation by the May Committee in 1979 to increase expenditures in the prison system. Militance was still evident among officers in 1980–81, when many participated in a 15-week job action. The officers refused to allow the number of prisoners to exceed capacity and, out of sheer necessity, many defendants detained awaiting disposition were simply diverted altogether by police (1984:29). Fitzgerald and Sim (1979:158) noted: "As soon as the dispute was settled, instead of using the ex-

perience . . . as an argument for a much reduced prison population, the Home Secretary sought a return to normal levels of imprisonment at the earliest opportunity."

Although economic restraints pushed corrections in England toward a standstill at one time during the late 1960s, the security and control crises undermined the effort because they encouraged expansion as a solution to the problems. The effort to hold population down was essentially abandoned in 1981 after a new conservative government sought increases in criminal justice resources and defeated automatic parole for short-term prisoners (Rutherford, 1984:55–56). The standstill policy itself may have contributed to later expansion in that "replacement" facilities for old prisoners became "additions" when old prisons were not closed (1984:57). This unintended form of expansion may also have been bolstered by various alternatives to imprisonment, such as community service orders (1984:158–159). Even "remission and parole, designed to reduce the amount of time served, eventually led to an increase in sentence lengths as judges inflated sentences" (1984:147).

Imprisonment in England today clearly intends to serve as the most serious punishment for the most serious offenses. The death penalty was abolished in 1969 (Fitzgerald and Sim, 1979:95). Nonetheless, many of those serving time in English prisons are property offenders. In 1981, nonviolent property offenders made up 56 percent of the prison population, violent offenders (including robbers) comprised nearly 30 percent, and 19 percent were those imprisoned for nonviolent crimes related to drugs, alcohol, or driving offenses (Rutherford, 1984:15). Length of stay is relatively short; 66.3 percent of all those released in 1978 served under six months, and only 10.7 percent served one year or more (1984:135).

Probation, fines, and community service orders are used with some frequency. Probation orders declined between 1970 and 1980, as community service orders became more popular (Pease, 1981). The fine, however, remains the most frequently used sanction for all serious offenses except robbery (Rutherford, 1984:153). In 1980–81, over one million pounds were collected as fines. One persistent problem with the fine system is that many offenders default and are subsequently imprisoned. In 1981, fine defaulters comprised nearly 25 percent of all prison receptions (1984:153).

JAPAN: A CASE OF EXCESS PRISON CAPACITY

Although the development of Japan's correctional system was influenced by the systems in European nations and in the United States (Kaiser, 1984:137), Japan has experienced certain unique trends in prison use. Perhaps the best known piece of Japan's correctional history is the 25-year period of decline in imprisonment which began in 1950 and eventually resulted in excess space (Rutherford, 1984: 131–135). The imprisonment rate dropped from 123 in 1950 to 40 in 1975 (1984:132). Since offenders under 20 years of age are under the jurisdiction of the juvenile courts in Japan, the figures are slightly lower than if training schools were included. Nonetheless, the decline was both steady and substantial. During that period, the physical capacity of the system and the size of the staff stayed relatively constant. Even in the 5-year period prior to 1950, when the prison population increased by 92 percent, capacity remained stable (1984:131–132). Since 1970, prison capacity has exceeded use by about 20 percent (1984:135). Rutherford observed: "Old prisons have been replaced by new construction without adding to new capacity, but there has been no attempt to reduce the prison system's overall physical estate" (1984:135).

Both a strong downturn in the crime rate and a conscious effort to effect changes at various points in the criminal justice process have contributed to the dramatic reduction in prison use. The number of recorded serious crimes dropped significantly from 1950 to 1970 (1984:122). This occurred in conjunction with rapid economic recovery after World War II; average Japanese income quadrupled between 1955 and 1978. It is interesting to note also that unemployment was generally on the rise during the period of reduction.

The drop in the crime rate does not account for all of the decline in imprisonment. Driven by a strong desire to avoid overcrowding, several strategies were implemented to reduce the use of imprisonment. It has been observed that in Japan, as in the Netherlands, prosecutorial decisions to dismiss cases "have been one of the most important mechanisms for achieving and sustaining reductions in prison population size" (1984:146). Prosecutors require restitution in some cases, in lieu of prosecution. Another tactic employed to reduce the prison population was to enlarge the availability of parole. This situation is an exception to a historical policy of granting parole quite sparingly (1984:135). Another method employed to reduce the level of imprisonment was the granting of mass amnesties on national occasions, such as upon the entrance to the United Nations in 1956 (1984:135).

Certain features of Japanese sentencing policy may also have contributed to the maintenance of low levels of imprisonment, although it is not clear that they were adopted specifically as a reductionist tactic. Prison sentences are often suspended, but unlike in England, breaches of suspension do not usually result in imprisonment (1984:134). Instead, those who breach suspension are often put under probation supervision. Fines are also prevalent. In 1978, fines accounted for about 85 percent of all sentences, and default was unusual. In contrast to England, defaulters comprised less than 0.2 percent of all prisoners in 1978 (1984:134).

Not all aspects of correctional policy and process in Japan would seem to aim toward reductionist goals. Prisoners typically serve longer sentences than many prisoners in Europe. In 1978, less than 20 percent of all those released served fewer than six months, compared to 65 percent in England (1984:134). About 30 percent served one to two years, but only 2.1 percent served more than four years (1984:135). The majority of prisoners in 1978 (69 percent) served their time in maximum security prisons, compared to 28 percent in England (1984:66). Finally, there is the traditionally cautious use of parole.

The decline of imprisonment in Japan ceased in 1975. From 1975 to 1978, the prison population increased 9 percent, although this might have been greater had it not been for renewed efforts to avoid use of custody. Part of the increase may be traced to a greater number of convictions for drug offenses and organized crime (1984:136). About one-quarter of all prisoners admitted to Japanese prisons in 1979 were connected with organized crime (Kaiser, 1984:140). Correctional policymakers have predicted an increase in prison population during the 1980s of between 3 and 10 percent, and plans to increase physical capacity are being considered.

THE NETHERLANDS: MORE CRIME AND FEWER PRISONERS

Of all the nations, the one most often recognized for a model system is probably the Netherlands. The primary reason for this lies with the fact that between 1950 and 1975, the Dutch prison population declined by 50 percent, despite a 300 percent increase in recorded crime (Rutherford, 1984:43). Holland's incarceration rate was 66 per 100,000 in 1955. By 1975, the rate had plummeted to 17 (1984:122). The prison population increased by approximately one-third by 1978, and the country is now experiencing pressure to expand capacity (Kaiser, 1984:86). Nevertheless, the extended period of reduction that ended in 1975 is worth close examination.

To identify the most important influences behind reduction is not a simple matter. Rutherford (1984:145) believed that the reduction was achieved as a result of confluent but unplanned changes. The following discussion includes some of the important factors identified by several authors.

Downes (1982) and Rutherford (1984) em-

phasized the police and prosecutorial practices that deflected cases from court. Prison populations became increasingly insulated from the rising crime rate because of such activities. The rate of crimes cleared by arrest fell from 60 to 30 percent between 1960 and 1975, diminishing potential inputs to the system (Downes, 1982:331). Additionally, an increase in the proportion of cleared cases not brought before the prosecutor facilitated the shielding effect (1982:349). Diversion by the prosecutors may have played an even stronger part in the program (Rutherford, 1984:26). The trend of dismissing cases gained momentum around 1960 (1984:139; Downes, 1982:349). The existence of a national prosecution policy helped to achieve this change. This policy included "structured consultation" between prosecutors and prison officials regarding the use of custody (Rutherford, 1984:27). As in Japan, dismissals may involve punitive consequences such as restitution, a written warning, or even probation supervision (Downes, 1982:332).

Deflection of cases also occurs at sentencing. The 25-year decline in prison use was almost entirely due to sentenced prisoners rather than those detained awaiting trial. In 1955, detainees comprised 36 percent of all confinements, but by 1975 this figure had grown to 50 percent. The crucial change in sentencing policy affecting prison population was a gradual shortening of both sentence length and time served. Downes contended it was largely the rising popularity of rehabilitation from 1950 to 1965 that triggered the move toward shorter sentences (1982:347, 355). Unlike the rehabilitation movement in the United States, reform in Holland focused on the negative effects of imprisonment (1982:345). In spite of a rising crime rate, sentence lengths dropped by 1965, and continued to drop in the next 10 years, while the crime rate doubled (1982:328).

One estimate of time served by male Dutch prisoners was 2 months in 1965. By 1975, this number had dropped to 1.6 months, and by 1977 it was 1.3 (1982:334). The decrease in time served is even steeper when only sentenced prisoners are considered. Less than 5 percent of all Dutch prisoners serve terms of one year or longer (Kaiser, 1984:87). The period of shortening sentences approached an end toward 1975, when the Opium Act of 1975 increased prison terms for dealing in heroin (Rutherford, 1984:180).

Another feature of sentencing practice that may have contributed to the reduction in prison use was the increased use of fines. In 1950, 58 percent of all sentences were fines, and by 1975 the figure had risen to 65 percent (1984:141). The final and perhaps most novel mechanism related to prison reductions was the use of the "waiting list." Convicted prisoners are informed when a certain space for them in prison becomes available, and are requested to arrive at a particular facility on a given data. About one-fifth do not appear and are arrested (Downes, 1982:331). The proportion waiting rose from 67 percent in 1965 to 75 percent in 1975. The buildup of the waiting list was so great that in 1975 a mass pardon was used to ease the backlog. The effect was short-lived, however, and plans are under way to expand capacity of the prison system (Rutherford, 1984:143).

Since 1947, there has been a statutory prohibition against placing more than one prisoner in a cell. This law, in conjunction with an actual reduction of the physical capacity of the system between 1960 and 1975, served to help constrain the prison population, but contributed to the buildup of prisoners on the waiting list (1984:143). This buildup, in addition to the increase in detained persons and longer sentences, have worked together against the dramatic reduction the Dutch had achieved earlier.

SUMMARY

1. In the United States, prison populations have generally increased since 1925, with exceptions during World War II and the Vietnam period. Only some of the increase is attributable to increases in the general civilian population.

2. Prison populations have increased faster than increases in prison space. In the 1980s, many prisons and jails are overcrowded.

3. Studies of prison incarceration and jail confinement rates permit the study of inmate populations across time or jurisdiction. By 1983, incarceration rates in the United States had hit an all-time high.

4. Probation data are less available than prison data. There are many more people on probation than in prisons and jails at any one time and it appears that probation rates have increased more rapidly than incarceration rates.

5. Prison and jail populations are determined by inputs and outputs. Inputs include the decision to incarcerate rather than use community sentences, and the frequency of new prison admissions. Output is governed by length of sentence and rates of release.

6. There is still some debate about whether prison use has increased in the long run. Some researchers have advanced a stability of punishment hypothesis, while others argue that rates have increased significantly.

7. A number of explanations exist for changes in prison use. Commonly cited factors include external or unplanned factors such as crime rate, unemployment rate, capacity of the prison system, and changes in the age composition of the general population. Internal or policy factors include changes in philosophy of punishment and specific sentencing and correctional policy changes reflecting philosophical trends.

8. There is tremendous variation in the use of punishments over time, among states, and across countries. In general, incarceration rates are higher in the southern and western regions of the United States. The rate of incarceration in the United States is higher than in many other countries. The United States uses longer and more frequent prison sentences than most European countries and Japan.

KEY WORDS

AGE COMPOSITION OF THE POPULATION. The breakdown of an entire population into age-specific categories. In criminological and correctional research, an important variable in the prediction of crime rates or incarceration rates, since younger groups are at greater risk of crime, violent crime, and incarceration.

JAIL CONFINMENT RATE. The number of persons confined in jails, both as detainees and as misdemeanants serving short sentences, per 100,000 people in the general civilian population.

PRISON INCARCERATION RATE. The number of persons serving sentences in federal and state prison, per 100,000 people in the general civilian population.

STABILITY OF PUNISHMENT HYPOTHESIS. The hypothesis that the rate of punishment in a given society will remain stable, despite fluctuations in the crime rate.

PROJECTS AND QUESTIONS

1. Find a recent *Sourcebook of Criminal Justice Statistics* and locate the table giving the most recent incarceration rate data for all the states. How does your state compare with others? How does it compare with the national average? With other states in your region? What do you think might cause these differences?
2. Review recent newspaper articles concerning the prison system in your state. Have claims been made that it is overcrowded? If so, which officials give what kinds of reasons for the overcrowding? How do they propose to deal with the problems?
3. Return to the *Sourcebook.* Locate two states with similar crime rates but very different incarceration rates. What kinds of questions would you want to ask in order to explain this kind of difference?
4. In recent New York State Sentencing Commission hearings, New York City's Mayor Koch testified that if he had to make a choice between spending money on prisons and spending money on schools, he would rather build prisons. He said if the streets were not safe, nothing else would matter. Do you agree? Do you agree with his strategy for crime reduction?

ADDITIONAL READING

Freda Adler. *Nations Not Obsessed with Crime.* Littleton, CO: F. B. Rothman, 1985. Adler examines five pairs of countries in different regions of the globe. Focusing on arrest rates, she concludes that "social solidarity" is an important feature of countries with low crime rates, and that unlike other countries, the United States is obsessed with crime.

M. Cahalan. "Trends in Incarceration in the United States Since 1880—A Summary of Reported Rates and the Distribution of Offenses." *Crime and Delinquency* 25 (1), 1979:9–41. Cahalan provides interesting historical data on the use of incarceration from 1880 to 1970. She examines possible influences on the use of incarceration.

Joan Mullen. *American Prisons and Jails, Vol. I.* Washington D.C.: United States Government Printing Office, 1980. This is the summary volume of the five-volume Abt census commissioned by the United States Congress as a means of understanding prison resources in the country. The most comprehensive data on prisons and jails available.

Nigel Walker. *Crimes, Courts, and Figures.* Baltimore: Penguin, 1971. This is an old book, but it is easy and informative reading on criminal justice statistics and their interpretation.

CHAPTER 3

INTERPRETATION OF PUNISHMENT IN AMERICAN SOCIETY

QUESTIONS

1. What are some of the common beliefs about society and punishment?
2. What is an ideology?
3. How does the dominant ideology support the punishment system?
4. What cleavages exist within the dominant ideology?
5. What happens to punishment ideology within correctional organizations?

PAINT THE TOWN DAY-GLO

Jim Horowitz, economist, was talking in such animated fashion that he was spilling his hot chocolate on the *Adams Evening News* as he pointed at the story. Jackson Greene seemed more concerned with avoiding the sailing liquid than following Jim's economic critique.

As Phil wandered into the lounge for his third cup of coffee, Jackson grinned and said "Hi, Phil. Jim has just found another absurdity in the world of criminal justice. Why don't you guys study something sensible once in a while?"

"Here, Phil. Look at this." Jim jabbed a finger at a small story at the bottom of the first page.

CRACKDOWN ON GRAFFITI ANNOUNCED

In preparation for the Adams bicentennial celebration, only three weeks away, Mayor Sam Leader and Chief of Police Alvin Wright announced a crackdown on graffiti on civic buildings. The get-tough policy goes into effect immediately, said Mayor Leader. Chief Wright reported that night-time patrols around the center city area and particularly along the Parkway will be stepped up immediately. "That is the route of the bicentennial parade. The parade will pass along some of the most beautiful public buildings in the world. We intend to keep them that way," said the Chief.

The Chief said that his department would press for full prosecution of anyone caught defacing public property and urged the public to cooperate by calling the 911 emergency number if they see suspicious activity. "This day-glo paint is particularly noxious," he said.

District Attorney Evan could not be reached for comment at the time of this report.

Phil shrugged. "So, typical stuff. You don't expect it to do any good, do you?"

Jim nearly choked. "Do you realize what it will cost the city to run extra patrols—let alone prosecute? Hell, man, they could resurface the entire downtown mall for what it will cost. Don't you realize how much cheaper it would be just to put on a couple of workmen to remove the paint, instead of trying to arrest people?"

"I'm sure you're right," said Phil. "But I think you're overlooking a few things."

Jackson Greene finally perked up. He loved the overlooked. "Why?"

"Well, to begin with, Jim forgets that criminal justice doesn't always work the way it sounds. It's one thing to announce a crackdown. Probably that's all that will really happen. The cops have better things to do than look for kids with spray paint, and the Chief knows that. He hopes the kids won't know it. So the real cost is the cost of the press conference. *But,*" said Phil with a proud smile, "I know more about it than that. I was down there yesterday, doing some work for the family court. You want to know what's really going to happen? It is a cost benefit analysis that's needed, but not the one you were doing. The issue is, how much more valuable the act of vandalism becomes now that the officials have labeled it bad business."

Jackson smiled, getting the picture. "I get it, Jim. Phil is saying that the crackdown will increase the graffiti, because it's now a more dangerous act. The kids will really be outdoing each other, to show how brave they are."

"Sure," said Phil. "All the probation officers know what's going to happen. One of them told me that two hours after the mayor hit the news, the hardware stores were sold out of day-glo. What the mayor didn't calculate is that not everyone in Adams is going to respond to threats the way he would. He wouldn't risk jail to do it anyway. The gang kids—this is playing right into their hands."

COMMON ASSUMPTIONS ABOUT PUNISHMENT AND SOCIETY

This time Phil knew what he was talking about, except that Jim's analysis turned out to be accurate as well. Within a week of the mayor's pleas, the marble walls decorating the familiar parkway stood in iridescent splendor as every youth within walking distance decided to take his turn avoiding the cops and adding his name, his gang's name, or his girlfriend's name to the bicentennial celebration. The Chief was forced to increase patrols, so to the cost of the massive cleaning job was added the cost of police manpower. One youth was caught, but when the prosecutor discovered the offender had a B average in ninth grade and no previous record, he was released to his chagrined parents. Deterrence backfired.

Phil's analysis was fairly accurate, but it might be helpful to dig deeper into the mayor's plan, the beliefs about society that sustained it, and some of the weaknesses in those beliefs.

Mayor Leader presumed that punishment would deter and that threats of more certain (and perhaps stiffer) penalties would increase the deterrent effect. He also assumed his plea for civic pride would find a sympathetic audience among most citizens. But, he knew that some people would have less civic pride than others. Thus the threat. Those who were less attached to his norms and more tempted to vandalism should have been deterred.

The youths were influenced by the mayor's threat, to be sure; they found it a challenge. The increased risk enhanced the prestige of engaging in the activity. The threat increased the attractiveness of the conduct, because it increased the potential cost.

The mayor's beliefs about Adams society were too simple. He expected people to be controlled by an informal norm (civic pride) or a formal sanction (arrest and prosecution). Norms are group pressures. If individuals are not part of the group which shares those norms, increased social controls, such as symbolic pleas or formal threats, may actually increase resistance rather than conformity (Coch and French, 1948). Adams, like other large cities, is made up of a number of social groups that have varying relationships to its formal control system. Many young people in the area did not perceive the mayor as their legitimate spokesperson. Since deterrence depends on a socially based calculation of costs and benefits, this calculation must be based upon the norms of the group whose behavior is to be controlled. If a respected gang leader had voiced a negative opinion about graffiti, that opinion might have had considerably more impact than any threats from the mayor. (For research that supports this case, see Jensen and Erickson, 1978.)

Our example is a fairly simple one concerning a rather trivial deviance, but the case does exhibit a number of typical beliefs about society that appear to support criminal punishments. Highlighting these beliefs may allow us to appreciate some of the difficulties correctional agencies face as they attempt to implement punishments.

ASSUMPTION 1. SOCIETY IS A SINGLE GROUP WITH ONE SET OF VALUES

One common belief is that society is a simple social system, much like a small group, with a leader at the core and followers displaying varying degrees of loyalty and conformity to a single set of values. This is the most important of all the beliefs underlying criminal punishment. If members of all social systems, regardless of size and heterogeneity of population, share the same values, then social control practices should have the same effects in any size system.

This belief implies that formal social controls, such as criminal punishment, operate in the same way as informal controls, such as approval or ostracism. If everyone in a society had the same values and followed the same norms, all would respond to punishments in the same way. The negative sanction would reinforce the norms of the group and reduce deviance, since all members would value membership in that group.

ASSUMPTION 2: DEVIANCE IS CHARACTERISTIC OF INDIVIDUALS

A second common belief builds on the first: that deviance is explained by characteristics of a particular individual which make it difficult for that person to follow the norms of the group. This belief recognizes that not all members of a group will follow the norms to an equal degree. Some will be leaders who, in the eyes of the group, best express the standards of group performance. Others will not achieve the norms so well and from time to time will be judged by the group to have made mistakes. The mistakes are assumed to emerge from the nature of the individual who is having trouble achieving the standards. This belief rejects the idea that deviance may be traced to the structure of society rather than to the nature of individuals. If deviance is an individual problem, social controls should keep most group members in line most of the time, by correcting individual faults and reinforcing individual commitment to group norms.

Some group social controls are incapacitative or rehabilitative. For instance, Jones, age 8, may insist on throwing his baseball bat every time he hits the baseball, putting the other players in jeopardy. The other children may insist that Jones cannot play until he learns to control that urge. This control would incapacitate Jones. A more sympathetic team member might say: "Jones, I used to do that too, but I figured out that the fastest way to start running is simply to drop the bat. You'll get there faster if you do the same." If Jones tries this suggestion and it works, perhaps he has been rehabilitated. Other small group social controls are considered retributive and deterrent; they operate on other members of the group, rather than the rule breaker. For example, Smith, age 6, who is occasionally allowed to play in late innings, watches Jones's ordeal carefully and vows tht he will never break that rule: Not throwing your bat is part of being a team member—retribution—and the thought of being thrown out of the game is too much to bear—deterrence.

The second belief about society is that crime is also a problem of individuals, and therefore can be controlled just like deviance in a small group. If someone commits a crime, punishment of that crime will reinforce the rules to which everyone subscribes, and the lawbreaker will adopt behaviors more favored by the group.

ASSUMPTION 3: CRIMINAL PUNISHMENT KEEPS SOCIETY TOGETHER

The third common belief stresses the value of criminal punishment rather than the nature of the group or the source of deviance. According to this belief, criminal punishment represents the will of all the people in the group and benefits the entire group, rather than specific individuals or factions. The government of a people is presumed to be representative of and operating for the society in which that government operates.

This belief does not imply that all members of society benefit equally from the operation of the society. It does imply that the operation of the law provides all members with the greatest opportunity to benefit, to the extent allowed by their own individual skills, abilities, and backgrounds. Thus, while life may be more pleasant and rewarding for some than for others, criminal punishment ensures that the degree of pleasantness is distributed naturally, on the basis of individual differences, rather than unnaturally, on the basis of deviant acts. For example, perhaps Jones cannot hit the baseball as frequently as Appleton and therefore Appleton enjoys more prestige on the team. But Jones must still be allowed to hit, so long as he is part of the team; the rules say all members take their turn. By the same token, Jones can't argue for more swings at the ball than Appleton is allowed in order to increase his chances of hitting the ball. His skills may reduce his reward, but neither increase or decrease his opportunity. The third belief is that the criminal law keeps members of society from cheating to obtain rewards; it keeps the distribution of rewards as fair as possible.

PUNISHMENT IDEOLOGIES

A tightly knit set of beliefs like the three above may be called an **ideology** (Abercrombie, Hill, and Turner, 1984:104–106). One significant characteristic of an ideology is that it can perpetuate itself, and the actions it justifies, whether or not the beliefs about society are accurate. An ideology is extremely difficult to change, because it contains its own prescriptions about what should be done in times of trouble (Miller, Ohlin, and Coates, 1977). For example, Mayor Leader concluded that the law was not being applied firmly or consistently enough and that the solution was to increase the strength of the control system. Ideologies based on accurate beliefs about society may produce order. Ideologies based on inaccurate beliefs produce disorder, but reinforce the existing control strategy, rather than change it. (The classic description of this process is March and Simon, 1958).

In times of increasing deviance, there is no certain means to distinguish accurate assumptions that need better implementation from inaccurate assumptions that need to be changed. Imagine the dilemma of a group leader facing rising dissension and deviance within a group. Does he risk the possibility of changing the rules in order to preserve the group? Or does he decide that the only possible way to preserve the group is for him to become firmer and sterner? Two human inclinations tend to push leaders in the second direction. First, for the group leader to acknowledge that deviance may be a result of the group structure, rather than an indication of individual difficulty, is itself a deviant act. Second, if deviance has reached crisis proportions, it appears illogical to abandon the rules. The most common response in time of trouble is to become more conservative and more defensive.

THE DOMINANT IDEOLOGY

The three interlocking beliefs described above form the most commonly held ideology of punishment in American society. To repeat briefly, this **dominant ideology** contains the following beliefs.

1. The social system is a large collection of similarly motivated poeple who subscribe to a single set of values governing behavior, and informal and formal controls are simply two different but compatible behavior controls.
2. Deviations from normative behavior are caused by deficiencies in individual members of the group, rather than by problems in the social system itself.
3. The formal control system preserves the fair and natural distribution of social benefits and rewards on the basis of individual merits and skills.

The dominant ideology contains a number of variations on these basic themes which differ primarily in the choices for implementing formal control most effectively. For example, the four most common justifications of punishment can be understood as four different approaches to the design of criminal punishment. The retributive design stresses maintenance of values and norms and downplays concern for changing behavior. The utilitarian designs stress control of behavior, and use the retributive concerns about fairness and appropriateness only to place limits on the choice of controls. Retributive and deterrent designs place greater emphasis on the impact of punishment on persons not being punished now, while rehabilitation and incapacitation emphasize the punitive impact on the individual offender. The rehabilitation design seeks to implement punishments which reduce personal deficiencies that presumably make criminals less able to follow norms. The other three designs implement punishments which reduce the negative impact of these personal deficiencies on other people.

These choices among punishment techniques can be accompanied by vociferous, acrimonious debate and by major struggles for political control of the punishment system. We have witnessed

one such struggle in the last ten years, as the forces for rehabilitation gave way, in many areas, to the forces for retribution, deterrence, and incapacitation. This type of ideological in-fighting can lead to major changes in the resources and practices of correctional systems.

One of the most successful depictions of the constant tension within the dominant ideology of punishment is Herbert Packer's "Two Models of the Criminal Process" (1968). Packer analyzed the operations of the criminal justice system as a constantly shifting balance between the Crime Control Model and the Due Process Model. The actual operations of criminal justice were compromises worked out between the competing forces for controlling crime, on the one hand, and being fair and preserving rights, on the other. Table 3.1 compares a number of points between the two models.

The choices among implementation strategies are important choices. Liberal choices can reduce the numbers of persons incarcerated, as was the case with deinstitutionalization of the juvenile justice system in Massachusetts (see Chapter 19). Swings to conservative premises about implementation can lead to massive construction campaigns.

But a full appreciation of corrections also entails the realization that all these programs share the same basic beliefs about American society and the value of punishment in that society. In other words, these conflicting programs are based on the same ideology (Griffiths, 1970). Losers do not give up on the system; and their losses are only temporary. Supporters of out of favor implementation programs retain some influence and periodically reassert their choices (Warren, Rose, and Bergunder, 1974; Miller, Ohlin, and Coates, 1978; Packer, 1968).

OTHER IDEOLOGIES

In contrast to these struggles over the most effective *means* of punishment, other ideologies challenge the basic beliefs of the dominant punish-

TABLE 3.1   A Summary of Characteristics of Packer's Two Models of the Criminal Process

CRIME CONTROL	DUE PROCESS
1 Criminal justice process is positive guarantee of social freedom	Criminal process is most severe social sanction to be used on free citizens
2 Criminal acts are major threat to social order	Investigation and prosecution of crimes can lead to severe constriction of social freedoms
3 To ensure social order we need high rates of apprehension and conviction	To ensure freedom we need to guarantee that procedures of apprehension and conviction are of high quality
4 To achieve high rates we need a system that can process cases routinely with speed and finality of outcome	To ensure minimal abuse of coercive sanctions we must have highly visible decision process and means for review and challenge of outcomes
5 Speed can be gained through uniformity of procedures for all cases, and finality can be achieved through an informal, administrative decision-making process	To ensure visibility and care we must emphasize individuality of cases and high formality with a judicial decision-making process
6 The best way of implementing above needs is through an "administrative" assembly line structure	The best way of implementing above safeguards is through adversary process, with continual checks and balances to provide obstacle course to flow of cases
7 Successful conclusion is achieved by an early screening-out of people who are innocent or unlikely to be convicted, and gaining quick and inexpensive convictions of the rest, with little opportunity for challenge	Successful conclusion is full application of rights in adversary proceeding which is concerned with determining the criminal responsibility of the accused
8 This conclusion rests on a presumption of guilt, which is a prediction of likely outcome of the case	This conclusion rests on a "presumption of innocence," which is a directive about how to proceed regardless of the probable outcome
9 Focal point of process is the guilty plea, which holds need for judicial fact-finding to a minimum	Focal point is the trial, because adjudicative fact-finding is most accurate and fair
10 Reliability of the process is assured through high efficiency—processing cases as quickly and cheaply as possible, screening out weak cases prior to prosecution	Reliability of the process is through quality control on each case; more efficiency can be oppressive in individual instance
11 Correction of errors through administrative controls; criminals should never be released because of mistaken procedure by officials	Correction of errors through appeal; "self-corrective" mechanism applied on a case-by-case basis; release of offenders, as correction, deters official misbehavior in the future
12 There is basic confidence in the agency action and in the representativeness of the government that structured the executive agencies	There is basic doubt about the efficacy of punishment applied through formal governmental mechanisms
13 The validating authority in this process is legislative and statutory, where directives for action are set	The validating authority of this process is judicial and constitutional, where limits to allowable action are set

SOURCE: David E. Duffee and Robert Fitch, *An Introduction to Corrections: A Policy and Systems Approach*. Pacific Palisades, CA: Goodyear, 1976, 348–349.

ment ideology. These other belief systems are often labeled radical or **critical ideologies,** because their interpretation of punishment leads to criticism of the entire political control system. Three critical challenges to the dominant ideology are reviewed below: the Marxist, the anarchist, and the conflicted systems.

THE MARXIST IDEOLOGY

The most difficult ideology to describe is often identified as the Marxian interpretation of punishment. The difficulty stems from the fact that Marx himself had relatively little to say about criminal justice and criminal punishment (Groves, 1982). Persons seek to elaborate a **Marxist ideology** of punishment face two challenging tasks. First, they need to "update" Marx to include certain problems Marx did not address. Then they must proceed to an application of the updated principles directly to the operation of criminal justice. Two of the better-known examples of this attempt are Richard Quinney's work (1977) and Jeffrey Reiman's analysis (1979).

The Marxian interpretation of punishment rejects all three assumptions of the dominant punishment ideology. First, a capitalist society is not seen as a single group with a single set of norms, but as a system comprised of at least two classes, those of capital and labor. Capitalists control labor because they control the means of production and have an exploitive, coercive relationship with the working class, which sustains itself by selling its labor.

Second, although Marxists perceive deviance to stem from a number of specific causes, they generally argue that the underlying sources of crime arise from class conflict. They would argue that the criminal law preserves the property rights which protect the capitalist system. The enforcement of the law systematically excludes labor from control of its own future. As poverty spreads through the working class, demands for survival press individuals to compete in a number of ways, including victimizing others for economic gain.

Violent crime can be more complicated to explain, but a Marxist interpretation would point toward the ghettoization of labor, the alienation of workers from each other, and the emergence of violent subcultures as the family and other informal controls among the working class break down. Marxists might agree that specific acts of deviance stem from individual problems, but according to Marxists, class conflict is the source of those individuual problems.

Third, Marxists view the punishment system as benefiting the interests of the controlling class, rather than as an instrument that benefits the entire social group. Marxists would also argue that the visible attempts in capitalist systems to deliver "fair criminal justice" hide the deeper injustices. The due process and offenders' rights movements may temper state force, but by doing so merely strengthen the message that crime is an individual problem.

In some sense, the Marxian position on punishment may see criminal activity as "politically caused," but it does not interpret typical street crime as politically motivated or morally inexcusable. Instead, Marxists interpret criminal activity as the behavior of politically uninformed individuals who have become totally self-interested. The dominant punishment ideology, in summary, operates to perpetuate both crime and criminal identities as means of keeping the lower class disorganized and victimized (Cavender, 1984:203–213).

In the last several years, Marxian philosophers have struggled with the difficult question of which justification for punishment in our current society should be preferred, since a political revolution does not appear to be a solution to perceived social injustice. J. G. Murphy (1979:79) asserted that Marxian analysis would favor retribution, rather than utilitarian justifications. However, Marxists would argue that our current society may not have the right to dispense retributive justice because it is not a community of responsible individuals (Murphy 1979:102–110). Nevertheless, Marxists might conclude that a retributive scheme, even under conditions of social injustice, may be preferable to a deterrent or rehabilitative justification, because it provides a greater measure of respect for the individual and places more restrictions on the powers of the state (Murphy, 1979:102–110, Cavender, 1984; and Braithwaite, 1982a,786–789).

THE ANARCHIST IDEOLOGY

The **anarchist** position shares many beliefs with the Marxist position, particularly regarding capitalism. However, the anarchists disagree with Marxists on solutions to social conflict. And the anarchists oppose all complex social structures, rather than only capitalist structures. The anarchist position on crime and punishment is perhaps best represented by Tifft and Sullivan (1980) and Sullivan (1980).

Anarchists argue that complex formal organizations are fundamentally destructive of natural human inclinations toward cooperation and mutual aid. The class distinctions the Marxists trace to ownership of the means of production, the anarchists trace to the differential distribution of power. The fundamental conflict is between the managed and the managers. Increasing complexity, not simply of work organizations but of all aspects of life, pushes human beings toward narrow specializations and dependence upon organizational rules for governing their interactions with each other. People become alienated from each other, estranged from their own feelings, and unable to cooperate.

The anarchist reaction to the three assumptions that dominate punishment systems are as follows. First, modern society is not a simple system in which we all belong to the same group and subscribe to the same norms. It is composed of conflicting groups separated by formal roles differentiated in power. Second, deviance has its source in the inability of human beings to conform to the simple and narrow roles assigned to people in the world of complex organizations. Third, a system of punishment is a means of preserving

coercive social structures by forcing criminals to conform to the rules of competition and specialization. An anarchist belief system does not accept any form of punishment as satisfactory; it argues instead for a communal settlement of disputes and differences without resorting to roles or labels of "victim" and "offender."

THE CONFLICTED SYSTEMS IDEOLOGY

The last ideology we will review here is difficult to label. It is a view held by some systems analysts. And some people may object to the view being labeled an "ideology" rather than a "theory," because the **conflicted systems** view is derived from general systems theory, rather than from a politically motivated set of beliefs. However, the term ideology, as used in this chapter, can be applied to this position. The basic assumptions of the conflicted systems ideology are not directly testable; they form a set of interlocking beliefs. Two of the best examples of the conflicted systems view are the works of T. M. Mills (1959) and Leslie Wilkins (1965).

This ideology insists on a major difference between deviance and control in small groups and deviance and control in large, complex societies. Informal control is the application of informal group standards to behavior *within* a small group. Formal control, on the other hand, is the application of written rules by state officials to behavior *across* all groups in the society.

Formal controls are operated by complex control organizations. Each organization has only partial responsibility for the problems of human beings. Control of deviance is divided up among many different agencies: There are welfare systems, criminal justice systems, mental health systems, juvenile justice systems, and so on. None of the officials in any of the systems has the resources or the responsibility to deal with a whole individual. One system deals with lack of money, but not with crime. Another deals with crime, but not with mental anguish and confusion.

The specialization found in formal controls is not found in informal controls. In informal groups, attempts are made by the group to engage the whole individual whose behavior is deviant. The solution, if one is discovered, may have very little direct resemblance to the behavior that caught the group's attention in the first place. The control response reevaluates the deviant behavior in terms of underlying difficulties and attempts to deal with the causes of the deviant behavior. In formal control by complex societies, there may be some lip service to "root causes" but, since no one agency has the responsibility for root causes, the focus of any agency is on the behavior within its jurisdiction. Therefore, complex societies that rely on formal controls have difficulty matching deviant actions with control responses.

Moreover, the responses by formal control systems become even more complicated. The interpretation of agency jurisdiction and the definition of the behavior to be controlled can easily vary from one level of the agency to the next. There is often a difference between control agency policy and the behavior of the agents on the front line. Organizations tend to push officers to follow rules rather than control deviant behavior. Control organizations invest a great deal of effort in preserving the *image* that they provide effective control.

The conflicted systems ideology rejects all three assumptions of the dominant punishment ideology. (1) The conflicted systems ideology perceives society to be made up of many groups in varying degrees of conflict, both about abstract values and about implementation decisions. (2) Deviance has both individual and social sources, but the formal control agencies do not deal with all of an individual's problems and fail to recognize the system sources of deviance, such as conflicts among groups. (3) The formal control system is not similar in operation or in results to informal control systems. Instead, it is a complex system of specialized responses that has limited ability to control deviance. The conflicted systems ideology proposes that formal control systems, including punishment, have not been designed to control deviance in complex society and as a result may not be benefiting anyone.

THE RELATIONSHIP BETWEEN CRITICAL AND DOMINANT BELIEFS

The four punishment ideologies provide different interpretations of punishment history. The Marxist, anarchist, and conflicted system beliefs, which we can call "critical" ideologies, all claim that the dominant punishment ideology is "ahistorical"—in other words, that it ignores how the system of punishment evolved. Because it ignores the evolution of punishment, it is also blind to the development of feasible alternatives to the current system. In other terms, the critical ideologies claim that the dominant ideology does not recognize the ways in which the structure of society determines the forms of control found in that society. The dominant view of punishment, argue the critical ideologies, overemphasizes the extent to which ideas—such as the justifications of punishment—govern the control system. The rival positions assert that even the likelihood that an idea will get expressed is controlled to a large degree by the position of the holder of the idea in the social structure.

The punishment system may undergo small revisions, but the critical ideologies view these changes as trivial, as superficial adjustments that do not alter the basic operation of the system. For example, merits of retribution versus those of rehabilitation have been actively debated in the last ten years. The critical ideologies view this type of contest as relatively insignificant. Systems analyst Leslie Wilkins, responding to *Doing Justice*, an early retributive statement, said he could find little novelty in deciding that offenders were "bad" rather than "mad" (Wilkins, in Von Hirsch, 1976).

The contention that the dominant ideology is ignorant of history and uncritical of social struc-

Correctional organizations are complex. Staff perception of problems is partially dependent on the opportunities presented by the roles they perform. *Above:* New York State central office team deals with an officers' strike in 1979. *Left:* Officer in Elmira correctional facility supervises inmates. (New York State Department of Correctional Services)

ture is to some extent accurate, but also understandable. Remember that these rival ideologies are not actually operating control systems, but criticizing the one in force. Those who are operating our punishment systems are not seeking alternative courses of action, but are seeking to implement the system they are committed to. They are likely to adopt assumptions, accurate or not, which pose that system in a favorable light. The adoption of a favorable belief system may help the actors in the punishment system perform their roles. We can understand the dominant ideology as a set of beliefs that makes difficult action in our current system palatable to the actors, while we can understand the critical ideologies as counterpressure belief systems, whose existence makes change possible.

The dominant ideology is a defense of the system and of the integrity of its a actors. The rival ideologies may or may not criticize the integrity of the actors, but they do challenge the effectiveness of the system. The challengers often emphasize history to indicate that the leading ideas of a time arose from and are explained by a particular historical context. For them, the specific justifications of punishment are less important than understanding how the justifications help the system survive. The dominant ideology, however, is often less concerned with how a particular practice originated than to what uses it can now be put. Thus for those committed to the current punishment system, modifications in ideology and practice—while these may look like minor alterations to outsiders—appear to be major concerns to insiders. The difference in viewpoint can perhaps be understood by the analogy to two groups of people arguing about games. One group, committed to the game of chess, may spend a great deal of time debating the best opening gambit by which to win a game. A group of dissenters, however, may see the argument over these decisions to be mere diversions; they might prefer to argue over the selection of games and claim that chess is historically outdated and should be replaced by football. The chess players are more interested in how to play chess well

than in whether an analysis of its origins points to the possibility of other games. A brief overview of the four ideologies is provided in Table 3.2.

ALTERNATE INTERPRETATIONS OF HISTORY

SOCIAL ORDER WITHOUT PUNISHMENT

One major point of contention is the historical challenge to the first assumption in the dominant ideology. Spokesmen for the dominant view, such as Ernest van den Haag (1975), insist that any social system is dependent on a criminal punishment system in order to maintain order. (For more detail on van den Haag's position, see Insert 3.1. This viewpoint is consistent with the first belief, that all societies are essentially similar. The critical ideologies take exception to this belief. They rely on historical and anthropological evidence that some previous and some current societies do not depend on punishment systems to maintain order.

Simple societies, such as aboriginal tribes and subsistence nomads, often do not resort to distinctions between victim and offender. Instead, social dissension is handled in a restitutive, conciliatory manner. The objective does not seem to place blame on a particular individual, but instead settling the dispute so that the group can get on with its work. Schwartz and Miller (1965) suggest that this characteristic of simple societies may arise from the high value each member has for the survival of the group. In complex societies, individuals have become unnecessary for group survival. Therefore, the society can focus on symbolic controls, such as retribution, rather than on practical controls, such as settling the dispute.

Anarchists would use these data to suggest that society could return to nonpunitive sanctions, if people were able to settle their own differences rather than depend on complex organizations. Marxists would not consider a return to simple control systems, but they would argue

TABLE 3.2   Four Punishment Ideologies

CHARACTERISTIC	DOMINANT	MARXIST	ANARCHIST	CONFLICTED SYSTEMS
1. Nature of society	Contains a consensus on values which are maintained by both formal and informal means	Contains a conflict of values between capitalists and labor. Formal controls enforce the values which preserve superordinate interests.	Contains a conflict of values between the powerful and powerless. Formal controls preserve the status differential.	Contains a number of different groups with varying interests. Formal control systems aggravate differences.
2. Nature of deviance	Indicates moral, physical, or psychological deficiencies in the deviant person.	Indicates the deterioration of individuals caused by unequal distribution of resources.	Indicates the deterioration of natural human communal spirit caused by hierarchical power relations.	Indicates both individual and social system problems, but formal control system interprets all deviance as individually based and makes no provision for changes in group relations.
3. Nature of punishment	Focuses on controlling individuals by correcting their faults or enforcing norms. Major rifts in ideology concern the devices of how to handle deviants.	Preserves inequality by controlling deviants and reinforcing the belief in individual pathology.	Replaces cooperative conciliatory social interaction with rules of losers and winners.	Punishment reinforces the belief in the individual nature of deviance but punishment organizations are unequipped to reduce it; organizations invest in public relations to preserve their resources.

that the evidence indicates that when classes of persons are not alienated from the whole group by the nature of production, punishment is less likely to occur. The conflicted systems view uses such information to bolster the argument that punishment does not operate in the same way as informal controls.

PUNISHMENT AND PARTICULAR ECONOMIC SYSTEMS

The second point made by the critical ideologies is that punishment arose with the emergence of capitalism. All three critical ideologies concur

that the state role in punishment became stronger as a capitalist economy required stable relationships among persons and organizations. In particular, the notion of the state as victim emerged as the state assumed some responsibility for the protection of property rights and for the enforcement of order so that commerce and industry could flourish.

In precommercial states such as the Roman Empire, policing was done by branches of the army rather than by a separate civil police. The order that was of interest to the state was primarily threats to state sovereignty, so many crimes between people were not of interest.

Insert 3.1 SOCIAL AND CRIMINAL JUSTICE IN ERNEST VAN DEN HAAG'S *PUNISHING CRIMINALS*

One of the more influential books in reshaping ideas about criminal punishment in the 1970s was Ernest van den Haag's *Punishing Criminals* (1975). Van den Haag's positions on retribution, deterrence, and rehabilitation are presented in Chapter 1. This summary focuses on his key assumptions, rather than on the specific reasons that he favors a retributive/deterrent criminal justice system.

In conclusion, van den Haag reminds his readers:

> The task, then, as I saw it, was not to dream up an order that can do without punishment but rather to consider how punishment can be just and effective— neither less nor more harsh and certain than required to secure life, liberty, and the pursuit of happiness (1975:265).

Van den Haag seems himself as a realist. He admits that punishment is painful and that the infliction of pain by a civilized society must be done with the utmost caution. Punishment should never be done unless absolutely necessary. But van den Haag argues that punishment is quite necessary, in this or any society. He devotes the major portion of his book to detailing what punishments, and what threats of punishment, are required in order to maintain safety and ensure justice, in a limited sense.

Retributive justice is the work of criminal justice (1975:30). It is limited to punishing persons who have broken the criminal law. Social justice, writes van den Haag, if it ever exists, is the result of the fair distribution of rewards throughout society. Since criminal justice can do no more than reinforce whatever distributive order exists in society, criminal justice will preserve distributive injustices, if they exist.

But van den Haag defends criminal justice in a social system which others often perceive as distributively unjust (many people get more than they need and others far less, regardless of moral worth). He argues that a capitalist market system may well produce injustices, but that a political rather than an economic distribution of rewards would have equal if not worse problems. While persons who receive the least in a capitalist system may commit more crimes than those who receive more, the injustices of the distributive system do not explain or excuse criminal behavior. Most poor people do not commit crimes. The poor (and the rich) who commit crimes must be held individually responsible. Modern society may create the opportunity for crime, and produce some of the temptations to engage in it. Therefore modern society must also fashion a deterrent justice system that makes the opportunities less attractive, and a retributive system that helps control temptation. Ignoring crimes, or rehabilitating rather than punishing, both create added injustices to the lives of those who have not broken the criminal law. Asking the criminal justice system to be less than retributive and deterrent will not remove the social injustices from the social system, but will only create additional disorder and suffering.

French monarchies developed a distinction between high and low police. The high police dealt with threats to sovereignty, and low police handled the citizen-to-citizen complaints that today are the most common types of crimes.

The French monarchy was not very interested in maintaining internal order. A primarily agrarian economy did not depend on the smooth conduct of commerce. It was in the English state that policing of everyday behavior became of great interest to the state. All members of English villages were charged with keeping "the king's peace" by setting up night watches and reporting wrongdoing to the king's sheriff. It was also England that became commercialized and industrialized most quickly, and therefore where public order was of most concern to the maintenance of the economy.

The critical ideologies argue that it was only as the state became a mechanism for preserving economic order that punishment for crimes against the state incorporated common crimes in the daily life of communities. All three ideologies use this historical development to argue that beneath the debates about the purposes of punishment, the current system maintains a particular economic structure in which individual victims are far less important than orderly organized commerce. These ideologies claim that the retributive justification of punishment ignores the link between preservation of the moral order and the economic order which underlies that particular morality. The utilitarian justifications are criticized on the ground that punishment does not increase public safety, but instead maintains economic inequalities.

THE EMERGENCE OF THE PENITENTIARY

A final historical criticism concerns the selection of the prison as the preferred mode of punishment. Within the dominant belief system, the prison is viewed as a reform of previous punitive practices, such as corporal punishment and frequent use of the death penalty. According to this rendition of history, the prison emerged in the eighteenth century as human beings came to be understood as rational, self-controlled creatures rather than as inherently wicked and sinful. The penitentiary was based on the human's rational character. In the late nineteenth century, punishment underwent a second wave of reform in order to make prisons more humane and to incorporate increasingly sophisticated rehabilitative techniques. At the same time, the juvenile court and probation arose as a means of classifying persons who needed more or less state intervention or needed interventions of different sorts. (For a brief review of this view, see Martin, Sechrest, and Redner, 1981:4–5; and Ignatieff, 1981:161–170.)

This view of prison development as a gradual and rational process, responding incrementally to new social technologies, has been challenged by critical historians. Revisionist histories stress that prisons were not developed because they were more humane than the punishments they replaced, but because they better served the evolving economic and political order. For example, Marxists have argued that imprisonment performed two important functions in capitalist economies. Prisons controlled unemployed, unskilled labor during economic downturns and kept labor costs low by releasing workers to the labor market when the economy improved (Rusche and Kircheimer, 1939). A more recent Marxist history focuses on the psychological impact of imprisonment as an important means of producing disciplined workers (Foucault, 1978).

In either case, the revisionist histories propose that the institution of imprisonment was an effective means of controlling the lower class and an effective way to increase the intrusiveness of state power. A Marxist critique of deinstitutionalization in the twentieth century continues that line of reasoning by suggesting that community supervision has become popular not because of its effectiveness, but because it is cheaper (Scull, 1977).

A recent review article by Michael Ignatieff (1981) offers some important criticisms of both dominant and revisionist histories. Ignatieff complains that both versions are incomplete. Dominant ideology historians place too much confidence in the stated intentions of reformers, and critical historians place too much confidence in the notions of ruling class and state power (1092:173–180). The radical explanations, according to Ignatieff, may help to explain why punishment takes place, but they do not adequately explain the specific form of punishment. He claims that the ideological belief in the drama of repentance through imprisonment did play an important role in the development of prisons. But Ignatieff was not satisfied with the dominant view, either:

Instead of looking for some hidden function which prisons actually succeed in discharging, we ought to work free of such fuctionalist assumptions altogether and begin to think of society in much more dynamic and historical terms, as being ordered by institutions like the prisons which fail their constituencies and which limp along because no alternative can be found or because conflict over alternatives is too great to be mediated into compromise (1981:181).

Ignatieff prefers the conflicted systems approach. Prisons, and other punishments, cannot be understood as social instruments that serve either the whole society or a dominant group. Instead, our punishment system is part of our social structure, and does as much to order society as the other way around. This view of history is compatible with the conflicted systems belief that complex organizations become quite active in marshaling support for themselves, whether they serve society well or not. Traditional history views the prison as the most effective means of preserving order in society. Marxist and anarchist histories interpret the development of the prison as a more effective way for dominant groups to control subordinate classes. The conflicted system view turns these ideas around: It views the belief in prison as an effective strategy by prison bureaucracies for maintaining support.

Each of these interpretations of history has some empirical support; they differ more in their assessment of how facts are connected than in their selection of facts. Weighing these interpretations of the development of punishment and integrating their relative contributions can help us to understand current correctional operations and to predict when shifts may take place.

But these historical interpretations involve rather grand-scale theorizing about the scope and shape of criminal punishment in the long run. They raise lofty questions about how punishment supports society, or in the conflicted systems view, how society supports punishment. While these are important issues, they should not becloud the current issues of people working in punishment organizations or of people being punished. Immediate concerns are also important. Studying what happens to the dominant ideology during the course of daily correctional administration can help us keep the short-range and long-range issues in perspective. Let us listen in, then, on the exploits of Phil, John, and Ken as they try to disentangle the ideological position governing one correctional organization.

JUST WHAT ARE THE GOALS, ANYWAY?

Phil was on the road again, this time with his research assistants John and Ken, who were deep in conversation planning the upcoming interviews. They were studying the new prerelease centers in the Department of Correction.

Ken was thumbing through the department's proposal for the centers. "From the looks of this proposal," he said, "these guys have been reading those articles you and Professor Masters wrote on reintegration. I mean, they really have it all down—easing the transition from prison to parole, allowing offenders to test new behaviors in a real world setting, working closely with community leaders to provide new opportunities. Do you think they really do all this stuff?"

Phil shrugged. "That's the point of interviewing at every level in the organization, from the commissioner on down to the residents. It's nice to see those goals in a proposal, but it's another thing to put them into operation."

The central office building was as nondescript as the Dunmore prison. They found the director's office without trouble. George Jenison, the newly appointed director, greeted them warmly. Jenison looked quite proud to be in charge, but perhaps not quite ready to be in charge. The desk seemed confining.

Although Phil assumed Jenison had read the evaluation contract, he patiently explained the design of the study again. "We'd like to begin by asking you how you plan to implement the goals stated in your proposal to the State Planning Agency."

Jenison laughed and lit another cigar. "*My* proposal? What do you mean, *my* proposal? That was written by Baker before he was fired. It got us the money for this program, but that's not the way I see it operating."

Phil raised an eyebrow. "So you don't subscribe to the goal statement in here—" he waved the proposal—"about gradual reentry to the community, services aimed at establishing new behavior patterns for the residents. . . ."

Jenison waved. "Look," he said, "this is a prison system. These guys are being punished. Sure, the centers are supposed to be less rigid and less secure than the prisons, but the residents are still doing time. Baker's proposal might talk about all sorts of opportunity and job readiness and so on, but he forgot one important part of any penal system—and that's control."

The conversation went on for an hour and a half. Jenison did as much interviewing as answering questions. He promised Phil and his assistants every cooperation, but also made it clear that he had some new objectives for the evaluation, regardless of what the contract called for. "I want your help with ideas on how to get this program under control. The staff got the notion under Baker that just about anything goes. And they passed that attitude on to the residents. There's got to be some central direction here, and I'm going to provide it."

Back in the parking lot, John and Ken started to giggle. "So much for proposals," said Ken. "I mean, the program statement doesn't mean anything."

"That's what happens when administrations change," said Phil.

"But isn't he obligated to fulfill the contract?" asked John. "Can he just change the whole direction of the program, after he has the money?"

"I guess we'll find out, won't we?" said Phil. "It probably boils down to who has the most clout with the governor—the Department of Correction, which runs the program, or the State Planning Agency, which funds the program. Who would you bet on, the planners or the wardens?"

"The wardens!" Ken and John chimed in unison. They piled into the car and John read the directions to the Madison center. It was only ten minutes from the central office, but in a decidedly different world.

They walked along a littered sidewalk to Number 32 Greene Street. This was a large beige building, in no better shape than the others on each side of it. There was no sign on the structure. On the front stoop, a loud argument was attracting attention. A skinny young man with tattooed arms stood on the sidewalk and screamed up at the massive black woman in the doorway. The argument over, the man disappeared.

Phil, John, and Ken looked at the address on the paper, and then back at the number over the doorway, and then at the large woman, who was smoothing out her dress in preparation for ascending the stairs, her task done.

"Excuse me, ma'am," asked Phil quietly.

"Can I help you?" she asked politely.

"We're looking for the Madison Prerelease Center. We're from the University."

"You found it," she announced. "You want to see Director Sims?"

"I guess we'll start with him."

"I'll show you to his office. I'm Dora Robbins, the day shift house manager. We've been expecting you."

Director Sims met them inside. Apparently he had witnessed most of the argument between one of his residents and his house manager, but had done nothing to interfere. When his office door was closed, he smiled approvingly. "She can run a tight ship.

Wish I had two more like her. What can I do for you?"

Phil explained the purpose of the evaluation, and mentioned their morning visit with Jenison. Sims nodded. "Yeah, he'll shake the system up all right, but it won't happen the way he plans. Don't get me wrong. He's the boss now, and we'll cooperate as best we can. But there are limits. We're *not* running a prison here. This is a service center."

Phil perked up. "Then you're saying you are still committed to the goals in the proposal."

Sims looked around at his bookcase. "Proposal? What proposal? Oh, you mean the application to the State Planning Agency?"

Phil nodded. "I mean the original goals written for the program."

"Well, in a way. I take exception to some of that stuff," said Sims. "Is that really what you're looking for?"

Phil shrugged. "Not necessarily. That's only a beginning. We're not in favor of one set of goals or another. We're just trying to understand what the objectives of the program are."

Sims nodded. "Are you visiting each of the centers?" The researchers nodded. "Well, then, I think you've got your job cut out for you. You visit twelve centers, you will get twelve different answers. We each have different goals, when you get right down to it. I can only tell you what mine are."

"Okay," said Phil. "Why don't you focus just on that. Maybe you could start with what you take exception to in Mr. Baker's proposal."

"Sure. I knew Baker pretty well. I helped to write part of that. It was a pretty tight group when this program started. But you have to remember that Baker was writing the proposal to attract the funds. I don't mean it's inaccurate, really, but things that make sense up there on Capitol Hill don't

always make sense down here on Greene Street."

"What would you say are the major differences?"

"The recidivism stuff, mainly. You look through that plan, it talks about reducing *crime.*"

"And you disagree with that?"

Sims shook his head. "No, no, reducing crime is fine. If you can do it. If you know how to do it. But I don't know those things. My counselors don't know those things. What does it mean, to say 'reduce crime?' Keep guys from going back to prison? I can do that by not reporting violations. But that might not reduce crime. My job is to get these kids straightened out and to upgrade their skills. I mean, *these* are my problems. My objectives. You can talk about reducing crime all you want, but my staff and I are here to provide services. If it reduces crime, okay; if it doesn't, it doesn't. The kids still need family counseling and better jobs."

Phil spoke up: "Well, specifically, I guess, and also in general, I need to know what objectives the residents think the program has. I mean, so far, we've seen one set of goals in the proposal, another set from Mr. Jenison, and now a different set from you. I was just wondering what kind of program goals the residents see.

"You're better off asking the residents," said Sims. "And I guess you will. But if you want my guess, I'd say 80 percent of them will probably say something different altogether. They'll say this program is here because they deserve it—they all did at least a year in the prison, they've had six months with no disciplinary reports, and the good behavior warrants this placement. For them, it's got nothing to do with services."

That evening, on the ride back to the university, the discussion was a good bit different than on the trip down in the morning. "So what *are* the goals of the program?" asked John. "The written goals talk about reintegration and crime reduction. The director talks about controlling people. The center director talks about services, and justifies them on the grounds that they are needed. And ten of the fifteen residents said they were being rewarded for good behavior. Is there something in common there?"

"They all come from the same system," Ken offered, half facetiously.

"That's not so silly," said Phil. "That is about what they have in common, at least relative to goals. No single belief system controls what goes on there, or at least it doesn't look that way."

"Do you think Jenison's goals will prevail, in the long run?" asked Ken.

Phil thought a minute. "In the long run, Jenison won't be there. He'll go the same way Baker did."

"Well, then, how about the proposal? Won't they eventually need to meet the contract goals, no matter who is in charge?"

Phil shrugged. "Probably not. Think of it. By the time we get recidivism results—whatever they are—the program will be three years old. If the results are good, the director will use them. If the results are bad, the director will blame them on some past director and claim they no longer reflect what the program is doing."

"Then what is this evaluation all about?" asked John.

"Maybe it will be about how goals and program operations don't stay still long enough to be understood. Or about how each level in the organization has its own objectives."

MUTLIPLE LEVELS AND MULTIPLE COMMITMENTS IN CORRECTIONAL ORGANIZATIONS

Several years later, Phil's conclusions on the prerelease center program turned out to be fairly

similar to his prediction after his first day of interviewing. In between, several directors had come and gone, hundreds of residents had passed through the centers and on to parole. About 10 percent of them, as it turned out, were returned to prison after two years of parole supervision, a much lower failure rate than for most parolees, but not necessarily a demonstration of program success. Phil and his assistants could not demonstrate that the "success" rate was due to the program rather than to the characteristics of the inmates selected for the program. But the program was called a success by the commissioner, and after six years the Department funded the program directly out of its state budget, and took the program off grant status with the State Planning Agency.

If Phil and his colleagues learned something from their examination of goals, it went something like this. The organization went through a series of stated goals in its first eight years of operation. The Central Office concern for control and rules waxed and waned, but did not much change the behavior of the staff in the centers. After a while, the centers simply became another accepted part of the system run by the Department of Correction. They succeeded in surviving.

From time to time, a new program administrator, or a new legislator, or a new governor would talk about altering the goals of the program. He or she would argue about how the program had to keep pace with the times. And as the public spokespersons for the program called upon new ideologies as a means of criticizing old ideologies, the prerelease program would change a bit. It changed the most at the top. New governors appointed new commissioners, and new commissioners appointed new directors. New directors talked about reshaping the program. But in the centers, the changes were less dramatic. And not all the changes occurred in unison. Sometimes counselors stuck to their own ideological position, regardless of the messages from their superiors. Some counselors insisted that they were too practical to worry about philosophies and ideologies. And some simply found new ways to justify their old behavior under the new belief system.

When Phil was pushed to describe the "goals" of the program, he stated that the center *eventually* settled on a fairly therapeutic, counseling-rich program which sought to help the residents make both economic and social adjustments to community living. But he denied that the goal was one with which everyone in the program agreed, or that it had been the goal which had guided program development. The operational goals of the program—the ends it actually achieved—seemed to derive from compromise, conflict, and incremental adjustments among politicians, administrators and counselors over a long period of time. The founder of the program, Mr. Baker, whom Phil knew only by reading his proposal, had been described by many as a charismatic, ideologically driven person, dedicated to reducing prison populations and increasing the use of community programs. The eventual program bore little resemblance to the goals Baker had proposed, but the operational goals never came to reflect George Jenison's get-tough attitude either.

Commenting on goals in corrections, Francis Allen (1964:35) observed:

> Experience has demonstrated that, in practice, there is a strong tendency for the rehabilitative ideal to serve purposes that are essentially incapacitative rather than therapeutic in nature.

Correctional organizations modify stated goals. Allen lamented that rehabilitative justification of punishment lost credibility because the organizations did not implement the stated intentions. But if Allen had examined the Jefferson prerelease system when Phil was conducting his evaluation, he could have observed the opposite: The system had the capacity to bend the incapacitative ideal of Director Jenison toward rehabilitative purposes. Correctional organization ability to modify goals does not operate in only one direction; it can modify both liberal and conservative values.

Observing this tendency in many correctional programs, Austin and Krisberg (1981:166) stated that the practical consequences of ideological reforms are the results of *interactive* and *dialectic* processes between outside political and economic forces and internal agency forces. The agencies may resist, transform, or destroy reformulations of goals, depending on the "perceived value of that reform to the agency's survival" (1981:166).

When we compare the changing ideological forces working on the Jefferson prerelease system, we could classify *all* the purposes as falling within the "dominant ideology." The reintegration, rehabilitation, and incapacitation aims of the various system leaders would be seen as fairly minor change, as far as Marxists or anarchists would be concerned. But of course we will rarely find a Marxist or an anarchist running a correctional organization. The conflicted system ideology would interpret the prerelease history as a case of a system finding the path of least resistance: People at the top of the organization changed the tune from time to time, in keeping with political and economic changes in the state, while the behavior of staff and clients down at the bottom remained reasonably stable, and structured by their daily problems rather than by the changing wisdom of their leaders.

SUMMARY

1. Four ideological positions, or belief systems, treat very differently the operation of punishment in modern society.
2. The dominant ideology focuses on the expressed goals of punishment. It stresses retribution, deterrence, incapacitation, and rehabilitation, sometimes alone and sometimes together. This ideology assumes that punishment in complex societies op-

erates in about the same way, and with about the same consequences as informal controls in simple social system.

3. The Marxist ideology argues that the real control function of the punishment system is subjection of the lower class to the upper class and the preservation of a capitalist economic order.

4. The anarchist ideology argues that reliance on formal control systems makes people dependent on the roles of superior and subordinate and makes the human group less capable of solving its problems in consensual, informal ways.

5. Finally, the conflicted systems ideology presents the formal control system, including punishment, as too fragmented and specialized to respond effectively to social problems in the modern world.

It sees the punishment system often creating conflict rather than reducing it. It also perceives correctional organizations as perpetuating the dominant view as a way of protecting organizational interest.

6. The dominant ideology represents the controlling political force; its adherents propose new goals and new programs. However, the complex organizations that implement punishment are so large and complex that they do not do precisely or only what political leaders believe should happen.

7. Emphasis on ideological positions probably has minimal relevance to the short term, here-and-now interests and problems at the front line of corrections, but they are important in long-term trends in correctional practice.

KEY WORDS

ANARCHIST IDEOLOGY OF PUNISHMENT. Contains the beliefs that modern society is based on structured power relationships, that deviance is a product of fitting human relationships into hierarchical rules, and that the current punishment system preserves the power system while reducing human capacity for cooperation.

CONFLICTED SYSTEMS IDEOLOGY OF PUNISHMENT. Contains the beliefs that modern society is composed of many diverse groups, that deviance is partially a product of formal control systems' inability to deal with social complexity, and that punishment organizations are more effective in maintaining their political support than in delivering effective social control.

CRITICAL IDEOLOGIES. Ideologies that challenge the dominant ideology, typically by analyzing social control systems as behaviors emerging from particular political and economic structures.

DOMINANT IDEOLOGY OF PUNISHMENT. The punishment ideology which is politically accepted. In the United States, the ideology which accepts punishment as a means of retribution, deterrence, incapacitation and/or rehabilitation. Essential beliefs include (1) That society has a consensus of values, (2) that deviance from those values indicates individual not system malfunction, and (3) that punishment protects a fair system of social rewards.

IDEOLOGY. A tightly knit set of beliefs, often with political implications, that justify a particular action system.

MARXIAN IDEOLOGY OF PUNISHMENT. Contains the beliefs that capitalist society has built in conflicts between capitalists and laborers, that deviance is a result of class structure, and that the punishment system protects the unequal distribution of resources.

PROJECTS AND QUESTIONS

1. This chapter has dealt with some fairly complex issues, such as the relationship between beliefs and behaviors. The dominant ideology tends to assume that beliefs and attitudes of a political group determine the actions it takes. The critical ideologies argue that people adopt beliefs that are consistent with and justify behavior. How do you stand on this issue? Why?

2. In the last decade, a number of communities have added dispute mediation centers to their conflict

resolution mechanisms. Investigate whether such a center exists in your town. If so, invite someone from the mediation center to explain its operation. If not, select one or two class members to investigate dispute mediation in the library. Do such centers operate as substitutes for the formal criminal punishment system? If so, in what ways and for what kinds of problems? Do these centers offer informal control? Or are they a new kind of spe-cialist organization in an expanding array of formal controls?

3. If the lesson that Phil and his graduate students learned about goals in complex organizations is at all accurate, why all the fuss about the appropriate philosophy of punishment? Do you think a philosophy of punishment could *include* some guidelines for dealing with program implementation? What would these guidelines look like?

ADDITIONAL READING

Herbert Packer. *The Limits of the Criminal Sanction.* (Stanford, CA: Stanford University Press, 1968). Generally considered one of the finest statements of the dominant ideology of punishment. Packer reviews the typical justifications for punishment, argues for a combination of retributive and utilitarian aims, discusses the conflicting goals in the criminal justice system, and proposes how he would limit punishment, given his aims and the problems of implementation.

Anthony Platt. *The Child Savers.* (Chicago: University of Chicago Press, 1969). Platt reviews the rise of the juvenile justice system in Illinois from a radical perspective. He argues that the reform movement which culminated in the juvenile court was more closely related to changing class structure than to concerns for rehabilitating youngsters, or for removing them from the adult correctional system.

Leon Radzinowicz. *Ideology and Crime.* (New York: Columbia University Press, 1961). Radzinowicz reviews the evolution of criminological theory and analyzes the impact of ideology on the practices for controlling crime and handling criminals.

Stephen Rose. *Betrayal of the Poor.* (Cambridge, MA: Shenckman, 1972). Nothing about corrections here, but instead a fine study of another social control system, concerned with poverty, and the attempts to change that system in the 1960s. A good introduction to ideologies, how they affect organizations, and how organizations tend to resist change that threatens their operations.

CHAPTER 4
THE PRECONVICTION PROCESS AND CORRECTIONS

QUESTIONS

1. How often does the commission of a crime result in arrest?

2. How many arrests lead to punishment?

3. What decisions intervene between arrest and conviction?

4. What are preconviction "correctional" activities?

5. Do preconviction decisions and programs affect sentencing?

"I DID IT, YER HONOR, NOW HARVEY SAID YOU'D LET ME GO"

Hollis Jones woke up with a splitting headache. The pain in his back was even worse. While he had a vague memory of collapsing on a cot, he was now prone on the cement floor.

"Hey, Hollis. Court's at ten. Want something to eat?"

Hollis cast a bleary eye at the young man on the other side of the bars. "Lo, Johnny. What are they sayin' I did?"

"Well, Hollis, there's talk of burglary this time. Found you in the back room of Philbin's liquor store."

"Oh, Lord. I didn't burgle nothin'!" Hollis stood and wobbled to the bars. "Do I have any money left? I got paid yesterday."

"Not yesterday, Hollis. This is Monday already. You got paid Friday. It's all gone, too."

Hollis shut his eyes and looked around the room. There was the drunk snoring on the cot which Hollis thought had been his. There were two college kids huddled in the corner, looking scared. There was a large stranger in a rumpled suit standing by the barred window and staring out toward the courthouse. The weekend catch in Cummings County.

"Johnny, I need some coffee."

The guard disappeared with a cheery "Comin' right up."

By court time Hollis was feeling somewhat better. He had filled himself with coffee, a little lukewarm oatmeal, some toast. His head was clear, but his back still ached. Judge Finney was not as agreeable as Hollis remembered him being before. The liquor store owner was apparently very angry about damage to his back door. Hollis insisted the back door must have been open and he had only come in to get away from

the early morning chill. But Hollis really remembered nothing. The district attorney
was angry too. He asked Hollis if he'd plead
to criminal trespass, "to get the thing over
with." Hollis insisted he was innocent. Finney set bail at $500 on the burglary
charges. The bondsman wanted $50 to write
the bond. Hollis, without a dime, was sent
back to jail to await trial. Judge Finney ordered assignment of counsel.

By lunch time, Hollis had been assigned
a regular cell. He passed his time reading
an old *Time* that Johnny happened to have.
At 2 P.M. Johnny came through with a piece
of paper and read Hollis the name of his
assigned lawyer. Cummings County had no
public defender; members of the bar were
chosen by the judge on a rotation basis to
represent the indigent. Hollis didn't recognize the name. He was told the lawyer
would see him the next morning.

Dinner time finally rolled around. The
other drunk was the only other one left
from the weekend arrests. The big stranger
in the rumpled suit had had his lawyer
present at initial appearance. He had been
released on bond. The two college kids had
paid fines for disturbing the peace and had
gone back to the university. Johnny led Hollis and six others from the cellblock to the
large room that doubled as dining hall and
indoor recreation room.

Hollis was carrying his tray of hot dogs
and beans over to the table when the door
to the front office opened, and in walked
Ernie Shavers with two other men. Ernie
spied Hollis and lit up with a happy smile.
He rushed through the line and grabbed the
place on Hollis' left.

"Hi, Hollis. Had you in the holdin' pen
all weekend, eh?"

Hollis ignored the questions. "You're in
a fine mood for someone arrested just in
time for dinner."

"No, no, no," said Ernie. "I'm doin' my
time for breaking John's nose in that brawl
two weeks ago."

"Where you been all day?"

"Working. I still got the job on Miller's
farm."

Hollis stopped eating. "You still got the
job? I been working too, in the orchards
pickin' apples. But *now* I'm *here*. How can
you be both places?"

"Work release," said Ernie with the air
of one in the know. "Guess it's new since
you were here last. Started in September.
Sheriff Stamford and some college professor
dreamed up this program."

Hollis was dumbfounded. He was determined to get hold of Harvey Stamford right
away.

Actually, he had to wait until eight that
night. Finally the cellblock door opened.
"Johnny said you were calling for me?"
asked the sheriff. Although Sheriff Stamford
has never been west of Ohio, he dressed like
Gary Cooper. But he was universally respected by the Cummings County denizens
who most frequently inhabited the jail.

Hollis stood and came to the bars. "Yes,
Harv. How do I get this work release business?" Stamford shifted in his cowboy
boots. "Work release is for prisoners who
have jobs, or who we can find jobs. You're
a detainee. You're not guilty yet."

Hollis mulled this over. "You mean if I'm
guilty, I can go out and work? But if I'm
not, I stay in here all day?"

Stamford calmed him down. "Not exactly. Your employer has to agree, and so
does Finney. But I can't see how they
wouldn't, if you promise to fix Philbin's
door."

"But I didn't *do* that, Harv."

Stamford shook his head. "I don't make
the judgment, Hollis. I just run the jail.
Right now it looks like you did. If you're
going to fight it, stay here and fight it. But
I'm warning you. If you stick with not guilty

and they get you on burglary, you go to Dunmore." Stamford tipped his hat and walked out.

The next morning, Hollis and his lawyer worked out the details of a guilty plea. Hollis would plead guilty to criminal trespass, and the D.A. would drop the burglary charge. The lawyer would ask Finney for work release for 90 days, backed up with a letter from Willy's Orchards promising continued employment. The D.A. would promise not to object, as long as Hollis promised to pay restitution for property damages.

On the following Thursday, Hollis was back in court with his lawyer. After a brief conference with the two attorneys, Judge Finney asked Hollis how he pled to criminal trespass.

Although Hollis had practiced his script with his lawyer, he forgot the lines and blurted out: "I did it, Yer Honor, now Harvey said you'd let me go."

DILEMMAS OF THE PRECONVICTION SYSTEM

These events took place in a rural county in October 1971. A professor from the university and a country sheriff collaborated on a State Planning Agency proposal and obtained funds to start a work release program. (Their operation will be discussed in Chapter 17.) Hollis faced a rather strange choice, on the face of it. He was confronted with several weeks of jail detention on a felony charge while he awaited trial, or the option of pleading quilty to a misdemeanor and receiving a sentence that, deserved or not, was one he could live with. He continued to work in the orchard each day, bussed back and forth from the jail in a van purchased on the grant. He spent his nights and weekends in jail. From his next paycheck, he repaid Mr. Philbin for the broken back door.

Had Hollis been arrested in 1986, he might have faced a different set of choices. Since 1971, a number of pretrial programs have been designed to deal with dilemmas like those faced by Hollis Jones. Now, if Hollis did not have the money for a bail bond, he might have been eligible for a number of other options which could have secured his release from jail. Perhaps he could be released on his own recognizance, if he met certain criteria established in Cummings County for such releases. Failing that, he would have faced the possibility of supervised pretrial release. In Cummings County, this would mean that a probation officer would have kept track of Hollis during the pretrial period.

These programs have emerged for a number of reasons. One impetus for them has been to resolve the kind of dilemma faced by Hollis Jones: that his treatment as an unconvicted defendant appeared harsher than his treatment as a convict. Another impetus has been the desire to reduce the impact of poverty on the conditions experienced before trial. Hollis had had to stay in jail because he could not raise $50 for the bond. Other changes have occurred in the last fifteen years in the kinds of pretrial options available to judges and prosecutors. A number of diversion programs are available in many jurisdictions. If defendants are eligible for these programs and complete them successfully, prosecution on criminal charges may be dropped. Unlike release on recognizance and supervised pretrial release, which are usually justified as means of reducing the differential impact of prosecution on the poor, diversion is often justified as a means of reducing the court and correctional workloads.

These and other changes in the preconviction process have resulted in changing the shape and purpose of the preconviction system. Many of the options that have emerged appear remarkably similar in operation to more traditional postconviction sentences. In many jurisdictions, the same officials are involved. In other jurisdictions, new agencies have been constructed to handle the expanding workload, but these agencies often employ workers whose credentials and skills re-

FIGURE 4.1   Estimated Percentage of Personal Victimizations Not Reported to Police, by Type of Victimization, United States, 1973–1982

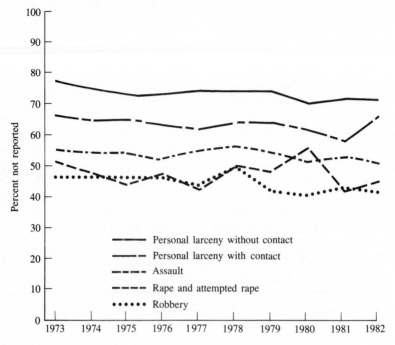

SOURCE: Edmund McGarrell and Timothy Flanagan (eds.), *Sourcebook of Criminal Justice Statistics—1984*. Washington, DC: Bureau of Justice Statistics, 1985. Figure constructed by *Sourcebook* staff.

semble those of correctional workers. In many respects, the preconviction process has become "correctionalized," in the sense that it involves the kinds of programming and supervision that also occur in probation and parole.

This chapter reviews the justifications for decisions, the programs, and problems in the preconviction process and examines, to the extent that the data allow, the relationship between these pretrial options and the selection of persons for punishment. Our attention will focus on pretrial detention and alternatives and on diversion programs. However, before we can study these, it will be useful to review the entire preconviction decision process, a series of decisions that have been called the "corrections funnel." Our corrections system is heavily influenced by previous decisions about how often, for what, and against whom punishment will be invoked.

FROM CRIME TO PUNISHMENT:THE CORRECTIONS FUNNEL

THE DECISION TO REPORT A CRIME

It is now well known that only a fraction of alleged offenses are reported to the police. Since 1973, some information about the amount of unreported crime is available in the United States because of the National Crime Survey, sponsored by the Bureau of Justice Statistics and conducted by the U.S. Bureau of the Census. Working from a carefully chosen panel of respondents, the National Crime Survey provides annual estimates of the number of crimes of specific types committed in the United States. Among the data collected is information about the number of victimizations which are not reported by the victim to the police. Figure 4.1 presents estimated percentages of five

TABLE 4.1   Percent of Personal Victimizations Not Reported to Police, by Type of Victimization and Reasons Given for Not Reporting to Police, United States, 1982

TYPE OF VICTIMIZATION	TOTAL VICTIMIZA- TIONS NOT REPORTED	REASON FOR NOT REPORTING VICTIMIZATION TO POLICE								
		NOTHING COULD BE DONE	VICTIMIZATION NOT IMPORTANT ENOUGH	POLICE WOULDN'T WANT TO BE BOTHERED	DID NOT WANT TO TAKE TIME	IT WAS A PRIVATE MATTER	FEAR OF REPRISAL	VICTIMIZATION REPORTED TO SOMEONE ELSE	OTHER	NOT ASCERTAINED
Rape and attempted rape	69,071	—	—	—	—	—	—	—	—	—
Robbery	553,511	23	15	12	5	20	5	9	32	3
Assault	2,552,949	5	26	7	3	34	6	13	17	2
Personal larceny with contact	381,169	31	25	6	3	6	1	18	35	4
Personal larcency without contact	10,696,939	20	34	8	3	4	0	21	28	2

SOURCE: Edmund McGarrell and Timothy Flanagan (eds.), *Sourcebook of Criminal Justice Statistics—1984*. Washington, DC: Bureau of Justice Statistics, 1985, p. 284.

types of personal victimization not reported to the police. Note that even in very serious crimes, such as robbery, nearly half the events are not reported. Table 4.1 provides information given by the victims on why they decided not to report the incident. The most common reasons for not reporting were the belief that nothing could be done, the belief that the victimization was not important enough, and the belief that the incident was a private matter. The last response is particularly frequent in assault cases.

Once a report is made to the police, a number of other decisions intervene before punishment is a possibility. The reporting victim may have been mistaken, and the police may decide not to count the report as a crime. Or a victim may report a burglary which the police decide is only a theft. Police reporting policy may affect greatly both the numbers and kinds of crimes officially recorded and sent on by the police to the Federal Bureau of Investigation as "crimes known to the police" (for a very interesting study of the impact of reporting practices on crime reports, see McCleary, Nienstedt, and Erven 1982).

After this additional filtering, the police department officially reports a crime as known. Additional investigation may ensue, if there are any leads to pursue. The vast majority of crimes reported do not result in arrests. Figure 4.2 provides data on the percent of index crimes cleared by arrest in 1983. In comparing reported victim-izations with clearance rates, we can see that roughly only half to a quarter of victimizations lead to a report, and that only a fraction of reported crimes are "cleared." (In the case of robbery, for instance, about one-half are reported and only one-quarter of that half are "solved" by an arrest.) One should remember also that many offenses cleared are not arrests for that particular crime, but offenses admitted by a defendant charged with something else (see Skolnick, 1966, for one example of the police practice of clearing open cases by having a suspect confess to other crimes during interrogation).

DECISION TO PROSECUTE

For punishment to become a possibility for an act, the system needs to amass considerably more evidence of greater quality than it needs for reporting a crime. Officials need to transform the report of an event into a case against a person. The police need to gather evidence that the event was indeed an act proscribed under the rules of the criminal law, and they need evidence attaching responsibility to a particular person for that act. Once the police have determined that they have a suspect for a crime, the prosecutor must agree to prosecute the case, and the court must determine that the prosecution is warranted and the available evidence substantiates that state claim.

FIGURE 4.2   Percentage of Offenses Known to Police That Were Cleared by Arrest, by Offense, United States, 1983

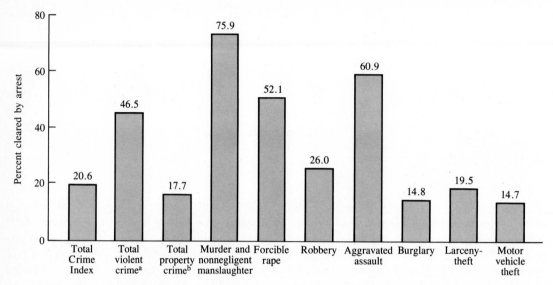

[a]Violent crimes are offenses of murder, forcible rape, robbery, and aggravated assault.
[b]Property crimes are offenses of burglary, larceny-theft, and motor vehicle theft. Data are not included for the property crime of arson

SOURCE: Edmund McGarrell and Timothy Flanagan (eds.), *Sourcebook of Criminal Justice Statistics—1984*. Washington, DC: Bureau of Justice Statistics, 1985, p. 518. Figure constructed by *Sourcebook* staff.

Before the early 1970s, we knew very little about this process of transforming an arrest into a conviction. One major breakthrough in examining the process was a study conducted by the Vera Institute of Justice in New York City (1981). It tracked 1,888 felony cases from arrest to disposition. These kinds of studies are now becoming more numerous (see Chen, 1981; Petersilia, 1983; Boland et al., 1983; Boland and Brady, 1985). Each jurisdiction in the United States has a slightly different pattern of decision-making, and the rate with which a case is passed on from one decision point to the next varies both by type of crime and by jurisdiction. But Hans Zeisel (1981:462) claims that the overall attrition of cases from arrest to conviction has not changed much in a dozen years, and that the pattern of fallout described in the original Vera study is fairly similar to what we find in other jurisdictions.

The Vera study found that 20 percent of felony arrests did not reach the criminal courts. Thirteen percent of the cases were transferred to family court; in 6 percent of the cases the defendant jumped bail, and in 1 percent the defendant died or the case was dropped for other reasons (Zeisel, 1981:421–423). Of the remaining 80 percent of felony arrests, 55 percent resulted in a conviction, and 45 percent ended in dismissals or acquittals. Twenty-eight percent of the original arrests resulted in sentences or fines, conditional discharges, or probation. Twenty-seven percent of the arrests resulted in some form of incarceration, but only 5 percent of the arrests for felonies resulted in prison sentences (Zeisel, 1981:424). Zeisel says that 45 percent of the arrests which did not result in conviction is similar "in all legal systems that distinguish between the amount of proof sufficient for arrest and the amount of proof required for conviction" (1981:424).

FIGURE 4.3   Outcome of 100 "Typical" Felony Arrests

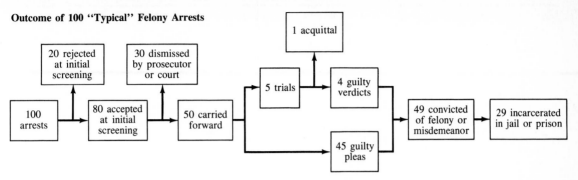

Outcome of 100 "Typical" Felony Arrests

SOURCE: Barbara Boland et al., *Prosecution of Felony Arrests, 1979*. Washington, DC: Bureau of Justice Statistics, 1983, p. 2.

Figure 4.3 presents data from a study of 14 jurisdictions in 1977 and 1979 (Boland et al., 1983). While the data are slightly different than those reported in the original New York City study, Zeisel appears to be correct that the pattern is fairly similar. Table 4.2 examines the reasons for rejection of cases at initial prosecutorial screening, and Table 4.3 the reasons for dismissals by the judge or prosecutor (the first two attrition points in Figure 4.3).

In Table 4.2 reasons for declining to prosecute are provided for seven sample jurisdictions. Notice that the most frequent reasons to refuse to prosecute are that the evidence was insufficient, that there was a witness problem, or that the case lacked merit. The reasons for dismissal are the same, but the percentages change (Table 4.3). Lack of evidence is less of a problem at this stage. Witness problems remain about the same, as does the contention that the case lacks merit. But now some other reasons for attrition become more important. Note, for example, that a significant number of cases are dismissed because the defendant has been diverted. Dismissals for this reason do not imply that the defendant has avoided any intervention. (We examine the op-

TABLE 4.2   Declination Reasons at Screening

| JURISDICTION | NUMBER OF DECLINED CASES* | PERCENT DISTRIBUTION OF CASES DECLINED BY REASON | | | | | | | |
		EVIDENCE	WITNESS	LACKS MERIT	DUE PROCESS	OTHER PROSECUTION	DIVER- SION	PLEA BARGAIN	OTHER
Golden	41	59	27	5	2	2	2	2	0
Greeley	235	52	7	38	0	2	1	0	0
Indianapolis	433	44	10	28	0	18	0	0	0
Los Angeles	33,154	42	8	3	4	38	1	0	5
Manhattan	1,088	60	22	4	7	0	3	0	4
Salt Lake	1,021	57	13	9	1	16	1	0	2
Washington, DC	917	38	30	29	0	2	0	0	0

* Excludes cases where reasons are unknown.
NOTE: Declined cases include diversions and cases referred for other prosecution. These cases are excluded from counts of rejected cases in other tables.
SOURCE: Barbara Boland and Elizabeth Brady, *Prosecution of Felony Arrests, 1980*. Washington, DC: Bureau of Justice Statistics, 1985, p. 13.

TABLE 4.3   Dismissal Reasons (Cases filed or indicted)

JURISDICTION	NUMBER OF DISMISSED CASES[a]	PERCENT DISTRIBUTION OF CASES DISMISSED BY REASON							
		EVIDENCE	WITNESS	LACKS MERIT	DUE PROCESS	OTHER PROSECUTION	DIVER- SION	PLEA BARGAIN	OTHER
Brighton	443	16%	7%	10%	1%	2%	21%	43%	0%
Colorado Springs	675	13	11	3	2	14	16	40	0
Fort Collins	257	4	5	5	1	15	27	41	0
Geneva	567	13	23	17	4	5	10	25	2
Golden	709	14	14	7	1	9	17	38	0
Greeley	207	12	25	4	1	20	20	18	0
Indianapolis	573	27	13	31	2	8	1	10	9
Los Angeles	7,196	26	21	22	4	5	8	10	4
Louisville	202	28	25	20	8	7	11	0	0
Manhattan	9,265	20	30	9	7	0	1	5	28[b]
Portland	906	15	22	6	0	13	7	23	13
Pueblo	146	16	11	7	2	6	14	43	0
St. Louis	1,090	17	26	8	14	6	0	11	18
Salt Lake	654	11	17	4	2	19	5	28	16
San Diego	1,443	28	16	5	6	10	17	17	0
Washington, D.C.	2,992	21	26	7	3	2	7	9	25

[a] Excludes cases where reasons are unknown.

[b] Includes cases adjoined in contemplation of dismissal.

NOTE: Dismissed cases in this table include diversions and cases referred for other prosecution. These cases are excluded from counts of dismissed cases in other tables.

SOURCE: Barbara Boland and Elizabeth Brady, *Prosecution of Felony Arrests, 1980.* Washington, DC: Bureau of Justice Statistics, 1985, p. 13.

eration of diversion in detail later in this chapter.) Across all jurisdictions, the most frequent reason for dismissal is that a plea bargain has been arranged. A plea bargain, like diversion, does not mean that the defendant has escaped the system. Dismissals for this reason indicate that a particular charge has been dismissed in return for conviction by plea to another charge.

When we compare prosecutorial and judicial reasons for declination and dismissal, we can see a continuation of some patterns that first appeared in the data concerning a victim's refusal to report a crime to the police. Victims often reported a belief that nothing could be done. In some of these instances, we are probably observing an earlier but similar decision to the one made in court when it is decided that evidence is insufficient. Also, when victims report that an event was not serious enough, the criteria for that decision are at least in some instances similar to

the "lacks merit" decision by prosecutors and judges. Although these similarities are speculative, the data would indicate that in many instances, private citizens and criminal justice officials are applying roughly similar rules to the question of what the criminal sanction can and should accomplish.

INFLUENCES ON CONVICTION

An even greater indication of this rough similarity between commonsense judgments by citizens and formal rule application by officials is evident in comparing victimization reports that an event was a private matter with data indicating that a major reason for declinations to prosecute and dismissals of cases is that the case encountered a problem with a witness. While there are many different reasons a witness may be a problem for a prosecutor, such as lack of credibility or difficulty in communicating effectively, one major subcategory involves a victim who reported a crime later refusing to testify. Both the original New York City study of felony arrests (Vera, 1981) and the cross-jurisdictional comparisons (Boland and Brady, 1985) find that a major determinant of case attrition, and of plea bargaining to lesser charges, is the prior relationship between the victim and the offender. Table 4.4 shows the association between victim-defendant relationship and likelihood of conviction. In most of the crime categories reported, conviction is most likely when the defendant is a stranger, rather than a family member or a friend or acquaintance. Such data led Gottfredson and Gottfredson (1980) to conclude that criminal punishment is reserved, in many cases, for persons not previously known to the victim. When a prior relationship exists, often punishment is not the control option chosen, by the person harmed or by the criminal justice system.

For the vast majority of cases which are neither screened out by the prosecutor nor dismissed, the result is a conviction by a plea of guilty. Table 4.5 provides the percentages of convictions obtained by plea in the 14-jurisdiction study by Boland et al. (1983:12). For years it has been assumed that the roughly 90 percent guilty plea rate was a function of overcrowded courts (Heumann, 1978:24–33). Others have argued

that the "court work group"—in particular, the prosecutor, defense attorney, and judge—press for cooperative methods of resolving cases rather than risking the uncertainty of trial (Blumberg, 1970; Eisenstein and Jacob, 1976). In either case, however, critics have often assumed that justice is reduced as the guilty plea is relied upon, both because it reduces the penalty the defendant is likely to face and because constitutional rights are denied (Boland et al., 1983:12).

In recent years, the case overload explanation has been attacked in a variety of ways. Lawrence Freidman's historical study of conviction suggests that pleading guilty has been the most common method of conviction since the late nineteenth century, rather than an invention of the modern urban court (1979). Heumann (1978) and Feeley (1979) have observed that both high-volume and low-volume courts resort to guilty pleas at about the same rate. However, other researchers have argued the resources available to the court, rather than volume of cases, is the crucial variable in deciding whether pleas or trials will result (Nardulli, 1979). The present evidence allows for no conclusions, but it does suggest that the traditional assumption that pleas are a new practice or a practice only in the busiest courts needs to be reexamined.

Much of the criticism about the high rate of

TABLE 4.4 Conviction Rate, by Victim-Defendant Relationship and Crime Group* (New Orleans)

CRIME GROUP	FAMILY		FRIEND/ ACQUAINTANCE		STRANGER	
	NO. OF ARRESTS	RATE	NO. OF ARRESTS	RATE	NO. OF ARRESTS	RATE
Robbery	14	7%	142	21%	446	37%
Violent	200	16	616	19	456	35
Property	88	19	603	37	1,709	53
Victimless	18	72	107	56	367	52
All other	42	14	79	35	183	50
All offenses	362	19	1,547	30	3,161	48

* PROMIS data, 1977–78; includes only cases in which the relationship between victim and defendant was recorded in PROMIS.
SOURCE: Brian Forst et al., *Arrest Convictability as a Measure of Police Performance*. Washington, DC: INSLAW, Inc., 1981.

TABLE 4.5 Percent of Convictions That Were Guilty Pleas

JURISDICTION	GUILTY PLEAS	NUMBER OF CONVICTIONS
Louisville	81%	1,221
Indianapolis	85	1,182
New Orleans	87	3,131
Washington, DC	89	3,884
Milwaukee	89	2,250
Salt Lake	90	1,139
Los Angeles	91	14,811
Kalamazoo	94	597
Geneva	95	466
Golden	95	872
St. Louis	95	2,293
Manhattan	96	15,694
Cobb County	96	1,778
Rhode Island	97	2,752
Average	92%	

SOURCE: Barbara Boland et al., *Prosecution of Felony Arrests, 1979*. Washington DC: Bureau of Justice Statistics, 1983, p. 12.

conviction by plea centers around the issue of plea bargaining, the practice of reducing charges or settling on a lesser sentence in return for a plea of guilty. Plea negotiations can be explicit, in which case defendant and prosecutor strike a specific agreement about charge reductions or sentence recommendations, or the negotiation can be implicit, in which case the defendant pleads guilty as charged, assuming he or she will be treated more leniently for having done so (Newman, 1966). A recent study by the Bureau of Justice Statistics suggests that a guilty plea may be less likely to result in a prison sentence and, for those sentencing to prison, may result in a shorter term (Table 4.6). However, as the data indicate, this is not the case across all conviction charges. The Bureau also points out, however, that contrary to popular belief, the plea process often does not involve a reduction in charges. The Bureau found that 83 percent of those pleading guilty plead to the highest original charge (BJS, May 1985:9).

TABLE 4.6 Sentences to Prison, by Method of Conviction

CONVICTION OFFENSE	PERCENT OF SENTENCES TO PRISON FOR THOSE CONVICTED BY:		AVERAGE PRISON SENTENCE LENGTH FOR THOSE CONVICTED BY:	
	TRIAL	GUILTY PLEA	TRIAL	GUILTY PLEA
Total	51%	44%	10.7 years	6.0 years
Violent				
Homicide	92	82	16.6	14.2
Rape	81	65	16.2	10.9
Robbery	66	65	12.7	7.3
Aggravated assault	47	36	9.8	5.6
Property				
Burglary	42	48	6.4	4.3
Larceny	24	30	4.2	3.1
Other				
Drug trafficking	27	21	5.7	3.8

NOTE: Table excludes those cases (9%) where the study could not ascertain how the person was convicted.
SOURCE: Bureau of Justice Statistics *Bulletin*. Washington, DC: Bureau of Justice Statistics, May 1985.

PRETRIAL RELEASE AND DETENTION

For many defendants, their first experience with a correctional organization occurs during the pretrial process rather than upon conviction. Most defendants spend somewhere between a few hours to many days in a local jail in **pretrial detention.** Indeed, Malcolm Feeley has argued that we have an "inverted justice system" because about four times as many people are incarcerated before disposition than after disposition of their cases (1979:236). Similarly, in Goldkamp's study of the pretrial process in Philadelphia, 43.4 percent of defendants detained for the duration of the pretrial process had their cases dismissed or dropped, or were acquitted. Consequently, Feeley states that the pretrial process is the "punishment," in the sense that greater social control is exerted prior to conviction, in many cases. Using national data from the United States Bureau of the Census for the 1972 Survey of Inmates in Local Jails, Goldkamp (1979) found that 30 percent of the local jail population were detained rather than convicted persons. The percentage of jail inmates who are detainees has gone up in the succeeding fourteen years, and in some urban jails constitutes a majority of those incarcerated.

Few issues in American criminal law are so controversial and ambiguous as the right to pretrial release. Not only ordinary people, but many courts and standard-setting bodies have presumed that detention prior to trial is inconsistent with the presumption of innocence until proved guilty. Those taking this position have argued that incarceration prior to trial is like punishment without due process, a practice prohibited by the Fifth and Fourteenth Amendments to the United States Constitution. Nevertheless, the United States Constitution is absolutely silent on the right to release pending trial. The only related wording occurs in the Eighth Amendment, which

Jails are often constructed to allow convenient transport of pre-trial detainees to court, as evidenced by the bridge between the Schenectady County Jail and the County Court. (David E. Duffee)

prohibits excessive bail. But the Constitution does not state that bail is a right, let alone suggest that those who cannot afford cash bail should be released in another way. The Supreme Court of the United States has never ruled directly on whether there is an implicit right to bail or to release. However, the leading case on conditions of pretrial confinement, *Bell* v. *Wolfish*, takes the position that the "presumption of innocence" standard is essentially a rule of evidence and trial procedure, and does not imply the right to pretrial freedom or the extent of rights enjoyed by pretrial detainees (see Gill, 1981:470).

Without an ultimate resolution in the courts, current legislation and current practice relating to pretrial release is proceeding on the grounds that release may be denied, under certain conditions, so long as the purpose of detention is not punishment. The two alternate purposes of controlling pretrial release which have presumed legitimacy at this point are (1) ensuring the defendant's appearance at trial, and (2) preventing harm to other persons or the community (Goldkamp, 1979:55–74; Bragg, 1984). Although some writers still assume that the sole purpose of the release decision in the adult criminal law system should be to determine whether the defendant will appear for trial (*University of Pennsylvania Law Review*, 1983:96), a number of states and the federal government have passed legislation allowing a determination of dangerousness to play a part in the release decision.

Even if these two nonpunitive purposes of the pretrial release decision are permissible, considerable controversy remains. What evidence is to be used to determine risk of flight from prosecution or risk of danger to the community? To what extent must that evidence be validated against the actual behavior of persons released or detained? Which release mechanism, bail or an alternative, is the best method of assuring presence at trial or protecting the community? Since the Federal Bail Reform Act of 1966, across the country a large number of agencies have appeared which attempt to secure the release of as many persons as possible prior to trial, while preserving the two goals of reducing flight and protecting the community.

BAIL REFORM AND PRETRIAL RELEASE

In 1967, the President's Commission on Law Enforcement and Administration of Justice strongly criticized the practice of pretrial detention. Observing the plight of the incarcerated defendant the commission said:

> He may be confined for something he did not do; some jailed defendants are ultimately acquitted. He may be confined while presumed innocent only to be freed when found guilty; many jailed defendants, after they are convicted, are placed on probation rather than imprisoned (1967:131–133).

The commission advocated the use of systematic information gathering about defendants to provide the magistrate making the release decision with sufficient information for an informed decision about which pretrial option was the least restrictive way to preserve the state's interest (1967:131–133). Specifically, the commission recommended the practice of pretrial release interviews and recommendations pioneered by the Vera Foundation in New York City in 1963 (Ares, Rankin, and Sturz, 1963).

The systematic gathering of information about defendants would, it was hoped, reduce the discretion of bail officials, the police, the prosecutor, and bail **bondsmen,** who often determine the likelihood of release based upon tradition, whim, pecuniary interest, and hidden desire to punish (see Feeley, 1979:209–215). One of the major targets of criticism was the **bail system,** the practice of releasing a defendant who could put up an amount that was to assure reappearance. This practice was seen as especially unfair because

> . . . it denies pre-trial freedom to those defendants who are least capable of forfeiture, while granting release to those defandants who are actually most likely to be able to afford leaving the jurisdiction and escaping prosecution (Wice, 1974:159).

Bail was seen as unfair to the poor and a method of release that did not fulfill its intended purposes.

In response, a number of reform projects have been designed, many following the lead of the Vera Foundation. These projects sought to gather information from and about the defendant (usually through interview) in order to determine if the defendant could be recommended for **release on his own recognizance (ROR).** If the judge accepted the recommendation, the defendant could be released on promise to reappear, rather than on payment of bail or a fee to a bondsman.

The difficulty with ROR programs is that they have often failed to secure the release of the defendants who suffer most from the cash bail system. These programs often use point systems based on characteristics of the defendant, such as length of time in the community, stable residence, family ties, and employment. The result, says Wice in his national evaluation of bail reform projects, is that the projects systematically exclude the poorest defendants (1974:102).

Consequently, many pretrial service agencies, which conduct ROR programs, have expanded their services in the last decade to provide alternatives. Among the alternatives now used are release to a third party or to an organization which promises to vouch for the defendant, and **pretrial diversion** (Wice, 1974:108–113). While it is not always easy to do so in practice, we shall try to separate supervised pretrial release, which has the objective of returning the defendant for trial, and diversion, which has the objective in most cases of substituting pretrial supervision for prosecution altogether. However, both pretrial supervision programs and diversion supervision are often administered by the same agencies.

SUPERVISED PRETRIAL RELEASE

With the advent of pretrial supervision, if not with ROR programs, the preconviction process has begun to resemble the post conviction process. As Wayne R. Lafave pointed out:

The supervision of persons at liberty to insure against violation of the conditions upon which that liberty is granted is not a problem at all new to American law; for years we have faced this problem with some measure of success as to those already convicted of crime (1965, cited in Remington et al., 1968:500).

The types of services to be offered and the type of supervision required of persons released prior to trial is in large measure based upon the practice of probation supervision. Indeed, a recent trend in the administration of such services is a department of court services, which administers ROR, supervised pretrial release, probation, diversion, and perhaps the local jail or residential alternatives to the local jail. The best-known example of this organization is the Department of Court Services for the Fifth Judicial District of Iowa at Des Moines (the department has recently been renamed the Department of Correctional Services; see Insert 4.1).

One of the earliest statutes establishing such supervision was the Federal Bail Reform Act of 1966, which became a model for many state programs. Section 3146 of the Act, which describes release procedures in noncapital cases, provides, in part, for placement of a person in the custody of a person or organization that agrees to supervise the releasee, and if necessary to impose restrictions on travel, association, or residence, when release on recognizance is not sufficient to ensure appearance at trial.

The majority of pretrial service agencies arose in the 1970s and followed the lead provided by the federal legislation. Their services include the supervision of persons released by the court, providing the judge with specific recommendations that should apply to the supervised period, the development and monitoring of support services for released defendants, rehabilitation and crisis intervention, and mediation between the courts and law enforcement agencies for those who fail to appear (McCarthy and McCarthy, 1984:59).

Typical conditions imposed on released defendants include (1) regular reporting to the pretrial agency (often weekly), (2) maintaining a sta-

Insert 4.1 REEXAMINATION OF SUPERVISED PRETRIAL RELEASE IN DES MOINES

In 1973, the Law Enforcement Assistance Administration selected the Department of Court Services for the Fifth Judicial District of Iowa (Des Moines) as an Exemplary Program. LEAA proposed that the Des Moines Department should serve as a model for other jurisdictions because of its comprehensive and effective system of pretrial and community correctional programs (Borkman, Fazio, Day, and Weinstein, 1976). Many of the claims for effectiveness were based on a series of evaluation studies conducted by the National Council on Crime and Delinquency for the Department. Many of the claims were certainly deserved; others now appear to have been overly optimistic. In 1986, Paul Stageberg finished a lengthy study of the Des Moines programs in their formative years from 1969 to 1972. He had available considerably more data than NCCD evaluators had used. In particular, he examined relationships among the Des Moines programs of ROR, supervised pretrial release, and short-term residential programs for convicted persons. One of Stageberg's interests concerned the operation of the "Release With Supervision" program, which designers hoped would reduce detention populations by securing the release of persons ineligible for ROR and unable to make bail.

Stageberg examined Release With Services samples for the four years from 1969 to 1972. He used a number of means to control for the seriousness of charges and the seriousness of risk presented by pretrial defendants, in order to determine if the programs had differential impact on different types of clients. When Stageberg compared the pretrial status of different types of defendants, he discovered some interesting patterns. Over the four-year period, high-risk defendants were found to gain release more often than before the program, were slightly less likely to be released on bail bond, and were much more frequently released with supervision. For this group, the introduction of Release With Services appeared to work as planned. However, when Stageberg examined the pretrial status of lower-risk persons, he found that release on ROR decreased slightly over the four years, while use of bail bond went up, and the percentage detained went up.

Stageberg concludes that Release With Services did succeed in removing from detention some defendants facing serious charges and who had serious criminal records, but when considered against the total pattern of pretrial release options, the program may have produced some unwanted results. First, it is possible that rather than diverting persons from detention, it diverted persons from ROR. Second, it is possible that as attention to the most serious cases increased, those charged with the least serious crimes were often left to the old bail bond route, and in some cases left in detention. He also points out that persons left in detention often scored better on risk and seriousness ratings than those on Release With Services. Thus, even if the introduction of Release With Services had some positive impacts, it may also have had some negative repercussions, and at least was not used as frequently as would have seemed possible.

ble residence, (3) finding and maintaining employment, (4) avoiding complaining witnesses, (5) obeying a curfew, (6) refraining from criminal activity, and (7) participation in alcohol, drug abuse, or mental health treatment, if deemed necessary (McCarthy and McCarthy, 1984:76; Hall, 1984:8–9).

Such conditions, as we shall see in Chapter 8, are also common to probation supervision. It is likely that a person released under these conditions prior to trial will encounter the same regimen if sentenced to probation. Moreover, a person who is considered a success under these pretrial release conditions will probably be considered a good candidate for probation by both the judge and the probation department.

Supervised pretrial release raises some difficult and unsettled legal questions. Since many of these are similar to those raised by diversion programs, we will take them up in more detail here. However, the crux of the matter involves the allegedly different purposes of probation and supervised pretrial release. While there are some limitations on the nature of what a probationer can be required to do, discretion about the appropriateness of probation conditions is rather broad. Any number of required educational, vocational, and treatment programs can be ordered as reasonably related to the purposes of punishment. The pretrial defendant, however, is not being punished. Presumably, all the conditions imposed in pretrial supervision must relate to the government's interest in (1) ensuring appearance at trial or (2) protecting the community. Just what range of release conditions can be imposed under these purposes is an open question.

Requirements about limiting associations with other people, imposing curfews, and requiring treatment participation would be rather farfetched as mechanisms to assure appearance. Can they be justified under the goal of protecting the community? As a legal question, protection of the community is a less settled issue than ensuring appearance. However, many jurisdictions are pursuing preventive detention as constitutionally permissible. If it is permissible to lock someone up to provide protection, then requiring certain conditions of pretrial release that seek the same end would be seen as less restrictive, and therefore legal. Possibly the requirement to seek treatment will be justified on these grounds. However, correctional evaluations provide a rather dim picture of the effectiveness of treatment in reducing further crime by convicted persons. Will the courts permit the requirement of such treatment from persons who have not been convicted? To cover themselves in this ambiguous area, most pretrial supervision programs require the defendant to make a statement that treatment participation is voluntary. But how voluntary is a choice between conditional release and detention in jail pending trial?

PREVENTIVE DETENTION

Another important question in recent bail reform involves not how and when to release defendants, but whether defendants can be denied release on grounds other than predicted failure to appear for trial. This is the conservative swing of bail reform. The model for the increasing practice of detaining on grounds of dangerousness is the District of Columbia Preventive Detention Act.

THE LEGALITY OF PREVENTIVE DETENTION

How can **preventive detention** be seen as bail reform? Two separate, nearly opposite arguments are made. The D.C. legislation, promoted by Attorney General John Mitchell under President Nixon, presented the direct, conservative reasoning. The argument is that some defendants, both quite capable of making money bail and unlikely to flee, present considerable risk to the community if released. Some will commit more crimes while on pretrial release, sometimes to threaten witnesses or jurors in the previous crime, sometimes to finance their defense, or to continue their criminal livelihood. The conservative argument is that such persons should not be admitted to bail if the prosecutor can make a "clear and convincing case" that new crimes are likely.

There is, however, also a liberal, due process argument for preventive detention. That is that bail judges and prosecutors will always be concerned about prevention of future crimes, even if they do not say so. If denying release on preventive detention grounds is not allowed, bail officials will pursue this aim anyway by raising the bail required to such a high level that most defendants cannot afford it. These due process advocates suggest that it is better to bring preventive detention concerns into the open, rather than have them operate beneath an artificial risk of flight argument. If the officials are concerned about danger, it would be better to have them admit it and provide the defendant an opportunity to contest the evidence.

The problem of preventive detention, then, is very similar to the selective incapacitation justification for punishment. Preventive detention requires prediction of future behavior and justifies incarceration on the basis of a prediction that someone is dangerous. While the Supreme Court of the United States has not ruled directly on the constitutionality of preventive detention for adults in the criminal system, it has done so in the juvenile justice system. *Schall* v. *Martin* (1984) held that the detention of juveniles prior to the adjudication of delinquency was permissible for the protection of the juvenile or the community. The Court did so on the grounds that the court could act as a surrogate parent (parens patriae) to protect the interests of the child (*University of Pennsylvania Law Review,* 1983:96). While the court could not use the same reasoning in the adult system, the Schall case suggests that the current Supreme Court would be sympathetic to a nonpunitive protection argument for detention. (Another parallel for preventive detention would come from involuntary mental health commitment, which is permissible if the patient is deemed dangerous to himself or others, or unable to care for himself.)

THE PREDICTION OF DANGEROUSNESS

While the likelihood of upholding the state's interest in protecting the community seems strong, another important question is whether the courts have the capacity to carry it out. Do the courts have the proper criteria by which to determine who may be dangerous? How many nondangerous defendants would be detained because of poor criteria or faulty application of them (Goldkamp, 1983:1559; Wice, 1974:163)?

In 1978, the National Association of Pre-Trial Service Agency Administrators adopted standards recognizing protection of the community as a valid concern in pretrial release decisions. Interestingly, the kinds of evidence to be used in making the determination of dangerousness is very similar to those used for determining risk of flight (Goldkamp, 1979). In practice, the most common criteria used are the seriousness of the charge in the instant offense, previous criminal record, and evidence of violence or use of weapons.

Whether the criteria of dangerousness in use are actually valid predictors of future criminal behavior has been difficult to determine, since the persons predicted to be dangerous are locked up and their propensity to reoffend cannot be studied. Therefore, most studies of criminal activity among pretrial subjects have been conducted only on those defendants admitted to bail or to bail alternatives. Reoffending by this group during the pretrial period is generally very low, normally estimated at between 5 and 15 percent (see the review of these studies in Goldkamp, 1979). However, this is the group of defendants judges have already predicted to be relatively safe (Goldkamp, 1983:1561).

A recent study by Goldkamp shed some light on the predictive ability of the operating pretrial release decision process. The study was made possible by a court decision (*Jackson* v. *Hendrick,* 1982) which required the emergency release of some defendants detained in the Philadelphia county jail. Goldkamp studied the detainees, the detainees released through court order, and a sample of defendants released normally. He found that on attributes such as felony charges, prior felony convictions, prior failures to appear for court hearings, and pending charges, the detained and released defendants had much more serious criminal histories. He concluded:

> The implications of these results for the use of detention in a general sense are straightforward: not only is detention in Philadelphia selective, but the dividing line between released defendants and the "most releasable" detained defendants appears to have predictive merit. (1983:1575)

Catherine Bragg (1984) asked what would happen to the size and nature of the detained population in our jails if preventive detention statutes were fully implemented. She applied the preventive detention criteria from eight different statutes and constitutional amendments to a sample of the jail population in ten different jurisdictions to determine who and how many defendants would be detained under this legislation rather than the present bail system. The findings are that the detained population could decrease by as little as 0.3 percent or increase by as much as 26.6 percent, depending on how broadly or narrowly the legislation is worded. Most of the preventive detention statutes, if fully implemented, would result in populations similar in size to those we now experience—evidence, perhaps, that judges are already using similar decision criteria anyway. However, Bragg also discovered that a number of the statutes would significantly change the nature of the detained population, with as much as 20 percent more minority defendants being detained than is now the case (1984:62). She raised the important question of whether, given the sorry state of our predictive skills, such a change in the detention population would be defensible.

THE IMPACT OF THE RELEASE DECISION ON PUNISHMENT

One of the more important questions concerning pretrial release is the concern that detention prior to trial may affect the defendant's chances of avoiding conviction and increase the chances of being punished or being punished more severely upon conviction. For many reasons, the detainee is at a disadvantage compared to those released before trial. For example, detained defendants may lose employment, may experience fractured family ties, may have difficulty communicating with a lawyer in order to marshall an effective defense, and may, because of the simple fact of detainee status, appear to the judge to be ready candidates for incarceration, in comparison to defendants who have been free pending trial. Should any of these disadvantages actually result in greater likelihood of conviction or more severe punishment, detention practices would be hard to justify. They would imply, on the one hand,

that detainees are being punished because of their pretrial status rather than their criminal behavior. On the other, they would imply that our correctional system could not support any of the current justifications for punishment because selection for the system was not based on any of the accepted goals for punishment.

The position that detention status negatively affected a deefendant's chances for conviction and punishment was championed by Caleb Foote in a series of articles about bail (1954; 1965a; 1965b). Other studies claiming a negative impact for pretrial detention on case outcome are those of McCarthy and Wahl (1965) in Washington, D.C., Ares, Rankin, and Sturz (1963) in New York City; Single (1972) in New York City; and Bing and Rosenfeld (1970) in Boston.

By 1975, these and other studies had succeeded in leaving the widespread impression that detention status had a significant negative impact upon the case disposition of persons detained. Also, these studies suggested that the factors used by bail decision-makers were unfair because they were irrelevant to the legal purposes of pretrial release. The studies proposed that many demographic factors, such as race, sex, and financial condition, were influencing bail and release decisions. However, doubt remained because there were methodological problems with all these studies. It was not until Goldkamp's remarkable study of pretrial release in Philadelphia that some of these doubts could be settled. Goldkamp's sample design allowed him to estimate the characteristics and outcomes of all persons released or detained at preliminary hearing. His research design permitted Goldkamp to address a number of questions.

THE IMPACT OF DETENTION ON DISMISSALS

A first step in Goldkamp's examination of the impact of detention on outcome is the question of whether the detained are less likely to have their cases dropped or dismissed than those who are released prior to disposition of the case. The answer is No. While those in detention suffer the obvious interference with their lives not experienced by released defendants, about one-third of both groups had their cases dismissed or dropped. Thus the fact of detention, by itself, does not seem to place defendants at a disadvantage on this issue.

THE IMPACT OF DETENTION ON DIVERSION

The next question was whether the detained defendant has less chance of receiving diversion than defendants released at initial appearance. Goldkamp discovered that detention status has no appreciable effect on the likelihood of diversion, when seriousness of the charge and prior record were controlled.

THE IMPACT OF DETENTION ON CONVICTION

A third question was whether those detained were less likely to be found innocent than defendants not detained. Goldkamp discovered that none of the charge, prior record, and detention status variables enabled him to predict who was found guilty. Presumably, other variables related to conviction, such as strength of the evidence, affected this decision.

THE IMPACT OF DETENTION ON INCARCERATION

Next, Goldkamp asked whether detention had an impact on receiving incarceration. Without controlling for other factors, there is a very strong association between pretrial detention and incarceration after conviction. For example, only 10.5 percent of the convicted who were released within twenty-four hours of arrest received incarceration sentences, while 74.2 percent of the convicted who were detained throughout prosecution received incarceration (Goldkamp, 1979:202). This is the relationship that previous researchers were so convinced indicated the unfairness of the pre-

trial release system. Goldkamp's analysis was designed to determine how much of the apparent relationship between detention and postconviction incarceration remained when other important variables, such as charge seriousness and criminal history, were controlled. Goldkamp stated his findings:

> Although the relationship in question was noticeably diminished once controls were exercised, this analysis has been unable to "write off" the entire relationship as wholly an artifact of spuriousness. (1979:205)

In fact, Goldkamp discovered that detention remained the strongest predictor on the decision to incarcerate among the variables he measured. He points out that perhaps other variables not measured or recorded had an impact on both detention and incarceration. However, the largest and most carefully done study of pretrial status and punishment seems to indicate that convicts who were previously detained as defendants are more likely to be sentenced to jail or prison than convicts who were released during prosecution.

THE IMPACT OF DETENTION ON LENGTH OF INCARCERATION

The final question addressed by Goldkamp is whether pretrial detention has an effect on the length of time a convict is to spend in prison or jail. Goldkamp found a small positive relationship, one he was willing to dismiss as inconsequential. Goldkamp's conclusion is that the relationship between the pretrial process and the disposition of cases or the kind of punishment received is a far more complex question than previously thought. Detention prior to trial, in this Philadelphia sample, affected some but not all the decisions in the process. Relative to release policy, the two most troubling findings are (1) that a large number (one-third) of detained defendants had their cases dropped or dismissed, and (2) that among the convicted, detention appeared to play a part in the decision to incarcerate. This second finding has recently been replicated by Petersilia et al. (1985) in California.

One correctional organization, the jail, plays a major part in the preconviction system. As a place of detention, it figures as an important social control in the lives of many persons who after that experience will not be punished. Also, it would appear that its use for the purposes of detention may have an effect on the distribution of punishment among those who are found guilty.

PRETRIAL DIVERSION

Diversion programs vary from one jurisdiction to another, but they often have the following characteristics:

1. Formal criteria for entry to the program
2. A statement from the defendant claiming voluntary participation
3. The provision of services either directly by a pretrial services agency or by referral to other agencies
4. Dismissal of charges upon successful completion of the program (Rovner-Pieczenik, 1976:5)

TYPICAL PROGRAMS

One example of legislation establishing pretrial diversion is the Connecticut General Statutes, section 54, defining "pre-trial rehabilitation programs." In Connecticut, the judge may assign to such a program an accused who, the court believes, " . . . will probably not offend again and who had no previous record of crime. . . " The statute does not permit pretrial rehabilitation for those charged with more serious felonies. Section 54 provides for the release of eligible defendants to the custody of the state department of probation "for such period, not exceeding two years, and under such conditions as the court shall order . . . ". The principal advantage provided to defendants for their participation is the provision

that "if such defendant satisfactorily completes his period of probation, he may apply for dismissal of the charges against him . . . ".

Another example of diversion is the Citizens Probation Authority in Michigan. This program requires the defendant to admit his guilt, pay a sentencing fee, if able, accept probation supervision for up to one year, and sign a treatment contract to engage in rehabilitation or other self-improvement programs. Restitution may be ordered. If the defendant is deemed successful, his record will be expunged and prosecution dropped (McCarthy and McCarthy, 1984:35).

Rovner-Pieczenik describes the usual process of determining diversion as follows (1976:6–8). The decision to divert begins when charges are filed. Court staff will review records on the defendant, followed by a personal interview, in order to determine eligibility. The most common reasons for exclusion are the seriousness of the present charge and prior criminal history. Confession of guilt to the charge in question is generally not mandatory, although many programs ask the defendant to admit or assume responsibility. In order to gain access to the diversion program, the defendant must waive the right to a speedy trial. Participation is voluntary, in the sense that the defendant can refuse to participate and continue with the prosecution. Program staff will seek agreement for diversion from either the prosecutor or the judge (depending on jurisdiction).

If the appropriate officials agree, the defendant enters the diversion program for an established period of time. Many programs are set to run for three to six months, but may last up to two years in some places. After entry, there will be an intake conference between program staff and defendant in which needs will be assessed, goals for supervision established, and a service delivery plan designed. Staff may deliver some services directly and may refer the defendant to other community agencies for other needs. Many programs stress employment, vocational training, and remedial education as primary goals. Counseling, financial assistance, housing, and medical services may also be offered if appropriate. At

Insert 4.2 EXAMINATION OF ORGANIZATIONAL FACTORS IN BAIL POLICY

Roy B. Flemming's *Punishment Before Trial* comes to grips with the pressures influencing judges and bail commissioners as organizational participants. Flemming begins his analysis with the observation that bail policies, which he defines as the percent of defendants detained and the percent released on their own recognizance, differ considerably from city to city. Using Wayne Thomas' data (1976), Flemming identifies one cluster of cities with punitive pretrial release policies and another group with liberal pretrial release policies.

The two cities used in Flemming's research, Baltimore and Detroit, are representative of these punitive and liberal policy cities. At the time Flemming gathered his data (1972), Detroit released 48.8 percent of its accused felons on ROR, while Baltimore released only 11.8 percent. Cash bail was the means of release for 48.2 percent of the cases in Detroit and for 75.3 percent in Baltimore. Detroit judges remanded only 3 percent of the cases before them, while Baltimore judges remanded 12.9 percent. The median amount of bail in Detroit was $2,000, while the median amount in Baltimore was $4,650. The differences in bail policies are not due to a greater proportion of more serious crimes in Baltimore. Baltimore had a larger and more active pretrial release agency and operated under a more liberal state bail law than Detroit. Flemming argues that the reasons for the harsh pretrial policies in Baltimore and the liberal policies in Detroit are not a product of individual crimes, nor of state law, but rather result from the interorganizational pressures influencing the two courts.

Flemming argues that court organizations are open systems seeking to maintain a reasonable equilibrium between external pressure and internal practice. Bail decision-makers attempt to control risks and uncertainties in their work by manipulating resources. The resources most commonly relied upon are the points of slack in the system, including the capacity of the jail (will the community tolerate overcrowding in the jail?) and the capacity of the disposition process (can actors dispose of cases more quickly, if need be, to accommodate changes in inflow to the jail?). Other resources include modes of interaction among officials, the quality and quantity of information, and the size and mix of the bail docket. The mix of uncertainties, risks, and resources, according to Flemming, will determine the kind of bail policy evident in a court. As it turns out, the most significant resource in the quality of bail policy is jail capacity, which is notoriously elastic and elusive (Mullen, 1980).

Flemming's policy implications deserve serious consideration. Among the most provocative of his conclusions are the following: (1) Crisis is important in engendering reform, but only if the crisis is politicized; (2) pretrial release agencies have little leverage in altering the political risks in freeing felony defendants; the effectiveness of these agencies as change agents is small; (3) the quickest and most direct means of changing pretrial detention policy is to reduce the capacity of the jail. Despite a liberal bail law and a large pretrial service agency, Baltimore officials were conservative, using ROR only for misdemeanants and relying on jail overcrowding. Detroit judges released more felony defendants because of a court-imposed cap on jail capacity and more trustworthy information about felony defendants.

---

the end of the program, the defendant will return to court facing one of four possible outcomes: The case may be dropped; prosecution may continue on reduced charges; the program may be extended; or full prosecution may be resumed.

FREQUENCY OF DIVERSION

Data presented in this chapter suggest that diversion is a frequent disposition. Table 4.3 shows that diversion is the reason for dismissal in up to

27 percent of *felony* arrests in 14 jurisdictions. Goldkamp's study indicates that diversion was the outcome in 31 percent of *all* Philadelphia arrests in his sample. Goldkamp found that he could explain 32 percent of the variation in the decision to divert by using six variables, all of which were related to the present charge or past criminal history. The most powerful predictors were the seriousness of the present charge and the number of prior arrests. In his study, the decision to divert appeared heavily related to two intertwined concerns: the desire for retribution and the desire to protect the community. Either of these would be particularly sensitive to seriousness of the crime charged and prior record. Thus diversion seems to be a means of speeding up a nonincarcerative disposition for persons the judge or prosecutor predicts would not receive a severe punishment if convicted.

RIGHTS AND DIVERSION

One traditional means of circumventing the more rigorous legal procedure of the criminal process has been to devise a new social control process that is not labeled "criminal." A. A. Stone (1975) suggests that diversion is merely the newest in a number of attempts to avoid the procedural limits in the criminal process. Austin and Krisberg (1981) seem to agree. In an important article highly critical of the outcomes of criminal justice reform attempts in general, they observe that the typical response of diversion programs to criticism about infringement of rights has been to have the diversion client enter into a formal contractual relationship with the program. Austin and Krisberg point out that the result of this formalization of diversion actually results in enmeshing the diversion client in a new set of formal rules and procedures without any determination of guilt. They conclude that diversion programs "represent an erosion of due process and increased formal intervention . . . " (1981:171). Although McCarthy and McCarthy are somewhat

narrower in their criticism, they also perceive a problem.

> . . . when divertees are required to admit guilt as a prerequisite to diversion, they may suffer an irretrievable loss of due process guarantees under current diversion operations. (1984:28)

Among the many legal issues which arise in the operation of diversion, concern about the admission of guilt provides one of the starkest portrayals of the legal dilemmas of diversion. Diversion is proposed as an alternative to prosecution. If there is nothing to prosecute, the rationale for diversion falls apart. Thus, while these programs continue to grow in number and use, they are caught between their own rationale and the rights of the defendant.

EVALUATING DIVERSION

Reviewing an array of diversion programs arising in the 1970s, Miller (1980:39–40) perceives diversion as the countermovement to the just deserts/retribution movement. Persons in favor of diversion have argued that the failure of treatment and rehabilitative efforts has not been documented as well as some would claim. In this view, diversion is the reflowering of rehabilitation.

If so, it would appear to suffer from some of the same legal problems that angered retributivists about treatment in the context of punishment. Diversion evaluations have uncovered other problems that also seem to resemble the criticisms of rehabilitation in punitive settings. Perhaps the greatest of these is that diversion, whether intended as rehabilitative or not, has not reduced the numbers of persons coming under the "net" of social control, but instead:

> Placed under the control of the criminal justice system, diversion programs have been transformed into a means for extending the net, making it stronger, and creating new nets. (Austin and Krisberg, 1981:170)

Diversion has not enabled rehabilitation to escape the shroud placed on it by association with coercive or apparently coerced alternatives.

Diversion has had other goals besides the provision of rehabilitation, and reduction of prosecution and correctional caseloads. In addition, it has promised lesser cost. Diversion has not fared well on this dimension either, in part because it faces other dilemmas. Pressure to cut costs, observes Rovner-Pirczenik (1976:143) has led some programs to depend on referral rather than direct services, hire less specialized staff, increase client turnover (or shorten the period of supervision), increase staff caseloads, decrease vocational and employment efforts, and compete for funds with probation programs.

In other words, paying attention to the cost-containment objective may weaken still further the argument that diversion is rehabilitative. Additionally, McCarthy and McCarthy report that some diversion programs, which have not been able to generate sufficient referrals from the courts, have begun to accept pretrial releasees (on supervised pretrial release), probationers, and even parolees. Such client combinations may reduce the strength of the claim that clients are being diverted.

SUMMARY

1. We have examined the preconviction criminal process to determine: (a) how the sequence of decisions prior to conviction may influence the selection of persons for punishment, and (b) how changes in the preconviction process itself have "correctionalized" the prosecution stage of criminal justice systems.
2. Pretrial reform has several rationales, including: (a) preconviction conditions are often worse than those experienced by punished persons; (b) the traditional procedures for releasing persons prior to trial are unfair to the poor; and (c) the courts and correctional systems are overloaded. These criticisms have led to release on recognizance programs, supervised pretrial release, and diversion programs.
3. Victims may decide not to call the police for roughly similar reasons that prosecutors and judges decide to decline prosecution or dismiss a case. Reporting a crime and full prosecution are more likely when charges are serious and when the victim and offender have no prior relationship.
4. Recent evidence suggests that guilty pleas are common in both busy and not busy courts and that the plea has been the most common means of conviction for many years. Some evidence suggests that a guilty plea may not imply the kind of bargaining that is often assumed. Nevertheless, persons who plead guilty may receive somewhat lighter sentences than those who do not, although this is not true in all cases.
5. Many more persons in this country experience detention in a correctional agency than experience incarceration for a conviction.
6. Release on recognizance programs permit release of some defendants without the requirement of bail. ROR does not succeed in reaching the poorest defendants.
7. Supervised pretrial release has emerged as an option for persons not eligible for ROR programs.
8. The most exacting study of pretrial detention shows that the impact of detention on punishment is probably less than had long been assumed. However, detention does appear to have an affect on the likelihood of incarceration after conviction.
9. Many persons detained prior to trial are subsequently released without conviction.
10. Diversion has become the final outcome for a significant proportion of cases in many jurisdictions. Many critics of diversion claim that the practice actually increases social control rather than reduces it, because diversion is often used as an alternative for cases that would not culminate in conviction.

KEY WORDS

BAIL SYSTEM. The practice of releasing, pending trial, a defendant upon placing a financial guarantee with the court to ensure appearance. The defendant may place the entire amount with the court, or pay a bondsman a premium.

BONDSMAN. A person who provides a financial guarantee that a defendant will appear at subsequent hearings in return for a nonrefundable payment from the defendant.

PRETRIAL DETENTION. The practice of detaining in jail a defendant who cannot make bail or obtain other release pending trial.

PRETRIAL DIVERSION. Formal programs that provide community supervision of a defendant for a specified period of time, typically with the promise to drop prosecution if supervision is completed successfully.

PREVENTIVE DETENTION. The practice of detaining a defendant prior to trial on the grounds that the defendant will commit a new crime if released.

RELEASE ON RECOGNIZANCE (ROR). A program of releasing a defendant prior to trial without bail, upon a promise to return for future hearings.

SUPERVISED (PRETRIAL) RELEASE. The release of a defendant without bail, but under supervision of a pretrial release agency or other supervising party.

PROJECTS AND QUESTIONS

1. The study *Felony Arrests* by the Vera Institute of Justice (1981) contains excellent descriptions of the kinds of cases which "fall out" at various points in the system. Choose students to focus on what happens during the prosecution of various kinds of charges, such as assault, murder, rape, and burglary. In what types of cases is full prosecution most likely? Least likely? Why?

2. In his study of the lower criminal courts of New Haven, Connecticut, Malcolm Feeley (1979) discovered that the cost of the bail bond charged was often greater than the amount of the fine defendants would pay if convicted. Additionally, he calculated the loss of wages during detention and court appearance to be five times greater than the amount in fines collected by the court (1979:238–240). While these costs are not punishments, what do they imply about the presumption that the criminal sanction is the most serious state intervention in the lives of its citizens?

3. Feeley also provides an interesting comparison between the broader concept of social control and the narrower concept of punishment. He points out (1979:199–201) that many persons arrested do not find the stigma of conviction to be a significant sanction because many of them have criminal records already and do not value conventional rules in the first place. What would this observation suggest about the retributive and deterrent rationales for punishment? Is it possible that the preconviction system, as Feeley claims, has been constructed to be the real (although illegal) punishment because the punishment itself is not perceived to be a significant social control under these conditions?

4. In the juvenile detention case of *Martin* v. *Stasburg*, a family court judge testified that many juveniles originally detained before adjudication are not given dispositions of incarceration once adjudicated delinquent because the pretrial detention was considered "punishment enough" (*University of Pennsylvania Law Review*, 1983:109). Undoubtedly some judges in the adult system feel the same way. While there are no arguments that legitimate such a detention objective under our Constitution, can you think of ways to prevent decision-makers from acting in this way? Independent of the failure to appear and danger to community arguments, could this desire to punish be an explanation for the significant role played by charge seriousness and prior record in the detention decision?

ADDITIONAL READING

Jonathan Casper. *American Criminal Justice* (Englewood Cliffs, NJ: Prentice-Hall, 1972). Casper interviewed a number of prisoners in the Connecticut prison system about their preconviction experiences. Easy and interesting reading that provides a number of important insights into the relationship of convicted offenders and the prosecution process.

James Eistenstein and Herbert Jacob. *Felony Justice* (Boston: Little, Brown, 1976). A study of the court process in three jurisdictions. One of the studies which advanced the idea that prosecution is controlled not so much by the law, but by the norms and working relationships of the "court work group."

Donald J. Newman. *Conviction* (Boston: Little, Brown, 1966). This is still the classic work on the guilty plea and the negotiation of pleas. Part of the American Bar Foundation field study of criminal justice practices in the United States.

Wayne Thomas. *Bail Reform in America* (Berkeley: University of California, 1976). A national evaluation of the impact of bail reform in the United States.

CORRECTIONAL PROCESS AND CORRECTIONAL SYSTEMS

QUESTIONS

1. What is the correctional process?
2. What are the problems with defining a system?
3. Does the correctional process have system characteristics?
4. What is a correctional network?
5. What steps are being taken to coordinate networks?

A MASTER PLAN FOR JEFFERSON

In the spring of 1969, Phil accompanied Professor Masters to a planning meeting in the new Jefferson Department of Correction. The Jefferson legislature had finally created a Department of Correction in 1967, and a lengthy search for the first commissioner had just been completed. As one of his first executive decisions, Commissioner Rush had contracted with Professor Masters to conduct an executive development program for his new central office staff. Commissioner Rush had a number of legitimate concerns about the operation of the new department. How could the new central office executives interact most effectively to make and oversee the implementation of policy? How could the central office deal with the predicted resistance from the

institutional executives who, until the creation of the department, were in direct communication with the governor? What correctional policy made the most sense as the state entered the 1970s? How could the department best use its resources?

After a brief group meeting, Professor Masters asked Commissioner Rush for a private conference.

Professor Masters began: "If you want real system development, then we have to begin right now with your overall strategy for this department."

Rush settled in a new easy chair in the corner. "This state has real advantages over most. What attracted me here is the possibility of really putting a coherent strategy in place. This state is small and compact enough to be manageable. I can visit every institution in the state in a two-day trip.

The important facilities are brand new, and we're not hurting for space. I want to develop a model system, and we've got the pieces to do it. The only problem is putting them together."

Rush ticked off what he saw as the special attractions of the Jefferson Department of Correction. "One, we've got the institutions and parole in one department. So, I can develop a field supervision program integrated with programs in the institutions. Two, this department controls the jails in this state. That means we can use the jails not only for detention and misdemeanants, but also as work release centers for felons. Imagine the advantages compared to a state like New York. Six months before our inmates are released, we can move them from Dunmore or Mulwan back into the cities. We'll develop work release wings in each of the jails. The parole staff can supervise employment and social services for the work-release centers, not just for parolees. The maximum security and minimum security institutions are close together; transfer is no problem. The only piece we're missing is probation. So most of the pieces are in place for a graduated series of transfers from reception and diagnosis, through maximum security, on to minimum for about a year, and then back to the jails for the last six months. The majority of our inmates, when they are ready for parole, will already be working in the community. They'll just move out of the jail and go back home. So I see the whole thing as a tightly organized giant release system, from beginning to end."

CORRECTIONAL SYSTEM PROBLEMS

Commissioner Rush remained in Jefferson for only one term. The governor elected in 1972 was of the other party, and Rush accepted the commissionership in a larger state. His staff development program came off pretty well; in fact, it

lasted three years. His plans to transform the jails into multipurpose correctional centers were, with modifications, adopted. But his intentions to move inmates quickly through maximum security and on to less secure settings were never fully implemented. By 1976, Mulwan was full to capacity. The plans for a "giant release system from beginning to end" proved futile in light of sentencing changes. The department became busy deciding where to put the next body, rather than in deciding how to coordinate reception, graduated reduction in custody, and graduated reentry to community living. The master plan for the Jefferson Department of Correction had some holes in it.

The partial fulfillment of Commissioner Rush's strategic plan is a good example of the difficulties with correctional systems. Commissioner Rush had control over the pieces of the correctional system *within* his department, but he lacked control over some other major system components, such as judicial and legislative decisions, which by the mid-1970s had drastically altered the department. Every state in the United States and the federal government has a centralized department of correction that controls and coordinates portions of the decision process. But no correctional organization controls all the decision points. How corrections operates in this country, and in many others, can only be understood in the context of the systemic relationships among the various decision-makers, agencies, facilities, and programs.

Eric Steele and James Jacobs (1975) observe that a **systems approach** to corrections has become increasingly important, because the various decisions within and among correctional organizations are increasingly interdependent. For example, prisons have often been studied as autonomous social systems. But single prisons are rarely autonomous. Commissioner Rush's plan to use the Dunmore minimum security prison as a midway point between maximum security and work release would be essential to any analysis of operations in Dunmore prison. It could not be accurately understood as a separate entity.

The New York State Department of Correctional Services Masterplan Advisory Committee meets in 1980. (New York State Department of Correctional Services)

Steele and Jacobs argue that many correctional programs have failed because they were expected to coexist with other programs that operated under contradictory principles. In Jefferson, the plan for an integated system of correctional programs that prepared inmates for eventual release was inconsistent with legislative and judicial decisions that rapidly filled the institutions and made orderly transfers from one program to another very difficult to accomplish. The purposes Commissioner Rush wanted to pursue in his part of the correctional system were contradicted by purposes sought in other parts of the system.

SYSTEMS ANALYSIS

The term **system** in criminal justice is applied very freely; no one stops to ask if the entities under consideration really constitute a system, or under what conditions they might be a system, or what type of system they happen to be. Dan Freed (1970) once characterized the collection of agencies that administer the criminal process as a nonsystem, because in his view, none of the agencies worked together to accomplish particu-

lar goals. But at nearly the same time that Freed was writing, the President's Commission on Law Enforcement and Administration of Justice (1967a) proposed that the most effective way of examining criminal justice was to examine it as a system. Why were Freed and the commission so far apart?

C. West Churchman (1968:29) defined a system as "a set of parts coordinated to accomplish a set of goals." If we accept this definition, we cannot identify a system by examining its parts. We must begin with the bigger picture. We must observe accomplished goals, notice the coordination, and only then become interested in the parts themselves. But what do we consider evidence of goals? How much accomplishment of them is necessary? How much coordination is required before we say that certain elements are interconnected and together produced that observed achievement?

Systems analysts give a rather complicated "it all depends" answer to these questions:

Any system has an unlimited number of properties. Only some of these are relevant to any particular research. Hence, those that are relevant may change with changes in the *purposes of the research*. (emphasis supplied; Ackoff and Emery, 1972:18)

What we consider to be a correctional system is to some extent dependent on *our* purposes as we analyze them. An example might help to make the point. When Commissioner Rush was outlining his plans for his department to Professor Masters, he was describing as a system only those persons and facilities that fell under his direct authority. For him, the "correctional system" was his department. Also, the system he perceived did not yet exist—it was a plan. The plan was anchored by an overarching purpose for all the various pieces—a graduated release system that would have as its primary goal the easiest transition to parole that he could manage to bring about. The parts of the system were defined in relation to this purpose.

When Commissioner Rush looked at the jails under his control, he did not see what a sheriff or jail warden might see. Instead, he saw the potential for community correctional centers which would not only hold detainees and misdemeanants, but would also hold felons during the last part of their incarceration. A different commissioner might have seen quite a different system. What if the governor had appointed a commissioner interested in maximizing the protection of the public? To this commissioner, the characteristics of greatest concern to Commissioner Rush would have been irrelevant or even negative. The location of the jails in the major employment centers of the state, so important to a work release system, would have been irrelevant to someone concerned about security.

Consequently, decisions about the nature of a system are partially dependent upon the purposes of the observer. But does this mean that the "system" is totally in the head of the analyst? No. If Commissioner Rush had remained in office for another term, he might have noticed some problems with his notion of a graduated release system. He would have discovered that regardless of his purposes, other actors had a major say in determining how his facilities were to be used. By 1976, judges had filled up all the empty

space. The commissioner's purposes could not be implemented because his analysis had left out parts of correctional reality. Deciding on purpose is crucial to the analysis of human systems, because people act on their ideas. But purposes may not be achievable because of an insufficient supply of resources or an inhospitable environment.

Commissioner Rush had not taken his systems analysis far enough. His plans were dependent on accomplishing one of two things. He had to find a way to include judges' sentencing decisions in his system, so that he could control their purposes, or if judges remained outside his control, he had to make sure that their decision patterns were not about to change. As it turned out, neither step was taken. Therefore, the commissioner was not able to "coordinate all the parts to accomplish a set of goals."

THE ELEMENTS OF SYSTEMS ANALYSIS

C. West Churchman (1968:29–30) provides a checklist of minimal elements in systems analysis that might have helped Commissioner Rush. These are: (1) total system objectives, as measured by performance; (2) the environment of the system, or the fixed constraints which affect the system but cannot be affected by it; (3) system resources, or the supply of material and persons the system can use to meet its objectives; (4) the components or parts of the system, as indicated by their activities and goals; and (5) the management of the system, or the means by which resources are deployed and parts coordinated to meet system objectives.

The procedures for identifying these elements are often ignored when correctional systems are described. In this chapter we have space only to indicate some of the most important issues to be kept in mind when correctional systems are discussed.

DETERMINING OBJECTIVES

One problem with the definition of correctional systems is that of determining total **system ob-**

Correctional objectives are complex, as indicated by the custodial, industrial, and agricultural activities evident at Elmira Correctional Facility. (New York State Department of Correctional Services)

jectives. Can we identify a system on the basis of purposes such as retribution, deterrence, incapacitation, and rehabilitation? How do we measure these objectives in terms of actual performance?

A quick but inaccurate approach is to listen to what correctional officials claim are the objectives of the system. Should we believe these claims? Recall Phil's problem with evaluating the objectives of the prerelease centers in Chapter 3. Could he believe Director Jenison's stated objectives? Or those in the proposal which spoke of recidivism reduction?

Systems analysts are inherently suspicious of stated or believed objectives for a number of reasons. First, a spokesperson for a system does not necessarily know what the system is actually doing. Second, the publicly stated objectives enunciated by a spokesperson must be evaluated against the context of the statement. Director Jen-

ison was appointed to reduce costs, reduce staff discretion, and place greater controls on the residents. Under these conditions, he was unlikely to boast of rehabilitative potential, even if he knew that his counselors were more concerned about the delivery of services than they were with control. Consequently, systems analysts demand measures of system performance rather than statements of them.

But, as we already know, measures of system performance in corrections are rather difficult to come by. It may be some time in the future before the actual consequences of correctional activity can be specified. In the meantime, we may have to settle for rather crude measures. Churchman suggests one simple test of objectives that may be helpful:

The scientist's test of the objectives of a system is the determination of whether the system would knowingly sacrifice other goals in order to obtain the objective. (1968:31)

Using this test of objectives, systems analysts have concluded that correctional systems generally do not have rehabilitative objectives. As the National Academy of Sciences panel on rehabilitation put it, we cannot expect one hour of counseling a week to have effects when the remainder of the inmates' experience is purely custodial in nature (Sechrest, White, and Brown, 1980). Using the same test of objectives, someone could have told Commissioner Rush that his plan was unrealistic. His system could not legally reject the goal of taking all sentenced offenders in order to accomplish the objective of graduated release.

Because of the complexity and the ambiguity in correctional objectives, systems analysis has not proceeded very far in the definition of correctional systems. The system analysis position is often relegated to objectives that can be measured, despite the recognition that unmeasured and perhaps unimagined consequences are actually far more important than those which can be observed. A systems analyst approaching corrections is often left with conservative statements about the observable consequences, such as "the objectives of the Jefferson Department of Correction are to house at an allocated cost a certain number of felons and misdemeanants, as well as defendants awaiting trial." Housing inmates is considerably more observable than intangible objectives such as retribution, deterrence, and rehabilitation.

To date, system analysts have probably made the greatest progress with measuring the claimed objective of rehabilitation. The usual conclusion is that it does not happen (Greenberg, 1977b). Highly sophisticated statistical techniques are also being used to measure the claimed consequence of incapacitation. Measures of deterrence lag far behind, and satisfactory measures of retribution have not even been conceived.

Since systems analysts are generally more able to measure consequences involving persons actually under custody than to measure conse-

quences for the social system in general, it is possible that the limitations of systems analysis may have a constraining effect on our ability to conceive of correctional systems. For instance, an incapacitative system is often proposed as a means of reducing danger to society. But the popularity of this proposal may rest in part on the comparative simplicity of the idea of incapacitation compared to retribution or deterrence. Although it is difficult enough, it is still easier to study the effects of correction on the offender than it is to study the effects of correction on other people.

FINDING SYSTEM BOUNDARIES

Beyond the difficulty in measuring performance, another critical problem in describing correctional systems is determining **system boundaries.** "Bounding the system" is often considered a critical step. So what is the problem? you might say. Boundaries are pretty easy to spot. A frog is a frog. Where the skin ends, so does the frog. Well, that might be convincing to someone who wishes to dissect the frog. But what about the ecologist? To him, the frog is only part of a system that includes swamps, mosquitoes, and muskrats. In other words, definition of system boundaries can lead us right back to the purposes of analysis again. What is a system to one analyst is merely a component in a larger system to another analyst.

The boundaries of human systems, such as correctional systems, can become particularly fuzzy. For example, in the case at the end of Chapter 3, how should Phil set out to bound the prerelease system? Should he simply count all the personnel designated as prerelease center employees by the Department of Correction? If he were a personnel analyst for the department, that rule might suffice. But Phil is a social scientist concerned with the prerelease system as a means of releasing inmates. Counselors in this system spend tremendous effort convincing local employers to hire center residents. Are these employers in or out of the prerelease system, relative to the purposes of releasing inmates?

If the counselors are successful in convincing employers to commit jobs to residents, then these employers, or at least certain positions in their enterprises, are *in* the prerelease system, and function as resources in the release process. If, on the other hand, employers are relatively indifferent to the overtures of the counselors, they might better be described as *outside* the system, as part of its environment. The same is true with Commissioner Rush's problem of designing his giant release system. Are judges an environmental constraint, or part of the system? Commissioner Rush had no direct control over their decisions. They were not part of his department. But could he somehow affect their purposes in sentencing so these were consistent with his desires? If not, they had to be considered part of the environment and the system had to adjust to them.

As should be clear in these examples, the boundaries of correctional systems are not well defined. Indeed, the functioning of correctional systems, as political systems, is partially dependent upon the power of influence of stakeholders and the limits of their imagination. If Commissioner Rush never attempts to influence judicial sentencing policy, he will never know if judges can be considered resources or must be accommodated like the weather. Counselors in the prerelease system can change the boundaries of the system by the means they use to exert influence. If the counselors' means of assisting with employment is counseling residents on how best to approach employers, then the prerelease system remains fairly limited by the walls of the prerelease centers. Employers are not being treated as directly approachable. However, if the employers are somehow directly influenced, such as by counselors making presentations at business club meetings on the advantages of hiring ex-offenders, then perhaps the boundaries of the system have expanded to include sympathetic employers. In other words, in corrections, system boundaries are partly a matter of will and intent, rather than merely of legal authority or location of facilities.

DETERMINING RESOURCES

"**Resources** . . . are the things the system can change and use to its own advantage" (Churchman, 1968:37). The most visible resources in correctional systems are facilities and personnel. However, estimating the resource potential of facilities and personnel can be tricky. A resource is something the system can convert to obtain its objectives. In Commissioner Rush's proposed system for Jefferson, the size of the Mulwan maximum security prison was not a resource. For Rush's purposes, the facility was too large. He was afraid that a large maximum security facility would dominate the system, and he perceived it as a hindrance or a constraint. An effective commissioner would also need to be careful when estimating personnel resources. The number of persons on the payroll may not be a good indicator of resources, since the available laborpower is really measured by the amount of energy exerted by the workers to reach objectives. A recalcitrant, alienated guard staff, no matter how large, is not an indication of a wealthy correctional system. Consequently, when Commissioner Rush approached Professor Masters for an executive development program, he was really seeking help in increasing his labor supply. How could he convert potential person power into coordinated, committed team members? Todd Clear makes the point that correctional personnel policies have been deficient for years (1985). Staff are often underpaid, poorly trained, and poorly directed. Under these conditions, mere numbers of personnel may not be a good indication of available resources.

A crucial resource in corrections is not an easily measured item. How much *legitimacy* does the organization have? A number of organizational researchers treat legitimacy, or the perceived credibility of the system in the environment, as just as important as financial resources (Meyer, 1975; Benson, 1975). When evaluations indicated that rehabilitative claims by correctional departments were not being achieved, these departments lost credibility, and therefore lost legitimate claim on some resources.

IDENTIFYING SYSTEM COMPONENTS

The fourth element of systems is its components. The most important criteria in distinguishing system components are the activities, or functions, of the parts rather than the visible structure. Official departmental structures often have little to do with actual contributions to system objectives and can therefore be very misleading indicators of system components (Churchman, 1968:40). In the Jefferson case, the decision to identify the separate facilities as system components could have been harmful to the proposed purposes. In Commissioner Rush's view, the city correctional centers were not to be treated as jails, but instead were to perform several functions. In the commissioner's plan, these units were to contain pieces of several components. The work release portions of the centers were connected to operations in the minimum and maximum security prisons. For his plan to work, he could not manage the centers as separate components of the system; at least portions of those buildings and portions of their staff would have to be organized as part of the graduated release system spread across the state and including counseling staff at both prisons and the classification staff in the reception center. Similarly, he did not want to consider his parole division as a separate component. He wanted his parole officers to supervise work release inmates and marshall employment resources for the whole system. No matter what their official departmental name, these officers were not merely supervisors of persons paroled from prison.

Measuring system components by contribution to objectives can result in a very different picture of the system than we would derive by depending on the official nomenclature used in the system. For example, in his 1964 study of federal prison and parole, Dan Glaser assessed the relative contribution of guards and counselors to the rehabilitation of inmates. Although the measures were necessarily crude, Glaser indicated that occasionally guards, and very often prison work supervisors, contributed far more to an inmate's change of behavior than did prison counselors, despite the fact that counselors were supposedly in charge of treatment. If federal planners had wanted to portray accurately the treatment component of the federal prisons, they would have had to include some guard or work supervisor activities, rather than just the persons paid to be counselors. We will return to this important issue in Chapter 14.

MANAGING THE SYSTEM

The final element in the analysis of systems is the **management component.** It establishes the goals of other components, distributes resources, and monitors system performance (Churchman, 1968:44). When Dan Freed declared that criminal justice did not qualify as a system, he was arguing that it had no management component. Freed and Malcolm Feeley (1973) concur that criminal justice agencies do not share a common managerial control, but act independently of each other and are therefore not systems in Churchman's sense of parts coordinated toward a set of objectives. Can the same criticism be levied at correctional systems? Or can this "component" of the criminal justice system manage its affairs through goal setting, resource distribution, and performance monitoring? This is a controversial point. Optimistic and assertive managers such as Commissioner Rush believe that they are at the helms of their systems, controlling and coordinating performance. What behavior on their part might make us agree with them?

Like the management of other public organizations, the management of correctional systems is fragmented, when compared to private organizations. With the exception of some probation chiefs who are appointed by judges, the ostensible managers of corrections departments are officials in the executive branch of government. Governors appoint state commissioners, and county executives appoint many probation directors. The director of the Federal Bureau of Prisons is appointed by the president. The sheriffs who often run local jails are elected. However, these official administrators do not have the same kind of control over resources and over selection of goals that would be true of the chief executive officer of a private corporation. The chief executive of a correctional organization must present a budget request to an independent legislature at every government level. Key decisions about programs, at least to the extent that programs are determined by appropriations, are determined by the legislative branch.

But this is not the end of the managerial fragmentation. The judicial branch of government plays an important managerial role in two respects. First, sentencing judges retain considerable control over the input to correctional systems. Their goals for punishment can often contradict those of the persons operating the correctional department. The judge's determination of appropriate punishment, and in particular the decision to use probation or incarceration, plays a crucial role in setting the objectives of the correctional system. Second, appellate courts have taken an increasingly active role in the administration of corrections. (Judicial activism will be discussed in detail in Chapter 13.)

Under these conditions, how do we identify the management component of correctional organizations? The chief executives often lack the authority to determine system components, to distribute resources, or to monitor and control system performance. There are, of course, plenty of reasons to maintain this fragmented control. Our three-branch system of government is based on the principle that too much power in the hands of the executive can lead to evil consequences. The atrocities committed by a rather autonomous management of the Tucker Prison Farm in Arkansas is evidence of the need for a balance of power (see Murton and Hyams, 1969).

Under these conditions, there is no simple answer to the question of whether our correctional systems are true systems, as defined by Churchman. Another analyst, Walter Buckley, may provide us with a solution. Buckley (1967) makes a distinction between **goal-directed** and **goal-oriented** systems. He proposes that some systems

lack sufficient control to actually achieve or set goals; they are oriented toward particular values. This orientation provides some general direction and structure, but such systems lack the capacity to direct their components to specific objectives. In this view, shared by Freed and Feeley, among others, correctional systems may be seen as goal-oriented rather than goal-directed systems. But there is another perspective. One could argue that the system management component is a combination of executive, legislative, and judicial activity. In this view, the fact that the chief administrator of a particular organization lacks all the tools to manage the system does not necessarily mean that the system is adrift. The system may be managed by a combination of forces and actors from different branches of government.

The hard-nosed systems analyst would probably respond that management exists to the extent that it works, regardless of its structure or the name on the door. To the extent that judicial, legislative, and executive branches work together, control of the system may be achieved. A number of observers have commented that the late John Manson, commissioner of corrections in Connecticut from 1971 to his death in 1984, succeeded in bringing legislative, judicial, and executive leaders together in sufficient harmony to produce a system. In New York State, Governor Carey's administration created a new position in that state criminal justice administration, director of criminal justice. The position was created to coordinate not only correctional organizations, but judicial administration and police operations as well. All budget requests from all New York State criminal justice agencies pass through the director's office. The intent is to consolidate and therefore better coordinate criminal justice policy so that a system can be produced. But whether such a structural solution can achieve the hoped for result remains to be seen.

We can ask once again: Do we have correctional systems? Do we have a set of parts coordinated to achieve a set of objectives? In most cases, probably not. It is possible that some systems are under control some of the time. It is also possible that some institutions or some community correctional agencies are reasonably well managed and can be considered systems in the true sense. However, it is likely that most of the agencies and networks of agencies we designate as "correctional systems" in the United States fall rather short of the mark.

THE CORRECTIONAL PROCESS

That portion of the criminal justice process which occurs after conviction is commonly referred to as the **correctional process.** It encompasses the sequence of decision points through which convicted offenders may pass. Figure 5.1 is a schematic presentation of three correctional processes, one for persons convicted of felonies, one for persons convicted of misdemeanors, and one for persons adjudicated delinquent. The juvenile correctional process, which operates under separate law, will be discussed in Chapter 19. The adult felony and misdemeanant processes and the agencies responsible for these decisions and activities are described in Chapters 6 through 18.

No single authority has control over this process, but behavior at any one point can affect behavior at any other point. Successful implementation of the goals of punishment is contingent on whether those interactions are coordinated. The mutual interdependencies in the correctional process prompted the President's Commission on Law Enforcement and the Administration of Justice (1967a) to use a systems approach to correctional problems. As we noted in Chapter 3, the dominant ideology since 1967 favors the creation of a more coherent, managed system by finding ways to control the interactions in the process. Other ideologists reject unification as either not feasible or damaging to social order. Understanding contemporary correctional practice requires some knowledge of what unification would mean and why its achievement is such a problem. In the remaining sections of this chapter, we review the stages of the correctional process and their interconnections. Then we examine four goal-directed systems which could be created, and finally describe some of the changes required to improve coordination.

SENTENCING

Sentencing officially occurs at a sentencing hearing where the judge pronounces the chosen punishment for the conviction. The variety of sentencing options was described in Chapter 1. These options are predetermined by the legislature. As we will see in Chapter 6, legislatures can give judges varying degrees of freedom in selecting a sentence. In most jurisdictions and for most crimes, the judge has sufficient discretion that his or her decisions greatly affect the rest of the process. Typically, the prosecution and the defense have an opportunity to influence the judge prior to pronouncement. In addition, before many sentencing hearings, a probation officer will conduct a presentence investigation and report the findings.

Most experts agree that the crucial choice in sentencing is selecting probation or incarceration. For the individual defendant, this decision has as much bearing on his or her immediate future as any other. While the choice in any individual case has little impact on the rest of the process, the *rate* with which incarceration is chosen has a tremendous influence because it distributes the workload among the different agencies.

The extent to which conditions later in the process do and should influence the judge is controversial. Will fewer incarcerative sentences be chosen when prisons and jails are overcrowded? This question is one of **feedback.** Do behaviors later in a system feed back to influence behavior at earlier stages? Some judges admit they consider this issue when sentencing, while others insist it should not have a bearing on their choices.

When a judge chooses incarceration for a felony, he or she can usually also influence later decisions about that felon. By selecting a lower or higher minimum term, the judge can alter the

FIGURE 5.1   The Correctional Process

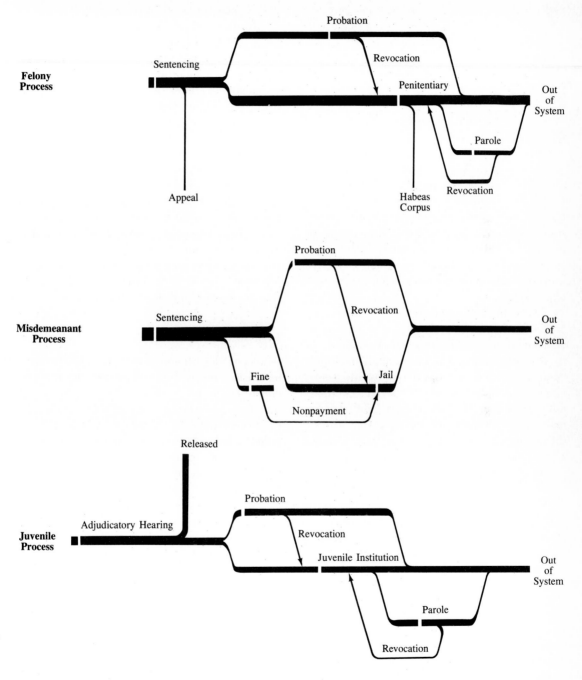

SOURCE: Adapted from President's Commission on Law Enforcement and Administration of Justice, *Challenge of Crime in a Free Society*. Washington, DC: United States Government Printing Office, 1967, p. 9.

proportion of an inmate's sentence over which the parole board can exert authority. Parole is generally not available in the misdemeanant process, although some sentence options, such as the split sentence, can approximate parole for misdemeanants.

PROBATION

Probation is usually available in both felony and misdemeanant processes. Probation is both a punishment option and a subprocess that contains other decisions. When a probation department receives a case, a classification and assignment process begins to determine how much and what type of supervision a probationer will receive. Some departments make these determinations using only tradition and rudimentary information. Others use complex measurement and predictive instruments to place the probationer in a particular program.

Probation is a **conditional sentence;** the probationer's retention of freedom is contingent on conformity to imposed conditions. Many of these conditions are general and apply to all probationary sentences handed out by the court. However, a judge can order special conditions for a particular case. Prosecution and defense may have a hand in shaping these special conditions, as may the probation department through a presentence investigation report.

If the conditions of probation are not observed, the probation department may file for revocation. At a revocation hearing, the judge will determine whether a violation has been factually substantiated and whether to revoke. The probationer, often with counsel, may challenge the accuracy of the revocation request or may argue that probation should be continued, with new conditions, despite the violation. If the judge determines that conditions have been violated, he or she may resentence the probationer to prison in the felony process, or to jail in the misdemeanant process.

The rate of probation revocation in a jurisdiction can have an important impact on prison or jail populations. Current institutional conditions and the current rate of new convictions may influence how frequently revocations occur.

Revocations are usually divided into two types, technical and new crimes. Technical violations involve breaking of probation conditions, such as timely reporting to the probation officers, which are not crimes. A violation for a new crime involves breaking the condition that probationers do not engage in new criminal activity. It is difficult to determine how many technical violations are simple rule violations rather than substitutes for a new prosecution. Probation officers, particularly if they are pressured by police or prosecutors, may seek a technical violation when a new crime is suspected but cannot be proved in court. To some extent, probation revocation policy may depend upon prosecutorial decisions about whether to seek a new conviction against a probationer or to save resources by relying on revocation for technical violations.

JAIL SENTENCES

In the misdemeanant system, the incarcerative option is sentence to a jail, usually for a determinate period not to exceed one year. Since jail sentences are short and inmate turnover is high, the decision-making sequence in most jails is rather simple. The jail process usually includes some form of reception and classification. Often jail classification involves only superficial screening for the most observable medical and mental health problems and may result in segregation of prisoners only by age and sex. Many jails also attempt to separate the convicted from those awaiting sentence. Large urban jails, however, may have more sophisticated classification processes and more placement options. Some correctional departments for misdemeanants will have options for releasing inmates after a portion of the sentence is served (see, for example, the discussion of home arrest in Chapter 9). Others may have programs of intermittent confinement, releasing some inmates during the day to work, or locking up others only on weekends. Some of these options depend upon prior judicial sentencing approval; others may be implemented at the discretion of the jail administrator.

PRISON SENTENCES

Felons are usually sentenced to prisons for more than a year. Since sentences are longer, a more complex decision sequence usually unfolds during a prison sentence. A felony prison sentence involves transfer of jurisdiction to the state or federal executive branch from the sentencing court. Most departments can choose from a number of facilities and programs to implement the sentence.

Most felony incarcerations will involve initial classification decisions and then a series of program and/or facility transfers during the course of the sentence. The later transfers are usually called reclassification decisions. Some of these may be initiated after disciplinary infractions; some may be considered purely administrative (such as keeping prison populations under control); and some may be initiated to make available to an inmate other programs or conditions. The amount of discretion prison officials have in this part of the process depends on the resources they have for the number of inmates under their control. Consequently, sentencing policy and revocation policy can severely limit choices in the prison.

In this regard, the correctional process differs considerably from the preconviction decision process. Police, prosecutors, and judges all exert some control over the numbers and types of cases they choose to deal with. Correctional officials generally cannot. As long as a particular sentence is within legal limits, correctional authorities must accept supervision responsibility.

CONDITIONAL RELEASE

In the felony process, there are several alternative forms of release. The most common is parole, a discretionary release decision by a board. Like probation, parole is conditional. Paroling authorities vary considerably in the rate with which they grant parole. This rate will not only influence the prison process, but may also influence sentencing decisions.

Some states also provide for the conditional release of persons not paroled. This option is variously called mandatory release, conditional release, or good time release. It may not be available for all inmates. This form of release does not involve a board decision, but rests on statutory provisions for releasing prior to the end of sentence inmates who have displayed "good behavior" in prison. Whether prison officials have discretion in awarding or taking away good time credit depends on good time statutes. Mandatory releasees are generally subject to the same conditions as parolees and may also be revoked.

Parole revocation process is very similar to probation revocation process, although the findings of fact and determination of outcome are made by an administrative board rather than a sentencing judge. In some jurisdictions, a major proportion of yearly prison admissions are conditional release revocations. The revocation rate may be influenced not only by board policy and rigor or release supervision, but also by interactions among police, prosecution, parole supervision officers, and prison officials.

TERMINATION OF SENTENCE

At the expiration of sentence, legal control of the convicted offender ends. The majority of offenders are already in the community when their sentences expire. They are simply removed from probation or conditional release supervision, or they complete the payment of a fine or a restitution order. A small percentage of inmates remain incarcerated until the expiration of the maximum sentence. Inmates who "max out" are then released without supervision. Only in rare instances are convicted offenders never released: A small but growing number are executed. A few are sentenced to life imprisonment without parole. A few die in prison prior to parole or expiration of their term. A number of jurisdictions provide for termination of supervision prior to expiration of the sentence. Parolees who have obeyed all conditions for a specified period of time may be told to report in writing once or twice a year. Other jurisdictions may use a pardons or commutation board to reduce the length of a sentence.

In many jurisdictions, the termination of a felony sentence does not result in automatic restoration of all rights enjoyed by free citizens. Many states deny convicted felons the rights to vote, to serve on a jury, to hold public office, to enter into contracts, or to sue in court. There may be a number of restricted occupations exfelons may not enter. Very often these collateral consequences are permanent. Some states have experimented with procedures to expunge the records of certain offenders after termination of sentence, but the procedures have not worked very well. Other states provide for a process of full pardon and full restoration of rights if the exoffender has remained free of arrest for a specified period of time. However, the pardon process is lengthy and expensive, and it must be initiated by the ex-offender.

These losses and restrictions are probably less important to many ex-offenders than informal barriers, such as suspicion and fear, that may exacerbate the difficult tasks of finding a job and a decent place to live, and resuming family life. While the vast majority of ex-convicts return to community life after the correctional process is completed, a significant number of hurdles may stand between them and productive citizenship. Most correctional processes include great expenditure of resources to separate the convicted offender from other people. Far less investment is made in ceremonies and procedures to mark the end of punishment.

FROM PROCESS TO SYSTEM: MODELS OF CORRECTIONAL POLICIES

The correctional process, even as it currently operates, is in some sense a "system." It is a series of interlocking, interactive decisions and activities that achieve the implementation of punishment. As we can see in the brief description above, or in the detailed descriptions that follow, a diverse set of agencies and actors contribute to the completion of the process and shape its character in any particular jurisdiction.

Starting in the 1960s, a number of steps were taken to exert greater control over this process. The aim has been to make the process more of a system, in Churchman's sense of that term. These control efforts have not been very effective, and many initiatives launched to produce greater cohesion and consistency have backfired. Nevertheless, the push to increase control, particularly to permit the executive branch of the government to manage the system, has had important effects on the correctional process.

If executives want to exert greater control, the first step, according to systems analysts, is clarification of goals. There are a number of ways to increase clarity, but a statement of system goals widely used by correctional practitioners was developed by Vincent O'Leary (1967; 1970; O'Leary and Duffee, 1971; and Gottfredson and Gottfredson, 1980). O'Leary's conceptual framework, called the correctional policy model, permitted the identification of consistent assumptions, strategies, and programs across the various stages of the correctional process.

The correctional policy model is based on two major assumptions. First, the model assumes that goals can be clarified if correctional activities are measured on their orientations toward planned individual change. Many correctional decisions and processes have the aim of influencing the behavior of individual offenders. Thus, commonalities can be found by asking whether such influence is intended and how it is exerted.

Second, the model assumes that decision-makers, such as judges, prison classification officials, and parole boards, and agency executives, such as probation chiefs, and commissioners of correction, are influenced by various pressures both inside and outside their organizations. The correctional policy model simplifies the nature of these complex pressures, but it does depict major sources of concern to correctional decision-makers. The model proposes that the two important concerns of these officials are (1) the degree to which they are responsive to individual differences among offenders, and (2) the degree to which they are responsive to community standards and norms.

By elaborating on common correctional change strategies, on the one hand, and combining the concerns for the community and the individual offender on the other, the model identifies four coherent correctional policies. In other words, the model depicts how the correctional process would operate if the assumptions and pressures at one decision point were consistent with assumptions and pressures at other decision points. The dimensions of the model are summarized in Table 5.1.

REFORM POLICY

Policymakers displaying a high concern for the community and a low concern for the individual offender have a **reform policy.** The approach to changing offenders is one of "compliance," and there is heavy emphasis on protecting society by demanding that offenders conform to rules. Offenders are rewarded for conformity and punished for deviation from the rules. Control is exerted by maintaining surveillance. Sentencing criteria include the perceived danger or damage of an offender's previous behavior. Probation and parole officers adopt law enforcement investigative postures, rigorously enforcing conditions and us-

ing revocation to make sure conditions are observed. Prison classification relies primarily on security criteria, and inmate behavior is controlled by holding out more attractive conditions or early release for those who behave. Prison programs stress habit formation through regimentation and repetition. Parole board policy stresses maintenance of prison discipline by rewarding good behavior and enforcement of community norms by releasing inmates who display industriousness and obedience.

REHABILITATION POLICY

Rehabilitation policy is characterized by high concern for the individual offender and a low concern for the community. Change in offenders is accomplished through a process of "identification." This policy assumes that criminality is the result of an offender's internal problems. Correctional programs must therefore supply a supportive atmosphere and congenial relationships with therapists. Offenders who identify with these therapists and value relationships with them will mature. Rehabilitation sentencing focuses on appropriate diagnosis and linking an offender with the right therapy. The prison is viewed as a sort of hospital where the offender can overcome critical character deficits. Rehabilitation policy poses a sharp division of labor between treaters and support staff. Custodians should maintain a therapeutic atmosphere in a prison but leave treatment to professionals. A parole board in this system functions like a clinical review team, determining the stages of treatment. Probation and parole officers are selected and trained for their therapeutic expertise. They are expected to recognize when offenders require a more supportive environment and more intense therapy than the community can provide.

RESTRAINT POLICY

Restraint policy displays low concern for the individual inmate and low concern for the community. Correctional activity does not include changing motives, but instead is designed to hold

TABLE 5.1   Models of Correctional Policies

		EMPHASIS ON THE COMMUNITY	
		LOW	HIGH
EMPHASIS ON THE OFFENDER	HIGH	Rehabilitation (Identification focus)	Reintegration (Internalization focus)
	LOW	Restraint (Organizational focus)	Reform (Compliance focus)

offenders securely. This policy limits correctional officials to the enforcement of orders determined by sources outside the system. Inside the system, workers are expected to maintain order. Thus most staff, including probation and parole officers, perform monitor roles. Officers are left to choose whether or not they should conform to rules; staff do not attempt to influence offender behavior.

REINTEGRATION POLICY

A **reintegration policy** displays high concern for the community and for the individual offender. The change strategy is one of "internalization." Crime is perceived as ineffectual problem-solving behavior. The goal of correctional decisions and programs is to link offenders with skills and resources that will enable them to accomplish their goals legitimately. If the new behavior is effective, it will be internalized. Sentencing policy stresses community settings rather than institutions because offenders must ultimately learn behaviors that work in community settings. Imprisonment, when used, should occur close to the offender's home community, so that positive links can be preserved or developed. Teamwork among staff and between staff and inmates is stressed because no single staff type is likely to be effective with all offenders. Parole and probation officers are expected to act as advocates for offenders and as mediators of community resources. In return for supplementation of skills and brokerage of resources, offenders are expected to conform to community standards and expectations. If entrance to that community is facilitated, the new entrants are to behave in accordance with the rules of membership. More specific characteristics of this policy, and the other three, at various stages of the correctional process, are compared in Table 5.2.

MANAGING CORRECTIONAL NETWORKS

When the President's Commission on Law Enforcement and Administration of Justice used the term correctional system, it was referring to the activity of a **correctional network,** rather than to the activity of specific correctional organizations. Any correctional network would include that collection of agencies and decision-makers which legislates, funds, manages, and regulates pretrial release, detention, diversion, sentencing, and punishment. Networks generally include at least two levels and all three branches of government. If corrections is to become more systematic, change must occur at the network level. Consistent correctional policies, for example, are achievable only if the same policy is adopted throughout the network.

Network connections have always existed, but they have become easier to see as overcrowding has increased. For example, in New York State, local jails became overcrowded when prisoners already sentenced to state prisons could not be transferred because the Department of Correctional Services had no space. When both local and state organizations in a network have slack resources, the connections are less visible, and perhaps less important.

When people criticize the fragmented nature of the correctional system, they are observing that there is no centralized authority. Since a number of autonomous agencies participate in networks, the flow of offenders, the allocation of resources, and attempts to structure networkwide programs are often matters of compromise and conflict. Traditionally, management of the correctional network, to the extent that it was managed at all, was the product of interagency give and take, rather than unified policy direction. Only recently has the management of correctional networks become a high-priority issue. Many governments at all levels are now attempting to restructure network connections to make policy more coherent. Some of the changes that are aimed at systematizing the correctional process are described below.

CHANGING STATE-LOCAL NETWORKS

In the early 1960s, the State of California devised a new network relationship called the probation subsidy. Some officials argued that the main function of the subsidy was the improvement of probation services through increased staffing and training. Others argued that the subsidy was an attempt to decrease commitments to the state department of correction, saving state tax dollars by keeping offenders under local supervision (Lerman, 1975). Because the subsidy had ambiguous purposes, it also had ambiguous effects, and the original subsidy was repealed. However, the California probation subsidy is an early example of an attempt to manage the connection between local probation and state prison commitments through a unified policy applying to both.

Based on the California subsidy heritage, what is now the model for changing local-state punishment networks was established in Minnesota by the Community Corrections Act (Blackmore, 1978; Ku, 1980). The Minnesota Community Corrections Act (CCA) is an excellent example of a network management attempt. The act was initiated by Corrections Commissioner David Fogel and brought to fruition by his successor, Ken Schoen. While it was called a "community corrections" act, it was in fact an innovation by the state corrections executive which sought to change the proportion of convicted offenders committed to the state from local courts. Typical of this kind of network change, the CCA utilized a carrot and stick approach to make local decision-makers more responsive to state priorities.

The CCA, unlike the California subsidy, involved not only management of the state-local connection, but also creation of new management activity to coordinate agency interaction at the local level. The CCA required interested counties to create Community Corrections Advisory Boards which would bring together most of the significant actors in the local network to establish a unified plan for handling all offenders sentenced to less than five years. If these plans were approved by the Minnesota Department of Correction, the state would fund the new local correctional programs. The CCA did not prescibe the particular programs or policies the local networks should adopt. The local advisory boards were free to determine the

mix of public and private, institutional and non-institutional programs they felt were appropriate to the area. Thus, the CCA was not intended to guarantee that community supervision would be used more frequently than institutions.

A number of counties have used CCA funds to improve jail facilities and expand jail populations. While the program originators may have hoped the CCA would lead to greater use of probation or low-security residential settings, such as halfway houses and group homes, it did not require this. The CCA is a significant step in managing network connections: (1) It explicitly recognizes the connection between local and state punishment. (2) It attempts to separate the issue of state funding from the choice of correctional options (such as using the jail rather than probation). (3) The plan correctly assumes that a change in the state-local network required a *simultaneous* change in the local network. In a number of participating counties, the local advisory boards have created more cooperative relationships than existed previously. It has, in other words, reduced the extent to which the local network is managed by interagency conflict and competition and increased the likelihood of joint management by interagency agreement.

CHANGING NETWORKS AT THE SAME GOVERNMENTAL LEVEL

Another important network connection is the one between two correctional agencies at the same level of government. Perhaps the most well known network links of this type involve state prisons and parole supervision in states where these are separate departments. Since these two state agencies must process the same offenders, a certain amount of cooperation must take place. For example, state parole officials are housed in state prisons in order to prepare parole plans. State parole board officials conduct hearings in state prisons. While these network links would seem to be fairly simple, they are often contentious. Prison and parole officials may disagree on which inmates are appropriate for consideration, and they may disagree on release policy. As prisons

TABLE 5.2   Summary of Correctional Strategies Based on Correctional Policy Model

COMPONENT OR PROGRAM	REINTEGRATION	REHABILITATION	REFORM	RESTRAINT
1 Change philosophy	Offender has learned crime as a solution to problems; more effective solutions are possible that are congruent with offender's value system.	Offender has committed crime as outgrowth of antisocial attitude and dysfunctional psychological developments. Offender needs to be changed internally so that he can adapt in suitable ways.	Offender has committed offense as direct result of disobedience to formally prescribed codes of conduct. This misconduct is willful, and this immoral stand should be punished.	Offender has committed crime in eyes of society and should be shown the negative consequences. He will not change unless he wants to, but he can be housed efficiently until he has served his time.
2 Change strategy	Internalization	Identification	Compliance	None, or maintenance of rules that have internal organizational benefit.
3 Sentencing policy	Light sentences, emphasis on controlling offender in community.	Indeterminate sentences in which judge passes on decision to therapeutic experts in correctional system. Use of additional sentences for dangerous offenders, or civil commitment of addicts, or offenders with other special needs.	Stiff sentences determined by judge on basis of severity of the crime.	Sentence that satisfies the statutory requirements; judicial responsiveness to community desires is important.
4 Presentence investigation	Concentration on offender's social relationships in community, employment history, desires for other opportunities. Identification for probation of offenders with good work records and social ties that should not be disrupted.	Concentration on diagnosis of internal problems, motivations for crime, familial history. Identification of offenders for probation not in need of continual staff support and care.	Concentration on past record aggravating or mitigating circumstance—demonstration of degree of guilt. Identification of offenders for probation who are deserving.	Concentration on judicial and probation office requirements. Selection of good risks for probation who will not cause trouble.
5 Probation supervision	Advocacy of offender who needs help with employment, relocating residence, etc. Intervention in community relationships to promote offender goals legally.	Counseling of offenders on pressures of social demands, concern for developing offender's insight into problems.	Concentration on protecting community by policing probationers, enforcing probation requirements such as demand visitation.	Concentration on reducing "flak" from community. Adjusting probationer's behavior to meet staff needs.
6 Probation revocation	On full hearing about facts. Probationer with lawyer to challenge legality of revocation and its efficacy as a correctional strategy.	Clinical staff reviewing offender's problems in community decision as to whether stronger, more concentrated support needed to promote maturity, ability to adjust.	Pro forma hearing establishing probation officer's prima facie case, revocation of privilege for undeserving offenders.	Verification of rule breaking to justify imposition of originally suspended sentence.

TABLE 5.2 *(Continued)*

COMPONENT OR PROGRAM	REINTEGRATION	REHABILITATION	REFORM	RESTRAINT
7 Probation officer type	Community organizer skilled in advocacy techniques, use of ex-offenders and volunteers whose skills are integrated to maximize goal attainment.	Skilled therapist who combines rapport with individual case planning, establishing procedure for supporting emotional growth.	Skilled investigator able to deter law- or rule-breaking through firm but fair imposition of rewards, sanctions, or threat of them.	Trained organization man familiar with judge's desires, probation rules.
8 Jail facilities	Jails used as community centers for work release, study release, dialogue with community leaders, recruitment and coordination of volunteers.	Outpatient clinic for offenders in need of institutional stay before or during probation or parole period.	Place of punishment for minor offenders, emphasis on simple vocational skills, work release possible emphasis.	Place of restraint for minor offenders in accordance with statutory regulations.
9 Felony reception	Heavy dependence on coordination with probation staff reports and assessments; reception directly to community facilities wherever possible.	Heavy reliance on medical and psychological testing for diagnosis of need, psychological type, and suggestion of therapeutic program.	Major decisions based on security risk, vocational ability, and moral merit. Housing and work assignments major issue.	Major decisions based on system capacity—where will offender fit with least disruption and most contribution to institutional maintenance goals?
10 Prison types	Infrequent use of traditional custodial prisons, frequent use of small residential units based in or close to communities.	Large minimum security facilities usually isolated from community. Isolated to prevent inmate from being pressured by outside interests during intensive counseling phases.	Large maximum security prisons isolated from community to protect, and to provide visible symbol of regimentation.	Most common in large city jails and other traditional custodial units.
11 Prison staffing patterns	Small staff team with diverse backgrounds and complementary skills, use of ex-offender, volunteers, active participation by inmates in their own program and in aiding other inmates.	Bifurcation of custody and treatment functions. Guard force less militaristic but responsible for maintaining order. Professional treaters in management positions and in charge of inmate activities, milieu, and clinical arrangements.	Large custodial force, dependence on common officer to provide model of legal behavior and to enforce rules. Counselors in minority and out of power, provide staff services, aid in custody and regimentation by reducing inmate tensions. Emphasis on vocational skills among staff.	Primarily custodial, with less emphasis on inmate or staff regimentation. Maintenance of physical rather than social order.
12 Prison program	Varied, emphasis on vocational training. Active seeking of new opportunities for offenders to prerelease. Concentration on practical matters of reintegration.	Emphasis on various soft services, counseling in groups or individual emphasis on emotional support, self-expression, gaining insights.	Emphasis on regimented labor, gaining rudimentary skills, more sophisticated behavior modification a possibility.	Emphasis on busy work that will release tension. Hobbies, institutional repair and maintenance.

(Continued)

TABLE 5.2 *(Continued)*

COMPONENT OR PROGRAM		REINTEGRATION	REHABILITATION	REFORM	RESTRAINT
13	Preparation for release	Work release, study release, halfway houses, other means of actually introducing offender to community roles before parole.	Halfway houses, institutional prerelease, concentration on discussion of stigma, dealing with emotional pressures.	Release programs a reward for good institutional behavior. Maintenance of custody until man proves himself dependable.	No preparation that may disrupt routine.
14	Parole board decision	Review of institutional decisions and outcome, release as soon as possible of as many men as possible. Emphasis on community parole plan.	Clinical staffing of offender's progress. Attention to change in attitudes, ability to relate and adjust.	Review of inmate institutional record, emphasis on obedience, worthiness for privilege of parole.	Review of community pressures, predictive of offender's nontroublesome status in community.
15	Parole board members	Mixed skills and background, inmate participation, or legal counsel.	Professional therapists and medical doctors.	Community leaders able to recognize productive citizens.	Political appointees sensitive to the climate of the times.
16	Parole supervision	Advocacy of offender's needs, acting as counsel to offender, helping to review goal accomplishment.	Therapist skilled in investigating emotional trouble, regression to former attitudes.	Investigator, surveillance to maintain viability of negative sanctions, community protection.	Bookkeeper, maintaining records on established parole regulations.
17	Use of volunteers	Frequently, seeking integration of skills and interests.	As aides to professionals or seeking outside professional group support.	Sometimes, seeking community business leaders' support.	Hardly ever, too risky and disruptive.
18	Attitude toward legal intervention	Invited, as aid to offender in challenging decisions and negotiating program.	Avoided, legal argument seen as conflicting with needs of therapy.	Avoided, offenders rights seen as lost at conviction.	Avoided, litigation does not contribute to smooth flow of operation.
19	Relations to universities	Encouraged, particularly applied interdisciplinary research, increasing skill and competency range, opportunities for offenders.	Encouraged, for use of psychological and other clinical resources and consultant services. Research on offender personality types.	Approached cautiously, seeking management consultant help.	Avoided as disruptive.
20	Evaluation	Data-based, democratic feedback process. Inside and outside evaluation for constant program modification.	Clinically based, emphasis on offender personality change, how to create effective therapy situations.	Belief-based, or action-based in terms of low crime rate, satisfaction of community norms.	Experience-based in terms of lack of negative repercussions, satisfaction of political support.

SOURCE: David E. Duffee and Robert Fitch (1976), *An Introduction to Corrections: A Policy and Systems Approach.* Pacific Palisades, CA: Goodyear, 322–327.

become overcrowded, there may also be disagreement over how parole organizations should handle supervision and revocation. If revocation rates are high, prison populations rise even if sentencing has not increased.

One common method of managing this kind of network interaction is the interagency memorandum of agreement, which spells out the joint responsibilities of the staff from both agencies for a common program or a common problem. For example, in New York, prerelease centers in each of the state institutions are now administered by a memorandum between the Department of Correctional Services and the Division of Parole. Interagency agreements attempt to make joint programs the target of explicit interagency policy, rather than an informal compromise. These agreements do not always succeed. For example, in Pennsylvania, Community Service Centers now run totally by the Bureau of Correction were originally established by joint memorandum between the bureau and the Board of Probation and Parole. The bureau was to supply the security personnel; the board was to select residents and supply counseling services. However, this agreement broke down rather quickly, with both agencies complaining that the other had violated the terms of the agreement (Duffee, 1985).

CHANGES IN PUBLIC-PRIVATE NETWORKS

Another major change occurred in the relationships between public and private agencies. To date, the most famous example of such a change has occurred not in adult corrections, but in the juvenile justice system of Massachusetts. It will be discussed in detail in Chapter 19. While the Massachusetts deinstitutionalization movement occurred in another (but closely related) social control network, in many respects it serves as a model for network changes in adult corrections. When Jerome Miller closed most of the secure institutions in Massachusetts, the Department of Youth Services took on a different function than it had had when it ran training schools. It became a contract agency overseeing a number of private organizations, which then became responsible for direct service. The principles behind this new arrangement were: (1) The private providers would know better the communities in which youth were to be supervised; (2) the small private organizations would increase the diversity of programs available for the placement of youth with different needs; and (3) the contract network would provide Massachusetts with greater flexibility in its youth services, since program funding

could change as needs changed (Coates, Miller, and Ohlin, 1978).

Similar changes have been made in some correctional networks, although not on so massive a scale. In the neighboring state of Connecticut, the Department of Corrections contracts with private service providers for all community services. Similar arrangements exist in the South where the Salvation Army and other private organizations provide probation services for misdemeanants.

The most controversial change in public-private networks involves the operation of prisons by private contractors. The Correctional Corporation of America has proposed to operate all the institutions in Tennessee. The Federal Bureau of Prisons has contracted with private agencies to run several of its facilities. (This development will be discussed in detail in Chapter 20.)

The presence of private agencies in correctional networks is nothing new in the United States. Private contractors operated the industries in the earliest American prisons (Beaumont and de Toqueville, 1964). What does appear to be new is the extent to which privatization is taking place, and the fundamental changes in the public agencies as these new networks form. As public correctional agencies become contractors rather than direct service providers, they are required to develop new skills, particularly in the channeling and monitoring of funds, and in the evaluation of the work of the private providers. Correctional agencies which for years did poorly in evaluating their own activities may become more attentive to evaluation when they give up the direct provision of service.

CHANGING SOCIAL CONTROL NETWORKS

These network changes involve two or more correctional agencies. There are also occasions for managing networks that connect agencies in two or more different types of social control activity. At the present time, perhaps the best known of these interindustry networks connects mental health with prisons and jails. (These connections will be discussed in some detail in both Chapters

10 and 14.) One such network is a cooperative arrangement between the New York Division of Mental Hygiene and the New York Department of Correctional Services. DMH runs forensic centers in the major prisons of the state (Adams, 1984). Similarly, a fully staffed, complete-service mental health hospital operates within the walls of the Philadelphia county jail.

Such interindustry networks are, in large measure, the result of judicial decisions about particular correctional networks. A number of appellate courts have ruled that punishment does not limit an inmate's rights to medical care. As the courts have narrowed the boundaries of punishment, they have required greater interaction between different social control industries, so that persons with multiple problems are not isolated in one control industry. Similar interactions occur between corrections and public welfare and corrections and organizations concerned with unemployment.

SUMMARY

1. A system is defined as a collection of interrelated parts coordinated to achieve a set of objectives. Systems are composed of five elements: objectives, boundaries, resources, components, and management.
2. Each of these elements can be difficult to identify and measure, particularly when the system is a dynamic human system. Applying the concept of system to corrections is particularly difficult because objectives are ambiguous and difficult to measure, because the distinction between environmental constraints and resources is not firm, and because management is fragmented.
3. Within the social control sector there are a variety of social control industries; corrections is only one. Within the corrections industry, networks of organizations carry out the activities of any actual correctional process.
4. Specific correctional organizations have responsibilities for a particular part of network operations and often for the intersection of networks.
5. Networks rather than single organizations must be managed to achieve the objectives usually discussed in contemporary corrections.
6. In recent years, a number of significant changes have been made in the attempt to manage networks. These changes have implications for local-state networks, for networks involving two agencies at the same level of government, for networks involving public and private agencies, and for networks that connect different social control industries. Recent changes are based on the increasing realization that specific correctional organizations generally do not have sufficient managerial control to affect objectives without coordinated action by other organizations in the network.

KEY WORDS

CONDITIONAL SENTENCE. A sentence, such as probation, that can be revoked if certain supervision rules or conditions are not obeyed.

CORRECTIONAL NETWORK. That collection of agencies and decision-makers which funds, manages, and regulates the correctional process.

CORRECTIONAL PROCESS. The sequence of decisions and activities through which convicted offenders are processed until the completion of sentence.

FEEDBACK. Output from a system or system component that loops back to become input to earlier components in the system.

GOAL-DIRECTED SYSTEMS. Managed systems, or systems that effectively set, change, and reach objectives.

GOAL-ORIENTED SYSTEMS. Systems lacking a management component.

REFORM POLICY. In the correctional policy model, a correctional system with high concern for community, low concern for the individual offender, using compliance strategies to maintain conformity.

REHABILITATION POLICY. In the correctional policy model, a correctional system with high concern for the individual offender and low concern for the community, using identification strategies to help the offender mature.

REINTEGRATION POLICY. In the correctional policy model, a correctional system with high concern for the offender and the community, using internalization change strategies.

RESTRAINT POLICY. In the correctional policy model, a correction system with low concern for the offender and the community, using no strategy to influence offender behavior; a holding strategy.

SYSTEM. "A set of parts coordinated to accomplish a set of goals" (Churchman, 1968:29).

SYSTEMS APPROACH. An analytical method that focuses on systemic properties and processes.

SYSTEM BOUNDARIES. The division between a system and its environment. In human systems, the boundary is often permeable and changing.

SYSTEM COMPONENTS. The separate subroutines or activities that contribute to total system objectives.

SYSTEM MANAGEMENT COMPONENT. The portion of a system that designs other components, distributes resources to them, coordinates activities, and evaluates system performance.

SYSTEM OBJECTIVES. The measured performance of a total system, rather than of its parts; the joint products of system components.

SYSTEM RESOURCES. Items a system can change and use to achieve objectives.

PROJECTS AND QUESTIONS

1. Study the local correctional network in the immediate vicinity of your school. Determine the extent to which there are system objectives for the network and how the agency executives and other decision-makers seek to coordinate their activities for the achievement of these objectives. The class can invite a panel consisting of a local trial judge, pretrial services director, jail manager, and probation chief, or assign particular students to go out and interview these officials separately and then hold a seminar on the findings. Questions should be decided upon beforehand, although they need not be highly structured. To what extent do the separate agencies have compatible goals? Over what points does there appear to be the most friction? Do the separate actors ever meet on a formal basis in an attempt to coordinate activities, or is the system a product of separately determined actions?

2. Debate the advantages and disadvantages of administering the correctional process through a network rather than a system with central control. Assign one team to argue for maintenance of separate agencies and another to argue for centralization and unification. Which types of problems and solutions seem to be associated with each side of the argument?

3. Invite an expert from another department or from a private corporation to discuss business management systems. Compare and contrast the conceptions of control systems in business and corrections.

4. The correctional policy model has been used in a wide variety of correctional settings; some examples are given in Chapter 18. Correctional managers attest to the descriptive accuracy of the model; it helps them to confront problems and pose issues they deal with all the time. But how does the policy model view of correctional goals relate to the common goals of punishment? Can you see relationships between retribution, deterrence, incapacitation, and rehabilitation and the four policy systems described by O'Leary?

ADDITIONAL READING

Stafford Beer. *Management Science* (Garden City, NY: Doubleday, 1968). Stafford Beer is one of the pioneers in operations research and systems analysis. This book is a simplification of his major treatise on systems analysis, *Decision and Control*, and provides an easy but exciting introduction to key concepts and uses of systems analysis in the management of organizations.

Michael Gottfredson and Don Gottfredson. *Decision Making in Criminal Justice* (Cambridge, MA: Ballinger, 1980). This book is one of the leading attempts to utilize the principles of decision analysis and systems analysis in studying the criminal process.

Martin Grozdins. *The American System* (Chicago: Rand McNally, 1963). This important work examines the arrangement of public network systems in the United States. One of the focuses is the interconnection of local, state, and federal agencies to create one network system in any particular control sector. While Grozdins does not study corrections, he does use the extended example of network connections in policing.

Alfred Kuhn. *The Study of Society* (Homewood, IL: Irwin-Dorsey, 1963). Regarded by many as the finest introduction to systems analysis applied to social systems. The first 100 pages provide a simple but exacting introduction to system behavior, system components, and types of systems.

6 SENTENCING

QUESTIONS

1. What is sentencing policy?

2. How is sentencing structure related to policy?

3. How has sentencing structure changed?

4. What are the differences between legislative and commission control of sentencing policy?

5. Which criminal justice actors influence sentencing at the case level?

6. What are the consequences of current sentencing practice?

7. Do current sentencing patterns demonstrate racial discrimination?

"HAMPTON'S NOT LENIENT—MCGRAW'S TOUGH"

Felony trial court duties in Madison are shared by two judges. Until 1984, Judge McGraw and Judge Lacy were among the most popular political figures in Madison, with each carrying more than 70 percent of the vote in the two previous elections. Part of their popularity was apparently related to their sentencing policies. Known as nononsense judges, McGraw and Lacy at times seemed engaged in a contest to see which of them could pronounce the stiffest sentences. Lacy was nicknamed "Maximum Marilyn" because she generally avoided community options. Officials in the Department of Cor-

rections and in the state planning office secretly complained about both judges. One planner once pulled a sheet of sentencing statistics off a shelf and in frustration tossed them at Phil. "Look at those numbers," he said. "Those columns give you felony sentencing in Jefferson for 1983. Lacy and McGraw sent the department more inmates who were eligible for probation than any other judge in the state. It's deplorable. We're full up in corrections, and these two can't keep a burglar in the community."

Then, in 1984, Marilyn Lacy stunned the Madison community by resigning in the middle of her second ten-year term. As provided by the state constitution, the governor appointed a judge to finish the term. He took his advice from state officials and politicos, rather than from the Madison electorate. His choice, John Hampton, had once been the Madison district attorney. Since then he had been both a law professor and a senior partner in a public interest law firm. Within weeks the *Madison Current* was on the attack, with headline after headline about Hampton's sentencing practices. "Hampton Lenient on Lawbreakers!" screamed one. The story compared sentences by Hampton and McGraw for eight different burglary convictions. Hampton had ordered restitution and three years' probation in his cases. McGraw had sentenced his four burglars to prison terms of two to six years. "Hampton Lets Thieves Go!" said another two weeks later. "Letting them go," it turned out, meant Hampton had placed two young car thieves on probation, with 40 hours of community service washing police vehicles, and full restitution for the damage to the car they had stolen.

Phil was in the probation department on the morning of the second headline. Assistant Director Jenny Hague was groaning in agony, coffee in one hand, paper in the other. "What's the matter, Jenny, Kulack make the coffee again?"

Hague was in no mood for jokes. "Have you seen this?" she said, waving the paper. Phil nodded. "I can't believe it. For the first time in fifteen years we get a judge we might be able to work with, and this paper is going to lynch him for being rational. Hampton's not lenient—McGraw's tough."

"You know where I stand," assured Phil. "But who's to judge—excuse the pun. The voters in this district apparently like the tough approach."

"The voters in this district don't know what they want."

"Well? How else do we determine what punishment matches the crime?"

Hague looked surprised. "I thought you were the criminal justice expert."

Phil smiled. "Sentencing isn't my line. What would you suggest?"

Hague threw him a report from Minnesota. "That. We need a rational guidelines system in this state. It's just not fair to have individual judges—or local electorates for that matter—determining penalties on the basis of their own narrow views. We should have a sentencing commission like Minnesota's to provide guidelines across the state. Then we would know who was lenient and who was tough."

Phil looked through the report. "A number of states are doing this. But how does it make sentencing more rational? Isn't it possible that the legislature or the commission might make even bigger errors than a few local judges? And why should a state group determine what local communities should do about punishment?"

TWO LEVELS OF SENTENCING DECISIONS

For years, sentencing was one of the more invisible of correctional decisions. However, the furor over the proper focus of punishment has changed this low-visibility, high-discretion activity. As court decisions and correctional problems have become more clearly linked, as the tremendous variety of sentences for similar crimes has been interpreted as evidence of arbitrariness and unfairness rather than individualized justice, and as any number of groups have clamored that the courts are too easy on crime, sentencing has become a central issue in punishment and corrections.

THE BASIC OPTIONS

The basic sentencing options are discussed in Chapter 1. They are reviewed in a presumed sequence of occurrence in Figure 6.1. The most critical sentencing decision is in or out? Secondary decisions flow from the this initial decision.

FIGURE 6.1   Sentencing as a Bifurcated Decision-Making Process

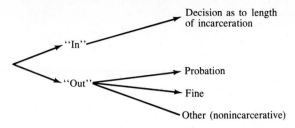

SOURCE: L. T. Wilkins et al., *Sentencing Guidelines: Structuring Judicial Discretion*. Washington, DC: United States Department of Justice, 1978, Figure 1, p. 1.

If the offender is to be punished in the community, the judge must determine the conditions of probation, or the alternative to probation. If the judge determines that justice is served only through an incarcerative sentence, two decisions remain: where (jail or prison), and for how long? Naturally, the judge is not free in these decisions. In some instances, the judge has no room to maneuver at all—there may be mandatory sentencing provisions or a sentencing agreement worked out as part of a plea negotiation.

This chapter examines the variety of actors who have some influence on individual sentencing decisions. But it must begin at a more abstract level. While we often think of sentencing as occurring when the convicted individual stands before the bar to hear the decision of the judge, this **case level sentencing** is constrained by previous, higher-level decisions. In the case above, Jenny Hague was essentially arguing that the state gave its individual trial judges far too much discretion in why and how to sentence. She was calling for decisions at a **policy level** to rectify what she saw as undesirable variation at the case level.

SENTENCING POLICY

We will use the term sentencing policy to refer to the decisions made by the state (or federal) legislature to prescribe or guide decisions at the case level. It is ultimately the state legislature which determines how much freedom the actors

in the correctional process have. While one state may provide judges with tremendous discretion and another with far less, both states have adopted a sentencing policy. The first state has taken the position that criminal punishment by and large cannot be predetermined because the relevant variables are not knowable by the legislature. The second state has taken the opposite position, that the information relevant to determining penalties for specific crimes is generally knowable before the occurrence of a specific act. It is also likely, under these circumstances, that these states have taken very different positions on the purposes of criminal punishment.

Implict and Explicit Policy. Sentencing policy need not be a formal set of statements about the nature and purpose of punishment and rules for carrying it out. Sentencing policy can be **implicit** rather than **explicit**.

An implicit sentencing policy would be a set of goals and rules that must be inferred from other decisions made by the legislature. For example, its sentencing policy might be inferred from the types of penalties it attached to individual crimes, or from the level of resources it supplied to its department of correction. The problems with implicit policy are many: Different decision-makers at the case level may make different inferences; the legislature itself may have difficulty being consistent as it considers individual crimes or reconsiders budgets; the goals of implicit policy may be ambiguous; changes in policy will be

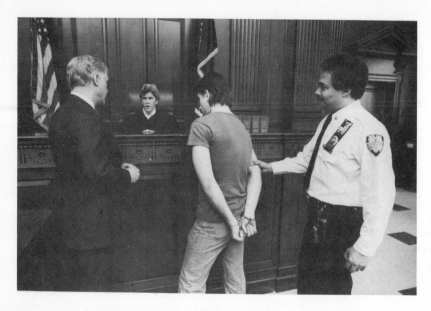

The judge makes critical correctional decisions, including the decision to release pending trial and the sentencing decision. (Russ Kinne/Comstock)

made piecemeal, and over time consistency becomes impossible. The advantage of implicit policy is that it avoids debate on controversial issues. Legislatures have often been called poor policymakers because the desire to satisfy conflicting interests often leads to inarticulate, inconsistent, and unfair policy.

Explicit policy requires a legislature to take a stance. Explicit sentencing policy would include a statement of goals to be achieved through sentencing, a codification of criminal penalties consistent with those goals, and a structure and process for implementation. While explicit policy has many advantages, including greater chances of consistency, fairness, and efficient distribution of resources, it is difficult to accomplish. Explicit sentencing policy, for example, requires the legislature, or its delegate, to take a stand on the fundamental goals of punishment. It also requires the adoption of articulated structures and procedures for sentencing at the individual level.

Individual actors in the correctional process, particularly judges and prosecutors, jealously protect their decision-making discretion. They make momentous decisions, and for that reason often feel safer if they have as much room as possible for considering different options. Moreover, these actors are often powerful political actors in their own right. Explicit legislative policy requires the legislature to come to grips with these interests, to satisfy as many claims as possible, but to craft coherent goals and procedures despite powerful objection.

Direct and Delegated Policy. In sentencing the buck stops with the legislature, because criminal penalties are the province of the rulemaking body of government. But the legislature need not make **direct policy.** Traditionally, legislatures in the United States have **delegated** a tremendous amount of sentencing policy both to the executive branch, where parole boards have had large discretion in setting prison terms, and to judges, who often have had vast discretion in choosing specific sentences within wide ranges provided by the legislature. Often, this delegation resulted in implicit policy, since parole boards and judges rarely promulgated statements of goals and rules that would apply to all their decisions. Recently, this has changed. The Federal Board of Parole, now the Federal Parole Commission, led the way by adopting parole guidelines (Wilkins, 1981).

More recently, some states have adapted this delegated policymaking form to judicial sentencing decisions by setting up **sentencing commissions.** These new forms of delegated authority may have several advantages over direct, explicit policymaking by the legislature. Commissions, it has been argued, are less susceptible to the political pressure that faces legislatures. Second, commissions are specialized policymaking bodies; they concentrate on sentencing. Third, their specialization and buffering provide them with more time to consider the issues, and with more expertise than would be found in the legislature as a group. These characteristics may enable commissions to articulate goals and elaborate a structure for implementing goals more effectively than a legislature (von Hirsch and Hanrahan, 1984:298–305).

SENTENCING STRUCTURE

A MEANS OF CONTROLLING DISCRETION

Sentencing structure is the division of decision space at the individual case level. It is the setting of limits on the actors in the correctional process who influence individual outcomes. Structure is the division of sentencing authority among the legislative, judicial, and executive branches of government. Sentencing structure is the creation of formal relationships through which to implement policy.

Many of the recent changes in sentencing have been spurred on, in part, by concerns for **sentencing disparity.** Sentencing disparity is difficult to define, and more difficult to measure. As concern about sentencing has increased, the general definition of disparity which appears to be gaining acceptance is differences in sentencing not attributable either to differences in the criminal history of offenders or to differences in the current offense. It is important to emphasize that this definition includes sentencing differences which can be explained by disagreement

in goals at sentencing. Some years ago, many sentencing experts may have excused sentence differences among offenders with similar histories and convictions if they could find legitimate differences in goals. For example, perhaps one judge had selected rehabilitation as an objective and placed on probation on offender whom another judge, more interested in deterrence, would have incarcerated. Currently, disparate sentencing outcomes for similar offenders, on the basis of different sentencing rationales, is no longer considered a legitimate difference, but a major reason for disparity.

The manipulation of sentencing structure is widely perceived as a primary means of controlling disparity in sentencing. It is argued that structures which permit case-level decision-makers wide latitude in sentencing options allow those decision-makers a greater use of uncontrolled discretion in selecting a sentence. Under these conditions, decision-makers are more susceptible to idiosyncratic influences, and their decisions will differ in inexplicable ways from decisions by other sentencers. In contrast, structures that provide case-level decision-makers with less unfettered discretion are more likely to yield more equal sentences for offenders committing similar offenses and having similar criminal history backgrounds.

THREE STRUCTURAL MODELS

Sentencing structures can be classified in a number of ways. One of the more common divisions is three models, named for the branch of government that has the greatest amount of discretion for individual sentences within the model.

The **executive model,** for years the most common, delegated considerable discretion in the setting of prison terms to an executive board, often called the parole board. The legislature in this model provided for each crime an **indeterminate sentence,** a range of permissible years in prison expressed in minimum and maximum terms. In the states with the greatest indeterminacy, such as California before 1976, the minimum sentence was usually zero and the maximum very long. Six months after sentencing, the California Adult Authority would set the minimum term to be served before the offender was eligible for parole.

In other states such as Pennsylvania, the degree of indeterminacy, or the amount of discretion left to the parole board, could be restricted by the judge, who could set the minimum term higher if he or she did not want the parole board releasing an inmate earlier than a particular date. The judge could reduce the maximum term, if he or she did not want the inmate retained beyond a certain date. In many states with modified indeterminate sentences, the legislature would restrict the judge's ability to change minimums and maximums within some outer limits. For example, the legislature might require that a minimum could be no more than one-half or one-third of the maximum sentence, so the judge could not take the parole board out of the picture altogether by making the minimum equal that of the maximum term. The executive model is usually associated with a rehabilitative policy. It gives correctional administrators maximum flexibility to control the sentence based on the behavior of the offender.

The **judicial model** provides more discretion to the judge, and narrows or eliminates the discretion of executive authority. In the executive model, it is questionable at what point indeterminacy becomes so modified that major sentencing power has shifted to the judge. Some modified indeterminate sentences may provide a structure with mixed authority that is hard to classify.

Perhaps the purest form of judicial sentencing was adopted in Maine in 1975. Its essential characteristic is that it places control of time to be served directly in the hands of the judge. The legislature provides the judge with wide latitude in fixing a **flat prison term** (rather than a minimum and maximum). The inmate serves the entire sentence with no discretionary release by a parole board. In most states, judges have retained one extremely important sentencing decision, regardless of the sentence structure that controls prison terms: Judges usually admit people to probation at their discretion. In other words, the in-out decision is usually governed by the judicial model.

This need not be the case, as we will see later. However, legislatures have rarely taken this discretion away from judges. The sentencing policy associated with a judicial structure is hard to determine. Frequently, judicial grants of probation are associated with rehabilitation. But the flat term of imprisonment, when controlled by the judge, is more often associated with incapacitation, deterrence, or retribution.

In the **legislative model** of sentencing, the legislature retains control of sentencing policy. It may provide the judge with some choice, and it may provide for some executive involvement in discretionary release from prison, but it narrows considerably the maneuvering room of judge and administrator. One of the best examples of legislative sentencing is the California law adopted in 1976. The legislature grouped all crimes into five classes, and provided a **presumptive sentence** for each class of crimes. The presumptive sentence was flat, as in Maine, but unlike Maine, it was also **determinate,** meaning that one could determine the penalty for a particular crime prior to the individual sentence hearing. Legislative structures often have explicit goals of retribution, but many legislative structures appear oriented toward incapacitation.

PIECEMEAL CHANGES IN STRUCTURE

Prior to the wave of policy and structural reform that began in 1975, there were a number of attempts to control discretion through less drastic means than removal of executive or judicial authority. Many of these earlier attempts focused on what were perceived as excessively harsh or lenient sentences. Some of the reforms consisted of minor tinkering with structure, or changes in communication at the individual sentencing level. None of them was sufficiently broad to make policy explicit.

SENTENCING COUNCILS

One of the major criticisms of modified indeterminate sentencing was the disparity in sentences from different judges for relatively similar offenses. Such differences were often justified on the grounds that rehabilitation was the purpose of punishment and that each judge had to pay attention to the unique characteristics of the offender. However, such rationales could not withstand evidence that offenders with similar backgrounds were sentenced quite differently by different judges. Nor could they withstand evidence that individual judges had their own sentencing patterns—they were not tailoring their sentences to the offender, but to their own preferences.

One means of reducing this interjudge disparity in large courts was the **sentencing council.** It operated on the presumption that if judges shared their thinking with other judges, final sentencing decisions would tend to gravitate toward the norm of the group, and sentencing would not vary so much from one judge to the next. In a sentencing council, several judges from a multi-judge court would meet periodically to discuss the dispositions of pending cases. Judges shared presentence reports and other relevant data and discussed the various factors they thought were significant in arriving at decisions.

The judge to whom the case had been assigned was still responsible for the individual decision, but he or she heard the opinions of other judges before making the decision (President's Commission on Law Enforcement and Administration of Justice, 1967a:145). The sentencing council was a significant advance at the individual level. The idea of influencing judges by exposing them to the ideas of a group was one of the forerunners of sentencing guidelines. However, councils were very costly and still too narrow. They could temper aberrant sentences within one court, but not across a state.

SENTENCING CONFERENCES

Other judges hold **sentencing conferences** prior to the sentencing hearing. Participants may include the probation officer, prosecutor, defense attorney, and on rare occasions, the victim. Such conferences provide an opportunity to hear recommendations from all parties prior to the formal hearing. Conferences can be used to clarify plea bargaining promises, or to disclose presentence report information supplied by the probation officer. Such conferences may serve to avoid confusion and surprises in the open courtroom.

JUDICIAL SENTENCING INSTITUTES

Judicial sentencing institutes became popular in the late 1950s and 1960s to help train judges in sentencing goals and options and to expose them to information about the correctional programs they were using. These training conferences were pioneered in the federal judiciary, and have since been institutionalized for a number of state trial judges as well. Institutes are not a direct structural change in sentencing, nor an explication of sentencing policy for a real jurisdiction. Instead, they provide an opportunity for career development in an area where judges are typically undertrained. Their educational function is adaptable to any sentencing system, but their impact on sentencing is probably limited. They are based on the assumption that education can improve sentencing, as if the "ideal" sentence could be discovered through education. But institutes cannot alter the specific pressures influencing the judge in an actual sentencing situation. Behavior change may require structural change.

APPELLATE REVIEW OF SENTENCES

Another device that has contributed to the reduction of sentencing disparity and inappropriate sentences in some jurisdictions is a structural change: the **appellate review of sentences.** The laws of most states have not provided for appellate review of the sentence, as opposed to appellate review of the conviction. In most jurisdictions, as long as the sentence pronounced by the judge is within legislative limits and meets constitutional standards, it is a binding and nonreviewable decision. Appellate review of sentences, it has been argued, is one way to reduce excessive sentences, and to slowly arrive at judicially enunciated sentencing policy for an entire jurisdiction. It is, however, a cumbersome and backward way of making policy, since issues can be discussed only in terms of one allegedly bad sentence at a time; it is not a proactive means of shaping sentencing policy prior to individual decisions. Appellate review of sentences has been recommended by the American Bar Association, and has been available in the federal system and a few states for some time. Some of the new sentencing reforms to be discussed below have included appellate sentence review, or some other means of modifying unusual sentences.

MANDATORY SENTENCES

One of the older piecemeal structural changes still very much alive today is the mandatory sentence. In general, a **mandatory sentence** is a specific sentence or a specific limitation on a sentence that must be followed by the judge when pronouncing sentence. There are several variations on this basic theme. For example, the legislature can rule that certain convictions are not probationable. In other words, the legislature can mandate a prison term, but not specify the length of that term. In indeterminate states, the legislature can mandate a specific minimum sentence, mandate a nonparolable term, or a life term. In determinate sentencing states, mandatory terms would seem to be less necessary, since prison terms are specified anyway. However, as we will see, even determinate states can provide a judge with sufficient leeway that some offenses may

carry mandatory terms. An overview of mandatory sentencing is included in Table 6.1.

Mandatory sentences can have many unintended effects. Legislatures can use them to ensure that a judge or parole board cannot deviate from the legislature's choice of sentence, but this discretion-reduction mechanism overlooks the prosecutor. Mandatory sentencing provisions apply to conviction charges. Prosecutors often avoid these strictures by simply charging on a different or lesser offense. For example, the American Bar Foundation survey of criminal justice discovered that mandatory sentences for armed robbery in Michigan were avoided by charging with unarmed robbery. Prosecutors explained the mandatory sentence was so severe that no one would plead to it, and juries would rarely convict. For these or similar reasons, mandatory sentences often become bargaining chips—threats used by the prosecutor to obtain conviction by plea to another charge.

Recently, mandatory sentencing has seen a resurgence. Many of the new mandatory terms are broader than specific charges at conviction. For example, there may be mandatory terms for repeat offenders, or for persons convicted of designated dangerous felonies. These broader mandatory statutes may be harder for prosecutors to avoid, on the one hand, and may provide them with less trouble on the other. Moreover, given the present mood of the country, convictions on still mandatory terms may be easier to obtain than was the case twenty years ago.

RECENT SENTENCING REFORMS

The major arguments against the executive model and the indeterminant sentence include (1) the perceived failure of discretionary release to contribute to rehabilitation, (2) the great deal of disparity generated in the name of individualization, (3) the presumed stress and anxiety placed on inmates because of the uncertainty of release dates, and (4) the propensity of discretionary release to coerce inmates into treatment in order to impress the sentencers (Goodstein, et al., 1984:8–11). These complaints led rather quickly to positive statements about alternative sentencing structures.

Sentencing reform was accomplished because an unusually diverse set of interests was mobilized in the same direction. An "unholy alliance" of liberals and conservatives hammered out new sentencing policy and new structures to implement it in a number of states. Liberal groups, including a number of inmate and ex-inmate organizations, were in favor of change because they opposed the disparities and arbitrariness associated with indeterminacy (Goodstein et al., 1984:11). Liberal coalitions also believed that determinate sentences would generally be less severe than the lengthy sentences often served under discretionary release (von Hirsch, 1975; Fogel, 1975). Conservatives also favored determinate sentences, but for different reasons. They saw parole boards as being too soft and perceived less discretion in individual cases as a means of guaranteeing prison time of particular duration (Goodstein et al., 1984:11).

The number of sentencing schemes that fall under the label "determinate" are far too diverse to lump together (von Hirsch and Hanrahan, 1981:290). The new sentencing systems vary in rationale, scope, format, severity, and location of the rulemaking body (1981:297–98). In other words, they differ in the location and structure of policy, and they also differ in substance. One critical characteristic is **scope** of the sentencing policy. Many of the new systems do not govern the awarding of probation, but only decisions on sentence length. Ignoring probation is a critical oversight, especially for sentencing policy that seeks to implement retributive goals.

Sentencing reform will doubtless continue for some time to come, and future revisions will benefit from the errors made in the first systems to change. As of 1986, nine states have revised their sentencing practices to adopt some form of determinate sentence (see Table 6.1). These are often referred to as first- and second-generation sentencing schemes. Among the first are California, Indiana, and Illinois. The best example of a second-generation state is Minnesota, whose new system is generally regarded as the best (von Hirsch and Hanrahan, 1981:316). In first-generation states, policymaking usually was done directly by the legislature, and various versions of the legislative model of sentencing were adopted. In the second wave of reform, the legislatures more often delegated policymaking to a commission.

THE FIRST FALTERING STEP: MAINE

The first state to venture toward determinate sentencing was Maine. The result was so strange that von Hirsch did not include the new Maine system within his definition of determinate. A new sentencing commission is currently drafting a second set of changes, since the first set, adopted in 1975, has already proved unsatisfactory.

Sentencing in Maine was altered by the same group, the Revision Commission, that was revising the Maine criminal code. Their work preceded the classic determinate sentencing works by von Hirsch (1976), Dershowitz (1976), and Fogel (1975). Thus, in many respects the commission worked with little guidance (Kramer et al., 1978:6–8). The commission failed to adopt a coherent goal statement; it continued to see all punishment goals as legitimate (1978:12).

The new sentence provisions abolished the parole board and parole supervision. Offenders were sentenced to flat terms by the judge. However, the judge had vast discretion in setting the flat term. For example, for robbery, the judge could select any term of years up to ten. The code called for minimum, nonprobationable sentences for persons who had committed any of the top four classes of felonies with a firearm. But the judge retained discretion to grant probation for any other convictions. Probation could include any term of confinement, except in the Maine State Prison, where the limit was 90 days. Per-

TABLE 6.1   Sentencing Schemes and Mandatory Sentencing Provisions

	TYPE OF SENTENCING	MANDATORY SENTENCING	MANDATORY OFFENSES
Alabama	Determinate	Yes	Repeat felony
Alaska	Determinate, presumptive	Yes	Murder, kidnaping, firearms, repeat felony
Arizona	Determinate, presumptive	Yes	Firearms, prior felony convictions
Arkansas	Determinate	Yes	Robbery, deadly weapons
California	Determinate, presumptive	No	
Colorado	Determinate, presumptive	No	
Connecticut	Determinate	Yes	Sex assault with firearm, burglary, repeat felony, assault on elderly
Delaware	Determinate	Yes	Murder, kidnaping, prison assault, robbery, narcotics, deadly weapon, habitual criminal, obscenity, others
Florida	Indeterminate	Yes	Drug
Georgia	Determinate	Yes	Armed robbery, burglary, drugs
Hawaii	Indeterminate	No	
Idaho	Determinate	Yes	Firearm, repeat extortion, kidnap or rape with bodily injury
Illinois	Determinate	Yes	Major offenses, specified felonies and offenses, repeaters, weapons
Indiana	Determinate, presumptive	Yes	Repeat felony, violent crime, deadly weapons
Iowa	Indeterminate	Yes	Forcible felonies, firearms, habitual offenders, drugs
Kansas	Indeterminate	Yes	Sex offense, firearms
Kentucky	Indeterminate	No	
Louisiana	Indeterminate	Yes	Drugs, violent crime
Maine	Determinate	No	
Maryland	Determinate, guidelines	Yes	Repeat violent offenders, handgun
Massachusetts	Indeterminate	Yes	Firearm, auto theft, drug trafficking
Michigan	Indeterminate	Yes	Murder, armed robbery, treason, firearms
Minnesota	Guidelines	No	
Mississippi	Determinate	Yes	Armed robbery, repeat felony
Missouri	Determinate	Yes	Dangerous weapon, repeat felony
Montana	Indeterminate	Yes	Firearms

TABLE 6.1 *(Continued)*

	TYPE OF SENTENCING	MANDATORY SENTENCING	MANDATORY OFFENSES
Nebraska	Indeterminate	No	
Nevada	Determinate	Yes	2nd degree murder, 1st degree kidnaping, sexual assault, firearm, repeat felony
New Hampshire	Indeterminate	Yes	Firearms
New Jersey	Determinate, presumptive	Yes	Sexual assault, firearms
New Mexico	Determinate, presumptive	Yes	Firearms
New York	Indeterminate	Yes	Specified violent and nonviolent felonies
North Carolina	Determinate, presumptive	Yes	Armed robbery, 1st degree burglary, repeat felony with firearm
North Dakota	Determinate	Yes	Firearm
Ohio	Indeterminate	Yes	Rape, drug trafficking
Oklahoma	Determinate	Yes	Repeat felony
Oregon	Guidelines, indeterminate	Yes	Drugs
Pennsylvania*	Guidelines, indeterminate	Yes	Selected felonies with firearms, within 7 years of prior convictions, in or near public transportation
Rhode Island	Indeterminate	No	
South Carolina	Determinate	Yes	Armed robbery, drugs, bomb threat
South Dakota	Indeterminate	No	
Tennessee	Determinate, indeterminate	Yes	Specified felonies, firearms, repeat felony
Texas	Determinate	Yes	Repeat felony, violent offenses
Utah	Indeterminate	No	
Vermont	Indeterminate	Yes	Drugs, violent crime
Virginia	Indeterminate	No	
Washington	Indeterminate	Yes	Firearms, rape, repeat felony
West Virginia	Indeterminate	Yes	Firearms in felony
Wisconsin	Indeterminate	No	
Wyoming	Indeterminate	No	

* Pennsylvania updated as of December 1982.

SOURCE: Bureau of Justice Statistics, *Report to the Nation on Crime and Justice.* Washington, DC: United States Department of Justice, 1982. p. 72.

sons who were sentenced to more than 20 years were permitted to petition for release after serving 80 percent of their sentence (Hussey and Kramer, 1978:117). Maine created a hodgepodge (Kramer et al., 1978:13–14):

> Inequalities in sentences are deplored but individualization is encouraged. Parole is eliminated, but the possibility of reduced sentences is preserved. Flat sentences are required, but the discretionary powers of the judge have been increased to an extent unknown in other American jurisdictions.

THE FIRST DETERMINATE SYSTEM: CALIFORNIA

California changed its sentencing system one year after Maine, in 1976. Change in this state represented the operational overthrow of the executive model of indeterminate sentencing. California's old sentencing policy has been a benchmark for rehabilitative corrections. So this change occurred in a glass house, as the rest of the country studied the change process, the rationale for the new system, and its first years of implementation. In general, observers agree that the California approach demonstrates the hazards of the liberal/conservative alliance, and the tremendous uncertainty that occurs when sentencing policy is made directly by the legislature.

California's new scheme is called presumptive sentencing because the legislature sets a flat term that is presumed appropriate for the offense. Specified aggravating or mitigating factors permit the judge to raise or lower the term, but only slightly. In addition, there are specific and general enhancements. Specific enhancements are additional years for features of the offense, and general enhancements are additional years for features of the criminal record (von Hirsch and Mueller, 1984:270–271). The parole decision has been abolished, but good time reductions are provided. The good time law has changed to reward participation in work and educational programs. Von Hirsch and Mueller observed that this use of good time still coerces rehabilitation, despite the explicit rejection of coerced treatment

participation in the new law (1984:290). Finally, a standard parole supervision period is added to the end of each sentence. Standards for parole revocation are not clear (1984:292).

The enunciated goals of the presumptive sentence were equity among offenders and proportionality of punishment to the crime (1984:256). The law may not have accomplished these aims. The major problem is that the scope of legislative policy is too narrow; it does not include probation, but only the length of the prison term. The State Judicial Council was supposed to write guidelines for awarding probation, but apparently did a poor job:

> The absence of meaningful "in-out" standards drastically restricts the extent to which California's determinate sentencing scheme can achieve its stated goal of proportionate punishments. (1984:267)

There are a number of other problems with the law. California failed to consider prison capacity when drafting the law. Inability to control prison capacity is partly related to the in-out deficiency, but it is also related to the legislature's proclivity to increase the presumptive terms for specific crimes in response to particular incidents (1984:265). The result of this direct but unsystematic policymaking is that proportionality has been sacrificed. For example, night time residential burglary, arson, assault, and sale of marijuana all receive three years (1984:272). Additionally, the invocation of aggravating and mitigating factors is discretionary with the judge, so persons committing similar crimes can receive disparate sentences (1984:280). Von Hirsch and Mueller (1984) and Davies (1985) concluded that just deserts has not been well served in this law, and that many of its characteristics, such as general enhancements, are more closely related to incapacitative goals than to retributive ones.

Despite these problems, a number of states have followed California's lead. Sentencing systems similar in structure appeared in Illinois, Indiana, and Connecticut (Goodstein et al.,

1984:19–22, Lagoy, Hussey and Kramer, 1978). These states vary in the amount of freedom the judge has in selecting the flat term. Indiana is perhaps the most severe, Illinois the most flexible. However, each of these states has ignored the in-out decision, abolished the parole decision, and, except in Connecticut, provided for postprison supervision during a period set by the amount of good time credit.

THE SECOND WAVE: MINNESOTA

Minnesota's new sentencing scheme differs from the first wave reforms in a number of significant ways. Perhaps the most important is that Minnesota rejected direct policymaking by the legislature and established a Sentencing Guidelines Commission in 1978. The Minnesota legislature accepted the guidelines in May of 1980 (Martin, 1984).

Guideline sentencing developed from parole guidelines pioneered by the Federal Parole Board in collaboration with the National Council on Crime and Delinquency. The board had been seeking a means of structuring discretion in parole decisions for individual cases (Wilkins, 1981:19–20). Wilkins reports that the breakthrough in the parole project was the realization that the board was not actually making an absolute parole/no-parole decision, but instead was determining *when* to parole. When the parole decision was reenvisioned as a time-setting decision, it was a short jump to consider application to the judicial sentencing function (1981:23).

While the developers of the guidelines originally intended to set guidelines for the federal district courts, the National Institute of Justice decided that it could fund only state-focused projects. Eventually, the sentencing guidelines project was funded with courts in several states collaborating in the feasibility study (1981:24). Wilkins summarizes the guidelines construction process as follows (1981:25–26):

1. Obtain a database on crime, the accused, and the disposition rendered.

2. Using the information on the crime and the accused, predict the dispositions.
3. Discuss the results with the judges.
4. Modify the prediction equation to include or exclude certain variables, based on the decision-maker's reactions.
5. Transform the final prediction equation into a set of decision rules so that between 75 and 85 percent of the sentences will fall within the guidelines.
6. If too few of the sentences fall within the guidelines, discuss the outliers with the judges to determine what factors they might be using that have not been accounted for in the guidelines. If necessary, add new data and repeat the process.

The general result is usually a matrix: a two-dimensional grid, with scores derived from offender background variables on one dimension and scores for crime severity on the other dimension. Each juncture of scores on the two dimensions forms a cell. Within each cell, the decision-maker will find a fairly small range of sentences, usually in months, which represent the sentence usually given for that level of crime by that type of offender.

Wilkins stresses that the original guidelines system was set up to ensure that a certain percentage of sentences given would fall outside the guidelines. When judges did deviate from the norm, they were asked to explain the reason for the deviation in writing. These data were then analyzed as a means of updating the guidelines. Over time the guidelines could change to reflect changes in crimes or criminals, or changes in sentencing patterns. Unlike the legislative sentences developed in California, a guideline system has built-in procedures for change. These internal change procedures ensure that the system continues to be coherent and consistent when change takes place (1981:5).

The major difference between the guidelines approach in Minnesota and the guidelines developed by Wilkins and his colleagues is that the original model was **descriptive,** while the Minnesota Sentencing Commission took a **prescriptive** approach (Minnesota Sentencing Guidelines Commission, 1982:8–9). The descriptive approach basis the initial matrix on past judicial decisions. The guidelines are a statement of the most common sentences given out in the past. The prescriptive approach may begin with analysis of past sentences, but the actual guidelines are based on normative arguments (prescriptions) about how sentencing should be done.

The commission was empowered by the legislature to determine when imprisonment was proper (in-out decision) and the length of prison terms. Additionally, the commission took very seriously the charge from the legislature to consider prison capacity when setting the guidelines (Martin, 1984:101). The commission approach to this issue was to define the severity of punishment to be given in terms that would not exceed prison capacity (von Hirsch and Hanrahan, 1981:297–298). This principle has included procedures to reset the sentencing values in the matrix if the system approached capacity (Knapp, 1984:184).

The Minnesota sentencing grid contains 70 cells for different combinations of offender and offense characteristics (see Table 6.2). In the case of probation, the cell identifies both the length of the prison term and notes that the term is to be suspended. The cells contain presumptive sentences as well as a range of months above and below that prescription that judges can select without needing to file an explanation for deviation. Sentences outside that range must be explained in writing and are reviewable. Parole decisions are abolished, and prisoners are released to supervision for a length of time determined by good time.

The guidelines also contain rules for choosing between concurrent and consecutive sentences (Goodstein et al., 1984:22–24). **Concurrent sentences,** the most common choice, provides for separate sentences on multiple convictions to be served at the same time. **Consecutive sentences** provide for these separate penalties to follow each other. While rarely used, consecutive

sentencing obviously increases time served tremendously and therefore should not be a totally discretionary choice. The new sentencing system includes a right to appeal. Appellate review of sentencing so far has upheld the guideline norms and stressed the instant offense rather than offender background as the key dimension (Knapp, 1984:183). More than any other state, Minnesota has apparently achieved a retributive system that accomplishes equity and proportionality (see Table 6.2).

THE SENTENCING PROCESS

At the individual case level of sentencing, the key actors are the prosecutor, the defense attorney, the probation officer, and the judge. Research indicates that their relative influence over individual sentences has changed to some extent as the policy and structure of sentencing have changed. The attorney's influence on sentencing precedes the sentencing stage of the correctional process. Many sentencing decisions are severely constrained by decisions and negotiations occurring during prosecution, as discussed in Chapter 4. This predetermination of the sentencing process has led Hagan and his associates (Hagan, 1975, Hagan, Hewitt, and Alwin, 1979) to describe the sentencing process as largely ceremonial rather than practical in its consequences, particularly as far as the involvement of the probation officer is concerned.

THE PROSECUTOR

The interests of the state are represented at all sentencing hearings by a representative of the prosecutor's office. The prosecutor is usually asked by the judge to give a recommendation of sentence. If a plea bargain has been struck prior to conviction, the prosecutor's recommendation is often determined in those negotiations. Supreme Court cases acknowledging and supporting the plea negotiation process have required that a

TABLE 6.2   Minnesota Sentencing Guidelines Grid

Severity levels of conviction offense		0	1	2	3	4	5	6 or more
Unauthorized use of motor vehicle Possession of marijuana	I	12*	12*	12*	15*	18*	21*	24 *23–25*
Theft-related crimes ($150–$2500) Sale of marijuana	II	12*	12*	14*	17*	20*	23*	27 *25–29*
Theft crimes ($150–$2500)	III	12*	13*	16*	19*	22 *21–23*	27 *25–29*	32 *30–34*
Burglary-felony intent Receiving stolen goods ($150–$2500)	IV	12*	15*	18*	21*	25 *24–26*	32 *30–34*	41 *37–45*
Simple robbery	V	18*	23*	27*	30 *29–31*	38 *36–40*	46 *43–49*	54 *50–58*
Assault, 2d degree	VI	21*	26*	30*	34 *33–35*	44 *42–46*	54 *50–58*	65 *60–70*
Aggravated robbery	VII	24 *23–25*	32 *30–34*	41 *38–44*	49 *45–53*	65 *60–70*	81 *75–87*	97 *90–104*
Assault, 1st degree Criminal sexual conduct, 1st degree	VIII	43 *41–45*	54 *50–58*	65 *60–70*	76 *71–81*	95 *89–101*	113 *106–120*	132 *124–140*
Murder, 3d degree	IX	97 *94–100*	119 *116–122*	127 *124–130*	149 *143–155*	176 *163–184*	205 *195–215*	230 *218–242*
Murder, 2d degree	X	116 *111–121*	140 *133–147*	162 *153–171*	203 *192–214*	243 *231–255*	284 *270–298*	324 *309–339*

First degree murder is excluded from the guidelines and is punished by life imprisonment.

The italicized numbers represent the range within which a judge may sentence *without* the decision being deemed a departure from the presumptive sentence requiring explanation or appeal.

The * represent sentences which are suspended, with offender placed on probation.

SOURCE: Minnesota Sentencing Guidelines Commission.

promise involving sentencing recommendations must be honored at the sentencing hearing (*Santobello* v. *N.Y.*). In the rare event that the prosecutor breaks that promise, as can happen when new information about the defendant is obtained between plea and sentencing, the defendant must be given the opportunity to withdraw the plea and go to trial.

Under the rehabilitative ideal, it was fre-quently argued that the prosecutor did not have the training or experience necessary to participate in the sentencing process, since sentencing was often perceived as an individualized decision that should focus on the treatment needs of the offender. The prosecutor's role was often seen as a check on sentencing, so that public safety and retribution were not damaged in the sentencing process. This perception of the prosecutorial role

Insert 6.1 THE TRAVAILS OF A SENTENCING GUIDELINES COMMISSION

Once a state decides to use sentencing guidelines as a method for structuring sentencing, the policymaking process has just begun. Studying the evolution of the Pennsylvania Sentencing Guidelines Commission (PSGC), Kramer, McClosky and Kurtz (1982) described the path of policy as it was shaped and reshaped by legislative, judicial, and public opinion.

In 1978, despite the fact that one group of legislators was already working on legislation for mandatory sentencing, the Pennsylvania General Assembly passed the legislation to establish the PSGC by an overwhelming majority. As the work of the commission unfolded, however, it became increasingly evident that the debate between guidelines and mandatory sentencing had not been resolved. Legislators and other groups in favor of the mandatory option withdrew their support for the guidelines during public hearings on the commission's initial proposals. Upon submission to the legislature, the guidelines were rejected.

During the first of the hearings, it was evident that the commission had not made sufficient contact with groups opposed to the concept. Much of the testimony at the hearings concerned the principle of guidelines sentencing, even though the principle had already been approved. Many criticisms focused on the apparent leniency of the guidelines, the prescriptive language in the guideline rules, and their failure to accommodate community differences. At the same time, John Hinckley's attempted assassination of President Reagan appeared to increase demands for stiff sentences.

After the rejection of the first submission, the Assembly passed a resolution permitting their revision. The Commission was reconstituted, with three Republicans replacing three Democrats on the PSGC. The guidelines were revised in close accordance to the changes suggested by the legislature. The most substantial change involved increasing the upper limits of permissible sentences. At a second round of public hearings, the new, more conservative policy was well received. The guidelines were resubmitted and accepted by the legislature in July 1982. Earlier in the same year, the mandatory proposals that had served as a roadblock to the first submission were also enacted. Their passage eliminated one obstacle to passage—while also diluting the consistency of sentencing policy. Kramer, McClosky, and Kurtz, echoing Wilkins' (1981) sentiments, concluded their history with the observation that establishing guidelines is a political rather than a technical exercise.

---

at sentencing has reversed itself in the last ten years. The prosecutor's interest in safety and retribution are now seen as legitimate driving concerns in the sentencing decision.

Research on the sentencing process has indicated that the prosecutor may *always* have been the driving force, regardless of the rhetoric of rehabilitation. This research found that the prosecutor's recommendations for sentence were among the most powerful influences on sentencing outcomes, far more influential than probation recommendations even when indeterminacy and treatment were still alive. Hagan and associates found that the prosecutor's recommendation appeared, in turn, to be influenced by three variables: use of weapon, prior record, and the presence of a plea (Hagan, Hewitt, and Alwin, 1979; and see Blumberg, 1970).

As is the case with most organizational actors, the prosecutor seeks to balance competing objectives during the sentencing process. Many have argued that prosecutorial concern with rewarding pleas reduces concern for deterrence, incapacitation, and retribution. However, the research reviewed in Chapter 4 demonstrates that in general, prosecutors do not give away a great deal in return for pleas. They generally obtain conviction on the highest original charge, and sentences following pleas are, on the average, only six months shorter than those following trial.

THE DEFENSE COUNSEL

Defendants are usually represented at sentencing. The Supreme Court has determined that sentencing is a critical stage in the prosecution process, and that the general right to counsel established in *Gideon* v. *Wainwright* applies at sentencing (*Mempa* v. *Rhay*, 1967). The Court pointed out that although conviction has already taken place, there are many important defense duties at sentencing or shortly thereafter. These include ensuring that plea bargaining promises are kept and that arguments for stringent sentencing, based on prosecutorial or probation information, are challenged. If an appeal is to occur, it usually must be filed at or shortly after the sentencing hearing. Defense counsel can also argue for continued release, on bail or other assurance, between conviction and sentencing, or while an appeal is pending.

Role of Defense Counsel. At sentencing, it is the defense lawyer's duty to continue to protect the defendant's interests. In most cases, this duty translates into obtaining the most lenient sentence possible, and avoiding incarceration when that can be done. In instances where a plea has involved discussions with sentencing implications, much of the defense attorney's work is actually done before conviction. In instances where that is not the case, a well-prepared defense lawyer can have a significant impact on sentencing decisions, particularly in instances where judges have more discretion.

Client-Specific Planning. When indeterminacy and rehabilitation were strong, defense work often focused on obtaining knowledge about the probation officer's presentence report. A more recent innovation is **client-specific planning,** a concept developed by Jerome Miller as director of the Center on Institutions and Alternatives. Miller's organization has taken the position that

defense can better serve the client by preparing its own community treatment plan rather than by relying on the probation plan. Client-specific planning centers now operate in a number of cities. Their staffs assist defense attorneys with the preparation of a sentencing package tailored especially for the client. The defense lawyer and the planning staff attempt to build a network of support and supervision services, often involving community service and restitution, that will convince the judge to use a community sentence rather than to incarcerate. The planning staff and the attorney attempt to line up commitment from third parties and service agencies before the sentencing hearing in order to document the plan.

Part of the rationale for this approach is simply to avoid institutions as much as possible. However, the focus on attorney involvement is based on the assumption that the attorney knows the client better than any other official in the sentencing process and can therefore make the best case for a community sentence. It is also assumed that the client-specific plans are likely to be fairly influential with judges in an era of prison overcrowding. The Center on Institutions and Alternatives believes that the prosecutor will not balk at a community placement and that the judge will welcome alternatives to incarceration, if the plans are well designed and offer greater control than traditional probation supervision.

THE PROBATION OFFICER

Before the rise of the positive school of criminology, judges required little information about the offender at sentencing. Following the tenets of the classical school of criminology, sentencing relied primarily on information about the offense. With the advent of the positive school, sentencing changed to focus more on the offender. Sentencing was supposed to be individualized. Probation arose as a means of reducing overly harsh sentences within the classical tradition (see Chapter 8), but was rapidly transformed by the positive emphasis on the nature of the offender. Probation became the structural change to implement a policy of individualized justice in the criminal court. The probation officer, using social work methods, became an active member in the determination of sentence by providing information about the offender to the judge through a **presentence investigation (PSI)** report (Hagan, Hewitt, and Alwin, 1979:507).

The original function of the presentence investigation was to help the judge understand the basic personality of the offender, his or her social environment, and previous criminal involvement. This information was to be used by the judge to determine whether probation rather than incarceration was possible. While this is still a primary function, the PSI has come to serve other uses. For offenders placed on probation, the report may help to determine probation conditions and other aspects of a supervision plan. For those sentenced to prison, the PSI is often relied upon for initial classification decisions and for parole release and supervision plans. Over time, the PSI has also become a basic correctional research resource, providing in one document information about the offender and the disposition (Hussey and Duffee, 1980).

PSIs and the reports vary in length and quality. A typical report contains information on the following: (1) present offense, (2) prior criminal history, (3) family history, (4) education, (5) employment history, (6) military service, (7) current financial situation, (8) medical history, (9) psychological and psychiatric evaluations, if available. After reporting this information, the probation officer will usually write (10) an evaluation summary. PSI reports often conclude with (11) a sentence recommendation by the officer, although some judges do not request officer recommendations or prefer not to have them.

The PSI was traditionally treated by judges and probation officers as neutral, detached, and scientific. However, the information incorporated in the report is influenced by the biases and prejudices of the investigating officer. It also often contains a good deal of hearsay and unsubstantiated claims by interested parties such as friends, relatives, and victims of the offender.

Moreover, the probation officer relies heavily on records prepared by the prosecutor. Much law enforcement information, such as rap sheets, is notoriously inaccurate and incomplete. As a result of these sources, PSI reports frequently contain factual errors as well as opinions from parties who are rarely detached and objective.

Disclosure of the Presentence Report. Such problems led to a controversy over **disclosure** of the report. Defense counsel often argued that adequate assistance of counsel was effectively denied if there was no access to the report. Probation officers frequently retorted that the PSI should be "privileged," just as doctor-patient or lawyer-client communications are privileged. Additional arguments against disclosure included the claim that the probation officers' sources would dry up if informants knew the defendant would see the report and that a positive relationship between the probation officer and the client might be jeopardized if the client reacted negatively to evaluative judgments that he misunderstood (Dubois, 1981).

The American Bar Association, the American Law Institute, the National Council on Crime and Delinquency, and the National Advisory Commission on Criminal Justice Standards and Goals all recommend disclosure of PSI reports. Their primary argument was that the defendant has a right to challenge inaccuracies or adverse recommendations. These professional associations have generally agreed that the judge could withhold portions of the report to protect the safety of sources or to protect a rehabilitative program. In the event that the judge does withhold some information, the standards recommend that he summarize the contents of the undisclosed portions.

Despite these recommendations, PSI report disclosure has remained highly discretionary with the individual states. The courts have rarely joined the debate. For years, the key case was *Williams* v. *New York* (1949). In this case, a judge decided on the death penalty for Williams, despite a jury recommendation for life imprisonment. The judge's decision was influenced by undisclosed PSI material. The Supreme Court held that Williams had received adequate assistance of counsel, despite the lack of disclosure. Accompanying opinion spoke highly of the PSI as a treatment advance and supported its confidential nature. In 1977, the Court determined in *Gardner* v. *Florida* that in capital cases incomplete disclosure denied effective right to counsel. In that case, the Court took the position that the most accurate means of determining aggravating and mitigating circumstances was an adversary proceeding in open court.

Neither case controls noncapital cases, but the trend is toward disclosure. Sixteen states have required full disclosure by statute (Allen, Carlson, and Parks, 1979:121). Other states and the federal government provide for partial disclosure, with the editing of the report determined by the judge. Jurisdictions with a practice of full disclosure report positive rather than negative effects (Zastrow, 1971; Larkins, 1972; Dubois, 1981).

The Use of the PSI. While many persons predicted that the utility of the PSI would decline with the advent of determinant sentencing, the PSI is still widely used. The most recent information indicates that 22 states and the federal government require PSI in felonies. Other states require the PSI in felonies only when probation is being considered, while a third group leave the request for a PSI to the judge (Allen, Carlson, and Parks, 1979:106–107). PSIs in misdemeanant cases are rarely required. Since, as we have seen, most determinate systems still provide the judge with vast discretion in the in-out decision, an investigation of potential adjustment to probation has merit. However, there are strong doubts about the effectiveness of current PSI practice.

The Effectiveness of the PSI. Hagan, Hewitt, and Alwin (1979), Abraham Blumberg (1970), and others argue that the probation officer's involvement in the sentencing process is not what it appears to be. Hagan's position is that the PSI is a largely ceremonial duty. The court pays lip

service to individualization while continuing to rely on the prosecutor's recommendation (1979:509). Hagan also suggested that PSI work serves prestige needs in the probation department by permitting senior agents to get away from the dirty work of supervision and providing them with the prestige associated with making sentence recommendations (Hagan, 1975:623). Hagan argued that this profession-building function may have advantages for probation staff, but not for clients.

Empirical evidence does suggest some problems with PSI practice. Hagan's 1975 Canadian research warned that probation officers were influenced by race and susceptible to probation recommendations based on the demeanor of the defendant during PSI interviews. His 1979 research in the state of Washington found that probation officers' and prosecutors' recommendations were both influenced by weapon use and prior record and that the prosecutor's recommendation was far more influential than the PSI recommendation (Hagan, Hewitt, and Alwin, 1979).

These studies were conducted prior to determinate sentencing changes and arguably indicate the negative consequences of the greater discretion permitted under indeterminate structures. However, very recent research in California continues to indicate problems. Petersilia et al., (1985) found that lengthy clinical probation reports were poor predictors of recidivism in felony cases. PSI recommendations did not distinguish good risks from bad (1985:40). Moreover, this research found that judges frequently ignored the probation officer's recommendation. Petersilia observed that previous plea negotiations often overrode the PSI in determining probation (1985:41). Such research would suggest that to the extent that probation is determined on the basis of risk, a few variables coded in quantitative fashion would be more effective than a long PSI report. Some probation departments have gone in this direction (see the discussion of risk assessment in Chapter 8).

However, these criticisms overlook some important features of the PSI. First, if merit rather than risk is an issue, then more information about the offender and the crime may be required than is helpful in predicting risk. Second, the detailed information in the PSI may be essential to drafting specific probation conditions. Third, the PSI may provide the supervising probation officer with important clues to supervision. Criticism of the PSI on the basis of its poor predictive power is important, but certainly not the controlling issue.

THE SENTENCING JUDGE

Judges have traditionally defended their discretion in sentencing, and in that posture have generally not been available for research about sentencing. Wilkins (1981) observed that part of this reticence on the part of judges is an understandable reaction to some of the uses of sentencing research. Judges have occasionally been attacked personally for their decisions rather than provided with information that would help to improve the sentencing process. Judges have also learned that enunciation of their reasons for particular sentences in open court could get them into trouble. Since sentencing is a controversial activity, someone is bound to disagree with their stated reasons. Judges have often felt safer saying as little as possible about the rationales for sentencing decisions.

Much of what we know about judges' sentencing decisions comes from sentencing institutes, observation, and anecdotal accounts by judges (Frankel, 1972). More systematic information is available in statistical models of sentencing outcomes. These models suggest that the best prediction of sentencing decisions usually involves data on the offender's criminal history and on the seriousness of the offense. However, these models do not tell us whether this is really the information judges use, nor can they suggest by what internal thought processes judges produce a decision (Wilkins, 1981).

It would appear from trends in the last dozen years that judges across the country have altered their goals in sentencing. Rehabilitation would appear to be less of a factor, and some combination of deterrence, incapacitation, and retri-

bution would appear to be more important. Ironically, these changes have not reduced public criticism of the courts. Public opinion surveys taken since 1972 indicate that the percentage of persons believing that the courts in their area do not deal harshly enough with criminals increased from 66 percent in 1972 to highs of 86 percent in 1982 and 1983. The greatest single-year increase in this opinion occurred in 1973 and 1974, almost simultaneous with the judicial swing toward more frequent use of incarceration (Flanagan and McGarrell, 1986:187–188). It is strange that that opinion continued to increase in frequency as sentencing has become more severe.

Some research indicates that judges with different backgrounds, or enmeshed in different organizational contexts, may sentence differently (Hogarth, 1971). For example, Levin's (1976) comparison of Minneapolis and Pittsburgh found that judges elected by partisan politics in Pittsburgh often had law degrees from local, nonprestigious law schools, often had middle-class or working-class backgrounds, often ran rather informal courts, and often dispensed justice differentially by area of the city in which the crime occurred. Minneapolis judges, who do not participate in partisan elections and are seen as "good government" officials rather than party loyalists, were often from prestigious law schools, often came from upper-class backgrounds, often ran more formal courtrooms, and applied the same formal rules across all areas of the city. One result, found Levin, is that poor and minority offenders often fared worse in Minneapolis than in Pittsburgh. But another result was that sentencing for the same crime was far less uniform in Pittsburgh than in Minneapolis.

Flemming's study of criminal courts in Baltimore and Detroit (1982), while focused on bail decisions rather than sentencing, suggests that patterns of judicial decisions are shaped by a number of organizational factors, such as vulnerability of the judge to political criticism, the kinds of resources available to the court for dispositions, and the extent to which judges trust the information about the offender.

Like the prosecutor, the judge faces a number of competing pressures when sentencing, no matter what the sentencing structure in the jurisdiction. Often the more controversial of these pressures concern the judge's role as a manager of the criminal process. The judge must oversee the fairness of the procedure. This includes assuring that plea bargains are honored and that defendants understand the possible consequences when they plead guilty (Newman, 1966).

As the Supreme Court has increasingly recognized and supported the bargaining process, judges have become more active in plea bargaining. This direct influence on negotiation is probably enhanced in determinant structures that provide the judge with little leeway in choosing a sentence. Under these conditions, a judge is probably freer to discuss possible sentences without appearing to be threatening a defendant for demanding a trial. However, there is still considerable controversy over awarding defendants who plead guilty less severe sentences than defendants who go to trial. Another controversial management issue is the extent to which judges do and should consider prison and jail conditions when deciding an individual sentence. Some judges admit to using prison less when they know prisons and jails are crowded, especially for less serious cases. Other judges insist that prison population is totally irrelevant to the individual case (Johnson, 1986).

CURRENT SENTENCING PRACTICE

FELONY SENTENCING IN 18 JURISDICTIONS

An overview of felony sentencing is available in a recent BJS report (May 1985). The project studied 15,000 felony convictions in 18 jurisdictions in 1983. The study is representative of current practice in those jurisdictions, but may not be representative of practice in other jurisdictions. Indeed, the variations found within the sample counties indicates that sentencing practices vary

considerably from place to place. Nevertheless, the study included a sample of counties from all regions of the country, and included counties in determinate and indeterminate states. The study sampled the convictions for homicide, rape, robbery, aggravated assault, burglary, larceny, and drug trafficking (May 1985:2). It provides an important comparative perspective on current felony sentencing.

A summary of 100 hundred typical sentences for these seven felonies is provided in Figure 6.2. Seventy-one percent of the felony convictions resulted in some form of incarceration (46 percent to prison, 26 percent to jail). Twenty-eight percent of convictions led to sentences of straight probation (May 1985:2).

BJS noted that in one-quarter of felony sentences, the local jail rather than a state prison was the place of incarceration. The heavy involvement of the jail in felony punishment appears to be relatively new. When the jail was used, 68 percent of the offenders were also placed on probation at the end of their jail term. Thirty percent of the jail sentences entailed no additional conditions, and 2 percent of jail terms were sentences to time served while awaiting trial (May 1985:2). Felony offenders who did straight jail time were typically given longer sentences than those serving probation terms after the jail sentence.

Considering both sentences to straight probation and split sentences, probation was involved in about half the felony sentences. The average probation term was three years and one month for straight probation and only one month longer for those who also served time in jail. BJS noted that the length of the probation term did not vary by seriousness of crime, unlike prison and jail time. However, it also noted that possibly the conditions attached to probation did vary with seriousness, although data to verify this were not reported (May 1985:2).

As we would expect, the likelihood of receiving a prison sentence varied with the seriousness of the crime. Prison was the sentence in 85 percent of homicide cases, 69 percent of rape cases,

FIGURE 6.2   A Typical 100 Sentences in Felony Court

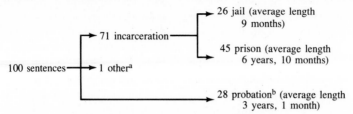

a Other includes such sentences as restitution to the victim or a fine.
b Probation refers to probation only and does not include sentences to
a split term of incarceration and probation.

SOURCE: Bureau of Justice Statistics, *Felony Sentencing in 18 Local Jurisdictions*. Washington, DC: United States Department of Justice, 1985, p. 2.

and 65 percent of robbery convictions. The convictions least likely to lead to prison were drug trafficking (23 percent), which in most instances were minor drug selling, and larceny (29 percent). Jail was the common punishment for aggravated assault, burglary, larceny, and drug trafficking, while straight probation was the most common sentence for larceny (see Table 6.3).

BJS attempted to compare prison sentence lengths in determinate and indeterminate states (May 1985:3). Unfortunately, comparisons are exceedingly difficult—one does not know whether to compare the flat term in determinate states with the minimum or the maximum sentence in states with discretionary release. BJS chose the maximum sentence, and found that median sentence length in determinate states was considerably shorter than median maximum sentences in indeterminate states. However, actual time served was probably very similar.

Comparisons across jurisdictions provide some rather surprising differences in sentence length (across both types of structure). See Figure 6.3 for comparisons of burglary sentences. While the severity of sentencing in the 18 counties clearly differed, they appeared to agree on the relative ranking of penalties. (For example, homicide received more serious penalties than rape, and rape more serious penalties than robbery (May 1985:3–6).

Sentences were more severe for completed crimes, and more severe when aggravating circumstances were present. Offenders convicted on multiple charges were given stiffer sentences than those convicted on one count. The majority of offenders were convicted on only one charge. Consecutive sentences were very rare (only 2 percent of the sentences). When consecutive sentences were given for conviction on multiple charges, sentence lengths were extremely long—suggesting that courts reserved this option for unusual crimes. BJS continued to find the prosecution process effects reported in Chapter 4: Pleas received slightly less severe sentences than convictions following trial, in most instances.

SENTENCING REFORM IN PRACTICE

The shift in sentencing structure is still so new that evaulations of its impact on actual practice are still preliminary. We will sample a few impact studies with an eye on (1) changes in sentencing process, (2) changes in sentencing and time served, and (3) changes in behavior within prisons.

Process Changes. Most of the observations about changes in the relative influence of the various criminal justice actors comes from California. Casper, Brereton, and Neal (1983) ex-

TABLE 6.3   Sentencing Outcomes by Conviction Offense

CONVICTION OFFENSE	PRISON	JAIL ONLY	JAIL AND PROBATION	PROBATION ONLY	OTHER	TOTAL
Total	45%	8%	18%	28%	1%	100%
Violent						
Homicide	85	1	5	9	—	100
Rape	69	2	10	18	1	100
Robbery	65	4	12	17	1	100
Aggravated assault	39	11	19	31	2	100
Property						
Burglary	46	8	17	28	1	100
Larceny	29	15	17	38	2	100
Other						
Drug trafficking	23	6	35	35	2	100

NOTE: May not add to 100% because of rounding.
— Less than 0.5%.
SOURCE: Bureau of Justice Statistics, *Felony Sentencing in 18 Local Jurisdictions*. Washington, DC: United States Department of Justice, 1985, p. 3.

amined the rate and timing of guilty pleas and the plea bargaining process in three counties after the switch to presumptive sentencing. They reported that control of the sentencing process in California shifted to the prosecutor, who could determine sentence lengths through manipulation of number of charges filed and use of sentence enhancements. They observed that judicial power also increased. Sentence bargaining greatly increased, since the actors had greater control over sentence and more incentives to bargain over time (1983:410). A study of Indiana observed the same phenomenon. Discretion in sentencing did not disappear, but was transferred to the prosecutor through charge and sentence bargaining, and to prison officials, who gained discretion in the timing of release through good time (Clear, Hewitt, and Regoli, 1978). Casper and his colleagues caution us that perhaps not all of the increased sentence bargaining can be attributed to the new structure. They observed that in California, the bargaining trend began prior to the change in the sentencing law (1983:425).

Changes in Sentencing. Changes in sentencing patterns vary considerably from state to state,

as one would expect, with specific sentencing structures varying considerably. In California, both Casper, Brereton, and Neal (1983) and Brewer, Beckett, and Holt (1981) have reported increased commitments to state prison. Again, both are cautious about making causal assumptions. The Casper group observed that the commitment rate had begun to climb prior to the change in the law. Brewer and associates point out that the drastic reduction in state support for probation could by itself have resulted in increased commitment rates, without any changes in sentencing law (1981:211). Trying to predict actual time served based on sentences handed down in the first year of the presumptive sentencing, Brewer et al. suggest that men would serve shorter terms and women longer terms under determinant sentencing, provided most good time was actually handed out (1981:218–226). Sentences in California have become longer since that study, but good time provisions have also become more liberal.

The Minnesota Sentencing Guidelines Commission has issued regular reports about sentencing in that state, comparing sentences under the matrix guidelines to sentences just prior to the

FIGURE 6.3   Average Burglary Sentence Lengths and Potential Reductions in Eighteen Jurisdictions

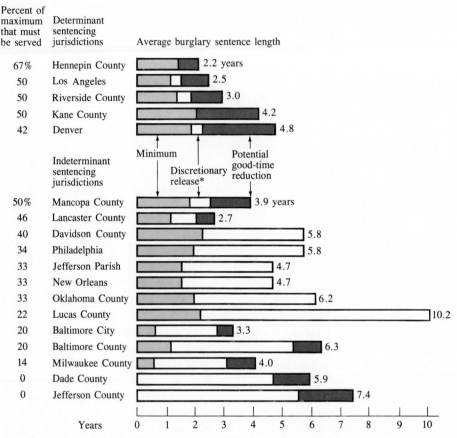

*Discretionary release included earned-time credits as well as the parole board's authority to release.

SOURCE: Bureau of Justice Statistics, *Felony Sentencing in 18 Local Jurisdictions*. Washington, DC: United States Department of Justice, 1985, p. 6.

sentencing change. The commission's general finding is that disparity in sentences for offenders with similar histories and convicted of similar crimes has indeed gone down (1982:20–36). The guideline system in practice appears to favor the instant offense over criminal history. Reviewing cases from 1980 and 1981, the commission reported a 73 percent increase in prison sentences for persons who had committed serious crimes but had low criminal history scores, and conversely, a 72 percent reduction in prison for of-

fenders with high criminal history scores but whose instant offense was of low severity (1982:16–17). The commission also observed that the prison population has stayed within capacity in the first three years, although this accomplishment required adjustments in the matrix in the third year.

Unlike California, commitment rates are down, while persons sent to prison are serving more time (1982:43). The director of the commission observed that judges and prosecutors are showing an increasing tendency to avoid proportionality of sentence to crime. In 1982 there was excessive use of aggravating factors, and in 1983, excessive use of mitigating factors (Knapp, 1984:186–189). She also reported a surprising finding from 1982: In that year many defendants reportedly requested a prison sentence rather than a community alternative because they perceived the community alternatives in Minnesota to be more onerous than prison.

Changes in Correctional Practice. Two interesting studies have examined the impact of determinate sentencing on life in prison. This would appear to be an important inquiry, particularly since many liberal sentence reformers (including inmates) argued that determinate sentencing would improve prison conditions. Goodstein et al., (1984) studied prisons in three determinate states, Minnesota, Connecticut, and Illinois, using interviews with inmates and staff and self-report questionnaires with random samples of inmates. The researchers cautioned their readers that some of the postsentencing indeterminacy which was attacked in the sentencing reforms still remained, but in different forms. One important possibility is that the sentencing reforms, as implemented, have not altered the "time game" syndrome.

Goodstein and colleagues indicated that three mechanisms operating to reduce release predictability are (1) new good time laws and procedures, (2) new release programs, such as work release, and (3) discretionary postrelease supervision policies. They also reported that coerced treatment was still a staple, partly out of the habit of treatment staff. They could find no significant effects of sentencing change on prisoners' attitudes toward the law or toward prison staff. Inmate stress levels and anxiety appeared unaffected. However, inmates who had been sentenced after the sentencing changes believed that they had been more equitably sentenced, and the majority of all inmates preferred determinate sentencing (1984: 44–63).

A far less sophisticated study of the California system was conducted by an English observer (Davies, 1985). He agrees with the Goodstein group that in general, the sentencing change has had remarkably little effect on prison life. However, there appeared to be some negative consequences in California that are not stressed in the Goodstein study. Davies reported that staff believed inmate attitudes toward staff worsened, since they felt no need to impress staff (1985:13). Custody staff, in particular, complained that the fixed release dates reduced ability to control inmate behavior. Davies reported that California altered the original good time provisions as a means of dealing with this situation. As of 1983, inmates are offered one day off the term for each day worked, and other privileges are tied to prison labor. In effect, Davies suggested, coerced treatment had been replaced with coerced labor, and despite the retributive goal statements of the California legislature, punishment in practice appears more concerned with incapacitation than retribution.

RACIAL DISPROPORTIONALITY*

Prison populations in the United States contain a far greater proportion of minority persons than their numbers in the general population can explain. Many persons have assumed that the racial mix in our prisons indicates racial discrimination in the preconviction and sentencing parts of the criminal process. Although the focus here is sentencing, the factors associated with disproportionality and discrimination are so intertwined that we must discuss the entire criminal process.

The disproportionate incarceration of minorities is a weak indicator of racial discrimination (Blumstein, 1982; Dehais, 1983; Garofalo, 1983). Blumstein illustrates the basic weakness of the argument with an analogy to disproportionate incarceration by gender. Many more men than women are incarcerated, although there are about

---

* This section was written by Shelley L. Kath.

equal numbers of both sexes in the general population. Does this disproportionate locking up of men indicate sexism in criminal justice decisions? While there may be some element of sexism in criminal justice processing, it often tends to work against women, not for them. The major explanation of sexually disproportionate incarceration rates is that males have much higher crime rates than women, rather than biases in the decisions made about the two sexes (Blumstein, 1982: 1262).

Blumstein argued that a great deal of racially disproportionate incarceration could be due to the same explanation—differential involvement in the crimes that lead to prison sentences. We must examine factors such as offense rates and arrest frequencies in order to surmise how much, if any, of the disproportionality in prison populations may result from legitimate processing factors rather than from racial discrimination (1982:1262). The proposition that disproportionate incarceration rates by race are explained by race-specific crime rates rather than decision discrimination is the **differential involvement hypothesis.**

Research on the hypothesis is limited. In the first major study of its kind, Blumstein compared the black-white arrest ratio with the black-white incarceration ratio by type of crime. He assumed that if there was no racial biasing in the criminal process, the proportion admitted to prison should mirror the proportion arrested for various crimes (1982:1264). He found that approximately 80 percent of the disproportionality between black and white incarceration rates could be accounted for by racial differences at arrest (1982:1267). Similar findings of a mirroring from arrest to incarceration were reported by Garofalo (1983) and Petersilia (1983). However, Christianson (1982) reported finding significantly greater proportions of blacks in inmate populations than in arrest populations for most types of crimes.

These findings tend to suggest that racial bias, if it exists, occurs prior to arrest, rather than in prosecution or sentencing. Blumstein (1982) argued that there is probably little racial discrimi-

nation in arrest. He based his argument on research such as that of Hindelang (1981) demonstrating that racial distribution in arrest data parallels that in victim self-report data. Petersilia (1983) also found that prisoner self-report data supported the conclusion that minorities were not overrepresented in arrests, relative to the offenses they committed. She also found no evidence of racial disparity in the probability of arrest (1983:46). Still, some assert that higher arrest rates for minorities may be due to such factors as heavier police patrols in urban areas where minorities live (Geis, 1972), or police consideration of black arrests as "safe" arrests (less likely to be challenged than arrests of whites) (Christianson, 1982:71).

Although Blumstein's explanation of the bulk of incarcerations in terms of arrests is persuasive, it can be argued that the mirroring of black arrests in incarcerations does not necessarily preclude the existence of racially disparate processing. Some evidence, for example, shows that unequal treatment is more likely when more discretion is used in decision-making, as is the case in less serious offenses. Blumstein's "20% unexplained" figure for disproportionality ranged from 2.8 percent for homicide to 33 percent and more for burglary and less serious property offenses (1982:1274). Petersilia also found that the parallel between arrest and imprisonment populations existed only for serious crimes (1983:97). A related finding by Zalman (1979:278), in his study of Michigan sentencing, is that while sentence length seemed most strongly influenced by offense type for violent crimes and drug offenses, offender characteristics relating to race were more influential in other crimes. Although it seems that more racial bias may occur in the processing of lesser offenses, it must be noted that blacks are heavily represented among offenders committing the more serious crimes (Blumstein, 1982:1266).

Comparing racial distributions at arrest and imprisonment, Blumstein inferred that whites and minorities were accorded roughly the same treatment from arrest on (1982:1264). Research on case processing at stages such as release by the prosecutor prior to filing charges and by judges at sentencing suggests that this inference may not be wholly accurate. Blumstein's method permits a good deal of decision-specific bias to occur, without showing up in the incarceration-arrest comparisons (Blumstein, 1982:1280).

DISCRIMINATION AT SENTENCING

Reviews focusing specifically on sentencing disparity find that studies showing discrimination are generally outweighed by those showing no discrimination. Early studies finding discrimination at sentencing generally failed to control for seriousness of offense, length of prior record, and other variables judges can legitimately consider when determining whether to incarcerate or how long to imprison. However, more recent studies with much more sophisticated controls for "legal variables" are still contradictory (Pertersilia, 1983:18; Hagan and Bumiller, 1983).

Hagan and Bumiller reported that the more recent and more sophisticated research on sentencing is uncovering more, not less, racial discrimination in sentencing, although the effect of race on sentence is generally weak (Hagan and Bumiller, 1983). Petersilia's 1983 study concluded that, controlling for other factors, minorities received harsher sentences and served longer prison terms (1983). The Minnesota Sentencing Guidelines Commission (1982, 1983) reported that minority offenders received more severe sanctions than whites when crime and criminal history were controlled. The commission observed that aggravating circumstances were more often applied against minorities (1982:37–40). Zatz (1984) found that the effect of race was subtle and indirect in the first year of the new California sentencing system. She found that Chicanos were particularly disadvantaged by the use of prior record.

In her more recent probation research, Petersilia continued to find an impact of race on felony sentencing in two California counties (Petersilia et al., 1985:30–31). In general, the research on sentencing indicates (1) that more sophisticated

controls have not reduced the claims of discrimination, (2) that contradictory and inconsistent results are probably partially a result of discrimination in some areas and not in others (with rural areas apparently more discriminatory) (Hagan and Bumiller, 1983), and (3) while race may have some effect on sentencing some of the time, it is rarely the major reason for the disproportionate representation of minorities in prison.

DISCRIMINATION AT OTHER DECISION POINTS

Most of the research on case proceeding has focused on sentencing; relatively little has been done on disparity of treatment before arrest or after sentencing. Because greater discretion and decreased visibility often characterize decisions occurring earlier than and later than sentencing, discrimination may be more likely at these other stages (Petersilia, 1983:6; Carroll and Mandrick, 1976). Also, the analysis of only formal or recorded decisions can prevent the finding of discriminatory practices that may occur in less formal ways (Frederick and Zimerman, 1983:23). Finally, even if all processing points between arrest and sentencing involved no racial discrimination, it could be argued that disparate treatment occurring prior to arrest or during incarceration and parole might contribute to racial disproportionality in prison populations.

Discrimination against minorities in prison could result from procedural biases in such areas as computation of good time and jail credit, security level assignment, and disciplinary reports (Christianson, 1982:82–85). If racial bias in such procedures serves to extend times served by minority offenders, racial disproportionality of the prison population could be exacerbated. Some evidence suggests that use of presentence investigation reports by prison administrators and parole officials may not favor racial minorities (Schmolesky and Thorson, 1982; Petersilia, 1983; Carroll and Mandrick, 1976). The underlying reason for this may be that the presentence investigation report serves as a source of information for indicators of recidivism such as employment history and unstable family relations, that may be more prevalent among minority offenders (Petersilia, 1983; Carroll and Mandrick, 1976, Hagan, 1975).

Hagan's study of sentence recommendations by probation officers in a western Canadian province offers some support for these arguments. Hagan proposed that (1975:628):

> . . . [the] social work orientation of probation officers will lead them to emphasize extra-legal factors, particularly racial background, in making recommendations.

His analysis suggested that the presence of sentence recommendations in the presentence report did provide a channel for extralegal factors. Sentences that followed recommendations showed more influence of race and offender class and demeanor than sentences which did not follow a sentence recommendation. The result was adverse for Native Americans (1975:634–635). It would seem quite likely that these factors could also influence prison and parole officers, even if ignored by the judge. Finally, the subtle and low-visibility influences of race can come around again and influence sentencing indirectly, through their impact on previous criminal history.

Efforts to reduce discrimination within the criminal justice system have not had the desired effect on racial disproportionality. The most frequent effort has been to structure discretion, such as through determinate sentencing schemes. Generally, racial disproportionality has increased rather than decreased after the use of guidelines.

A recent report by Petersilia and Turner (1985) examined the impact of guidelines on racial disproportionality. After reviewing each of the items used in the guidelines and their relationship with race, they concluded that the items are not racially discriminatory. Use of guidelines results in a higher proportion of blacks going to prison because blacks are more likely to commit the more serious crimes and have the lengthier criminal records which are built into the guideline matrices. Thus guidelines reflect the greater involvement of minorities and the lower classes in serious street crime, but they do not, in and of themselves, discriminate on the basis of race. (However, as the Minnesota Sentencing Commission discovered, while the guidelines do not discriminate, the decision-makers using the guidelines may still decide to deviate from the guidelines in ways that are discriminatory.)

While such practices should be stopped, the data would strongly suggest that the major reasons for the racial disproportionality of our prisons are beyond the control of criminal justice decision-makers. Blumstein suggests that only changes in the social conditions that cause crime will be effective (1982:1281).

SUMMARY

1. Sentencing decisions occur at two levels. Sentencing policy decisions originate with the legislature. Policy concerns include basic purposes of sentencing, severity, linkages between severity and resources, and structure. Individual case-level decisions involve prosecutors, defense attorneys, probation officers, judges, and where permitted, officials in charge of discretionary release.
2. Sentencing policy may be explicit or implicit, and it may be made directly by the legislature or delegated to another agency, such as a sentencing commission.
3. There are three basic types of sentencing structure: (a) the executive model, associated with indeterminate sentencing, (b) judicial, and (c) legislative, both usually associated with incapacitation and retribution.
4. Prior to the sentencing reforms of the 1970s, a number of partial structural changes were employed in an attempt to control discretion. These controls included sentencing councils, sentenc-

ing conferences, and appellate review. Mandatory sentences, which were used in an attempt to eliminate discretion in certain cases, are still popular.

5. In the 1970s a number of major structural reforms were initiated in an attempt to reduce disparity, to reduce the influence of rehabilitative justifications, and/or to increase certainty and severity. The most common types have been legislatively controlled presumptive sentences, such as in California, or sentences controlled by guidelines overseen by a sentencing commission, as in Minnesota.

6. The sentencing process at the case level varies somewhat, depending on the sentencing structure in the state. Research indicates that prosecutor's recommendation is very influential. Major variables influencing sentence choices include seriousness of charge, weapon use, history of the offender, and type of conviction (plea or trial).

7. The presentence investigation is often done in felony cases. While PSIs do not seem to predict recidivism well, they remain a major planning document for probation supervision and prison classification.

8. A recent survey of felony sentencing indicates that 71 percent of felony convictions result in some type of incarceration. Jail sentences appear more common for felony sentences than was previously thought to be the case. Probation, with or without jail time, was involved in roughly 50 percent of all sentences. Severity of punishment varies considerably from jurisdiction to jurisdiction.

9. Determinate sentencing reform has probably affected the sentencing process, but research to date has been unable to tease out its effects from those of other influences. It appears that bargaining has increased, that commitment rates have increased, and that life in prison has remained unchanged.

10. While the tremendous overrepresentation of minorities, especially blacks, in the prison system has led to criticism of discrimination in sentencing, the bulk of the evidence suggests that sentencing discrimination is present, but is not the major explanation of racial disproportionality.

KEY TERMS

APPELLATE REVIEW OF SENTENCING. The practice of reviewing sentences per se (rather than convictions) in appellate court.

CASE-LEVEL SENTENCING. The sentencing of specific offenders.

CLIENT-SPECIFIC PLANNING. A new form of private presentence report done on behalf of the defendant.

CONCURRENT SENTENCES. The practice of ordering separate sentences for convictions on multiple charges to be served at the same time.

CONSECUTIVE SENTENCES. The practice of ordering separate sentences for convictions on multiple charges to be served in sequence.

DELEGATED SENTENCING POLICY. The practice by the legislature of permitting or authorizing the development of sentencing policy by a group other than itself.

DESCRIPTIVE GUIDELINES. Sentencing guidelines in which the sentencing values are determined by studying the normal patterns for certain offenses and offender types. The sentence values in this case describe past practice.

DETERMINATE SENTENCE. A flat sentence specified in advance of the specific conviction.

DIFFERENTIAL INVOLVEMENT HYPOTHESIS. The hypothesis that racially differential incarceration rates are caused by the different levels of involvement of different racial groups in specific types of crimes.

DIRECT SENTENCING POLICY. The construction of sentencing policy directly by the legislature.

DISCLOSURE OF PSI REPORT. The practice of sharing the PSI report with the defendant and counsel.

EXPLICIT SENTENCING POLICY. A formal statement of goals, a codification of criminal penalties consistent with the goals, and an explicit structure and stated process for implementing sentencing goals.

EXECUTIVE MODEL OF SENTENCING. A sentencing structure which gives most discretion to the executive branch of government, usually to a parole board.

FLAT TERM. A specific, definite term for a conviction, not necessarily known in advance of sentencing.

IMPLICIT SENTENCING POLICY. A legislative orientation to sentencing that must be inferred from its other actions.

INDETERMINATE SENTENCE. A sentence that permits discretionary release, sometimes based on factors unknown at sentencing, such as prison adjustment. Expressed in two figures, a minimum term (which may be zero) and a maximum term.

JUDICIAL MODEL OF SENTENCING. Sentencing structure that provides the judge with more discretion in fixing a term than either the legislature or the executive branch.

JUDICIAL SENTENCING INSTITUTE. An educational or training session for judges on issues relevant to sentencing.

LEGISLATIVE MODEL OF SENTENCING. A sentencing structure in which the legislature retains most discretion, and does not permit a great deal of judicial or executive flexibility in fixing terms.

MANDATORY SENTENCE. A statutory requirement of a specific sentence, or a proscription of certain sentencing options.

POLICY-LEVEL SENTENCING DECISIONS. Sentencing decisions by the legislature or its delegate about the goals and structure of sentencing.

PRESCRIPTIVE GUIDELINES. Sentencing guidelines in which the sentences are determined on the basis of value judgments about appropriateness rather than on the basis of past practice.

PRESENTENCE INVESTIGATION (PSI). An investigation by a probation officer prior to sentencing. The PSI report is one source of information used by the judge in determining sentence, especially in the decision to grant probation.

PRESUMPTIVE SENTENCE. The sentence presumed to be appropriate, by the sentencing policymaker, and that therefore must be selected by the judge unless there are compelling reasons to sentence otherwise.

SCOPE OF SENTENCING POLICY. The breadth of sanctions covered by sentencing policy. The most important distinction is between broad policies that address probation as well as prison terms and narrow policies that address only length of incarceration, but not whether to incarcerate.

SENTENCING COMMISSION. A group commissioned by the legislature to determine sentencing policy and usually to monitor implementation of that policy.

SENTENCING CONFERENCE. An informal meeting prior to the sentencing hearing involving judge, prosecutor, defense attorney, and probation officer to discuss sentencing recommendations.

SENTENCING COUNCILS. The meeting of a panel of judges in a multijudge court to discuss sentencing of pending cases. Designed to temper individual decisions by comparison to group norms.

SENTENCING DISPARITY. Differences in sentencing not attributable to differences in criminal history of offenders or to differences in the current convictions.

SENTENCING GUIDELINES. Determination of sentences based on decision rules that apply to all sentences. Typically the rules are based on severity of crime and length of criminal record.

SENTENCING STRUCTURE. The division of decision authority at the individual case level of sentencing; provides the formal relationships by which to implement policy.

PROJECTS AND QUESTIONS

1. One complaint about client-specific planning is that clients often have to pay for it, and therefore it is an advantage to the well-off. Another complaint is that sentencing reports should not be made by advocates for the defense. What are some possible answers to these criticisms?
2. Probation officers have often claimed that the PSI report should be privileged information. What is the difference between the privileged doctor-patient relationship and the defendant-officer relationship?
3. The Minnesota Sentencing Guidelines Commission preferred prescriptive guidelines to descriptive ones. The commission stated that descriptive guidelines institutionalized past mistakes and failed to make goals explicit. Wilkins argued that descriptive guidelines were better, at least initially,

because "We do not know how to program a computer to decide the right sentence (nor could we draft legislation to the same end)" (1981:68). In other words, Wilkins thought we should profit from the judges' sentencing expertise by using previous decisions to set the norms for future sentences. Which approach do you prefer, and why?

4. Wilkins (1981:67–68) observed that one major problem with any current grading of penalties by seriousness of offense is that penalties of different types cannot be graded. What do you think would be the breakeven point between prison, jail, probation, and a fine? That is, at what level of each penalty would an offender not care which was imposed? If you cannot come up with an answer (which is very likely) how would you propose that we approach the problem?

ADDITIONAL READING

David Fogel. " . . . *We Are the Living Proof* . . . " Cincinnati: Anderson, 1975. This is one of the most often cited and discussed of the arguments for sentencing reform. This description of a "justice model" had an influence on reforms in Illinois and a number of other states that chose a legislative model of sentencing.

Paul Keve. *The Probation Officer Investigates*. Minneapolis: University of Minnesota Press, 1960. This is an old book, but still the classic rendition of the PSI.

Andrew von Hirsch. *Doing Justice*. New York: Hill and Wang, 1976. Another of the classic sentencing reform tracts. This one argues for a matrix format with guidelines.

Leslie T. Wilkins. *Developing Sentencing Guidelines*. Washington DC: U.S. Government Printing Office, 1981. A nontechnical discussion of both methodological and ethical issues in the development of the Albany guidelines project.

QUESTIONS

1. Do the guidelines that have resulted
   from *Furman* v. *Georgia* make imposition of the death penalty fair and consistent?

2. Does a retributive argument for the
   death penalty require empirical evidence?

3. Are the poor and the black who are
   found guilty of murder more likely to receive the death penalty than the equally
   guilty rich and white?

4. Does the fact that innocent people are
   executed make a valid argument against
   the death penalty?

5. What were the findings in *Gregg* v. *Georgia* regarding the constitutionality of the
   death penalty?

6. Is it more economical to execute an individual than it is to maintain him or her
   in prison for life?

HARD CHOICES

Phil and Morton Shaffley had just met with
Senator Givens and Marianne Shrievers,
chief staffer on the Senate Criminal Justice
Committee. Phil and Mort were trying to
drum up money for a new halfway house
they hoped to start near the university.

This chapter was written by Robert Fitch.

Mort, an ex-priest, was a local criminal justice gadfly, constantly calling to question the
criminal justice officials in the state and always seeking innovation in the system. He
earned his keep as the lobbyist for the Jefferson Citizens for Criminal Justice, a liberal coalition for policy change.

Senator Givens had listened attentively
to the halfway house proposal, but he left
Phil and Mort without much sign of encour-

agement. Marianne followed them out to the lobby.

"Hey, don't get discouraged. The proposal looks good. But I think you'll get a better hearing in the Assembly than over here. Going for lunch?"

Phil and Mort nodded, and the three set off for the Legislative Cafeteria. Not surprisingly, lunch conversation shifted quickly to bigger matters. Mort was gathering church and other reform group support behind Governor Kenney as he prepared to do battle with the legislature again over the death penalty.

"The way I count them, Kenney can still avoid an override this year. I think they'll fall five short in the Senate."

"Five," said Marianne. "The override last year failed by two votes. One of these years, it'll happen. Kenney is just prolonging the inevitable, and giving away the store to do it."

Mort flared instantly. For him, holding off the conservatives on this issue was worth all the other issues. "What do you mean giving away the store? The death sentence is not something you can trade off against something else."

"Oh, no?" said Marianne; "You want your halfway house to get some poor slobs out of that overcrowded zoo we call a prison? Do you know how much more leverage we would have with the conservative senators in return for the death penalty?"

Shaffley nearly choked on his coffee. "I can't believe you can think like that. You're supposed to be the support on this. How can you even think of trading off life for a halfway house? Sure I want lots of reforms. But if it means a few more inmates spend a few more days in prison before parole so we can keep this state from committing murder, well, then that's the way it goes."

Marianne was not easily brushed aside. "I don't think you down-to-the-wire, anti-death-penalty people have ever thought through who's suffering how much on this issue. You think a few little halfway houses are all we give up? Do you know just how many life sentences and mandatory prison terms have been traded away by the governor just to keep the death penalty off the books? For what? How many times would the death sentence be handed down anyway? Four, five times a year. Guess how many guys died in Mulwan last year alone. Six inmates and one officer. There's so little space up there, Robinson is bunking people in the hallways. Two officers have had stress-related heart attacks. Four more took early retirement last week. The union is threatening a walkout unless we pass a new construction bill this session. How many millions is that that could have gone into education or hospitals or something else a lot better than cement and iron bars? This issue is not going away, and I for one think Kenney and your group are actually causing a lot more suffering than the death penalty."

"Okay," said Mort, not wanting to alienate an ally. "You've got some good points there. But I know all those. You still can't weigh life against overcrowding and other prison problems. I don't believe for one second that giving the conservatives the death penalty would decrease the prison population. Look at Florida and Texas. They lock 'em all up with the death penalty. The death penalty can't be handled like any other political issue."

"You wanna bet? It's about the most political issue we can get. It's an issue of life against life. How else do you solve that conflict except politically? And as for avoiding tradeoffs—you can't do that either. I know we could have defeated the last mandatory sentencing bill in return for the death penalty. That's Kenney's whole strategy. He doesn't want to be seen as soft on crime, but he's morally opposed to the death penalty. So he pushes incarceration. The fact that other states have overcrowding and the death penalty is irrelevant to the issues in this state. Sure, I'll help lead the fight against the override one more time. But I'm doing it because Givens does what Kenney asks. Personally, I'd rather take my fight elsewhere."

Mort shook his head. "We're never giving up."

ORIGINS OF CAPITAL PUNISHMENT

As a method of punishment, the death penalty is not unusual: it has been applied to individuals convicted of crime since the dawn of history. In primitive society, for example, public crimes, such as the breaking of the incest taboo and sorcery, were punished with great severity in order to placate the gods. The offender might be hacked to pieces by a frenzied mob, stoned, burned, banished, even eaten. These punishments were not administered necessarily in the name of retribution or to inflict pain on the victim, but to prevent the entire clan from being harmed by an outraged god.

In ancient times **capital punishment** was carried out for a variety of crimes. Under the laws of ancient Athens, almost any kind of offense was liable to the death penalty. It was a capital crime, for example, to be idle and to steal fruit and vegetables (Aristotle, 147). Under the laws of Justinian in ancient Rome, the death penalty was applied to individuals convicted of treason, adultery, sodomy, publicly selling deadly drugs, ravishing virgins and widows, and carrying weapons for the purpose of homicide. Indebtedness, under certain conditions, could also be a capital offense.

Capital punishment continued into medieval times. The punishment for all felonies was death. Medieval common law imposed death for such crimes as treason, blasphemy, witchcraft, mayhem, burglary, robbery, grand larceny, rape, and arson. In the Middle Ages, execution was by torture (Hunnisett, 1972). For example, in the fifteenth century, in what is now Romania, a king

called Vlad the Impaler, who later became known by the name of Dracula, was extremely brutal in his punishments for the purpose of keeping order and preserving the law. Some of his punishments have been described as follows (McNally and Florescu, 1974):

> He killed some by breaking them under the wheels of carts; others stripped of their clothes were skinned alive up to their entrails; others placed upon stakes, or roasted on red hot coals placed under them; others punctured with stakes piercing their head, their breast, their buttocks and the middle of the entrails, with the stake emerging from their mouths; and in order that no form of of cruelty be missing he stuck stakes in both the mother's breasts and thrust their babies into them.

During the sixteenth and seventeenth centuries, the belief in witchcraft was so widespread in Europe that many individuals suffered deaths by torture. Those especially prone to undergo summary trials for witchcraft were the eccentric, epileptic, senile, or mentally disturbed (Hunnisett, 1972).

The American colonies established a pattern of punishments directly imported from Europe. Death was prescribed for such crimes as murder, copulation with animals, homosexuality, rebellion, striking one's parents, and atheism. The Pennsylvania Prison Code of 1718 punished all felonies except larceny with death (Barnes and Teeters, 1951).

A draconian code of law again emerged in England during the early nineteenth century. It became known as the Bloody Code. Under this code there were more than 220 offenses punishable by death. The death penalty was applied to such offenses as the stealing of turnips, associating with gypsies, cutting down a tree, forgery, and shoplifting (Koestler, 1957:7). Because the English lawmakers believed in the deterrent value of public executions, execution days became public spectacles comparable to football games and rock concerts. Thousands of citizens from all social classes would come to view the hangings. The condemned were sometimes hanged in batches of sixteen or more, and frequently both prisoners and executioner were drunk at the time. The crowds attending the executions were boisterous and rowdy. A collective hysteria filled the air. Although pickpocketing was a capital offense, pickpockets thrived at public executions (Koestler, 1957:8–9).

The United States also used public executions. Dr. Benjamin Rush delivered an address against public executions as early as 1787. Little was done until 1830, when the State of New York required sheriffs (at their discretion) to hold executions away from the public view. However, public executions continued until fairly recently in some states. The last public executions in the United States were carried out in Owensboro, Kentucky, on August 14, 1936, and in Galena, Missouri, on May 21, 1937. Over 20,000 people watched in Owensboro as a black man was hanged for rape. Many present for the hanging took away as a souvenir a piece of rope used in the hanging (Bedau, 1982:13).

With the reform of the criminal law in England in 1861, the death penalty was removed for all offenses except murder, treason, and piracy, and finally abolished for all crimes in 1967. Although the death penalty is not used as extensively as in the past, it is still provided by law in over 100 countries. During 1984, 2,068 people were reported sentenced to death by courts in 55 countries. In countries like China, Iran, and Iraq, where many executions took place throughout the year, official figures were not available (Amnesty International, 1985).

Many countries of Western Europe and Central and South America, as well as New Zealand, have abolished the death penalty. On January 17, 1986, the European Parliament adopted a resolution affirming its strong desire that the death penalty be abolished throughout the European Community. The resolution called on all member states of the Council of Europe to ratify the Sixth Protocol to the European Convention of Human Rights, which abolished the death penalty for peacetime offenses. The Sixth Protocol is the first binding international treaty prohibiting the death penalty (Amnesty International, 1986). In the past decade, certain countries such as the United States and Japan have increased their use of the death penalty (Amnesty International, 1986).

CAPITAL PUNISHMENT IN THE UNITED STATES

Since 1608 there have been more than 14,000 legal executions in the United States and American Colonies (ABA, 1985). Executions in the United States reached a peak in 1935, when 199 convicted felons were put to death at the hands of the state. Of the 14,000 executed, more than 360 were women and at least 320 were juveniles (ABA, 1985).

The death penalty achieved renewed life in the United States with the execution of Gary Gilmore by a Utah firing squad on January 17, 1977. Prior to Gilmore's execution, an official moratorium on executions had prevailed since 1967, while legal challenges to the death penalty were decided at various court levels. Since the execution of Gary Gilmore, executions in the United States have continued slowly, but threaten to accelerate in the future.

As of March 1, 1987, there were 1,874 inmates on death row, 1,855 males and 19 females (NAACP, 1987). Since Gary Gilmore was shot, 69 individuals have been executed (NAACP, 1987). The states that have actually carried out executions since 1967 are Florida, Texas, Alabama, Georgia, Mississippi, Virginia, Louisiana, North Carolina, Nevada, South Carolina, Indiana, and Utah. Texas leads in the number of executions with twenty, and Florida is second with sixteen (NAACP, 1987). Tables 7.1 and 7.2 show number of persons executed by jurisdiction, and prisoners under sentence of death by region and state.

According to Faye A. Silas (1985), some of the reasons for this revitalization of the death penalty are: (1) the exhaustion of long appeals in several cases; (2) the impatience of the courts with long appeals and therefore rejecting issues

TABLE 7.1   Number of Persons Executed by Jurisdiction in Rank Order, 1930–1984

STATE	SINCE 1930	SINCE 1977	STATE	SINCE 1930	SINCE 1977
U.S. total	3,909	50	District of Columbia	40	
			Arizona	38	
Georgia	372	6	Federal system	33	
New York	329		Nevada	31	2
Texas	307	10	Massachusetts	27	
California	292		Connecticut	21	
North Carolina	265	2	Oregon	19	
Florida	183	13	Iowa	18	
Ohio	172		Kansas	15	
South Carolina	163	1	Utah	14	1
Mississippi	155	1	Delaware	12	
Pennsylvania	152		New Mexico	8	
Louisiana	140	7	Wyoming	7	
Alabama	136	1	Montana	6	
Arkansas	118		Vermont	4	
Kentucky	103		Nebraska	4	
Virginia	96	4	Idaho	3	
Tennessee	93		South Dakota	1	
Illinois	90		New Hampshire	1	
New Jersey	74		Wisconsin	0	
Maryland	68		Rhode Island	0	
Missouri	62		North Dakota	0	
Oklahoma	60		Minnesota	0	
Washington	47		Michigan	0	
Colorado	47		Maine	0	
Indiana	43	2	Hawaii	0	
West Virginia	40		Alaska	0	

SOURCE: Bureau of Justice Statistics *Bulletin. Capital Punishment 1985*. Washington, DC: Bureau of Justice Statistics, Table 8.

brought up as defenses; and (3) the public opinion favoring the death penalty. To this list may be added a return to a model of corrections by lawmakers and chief executives that is based more on retribution than rehabilitation. In February 1985 the Gallup Poll reported that 75 percent of Americans favored capital punishment for murder, as opposed to 45 percent in 1965 (Silas, 1985:48). Henry Schwarzchild feels the United States is competing with such countries as the Soviet Union, Iran, the People's Republic of China, and the Union of South Africa in the extent of application of the death penalty (1985:38).

There are 37 jurisdictions in the United States with capital punishment statutes; 14 states are without capital punishment statutes (NAACP, 1987). The seven states having the most murderers sentenced to die as of March 1, 1987, are: Florida (259), Texas (242), California (195), Georgia (109), Illinois (103), Pennsylvania (87), and Alabama (81) (NAACP, 1987). Table 7.3 presents a profile of capital punishment statutes and legal changes during 1985.

METHODS OF EXECUTION

In early times a variety of cruel and inhuman means were used to execute people. The condemned person might have been boiled in oil, crucified, burned at the stake, pressed to death, sawed in half, drowned, stoned, or flayed and impaled. The devices employed to put people to death were gradually humanized and now consist mainly of beheading, electrocution, hanging, shooting, lethal gas, and lethal injection.

In the United States electrocution is authorized in fifteen states, with one state providing the alternative of lethal injection (U.S. Department of Justice, 1986:4). Electrocution was first used in Auburn Prison in New York, when William Kemmler was put to death on August 6, 1890 (Bedau, 1982:15). Eight states provide lethal gas as a method of execution, with three of the eight states providing the alternative of lethal injection (U.S. Department of Justice, 1986). Death by a lethal dose of cyanide gas was first applied in the execution of Gee Jon in the State of Nevada on February 8, 1924 (Bedau, 1982:16).

Sixteen states allow lethal injection, although seven of these provide alternative methods of execution, such as electrocution, shooting, lethal gas, and hanging (U. S. Department of Justice, 1986). In May 1977, Nevada became the first jurisdiction in the United States to authorize lethal injection as a method of execution (Bedau, 1982:17).

Hanging is authorized in four states, with two of these providing the alternative of lethal injection. Throughout history, hanging has probably been the most widely used method of execution. Two states (Idaho and Utah) make the firing squad a legal method of execution, but offer alternatives such as lethal injection and electrocution (BJS, October 1986).

Many states authorizing lethal injection as a method of punishment provide alternatives because they are fearful that lethal injection may eventually be found unconstitutional. However, all other methods of execution applied in the United States previously challenged on Eighth Amendment grounds of cruel and unusual punishment have been found to be constitutional (BJS, October 1986). Table 7.4 lists method of execution by state.

THE CAPITAL PUNISHMENT CONTROVERSY

Arguments concerning the appropriateness of capital punishment date back to the eighteenth century. In 1764 Cesare Beccaria argued against

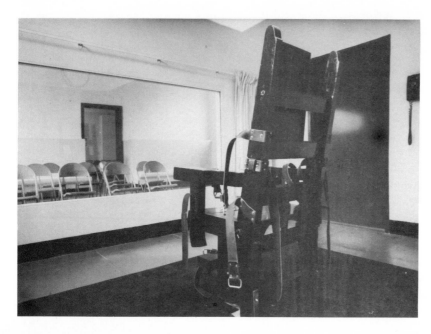

The electric chair, Rockview Correctional Facility. (Pennsylvania Department of Corrections)

TABLE 7.2   Prisoners under Sentence of Death by Region and State, 1985

REGION AND STATE	PRISONERS UNDER SENTENCE 1984	CHANGES DURING 1985			PRISONERS UNDER SENTENCE 1985
		RECEIVED UNDER SENTENCE	REMOVED FROM DEATH ROW (EXCLUDING EXECUTIONS)	EXECUTED	
United States	1,420	273	84[a]	18	1,591
Federal[b]	0	0	0	0	0
State	1,420	273	84	18	1,591
Northeast	59	20	6	0	73
Connecticut	0	0	0	0	0
New Hampshire	0	0	0	0	0
New Jersey	10	7	0	0	17
Pennsylvania	49	13	6	0	56
Vermont	0	0	0	0	0
Midwest	174	54	6	1	221
Illinois	70	15	2	0	83
Indiana	26	10	1	1	34
Missouri	29	8	1	0	36
Nebraska	13	0	1	0	12
Ohio	36	21	1	0	56
South Dakota	0	0	0	0	0
South	900	167	50	16	1,001
Alabama	68	13	2	0	79
Arkansas	23	6	1	0	28
Delaware	6	0	2	0	4
Florida	215	27	13	3	226
Georgia	112	8	10	3	107

capital punishment in his *Dei delitti e delle pene* (On crimes and punishment). Beccaria took a position that was radical for his day; he strongly opposed the use of capital punishment. He stated that the death penalty was neither legitimate nor necessary. He believed that men in forming a social compact did not deposit with the sovereign their right to live. For Beccaria, life was the greatest of all human good; no man willingly gave to another man the authority to deprive him of his life (Mannheim, 1973). Beccaria also felt that the death penalty did not deter. The death of an offender was a passing spectacle, leaving no en-during impression upon those who witnessed the execution. He also stated that the death penalty was unreasonable in that it was an act of barbarity. Its infliction was no more than homicide, even though it was in repayment of homicide (Mannheim, 1973). Arguments for and against the death penalty have continued, with no settlement yet in view.

RETRIBUTION AS A JUSTIFICATION

It is believed by some exponents of the death penalty that retribution in and of itself is suffi-

TABLE 7.2   *(Continued)*

REGION AND STATE	PRISONERS UNDER SENTENCE 1984	CHANGES DURING 1985			PRISONERS UNDER SENTENCE 1985
		RECEIVED UNDER SENTENCE	REMOVED FROM DEATH ROW (EXCLUDING EXECUTIONS)	EXECUTED	
Kentucky	20	6	1	0	25
Louisiana	31	10	1	1	39
Maryland	19	0	2	0	17
Mississippi	39	5	3	0	41
North Carolina	37	20	1	0	56
Oklahoma	50	14	6	0	58
South Carolina	35	9	1	1	42
Tennessee	37	11	2	0	46
Texas	180	36	4	6	206
Virginia	28	2	1	2	27
West	287	32	22	1	296
Arizona	56	4	4	0	56
California	167	16	13	0	170
Colorado	1	0	0	0	1
Idaho	14	1	1	0	14
Montana	4	1	0	0	5
Nevada	28	7	3	1	31
New Mexico	5	0	0	0	5
Oregon	0	0	0	0	0
Utah	5	2	1	0	6
Washington	4	1	0	0	5
Wyoming	3	0	0	0	3

[a] Includes 1 inmate in Ohio who committed suicide, 1 each in Missouri and Tennessee who were murdered by another inmate, and 1 in Louisiana who died of natural causes.

[b] Excludes one male held under Armed Forces jurisdiction with a military death sentence for murder.

SOURCE: Bureau of Justice Statistics *Bulletin. Capital Punishment 1985.* Washington, DC: Bureau of Justice Statistics, 1985, Table 4.

cient justification for taking the life of someone who has committed a crime such as murder. Retributivists argue that it makes no difference whether infliction of the death penalty serves as a general deterrent or is reformative.

All the great philosophers, with the exception of Spinoza, seem to have approved of retribution as a justification of punishment. Philosophers such as Hobbes, Locke, Rousseau, Hegel, and Mill supported the death penalty. Perhaps Immanuel Kant was the most explicit in his defense. Kant stated that a criminal must never be released from punishment, nor must the punish-

ment ever be reduced for reasons concerning the individual or society. The penalty had to fit the crime. If the penalty was death, life imprisonment could not be a substitute:

> If a person commits murder . . . he must die. In this case there is no substitute that will satisfy the requirements of legal justice. There is no sameness of kind between death and remaining alive, under the most miserable of conditions. The judicial authority must will death to the murderer in accordance with universal laws that are grounded *a priori.* (Kant, 1973:37)

TABLE 7.3   Profile of Capital Punishment Statutes and Legal Changes during 1985

JURISDICTIONS AUTHORIZING CAPITAL PUNISHMENT AT SOME TIME DURING 1985	REVISED OR REPLACED BY LEGISLATURE	AUTOMATIC APPEALS REQUIRED	CAPITAL OFFENSES
Federal			Aircraft piracy
Alabama		Yes	Murder
Arizona	Yes	Yes	First degree murder
Arkansas	Yes		Aggravated murder; treason
California		Yes	First degree murder with special circumstances
Colorado	Yes	Yes	First degree murder (includes felony murder); first degree kidnaping
Connecticut	Yes	Yes	Murder
Delaware		Yes	First degree murder with statutory aggravating circumstances
Florida			First degree murder
Georgia		Yes	Murder; treason; aircraft hijacking; kidnaping with bodily injury; armed robbery or rape in which victim dies
Idaho		Yes[a]	First degree murder, aggravated kidnaping (except where victim released unharmed)
Illinois		Yes	Murder
Indiana		Yes	Murder
Kentucky		Yes	Aggravated murder; kidnaping when victim is killed
Louisiana		Yes	First degree murder
Maryland		Yes[a]	First degree murder
Mississippi	Yes	Yes	Capital murder, capital rape
Missouri		Yes	First degree murder
Montana	Yes	Yes	Deliberate homicide, aggravated kidnaping (resulting in death)
Nebraska		Yes	First degree murder
Nevada	Yes	Yes	First degree murder
New Hampshire		Yes	Contract murder or murder of a law enforcement officer or kidnaping victim

If he were alive today, Kant would probably say that even if it were known that a nuclear war would break out tomorrow and our society be destroyed, those awaiting death in prison must first be executed to absolve us of guilt in not carrying out the moral law or our legal duty.

When Adolf Eichmann was executed in Israel for the crime of helping exterminate some 6 million Jews, the authorities were not in the least concerned with whether or not his execution would deter other individuals from committing such a crime. At the time of his arrest, Adolf Eichmann was an old man who had lived peacefully in his community for many years; he was no longer a threat or a danger to anyone. His execution did not protect society from some dangerous criminal. Killing him was unlikely to have had a deterrent effect on any other individual who might ever have a position of power. However, the crimes Eichmann had committed were

TABLE 7.3   *(Continued)*

JURISDICTIONS AUTHORIZING CAPITAL PUNISHMENT AT SOME TIME DURING 1985	REVISED OR REPLACED BY LEGISLATURE	AUTOMATIC APPEALS REQUIRED	CAPITAL OFFENSES
New Jersey	Yes	Yes[b]	Kidnaping or purposeful murder or contract murder with aggravating circumstances
New Mexico		Yes[a]	First degree murder
North Carolina		Yes	First degree murder
Ohio			Aggravated murder
Oklahoma		Yes	Murder
Oregon		Yes	Aggravated murder
Pennsylvania		Yes	First degree murder
South Carolina	Yes	Yes	Murder with statutory aggravating circumstances
South Dakota		Yes	Murder, kidnaping (with gross permanent physical injury inflicted on victim)
Tennessee		Yes	First degree murder
Texas	Yes	Yes	Murder of public safety officer, fireman, or correctional employee; murder during specified felonies or escapes; contract murder; multiple murders
Utah		Yes	First degree murder; aggravated assult by prisoner sentenced for first degree felony where serious injury is caused
Vermont			Murder of police or corrections officer, kidnaping for ransom
Virginia	Yes	Yes	Capital murder
Washington		Yes	Aggravated, premeditated first degree murder
Wyoming		Yes	First degree murder

NOTE: Jurisdictions without capital punishment statutes are: Alaska, District of Columbia, Hawaii, Iowa, Kansas, Maine, Massachusetts, Michigan, Minnesota, New York, North Dakota, Rhode Island, West Virginia, and Wisconsin.

[a] Sentence review only.

[b] Automatic review after January 17, 1986.

SOURCE: Bureau of Justice Statistics *Bulletin. Capital Punishment 1985.* Washington, DC: Bureau of Justice Statistics, Table 1.

so repugnant and heinous that the government of Israel felt retribution in the form of the death penalty was the only possible sentence that could be handed down. It is quite easy to find sympathy for this point of view in the case of Eichmann. Other heinous crimes, although not committed on such a grand scale, evoke similar feelings on the part of individuals.

Retributivists believe there is no crime more repugnant than murder. Since murder differs from other crimes in both magnitude and kind, it ought to be punished in a different manner than other offenses. In order to balance the scales of justice, the punishment for murder should be death. Further, those supporting the death penalty on the grounds of retribution feel that retribution is part of the nature of human beings and that the death penalty serves the important function of allowing individuals to express their outrage and frustration through the criminal justice system.

TABLE 7.4   Method of Execution by State, 1984

METHOD	STATES THAT USE METHOD
Electrocution	Alabama, Arkansas,* Connecticut, Florida, Georgia, Indiana, Kentucky, Louisiana, Nebraska, Ohio, Oklahoma,* Pennsylvania, South Carolina, Tennessee, Vermont, Virginia
Lethal injection	Arkansas,* Idaho,* Illinois, Mississippi,* Montana,* Nevada, New Jersey, New Mexico, North Carolina,* Oklahoma,* Oregon, South Dakota, Texas, Utah,* Washington*
Lethal gas	Arizona, California, Colorado, Maryland, Mississippi,* Missouri, North Carolina,* Wyoming*
Hanging	Delaware, Montana,* New Hampshire, Washington*
Firing squad	Idaho,* Utah*

* Provide two methods of execution.

SOURCE: Bureau of Justice Statistics *Bulletin. Capital Punishment 1983*. Washington, DC: Bureau of Justice Statistics, 1984, Table 3.

Those who argue against the death penalty state that very few individuals who commit such crimes as murder receive the death penalty. Since the great majority of offenders who commit serious crimes do not receive the death sentence, the retribution factor is a meaningless gesture applied to a very few. However, the supporters of retribution could counter, along with van den Haag (1982) that never to execute a person who commits a serious and heinous crime is to proclaim that no human being can commit a crime so repugnant as to be deprived of life. Society, according to van den Haag, affirms its values through the types and degrees of punishments it proclaims for certain offenses. The refusal to punish any crime with death is to imply that the negative weight of a crime can never exceed the positive value of the life of the person who committed it. For example, can the negative weight of the assassination of John F. Kennedy exceed the positive value of the life of assassin Lee Harvey Oswald to a degree to justify the death penalty in this case?

Is the argument from retribution a purely philosophical or metaphysical argument that cannot be settled through any kind or amount of empirical data, or is there some foundation for using retribution as a justification for punishment in the very nature of human beings? Can it be said that retribution is bad in and of itself? Is there some mysterious moral law denouncing the application of retribution as a reason for punishment? These are questions that have yet to be answered.

DETERRENCE AS A JUSTIFICATION

There is no question as to whether the death penalty acts as a specific (individual) deterrent. A person once executed will never again commit another crime. The deterrence argument questions whether or not the death penalty acts as a general deterrent. Does the execution of a few individuals instill a fear in the general public sufficient to keep them from committing a capital offense? Unfortunately, up to this time all the data available concerning the deterrent effect of capital punishment on the general public have been inconclusive.

Much research has been conducted to discover whether or not the death penalty has as much deterrent value as the prospect of spending a lifetime in prison. The early findings of Thorsten Sellin indicated that the threat of the death penalty was not a better deterrent than the threat of long-term imprisonment (Sellin, 1980). New research by Isaac Ehrlich, using econometric methods, found that an additional execution per year during 1933 to 1969 may have resulted, on the average, in seven to eight fewer murders (Ehrlich, 1975:414). Ehrlich made another study in 1977 in which he examined cross-sectional data for 1940 and for 1950. He came to the same conclusions as in his earlier study—deterrence works. Ehrlich's results have been reviewed by several other investigators using essentially his methods and identical or comparable data. Both of Ehrlich's studies have been thoroughly discredited by other researchers in the field (Klein et al., 1982).

A study resulting in different findings from those of Ehrlich was made by William C. Bailey (Bailey, 1983:827–859). He concluded that to some degree, and for some segment of the population, executions may deter killings. Conversely, to some degree, and for some segment of the population, executions may encourage killings. The new effect of executions may well have been to increase first degree murders and total criminal homicides.

Archer, Gartner, and Beittel, taking a cross-national sample, found that abolition of the death penalty was followed, more often than not, by absolute decreases in homicide rates. The authors looked at Austria, Canada, Denmark, England, Finland, Israel, Italy, The Netherlands, Antilles, New Zealand, Norway, Sweden, and Switzerland and found that the evidence is against capital punishment as a deterring agent (1983:991–1013).

Sam G. McFarland conducted a study to discover whether or not capital punishment acted as a short-term deterrent to homicide in the United States (1983:1014–1032). His study examined possible short-term effects after the first five executions which took place at the ending of the ten-year moratorium on the death penalty. Each of these executions received extensive news coverage. The study failed to find any evidence that capital punishment served as a short-term deterrent or had a rebound effect on homicide.

Studies have been conducted to determine whether capital punishment will deter a prisoner convicted of murder or serving a life sentence for some other crime from killing another inmate or a correctional worker. No research has shown that the threat of capital punishment will necessarily

deter an inmate from committing murder while in prison. It appears, from an analysis of contemporary studies, that the correctional personnel in prisons are not protected by capital punishment sanctions. Usually prison homicide is spontaneous, usually provoked by an altercation or precipitated by the victim. A prisoner is not likely to consider the risk of apprehension and threat of punishment at the time of the offense, as these notions are for him distant and abstract (Wolfson, 1982:159–173). Studies also indicate that police officers are no better protected by a statutory provision for capital punishment than they are by a threat of life imprisonment (Bedau, 1982:99–100).

The research to date that seeks to determine whether or not capital punishment deters in and of itself, or has more value as a deterrent than the threat of life imprisonment, does not give conclusive answers. The findings do not strongly favor either side and therefore cannot resolve the fundamental dispute over whether to favor or oppose the death penalty on deterrent grounds. Richard Lempert argues that we probably will be unable to find a conclusive answer as to whether capital punishment deters through recent research or in research likely to be done in the near future (1983:1101–1104).

Even if science could answer this question, would the debate about the death penalty fade away? Probably not. If it could be shown, without doubt, that the death penalty deters, most abolitionists would still be against it on moral, religious, or humanistic grounds. On the other hand, if all the evidence showed that capital punishment did not deter, many of those who support it would still do so on retributive grounds.

IS THE DEATH PENALTY ARBITRARY?

One of the major arguments against the death penalty is that it has been applied inconsistently and unfairly for such crimes as murder and rape. The Supreme Court took this argument into consideration in *Furman* v. *Georgia* (1972), and attempted through this and later cases to make the imposition of the death penalty fair and consistent. Has the Supreme Court achieved this goal?

Supreme Court decisions in the 1970s established that the Eighth and Fourteenth Amendments require fairness and consistency in capital sentencing. Pascussi, Strauss, and Watchman state that there are two methods by which states can attain fairness and consistency in application of the death penalty. One method is for the state to provide detailed statutory sentencing guidelines for judges and juries. Another method is to provide for appellate review of death sentences. A third remedy is provided by federal *habeas corpus* (Pascussi et al., 1984:1132–1133). In the case of *Furman* v. *Georgia* (1972), the Supreme Court ruled that ungoverned sentencing discretion in cases where the death penalty is applied violates the Eighth and Fourteenth Amendments (Pascussi et al., 1984:1134). However, the Court later rejected the other extreme of mandatory sentences for certain crimes.

In the cases of *Woodson et al.* v. *North Carolina* (1976) and *Roberts* v. *Louisiana* (1977), the Court held that mandatory death penalties for murder are unconstitutional. Even though a state has objective standards to guide, regularize, and make rationally reviewable the process for imposing a sentence of death, the state must also provide standards to guide the jury in the exercise of its power to determine which murderers shall live and which shall die.

Recent cases (after 1977) have been allowing more discretion again, thus shifting away from *Furman* v. *Georgia*. Most post-*Furman* statutes include a list of aggravating circumstances and allow the sentencing authority to impose the death sentence only if it finds at least one such circumstance. Most states also provide a list of mitigating factors (Pascussi et al., 1984:1135). In 1983, the Supreme Court upheld death sentences in which one of the aggravating circumstances involved was invalid (*Zant* v. *Stephens*, 1983).

Pascussi, Strauss, and Watchman argue that the Supreme Court has strayed away from *Furman* in recent years (1984:1138).

By tolerating death penalty statutes that provide greater capital sentencing discretion, while also restricting a condemned person's opportunity for meaningful appellate review, the court has paved the way for procedural schemes that violate the 8th and 14th amendments' demand for fair and consistent capital sentencing guidelines.

They further argue that increased discretion of the sort that allows for consideration of invalid aggravating circumstances "increases the likelihood of capital sentencing errors that result in unconstitutional executions" (1984:1215). It is questionable, therefore, whether new capital sentencing statutes that permit great discretion once the prosecutor has established a statutory aggravating circumstance provide "no more guidance than the death penalty statutes struck down in *Furman*" (1984:1215).

DISCRIMINATION AND THE DEATH PENALTY

Are the poor and black who are found guilty of murder more likely to be executed than the equally guilty rich and white? Although blacks represent approximately 11 percent of the population of the United States, blacks, as of December 20, 1986, represent 41.62 percent of inmates presently on death row awaiting execution (NAACP, 1986). As of April 22, 1986, 3,915 executions have been carried out in the United States since 1930 (BJS, October 1986). Of this number, 50 percent have been black or members of other minority groups (NAACP, 1986). All those presently sentenced to death have been convicted of murder. Wolfgang and Riedel state that of 455 individuals executed for rape since 1930, 89.5 percent have been nonwhite (1982:194). These differential rates by themselves are incomplete methods of exposing elements of judicial bias in the administration of criminal law. Blacks appear to have a criminal homicide rate between four and ten times that of whites (Wolfgang and Riedel, 1982:194). The question that is of interest here is whether, among individuals who have been convicted of capital crimes, a statistically significant higher proportion of blacks are differentially sentenced to death.

According to Bowers and Pierce (1982:208), "by far the most substantial and consistent extralegal basis of differential treatment under pre-*Furman* statutes was race." Under post-*Furman* statutes, the findings are similar. Black killers and killers of whites are substantially more likely than others to receive a death sentence in such states as Florida, Georgia, Texas, and Ohio (Bowers and Pierce, 1982:210). (Table 7.5 shows executions since 1977 by race of defendant and victim.) Further, "among the killers of whites, blacks are five times more likely than whites to be sentenced to death" (Bowers and Pierce, 1982:210). Bowers and Pierce conclude that (1982:220):

> . . . race is truly a pervasive influence on the criminal justice processing of potentially capital cases. . . . It is an influence revealed not only in the movement from one stage to the next, but also in the decisions about circumstances accompanying charges, and sentencing findings within the respective stages of the process. And it is an influence that persists despite separate sentencing hearings, explicitly articulated sentencing guidelines, and automatic appellate review of all death sentences. . . .

Based upon a refined statistical analysis of rape convictions where rape has been an offense punishable by death, Wolfgang and Riedel showed that "there has been a patterned, systematic, and customary imposition of the death penalty. . . . Sentences of death have been imposed on blacks, compared to whites, in a way that exceeds any notion of fortuity" (1982:205).

In an empirical study of 300 homicide cases involving an aggravating felony in South Carolina from June 1977 to December 1981, Raymond Paternoster found that race of the victim was significantly related to the decision of the prosecutor to seek the death penalty (1984:437, 438). In South Carolina, the prosecutor has unbridled discretion in whether or not to seek the death

penalty. Black killers of whites were more likely to get the death penalty than black killers of blacks. When homicide victims were black, a death penalty was requested only when the crime crossed a threshold of aggravation that was higher than that found in white homicide (Paternoster, 1984).

Ernest van den Haag has argued that no injustice is done by executing a black man for murder just because a white man has escaped punishment (van den Haag, 1985:38–42). He states that even if the death penalty is "capriciously distributed among the guilty as though by lottery," the guilt of those selected by the lottery is not diminished because others were not selected (1985). He implies that the solution to this problem is to try harder to catch and execute more whites who commit murder.

In the recent case of *Sullivan* v. *Wainwright* (1983), the Supreme Court would not grant a stay of execution to review a claim that the death penalty discriminated against blacks. The reason given was that the case had been in litigation for a full decade and had been reviewed carefully many times by state and federal courts.

In an even more recent case (*McClesky* v. *Kemp,* 1985), the Federal Court of Appeals in Atlanta rejected charges that Georgia's death penalty was racially discriminatory. The Appeals Court held that, unless statistical statewide studies reflected a disparity so great as to compel the conclusion that there was systematic discrimination, only proof of deliberate racial prejudice in a particular case would demonstrate a constitutional violation.

MISCARRIAGE OF JUSTICE AND THE DEATH PENALTY

Opponents of the death penalty have voiced a great deal of concern over the possibility that an innocent person may be put to death. From the period 1930 through 1980, there were miscarriages of justice in capital cases in at least 124 cases (Bedau, 1982:234). As a result, eight innocent people were executed. The last execution

TABLE 7.5 Executions since 1977, by Race of Defendant and Victim

DATE	DEFENDANT	STATE	RACE	RACE OF VICTIM(S)
1/17/77	* Gary Gilmore	UT	W	W
5/25/79	John Spenkelink	FL	W	W
10/22/79	* Jesse Bishop	NV	W	W
3/9/81	* Steven Judy	IN	W	W
8/10/82	* Frank Coppols	VA	W	W
12/7/82	Charlie Brooks	TX	B	W
4/22/83	John Evans	AL	W	W
9/2/83	Jimmy Lee Gray	MS	W	W
11/30/83	Robert Sullivan	FL	W	W
12/14/83	Robert Wayne Williams	LA	B	B
12/15/83	John Eldon Smith	GA	W	W
1/26/84	Anthony Antone	FL	W	W
2/29/84	John Taylor	LA	B	W
3/14/84	James Autry	TX	W	W
3/16/84	James Hutchins	NC	W	W
3/31/84	Ronald O'Bryan	TX	W	W
4/5/84	Arthur Goode	FL	W	W
4/5/84	Elmo Sonnier	LA	W	W
5/10/84	James Adams	FL	B	W
6/20/84	Carl Shriner	FL	W	W
7/12/84	Ivon Stanley	GA	B	W
7/13/84	David Washington	FL	B	W/B
9/7/84	Ernest Dobbert	FL	W	W
9/10/84	Timothy Baldwin	LA	W	W
9/20/84	James Henry	FL	B	B
10/12/84	Linwood Briley	VA	B	W
10/30/84	Thomas Barefoot	TX	W	W
10/30/84	Ernest Knighton	LA	B	W
11/2/84	Velma Barfield	NC	W	W
11/8/84	Timothy Palmes	FL	W	W
12/12/84	Alpha Otis Stephens	GA	B	W
12/28/84	Robert Lee Willie	LA	W	W
1/4/85	David Martin	LA	W	W
1/9/85	Roosevelt Green	GA	B	W
1/11/85	Joseph Carl Shaw	SC	W	W
1/16/85	Doyle Skillern	TX	W	W
1/30/85	James Raulerson	FL	W	W

of an allegedly innocent person was in the 1930s. The proponents of the death penalty argue that the eight wrongful executions out of several thousand supports the contention that the system under which the death penalty is applied is reliable and nearly infallible. However, the eight wrongful deaths do not include instances where an individual on death row was spared through luck and favorable circumstances.

There have been some notorious miscarriages of justice, such as in the Mooney case in California and the Scottsboro Boys case in Alabama (Bedau, 1982:234). There are highly controversial cases where presumption of error is based on

TABLE 7.5   *(Continued)*

DATE	DEFENDANT	STATE	RACE	RACE OF VICTIM(S)
2/20/85	Van Roosevelt Solomon	GA	B	W
3/6/85	Johnny Paul Witt	FL	W	W
3/13/85	* Stephen Peter Morin	TX	W	W
3/20/85	John Young	GA	B	W
4/18/85	James Briley	VA	B	B
5/15/85	Jesse de la Rosa	TX	H	W
5/29/85	Marvin Francois	FL	B	B
6/25/85	Charles Milton	TX	B	B
6/25/85	Morris Mason	VA	B	W
7/9/85	Henry Martinez Porter	TX	H	W
9/11/85	* Charles Rumbaugh	TX	W	W
10/16/85	* William Vandiver	IN	W	W
12/6/85	* Carroll Cole	NV	W	W
1/10/86	James Terry Roach	SC	W	W
3/12/86	Charles William Bass	TX	W	W
3/21/86	Arthur Lee Jones	AL	B	B
4/15/86	Daniel Thomas	FL	B	W
4/16/86	* Jeffrey Allen Barney	TX	W	W
4/22/86	David Funchess	FL	B	W
5/15/86	Jay Pinkerton	TX	W	W
5/20/86	Ronald Straight	FL	W	W
6/9/86	Rudy Esquivel	TX	H	W
6/18/86	Kenneth Brock	TX	W	W
6/24/86	Jerome Bowden	GA	B	W
7/31/86	Michael Smith	VA	B	W
8/20/86	Randy Woolls	TX	W	W
8/22/86	Larry Smith	TX	B	W
8/26/86	Chester Wicker	TX	W	W
9/19/86	John Rook	NC	W	W
12/4/86	Michael Wayne Evans	TX	B	H
12/18/86	Richard Andrade	TX	H	H
1/30/87	* Ramon Hernandez	TX	H	H

Total executions to date: 69

* = Voluntary.
SOURCE: NAACP Legal Defense and Educational Fund, Inc., *Death Row, U.S.A.*, New York, March 1, 1987.

suspicion, such as those of Julius and Ethel Rosenberg in New York (espionage), the Haupmann case (the alleged Lindberg baby kidnapper now thought to be innocent), and Sacco and Vanzetti (convicted of murder). There are other lesser-known individuals who have been executed wrongfully, or who have been able to escape ex-ecution only because of the help of concerned and determined investigators.

For those already executed, it is very difficult to set the record straight. It is true that in most of the 124 miscarriages of justice, convictions were ultimately reversed and the person's life was spared. It is a well-known fact, however, that wrongful convictions do happen, and perhaps more individuals have been wrongfully executed than we will ever know. Although it seems apparent that no person has been executed recently because of errors of justice, the possibility always remains.

Van den Haag, in reference to the irrevocable nature of the death penalty, states: "But in the long run nearly all human activities are likely to lead to the unintended death of innocents" (van den Haag, 1985:42). He cites, for example, truck driving and even golfing. He argues that the death penalty's usefulness "outweighs the harm done by the miscarriage" (1985:42). The question still remains as to whether or not the death penalty should be eliminated because miscarriages of justice sometimes take place.

IS THE DEATH PENALTY IMMORAL?

To demonstrate that the death penalty is immoral it would be necessary to show that absolute or intrinsic moral standards exist by which we can be guided. This is a philosophical issue that has never been resolved. Is there some Kantian categorical imperative, some Platonic form of good, or some other type of religious or metaphysical objective moral law or standard by which we may evaluate the behavior of people? Are all value judgments reducible to assertions or expressions of preference and therefore relative to an individual's feelings and pronouncements? Those who argue that the death penalty is immoral believe they can justify their belief on metaphysical or religious grounds. Actually, Kant, as we have seen, based his justification for capital punishment on the basis of a moral universal law which required that retributive action be taken for committing a crime.

The question of whether or not we can justify abolishing capital punishment on moral grounds is not a scientific one, but a moral judgment. No amount of empirical data will tell us whether or not capital punishment is immoral or whether or not human life is sacred.

IS THE DEATH PENALTY CRUEL AND UNUSUAL PUNISHMENT?

The United States Constitution and the Bill of Rights take for granted that life may be forfeited by punishment (Bedau, 1982:247). Further, the Eighth Amendment to the Constitution prohibiting cruel and unusual punishment was adopted when the death penalty was lawful punishment for many crimes. The issue of cruelty in regard to the death penalty was first questioned by the Supreme Court in 1878, in the case of *Wilkerson* v. *Utah*. In examining whether or not it was cruel in the State of Utah to punish premeditated murder by shooting the murderer at a public execution, the Court ruled that it was not cruel in the context of the times when frontier practices were in vogue. The issue of cruel and unusual punishment was brought up again in the case of *in re Kemmler* (1890) in which the Supreme Court found that it was not cruel and unusual punishment for New York State to use the electric chair as a mode of execution.

In many cases involving the death penalty, the Supreme Court has refused to intervene at all. Finally, in 1972, in the case of *Furman* v. *Georgia*, the Supreme Court found, in a five to four decision, that the death penalty as then administered, with trial juries free to sentence to death or life without any standards or guidelines to help them make rational and uniform sentencing choices, was "cruel and unusual punishment in violation of the Eighth and Fourteenth Amendments." The Court felt that in the arbitrary manner in which the death sentence was administered at the time, the punishment did not serve any legitimate social purpose such as deterrence or retribution any better than a less severe punishment.

It should be noted that prior to *Furman* v. *Georgia*, lower courts had held that the death penalty was cruel and unusual. The Federal Circuit Court of Maryland found in the case of *Ralph* v. *Warden* (1970) that it was cruel and unusual punishment to apply the death penalty in the case of rape. The California State Supreme Court held in the case of *People* v. *Anderson* (1972) that the death penalty was cruel and unusual punishment in violation of the Constitution of the State of California.

After the Furman decision there was much controversy among the various states. Many legislatures redrafted and reenacted death penalty statutes that they believed would meet the requirements of the Fourteenth Amendment. They passed death penalty legislation making the penalty mandatory or a consequence of guided discretion (Bedau, 1982). In *Woodson* v. *North Carolina* (1976), the Supreme Court held that state laws that make the death penalty mandatory for first-degree murder are unconstitutional. In *Roberts* v. *Louisiana* (1977), the Court held that making the death penalty mandatory for the killing of a police officer during the performance of his or her duties was unconstitutional.

In the case of *Gregg* v. *Georgia* (1976), the Supreme Court found that the death penalty is not in itself cruel and unusual punishment. It further argued that a two-part proceeding, one for the determination of innocence and/or guilt, and the other for determining the sentence, is constitutional and meets the requirements of the Fourteenth Amendment. The Court's ruling required the judge or jury to consider any aggravating or mitigating circumstances in life-death decisions and to identify at least one aggravating factor before imposing the death penalty. The Court felt that this ruling would channel the jury's discretion so that it could no longer impose death "wantonly and freakishly" (*Gregg* v. *Georgia*, 1976). In recent years the Supreme Court has tolerated death penalty statutes that provide capital sentencing discretion, while at the same time restricting a condemned person's opportunity for appellate review.

In cases where homicide was not a factor, the Supreme Court has not been so supportive. The Court ruled in *Coker* v. *Georgia* (1977) that the death penalty was not appropriate for rape, and in *Eberheart* v. *Georgia* (1977) that the death sentence for kidnapping was not proportionate to the crime.

CAPITAL PUNISHMENT AND THE JUVENILE OFFENDER

"On September 11, 1985 in Texas, Charles Rumbaugh became the first juvenile offender to be executed in the United States since 1964. . . . Two more juveniles were executed in 1986. Both were seventeen years of age when their crimes were committed" (Amnesty International, 1987). As of October 1986, at least 32 juvenile offenders were under sentence of death in fifteen states for crimes they committed when they were between 15 and 17 years of age (Amnesty International, 1987). These offenders were sentenced to death for murder, usually in connection with some other crime (*Parade* Magazine, 1986). Several have spent more than eight years on death row (Amnesty International, 1987). Should juvenile offenders be subjected to capital punishment? In 1983, the American Bar Association officially opposed subjecting juvenile offenders to this penalty. The Supreme Court has felt it appropriate to consider whether or not the execution of minors is contrary to the United States Constitution. No decision has yet been forthcoming.

Throughout its history, the United States has executed 281 juvenile offenders (*Parade* Magazine, 1986). A juvenile is usually specified as someone under the age of eighteen. A total of 23 states specify a minimum age at which the death penalty may be imposed. The most frequently specified minimum age for receiving the death penalty is 18 (9 states). Fourteen states specifically set the minimum age for receiving the sentence of death under the age of 18. For example, 10-year-olds can be subjected to capital punishment in Indiana and Vermont, and 13-year-olds can receive the death penalty in Georgia and Mississippi. Fourteen states and the federal system have no minimum age at which a person can be executed (U.S. Department of Justice, 1986).

Some of those who oppose the execution of juvenile offenders do so on the grounds that, because of their youthful age, they can still be rehabilitated. Children appear to be more malleable than adults and are therefore treatable (*Pa-*

rade Magazine, 1986). Further, children and adolescents are more liable than adults to act on impulse, without thought of the long-range consequences of their actions. They also tend to act under the influence of others (Amnesty International, 1987).

Should we protect juvenile offenders from the death penalty because of reasons similar to those mentioned above? This is a question that is currently at issue in the United States. Elsewhere, "more than 40 countries that retain the death penalty have statutes specifically prohibiting the imposition of the death sentence on people who are under eighteen at the time of the crime" (Amnesty International, 1987).

IS THE DEATH PENALTY ECONOMICAL?

Most people believe that execution is far less expensive than maintaining a prisoner behind bars for life. Upon further examination, however, it can be shown that the judicial and correctional process would be less expensive without the death penalty (Nakell, 1982:241). The trial process is more expensive in a capital case. All capital cases require jury trials, and the trials are longer and more complex than those in other cases. Most defendants will not plead guilty to capital murder unless it is a result of making some sort of deal with a prosecutor (Nakell, 1982). Even for those who do plead guilty, a jury trial still must be held on the penalty issue.

Normally, capital cases will automatically be appealed to the state supreme court. In a recent case, the United States Supreme Court ruled that there is a right to review of sentence in every death penalty case before the sentence is carried out. Persons cannot be executed before the review is completed (*U.S.* v. *McDonald*, 1984).

These appeals are usually more complex and expensive than other types of appeals. Appeals are usually carried to the United States Supreme Court for review. Postconviction petitions can be filed in the state courts, *habeas corpus* petitions filed in the federal courts, and governors asked for commutation. The expense involved in all this is enormous (Nakell, 1982:243–245). For example, it is estimated that in the case of Caryl Chessman, the State of California spent more than half a million dollars over many years during the appeals process prior to his execution (Inciardi, 1984). In the 78 days preceding Gary Gilmore's death, it cost the State of Utah at least $98,568: "Over $60,000 to keep him alive during his suicide attempts and another $18,330 for convalescent care, $19,000 in overtime payments for secretaries and deputies on execution day, $513 for a charter flight to Denver where a last minute stay of execution was overturned, and $725 to pay for a six man firing squad" (Inciardi, 1984).

The cost to the prison system is also significant. Prisoners under sentence of death must be maintained in a special area of a maximum security prison with special security precautions and under 24-hour surveillance. The expense of administering a death row unit is substantially greater than the cost of retaining a person in prison for the remainder of his or her natural life (Nakell, 1982:245). One expert has argued that a lifer in prison who can learn a trade and become an efficient worker in prison industries would eventually pay for his own subsistence.

It seems evident that executing an offender under our present system is not necessarily cheaper than imprisoning an individual for life.

JURY SELECTION AND THE DEATH PENALTY

Does the exclusion of jurors with anti-capital punishment sentiment lead to a conviction-prone jury? Many scholars feel that it does (Haney, 1984a). Craig Haney states that dismissing prospective jurors in a capital case because they are opposed to the death penalty can result in the jury forming expectations in their minds that the law disapproves of death penalty opposition,

Death row inmates. (David Burnett/Woodfin Camp & Associates)

which can result in their voting for the death penalty in certain cases (1984:122). An empirical study by Haney supports the notion that the "death qualification" is a biasing process. There is also a recent argument that a defendant is being denied his constitutional rights by denying jury status to those who voice opposition to the death penalty.

Prior to the case of *Wainwright* v. *Witt* (1985), the standard often relied upon for excluding jurors from capital cases was whether or not the juror made it clear that he or she would automatically vote against the death penalty. The Supreme Court dispensed with this requirement in *Wainwright* v. *Witt*, and held that the proper standard is whether a juror's views would prevent or substantially impair the performance of his or her duties as a juror in accordance with the instructions and oath.

DEATH ROW AS CRUEL AND UNUSUAL PUNISHMENT

There are those who believe that being on **death row** itself constitutes cruel and unusual punishment. Inmates on death row are housed in separate sections of maximum security institutions. They are isolated from the general population, and, to a large extent, from one another. They are denied participation in prison programs and have few of the privileges most inmates take for granted. They sometimes are treated with disrespect by correctional officers guarding them, as well as by other prison employees, including the chaplain. They are under 24-hour surveillance and live in an environment of drab and boring isolation. Because these conditions can continue for many years, they can be a kind of living death.

The death row in Alabama's Holman Prison and the condemned who live in it have been studied by Robert Johnson (1980:545–562). He described the physical setting of death row:

> [A]s intimidating . . . like a tomb. Even communication between tiers in the same cell block is ruled out. . . . In a sense, each tier is a miniature death row, with its own prison population, social climate, cultural history and character . . . the cells are narrow and close; even the toilets are small and cramped, little more than metal pipes wedged into the cell floors, which flush poorly and resist attempts at cleaning. (1980:546–547)

In regard to programs and privileges in the Holman death row, he reported (1980:549–550):

> Custodial regulations include restrictions on mail, visitation, and other intrusions from the outside world . . . purchases from the store are limited to one day a week and are carefully monitored by the staff . . . they are restricted to one hour per month on contact visitation. . . . The condemned prisoner spends twenty-three and one-half hours alone in the cell punctuated by thirty minutes of private exercise in a closely guarded outside cage.

He described the security as tight and oppressive. The guards were abusive and continually tormented the weaker, disturbed, or shy inmates. Medical care was difficult to obtain, and doctors treated the inmates with indifference. Psychological treatment was largely unavailable. The prison ministers treated death row prisoners in the same perfunctory manner as did the guards (Johnson, 1980:552–553).

A class action lawsuit has been filed by ten inmates on death row at the State Correctional Institution at Graterford, Pennsylvania, contending that the restrictive conditions constitute cruel and unusual punishment (Woestendiek, 1986). Neil Ferber, a former inmate on the Graterford death row for fourteen months prior to his being released from prison, stated that on death row "you lose all emotion . . . and there are times you just think you're going to explode inside, just going to crack up." He described the cells on death row as "poorly ventilated, saying they get so hot in the summer 'that you couldn't lay down on the bed' and so cold in the winter that 'you just didn't want to get out from under the covers.'" He stated that he was hospitalized for psychiatric treatment after his release from Graterford and "claims to still hear the noises of death row and sometimes sees a blank wall before him" (Woestendiek, 1986).

There are now over 1,700 men and women on death row in the United States, and the number continually grows. Nobody in the field of the administration of justice seems to know what to do about the backlog or the imminent executions of the future. Many correctional systems are not equipped to handle the death row bulge efficiently and effectively.

SUMMARY

1. The death penalty has been applied as a method of punishment from primitive times to the present. Perhaps the application of the death penalty reached its peak during the nineteenth century in England, when over 220 offenses were punishable by death. Since that time the death penalty has been abolished in England and limited to the most serious offenses in the United States.

2. There was a moratorium on the death penalty in the United States from 1967 until the execution of Gary Gilmore in 1977. Since that time, 69 individuals have been put to death. There are pres-

ently 1,874 inmates on death row awaiting execution, and 37 jurisdictions in the United States with capital punishment statutes. The death penalty is still provided by law in over 100 countries. The methods of execution at present consist of beheading, electrocution, hanging, shooting, lethal gas, and lethal injection.

3. Arguments for and against the death penalty focus mainly on retribution and deterrence. Those favoring the death penalty feel that it acts as a general deterrent to murder and further believe that retribution in and of itself is sufficient justification for capital punishment. Opponents of the death penalty believe that it cannot be justified on retributive grounds, and further argue that capital punishment does not act as a general deterrent to murder. Opponents argue that the death penalty has been applied inconsistently and unfairly, discriminates against minority races and the poor, and is immoral. The United States Supreme Court in *Furman* v. *Georgia* attempted to make the death penalty fair and consistent by providing statutory sentencing guidelines for judges and juries. This attempt has not been altogether successful.

4. In *Gregg* v. *Georgia*, the Supreme Court ruled that the death penalty is not in itself cruel and unusual punishment. The Court advocated a two-part proceeding, one for the determination of guilt or innocence, and the other to determine the sentence. The Court's ruling also required the judge and jury to consider any aggravating or mitigating circumstances in life and death decisions.

5. Whether or not juvenile offenders should be subjected to the death penalty is presently a major issue in the United States. The United States Supreme Court is reviewing this issue, and a decision should be forthcoming as to whether or not the execution of minors is contrary to the Constitution.

6. It appears that the execution of offenders under our present system is more expensive than imprisoning an individual for life. The automatic appeals that follow a conviction in which the death penalty is pronounced and the maintenance of a death row are very expensive. Some inmates sentenced to death believe that the maintenance of a death row in and of itself constitutes cruel and unusual punishment.

KEY WORDS

CAPITAL PUNISHMENT. The imposition of the death penalty for an offender convicted of a capital offense.

DEATH ROW. Cell blocks in prisons housing inmates convicted of capital crimes and sentenced to death.

PROJECTS AND QUESTIONS

1. Can the death penalty be justified on the basis of retribution alone? Do certain individuals commit crimes so heinous that they deserve to die whether or not their execution acts as a general deterrent? In your answer, consider cases such as that of Adolf Eichmann, mentioned in this chapter.

2. If you were arguing for the abolition of capital punishment, which argument, of the several discussed in the chapter, do you think is most effective? Why?

3. If you were opposed to the execution of juvenile offenders, how would you reply to the following statement by Ernest van den Haag? "I see no reason why juveniles should not be executed. Ei-

ther a convict is competent (legally responsible) and knew what he was doing, or he is not. If he is competent, I do not believe his age should make any difference." In answering this question, take into consideration that in some states children as young as 10 can be subjected to the death penalty.

4. Jack Savage was convicted of first degree murder after killing his wife in a heated argument concerning her infidelity. He has never been arrested before for anything other than a traffic offense. He is thought of by his neighbors as a good member of the community and is described as an excellent father to his children. Assume, for the purposes of this case, that we are at a stage in knowledge

of human behavior that we can predict without error that Jack will never again commit a crime of violence. Assume further that the sentencing guidelines allow Jack to be sentenced to anything from probation to life imprisonment or death. Would you agree to his being released on supervised probation at the time of sentencing, without being ordered to serve any time in jail or prison? Why or why not?

5. As a project, invite two professionals in the field of criminal justice, one opposed to and the other in favor of capital punishment (for example, a member of the district attorney's office and an attorney for the ACLU), to come to your class in order to lead a discussion on the issue of whether or not the death penalty should be retained in the United States. Have a member of your class act as the moderator. Encourage class members to participate in the debate and challenge the professionals.

ADDITIONAL READING

Thorsten Sellin, ed. *Capital Punishment*. New York: AMS Press, Inc., 1967. This is a classic collection of articles concerned with the death penalty. Thorsten Sellin is one of the most prominent scholars of capital punishment. The articles in this book examine capital punishment from ancient Rome to contemporary America.

Hugo Adam Bedau, ed. *The Death Penalty in America*, 3rd ed. New York: Oxford University Press, 1982. This book attempts to bring together as much as possible the results of the best social science research on capital punishment. It is a collection of essays that cover all areas of the capital punishment controversy and one of the most comprehensive books in the field.

Arthur Koestler. *Reflections on Hanging*. New York: AMS Press, Inc., 1957. A historical account of capital punishment in nineteenth-century England during the era of the "bloody code." This book is a devastating attack on capital punishment and contributed to reform of the British criminal code.

Clinton T. Duffy. *88 Men and 2 Women*. New York: AMS Press Inc., 1962. The former warden of California's San Quentin prison describes the condemned men and women he encountered there, including Caryl Chessman. The title refers to the 90 individuals who were executed under Duffy's supervision. Duffy makes a case against the death penalty.

CHAPTER

8 PROBATION SUPERVISION

QUESTIONS

1. Why is probation currently in crisis?

2. How did probation develop?

3. What kinds of activities do probation departments perform?

4. What are the two major debates about the administrative location of probation?

5. What is the care vs. control debate?

6. Why is risk assessment becoming important to probation?

7. What is intensive supervision?

"IT WAS A SETUP!"

One morning, Phil walked into Helping Hand, the new Madison halfway house, to drop off some forms. He found the new director gloating over a newspaper story. Sherry North handed the paper to Phil. The front page news in the local section was headlined: "Probationer Absconds From Experimental Program."

Judge Harold McGraw informed the *Madison Current* this morning that his first placement in a new probation program has apparently gone awry. The judge reported that Martin Jackson, just convicted of burglary, has absconded from his presentence residential placement at Project Thrive, a local program for youthful offenders. McGraw had ordered Jackson to report directly to Project Thrive for a 30-day trial period

while Judge McGraw considered sentencing options. If Jackson had obeyed the regulations for 30 days, there was a good chance the judge would have accepted a probation recommendation, even though Jackson was convicted of a felony.

This presentence placement is part of a new program, Project CRISP, designed by the Madison Probation Office. According to probation spokeswoman Jenny Hague, CRISP stands for Community Restraint through Intensive Supervision Probation. "CRISP is designed to keep some low-risk property offenders away from the crowded prison system, while providing them with a tough and rigorous community sentence," said Ms. Hague. Under CRISP guidelines, a convicted felon who appears eligible will be placed on intensive supervision status during the 30 days between conviction and sentencing. If the probation report is favorable, the department recommends to the judge that the client be kept in the community under intensive supervision. Ms. Hague pointed out that Project Thrive is not directly related to Project CRISP. "That's a separate residential program. It happens to specialize in youthful offenders. Since Mr. Jackson was under 23, we thought we would use that program as a residential placement. It was part of the intensive component of the program, in this instance," said Hague. "But we could just as well place a client under house arrest, or use another residential placement in the area."

Judge McGraw expressed his displeasure with the new program. "I can't believe they'd let the first one get away. It just confirms my feelings that felons don't belong in the community. They belong behind bars." Ms. Hague said the probation department had no comment until an investigation was completed.

Phil looked at Sherry. "This will help us?"

Sherry shrugged. "Well, it doesn't hurt. It'll be a long time before they use Thrive again. I think it means they'll try us next."

"From the sound of the judge, it'll be a long time before they try any program again."

"Well, maybe, maybe not. It was a set-up."

"Explain that."

"Judge McGraw was dead set against Project CRISP from the start. Jackson was not selected for that program by the probation department; McGraw threw them that case to embarrass them. That's what I hear. Jenny Hague says Jackson is actually a plea bargain informer. McGraw had to put him on the street in exchange for some information. He didn't expect him to cooperate with anyone. So he thought he might as well embarrass the probation department while he was at it."

Phil shook his head again. "If that's true, I wouldn't touch the program with a ten foot pole, if I were you."

THE GOAL MUDDLE

Judge McGraw's attack is an extreme reaction, but his negative view of probation is shared by many people. The current lack of confidence in probation takes many forms. In Great Britain, use of probation dropped by 50 percent between 1960 and 1980 (Stanley and Baginsky, 1984:51). As we saw in Chapter 2, the use of probation in the United States has increased, but there are other signs that the increase does not imply confidence. While probation rates and caseloads have risen, expenditures have not kept pace.

Perhaps the worst circumstances are evident in California. In that state, between 1975 and 1983, total criminal justice expenditures went up by 30 percent, but probation expenditures decreased by 10 percent. There were 30 percent fewer probation officers in 1983 than in 1975. The result: Costs per probationer have decreased by 25 percent, and caseload size has skyrocketed (Petersilia et al., 1985). Petersilia and associates predict that unless some important changes take place soon, the staff will be overwhelmed, and the result may well be the same sort of reduced use that has already occurred in Great Britain.

One major source of these difficulties is the current goal muddle. Probation was once closely associated with rehabilitation. It has been severely shaken by the demise of rehabilitation as a preferred goal of sentencing. Probation departments have been slower than other correctional agencies to adjust to the reascendance of retribution. Probation has also been attacked by utilitarians as an ineffective community protection measure (Thomson, 1987).

To understand the current problems, we need to review the relationship of probation to common correctional goals. Is probation so different from other correctional measures that it cannot achieve the same goals? How would probation have to change to be consistent with retributive principles, or to meet demands for incapacitation?

PROBATION AND RETRIBUTION

Can retribution be accomplished without a prison sentence? Sherman and Hawkins (1981) postulate that in the United States, a resilient link has been forged between the concept of punishment and the use of prison (see Chapter 2). Retribution cannot be accomplished, some argue, without a prison sentence. Our current legal system also supports a strong link between prison and retribution. For example, although probation is the most frequent sentence given in the United States, legally probation is a suspension of sentence. Only in Illinois, Delaware, and Nebraska is probation itself defined as a punishment (McAnany, 1984:56). In all other states, probation is technically a suspension of punishment, rather than a punishment in its own right.

Recently, a number of probation departments have attempted to alter the public perception of probation as nonpunitive. Many of these innovations appeared first in California, where the crisis arrived sooner than in other states because of a real estate tax revolt known as Proposition 13. Since probation in California was a county function, its major revenue source was county real estate taxes. When these taxes were rolled back, probation suffered more than many other services. Observing probation departments responding to Proposition 13, Harlow and Nelson (1982) reported that a number of departments sought to regain public support by emphasizing the ways in which community supervision could be distasteful to the probationer or could protect the community. These departments were assuming that expenditures cut for rehabilitation might be restored for services to the public.

Both Harris (1984) and McAnany (1984) observed that probation began as a retributive measure. It emerged as courts sought something between doing nothing and imposing harsh prison sentences. Thus probation originated as a means of matching the sanction to the offense. McAnany

and Harris maintain that if probation is to be true to its retributive heritage, it would once again have to be imposed according to retributive principles. They recommend:

1. That probation would have to be recognized as a legal sanction rather than as a suspension of sentence
2. That probation conditions and length of probation supervision would have to be determined in relation to the severity of the offense
3. That neither services nor control could be exerted on the basis of predictions about risk
4. That all persons guilty to the same degree should receive similar probation sentences

Harris and McAnany recognize that these changes would be radical departures from standard practice. But they also perceive in some new practices elements of the retributive motive. For example, they view orders of restitution and orders of community service, as probation conditions, to be more closely related to the nature of the offense than other types of supervision. They also propose that levels of supervision, which are now decided on the basis of risk, could become an element of retributive practice. The probationer who commits the more serious offense would receive the most supervision.

PROBATION AND DETERRENCE

Whether probation can be congruent with deterrence is related to the problem of increasing its retributive value. To act as a deterrent, probation must be severe enough to dissuade people from crime. Like retributive probation, deterrent probation would not be served by conditions tailored to individual differences among convicted offenders. The issue would be whether probation as penalty can be made visible enough and sufficiently matched to the temptation of crime that it makes that crime unattractive.

Presumably the conditions that would punish individuals for crimes could be those most consistent with deterrence. Highly visible probation conditions, such as community work details (Krajick, 1982) or the publication of restitution orders, could conceivably be threatening enough to reduce the attractiveness of some offenses. Visible supervision by correctional officials, such as home or work visits, might serve as deterrents, as might the order that probationers wear identifying clothing or maintain a strict curfew.

PROBATION AND INCAPACITATION

Many people have assumed that incapacitation is possible only in institutions; community settings could not be sufficiently controlling. This view is now changing. The principal proponents of an incapacitative probation are Todd Clear and Vincent O'Leary (1983), who propose that probation supervision can be altered to control risk.

Probation departments in a number of states have begun changes to increase capacity to control offenders in the community. Since this is currently the most widely accepted direction for probation, the risk control technology will be reviewed in detail later in this chapter. For now it is sufficient to underscore two basic issues. First, the capacity of probation to reduce risk, and therefore to reduce crime by probationers, is consistent with the punitive justification of selective incapacitation, a policy now receiving great attention. The argument that probation can also incapacitate may strengthen the move toward incapacitation policy because it adds credence to the idea that this policy need not increase prison populations. Second, incapacitation as a probation policy suffers from all the objections to incapacitation in general. It is especially inconsistent with retribution.

PROBATION AND REHABILITATION

Probation has often been held out as the last hope of rehabilitation. Proponents have often claimed that community corrections is more effective than prison if rehabilitation is the objective. Rationales for this claim vary. They include the proposition that probation can be more individualized than prison; that community placement avoids the exposure to criminality associated with prison; that probation allows the offender to confront and overcome the forces that led to criminal behavior; and that the probation staff can be more effective than prison staff in providing advocacy for offenders, thereby increasing access to a legitimate livelihood.

Most evaluations of community sentences, including probation, suggest that these claims are inflated. Lipton, Martinson, and Wilks (1975) found no stronger evidence for the rehabilitative effectiveness of community sentences. Moreover, the same problems with rehabilitative research hamper our knowledge of what, if anything, community sentences may actually contribute to rehabilitation. In a recent article on parole effectiveness, Flanagan (1984) recites a litany of unknowns about the rehabilitative characteristics of community supervision. We usually do not know the problems of the offender; we do not know if the staff are responsive to these problems; we do not know if staff suggestions are accepted by clients; we do not know if the actions taken by staff and clients have any effect on the problems; and we do not know if the problems permanently disappear. With these unknowns—which apply as much to probation as to parole—we simply cannot say whether community supervision is rehabilitative, and we certainly cannot claim that probation is more effective than prison.

If rehabilitation continues to be used as a rationale for community sentences, then community supervision is likely to be in conflict with the emerging objectives for prison use. However, it is doubtful that rehabilitation will continue to do well as a justification for probation or other community forms of supervision. First, it is inconsistent with retributive and deterrent aims, which are not about to disappear. Second, it has not yet been shown to be effective. Third, the argument that coerced rehabilitation cannot be effective applies to community and to prison sentences.

THE DEVELOPMENT OF PROBATION

As a recognized legal option at sentencing, probation is a relatively recent development, although the origins of current probation practice can be traced back hundreds of years. Many probation practices widely advertised as new have actually been around for a long time. And the current goal conflict in probation appears to be equally old.

THE BENEFIT OF CLERGY

In an effort to allow members of the clergy to escape capital punishment and the other severe sentences in thirteenth-century England, a compromise permitted a member of the clergy convicted in a King's Court to be transferred to ecclesiastical courts. Since at the time the ability to read was generally restricted to the clergy, the defendant had to prove literacy in order to escape the King's Court. Thus the practice became known as **benefit of clergy** (Chute and Bell, 1956:12).

Through the fifteenth century, benefit of clergy exempted some persons from punishment for even serious crimes such as murder (1956:14). In order to cut down on abuses, repeat offenders were branded in open court with the letters *M* for murderer and *T* for thief (1956:14). By the eighteenth century, benefit of clergy was widely available regardless of sex, class, or ability to read. Judges often connived with defendants to avoid the injustice of reserving the benefit to those who could read. Clerks of the court, who were responsible for verifying reading ability, often provided incorrect information. Although the judge could reject statements by the clerk, in many cases false certificates of literacy were accepted without challenge (1956:13). Before ben-

efit of clergy was abolished in England in 1827, it had become widespread. Its principal use was to avoid the death penalty. However, benefit of clergy was also used on occasion to provide a defendant with time to marshall arguments for mitigation of other punishments.

This form of clemency was brought to America by English colonists, where it was used both before and after its abolition in England. It gradually fell into disrepute because of its uncertain legality and its discretionary and unequal application. Nevertheless, the practice was a harbinger of some later practices, such as suspension of sentence, and an investigation (however crude) to determine whether the defendant merited consideration.

JUDICIAL REPRIEVE

Under English common law, new trials and appeals to another court were impossible. In order to permit a convicted offender to apply for an absolute or conditional pardon, the court would grant a temporary suspension of sentence, called **judicial reprieve.** This device was used in cases where the judge was not satisfied with the verdict; when he felt that the evidence was suspicious or the indictment insufficiently supported; or occasionally when the judge felt the felony was of a minor nature or mitigating circumstances existed (*Commentaries on the Laws of England, 1765–1769*, 1900:1041). In the seventeenth century, judicial reprieves from capital punishment were often coupled with deportation. Offenders sentenced to death were granted reprieves if they agreed to be transported to the colonies. Although even these reprieves may have been intended as temporary, the suspension of sentence was often extended indefinitely.

The practice of indefinite suspension of sentence was adopted in American courts, first under this common law tradition, and later by statute. This type of reprieve is a close cousin of modern probation, and includes provisions for good behavior (Hussey and Duffee, 1980:39).

RECOGNIZANCE AND PROVISIONAL RELEASE ON BAIL

Another measure that influenced the development of probation can be traced back to fourteenth-century England. Originally used as a preventive measure with persons thought likely to commit crimes in the future, **recognizance** was a sworn statement by a defendant to the court that he would conduct himself in a law-abiding manner if released. Often, in addition to the promise, financial surety, or bail, was required. In this case, the person who had put up the surety had both the power and the duty to make sure the released person obeyed the release conditions.

The English Criminal Law Consolidation Act of 1861 extended this release device to persons convicted of any except capital felonies. The practice was the forerunner of the British probation service, which was enacted into law in 1907 (Stanley and Baginsky, 1984:52). English magistrates using recognizance with convicted persons often asked volunteers to provide the offender with advice and assistance in discharging the conditional release. The Church of England Temperance Society appointed court missionaries to oversee released convicts as early as 1876 (Hagan, 1975). The recognizance practice was adopted in the United States, and was particularly common in Massachusetts.

Recognizance was used extensively by Judge Peter Oxenbridge Thacher, a magistrate in the municipal court of Boston. In the case of *Commonwealth* v. *Jerusha Chase*, in 1831, the defendant pled guilty to stealing from a dwelling. After an agreement from the prosecutor, Thacher ordered that the indictment be "laid upon file," and Ms. Chase was released on recognizance with sureties. (Chute and Bell, 1956:33–35). The order of laying the case upon file was not a final judgment, but left Thacher with the power to take action on the case at any time, upon motion of either party (Newman, 1966:9). Ms. Chase later appeared on new charges and was sentenced on the old conviction to the House of Correction. This case is important for laying the legal prec-

edent in the United States for the enforcement of probation conditions (Chute and Bell, 1956:35).

Thacher apparently often combined recognizance with supervision by a sheriff or constable, especially for youthful offenders (Grinnell, 1941). The practice of suspension of sentence and conditional release, often with supervision, paved the way for the invention of probation, a term apparently coined by John Augustus (Chute, 1939).

THE WORK OF JOHN AUGUSTUS

John Augustus is generally recognized as the father of probation. He was the first probation officer, although he worked entirely as a volunteer rather than as an employee of the court. While much of the groundwork for probation was laid by people like Thacher, Augustus was the first to approach the practice of conditional release in a systematic fashion (Chute, 1939).

John Augustus was born in Woburn, Massachusetts, in 1784. He was a bootmaker by trade and moved from Lexington to Boston in 1827 after amassing some wealth (Hussey and Duffee, 1980:38). Augustus took a special interest in the poor, the young, and the alcoholic offenders in the lower courts of Boston. He bailed his first case, a common drunkard, in August 1841 and extracted a promise that the offender would refrain from drinking if released to Augustus's care. The lower court usually charged Augustus $30 bail for 30 days suspension of sentence, and reduced the penalty to one cent and court costs if the probationer behaved as promised (1980:39). By the time of his death in 1859, Augustus had bailed 1,152 men, 794 women, and about 3,000 girls.

Following Augustus's death, his work was carried on by John Murray Spear and Rufus R. Cook, who was paid by the Children's Aid Society of Boston to work with children in the Suffolk County Jail. Cook eventually became chaplain of the jail and extended his help to adults as well as children. He used strategies similar to those of Augustus. He reported that he bailed about 450 individuals in 1870 and estimated that 87 percent made good adjustments under probation supervision (Chute and Bell, 1956:55).

PROBATION BECOMES LAW

The first probation statute was passed by the Massachusetts legislature on April 26, 1878. The law provided a salaried probation officer for the courts of Suffolk County (Chute and Bell, 1956:59). The act required the mayor of Boston to select a suitable person. The first appointee, Henry Hemmenway, was a police lieutenant. After four months, he was replaced by Edward H. Savage, a former chief of police, who served for many years (1956:60–61).

In 1891, Massachusetts passed a second probation law requiring the criminal courts to appoint probation officers. This law transferred probation authority from the executive to the judicial branch. Under the second statute, Hannah Todd became the first salaried woman probation officer in the United States (1956:65). In 1898, Massachusetts extended to all courts in the state the authority to hire probation officers. Probation also became available, at the judge's discretion, to all convicted persons (1956:66).

Vermont and Rhode Island followed the Massachusetts example in the same year. Vermont was the first state to adopt the county form of probation commonly found in the United States today (1956:67–70). It permitted each county to hire its own officer and to establish its own standards. Rhode Island, in contrast, adopted the other currently popular approach, a statewide system. The Rhode Island Board of State Charities and Corrections was authorized to appoint a state probation officer and to hire other officers to serve all the courts in the state (1956:70–71).

Probation laws were gradually adopted by other states. By 1925, probation for juveniles was available in all states, but it was not until 1956 that probation was available for adults in all jurisdictions. The Federal Probation Service was established on March 4, 1925, although the first three federal probation officers were not appointed until two years later (Maher, 1981). (For

a discussion of the administration of the federal service, see Insert 8.1.)

One of the important lessons in the development of probation is the early appearance of several controversies that are still very much alive. The use of law enforcement officers as the initial probation officers in Boston signaled that the care versus control controversy, which has recently reached a boiling point, was embedded in probation from its beginnings. The transfer of probation authority in Massachusetts from the executive to the judicial branch is the earliest example of one of two administrative controversies. The second is the choice between locally administered probation, as in Vermont, or a state-administered service, as in Rhode Island.

PROBATION TASKS AND THEIR ORGANIZATION

Probation departments currently perform a wide range of pre- and postconviction services. Most of these involve decisions about or supervision of suspects or convicted persons. The kinds of tasks assigned to probation departments vary considerably from one jurisdiction to another. For example, the preconviction tasks done by probation departments in one area will be done by a separate agency in another area. Even within one department, the demands on probation officers can vary considerably from one judge to another, since judges often establish policies for their own courtroom that are not followed by other judges in the same court. Because of this diversity, it is difficult to make accurate generalizations about probation department functions or probation officer duties. Here we will describe briefly the activities most commonly associated with probation.

PRETRIAL FUNCTIONS

Some probation departments have recently assumed enlarged pretrial responsibilities. Probation departments are often assigned the task of

Insert 8.1
DUAL AUTHORITY IN THE FEDERAL PROBATION SERVICE

The Federal Bureau of Prisons and Federal Probation are often held up as exemplars for other correctional agencies to emulate. The high quality of the federal agencies is often presumed to be related to their structure. For example, Allen, Carlson, and Parks (1979) use Federal Probation as an example of "centralized" correctional services, which, they believe, are more effective than fragmented services. Thomas Maher's study of administrative complexity in Federal Probation (1981) demonstrated that the structure of this federal agency is often misrepresented. While Federal Probation has a central office and is responsible for the supervision of federal probationers and parolees across the country, it would be incorrect to assume that nationwide jurisdiction implies centralized management or unified practices across the 94 different Federal Probation offices.

Following the addition of 1,000 new officer positions in the 1970s, the General Accounting Office, an investigative and evaluative arm of Congress, called the probation system to account for its use of resources (Comptroller General, 1977). The report was highly critical of Federal Probation. In his letter transmitting the report to Congress, the Comptroller General held the Federal Probation Division of the Administrative Office of the U.S. Courts responsible for correcting these problems (Maher, 1981). The central office responded with several monographs on presentence investigation and probation supervision practices that were designed to increase uniformity and improve the standards of probation work. Many of the 94 district offices conformed to these new standards, but a number of offices reported that they would only partly comply.

Rejection of central office policy in a centralized system would generally be considered insubordination and grounds for serious disciplinary action. Maher points out that in Federal Probation, the legal authority of the central office is dubious. While the central office is responsible for promulgation of standards and rules, for keeping records, for maintaining evaluation procedures, and for operating the personnel system, its direction is not obligatory on the district offices. Federal district judges have the statutory authority to select and dismiss officers. The policy manual recognizes that the chief judge of the district has final authority on all probation matters (Maher, 1981). Matters are made more complex in districts with more than one judge. In multijudge districts, the chief judge is usually responsible for probation policy, but individual judges may require probation officers to follow their individual policy in their own courtrooms.

Federal Probation is an organization operating under dual authority, one central and one local. Since the chief district judge has the final say in matters affecting his court, district chief probation officers will defer to the judge in instances where central and local policy conflict. Moreover, a district chief who may disagree with central office policy may actively seek the support of his district judge as a means of avoiding compliance. This administrative arrangement certainly does not imply that Federal Probation is ineffective. But it does suggest that those impressed with its effectiveness should not attribute its achievements to centralized power in the system.

supervising those released under supervision in lieu of bail and of designing and overseeing diversion programs. In some instances, the probation department may also be responsible for selecting defendants for these programs. In other places, selection is carried out by a separate pretrial services agency. Large probation departments often have significant responsibilities for general court administration and courtroom liaison services with the judge.

When the interest in victims and restitution increased, some probation departments took on responsibility for services to victims and witnesses (Helbush and Mandell, 1977). Probation departments also have important screening functions in juvenile court. Although the practice is declining, most probation departments still perform juvenile court intake functions (see Chapter 19).

PRESENTENCING FUNCTIONS

The more traditional role of the probation department is assistance to the judge in the determination of sentence. The tradition of the presentence investigation has its roots in the historical antecedants of probation. Given his limited resources, John Augustus was methodical in making determinations of which defendants to bail. The presentence investigation became more systematic with the adoption of social work techniques at the beginning of this century.

As doubts about its rehabilitative effectiveness grew, and as the image of the probation officer as a neutral third party was tarnished (Blumberg, 1979), both the process and utility of presentence reports have been attacked. In addition, the introduction of determinant sentencing has reduced judicial discretion in sentencing and by some accounts has therefore decreased the importance of presentence reports in helping the judge arrive at a sentencing decision. However, some states with determinant sentencing systems have used probation officers as the new sentencing experts (Thomson, 1987).

In addition to the presentence investigation, some probation departments have now taken on the duties of presentence supervision. This innovation is a logical extension of pretrial supervision. If defendants can be removed from jail prior to conviction, they may also be supervised in the community between conviction and the sentencing hearing. This period may take from two weeks to two months, depending on the jurisdiction. Additionally, as was the case in the CRISP program, presentence supervision may be used as a test period prior to a recommendation for probation.

POSTSENTENCING FUNCTIONS

The postsentencing activities of probation departments are also diversifying. The most important and most common function is the supervision of offenders placed on probation. However, recent innovations in sentencing have increased the range of tasks included in probation supervision. Probation officers may be responsible for establishing and supervising restitution orders, for finding and supervising community service placements, and for collecting or at least accounting for the collection of fines paid in installments. As programs have sprung up for drug and alcohol abuse, probation departments have often become responsible for verifying the attendance of offenders assigned to such programs.

SPECIALIST AND GENERALIST MODELS

While probation often includes all the diverse functions described above, these functions do not necessarily fall to the same probation unit or the same probation officer. Variations exist in the distribution of duties at both the organizational and the job level. At both levels, the major distinction is between generalist and specialist forms of design. A generalist probation department would be responsible for all probation duties in a jurisdiction. A specialist department would have more limited responsibility for some of these tasks. Specialization can take several forms. For example, it is common to split juvenile and adult probation between two units. Another common organizational division gives one probation unit the supervision of felons and another supervision of misdemeanants. The current trend appears to be to collect all probation responsibilities into one department with several divisions. Some jurisdictions have gone much further: They have created local correctional departments in which probation is one division of an organization with responsibilities for jails, residential programs, and a variety of court services.

Employment in a generalist department does not mean that an individual officer will also have multiple responsibilities. Many larger departments divide up the tasks into smaller collections of closely related duties. For example, large urban departments may have specialists assigned to presentence investigations, supervision, and other court liaison duties. Some departments will utilize a combination of specialist and generalist work roles, with many probation officers carrying out multiple duties while a few are assigned to special projects, such as intensive supervision. There is a correlation between the size of the department and the tendency to internal specialization. In many rural departments, one probation officer must carry out all probation responsibilities (Thomson and Fogel, 1980).

HOW PROBATION AGENTS SPEND THEIR TIME

Since the organization of probation tasks is so varied, generalizations about the use of officer time are impossible. One of the most often cited problems is the limited amount of time probation agents have for the direct supervision of clients. One example of this problem is provided by Jean Jester (1981), who conducted a detailed time study of four parole agencies and four probation units. In this study, officers' work was sampled on three randomly selected days, from 6 A.M. to midnight. The distribution of probation officer time in these four departments is summarized in Table 8.1.

A number of commentators have observed that control and direction of probation tasks is one of the weakest aspects of probation organization (Clear and O'Leary, 1983; Baird, 1981). Typically, the organization of tasks is determined by tradition or convenience, rather than careful scrutiny of effects. Recent management innovations have finally begun to correct this deficiency in some departments. Probably the most widely recognized task design improvements have been

TABLE 8.1 The Distribution of Probation Officer Time (in %) in Four Probation Offices

TYPE OF ACTIVITY	PROBATION OFFICE				
	1	2	3	4	TOTAL
Officer/client interactions	41	36	26	26	32
Outside agency contact	11	16	19	22	17
Administration	41	42	49	46	45
Travel	5	5	5	4	5
Other	2	—	2	—	1

SOURCE: Jean Jester, *The Technologies of Probation and Parole.* Unpublished Ph.D. dissertation, State University of New York at Albany, 1981.

made by the Wisconsin Bureau of Community Corrections, which supervises both probation and parole. The Wisconsin model has four basic components: (1) risk and need assessment to determine the level of supervision to which cases will be assigned, (2) a case management classification system to determine the content of supervision, (3) a management information system tied directly to the offender classification system, and (4) a workload deployment and budgeting procedure that is a direct product of the classification and management information system (Baird, 1981). While most probation departments are far behind the Wisconsin example, it is only through careful assignment and evaluation of tasks that probation can answer some of the current complaints about its efficacy.

THE ADMINISTRATION OF PROBATION

The two most recurrent debates concerning the administration of probation have to do with its location in the correctional network. One of these debates involves the decision to place probation in the executive or the judicial branch of government. The other involves the decision to make probation a statewide service or to make it responsible to local government.

JUDICIAL OR EXECUTIVE AUTHORITY

The National Advisory Commission on Criminal Justice Standards and Goals (1973) recommended that probation in all states should be transferred from the judicial to the executive branch of government. The NAC summary of the debate listed the following contentions (1973:332).

Advantages of Judicial Administration

1. Probation would be more responsive to the courts.
2. Relationship of probation to the courts creates an automatic feedback mechanism on the effectiveness of dispositions.
3. Courts will have greater awareness of resources needed.
4. Courts might allow their own staff more discretion than they would allow to members of an outside agency.
5. If probation were incorporated into a department of corrections, it might be assigned lower priority than it would have as part of the court.

Disadvantages of Judicial Administration

1. Judges are not equipped to administer probation.
2. Services to probationers may receive lower priority than services to the courts.
3. Probation staff may be assigned duties unrelated to probation.
4. Courts are adjudicatory and regulative rather than service-oriented bodies.

Advantages of Executive Administration

1. Allied human service agencies are located within the executive branch.
2. All other corrections subsystems are located in the executive branch.
3. More coordinated and effective program budgeting as well as increased ability to negotiate fully in the resource allocation process becomes possible.
4. A coordinated continuum of services to offenders and better utilization of probation manpower are facilitated.

The most recent survey of probation administration found that in 23 states, probation was located in the executive branch, in 6 states and the federal system, it was located in the judicial branch, and in 21 states there was a mixture of executive and judicial authority (McCarthy and McCarthy, 1984:99). The preponderance of opinion favors the executive location, although empirical justification for either placement is nearly nonexistent.

The NAC position on executive placement appears closely tied to its perception of probation as a service to offenders. As a service organization, probation would be enhanced by closer relationships to other service organizations. Hussey has argued that courts are "commonweal organizations" designed to benefit the body politic and therefore ill-suited to service provision (Hussey and Duffee, 1980:132–135). Whether these arguments remain valid if probation is defined as a punishment rather than a service has not really been addressed. Both the NAC and Conrad (1984) do recommend that if probation becomes an executive function, current probation activities which are specifically court services (such as presentence investigations) should be retained by the courts.

LOCAL OR STATE ADMINISTRATION

The NAC also recommended that probation should be a state rather than local function, and ideally located within the state department of correction (1973:332). According to the most recent available survey, probation is a state-level organization in 24 states, a local organization in 7 states, and an organization with mixed state and local control in 19 states (National Council on Crime and Delinquency, 1981). Since 1931, the trend has been toward state takeover of probation. In that year the National Commission on Law Observance and Enforcement recommended state takeover as a means of avoiding local corruption.

The principal arguments for state control include these: (1) greater integration with other state-level correctional activities, (2) better planning and more flexible use of resources, and (3) greater uniformity, procedural regularity, and equity across all areas within a state. The principal arguments for local control include these: (1) greater responsiveness to local conditions and needs, (2) more effective linkage to service agencies, which are primarily local or private, and (3) less bureaucracy.

As is the case with the executive-judicial debate, the issue of state or local control has not received a great deal of empirical study. One report did attempt to examine the relative advantages and disadvantages of local and state-level location of unified corrections departments. The researchers concluded that state-level control led to greater accountability, better administration, and higher quality and compensation of personnel, but to no difference in correctional outcomes (Nelson, Cushman, and Harlow, 1980). More recent research has examined a related but slightly different issue: What are the advantages and disadvantages of states directly running or contracting with local and private agencies for community corrections in general (although not probation specifically)? This research tends to favor a state-contracted system rather than a state-run system (Coates, Miller, and Ohlin, 1978; Vinter, Downs, and Hall, 1975). Whether these findings hold true for probation is not known. The hypothesis would appear to be that in states which mix state and local control, the results may be more effective, at least on some dimensions. This research suggests that direct service should be a local activity, while research, planning, funding, and other managerial activities should be done at the state level.

The state-local controversy is often characterized as a choice between centralized and decentralized service, but this characterization oversimplifies the issue. For example, Maher (1981) demonstrated that Federal Probation, while supervising probationers and parolees for the entire federal system, has a very decentralized authority structure (see Insert 8.1). The same could be the case at the state level. A state probation organization does not necessarily involve centralization of control over all activities in that organization.

Likewise, the fact that a probation department is "local" does not mean that it is internally decentralized. A large city probation department may be run very autocratically, with all power concentrated in the hands of a few top officials, and little discretion or participation given to front-line officers. It may not recognize that probationers in different parts of the large city have different characteristics and face different problems. While the local-state arguments usually assume that local departments are less bureaucratic and more responsive while state departments are more bureaucratic and less responsive, these are not safe assumptions. One frequent advantage of state-level organizations is that they can be more responsive to groups (such as offenders of politically weak segments of a community) that are often ignored by local organizations.

THE CONDITIONS OF PROBATION

Conditions of probation vary from jurisdiction to jurisdiction. In most courts, general conditions are imposed upon all probationers, and special conditions are applied to particular offenders. The American Bar Association, in its Project on Standards for Criminal Justice (1970), recommended the following conditions as appropriate:

1. Cooperating with a program of supervision
2. Meeting family responsibilities
3. Maintaining steady employment or engaging or refraining from engaging in a specific employment or occupation
4. Pursuing prescribed educational or vocational training
5. Undergoing available medical or psychiatric treatment
6. Maintaining residence in a prescribed area or in a special facility established for or available to persons on probation

7. Refraining from consorting with certain types of people or frequenting certain types of places
8. Making restitution of the fruits of the crime or reparation for loss or damage caused thereby

The NAC standard 5.4 (2) relating to probation conditions states:

> The court should be authorized to impose such conditions as are necessary to provide a benefit to the offender and protection to the public safety. The court also should be authorized to modify or enlarge the conditions of probation at any time prior to expiration of sentence. The conditions imposed in an individual case should be tailored to meet the needs of the defendant and society, and mechanical imposition of uniform conditions on all defendants should be avoided.

Either set of recommendations explicitly adopts the position that this period of conditional freedom should benefit the offender and that the specific conditions imposed on an individual probationer should be tailored to meet his or her particular needs and circumstances. There are probably no better examples of the conflict between the traditional perception of probation and the principles of retribution. The recommendations of either the ABA or the NAC would be rejected by those seeking to make probation a penalty for a crime.

Probation conditions are to be imposed by a judge, not determined after sentencing by the probation officer (del Carmen, 1985:52). However, general probation conditions are vague enough that the probation officer has considerable discretion in determining the specific actions the probationer should take. Although judges retain wide latitude in the kinds of behaviors they can proscribe or require, there are some limits on probation conditions. In general, probation conditions must not violate a probationer's constitutional rights; must be clear and enforceable; must be reasonable; and must contribute to public safety or rehabilitation (del Carmen, 1985:52).

The constitutional freedoms of probationers are much narrower than those of free citizens. For example, searches and seizures at unspecified hours by probation officers are allowable if they relate to the enforcement of conditions (1985:54). However, probationers are protected from warrantless searches and seizures by police investigating new crimes (Schwitzgebel, 1972). It is widely accepted that probationers and parolees are subject to blood or urine tests (del Carmen, 1985:55). And probationers are generally not protected by the Miranda ruling during custodial interrogations by probation officers. However, the First Amendment freedom of religion is protected; a judge could not order church attendance as a probation condition. Conditions are also limited somewhat by basic Fifth and Fourteenth Amendment rights to reasonableness and fairness. For example, revoking probation for a probationer financially unable to pay restitution was deemed unreasonable (*Beardon* v. *Georgia*, 1983). A condition cannot be enforced if it is too vague to guide behavior or if the probationer was not aware of the condition. A condition cannot be too severe for the offense committed, or imposed without a reasonable connection to the offense. Table 8.2 provides some additional examples.

A condition receiving new attention lately is the imposition of a fee for probation supervision. In Georgia, the intensive supervision program discussed below is funded entirely by fees from probationers. A 1984 survey of 40 states found that 18 of them required probation fees. Table 8.3 summarizes the states with fees, the amounts charged, and the criteria for waiving collection. In addition to these fees, some probation departments charge the probationer for the cost of drug testing (Flanagan and McGarrell, 1986:87–88).

REVOCATION

Probation status may be revoked if the probationer violates the conditions of probation. If probation is revoked, the judge sentences the offender to prison or jail. If the pronouncement of sentence has been suspended, the probation re-

TABLE 8.2   Examples of Limits of Probation Conditions

1. Condition rejected as unrelated to objectives of probation [*People* v. *Dominguez*, 64 Cal. Rptr. 290 (Cal. App. 1967)]	Woman convicted of second degree robbery ordered not to live with a man when she was not married, or to become pregnant while unmarried.
2. Condition rejected as unwarranted intrusion of privacy [*Springer* v. *U.S.*, 148 F2d. 411 (9th Cir., 1945)]	Probationer convicted of refusing military induction ordered to give pint of blood within 30 days.
3. Condition violates First Amendment rights [*Jones* v. *Commonwealth*, 185 Va. 335 (1946)]	Two youths required to attend church and Sunday school and report attendance to probation officer.
4. Condition requiring separation of husband and wife for duration of probation upheld as unusual but reasonable in this case [*In re Peeler*, 72 Cal. Rptr. 254 (Cal. App. 1968)]	Woman convicted of marijuana possession, marrying student who faced drug charges, ordered to live with parents and not associate with known drug users.

SOURCE: Adapted from Ralph Schwitzgebel (1972), "Limits on the Coercive Treatment of Offenders," *Criminal Law Bulletin* 8:267–320.

vocation will entail a sentencing hearing. If the sentence had previously been pronounced and its execution suspended, the initial sentence may be imposed following the revocation hearing. Probationers do not usually receive credit for time served on probation prior to the violation—another conflict between retributive principles and the current practice of probation. The NAC recommended that this practice be changed so that revoked probationers do not end up facing longer periods of state intervention than persons initially sentenced to incarceration (1973:160).

Although the granting of probation is generally discretionary (for exceptions, see the discussion in the sentencing chapter), there are now

limits on the revocation of probation. The United States Supreme Court took the position in *Morrissey* v. *Brewer* (1972), a parole revocation case, that conditional freedom cannot be withdrawn arbitrarily. Once conditional freedom is granted, the offender has a substantial liberty interest protected by the Fifth and Fourteenth Amendments. Revocation is a "grievous loss," and procedures for it must conform to certain due process standards.

One year after the Morrissey decision, the Supreme Court addressed the procedures for probation revocation in *Gagnon* v. *Scarpelli*. In general, the Court found the freedom interests of probationers and parolees to be indistinguishable. Therefore the Court held that the minimum requirements for due process in parole revocations applied in probation revocation cases as well.

Morrissey and *Gagnon* do not provide an offender with all the protections available to a defendant facing trial and initial sentencing. However, these cases place considerable restriction on the judge and probation officials. The probation officer must make a case for revocation that can withstand a challenge from the probationer. Specifically, the Court decisions require a two-stage revocation process. A first hearing must be held to determine whether there is probable cause for revocation. The probationer must be given notice of when and why the hearing will take place, and the nature of the alleged violation. The probationer is permitted to speak in his or her own behalf and to introduce documents or witnesses. The judge must make a determination of whether there is probable cause to proceed to a revocation hearing, and a written record of the hearing must be made. If the probation officer's revocation request passes this initial hearing, a revocation hearing is held.

Minimal requirements at this hearing include:

1. Written notice of the claimed violation
2. Disclosure of the evidence against the probationer
3. Opportunity for the probationer to testify

TABLE 8.3   Probation Systems Using Fees from Probationers, 1984

STATE	AMOUNT	WAIVER
Alabama	$15/mo.	Judgment of sentencing judge
Florida	$20 to $50/mo.	Waived for unemployment, students, handicap, hardship, and extenuating circumstances
Georgia	$10 to $15/mo.	For undue hardship
Idaho	$30/mo.	For unemployment or handicap
Indiana	Initial fee of $25 to $100 and monthly fee $5 to $15	Not waived for felons, but waivable for juveniles or misdemeanants
Kentucky	$100 to $500 for misdemeanants, $500 to $2,500 for felons	Optional by court, waivable for students, handicapped, hardship, unemployment
Mississippi	$15/mo.	Inability to pay
Nevada	$12/mo.	Hardship
New Mexico	$15 to $85/mo.	Hardship
North Carolina	$10/mo.	—
Oklahoma	$15/mo.	Hardship
Oregon	At least $10/mo.	Hardship or in interest of rehabilitation
South Carolina	$10/mo.	Hardship
South Dakota	Amount based on ability to pay	Fees not mandatory
Tennessee	$35/mo.	Hardship
Texas	Up to $15/mo.	Judge's discretion
Virginia	$15/mo.	Hardship
Washington	$15 to $50/mo.	Unemployment, hardship, handicap

SOURCE: Flanagan and McGarrell, *Sourcebook of Criminal Justice Statistics—1985,* Washington, DC: United States Department of Justice.

and to present other witnesses and documentary evidence

4. Opportunity to confront and cross examine adverse witnesses, unless the judge determines there is good cause not to permit this

5. An impartial hearing officer

6. A written record of the facts and the reasons for revocation

The Supreme Court has not required that probationers be represented by counsel at revocation hearings, although it urged that counsel be permitted or appointed in the case of indigents, particularly if the evidence is doubtful, the case complex, or the probationer appears to have difficulty comprehending the proceedings. However, if the probation revocation is in effect at the first sentencing hearing, then the probationer has a right to counsel at sentencing (*Mempa* v. *Rhay,* 1967). The level of evidence required to support a revocation is less than that needed for conviction of a new crime. Rather than the beyond a reasonable doubt standard, typical evidentiary standards are "the preponderance of evidence," "sufficient to satisfy the court," or "substantial evidence" (see, for example, *Jackson* v. *State,* 1978).

Revocations are usually classified into two types: revocation for noncriminal failures to comply with conditions, or technical violations, and revocation for conviction of a new crime. The usual distinction between these two, as well as the difficulties in making the distinction, are discussed in Chapter 5.

A substantiated case of probation violation need not result in incarceration. The judge retains the discretion to alter probation conditions rather than to revoke. Recently, prison over-crowding has increased the pressure to expand alternative revocation outcomes. In some juris-dictions, for example, revocation from regular probation may result in assignment to intensive supervision rather than incarceration. In other cases, a judge may decide to assign a probationer to a halfway house or residential facility rather than to incarcerate.

DILEMMAS IN SUPERVISION

The ambivalent goals of probation result in some difficult practical problems for those who super-vise offenders. In Great Britain, the literature frequently refers to the tension between care and control. In the United States the same ambiguity is usually captured in the phrases "assistance and control" or "service and surveillance." In this section we review some of the assumed difficulties in correctional measures that seek to apply con-trols and provide assistance simultaneously and

examine some of the proposals for reducing the perceived conflict.

CONTROL, ALIENATION, AND SERVICES

Because the offender is serving a sentence forced upon him or her rather than voluntarily accepted, it is presumed that the conditions will not be obeyed willingly. Since the offender has been coerced, the argument goes, he or she will nat-urally be alienated from those imposing the con-ditions and uncommitted to the goals and norms of the correctional organization (Conrad, 1984). Implementation of punishment therefore requires control. But the same officials who are to impose control are also responsible, in many instances, for the provision of services to their clients, most of whom face life conditions where help would appear to be welcome. So many community cor-rectional staff people struggle with the twin re-sponsibilities of control and assistance. Many practitioners and most observers find these twin duties quite a burden.

Assistance and control are often simultaneous concerns of the single officer in charge of the case. (New York State Department of Correc-tional Services)

Probation is certainly not the only community sentence that struggles with the choice between gaining the offender's trust and commitment or forcing conformity through rule and surveillance. Krajick (1982:16) indicates that many community service programs depend upon the threat of incarceration to make sure that the community service offender will complete the service order (see also Pease, 1985:70). In contrast, Brennan and Mason (1983) describe a Chicago community service program in which the "defendant is to consent voluntarily to participate in the program." They also argue that the completion of community service enhances client self-esteem and therefore becomes a useful start to a productive casework relationship (Brennan and Mason, 1983:51). An interview study with 50 British probation officers seconds these sentiments. Fielding found that most of his respondents sought evidence of commitment to change by the probationer and believed that little change would take place without it (1984:13). The British Home Secretary, testifying about the need for community service programs in Great Britain, stressed the importance of the offender voluntarily accepting the work order. Said Maudling: "After all, if it's not done voluntarily, the work will not be good." (Pease et al., 1975.) However, the Home Secretary pointed out in the next breath that the alternative would be to go to jail. Warren Young, commenting on this choice between community service and jail, defends the voluntarism in the choice. He says that consent is not negated just because the alternative is less attractive (Young, 1979:28).

While the belief in an inherent conflict between care and control is widespread, it is certainly not universal. Some commentators, for example, do not find the emphases on control and care to be very pronounced in the daily interaction of clients and correctional staff (Willis, 1983; Irwin, 1970). Others suggest that client involvement in the selection of supervision goals is beneficial, but that objectives "reflecting incapacitative aims . . . can be established by the officer as required controls on behavior. . . ." without

client involvement or consent (Clear and O'Leary, 1983:96).

Research on treatment in noncorrectional settings should caution us that the criticism of coerced treatment can be overdone. For example, the leading researcher in alcoholism treatment in occupational settings suggests that companies in which policies permitted "constructive confrontations" and "mild punishments" were more effective in reducing alcoholism than companies which relied on strictly voluntary treatments or resorted immediately to very strong punishments such as suspension (Trice and Beyer, 1984). A physician in charge of alcoholism treatment in a large New York City utility company reported 80 percent success rates with employees urged to seek treatment by supervisors and only 5 to 10 percent success rates with employees who had volunteered (Priae, 1974).

Seymour Halleck (1971), a psychiatrist who has worked in correctional and university settings, has argued that the legal definition of voluntary treatment can be misleading. He asserts that many mentally ill persons in noncoercive settings have no more freedom to choose for or against treatment than those who are in coercive settings. Other leading researchers on psychological treatment would agree (Toch, 1977; Bandura, 1969).

Some community corrections observers propose that the dichotomy between care and control overemphasizes the ideology of community corrections rather than actual practice (Irwin, 1970, Duffee, 1984, Fielding, 1984). Fielding argues that both treatment and punishment are attempts to produce "controlled and controllable behavior" (1984:115) and that most community correctional staff vary their approach depending on the situation (1984:31). He believes that the juxtaposition of care and control as conflicting objectives does not accurately describe the perceptions of clients or the behavior of staff. One of the earliest caseload studies, of federal probation, found that clients and officers achieved a high degree of agreement on the needs of clients. However, the

Insert 8.2 BURNOUT AMONG PROBATION AND PAROLE OFFICERS

Christine Maslach (1982), H. Freudenberger (1974), and C. Cherniss (1980) have proposed that burnout is a significant problem in human service work. Burnout may be defined as (Kahn, 1978:61):

> . . . a syndrome of inappropriate attitudes towards clients and towards oneself, often with uncomfortable physical and emotional symptoms ranging from exhaustion and insomnia to migraine and ulcer. Deterioration of . . . performance is a frequent additional element in this syndrome.

In 1983, John Whitehead examined burnout among probation and parole officers. He surveyed 968 officers in New York, Indiana, Connecticut, and the Philadelphia Office of Federal Probation. Whitehead used the Maslach burnout inventory so that he could compare his results with samples of other types of human service workers. The inventory measures three separate dimensions of burnout: (1) emotional exhaustion, (2) depersonalization, and (3) personal accomplishment. Whitehead discovered that his sample of officers reported feeling emotional exhaustion and depersonalization less frequently than other service workers, but that when these feelings did occur, they were more intense. The probation and parole officers also felt less personal accomplishment than workers such as teachers and nurses (Whitehead, 1983:154). Officers were generally satisfied with their careers, reporting dissatisfaction with pay, promotional opportunities, and degree of participation in policy, but high satisfaction with the amount of variety and autonomy in their work and with the amount of feedback they obtained from doing the job (1983:159).

Whitehead examined the relationship between work characteristics and feelings of burnout. Although Maslach proposes that burnout is caused by constant contact with clients, there was little support for that proposition in that study. Whitehead found no association between most of his workload measures and burnout; in fact, officers who spent the most time with clients were less rather than more burned out. However, some types of clients, and some types of client interactions, appeared to be stressful. For example, officers who had filed the greatest number of technical and criminal violations in the previous three months reported higher exhaustion scores than other officers. Officers whose caseloads contained a high proportion of unemployed clients reported greater levels of exhaustion and depersonalization. And officers with mostly rural clients had higher indications of burnout (1983:177–187).

While quantitative indications of workload or client contact were not generally related to burnout, a very strong relationship was found with two psychological reactions to the work. Officers who felt that they did not have time to do their job well and officers who felt a high degree of conflict between enforcing conditions and providing services both reported higher levels of burnout (1983:205–210). Whitehead also found that level of burnout differed significantly from office to office. Highest burnout scores were reported by Connecticut probation officers and Indiana parole officers and the lowest by Indiana probation officers or New York probation officers. The federal officers fell in the middle. While the reasons for this are not certain, there appeared to be a strong association between the level of bureaucracy and degree of participation in policy in these different offices and the burnout scores (1983:202–203).

The last stage of Whitehead's analysis assessed the relative importance of these factors in producing burnout. The most important variables were career satisfaction and the feeling of having the time to do high-quality work. Workload and client contact items were relatively unimportant. Whitehead concluded that burnout was closely associated with the more traditional notion of job dissatisfaction, and that burnout, for probation and parole officers, derived from job characteristics and management practices in particular organizations, rather than from the stress of working with clients.

clients did not perceive the officers to be very helpful in achieving a successful adjustment (Adams, Chandler, and Neithercutt, 1971). For recent research on officer reaction to various workload situations, see the insert on Whitehead's burnout research.

THE STRUCTURING OF CONFLICT

Those who perceive the tension between treatment and control to be a dominant characteristic of community correctional practice suggest that this conflict takes particular forms in community settings that would not usually appear in prison settings. In prison, much is made of the conflict between custodial and treatment staffs. In community corrections programs, more emphasis is placed on the conflict within the role of the single officer who is usually in charge of supervision. Since the probation or parole agent usually has both service and condition enforcement responsibilities, the conflict is embedded within the officer's role rather than between two sets of staff with different functions. For example, Jester's (1981) study of eight probation and parole units found that officers spent 14.5 percent of their time in supportive counseling and casework, and 8.3 percent of their time in rule enforcement and risk evaluation.

A number of researchers have attempted to describe the roles or styles of correctional workers by depicting how the conflict between assistance and control can structure the approach the worker takes to the job. One of the most highly regarded of these studies was conducted by Elliot Studt (1972) in the California parole system. Studt reported four predominant approaches by parole officers. Some officers, whom she called "guardians," stressed service rather than surveillance and treated their clients as "wards" under their protection and guidance. Others, whom she called "insiders," placed equal stress on service and surveillance by providing to the parolees (or "outsiders") access to opportunities in return for conformity to basic rules and regulations. Still other officers, whom Studt called "prosecutors,"

stressed surveillance and conformity to rules above all else. The "prosecutor" officers sought to build a case against their clients, who were treated as "defendants." Finally, Studt observed some officers behaving like "superiors" in a bureaucratic relationship with their parolees, who were expected to respond as "subordinates." These officers, observed Studt, did not exert a great deal of energy in the provision of either service or surveillance. Instead, they simply gave their clients information, maintained records, and considered requests. Similar characterizations have been made of probation officer styles (see Duffee, 1984, for a review of supervision style typologies).

While Studt could see advantages and disadvantages to each of these roles, and could describe situations where each might be more appropriate than the others, she also concluded that each of these styles was a relatively fragile resolution of the basic conflict between service and surveillance. The prosecutor, guardian, and superior styles were all vulnerable to complaints that not all the officer's responsibilities were being adequately assumed. The insider role was fragile because officers frequently did not have the resources for adequate surveillance or sufficient access to services to make the demand for conformity in return for service a fair exchange.

RECOMMENDATIONS FOR RESTRUCTURING

A number of recommendations have been made for restructuring probation, parole, and other community corrections programs to reduce or resolve the conflicts embedded in the traditional supervision situation. These recommended changes fall into three broad categories of reform: (1) making services voluntary, (2) splitting care and control into two separate work roles, and (3) delegating the conflicting functions to separate organizations.

One British reform, based upon a paper by Bottoms and McWilliams (1984) proposed that care and control could be split by making sure that all probation conditions were set by the court rather than the officer, and that officers would provide services to clients only when clients asked for them. This change had the purpose of removing control (the conditions of the court) from treatment (the offering of service), and made it improper for officers to seek violation warrants for clients who refused service. While there may be some advantages in this kind of change, Stanley and Baginsky (1984:59) suggest that it could also have unintended negative consequences. Judges might find the purely voluntary acceptance of services less attractive than the traditional scheme because the judge would no longer be sure that the client would get the help they believed to be needed. Consequently, judges might use probation less often.

In other settings, a different kind of reform has been tried. This change also seeks to make the acceptance of service more voluntary, but it removes from the shoulders of one agent both the care and control roles. For example, in the community service order project run by the Vera Foundation in New York City, community service work supervisors have no responsibility for providing service to clients. Their sole task is to give the community service clients their work assignments and make sure the work is done. Service provision has been assigned to another worker, called a "support services supervisor," who provides services to clients upon their request (Krajick, 1982). The Intensive Supervision Project in the Georgia state probation system has attempted a similar change. In the intensive caseloads, correctional workers work in teams, one as a surveillance officer and one as a service provider. Officers working in this system, however, report that both agents carry both sets of responsibilities, despite formal role differences (Krajick, 1982).

The most ambitious proposal for restructuring comes from Conrad (1984). He suggests that the three primary functions in probation—investigation, surveillance, and service—are all necessary but are incompatible and will never be done well when assigned to one agency. He recommends the reassignment of these functions to separate organizations, with investigations remaining with the courts, services going to a service unit in the corrections department, and surveillance going to the local police.

TECHNOLOGY OF RISK CONTROL

Among the more significant changes in community supervision in the last decade are classification by risk and the assignment of probationers presenting different degrees of risk to different levels of supervision. In some systems, risk classification and levels of supervision have been coupled with the assessments of needs. The need assessment process is a separable correctional issue, however. We do not currently know if clients with more needs also present higher risk. We cover the risk prediction and supervision issues here; the needs assessment process is covered in the next chapter.

THE BACKGROUND FOR RISK CLASSIFICATION

Despite the increasing concern for retribution, correctional practice and policy still concentrate on reducing crime by offenders. This attempt can be consistent with incapacitative or rehabilitative goals, and perhaps with both. Differentiating offenders in community settings by the risks they present is a relatively new tactic by which correctional practitioners hope to reduce reinvolvement in crime.

Community correctional programs have long had the goal of reducing the risk of reoffending (McAnany, 1984), but by the early 1970s considerable doubt existed about the efficacy of current supervision measures in reducing risk. For example, the size of caseload research did not demonstrate the ability of correctional workers to reduce recidivism when they were given more time to supervise clients. Elliot Studt's important work (1972) discovered that the great majority of parole violations for new crimes were based on evidence supplied by the police, rather than by parole officers. Studt concluded that, although parole supervision was unavoidably conditioned by the officers' responsibility for surveillance, their surveillance was actually relatively ineffectual. Shortly after Studt's evaluation of parole, David Stanley of the Brookings Institution also condemned traditional parole practice as ineffectual. He calculated that parole officers provided just minutes a month to each client (1976), and he concluded that the chances of effective service or control under these conditions was very slim.

The most recent study of control in probation is the RAND Corporation study of felony probation in two California counties. In the first phase of this study, researchers followed a sample of felony probationers from Los Angeles and Alameda counties for forty months after sentencing. They found that during the follow-up period, 65 percent were rearrested, 51 percent were reconvicted (18 percent for serious, violent crimes), and 34 percent were reincarcerated. They concluded that probation rather than prison for felons was a serious threat to public safety (Petersilia et al., 1985).

In the second phase of the study, the RAND group compared the postsentence behavior of 500 probationers and 500 prison inmates matched on criminal and personal backgrounds. They found that the probation sample fared slightly better than the prisoners two years after completion of probation or prison sentence. Of the inmates, 47 percent were incarcerated again, and 53 percent had new charges brought against them. Of the probationers, 31 percent were incarcerated and 38 percent had new charges brought against them (Petersilia, Turner, and Peterson, 1986). The researchers concluded that prison delayed the return to crime for the period of sentence, but that released prisoners reoffended at a higher rate than probationers.

Both the RAND researchers and Thomson (1987) warn us that generalizing from the California findings is hazardous. These studies concerned only felons and examined the counties hardest hit by the California tax revolt. It would

appear unlikely that the large size of the California caseloads would have permitted a high level of surveillance or of service provision. BJS (1983) has reported that success rates for probationers varied widely in 24 states that were studied, from a low of 66 percent in Mississippi to a high of 95 percent in Vermont.

Under attack by such studies, a number of probation departments began to seek ways of making supervision more effective. One natural and probably overdue result of that search was the adoption of classification methodologies which had been developed and implemented in other areas of corrections, such as prisons, parole boards, and sentencing (see the discussions in Chapters 6, 14, and 17). In these other areas, researchers had discovered ways to take risk into account when making correctional decisions. But techniques for assessing risk had never been systematically applied to the decision of what kind or how much supervision an offender should receive once it had been determined that he or she would remain in the community.

THE APPLICATION OF RISK ASSESSMENT TO SUPERVISION

Beginning in the mid-1970s, classification technology began to be used in probation, parole, and other community settings. Classifications always vary by the purpose to which they are put. As community correctional agencies sought to improve their record in reducing risk, they sought classification methods that might increase the amount of control they could exert over offenders. Agencies wanted to reduce risk by classifying offenders by the amount of risk they presented and then matching supervision strategies to level of risk.

If resources were infinite, classification would not be necessary: The agency could simply watch *all* offenders closely. But resources are not infinite. If all clients are to receive an equal share of officer time, none of them will get much attention. Risk classification of community correctional clients is based on the assumption that all of them are relatively safe (compared to those who have gone to or have remained in prison), but that some are safer than others. If the goal of community supervision is control of risk, then resources can be distributed rationally only according to some scheme that is known to be related to risk (Clear and O'Leary, 1983).

The method of risk classification varies from one jurisdiction to another, as do the specific data elements used to predict risk. But in general, the strategy of risk classification involves a three-step process. Researchers first take a large sample of offenders and measure the associations among a large number of offender characteristics, called **predictor variables,** and the behavior of interest, recidivism measured in some particular way, called the **criterion variable.** A statistical winnowing process eventually leads to a smaller group of predictors, usually a half-dozen or so, that show the strongest relationship to the criterion variable.

The second step involves using these predictor variables to assign a score to each subject in the sample. The score will place each subject in a group with a particular likelihood of success or failure. Typically not too many separate groups are wanted, since not very many different supervision techniques could be devised anyway. Moreover, the data are usually not sensitive enough to provide for more than half a dozen groups with varying reoffense rates. The scoring scheme is useful if it is easy to apply with minimal instruction and results in the creation of groups that actually do vary in rates of reoffending.

Once this classification process is completed, the third step is the validation of the classification on a separate sample of offenders in order to demonstrate that the scheme has predictive power for offender groups other than the one on which it was developed. If the system is to be really effective, this validation process should occur periodically in order to take into account changes in the offender population. An example of one risk assessment instrument is provided in Figure 8.1.

Once the classification system has been developed, it needs to be applied in the field. Experience has shown that correctional officials may reject the adoption of classification instruments they do not understand or whose purposes they reject. Consequently, training in the use of the classification instrument is essential. Unfortunately, agencies often give more time to the technical development of the instrument than to its adoption and daily use. Agencies that currently appear to employ risk classification systems most successfully have invested heavily in building commitment to adoption and use. One of the more successful means of doing that is having line officers participate in the development of the instrument. These officers can then demonstrate its utility and help in training (Clear and O'Leary, 1983; Baird, 1981).

The use of risk instruments is spreading rather quickly. Both the National Institute of Corrections and the American Correctional Association have devoted resources to development and dissemination of risk classification instruments (Clements, 1986; American Justice Institute, 1979). If the efforts of these national organizations have the proper impact, agencies seeking to change supervision strategies would use the models as guides to develop their own instruments. Unfortunately, a number of agencies either do not have the resources for instrument development or do not understand that an instrument developed in another system may not be valid for their clients. Consequently, as risk classification has become more popular—and as it becomes known that "advanced agencies" use risk classification—some agencies will adopt an instrument without any effort to determine if it actually applies (Clear and Gallagher, 1985; Wright, Clear, and Dickson, 1985).

Properly used, risk classification instruments provide community correctional agencies with a number of options that did not exist before. While it is certainly not the only way, classification by risk is one method of making resource allocation decisions on a more rational basis than tradition has provided. Probation and parole offices have

FIGURE 8.1   Massachusetts Probation Service Assessment of Offender Risk

MASSACHUSETTS PROBATION SERVICE
ASSESSMENT OF OFFENDER RISK

Name _____
            (First)   (Middle)   (Last)

D.O.B. ___/___/___   S.S. ___/___/___   Sex _____   CT # _____

Date Assessed ___/___/___   Assessed by _____
                                  (First)   (Middle)   (Last)

Supervising Probation Officer _____

Offense(s) #1 _____   #2 _____

#3 _____   Probation From ___/___/___ to ___/___/___

	INITIAL	FOUR MOS.	TEN MOS.	TERM
	SCORE AT:			
1. PRIOR RECORD (ADULT OR JUVENILE) DURING PAST 5 YEARS 0=3 or more 1=two 2=one 4=none				
2. NUMBER OF PRIOR PERIODS OF PROBATION SUPERVISION DURING PAST 5 YEARS 0=2 or more 1=one 4=none				
3. AGE AT FIRST OFFENSE 0=16 or younger 1=17–19 2=20–23 3=24 or older				
4. NUMBER OF RESIDENCE CHANGES DURING PAST 12 MONTHS 1=2 or more 2=one 3=none				
5. EMPLOYED/SCHOOL ABSENCE DURING PAST 12 MONTHS EMPLOYED SCHOOL ABSENCE 0=2 months or less 0=26 or more days 1=3–4 months 1=21–25 days 2=5–6 months 2=16–20 days 3=7–8 months 3=11–15 days 4=9 months 4=10 days or less				
6. FAMILY STRUCTURE 0=currently resides away from family, few or no family ties 1=resides in one-parent home 2=parent not supporting children 3=single, emancipated from parental home, strong family ties, or married no children 4=resides in two-parent home 5=parent supporting children				
7. ALCOHOL OR DRUG USAGE PROBLEMS 0=frequent abuse, needs treatment 1=presently in treatment 2=occasional abuse, some disruption of functioning 3=prior problem 4=no apparent problem				
8. ATTITUDE 1.=rationalizes negative behavior; not motivated to change 2=dependent or unwilling to accept responsibility 3=motivated to change; receptive to assistance 4=motivated; well-adjusted; accepts responsibility for actions				
TOTAL RISK SCORE				

SOURCE: Donald Cochran and Ronald P. Corbett, Jr., *Manual for Risk/Need Classification System Report #3*. Boston: Office of the Commissioner of Probation.

rarely been able to present an argument for how many officers were needed for how many clients. Studies of the amount of officer time devoted to clients in different risk categories is one means of tying resource requirements to task demands (Baird, 1981). The same studies can also provide a basis for allocating workloads.

Assuming that more agency time should be devoted to higher-risk than lower-risk offenders, caseloads can be based on risk levels rather than numbers of clients. One agent might supervise a very large number (say 300 clients) known to present a very low risk of reoffending. Other agents might be assigned very small caseloads of those with very high risk scores (Clear and O'Leary, 1983). In Wisconsin, time studies have found that officers spent about three hours per month with maximum supervision clients, about one and a quarter hours with medium supervision clients, and about half an hour with minimum supervision clients (Baird, 1981:41).

ASSESSING THE MOVEMENT TOWARD RISK CONTROL

While risk classification is probably a significant breakthrough in community supervision, current assessments may be overly optimistic. Obviously, classification is only one part of the task if risk is to be controlled. The next question is what to do with offenders of varying risk. Most risk assessment schemes assume that high-risk offenders should receive a greater share of agency resources. But this is only a starting point. What sort of resources should they receive? Is more time from the supervising officer enough? Unlikely. We probably have to determine what the officer should do with the time devoted to the client. Addressing this question is the task of needs assessment, covered in the next chapter. Before we move to that, what do we know so far about risk classification itself?

One, there is ample evidence that we know how to do it. At this point in time, statistical procedures for predicting some kinds of risks are rather sophisticated. The rarer the event to be predicted, the more difficult and inaccurate the

predictions. But as long as probation and parole departments are concerned with the prevention of events relatively common to their clients, such as rearrests and revocations, differentiating can be done rather well.

Two, the fact that the technology exists does not mean that it should be used. As the risk-control proponents correctly point out, the agency must adopt risk control as a goal before the technology is rational. Community correctional agencies have not always been good at adopting clear goals, and some critics suggest that it is not their business to adopt goals. These agencies should do what public representatives decide. Unfortunately, public representatives at the county, state, and federal levels often want several things from their correctional agencies at once. Thus an important question in the adoption of risk assessment is the extent to which agency executives and public representatives actually understand the goal decisions implicit in adoption. Some correctional goals, such as retribution, may not be served through a risk-based system.

Three, it is important to understand that the risk-prediction technology, while effective, will always entail some degree of misclassification. The statistical technology employed assigns an offender to a group with a known group reoffense rate. But the method does not tell the agency which offenders in that group will reoffend. Errors will be made both in assigning some offenders to higher risk groups than they actually belong in and in assigning some high-risk offenders to low-risk groups. If supervision practices are varied by the risk level of the group, some offenders will receive more supervision than they need and others less. In the former case, the offender will receive unwarranted and perhaps unwanted intervention, and resources will be wasted. In the latter case, the community will be put in greater danger than if the classification had been more accurate.

Given these problems, some argue that risk classifications are unethical. The response, and a good one, is that empirically based classification is more ethical than many other methods of determining how to supervise offenders, as long as the goal involves risk control. However, it is also important that agencies use the risk classification as a guide, not as a straitjacket. The system should permit moving a particular offender from one group to another, against the statistical score, as long as the staff has a good reason for doing so.

Four, while there is some evidence that risk classification systems will be adopted by staff who understand their purpose, there is less evidence about the utility of the adoption. Currently, we have little evidence that agencies which have adopted a risk classification system control risk more efficiently than those that have not. Baird (1981) claims that reoffending in Wisconsin dropped after levels of supervision were assigned on the basis of risk.

INTENSIVE SUPERVISION

Probationers who are classified as high risks are to receive a greater share of agency attention. This greater attention is usually called **intensive supervision,** and it is not a recent innovation. However, the coupling of intensive supervision with risk classification *is* a recent development. Small caseloads, presumably providing time and resources for intense supervision of the clients assigned to them, have been studied off and on since the late 1950s. Early research in California indicated that clients on small or intensive caseloads fared no better, and often worse, than offenders assigned to regular supervision (Adams, Chandler, and Neithercutt, 1971; Nath, Clement, and Sistrunk, 1976). This research implied that giving probation or parole officers fewer clients to supervise did not necessarily increase the time allotted to direct supervision, or if it did, resulted in more technical violations, since officers came across more information about their clients.

A review of 46 intensive projects in 1976 led to the conclusion that at that point, comparative results were inconclusive or negative. However, the reviewers also pointed out that most evaluations were poor and that consequently we knew little about actual implementation. The reviewers

An Albany County, New York, probation officer operates electronic surveillance equipment. The machine at the left automatically dials persons on house arrest at random intervals. The officer can alter the program and instruct it to call at particular times. (David E. Duffee)

expressed doubts that intensive supervision could ever reach a level sufficient to make a difference (Banks et al., 1977).

Following these early negative results, the interest in small caseloads was dormant until recently, when the twin concerns for reducing prison populations and making community supervision tougher has rekindled interest (Petersilia et al., 1985). The Citizens Crime Commission of Connecticut (1984) recently recommended intensive probation supervision to reduce prison overcrowding and to provide another punitive alternative. In Texas, intensive probation supervision is targeted at probation violators, who in 1983 made up 43 percent of all admissions to the overcrowded Texas prisons. The goal is to maintain the violators on probation by increasing surveillance (Gettinger, 1983:8). In Georgia, which has developed one of the better known intensive supervision programs, state probation officers select clients from prison inmates and then seek resentencing. Thus, the Georgia program combines the split sentence and intensive supervision (Gettinger, 1983:10). Other states have coupled intensive supervision to parole rather than probation, hoping that offenders will be released earlier to intensive supervision than they would be to regular supervision (Talty, 1985; Fallen et al., 1981).

One new twist in intensive supervision is a high-technology version. Two forms of electronic monitoring devices now on the market indicate the presence or absence of a person within 150 to 200 feet of a telephone line (Berry, 1985). It is proposed that the electronic monitoring of an offender's whereabouts could be used as an alternative to incarceration and would provide elements of retribution, incapacitation, and rehabilitation (Berry, 1985). This technology could be used with work release and home furlough programs, as well as in conjunction with probation or parole. Moran and Lindner (1985) point out that the new electronic devices are only one of several new monitoring technologies that may allow correctional staff to keep better track of offenders with less effort. The negative conse-

quence, they fear, will be the abandonment of treatment in favor of simple monitoring and control. Technology could conceivably allow intensive supervision with very high caseloads and reduced labor cost and would, in their view, endanger any attempts to provide service. (See also Ball, Huff, and Lilly, 1988).

The consequences of this movement toward high-control community supervision are of great concern. While critics like Moran and Lindner can foresee the death of assistance, others see the chance of finally convincing judges to use probation rather than prison:

> And even if the increased control, loss of freedom and extra cost of small caseloads do not dramatically change the lives of probationers, they may be cost effective if they increase the punitiveness of probation and thereby convince judges to use it as an alternative sanction. (Gettinger, 1983:10)

Observing intensive supervision at work in Georgia, where two-man teams are in contact with all 25 people on their caseloads daily, Gettinger is not convinced that help or assistance is disappearing. He reports that many contacts made for control purposes are filled with conversations intended to help (1983).

The new round of intensive supervision has not yet yielded much in the way of supporting evidence. Failure rates and evidence of the actual extent of diversion are scant. (The diversion issue will be taken up in Chapter 9.) Regarding recidivism, a common finding is that revocations are high. But unlike the response in the 1960s, many jurisdictions are not interpreting frequent violations as evidence of ineffectiveness. A number of program administrators suggest that high violation rates, particularly for rule breaking rather than new crimes, is evidence that the intensive supervision is working (see Fallen et al., 1981; Smith, 1984). Interestingly, some intensive supervision evaluations imply some possible therapeutic effects, at least for certain groups of offenders. In England, the British Impact Study found that offenders with many needs but minor criminal records fared well on intensive supervision, while offenders with few needs but long criminal rec- ords did better on regular caseloads (Stanley and Baginsky, 1984:62).

SUMMARY

1. Probation is currently in trouble. It has been attacked both for violating retributive principles and for not providing sufficient protection to the public.
2. The goals of probation are currently in disarray. Current practices seem ill-suited to retribution and deterrence, and rehabilitation does not seem to be achieved with great frequency. The trend now is toward an incapacitative probation.
3. Antecedents of probation include benefit of clergy, judicial reprieve, and release of convicted persons on recognizance. John Augustus appears to have been the first to use the term probation. Between 1841 and 1859, Augustus bailed and supervised many persons appearing before the Boston courts.
4. The first probation statute was passed in Massachusetts in 1878. Probation did not become available in all states for adults until 1956.
5. Probation tasks vary greatly from department to department. Common tasks include pretrial supervision, presentence investigation, and supervision of convicted probationers. Some offices are internally specialized, with probation agents assigned to only a few of these tasks. In other offices, agents perform all probation tasks.
6. Controversy surrounds the administrative placement of probation. Debates concern (a) the placement of probation in the judicial or the executive branch of government and (b) placement at the state or local level of government. The trend is toward state-level executive control.
7. The conditions of probation are the rules a pro-

bationer must follow. A wide range of conditions is permissible, including abiding by all laws, submitting to drug tests, and reporting to the probation officer. Violation of conditions may result in revocation.
8. Revocation for commission of new crimes or violation of conditions cannot be arbitrary or unsubstantiated. The procedure for revocation includes two hearings, one to establish probable cause and the second to determine the facts and render a decision. The probationer has a right to notice of the charges and to be present at these hearings, to answer the charges and contest the evidence. There is no constitutional right to counsel.
9. A central dilemma in probation is the provision of care or assistance by the same agent who enforces conditions. Recent attempts to reduce the conflict include making services voluntary, using separate agents for service and surveillance, and allocating service and control to separate agencies.
10. Probation has sought to increase its capacity for controlling risk by developing classification schemes to predict which probationers are more likely to reoffend and providing higher-risk offenders with greater supervision.
11. High-supervision probation began in the 1950s. Evaluation of the first twenty years of intensive probation demonstrated no positive effects. Nevertheless, intensive probation has sparked renewed interest as a means of protecting the public while not adding to prison populations.

KEY WORDS

BENEFIT OF CLERGY. An early form of clemency originally intended for clergy convicted in King's Courts but transferred to church jurisdiction for punishment. Eventually extended to many nonclerics who could read, or who claimed to be able to read. Primarily an escape from the death penalty.

CONDITIONS OF PROBATION. Rules to which a probationer must conform while on probation.

CRITERION VARIABLE. The outcome variable, the presence of which is predicted by using other variables thought to relate to it. In corrections, the criterion variable being predicted is often some version of recidivism.

INTENSIVE SUPERVISION. The application in probation or parole of greater than normal supervision. There is no standard for intensive supervision, but it usually varies from two contacts per month to daily contact. Most often applied to high-risk offenders.

JUDICIAL REPRIEVE. In England, originally the practice of temporarily suspending sentence to give a convicted person time to apply to the king for pardon; eventually coupled with deportation. It set the precedent for suspension of sentence.

PREDICTOR VARIABLES. Variables used in prediction research to assess the likelihood of a particular outcome or criterion variable.

RECOGNIZANCE. A forerunner of both some current pretrial release practices (in this text referred to as ROR) and of modern probation. Recognizance was used in England and in the United States in the nineteenth century to release offenders on promise of good behavior.

PROJECTS AND QUESTIONS

1. Take a poll in the class. How many students believe probation should be considered punishment for a crime rather than a suspension of punishment? Why or why not?
2. If a probationer serves two years on probation before violating, upon revocation is it fair to impose the original prison term? Or should the two years count for something? How much should they count?
3. While intensity of probation is most often determined on the basis of risk, it could, as McAnany proposed, be determined by just deserts. Probationers could be assigned to levels of supervision on the basis of the seriousness of their crimes. What do you think of the merits of the two approaches?
4. Probation conditions should protect society, but also should not militate against the probationer's attempts to maintain legitimate employment. If you were a probation officer, would you visit a probationer at work to ascertain that he or she is employed? Why or why not?
5. Request from a local probation office a copy of standard probation conditions. What do the objectives of each condition appear to be? Do you agree with them?

ADDITIONAL READING

Todd Clear and Vincent O'Leary. *Controlling the Offender in the Community.* Lexington, MA: Lexington Books, 1983. A philosophical argument for risk control as the focus of probation and an empirical study of how risk-control strategies can be developed.

Patrick McAnany, Doug Thomson, and David Fogel. *Probation and Justice: Reconsideration of Mission.* Cambridge, MA: Oelgeschlager, Gunn, and Hain, 1984. A collection of essays on the justice model applied to probation.

E. K. Nelson, Howard Ohmart, and Nora Harlow. *Promising Strategies for Probation and Parole.* Washington DC: U.S. Government Printing Office, 1978. An overview of recent developments in probation and parole.

Joan Petersilia, Susan Turner, James Kahan, and Joyce Peterson. *Granting Felons Probation: Public Risks and Alternatives.* Santa Monica, CA: RAND Corporation, 1985. The first of two studies of felony probation in two California counties, concluding with a strong plea for intensive supervision.

CHAPTER 9

COMMUNITY CORRECTIONS: SOME GENERAL ISSUES

QUESTIONS

1. Why is it difficult to define community corrections?

2. Are the goals of community sentences different from those of institutional sentences?

3. How have community supervision strategies changed?

4. How do community service and restitution differ?

5. What are the purposes of the split sentence? What have evaluations of its use shown?

6. Are the needs of probationers, halfway house residents, and parolees similar?

7. How has needs-based supervision altered community corrections?

THEY MIGHT BE ON PAROLE, BUT THEY'RE LOCKED UP

Phil and Ken were finishing their second year of the Jefferson Prerelease Center Project. Despite Director Jenison's lack of regard for the issue of recidivism, they were attempting to address the impact of an inmate's stay in a center on later parole performance. Did those transferred to the centers recidivate less often than offenders who were paroled directly from prisons?

Right now they were engaged in the tedi-

ous but necessary task of calculating the actual length of time each person in the two samples had been free in the community, and therefore at risk of committing new crimes. If the two groups had not been free for equal periods of time, Phil and Ken would have to make adjustments for this when comparing failure rates. Right now they were poring over the parole status sheets Ken had copied in the central parole office. Getting used to the parole status codes was taking some doing.

Ken said: "What we need to do is decide

what combination of parole codes would represent a community status and what combination of codes would tell us that the guy had been revoked, right?"

"I guess," said Phil. "Unless we are missing something. Let's see the list again. 36s and 37s are the guys recommitted for technical and recommitted for new crime. So we know they are out of the community. What else—except for those who died?"

Ken scratched his head. "Well, one of the research staff in parole said to watch out for 31s."

Phil looked at a stack of coding sheets. "There's lots of 31s. Look, this guy was listed as 31 from the second month on parole right through to the fifteenth month; then he's back on 23 status. So he wasn't revoked. He's still on parole. What's a 31?"

Ken pointed to the definitions: "It says detained. He wasn't free for those months."

"He was detained for fourteen months, but not revoked?" Phil was doubtful. "What does that mean? Is he on parole or not on parole?"

Ken shook his head. "No, he's on parole—he's on parole until you hit a termination code or a recommitment code. He's just detained."

"How is that possible?" asked Phil. "You mean we'll have to subtract all these months when we calculate whether these guys are at risk or not?" Phil was suspicious, but he had been at this work too long by now to be surprised. "So if we just went by the caseload reports instead of these figures, we'd have missed all these detention cases? We would have counted them as successes because they are counted as on parole. But they obviously did something to get detained. You'd better call back and get an explanation of the 31 code."

When Ken came back the next day, Phil put away his notes and looked up. "So? What does code 31 mean?"

"It means that parole will carry a parolee on the active caseload, even if he's in detention, for up to 23 months without necessarily revoking. It means the guy is locked up in a local jail. Either the parole officer has issued a warrant for revocation and it's pending, or the guy has been detained or sentenced for a misdemeanor to do county time. Abrams told me that the Board will often carry a guy on state time while he is doing county time, and then let him back out to continue the state parole. They don't always revoke for misdemeanors."

Phil shook his head. "Oh boy. So in the State of Jefferson, you can be in jail and on parole at the same time?"

Ken nodded. "Abrams said if you see a 31 code for just a month, it was probably a bluff. The officer detained in order to frighten the guy, but didn't really have enough on him to send him back. But if you see the detention code for lengthy periods of time, it's probably a new misdemeanor conviction. They often don't revoke parole here unless it's suspicion of a new felony."

"So they might be on parole, but they're locked up!"

THE COMMUNITY, INCARCERATION, AND PENAL GOALS

What defines correctional supervision as community supervision? As Phil and Ken discovered, simply accepting a head count of those on parole might not be very revealing. Some parolees are occasionally locked up. Although Phil and Ken had been aware that a parolee could be detained pending a revocation hearing, they found out that at least two other reasons for detention existed. A parolee could be detained pending trial. Or a parole officer could detain for a short period of time under the threat of revocation, when recommitment was not really intended. In addition, the parole department counted as "detained" some parolees who had been sentenced to jail for short periods of time.

Phil and Ken were surprised to discover how frequently detention was used. While the vast majority of persons in the two samples remained free of any trouble for the first two years on parole, the absolute number of detention months logged by some of the subjects was high—a significant cost to the state. Some parolees served a majority of the first two years of parole in some county jail but were eventually returned to regular parole status.

As Phil and Ken thought about this a little more, they realized that in many other ways the line between community and incarceration had become rather fuzzy. For example, some parolees who were listed as "reporting regularly" were enrolled in intensive drug treatment programs. In several of these programs, a resident was forbidden to leave the residence for the first 90 days of treatment. One could argue that perhaps Ken and Phil should have subtracted these residential months from their calculation of days at risk. If a person is isolated 24 hours a day in a residential program, he isn't on the street. His chances of committing new crimes is certainly much smaller than the chances of a parolee who is on the street. This kind of isolation in a treatment program is usually counted as "community status" because the program is not a prison. But it removes persons from the opportunity to commit crime just as effectively as a prison term.

Additionally, Phil and Ken were aware that some people legally listed as inmates were frequently in community settings. For example, at one of the Jefferson institutions, 80 percent of the inmates were on work release status. They left in the morning for jobs in the city and returned to the institution at night. For approximately 10 hours each day, these "inmates" had greater access to the community than did some parolees.

Moreover, by 1980 judges in Jefferson had become fond of the split sentence. Many were put on probation on condition that they spend the first few weeks of the probation period in the local jail. Some judges considered this a "community sentence" because the offender was retained under local jurisdiction rather than committed to the state department of correction. But it did not mean they were free in the community for the entire sentence.

Most offenders serving sentences in the United States are doing so under some form of "community supervision." The proportions of those serving incarcerative versus nonincarcerative sentences has remained rather stable for some time—about one-third in prisons and about two-thirds in the "community." However, the line between these two groups has become less clear. Practices such as those described above have become more common, although probably not so common as to change the 1:2 ratio. Yet the blurring of the line between institutional and noninstitutional corrections requires some attention, because it suggests that commonsense definitions of "community corrections" may not be sufficient to help us understand community supervision.

Definitions of community corrections vary widely, depending on themes particular authors wish to stress in their coverage. For example, in a book called *Community Based Correction*, Vernon Fox (1977) excluded probation and parole, because, in Fox's view, probation and parole are "traditional" programs rather than innovative attempts to reintegrate offenders into communities. Hassim Solomon (1976), however, included all community programs in his coverage, not only probation and parole, but also therapeutic community programs in prisons. Paul Hahn (1975) argued that community-based corrections included any programs that reduced the use of institutions, including diversion programs and prison programs such as prerelease and work release which reduce the duration of confinement or reduce the distance between the inmate and the community.

Such variation in the definition of community corrections sounds like the blind men grabbing at different parts of the elephant. C. West Churchman (1968) used the tale of the blind men and the elephant as an example of system definition problems. In Chapter 5, we examined Churchman's guidelines for systems analysis. The second guideline was designation of system boundaries. It is the problem of determining the boundaries of community correction that appears to be the major difficulty in the definition of the term. Vernon Fox appears wedded to the issue of innovation as a boundary-defining characteristic, and so he excluded traditional programs. Solomon was apparently attracted to any use of the term "community" in corrections and therefore included programs that occurred in prisons but utilized the concept of community.

For Hahn, in contrast, "community-based corrections" did not refer to the location of the sentence, but to whether the design of the entire correctional system functioned to reduce isolation from the community. This last approach may offer us the best lead, since Churchman warned that official structures are less useful in defining a system than behaviors or functions. In Chapter 5, Commissioner Rush proposed a system design for his department that would have maximized the emphasis on reintegration of offenders. With his design, would it be appropriate to include the prisons in the notion of "community corrections"?

As we might suspect, the answer depends on our purposes. Part of the fuzziness in the distinction between community and noncommunity corrections is due to variations in purpose which various analysts assume should guide their descriptions of the system, and therefore its boundaries. On the issue of purposes, Commissioner Rush, a practitioner, is perhaps more helpful. Notice that Rush was not concerned about specific lines between institutional and noninstitutional forms of correction. He envisioned his jails being converted to serve a reintegration purpose through work release and preparation for parole. He envisioned his parole officers working closely with work release inmates to increase their employment opportunities. He was hopeful that his reception center staff, even though housed in a maximum security prison, would make initial classification decisions consistent with the system goals of gradually reducing custody and increasing the responsibility of inmates. Commissioner

Rush was concerned about purpose, not about place, and not about the formal titles of those who would do the work.

Certainly, not everyone would share Commissioner Rush's objectives. Some would not care at all about easing the transition back to community living. But if they are good commissioners, they also will define their systems in relationship to their overall goals. The roles that both noninstitutional and institutional resources play in these systems will depend on those goals.

While this position is consistent with systems analysis, it also merits inspection in correctional terms. Can "community corrections" programs serve the same goals as prisons do? There is debate on this point. However, the emerging opinion would appear to be not only that they can, but that they must. The realization that the prison may not be the only means to pursue particular objectives is one of the reasons that the boundaries between institutions and noninstitutional programs are breaking down.

THE DISINTEGRATING DISTINCTIONS BETWEEN PRISON AND COMMUNITY SENTENCES

Community corrections is not a separate system or a separate correctional function which operates independently of institutions. Particularly since the demise of the rehabilitative ideal in the early 1970s, the refocusing and clarifying of correctional goals has made the traditional distinction between institutional and noninstitutional corrections appear all the more arbitrary. Under retributive justifications, community supervision exists as simply a grade of painfulness in the scaling of sentences calibrated to match the scale of offenses. Under deterrent objectives, community supervision would be used for crimes deterrable by less severe methods than institutionalization. Under incapacitative objectives, community forms of control would be reserved for offenders whose risk potential did not warrant isolation from the community.

These similarities in purpose indicate some underlying continuums that relate community to institutional sentences. One can argue that isolation from the community is a continuum which extends from maximum security isolation cells to the minimal intrusion of nominal or unsupervised probation. Coates, Miller, and Ohlin (1978) call this a "normalcy" continuum.

One can also argue that *control* is a continuum which ranges from absolute, 24-hour supervision through offender self-reporting of location on a postcard once or twice a year. While the isolation and control continuums are closely related, they are not necessarily the same. As we saw in Chapter 8, some probation departments have been experimenting with electronic surveillance. It is arguable that such control techniques may make some community settings the equivalent of some incarceration settings on the control dimension, even though the degree of isolation would be different.

Finally, one can argue that in some sense *community* is also a continuum. If community is defined as a quality of life or as access to resources, it is possible that sentences which leave the offender on the street, to his or her own devices, have not necessarily placed that person in a community (Scull, 1977). Some institutions may provide a greater psychological sense of community than some noninstitutional settings. Some prison programs have been found to provide inmates with more social and environmental supports than some community programs (Moos, 1975; Jenkins et al., 1973). These underlying themes may be more important to understanding how offenders are supervised, and to appreciating the quality of the correctional experiences they undergo, than simple designations of the location of punishment.

THE NEWER COMMUNITY SENTENCES

In the last decade, a number of community programs, or new conditions attached to old programs, have emerged. While a number of these have been available and in use in a number of jurisdictions for some time, frequency of use has increased dramatically in the recent past. Although the specific goals of these new options vary, they all seem to spring from a general dissatisfaction with the traditionally uneasy marriage of care and control. Most of the new options tend to emphasize control more than service, in the sense that they make new demands on community correctional clients that are thought to increase the sternness of the community sentence. Some of them also take the emphasis on benefitting the offender out of the equation altogether and replace it with a concern for the victim or for repaying a debt to society.

COMMUNITY SERVICE

M. Kay Harris (1980:6) defines community service as

. . . a program through which convicted offenders are placed in unpaid positions in non-profit or tax supported agencies to serve a specified number of hours performing work or service within a given time limit as a sentencing option or condition.

The practice of ordering offenders to do work has a long history. In a historical review of English statutes, Pease found forerunners of community service dating back to 1547 (1985:56–57). Modern community service is a noncustodial sentence rather than a circumstance of custody or exile (Pease, 1985:57).

A number of accounts of community service consider it a type of restitution, but the leading authorities on restitution and community service disagree. Pease has stated that community service can be regarded as a purely retributive sentence: The offender pays back a debt to society by working a specified number of hours (Pease, 1985:52–58). Krajick (1982) indicated that the recent increase in use of community service is closely related to recent drunk driving legislation. Such a penalty for drunk driving would appear to have retributive motives, although it is arguably provided as a deterrent.

While community service would appear to focus on the offense, rather than upon improving the offender, the care or service concerns of community service programs are not hard to find. Krajick's survey (1982:10) of community service directors found that many of them believed the main benefit of community service was the personal change in the offender. Young suggested that community service can rehabilitate by:

. . . the fostering of social responsibility; contact with other workers; the constructive use of leisure time; the development of long term interests and skills, and even new employment opportunities; and the resumption of work habits by the unemployed and unemployable. (1979:47)

Young also observed that community service in Great Britain was intended as a way of fostering reintegration, rather than simply as a sterner punishment. The English proposers thought that the participation of community members in supervising the work of offenders would "engender community spirit from within" by making them participate directly in corrections, rather than leaving corrections to bureaucracies (Young, 1979:14–15).

Community service was formalized in England and Wales in the Criminal Justice Act of 1972 (Pease, 1985:55). The act required community service offenders (1) to be 16 years of age or older, (2) to be convicted of an offense punishable by imprisonment, (3) to be recommended for community service in the probation report, (4) to serve between 40 and 240 hours within one year, during leisure time, (5) not to be on probation, and (6) to be revoked if the work was not completed or if the person was convicted of another offense (Pease, 1985:55). Community service gained popularity quickly. In 1982, over 30,000 community service orders were handed down, representing 8 percent of offenders sentenced for more serious crimes (Pease, 1985:55).

In the United States, the earliest program was probably a 1966 Alameda County, California, program designed for female traffic offenders who could not afford to pay fines (Krajick, 1982:8). The now defunct Law Enforcement Assistance Administration (LEAA) provided a major impetus for community service. Between 1978 and 1981, LEAA provided $30 million to establish 85 community service programs. More than half of these went out of business when LEAA folded (Krajick:1982:8).

The kinds of work done by community service offenders varies widely, although much of it is manual unskilled labor. The Cook County (Chicago) program has included garbage collection, street repair, painting street lines, putting up and repairing street signs, maintenance of sewers, sweeping and mopping, mowing lawns, general painting, repair of refuse cans, picking up debris, and working with children in day care settings (Brennan and Mason, 1983:56). A number of community service programs promise that the services rendered by clients will not replace the employment of others. This is a difficult promise to evaluate, but Pease, a leading student of community service, was very doubtful. He complained that many public and nonprofit agencies replaced paid labor with the free labor from offenders and restructured their budgets around its expected continuance. Such practices could lead to unemployment and certainly to negative perceptions of the program by the workers who are replaced (Pease, 1985:82–83).

How is community service used as a penalty? Young tried to answer this question by examining the previous records, age, and community ties of those sentenced to community service. He found that community service appeared to lie midway between imprisonment and probation, although many community service offenders had been convicted of charges serious enough to justify imprisonment (Young, 1979:116–117). Like the English program, the Dutch community service program was designed to replace short-term confinement. It was intended to be a positive experience for the offender, but was perceived as a sanction for the offense. A 1982 evaluation found that the program was implemented with relative success. Community service offenders were con-

Insert 9.1 COMMUNITY SERVICE BY CORPORATIONS

The sentencing of corporations convicted of crimes has long been viewed as a difficult task with no satisfactory outcomes. Probation has frequently been considered impossible to supervise effectively, incarceration impossible to implement, and dissolution of the corporation (a corporate death penalty) too severe. In 1984, Frank Merritt reviewed some rather recent innovations in the sentencing of corporations. He suggested that community service (or in his terms, "community restitution") might be a feasible alternative that would both punish the corporation and provide some valuable services to particular communities.

In Merritt's view, corporate community service would involve sentencing the corporation to a very large fine, then suspending the payment, placing the organization on probation, and using community service orders as a condition of probation. The corporation could be ordered to make payments to charitable organizations, or to provide them with goods or expert services.

Federal district courts in the Eighth and Tenth circuits have recently attempted this approach, attracting opposite reactions from their Courts of Appeal. In the Tenth Circuit, a 1982 decision reversed a corporate community service order on the grounds that the federal probation statute permitted only restitution to the victim, not to charitable organizations. However, the Eighth Circuit accepted a corporate order shortly thereafter on the grounds that restitution to the community was just another condition of probation, and that federal judges have wide latitude in selecting appropriate probation conditions.

Merritt argued that appellate courts will increasingly interpret the probation statute broadly, since installment fines are now commonplace and community service as a condition of probation for individual offenders is well established.

victed of far more serious charges than fine payers, and their characteristics resembled those of persons in short-term confinement (Junger-Tas, 1984).

A survey of seven probation districts in England found that work sponsors, judges, and offenders agreed on the severity of community service, scaling it between fines and intermittent detention (Leibrich, Galaway, and Underhill, 1984). A number of surveys discovered that offenders sentenced to it have rather high regard for it as a sentence. Offenders generally saw the order to work as an appropriate punishment. They also said that it kept them out of trouble or had other desirable consequences (Pease, 1985:58).

Considering how quickly community service has gained popularity, we should not be surprised to find that there are many implementation problems. Examining the English programs, Pease reported that community service completion rates have remained stable and high (about 74 percent of offenders successfully completed their sentences from 1979 to 1982) and that only about 10 percent of offenders are convicted of another offense during the period of the order. Pease hypothesized that these stable rates indicated increasing laxness in supervision. The number of orders had increased dramatically, so there were many more offenders to supervise with the same number of staff. He suggested that to handle the increasing numbers, supervisors had become lenient in their definition of successful completion and lax in reporting violations.

Krajick's survey in the United States attested to similar problems. Particularly in California, where funding cuts have been large, community service directors complained that caseloads were too large to allow them to screen cases adequately or to seek out offenders who have committed serious offenses. Given such problems, many programs have put caps on the length of the work orders they would agree to accept, which in turn limited the seriousness of the offenses for which community service might be seen as appropriate

(Krajick, 1982:12–14). Two Canadian writers traced the problems of implementation directly to popularity. Community service appealed to both liberals and conservatives, although for different reasons, and the resulting programs suffered from the same kinds of goal conflicts and ambiguities found in more traditional programs (Perrier and Pink, 1985).

Pease noted that most of the persons who actually supervised the work saw the primary purpose of the programs as helping the offender. This orientation conflicted with the statutory intent of the English program (Pease, 1985:77–79). Goal ambiguities were particularly visible in the many disparities across program sites. Attitudes of supervisors and work organizers varied, as did the conditions of work and the kinds of offenders who were sentenced to community service in different jurisdictions (see Pease et al., 1975:67). Particularly troublesome was the finding that the length of the community service order varied with the employment status of the offender rather than with the seriousness of the crime committed. Working offenders were given shorter orders (Pease, 1985:74). Krajick noted that as of 1982, LEAA estimated that the costs of administering community supervision were greater than the value of the labor received from the offenders (1982:9).

Revocation from community service appears to be a particularly difficult area. Pease (1985:81) found convincing evidence that discretionary decisions by work supervisors were influenced by social characteristics of offenders, rather than by their behavior. Moreover, there appeared to be virtually no rules governing the decision not to return an offender to court, only rules governing revocation itself. Finally, Pease reported that revocation from community service might result in incarceration even if the original charge did not merit custody (Pease, 1985:72).

It appears doubtful that recidivism after a community service order is of prime concern to program designers. To the extent that retribution is the real goal, then the frequency with which offenders reoffend is irrelevant. Consequently, the impact of community service or recidivism

has not received great attention. The few studies that do exist are not very favorable. The Vera study in New York City found that 44 percent of community service offenders were rearrested within four months of completing the program. In England, Pease, Billingham, and Earnshaw (1977) reported a 44.2 percent reconviction rate within one year after the sentence. They found no evidence that community service had lower rates than other types of sentence. One study from Tasmania reported that persons for whom community service was a true diversion from a more severe sentence did fail less often, while persons put on community service as an alternative to another community sentence had higher rates of failure (Pease, 1985:87–88). Leibrich's study (1984) compared community service only to periodic (weekend or evening) detention. By classifying offenders into three risk categories, he found that the least and most risky groups were not affected by the type of sentence, while the moderate risk group fared better on community service than in periodic detention.

RESTITUTION

While restitution as a correctional measure has been around a long time, like community service, it has seen increasing formalization and growing popularity in the last decade. Pease (1985:59–60) and Harland (1983) have defined restitution narrowly as action by an offender that corrects the harm suffered by the victim. Since the victim has long been left out of the correctional system, restitution frequently conflicts with more established sentencing objectives. Harland (1983:176) observed that the judicial desire for retribution often is thought to require imprisonment and that imprisonment will generally make restitution impossible. He also argued that desire for rehabilitation often impedes the ordering of restitution. When officials see the primary purpose of restitution as rehabilitation of the offender rather than aid to the victim, the chances of repayment actually being made go down. In addition, unemployed offenders are often ordered to community service rather than restitution, since the benefit to the offender is thought to be the same (Harland, 1983:196).

Restitution can serve as a sole sanction, or it can be attached as a condition to some other sentence. In the United States, restitution is most frequently associated with probation (Harland, 1983:200), although it is also used as a condition of parole (Smith, 1984).

Direct restitution by offender to victim is reported to have benefits for both parties. Launay (1985) suggested that both victims and offenders deal with each other as stereotypes. Victims overestimate the criminal propensity of offenders, while offenders tend to downplay the harm they have done. Restitution programs that provide for some mutual agreement about actual damages may reduce the stereotyping.

Galaway urged that offenders should be actively involved in developing their own restitution plans, since the chances of true reparation increase with such involvement (1983:12). Given these perceived benefits of participation for both victim and offender, one of the better known restitution programs, the Victim Offender Reconciliation Program (VORP), encourages direct negotiation between offender and victim about amount of damage and method of repayment. VORP administrators claim that this direct involvement builds commitment on the part of the offender and reduces the chances that he or she will see restitution as just another sanction. This personal accountability, they assert, leads to higher than average repayment rates (Zehr and Umbriet, 1982:65–67).

Launay (1985) proposed that some of the benefits, for both victims and offenders, that are often sought from restitution programs can actually be achieved better without it. He compared the VORP program, which brings specific offenders and their victims together, with a Rochester program that brings unrelated victims and offenders together in group therapy. He reported that the Rochester program, while not providing for restitution, does reduce much of the psychological trauma suffered by the victims and the chances that offenders will rationalize their crimes. The VORP model, in contrast, was found to be more effective in providing the financial reparation than in helping offenders or victims psychologically.

Restitution programs do not always run smoothly. Galaway (1983) observed that probation officers, who are most often the correctional workers responsible for overseeing restitution, are not always trained in how best to implement it and do not always approve of it in the first place. Failure to pay ordered restitution can occur quite frequently, and does not necessarily result in violation of probation. A study by the Legislative Audit Bureau (1985) examined 2,592 probation cases where restitution was ordered and found that in 513 cases full payment was not made. Reasons for failure varied from rearrest, to unemployment of the offender, to disapproval of restitution by probation staff, to excusal from the original order because the other conditions of probation were met. Harland found that chances of completed restitution go down the more the restitution focuses on the offender rather than on the condition of the victim (1983). Giving the victim a formal role in decision-making in the correctional process is a new venture and is frequently ignored in practice, regardless of how much the plight of the victim is stressed in legislation or formal program statements.

As is the case with community service, recidivism is not a prime concern in the evaluation of restitution, if one is concerned about the victim. However, many restitution programs claim that restitution benefits society by reducing crime. The claims have not been evaluated frequently, and the existing studies suffer from design deficits. Schneider and Schneider reported that as of 1985, five studies reported results favorable to restitution and two studies reported that restitution had no effect on recidivism.

THE SPLIT SENTENCE

Some sentences include both supervision in the community and some incarceration, but unlike parole, the mixture of the two is determined by the sentencing judge rather than an executive board. A common term for such sentences is the split sentence, although Parisi (1981) referred to "hybrid" sentences. The practice of preceding probation with a short period of incarceration apparently originated in Belgium in 1883. It was introduced in California in 1927 and into federal sentencing in 1958. Currently, some form of split or hybrid sentence is available in all states, and its use is increasing (Boudouris and Turnbull, 1985:83).

Like restitution and community service, split sentences have the aim of making sentences sterner, but unlike the other two new sentences, goals do focus on the behavior of the offender. Parisi indicates that the predominant goal of hybrid sentences is specific deterrence. It is often assumed that the incarceration portion of the sentence will be a novel experience, that the incarceration will be shocking, that the shock will have effects quickly, and that based on the experience, the offender will avoid behavior that could result in reconfinement (Parisi, 1981:1110).

One particular form of the split sentence is shock probation. Vito distinguished shock probation from other split sentences by the fact that shock probation involves judicial resentencing to probation after an incarcerative sentence has already begun. (In other split sentences, the prison and probation portions of the sentence are pronounced at the same time.) Not all jurisdictions provide judges with this resentencing power. It is available in 11 states, although the length of incarceration permitted prior to the resentencing varies from several hours to one year, and the place of incarceration varies from the prison to the local jail (Boudouris and Turnbull, 1985:54).

The assumptions on which split sentences are based are not always borne out in practice. For example, Boudouris and Turnbull found that in 42 percent of the Iowa cases they studied, the offender had prior institutional experience, reducing the "shock" to be expected from the sentence (1985:58). Parisi's study of federal split sentences found that roughly one-third of the offenders had been incarcerated previously (1981:1121). Vito (1984:24–25) reported that Texas surveys of shock probationers find that

these offenders often accurately predict their resentencing to probation. This anticipation effect would also reduce the shock actually generated by the sentence. Reviewing these problems, Vito claimed that the "shock" intent should be abandoned. Such mixed sentences should be used instead as a reintegration device for those who would otherwise have spent longer terms in prison. Used this way, rather than as a specific deterrent, the split sentence becomes very similar to parole (Vito, 1984:24–27).

Boudouris and Turnbull reported that the use of shock probation in Iowa is also open to serious due process challenges. They found that the period of shock ranged from 1 to 241 days (with a mean of 77 days). They discovered that in 26 percent of their cases, the incarceration period had exceeded that allowed by Iowa statute (1985:57).

Since the primary impact of the spit sentence is to be found in the offender's behavior, recidivism studies are certainly relevant. Most of the evidence is not favorable to current practice. Parisi's study found that those offenders who had not been incarcerated before had lower recidivism rates than persons who had been incarcerated previously. However, she also found that the addition of incarceration did not make the split sentence any more effective than regular probation; it was overkill (1981:1122–1123). Vito reviewed three comparison studies of shock and regular probation and found that the regular probationers fared better or the same as the shock cases (1984:24). He also reported that the length of the incarceration period had no impact on recidivism; those serving the shortest periods fared at least as well as those serving the longest periods.

The Boudouris and Turnbull study from Iowa is perhaps the most sophisticated to date. They examined 820 shock probationers released between 1978 and 1982 and compared them to samples of offenders who had experienced straight probation, parole, and halfway house placements. They defined success as neither rearrested nor revoked, and found that 61 percent of their sample was successful (1985:55). In trying to distinguish the successes from the failures, they discovered that intelligence and ethnicity made no difference, but that the females, the married offenders, the employed offenders, and those who were older were more successful (1985:56–57). Sex offenders, substance abusers, and those committing crimes against persons were less likely to fail than property offenders. As they compared failure rates and offender characteristics among their samples, they determined that the shock sentencing was not more effective than the other options. They concluded that the shocked probationers could have been kept in the community without increasing the failure rates (1985:65).

HOME DETENTION

An even more recent development is the use of **house arrest** or home detention. Corbett and Fersch (1985) recommend house arrest for its incapacitative and punitive value and as a means of reducing jail overcrowding. Home arrest is the order that an offender stay at home during specified hours of the day. It can operate as a condition of probation or as part of a jail sentence.

Home arrest is in widespread use in Florida, California, and Illinois, where it is used as part of a jail sentence or as an alternative to release on recognizance ("Home Detention Gaining Support," 1983). A number of private foundations with an interest in reducing prison overcrowding have been funding home arrest programs on a pilot basis. In Massachusetts, the Shaw Foundation instituted a program of home confinement for offenders who would otherwise have been sent to the local jail. With similar motives, the Clark Foundation funded an experiment in Contra Costa County. There jail inmates who have served one-fourth of their sentences for nonviolent crimes are eligible for the program. Violation of conditions results in revocation of parole, which is supervised by the probation department ("No Place Like Home," 1983).

Home detention is probably being used by

different actors and agencies for different reasons. As an add-on to probation, it makes a typical community sentence much more confining. As an alternative to a jail sentence, the practice might be seen as both humane and lenient. Like the other new sentences, home detention probably owes its growing popularity to the ability to appeal to both liberals and conservatives. But as is the case with other innovations, the attraction is based on conflicting goals, and the actual uses and consequences of the program probably depend very much on actual implementation in a particular jurisdiction. The practice is so new that evaluations are not yet available.

INTERMITTENT CONFINEMENT

Somewhat older but similar to house arrest is **intermittent confinement,** a sentence that provides for incarceration during some periods, such as nights or weekends, and freedom in the community at other times, such as during work hours. Typically, persons sentenced to intermittent confinement are placed on probation, and their reporting to the institution at the specified periods is a condition of probation (Parisi, 1984:70). Like many of the other newer sentences, this one is liked by some judges because they can implement a retributive or deterrent objective without totally disrupting the life of the offender. Jail administrators, who are usually the hosts for the intermittent confinee, are not usually pleased with this sentence. It requires considerable bookkeeping on their part, as well as complex communications among the jail officials, the judge, and the probation department. Often, weekend, evening, or vacation jail sentences make the jail population extremely hard to predict. While this sentence is probably in widespread use for minor crimes, it has not received systematic study.

THE NEW SENTENCES AND DIVERSION

The sources of popularity for these new community supervision programs also provide them with a dilemma. Conservative forces are attracted because they hear the message that these programs offer tougher, more punitive, more controlling community sentences. Liberal forces are attracted because they hear the message that these programs may be a substitute for prison. The two different perspectives coalesce in a coherent program only if the conservatives are sufficiently satisfied with the enhancements that they would be willing to have offenders serve their time in the community rather than in prison. The alternative is that the new programs will be used to upgrade the penalties now given to persons receiving less intervention, and the people now going to prison will continue to go.

The programs most frequently promising diversion from prison are community service and intensive supervision. So far, the highest quality research on the diversion issue comes from the community service research. The dynamics at work there are likely to be found in the other programs as well.

Young (1979:6–7) reported that the main impetus for community service orders in England was the presumption that the program would reduce prison overcrowding. However, implementation of the program did not require adherence to strict guidelines about the types of offenders or offenses for which community service would be used. In addition, a number of people saw community service as helpful to the offender rather than as a punishment. These factors, taken together, commented Young, have resulted in reducing the seriousness of the crimes for which community service is seen as appropriate (1979:134). Pease, Billingham, and Earnshaw confirmed this problem. They found that only 45 to 50 percent of the offenders on community service in six districts would otherwise have gone to prison. In a related work, it was discovered that when judges refused a recommendation for community service, they rarely placed the offender in prison. Instead, they used another form of community sentence (Pease et al., 1975:25). Krajick's informal survey of community service in the United States led to the same conclusion: The new program is far more often an enhancement

of probation than a replacement for a jail sentence (1982:10).

There are several reasons for the use of such sentences diverging from the proposed purposes. Certainly one is that many people, including judges and prosecutors, believe that those now getting straight probation are being treated too leniently. As we saw in Chapter 8, there is some evidence to support this contention. Another reason is that many of the programs do not have sufficient control of intake to screen out minor offenders (Krajick, 1982:12). Young pointed out that the use of community service as a diversion varies widely from jurisdiction to jurisdiction. Courts that already are reluctant to use prison are more likely to use community service as a diversion than courts that frequently use prison. Hence, the overall impact of the program on prison population is low (1979:102). Pease concluded a recent review of community service by wondering whether its current popularity could survive public knowledge of its actual use (1985:85–86).

MEETING THE NEEDS OF OFFENDERS

Another significant change in supervision is occurring, often in conjunction with risk classification. This is a shift in the technology of the supervision process away from a predominant investment in counseling and toward a concern for meeting the specific needs of offenders. This change toward a "needs-based" or "objectives-based" supervision does not necessarily have to be employed with a risk classification system. Indeed, offenders could be classified on the basis of needs rather than risk, and in some instances this does occur. However, at the current time, there would appear to be a joint change in supervision practice in which risk classification is followed by supervision that concentrates on meeting particular needs. This coupling suggests that at least in some agencies, there is a presumption that meeting needs will reduce or control risk. Whether that assumption is justified will be addressed below; but first, we need a brief review of the development of the concern for needs.

THE BACKGROUND OF NEEDS-BASED SUPERVISION

The early 1970s saw many attacks on the effectiveness of correctional rehabilitation, and community programs did not escape the onslaught. The same research which suggested that community programs were not effective in providing control naturally were damaging to the claims that community corrections rehabilitated. If offenders were improved by the supervision process, they should not reoffend. But in addition to the doubts about correctional rehabilitation in general, and in addition to recidivism studies which suggested that community programs were no more effective than prisons, a number of researchers turned a critical eye, really for the first time, on the process of supervision itself.

By far the most influential of these studies was Studt's pathbreaking work, *Service and Surveillance on Parole*. Perhaps her most important contribution in this study of California parole was a series of investigations about the helping process. She asked parole officers which of their actions had been helpful to parolees. Then she asked parolees when they thought they had actually received help. Finally, she compared the answers.

One of her general findings was that the service technology of parole was sorely underdeveloped. Although she found many parole officers sincerely intending to offer help to clients, and sincerely believing that they had done so, she also found that many parole officers had difficulty conceptualizing how their particular activities were actually related to desired outcomes for the client. In other cases, the parole officers' beliefs about helpful action seemed irrational (such as beliefs that saying Hello and asking parolees how they were doing would cheer them up and was therefore helpful).

In the process of trying to catalog specific helpful actions, Studt began a new trend in community supervision. She asked parolees and parole officers to describe in specific terms the problems faced by parolees. She was interested in the extent to which offenders and officers agreed about the nature and frequency of these problems, and also in documenting what either party did about them. Studt's attempt to measure client problems and to relate parole officer actions directly to those problems can probably be considered the start of the **needs-based supervision** concept.

Following Studt's project, both research and changes in actual practice appeared with increasing frequency. Two of the more important works borrowing from Studt were Community Resource Management Teams (CRMT), designed by Dell'Apa and associates in Colorado (Dell'Apa et al., 1976), and the risk control supervision methodology, called behavioral objectives, developed by Clear and O'Leary (1983). CRMT is really a particular organizational design for implementing a needs-based supervision technology, one that allows correctional workers some degree of specialization by interest and expertise. The development of the specialties then leads to supervision of clients by teams of officers, each of whom handles different client problems. CRMT is one version of a more general approach to supervision, although it is notable as an early version to gain wide publicity and some agency adoptions. The Clear and O'Leary work, although developed in two probation agencies, seeks to express some more general principles for a needs-based system.

THE CONNECTION BETWEEN RISK AND NEEDS

Systematic measurement of risk and needs began about the same time. Some people believed that offenders with high risk scores would also have a greater number of specific needs than offenders with lower risk scores. Wisconsin, which routinely measures probationers and parolees on both dimensions, reports that parolees, who generally have higher risk scores than probationers, also have many more needs (National Institute of Correction, n.d.). However, Clear and O'Leary's study found little relationship between risk level and numbers of needs presented by probationers (1983:111–112). Thus the evidence on the association between risk and needs is meager and inconsistent. There is some evidence that high-risk offenders may have few measurable problems, and some evidence that offenders with many problems are unlikely to recidivate despite the problems they face.

Despite the weakness of the association, Clear and O'Leary propose to use a particular type of needs-based supervision as a means of reducing risk. They admit there is little empirical evidence of an association between risk and needs, but they feel that in the absence of evidence, we can only proceed logically and study the results of intervention attempts. Moreover, the correlation between frequency of needs and level of risk need not be strong for their plan to work. What is necessary is a relationship between meeting needs and reducing risk. And for this connection, there is some evidence: Many agencies using risk instruments include in those instruments some data elements that also indicate particular problem or need areas. For example, the Wisconsin risk instrument includes as risk predictors the extent of substance abuse and the duration of unemployment. Since these are validated predictors, we can assume that some offender needs may be associated with chances of recidivating. Stronger evidence comes from a Canadian study by Waller, who was able to demonstrate that five "situational" variables during the parole period could be used to predict parole failure when he controlled for other background and risk factors (1979:194–195). Waller suggested that if parole officers could target their intervention on these specific factors, perhaps the chances of failure could be changed.

Clear and O'Leary recommend the specification of "behavioral objectives," or particular ac-

tions desired of correctional clients by the correctional worker. These objectives should be logically related to keeping the offender out of trouble in the future. When all the objectives have been specified, the correctional agent should determine what resources are available to enable the client to reach those objectives. According to Clear and O'Leary (1983:66):

> Under this model, a resource is appropriate if (1) it is selected because the offender's risk to the community is such that attention to the case is required, and (2) there is some reasonable likelihood that the intervention strategy selected will control or reduce risk, so long as (3) the resource does not constitute a more severe intervention into the client's life than is justified by the seriousness of the offense.

THE MEASUREMENT OF NEEDS

The methods used for measuring the needs of offenders have not been very sophisticated, nor have methods varied greatly from one study to another. Clear and O'Leary developed their system by drawing on research in education. They asked correctional workers to perform a force field analysis for each client, specifying the forces working for and against law-abiding behavior. Based on the listed forces, workers were then asked to specify objectives. These objectives were to be measurable behaviors toward some target or goal performed in a particular time period. For example, they suggest that "needing an education" is much too vague to guide the client or to evaluate progress, while the objective "to enroll in X vocational training program at the start of the next session and attend classes regularly for three months" indicates specific action that can be accomplished (see also Cohn, 1982).

The behavioral objectives method does not, strictly speaking, indicate needs. The objectives selected imply certain needs. Other methods have attempted to indicate needs more directly by asking workers or clients to list them. Sometimes the person doing the rating is allowed to list whatever comes to mind, but more frequently the respondent is asked to select needs or problems from a list. Some systems ask that the need be simply indicated (yes or no), while other systems ask for a rating of the severity of the problem. An example of a typical needs assessment form is shown in Figure 9.1. In those systems which seek a specification of needs, rather than specific action steps for the client to take, either client or officer must take the additional step of asking how, if at all, that need can be met. Thus the behavioral objectives approach and the needs assessment approaches generally end up in the same position: specifying particular actions. This method has considerable advantages over traditional casework methods, since it provides for easier and more complete evaluation of both client and correctional staff.

A particular characteristic shared by most needs assessment systems is the attempt to separate the goals for clients from the correctional resources that will be used to meet those goals. For instance, it used to be common for correctional workers to speak of clients "needing" counseling. Counseling is not a need, but an action addressed to meeting certain needs. Supervision strategies that fail to distinguish between objectives or needs and the methods of response are likely to rely too heavily on one or two standard supervision techniques (such as talking to clients in the office) and to overlook problems for which the agency has not developed responses.

Most need assessments currently in place rely upon the correctional worker assigned to the case to make the assessment. Since that is the person responsible for monitoring client actions, using the correctional worker as the needs assessor may make sense. Moreover, it is probably the most economical method of making the assessment. However, there are some problems. Studt's research indicated that clients and parole officers did not always agree on the problems faced by clients. She also found that the likelihood of disagreement was patterned. Clients and staff were most likely to agree on economic needs, such as employment, gate money, or other financial assistance, or vocational training. The two groups showed less agreement on more subjective matters. Staff were more likely to report emotional problems, for example, than were parolees.

Duffee and Duffee (1981) replicated Studt's work by asking halfway house clients and their counselors to report the absence or presence of 28 different problems for each client. The results of this survey are shown in Table 9.1. While residents and counselors most often agreed on the problems faced by each resident, once again the researchers found fewer matches on problems such as "needed to work out some problems with family after return from prison" or "wanted advice or counseling about some emotional problem" than with more day-to-day concerns like transportation, clothing, and jobs. These data do not suggest that correctional staff are wrong or offenders are right. Other research has suggested that psychological and emotional problems may be the most difficult for clients to admit. Nevertheless, such data indicate that correctional staff need to be careful in making assessments and should, as much as possible, involve the client. It would seem likely that problems would be more often solved when clients and workers agreed on their existence than when they did not. Finally, these data do not support the belief that correctional clients and staff are in strong opposition when it comes to determining the objectives of community supervision.

What are the most common problems faced by offenders in community corrections? Do these problems vary among probationers, parolees, and halfway house residents? Since data from needs assessments are not yet widely published, these important questions can receive only tentative answers. Table 9.2 presents data from 10 separate needs assessment studies in three different types of community correctional programs. Four of these examined probationers; 2 examined halfway houses; and 4 examined parolees and mandatory releasees. There are actually twelve separate samples from ten different states.

While the different studies used different methods of measuring needs, a few tentative con-

FIGURE 9.1   Sample of Basic NIC Model

INITIAL INMATE CLASSIFICATION
ASSESSMENT OF NEEDS

NAME _____   NUMBER _____
        Last   First   MI

CLASSIFICATION CHAIRMAN _____   DATE _____ / _____ / _____

TEST SCORES:

                                                                                          I.Q. _____

                                                                                          Reading _____

NEEDS ASSESSMENT: Select the answer which best describes the inmate.   Math _____

HEALTH:

1. Sound physical health, seldom ill   2. Handicap or illness which interferes   3. Serious handicap or chronic illness,   _____
                                            with functioning on a recurring basis   needs frequent medical care   code

INTELLECTUAL ABILITY:

1. Normal intellectual ability, able to   2. Mild retardation, some need for   3. Moderate retardation, independent   _____
   function independently   assistance   functioning severely limited   code

BEHAVIORAL/EMOTIONAL PROBLEMS:

1. Exhibits appropriate emotional   2. Symptoms limit adequate functioning,   3. Symptoms prohibit adequate func-   _____
   responses   requires counseling, may require   tioning, requires significant interven-   code
                                        medication   tion, may require medication or
                                                                                     separate housing

ALCOHOL ABUSE:

1. No alcohol problem   2. Occasional abuse, some disruption   3. Frequent abuse, serious disruption,   _____
                            of functioning   needs treatment   code

DRUG ABUSE:

1. No drug problem   2. Occasional abuse, some disruption   3. Frequent abuse, serious disruption,   _____
                         of functioning   needs treatment   code

EDUCATIONAL STATUS:

1. Has high school diploma or GED   2. Some deficits, but potential for high   3. Major deficits in math and/or reading,   _____
                                        school diploma or GED   needs remedial programs   code

VOCATIONAL STATUS:

1. Has sufficient skills to obtain and   2. Minimal skill level, needs   3. Virtually unemployable, needs training   _____
   hold satisfactory employment   enhancement   code

SOURCE: Carl B. Clements, *Offender Needs Assessment*. College Park, MD: American Correctional Association, p. 47.

TABLE 9.1   Frequency of Problems Claimed by 148 Halfway House Residents and Their Counselors

FREQUENCY WITH WHICH MENTIONED BY RESIDENTS	RANK	PROBLEM OR NEED	FREQUENCY WITH WHICH MENTIONED BY COUNSELORS	RANK
72	1	Needed help in finding a job	79	2
70	2	Needed some money to get started with	101	1
60	3	Had a problem with transportation	57	6
51	4	Needed training or education to get a job or a better job	61	4.5
35	5	Had a problem getting a wardrobe together	13	19
32	6	Had a problem seeing family often enough	37	8
31	7	Needed to work out some problems with family after return from prison	62	3
29	8	Needed some help about legal matters	29	10
26	9	Had a dental or health problem that needed attention	32	9
23	10	Had a problem putting together a parole plan	38	7
21	11.5	Had a problem establishing credit	10	23
21	11.5	Wanted advice or counseling about some emotional problem	61	4.5
16	13	Had a problem paying for meals	15	16
14	14	Had a problem with center rules about spending your own money	5	26
13	15	Needed help with an alcohol problem	26	11.5
12	16	Felt out of place on the job because you were a center resident	8	24
10	17.5	Had a problem finding housing for family or for self on parole	23	13
10	17.5	Had a problem knowing what to do with spare time	26	11.5
8	19.5	Had a problem on the job with the type of work required	14	17
8	19.5	Had a problem with center rules about curfew	2	28
7	22	Had a problem with some of the people you work with	19	14
7	22	Had a problem with center rules about rent	11	21.5
7	22	Had a problem with another resident	18	15
6	24	Needed help in dealing with the police	13	19
5	25	Had a problem finding friends outside the center	13	19
4	26	Needed some help with a drug problem	11	21.5
3	27.5	Had a problem with center rules about weekend furloughs	5	26
3	27.5	Had a problem with day care for children	5	26
605			794	

NOTE: Totals exceed number of respondents because most respondents cited more than one problem. $r_s = .74$; $p = .0001$.

SOURCE: David E. Duffee and Barbara W. Duffee, "Studying the Needs of Offenders in Prerelease Centers," *Journal of Research in Crime and Delinquency* 18: pp. 248–249. Reprinted with the permission of Sage Publications.

TABLE 9.2   Needs Assessment of Offenders by Type of Correctional Supervision

TYPE OF NEED[a]	TYPE OF CORRECTIONAL SYSTEM			
	PROBATION	HALFWAY HOUSE[b]	PAROLE MANDATORY[c]	ROW TOTAL
Survival[d]		76 (247)		76 (247)
Financial	56[e] (18,701)[f]	71 (150)	32 (2,019)	54 (20,870)
Social	51 (21,341)	13 (150)	36 (2,016)	49 (23,507)
Employment	47 (21,846)	54 (397)	46 (1,990)	47 (24,233)
Emotional	44 (21,845)	13 (397)	60[g] (1,835)	45 (24,077)
Family	47 (21,341)	23 (397)	27[h] (1,604)	45 (23,342)
Alcohol	38 (21,339)	9 (150)	11 (56)	38 (21,545)
Education	33 (21,850)	34 (150)	28 (125)	33 (22,125)
Transportation		40 (150)	27 (1,793)	28 (1,943)
Stigma		22 (397)	28 (1,888)	27 (2,285)
Drugs	25 (21,346)	18 (397)		25 (21,743)
Mental ability	22 (17,777)			22 (17,777)
Legal	23 (1,006)	10 (397)	32 (181)	21 (1,584)
Crisis	20 (503)			20 (503)
Clothing		23 (150)	19 (1,838)	19 (1,988)
System rules	70 (421)	20 (397)	7[i] (1,960)	18 (2,778)

clusions are possible. The most common problems appear to be employment, financial, emotional, family, alcohol, social, housing, and education. Moreover, the frequency of these most common problems appears to be fairly similar across correctional settings, with the possible exception of financial, emotional, and social. The parolees in these samples were reported to have markedly fewer financial problems than the probationers or the halfway house residents. This finding, however, is likely to be an artifact of the studies, since many of the parolees in the Texas and Georgia surveys were participants in a special financial support project.

The two halfway house surveys report fewer social and emotional problems among those residents than appears to be the case among parolees and probationers. This difference could be due to the ability of halfway houses to ease residents back into community living, thus reducing stress. But it could also be explained by the tendency of controversial programs to "cream" or skim re-

TABLE 9.2 *(Continued)*

TYPE OF NEED[a]	TYPE OF CORRECTIONAL SYSTEM			
	PROBATION	HALFWAY HOUSE[b]	PAROLE MANDATORY[c]	ROW TOTAL
Medical	19 (4,070)	10 (397)	20 (181)	18 (4,648)
Housing	17 (4,063)	7 (150)	15 (1,957)	16 (6,170)
Leisure	16 (503)	5 (397)		11 (900)

Sources:
Probation
  Clear (1977); N = 231; New York City probationers;
    N = 190; Middletown, Connecticut probationers
  Cochran (1981); N varies by need (approximately 3,150); Massachusetts probationers
  Lichtman and Smock (1981); N = 503; Detroit probationers
  Wisconsin (1979); N = 17,777; Wisconsin probationers (statewide)
Halfway House
  Duffee and Duffee (1981); N = 150; preparole release
  Minnesota (1975); N = 247; post-prison release
Parole
  Erickson (1973); N = 56; San Diego parolees
  Rossi, Berk, and Lenihan (1980); N varies by need (approximately 1,000 in each state); mandatory releases in Georgia and Texas
    (statewide)
  Studt (1972); N = 125; California parolees (statewide)
[a] Percentages are listed only where a need was measured. Blanks indicate the study did not inquire about the existence of that
  need.
[b] In the Minnesota project, only the five most pressing needs for each resident were counted, hence percentages/needs area should
  be less than for studies without this restriction.
[c] The Erickson percentages are for offenders responding that a need was inadequately met (p. 68).
[d] Defined as food, shelter, and clothing.
[e] Percentage of respondents reporting need.
[f] Number of respondents asked.
[g] Rossi, Berk, and Lenihan indicate the number of respondents reporting "feeling depressed."
[h] Rossi, Berk, and Lenihan indicate the number of respondents responding that they "did not get along" with *either* spouse or girl/
  boy friend.
[i] Rossi, Berk, and Lenihan indicate the number of respondents reporting problem with "staying out of trouble."
SOURCE: Table 2 in David E. Duffee and David Clark, "The Frequency and Classification of the Needs of Offenders in a Community
Setting." *Journal of Criminal Justice* 15 (3) 1985, pp. 252–253. Reprinted with permission of Pergamon Press. Copyright 1985,
Pergamon Journals, Ltd.

ferrals, taking only the most promising. In general these data suggest that offenders in different settings and legal statuses face fairly similar problems, and therefore that similar supervision strategies are called for.

THE MANAGEMENT OF NEEDS-BASED SUPERVISION

The specification of objectives for supervision may not only be helpful to clients and correctional workers; it also has implications for the management of the agencies, and sometimes even for restructuring the basic roles in the agency. Perhaps the greatest asset of needs assessment is the ability of management to build the needs instrument directly into the reporting and supervision process. The documents that form the case record also become the basic documents for analyzing agency performance and for reporting purposes.

Needs-based supervision has encouraged some changes in agency structure. The Commu-

This urban probation officer displays a caseload book, with 130 active cases. Needs-based supervision, along with risk-control methods discussed in Chapter 8, were designed to provide more efficient and effective control of scarce probation and parole resources. (David E. Duffee)

nity Resource Management Teams mentioned in the introduction to this section are one example. In CRMT, agents specialize in the types of behavioral objectives or needs they seek to facilitate. Clients are given several officers to work with, rather than one. The presumption is that the specialist can be more effective in job hunting, or mental health referrals, or drug counseling, than the officer who must handle all client problems alone. Naturally, this team model can have its problems—clients can get lost in the shuffle between members of the team. Moreover, specialization is impossible in very small agencies (Thomson and Fogel, 1981) or in agencies where resources are meager.

The focus on needs can also influence the contracting and referral processes used by the correctional organization. Just as specification of needs can be used to keep individual agents more accountable, it also can be used to keep other agencies more accountable. For example, in Connecticut, private agencies contracting with the Department of Correction build the meeting of particular needs into their contracts. The needs assessment process can enable correctional and cooperating human service agencies to talk to each other about the performance they expect, rather than simply the number of clients expected to be served. Additionally, all community correctional agencies use referrals to human service agencies with some frequency. By tracking whether needs have been met after a referral to an outside service program, correctional staff can evaluate the relative effectiveness of one agency over another. Then referrals can be channeled to the more effective agency, or steps can be taken to determine why the ineffective agency is having problems with correctional clients.

THE ASSESSMENT OF NEEDS-BASED SUPERVISION

While the use of needs-based supervision appears promising, current data imply that the promise has yet to be fulfilled. Most of these programs have been implemented on the presumption that assessing and meeting the needs of the clients is one way to reduce risk. The few reports we have on that issue are inconsistent. Studying a California juvenile program, Cross-Drew (1984) found that the employment of resource developers for youths in group homes did indeed result in more of these youths being employed and in school than youths in a comparison sample. However, the project youths were also more frequently arrested and had more frequent undesirable official dispositions. Examining the connection between needs and recidivism among intensively supervised probationers, Lichtman and Smock found that additional services focused on needs made little difference in failure rates. Rossi, Berk, and Lenihan (1980) found some positive effects for providing parolees with financial support in reducing theft, but found no effect for provision of employment services. A study by the General Accounting Office (1976) of local probation indicates that clients who had two or more referrals were more likely to complete probation than clients who had fewer referrals, but the GAO could not say whether the two groups of probationers were similar in other respects.

This trend in supervision technology is, like some of the others discussed above, too new to be adequately assessed. Duffee and Clark (1985) point out that the degree of change represented by this technology can be overstated—it is not a basic change in the methods of supervision, but an attempt to systematize and measure some long-held objectives. Nevertheless, the attempt to specify what is expected of clients on supervision and what is expected of staff when they are supervising seems a step forward. If data do not support a connection between achieving these objectives and reducing recidivism, then at the very least another myth will have been exploded.

SUMMARY

1. The line between "community" and "institutional" corrections is very difficult to draw. Some community programs make heavy use of isolation and overt control of clients. Some institutions include programs that provide offenders with considerable freedom and responsibility.
2. The goals assigned to community correctional programs do not vary from those assigned to institutions. Just as retribution, deterrence, and incapacitation have gained currency in prison policy, the resurgence of these goals has reshaped the operations of probation and parole.
3. A variety of "new" sentences or conditions of sentence have appeared in the last decade, not for the first time, but with new saliency as means of implementing the emergent goals of correctional systems.
4. Community service orders, either as the sole sentence or as a condition of probation, have become increasingly popular. Often viewed as a form of restitution, community service orders are more appropriately considered a form of retribution.

Failure rates are high, but may not be very relevant to this sentence.
5. Restitution by offenders to victims for the damages incurred during a crime has recently been touted as a sentence serving multiple objectives, including rehabilitation and deterrence. Restitution is more likely to be paid when the focus remains on the victim rather than on presumed benefits to the offender.
6. The split sentence comes in a variety of forms, depending on the laws in specific jurisdictions. Most forms of split sentence are proposed as specific deterrent measures, but most evaluations of the split sentence find no such benefit.
7. Each of these programs still has some degree of goal conflict, as the subterranean tension between service to the offender and protection of society continues to be felt, even in programs originally designed to help victims rather than offenders.
8. Needs-based supervision, while it could stand alone, is most commonly implemented in conjunction with a risk assessment system. Needs-

based supervision assesses offenders for the types of problems they face, identifies concrete steps to be taken by both offender and correctional worker to resolve those problems, and provides a means of monitoring client and staff performance.

KEY WORDS

HOUSE ARREST. Also called home detention, a sentence or condition of sentence requiring an offender to be at home during specified periods of time. May also be a condition of release before trial.

INTERMITTENT CONFINEMENT. The provision for specific periods of incarceration interspersed with periods of freedom in the community, often on probation.

NEEDS-BASED SUPERVISION. A form of community supervision in which interventions by the correctional staff are designed to meet specific needs attributed to or claimed by the offender.

PROJECTS AND QUESTIONS

1. The advantages and disadvantages of general concepts such as restitution and community service always vary from one jurisdiction to another—and, incidentally, so do the practices based on the concepts. Invite the local probation administrator to class for a discussion of restitution, community service, intensive supervision, and home detention as these ideas affect his or her organization.
2. Interview probation and/or parole officers about conflicts between service and surveillance. If possible, interview probationers or parolees about the same issues. Better yet, see if a small group of correctional workers and clients are willing to hold a group discussion about these problems. Do they agree that assistance and control are incompatible? Do they have any ideas for how to handle the conflict?
3. Do you think it is fair for offenders considered high risk to be provided with services (and surveillance) by correctional workers while low-risk offenders do not get similar attention? What if the low-risk offender asks for assistance?

ADDITIONAL READING

Carl Clements. *Assessing the Needs of Offenders.* College Park, MD: American Correctional Association, 1986. Clements provides an easy and up-to-date introduction to the process of needs assessment. He includes examples of needs assessments from a number of states and discusses special applications and common problems.

Paul Lerman. *Community Treatment and Social Control.* Chicago: University of Chicago Press, 1976. Lerman's book reviews two famous programs in California, the Community Treatment Project and the Probation Subsidy. While Lerman limits his analysis to juvenile corrections, the issues he raises are germane to adult corrections. He juxtaposes the concerns of treatment and control and argues that in these two programs, control became the predominant aim.

Elliot Studt. *Service and Surveillance in Parole.* Washington, DC: National Institute of Correction, 1980. This version is identical to the original from 1972. Fortunately, the NIC chose to reprint this classic, which is regarded by many as the single most influential research study ever conducted on the practice of community supervision.

CHAPTER

10

AMERICAN JAILS AND LOCKUPS

QUESTIONS

1. What are the key differences between prisons and jails?
2. What are the key differences between jails and lockups?
3. What impact would the fee system have upon conditions in the jails?
4. What do we mean by new rules and old rituals?
5. In what ways are inmate programs helpful in managing a jail?

SUNDAY AT THE MADISON JAIL

Phil could not tell from the garbled accounts whether Dexter had actually gotten into some minor trouble, or whether as a high-profile, rabble-rousing, politically vocal parolee he had just been in the wrong place at the wrong time. Visitors' day was Sunday, and Phil made up his mind to visit Dexter at the jail.

Phil had not paid a great deal of attention to the Madison jail; he had concentrated on the Jefferson prisons. He was shocked at the difference. The Madison jail had been built by the county long before the state had abolished counties. Although they were now called Correctional Centers and

had work release wings for prerelease inmates from the state prisons, in all other respects the jails were still jails.

High above the double front doors, the façade carving proclaimed the Madison County Penitentiary. In the distance, airplanes whined down the county runway and off into the Sunday sky. Phil watched the other visitors arriving after church. Some were dressed in their Sunday best. From nearly every car, at least one passenger would drag out a rumpled bag with supplies for the family member locked inside. An old black woman struggled slowly out of a taxi. She handed a Sunday paper to the little boy at her side. The boy dutifully took the rolled up paper, comics on the outside, and clutched his grandmother with his other hand.

Phil sighed and headed toward the front

This chapter was written by David Kalinich.

doors. By the time he arrived, the line of visitors had already threaded its way along all three walls of the lobby and out the door. Phil stood in line. He was not at all sure of the procedure. He had been in many prisons, but had never been a visitor.

"Excuse me, ma'am." The old woman looked at him warily. "Could you tell me what we have to do in here to get a visit?"

She pursed her lower lip and pulled the child closer to her. Phil nodded and smiled down at Tyrone. "Well, once we get in, you tell an officer with the visitin' list who you've come to see, and he writes it down. Then you wait. Sometimes—and it could be a long time—he'll call the name of your friend and shout out a number. You remember the number, because when they let you through to the cages where the phones are, you go the phone with that number. Then you can talk for fifteen minutes. Sometimes, they give extra time, but not with this crowd."

Phil thanked her and looked around. The line behind them was now halfway down the steps to the parking lot. It was the sorriest, shabbiest crew Phil had ever seen. A few steps down the line, an old man wearing a striped, double-knit sport coat and checked trousers stooped to pick a cigarette butt off the cement steps. A huge tumor deformed his left ear. He begged a match from the man behind him. A few feet in front of him, a small girl holding a battered doll in her left hand stared timidly at Tyrone. Just in front of her, two well-dressed men with neatly trimmed beards were apparently discussing legal strategy. One of them kept waving at the officer, who Phil could barely see through the crowd. Beyond this pair were a half-dozen young women, more accurately girls. Phil guessed the youngest might have been 15, the oldest no more than 20. Their chewing gum clacked loudly between puffs of smoke that wafted toward the ancient, peeling ceiling. The girls were having

a good time trading stories with another group that Phil could hear but not see. Apparently they were all here to see boyfriends.

Doing a swift, informal poll, Phil estimated that 60 percent of the visitors were black, about 20 percent were frightened children, and about 80 percent were lower class. The vast majority of people in line seemed to know the procedure well, indicating that they had been here before.

Eventually, the officer left his podium at the front of the lobby and began the slow round. He asked each person whom they wished to see. He checked each request against another sheet. Occasionally he would tell a disappointed visitor that the person had been released the night before, or was in segregation and could not be seen. Eventually, Phil recorded his name.

The guard frowned. "You're the sixth person in line to see Dexter Wilson. You're gonna have to bunch up. I can't get him in there twice with this crowd." Phil nodded and waited again.

Eventually Dexter's name was shouted out, followed by a booth number. Phil, along with thirty other people, was led through the double electrified gates and the metal detector, down a shabby corridor to a tunnel. The visitors filed into the tunnel, passing each other awkwardly, to reach the right booth. Phil was one of six people clustered around booth 12. They said Hello to each other in hushed tones and waited patiently for the inmates to be led into the booths on the other side of the wall. Phil could see the inmate side only with difficulty. Between his phone and the other phone was a thick pane of plexiglass, yellowed with age. Finally Dexter's shadowy form appeared through the glass, and the six strangers took their turns speaking through the phone.

The other five tried to feign indifference to the separate conversations, but there was nowhere to hide and no way not to hear the visitor's side of the conversation. The three-sided booth was tattooed with years of graffiti, some in ink, some scratched into the tile with sharp instruments. The noise in the tunnel was disconcerting, and the air thick with cigarette smoke. Dexter was surprised to see Phil, whom he had met only several weeks ago. Trying not to steal time from the others who apparently knew him better, Phil said a few encouraging words into the mouthpiece and then left. On his exit down the tunnel, Phil watched the grandmother struggling to hold Tyrone up to the phone so the boy could say hello to his father.

JAILS AS CLEARINGHOUSES

The case we have just reviewed paints a bleak but real picture of a local jail. Most seasoned recidivists will gladly do a year in a state prison instead of six months in a local or county jail, especially in a jail of any size where an inmate becomes a number. The conditions of most jails coupled with the lack of activities for inmates make confinement in them a far more punishing experience than most offenders realize in prisons (Irwin, 1985).

The formal function of the jail is to house pretrial detainees and offenders convicted of misdemeanors (some states allow certain categories of felons to serve their sentences in the jail). But the use of the jail goes beyond its official role. In many respects, jails are the clearinghouses for the criminal justice system, sorting, categorizing, and labeling offenders so they may be effectively processed. For the criminal justice pratitioner, the jail is a file cabinet for pending work. The jail may serve as a winter haven for some of the poor who "volunteer" for incarceration by committing a 90-day offense. Ultimately, the jail becomes a mechanism for control over offenders, most of whom are poor, underemployed and undereducated, and members of minority groups (Flynn, 1973). An increasing number of jail in-

mates are drug dependent or mentally ill. Those who populate our nation's jails have been labeled society's rabble (Irwin, 1985).

Lockups differ from jails in many respects. For now, we will point out that lockups house only pretrial detainees for short durations, usually for less than 48 hours. Convicted offenders will not be typically sentenced to lockups. As we will see, lockups have a set of priorities and problems that differ from those of local jails.

In 1983, there were 3,338 jails across the country (Bureau of Justice Statistics [BJS], 1984a) and over 15,000 lockups (National Institute of Corrections, 1986). The average daily population of our jails was 223,552, but over *8 million* offenders were admitted to jails that year (BJS 1984a). Presently, there are no estimates about the average daily population or annual admissions in our nation's lockups. Although jails are functionally similar, they differ greatly in size or inmate capacity. The Los Angeles County, California, jail system houses over 6,000 inmates. Wayne County in Detroit, Michigan, houses over 1,400 inmates in its jail, and plans are being made to expand the capacity to 1,700. At the other extreme, 1,875 jails throughout the country house 25 or fewer inmates.

Many jail facilities were built prior to 1920 (BJS, 1983a, 78). Most facilities built since then have been constructed with the traditional design that serves to separate correctional officers from inmates to the extent possible. Jails are typically under the jurisdiction of a sheriff, an elected official. In six states, however, jails are run by the state, and the federal correctional system has five jail facilities under its jurisdiction. Lockups are usually under the control of city or township governments and managed by local police departments.

The composition of inmates varies greatly. To begin with, the sociodemographic characteristics exhibit a great deal of diversity in terms of inmate age, race, ethnicity, and so on. Table 10.1 shows the extent of the diversity of sociodemographic characteristics of inmates across the country. In addition, as Table 10.2 shows, the

TABLE 10.1 Sociodemographic Characteristics of Jail Inmates

Sex	
Male	93%
Female	7%
Race	
White	58%
Black	39%
Other	3%
Ethnicity	
Hispanic	14%
Nonhispanic	86%
Age at Survey	
Under 18	1%
18–24	40%
25–34	39%
35–44	12%
45–75	7%
Marital Status	
Married	21%
Widowed	1%
Divorced	16%
Separated	8%
Never Married	54%
Education	
Less than 12 years	59%
12 or more years	41%
Military Service	
Served	21%
Never served	79%

SOURCE: Adapted from Bureau of Justice Statistics, *Jail Inmates 1983*. Washington, DC: United States Department of Justice, November 1985, p. 2.

TABLE 10.2 Current Offense and Legal Status for Jail Inmates

Current offense	
Violent	30%
Property	38%
Drug	10%
Public order	20%
Other	1%
Convicted	59%
Awaiting sentence	13%
Sentenced	87%
Unconvicted	40%
Not yet arraigned	29%
Awaiting trial or on trial	71%
Bail status	
Not set	13%
Set	87%
Released and returned	6%
Not released	94%

SOURCE: Adapted from Bureau of Justice Statistics, *Jail Inmates, 1983*. Washington, DC: United States Department of Justice, November 1985, p. 4.

composition of jail inmates varies by crime and pre- and postconviction status.

Basically, the overwhelming number of inmates who are processed through local jails are charged with misdemeanors and crimes involving property, drunkenness, and public disorder. The inmates tend to be disproportionately black, male, unemployed or holding a marginal job, and poorly educated. Many are intoxicated at the time of booking (National Council on Crime and Delinquency, 1984).

A BRIEF HISTORY OF JAILS

American jails have their roots in the English system of government, as does much of our criminal justice system. The English jail can be traced back to the tenth century (Pollock and Maitland, 1952). Local or municipal jails existed along with county jails. It is common to place the responsibility for the growth of jails in England on Henry II, who constructed jails during the time of Azzises of Clarendon to see to the incarceration of thieves and vagrants during that period (Barnes and Teeters, 1959). Like today's jails, the primary purpose of confinement then was to detain an individual until his or her guilt was established. Until the establishment of the workhouse, in Bridewell, England in 1557, confinement was not the usual form of punishment. Fines, flogging, banishment, and hangings were the punishments typically given to offenders (Barnes and Teeters, 1959).

Jails were maintained with little or no thought to the health and welfare of inmates. The sheriff was technically responsible for the maintenance of the jail, but he was usually an individual with some political stature appointed to his job by the Crown. The sheriff appointed a jailer to tend the jail without benefit of any salary (Robinson, 1922). Instead, the jailer received his income from the "fee system." That is, each inmate was required to pay for food, bedding, or other services received from the jailer (Webb and Webb, 1963). Deplorable and often corrupt jail management practices continued until the appointment of John Howard as the sheriff of Bedfordshire in 1773. With the determination of a reformer, he attempted to bring about changes in England's growing prison and jail system (Barnes and Teeters, 1959). He petitioned Parliament and the judiciary to impose humane standards of treatment and management practices upon the system. Through his efforts, Parliament passed the Penitentiary Act, which attempted to establish a secure and sanitary jail structure, systematic jail inspection, elimination of the fee system, and a reformatory philosophy in the management of the jail and prison system. He recommended a classification system for jails and prisons that would separate felons from misdemeanants, women from men, and juvenile offenders from adult offenders (Barnes and Teeters, 1959).

The American colonists brought the English practice and philosophy with them. Jails were used as places of detention for those awaiting trial or punishment. Punishment did not consist of confinement, but took such forms as hanging, whipping, and banishment (Andrews, 1899). Imprisonment eventually became a form of punishment, especially for debtors. Later, confinement became the prescribed punishment for most offenders except for those convicted of serious offense requiring a sentence of death or banishment. Consequently, jails became a method for punishing offenders as well as for housing them prior to conviction or sentence (Robinson, 1922). The contemporary jail thus has its functional roots

in colonial practices. The first jail was established in "James City" in the Virginia colonies in the early 1600s. In the latter part of the 1600s, jails were established in Pennsylvania, along with a penal system (Hoffer, House and Nelson, 1933).

In the Pennsylvania system, county trustees or commissioners were responsible for maintenance of the jail. They raised money through taxation for the building and maintenance of the jail. Actual management of the jail was the duty of the sheriff. As in England, the sheriff appointed a jailer or undersheriff to actually run the jail. This system of administration continued and is our present mode of jail governance and management. Then, however, the sheriff and the sheriff's staff were compensated through the fee system (Hoffer, House, and Nelson, 1933).

Since the establishment of American jails, some changes have taken place. The fee system has been modified or done away with; it is now common for county governments to pay a per diem to sheriffs to feed and clothe inmates. In addition, sheriff and staff are paid salaries for their duties rather than depending upon a fee system (Kalinich and Postill, 1981). However, it is not uncommon for sheriffs to keep the difference between the per diem allotment for feeding inmates and the actual cost as income. It was also a common practice, which to some extent continues, for the sheriff's wife to be given a salary as matron in charge of female inmates and of meal preparation. Typically, a house adjacent to the jail was provided for the sheriff and his wife under this arrangement.

In the late 1800s and early 1900s, a rash of jail construction took place. Jails were built with concrete and steel rather than from timber. The early jail design plagues us today. They were built to last, and they did. Twenty-five percent of the jails that existed in 1970 were built prior to 1920 (BJS, 1983a: 78). Many of the jails that have been constructed in the last twenty years follow the traditional design developed at the turn of the century. However, the treatment of inmates has been improved in many ways, and the operations of jails are not subject to judicial review. In many jurisdictions, they are subject to inspection by the state.

THE FUNCTION AND ROLE OF THE JAIL

The function and role of jails today is similar in many respects to that of the jail developed by the American colonists, which is to confine pretrial detainees and convicted offenders (Pappas, 1972). An important function of today's jail is to keep inmates from escaping or rioting, and to deliver pretrial detainees to the local courts for judicial hearings, as was true historically. These are considered custody functions of the jail. Contemporary jails also emphasize inmates' health and general well-being while they are incarcerated (American Correctional Association, 1981), which was not a major concern historically. The policies and programs that are aimed at the gen-

In most states, sheriffs' departments usually supervise the county jail. In Greene County, Catskill, NY, the jail is attached to the sheriff's office, a common arrangement in smaller and older facilities. (David E. Duffee)

eral well-being of jail inmates is called the care function of the jail. It is routine now to describe the function of the local jail as the care and custody of inmates.

THE CUSTODY AND SECURITY FUNCTION OF THE JAIL

Intake and Booking. The local county jail has the duty to accept, as inmates, citizens under lawful arrest by local law enforcement officers or sentenced to the jail by courts of the same county jurisdiction. In addition, state and federal law enforcement agencies making arrests in the jurisdiction of the county jail will place the individual arrested by the agency in the local county jail. State agencies do not have detention facilities, and federal agencies have only five jails across the country. Jails also hold witnesses in protective custody, and serve as overnight "motels" for prisoners being moved from one jurisdiction to another. In jurisdictions without juvenile detention facilities, the local jail may confine juvenile offenders. Densely populated counties with several cities may have lockups located in some or all of the cities under the jurisdiction of the city government and serving the police departments of those cities. Lockups are for short-term incarceration, usually limited to 48 hours. Inmates are transferred from lockups to the local county jail if longer-term incarceration is warranted.

The local county jail is at the mercy of local courts and law enforcement agencies and, to a lesser extent, federal and state agencies. That is, the local jail can received citizens who have just been arrested, inmates transferred from city lockups, and offenders sentenced to the jail by the local courts as punishment. Certain procedures must be followed as inmates enter the jail: intake and booking. The minimal requirements for booking an inmate traditionally have been (Kalinich and Postill, 1981):

1. Verification of commitment under legal authority

2. Proper and accurate identification of the inmate
3. Removal of personal property and issuance of property receipt to offender
4. Strip search of arrestee
5. Assignment of cell to the new inmate

Proper booking, intake, and inmate classification for local jails require more sophisticated procedures than those shown here.

Pretrial Detainees. Pretrial or pre-adjudication detainees are individuals who have been charged with a crime—felony or misdemeanor—but have not been convicted. You may ask why someone who has not been convicted of a crime is kept in jail. For better or worse we cling to the historical common law proverb that an individual is assumed to be innocent until proven guilty, yet the system by which we process accused offenders causes us to keep people incarcerated until their cases are adjudicated. The United States Supreme Court has attempted to distinguish between pretrial and sentenced jail inmates (*Bell* v. *Wolfish*, 1979). The Court ruled that pretrial detainees were being held for trial and not for purposes of punishment. In effect, the Supreme Court upheld the need and right of the government to detain individuals awaiting trial. However, governments, through their detention facilities, may not do more than is needed to incarcerate pretrial inmates and may not impose restrictions upon them that have been traditionally, or retrospectively, considered sanctions or punishment for their alleged criminal act(s). As a practical matter, at least for those in custody, the distinction may be philosophical rather than real.

The historical purpose of the jail was to confine individuals until their cases were adjudicated because if they were not confined, they might flee and avoid punishment. Today, however, pretrial offenders usually can avoid detention by being released on bond, a form of guarantee put forward by the offender or the offender's family so the offender will appear before the court for hearings. Those who cannot arrange bond will remain in custody awaiting trial. Thus, pretrial detainees tend to be poor and unable to post a cash or property bond, have committed a major felony such as murder for which bond may be denied or is extremely high, or have extensive criminal records and would not be eligible for bond. Hence pretrial detainees, as well as all jail inmates, typically tend to be poor, or charged with a major felony, or have a lengthy criminal background (BJS, 1984a). The residue from those who do make bond leaves a jail population that provides particular problems for the care and custody function of jails.

An extremely important duty for the local jail is to physically transport pretrial inmates from the jail to the local courts for hearings. This is a function that is rarely discussed in depth in the jail literature, but one that poses an ongoing logistics problem for correctional officers and administrators. It is of special concern for the custody function of the jail, considering the possible potential escape risk for pretrial inmates on major charges or with lengthy criminal backgrounds, because both groups face severe sentences if convicted. The custody problem is often complicated by the rules of some courts that pretrial offenders appear in court in street clothes and without chains or handcuffs.

Such propriety is meant to protect the rights of the accused, but can cause a logistics and security problem for the jail staff. About 40 percent of jail inmates across the country are pretrial detainees (BJS, 1984a) Thus, a significant group of inmates must be taken to and from local courts and have their clothing changed before leaving the jail and after their return from court. Inmates must be searched before leaving the jail and after returning from court. If inmates miss a meal as a result of a court appearance, they still must be fed. To complicate matters further, the inmates must be taken to the courts on the judicial schedule, not at the convenience of the sheriff or jail administrator.

This primary duty is complex, and poses a security risk. Most jails have officers who specialize in transporting offenders to court hearings.

In spite of precautions and years of experience by jail staff in this function, occasionally inmates will attempt to escape or escape while being transported to court for hearings. In addition, the jail administrator and his or her staff is expected to secure the inmate during the court hearing even though the court will restrict the ability of the jail staff to perform the custody function by requiring that the inmate be temporarily free of handcuffs and other security devices. One final point for clarity is that courts are typically located contiguous to jails to facilitate the movement of inmates back and forth between jail and courthouse.

Sentenced Offenders. Approximately 60 percent of jail inmates are considered sentenced—that is, serving time in the local jail as the punishment for an offense (BJS, 1984a). The sentenced inmates are usually serving time for commission of misdemeanor offenses. Many states limit the use of the jail for sentencing to misdemeanants. However, other states allow sentencing of felons to local jails for a period of one or two years. In addition, a small percent, probably less than one percent, of the jail population is made up of "civil commitments." This category of inmate is there for being in contempt of court. While this sounds strange, this is the typical method of processing nonsupporters, individuals who have been ordered by probate court to pay child support for their children. Having failed to pay child support, such individuals are considered in contempt of court for not complying with the court order to do so.

Some jails may house juvenile offenders temporarily, while some states have banned the incarceration of juvenile offenders in adult facilities. Finally, a number of inmates have been convicted but are awaiting sentence. A delay between conviction and sentencing of offender is common. Usually, the sentencing court will require its probation department to prepare a presentence investigation of the offender. This report is initiated after conviction and may take two to five weeks to prepare (Smykla, 1984).

Jails therefore contain an array of inmates that pose different problems to jail security and to the safety of inmates themselves. Inmate management requires separate types of housing or different degrees of control over various types of inmates. The importance of separating inmates based upon certain characteristics has been recognized as early as the sixteenth century (Barnes and Teeters, 1959). For example, we routinely separate men and women, violent inmates from nonviolent inmates. The need to separate inmates based upon a classification system is necessary in a jail of any size. All states require physical separation of inmates by sex. Some states require the separation of civil detainees from criminal detainees. Often, jails separate pretrial detainees from sentenced offenders. One jail in the Midwest separated male inmates by size and race in an effort to reduce inmate violence and aggression. Other jails attempt to house inmates in single cells to prevent interactions, while other jails will attempt to house inmates who are classified as high escape risks or highly assaultive in single cells and house other inmates in multiple-inmate cells.

The jail population turns over at a rapid rate. Inmates are booked and released 24 hours a day, 7 days a week, especially for misdemeanor offenders. This rapid turnover creates problems for inmate management because new inmates, especially those just arrested, present the most potential for problems such as suicide. In addition, processing inmates in and out of jail is a lengthy and detailed procedure. The rapid turnover of inmates thus creates an administrative problem as well as a problem for inmate management.

THE CARE FUNCTION OF THE JAIL

The modern jail must be concerned with the physical and mental well-being of all inmates (Embert, 1986). It will be argued later that the mission of today's jail continues to be custody and security, but has expanded to include the continued well-being of inmates. Stated clearly, today's jails must see to it that inmates leave the jail in no worse physical or mental condition than when they entered. This may sound simple, but for some inmates the experience of incarceration may be extremely harmful unless programs are developed to help them cope with the jail environment. In this section we will discuss the programs that contribute to the care function of local jails. It can also be argued that inmate programs which relieve tension will make a major contribution to the custody function of the jail (Walakafra-Wills, 1983a; Kalinich and Postill, 1981).

TRADITIONAL PROGRAMS AND INMATE SERVICES

Even in the bleakest periods, jail inmates were provided with some basic privileges or programs. Some of these traditional programs are summarized here. Visitation is a traditional and important program. It allows an inmate's relatives and family members to visit with the inmate at the jail. Typically visits take place for 10 to 30 minutes once or twice a week, depending upon the policies of the jail. Visits may take place through wire mesh screens or some barrier that precludes any contact between inmate and visitor. Eliminating contact is done to prevent the exchange of contraband—weapons or drugs—between visitor and inmate. However, so-called contact visitation has become an acceptable form of visitation in many jails. With contact visitation, the inmate and his or her visitor are not divided by a barrier and usually sit together at a table. "Contact" such as kissing or hugging my be allowed during such a visit. The problem of contraband exchange is controlled by thorough searching of inmates before and after the visit.

Religious programs have always been at least a tacit part of jail programming (Walakafra-Wills, 1983b). Services are usually made available to inmates on appropriate days. Priests, rabbis, and ministers are almost always allowed in the jail to spend time with inmates.

While never labeled as therapeutic, work programs have also typically been part of the jail process. Inmates who are considered low escape risks and can be trusted not to deliver contraband to other inmates are granted "trustee" status and allowed to work in and around the jail with little or no supervision. Trustees have been assigned to kitchen work, cleaning and maintenance of official vehicles, painting and general repair of the jail, and janitorial work, as well as an array of other useful tasks. In fact, many sheriffs looked forward to well-known misdemeanor offenders (the "town drunks") who were skilled in plumbing, painting, and so on, to be sentenced to the jail to serve as trustee maintenance men.

It is hard to find documentation on the extent to which inmates received medical treatment in the past. As recent federal court civil cases have found medical treatment lacking in jails and prisons, one may freely speculate about the efficacy of medical service for jail inmates during the last century. However, jails did not lack medical treatment for short-term or emergency purposes. The county coroner, if a medical doctor, had limited responsibility for the inmates' health. Other jurisdictions would contract with a local physician to perform emergency or first aid work. Since jail inmates were considered short-term guests, no comprehensive medical system seemed justified. Such patchwork medical service for inmates is no longer considered sufficient (American Correctional Association, 1984; National Sheriffs Association, 1974). Ignoring the serious medical needs of inmates because of lack of available medical services can be construed, in effect, as imposing cruel and unusual punishment on inmates in need of medical treatment (*Estelle* v. *Gamble*, 1976).

Traditionally, feeding an inmate was a simple matter. The need for a proper diet was usually part of recommendations for reform. However, feeding inmates was an integral part of the fee system wherever it existed. Day-old donuts and coffee would suffice for breakfast. Sandwiches and coffee, milk, or Kool Aid made up supper. Lunch could be meat loaf or hot dogs with mashed potatoes. Not a bad menu perhaps, but such a menu may not be nutritionally sound and may have an adverse effect on long-term inmates.

Traditionally, recreation was created by the inmates. They would play cards, though they were not allowed to gamble, play checkers, "signify" at great length (a traditional slang term for mutual entertainment among inmates—telling jokes, tall tales, etc.), read when reading materials were allowed, or create other forms of recreation. These would be created to help pass the time and fight off the worst aspect of being in a local jail, boredom and idleness. Little importance was placed on providing inmates with programs or services. The functional emphasis was on custody.

CONTEMPORARY PROGRAMS FOR INMATES

In looking back at change and trends, it is difficult to identify a year or even a decade when serious changes in the philosophy of jail management began to evolve. A good guess, however, is that prior to the mid-1970s, creating comprehensive programs for jail inmates was not even a serious subject for discussion. The need for programs for prison inmates was an accepted fact among penologists. However, the short stay for jail inmates seemed to preclude that need. The prison reformers of 1870 suggested that jail inmates be given longer sentences to allow programs to reform inmates to function in the jail setting (Wines, 1871).

During the early 1970s, however, the National Institute of Corrections, the American Correctional Association, and the National Sheriffs Association began to see value in an array of programs for inmates. Courts, as we will see later in this chapter, began to rule that inmates had rights to proper medical treatment, proper diets, and so on. The courts reasoned that as an inmate, the person could not pursue options to care for or protect himself or herself. Therefore, the jail had to meet standards of care, at least for medical needs.

While custody remains the primary concern of jail administrators, growing emphasis is being placed upon care, at least by professional cor-

rectional organizations and often by the courts through civil rights and tort actions against jails. Relaying on American Correctional Association *Standards for Adult Local Detention Facilities* (1981), a series of programs and services that are considered crucial in running a model jail are recommended. The recommendations are summarized as follows:

1. Jails should provide comprehensive medical and dental programs for inmates which include medical staff when appropriate.
2. Medical training should be provided for all jail staff, especially for emergency situations.
3. An appropriate state agency should accredit or certify jail medical service programs and provide routine inspections of services.
4. Health care should be arranged in advance for special illnesses.
5. Food services that deliver proper nutrition should be a part of the medical program.
6. Social service programs that deal with inmate problems, especially drug and alcohol abuse and addiction, should be established.
7. Recreational opportunities, including physical fitness programs for all inmates, should be standard.
8. Library services, including an up-to-date law library, are recommended for inmate use.

As evidence of the growing emphasis on the care function, some jails have gone beyond requirements and standards. There are jails that have installed telephone services in cellblocks with which inmates may make calls during certain time periods. A recent U.S. Supreme Court decision (*Block* v. *Rutherford*, 1985) concluded that jail inmates do not have a constitutional right to contact visits. However, many jail administrators are continuing contact visits even though they present a custody problem. What administrators often come to believe after some experience with comprehensive inmate programs is that the care function can greatly assist the custody function.

There appear to be two reasons why inmate programs and services make custody and security easier. First, inmates' time is occupied with activities they find useful and that help minimize some of the psychological pains of imprisonment (Sykes, 1958). Hence, tension levels tend to be reduced. Second, granting inmates a series of privileges can be used to reward those who conform to jail rules and regulations and taken away from inmates who violate jail rules.

While this sounds promising, most jails have limited resources and are not able to implement comprehensive programs, even when sheriffs and administrators find such programs desirable. Even jails that are under court order to make substantial changes and upgrade their care function are slow to comply (Schafer, 1986). It is very likely that modern jails as described here are few and far between.

PERIPHERAL SERVICES AND ACTIVITIES

In addition to inmate-specific programs, the jail must provide services to the police, courts, legal system, social service organizations, and state and federal parole systems. Inmates are interviewed with regularity by police detectives, defense attorneys, probation and parole officers, and members of social services agencies. These individuals are usually accommodated by the jail administrators, and lawyers and police officers require the use of private rooms to conduct their business. Inmates must be moved from the cell areas to interview rooms to facilitate this process.

Local probation officers and state and federal parole officers will use the local jail to detain probationers and parolees suspected of violating the terms of their parole. This process is referred to as holding an offender on a probation or parole detainer.

In addition, when convicted felons are sentenced to the state corrections system, the local jail has the responsibility of transporting the of-

fenders to the proper institution. This function is usually given to deputies designated as **transportation officers.** This may be an occasional assignment in small jails; in large jails, the assignment to transportation officer may be permanent. This function differs from taking inmates to and from court for judicial hearings.

GOVERNMENTAL AND ADMINISTRATIVE STRUCTURE OF JAILS

There are six states in which jails fall under the control of the state government: Alaska, Delaware, Connecticut, Hawaii, Rhode Island, and Vermont. As with other states, their local jails were historically under the control of county governments. These states gradually took over the jail functions. Hawaii was the last state to take over its local jails, in 1975. In Pennsylvania, counties fund jails as well as the police function of the local sheriff. However, the state appoints and controls the jail administrator for each of the state's local jails. For the remaining states, county jails are governed and funded by county governments. (Lockups, which will be discussed briefly at the end of this chapter, are funded and governed by city, municipal, and township governments.) Five jail facilities are under the jurisdiction of the federal government and serve the federal criminal justice system. They are located in Chicago, Illinois; Miami, Florida; New York, New York; San Diego, California; and Tucson, Arizona.

The majority of jails throughout the country are under the legal jurisdiction of the county sheriff. Historically, reformers have held the political nature of the sheriff to be a major impediment to reform (Barnes and Teeters, 1959; National Commission, 1973). Currently, the political nature of the sheriff does not seem as crucial an impediment to developing sound management practices as does the law enforcement role sheriffs emphasize in the performance of their duties. The law enforcement priority places

Connecticut is one of six states without county governments. The Bridgeport Correctional Center therefore serves more functions than is often the case of county jails. The facility may house pre-trial detainees, but is also used for work release and other programs for felons returning from state prison sentences. (Arthur, Inc.)

jail management and resource allocation second to police work. In large jails, sheriffs delegate jail management to an undersheriff or jail administrator. Small jails with limited funding are left to the sheriff's direct control and responsibility.

Traditionally, in jails under the control of county sheriffs, correctional officers and deputies worked at the will of the sheriff, without civil service or union protection. In the event a sheriff lost his office in an election, the new sheriff would fire all deputies who worked for the former sheriff and belonged to his or her (almost always his) political party. The new sheriff would then appoint people who supported him or her in the election and belonged to the new sheriff's political party. To the victor go the spoils was an accepted form of American politics at the local level, even though civil service and tenure for public employees was established at the federal and state and city levels for many employees, especially members of criminal justice agencies. Civil service procedures and unions have been making inroads into county sheriffs' departments in urban areas, while most rural departments still often handle personnel in the traditional way. The majority of jail correctional officers, however, still receive low pay and little training while being

given expanded responsibilities (American Correctional Association, 1981; Kerle, 1985).

For those departments with a police system (road patrol) and a jail, the road patrol get first priority for personnel. In small jails, deputies who can no longer function on road patrol are assigned to jail duty. A traditional form of punishment for a road patrol officer is temporary jail duty. In larger systems, deputies are often hired to work as road patrol officers but begin their service as correctional officers in the jail. Unfortunately, the pay grade for correctional officers in such a system is often lower than for road patrol officers. Recognizing this inequity, the American Correctional Association (1981) recommends that pay for correctional officers be equal to that of road patrol officers of the same jurisdiction because the jail officer job has become highly complex and responsible.

Finally, the sheriff with a strong police orientation will bargain more vigorously for the road patrol budget with the county government than for the jail side of his or her operation. Ironically, during the economically troubled times that local governments have faced since the late seventies, road patrols have frequently been eliminated in favor of the jail function, which is typically mandated as the sheriff's primary duty by state constitutions.

Reformers have argued historically that the governmental structure of the jail be changed, placing control and funding in the hands of state government and taking the administration of jails away from the sheriff, an elected official (Barnes and Teeters, 1959). Current prescriptions no longer call for such an extreme change, perhaps in reaction to conditions in state correctional institutions. However, prescriptions calling for accreditation and state control of jails through inspection are presently being offered as alternatives to local control. Also, consolidation of jails from several small counties into a larger multicounty institution with greater efficiency in resource management is prescribed as an alternative to small, poorly funded jails (QRC Research Corporation, 1982).

TRADITIONAL INMATE MANAGEMENT AND CURRENT STANDARDS: NEW RULES AND OLD RITUALS

Jails are being operated with an old set of rituals in the face of a new set of rules (Kalinich, 1986). The gap between where most jails are in terms of inmate management and where they should be is clear from the comparison we will draw in this section.

TRADITIONAL JAILS

The mission of the traditional jail focuses on custody and security. The major concerns are to (1) keep inmates from escaping; (2) get them to court on time to keep the judges happy; (3) to keep inmates from becoming unruly or noisy; (4) to protect the deputies acting as correctional officers from abuse or harm from inmates; (5) to see to the basic food and shelter needs of inmates during their stay in jail. Policies and procedures evolve or are developed around those concerns.

In such a jail, deputies are recruited as future road patrol officers and perceive themselves as police rather than correctional officers. Formal training, when offered, pertains to police work. In Michigan, for example, jail correctional officers typically have formal police training, which is required before one can be certified as a police officer. However, until 1986 formal training for jail correctional officers was not required. Correctional training is "on the job" training; experienced officers are required to pass on their knowledge of the job to junior officers.

The physical plant, the jail building, is designed to eliminate contact and communication between guards and inmates. It is designed with two thoughts in mind: (1) security (prevention of escape) and (2) minimal staffing. These basic concerns will result in furniture being bolted or welded to the floor. Generally, the jail is a stark, functional environment lacking all but the bare necessities.

Jails have been built with this type of design during the last twenty years, even though the design was conceived around the turn of the century. Newly constructed jails following this plan are century-old jails built with new concrete and steel (see Figure 10.1).

In a traditional jail, low concern for inmate safety and welfare is the norm. Inmates can be added to the jail without real regard to capacity or number of beds. They can be allowed to sleep on the floor with bedrolls or sleeping bags. No responsibility on the part of the jail staff is assumed if an inmate dies as a result of a health problem, while withdrawing from drugs or alcohol, or as a result of suicide. Booking procedures require only certain basic steps. The old beliefs and methods of running a jail, the old rituals, are concerned with performing the security and custody function efficiently. They intentionally limit contact between inmates and staff and have little to do with the well-being of the inmates.

In addition, traditional jails have been staffed predominantly by male personnel. Women have been used as "matrons" and have been given sole

FIGURE 10.1   Linear/Intermittent Surveillance

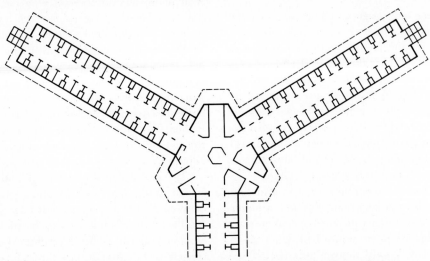

The most common design of jails is the linear/intermittent surveillance design. Generally rectangular, with corridors leading to either single or multiple occupancy cells. In this design correctional officers must patrol to see into cells.

In this common structural design, the frequency of correctional officer patrols is critical. For example, in the case of a high suicide risk, random patrols on a 30 minute or more schedule will be ineffective since a prisoner can hang him or herself in less than 10 minutes.

SOURCE: National Institute of Correction, *New Generation Jails*, Washington, DC: United States Department of Justice, December 1983.

responsibility for the supervision of female inmates. Men are kept out of the female section. In effect, female inmates are "hidden" deeper in the traditional jail facility than are male inmates.

REQUIREMENTS FOR CONTEMPORARY JAILS

The mission of jails still includes concerns for custody and security. However, administrators must be aware of the new rules of jail management: running a **constitutional jail** and taking an active part in maintaining the health and welfare of inmates (Kalinich, 1986).

Running a so-called constitutional jail requires knowledge and acceptance and application of inmates' basic constitutional rights. To run a constitutional jail, the sheriff or jail administrator must make every effort to insure:

1. That inmates are not subjected to cruel and unusual punishment
2. Inmates' personal safety (suicide potential, fire and safety hazards)
3. That inmates are provided with adequate medical and mental health care, including proper diet
4. Proper sanitary conditions throughout the jail
5. Due process for inmates prior to disciplinary actions
6. Inmates' rights to mail, phone calls, and visitation
7. Freedom of religion

8. That inmates are not abused by correctional officers

9. That inmates are not assaulted by fellow inmates

10. That the jail does not exceed capacity and become overcrowded (Embert, 1986: 73)

This set of new rules is based upon prisoner rights case law stemming from civil suits resolved by federal courts during the past two decades (Embert, 1986). The new set of rules conforms to a great extent to jail standards promulgated by the American Correctional Association. To manage a jail based upon the new rules requires the development of policies and procedures that facilitate their implementation. More important, jail administrators must be aware of their constitutional responsibilities as well as the body of law that has created inmate rights. Administrators should be committed to the new standards of care resulting from inmates' rights litigation.

To comply with the new rules, correctional officers should be hired and trained as correctional officers and accept that work role. In addition, comprehensive inmate programs and services must be established as a routine part of the jail system. The intake process should include screening and classification procedures that go beyond traditional concerns for custody. The procedure should help correctional staff diagnose potential medical and mental health problems for which an inmate may require special attention or care, including the identification of suicidal inmates. The orientation for correctional officers must be actively to observe inmates to detect and deter problems. Female inmates cannot be "hidden" from the view of jail staff because of traditional sex role propriety. The most important ingredient for compliance to new rules is a jail staff that is care- as well as custody-oriented and is willing and able to observe and interact with inmates. Old rituals basically deter jail staff from active, direct supervision of jail inmates.

The design of the physical plant will have a major impact on the staff's ability to observe and interact with inmates. The design shown earlier in this chapter shows how the physical structure can build physical and psychological barriers between staff and inmates. The design was intended to do just that. The National Institute of Corrections (NIC), jail division, under the leadership of former jail division Director Ray Nelson (1986), has developed a design concept referred to as the "new generation" jail. The plan allows maximum and continuous visibility of inmates by correctional officer staff. The **podular indirect** plan allows for total visibility with limited personal interaction between inmates and staff. The **podular direct** scheme places jail staff in direct contact with inmates and facilitates interaction with as well as visibility of inmates. Staff working in direct supervision jails experience greater job satisfaction than in traditional jails (Zupan, Menke, and Lovrich, 1987). Inmates in direct supervision jails seem more positive about the jails' climate and jail staff, and report less psychological and physical stress than inmates in traditional jails (Zupan and Stohr-Gilmore, 1987). Floor plans for podular direct and indirect jail designs are shown in Figures 10.2 and 10.3.

REGULATION OF LOCAL JAILS

The current standards of care are not readily enforceable. The American Correctional Association (ACA) as a professional organization can only recommend standards and goals for the correctional system; it has no enforcement power. Through an accreditation process, the ACA does attempt to upgrade correctional operations in jails and other adult institutions. In addition, several states have given state agencies regulatory powers over jails; and jail standards have been promulgated in some states (Franklin and Peters, 1981). However, regulatory efforts have not been effective in upgrading jail operations. Standards and goals created by professional organizations such as the American Correctional Association and state regulations do play a part in civil suits that are filed against jails.

FIGURE 10.2   Podular/Direct Supervision

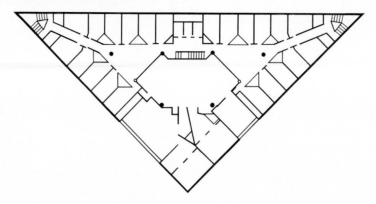

The podular/direct architectural/management relies on staff ability to supervise inmates, rather than on structural barriers or technological devices. In this model, one officer has direct control of 40 to 50 inmates. From a central position the officer has direct observation of all inmates in the pod, and a clear field of vision for 360 degrees. The correctional officer is free to move about, and inmates have ready access to the officer. This concept fosters a pro-active style of inmate management.

SOURCE: National Institute of Correction, *New Generation Jails*, Washington, DC: United States Department of Justice, December 1983.

Civil suits are filed against jails for two reasons. First, a tort or civil rights suit may be brought against a jail after an inmate is harmed as a result of his or her incarceration. The harm may be suffered as a result of an action on the part of the jail staff. For example, an inmate may be harmed by correctional officers trying to control the inmate. An inmate may also be harmed as a result of an omission of action on the part of a staff member or jail administrator.

Class action suits can be brought on behalf of a group of individuals who can claim that they are being deprived of their constitutional rights by correctional administrators. Such a suit will claim that either an act or failure to act on the part of administrators has deprived the group of basic constitutional rights.

Civil suits against jails have become common and costly. During such suits, standards of professional organizations and state regulations are typically reviewed and have a significant impact

on case law decisions (Sechrest, 1978). As a result of class action suits, federal courts have often directed communities to make substantial changes in the way jails are managed. It is not unusual for courts to put population limits on jails and order jails to refuse new arrests if they are at court-mandated capacity. Courts have gone so far as to write policy manuals and mandate the creation of comprehensive inmate services (*O'Brian* v. *County of Saginaw*, 1978). In one instance at least, the federal district court took over the operation of a jail and had a new facility built with local funds while it was under federal control (*Jones* v. *Wittenburg*, 1971).

While no direct, effective regulation over local jails exists, courts will intervene and put jails under court order (BJS, 1984a; Kerle and Ford, 1982), but usually only after someone is harmed and suit is filed or after a class action suit is filed. Except for those instances where courts literally take over the operation of a jail (Cham-

FIGURE 10.3   Podular/Remote Surveillance

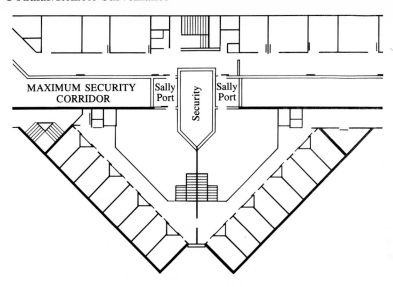

In the podular/remote system of surveillance and management, inmate housing areas are divided into "manageable-sized" units or pods. Unit size rarely exceeds 50 beds. This style of architecture facilitates a reactive management style. From a secure observation booth the staff has minimal contact with inmates, but can readily observe problems and call for help.

SOURCE: National Institute of Justice, *New Generation Jails*, Washington, DC: United States Department of Justice, December 1983.

pagne, 1983), there is no persuasive evidence that court action has brought sweeping reform to the jail system or even the promise of upgraded operations. Even direct court intervention in a jail may take years to begin to bring about reasonable change (Schafer, 1986).

Will state legislation and regulation help? Recommendations for state control began in 1870 (Wines, 1871) and have been repeated consistently since (Barnes and Teeters, 1959; National Advisory Commission [NAC], 1973). The constant battle to improve state institutions makes one pessimistic about the state's ability to improve jail operations. Experience in Michigan with state regulations governing jails has not seemed to have a significant impact on upgrading jail operations. On the positive side, there are states that are mandating training and a certifi-

cation process for local jail correctional officers. This may have some impact on jail operations if jail administrators for whom the newly trained correctional officers will work have a progressive management philosophy.

SOME CURRENT ISSUES

JAIL OVERCROWDING

The conventional definition of overcrowding is having more inmates than planned capacity. That is, if a jail is built to house 100 inmates, and more than 100 inmates are incarcerated, the jail is technically overcrowded. As a practical matter, overcrowding becomes an issue when a large inmate population is a chronic and unmanageable condition. Having 101 inmates one or two days a year in a jail designed to house 100 may not constitute a problem. Having a relatively large number of inmates over capacity for long periods of time will create management problems, and overcrowding becomes a real rather than a numerical problem. Overcrowding as a problem is exhibited when inmates are forced to sleep on floors in hallways and visiting rooms. Overcrowding exists when jails, with finite or limited capacities, are given growing numbers of sentenced and pretrial detainees by the local criminal justice system, which typically has little regard for the capacity of local jails (Taft, 1979; Finn, 1984). Jail administrators take responsibility for overcrowded conditions while having no direct control over the jail population or jail capacity (Cromwell, 1975; Pearlman, Price, and Webber, 1983).

Jail overcrowding has been a problem for jails during the last decade and has been considered a national epidemic (Allison, 1982). As we have shown earlier in this chapter, an overcrowded jail may be considered an unconstitutional jail, meting out cruel and unusual punishment to its occupants. An overcrowded jail will certainly interfere with both the custody and care functions of a jail system. According to the 1983 Jail Census, unused bed space decreased from 13 to 4 percent within those years. In some regions, occupancy rates peaked at 102 percent (BJS, 1984a). Jail overcrowding is not a problem just of the last decade. Barnes and Teeters (1959) discuss overcrowding in their classic work and describe jail inmates sleeping on the floor of an overcrowded jail. They cite recommendations put forward by the *National Jail Committee of the American Correctional Association* in 1937. Basically, the committee recommended more liberal use of the bail system, including measures other than cash bond, a system to collect fines rather than incarceration of individuals for failure to pay fines to the courts, and a probation system to supervise inmates released from jail. In addition, shorter sentences and regional work camps as alternatives to traditional facilities were recommended.

In an effort to deal with overcrowding in jails, The Law Enforcement Assistance Administration (LEAA) funded a number of programs aimed at reducing overcrowding during the late 1970s. A number of pretrial release programs were developed in several jurisdictions. Evaluations of such programs by LEAA (Dale, 1980) concluded that the average inmate population of the jails involved did not decrease. However, when viewed against increased arrests and bookings during that time period, the lack of reduction may be viewed as a positive sign. There have been instances where federal district courts have put population limits on jails and ordered local sheriffs not to accept *any new inmates under any circumstances* if the limit has been reached. Table 10.3 shows jails larger than 100 capacity under court order as of 1984. Of the 621 jails shown, 134 were under order to reduce capacity, and 150 were under court order for conditions of confinement (BJS, 1984a).

As we can see, overcrowding is not just a problem for reformers or jail administrators. It is now a problem that can place a jail and its administrators under legal control, if not legal jeopardy. Local officials can choose between living with an overcrowded jail and hoping to go unnoticed, without harming the security and care jail functions, or they can make efforts to alleviate overcrowding. But if the latter course is chosen, the causes of overcrowding must be discovered.

Hence, one must ask, is overcrowding due to insufficient jail capacity or too many inmates? We can address this question by comparing jails by county population, overall crime rate in the county, and jail capacity (Klofas, forthcoming). For example, if two counties have similar population and crime rates, but one of the counties had a jail with half the capacity of the other, we would expect the jail with the lower capacity to be overcrowded. If that were true, and the larger jail was not overcrowded, we could argue that the

TABLE 10.3   Jails in Jurisdictions with Large Jail Populations: Number under Court Order and Subject of Court Order, 1984

	NUMBER OF JAILS
Jails in jurisdiction with large jail populations	621
Jails under court order:	
To reduce populations	134
For conditions of confinement	150
Subject of court order:	
Crowded living conditions	122
Recreational facilities	81
Medical facilities/services/visitation	70
Disciplinary procedures/policies	54
Food service (quality)	51
Administration segregation policies/ procedures	50
Staffing patterns	48
Grievance procedures/policies	46
Education/training programs	43
Fire Hazards	41
Counseling programs	36
Other	35

NOTE: Data are for June 30, 1984, and cover all jails in jurisdictions with an average daily population of 100 or more in the 1983 jail census. Some jails were under court order for more than one reason.
SOURCE: *Jail Inmates 1984.* Washington, DC: United States Department of Justice, May 1986, Table 8, p. 3.

overcrowded jail was a function of size or inmate capacity. The solution to overcrowding in this case would be to increase capacity by building an additional or new facility.

Conversely, if both counties have similar capacities as well as similar population and crime rates but one was chronically above inmate capacity, we might conclude that the jail is overcrowded due to system problems. That is, the criminal justice policymakers in that county need to look at their policies and procedures for offender processing, pretrial release, and sentencing alternatives. Comparing the number of inmates to the capacity of a jail will tell us if that particular jail is overcrowded. However, the pop-ulation to capacity ratio does not tell us if a bigger jail is needed or if the present facility can be used less frequently.

Overcrowding is a problem that seems to plague large jails. The 100 largest jails are at 4 percent over capacity, while the smaller jails are typically underutilized. It seems, therefore, that smaller jails have too small an inmate population to justify expenditures for improvement, and large jails seem always to operate inefficiently (Mays and Thompson, forthcoming).

MENTALLY ILL INMATES

A current problem faced by jail administrators and correctional officers is the increasing number of inmates who are considered mentally ill. There is evidence that this is a real and growing problem (Gibbs, 1982, 1986; Steadman et al, 1984; Teplin, 1984). In the recent past, criminal offenders who were legally defined as mentally ill would be transferred from the jail or prison system and placed in an institution for mentally ill offenders. The process kept mentally ill offenders out of jails and prisons. Now deinstitutionalization of the mentally ill contributes to the placement of more mentally ill persons in jails (Johnson, McKeown, James, 1984).

Hardly any plans existed in local jail systems to deal with inmates who showed signs of being mentally ill. The old rituals ascribed skills only to trained professionals—psychiatrists, psychologists, social workers. Only they could deal with those who were considered mentally ill. However, during the early 1960s, drastic legal changes resulted in an influx of mentally ill individuals into jails (Steadman et al., 1984). However, correctional officers and even prison and jail counselors were not trained to deal with inmates who were psychologically disturbed.

In many respects, local jails today are still not prepared to deal with the increasing numbers of mentally ill inmates. That is, jails are not being given additional funds with which to hire professionals who are trained to deal with psychologi-

Mentally ill inmates have always been a problem in jails. The prisoner's ward at Bellevue Hospital, New York City, in the 1890s separated the disturbed inmates from regular inmates in the city jail. (North Wind Picture Archives)

cally disturbed individuals (Steadman et al., 1984). Yet the new rules of care apply to all inmates whether or not the jail staff has the credentials or training to care for them. This dilemma can be solved by changing the current laws on mentally ill offenders and placing them in mental institutions, as was done in the past. But this is contrary to current thinking on dealing with mentally ill individuals.

Current thinking in the field of mental health is to keep individuals out of traditional institutions because their problems must ultimately be resolved in their communities, with their families. However, existing jail staff can be given basic concepts for dealing with mentally ill inmates through training programs. In addition, local mental health agencies can provide services to mentally ill clients by entering into cooperative ventures with the local jails. Both New York and Michigan are making efforts to require, and as-

sist, local mental health agencies to provide assistance to mentally ill inmates in local jails. Mental health workers are being trained to work in a jail environment, and correctional officers are being trained to recognize symptoms of mental illness and interact with inmates who are psychologically disturbed.

In the final analysis, the responsibility for providing proper care for mentally ill inmates will fall upon administrators of local jails and their staff, whether or not they are given support from mental health workers, additional training, or resources. They must accept the role and utilize and develop the resources available, rather than wait for assistance or additional resources to deal with the problem.

In addition, mental health problems on the part of inmates are to some extent the result of being placed in custody and having one's life temporarily disrupted. Research shows that it is common for inmates to show symptoms of psychological disturbance for brief periods shortly after being arrested (Gibbs, 1986). As we will see in the section on suicides in jails and lockups, the potential for suicide is extremely high for several hours after initial incarceration. The importance of the research is that it shows that correctional officers have always dealt with inmates who have mental problems and usually the correctional officers have not had any special training. While having a group of clinical psychologists on staff in a jail sounds like a reasonable resource to cope with the increase in mentally ill inmates, realistically, correctional officers will continue to be the humane service delivery agents for such inmates. It is important, therefore, to assume that inmates with problems are going to be the responsibility of the jail. Correctional officers' skills should be upgraded to help them deal effectively with these inmates (Gibbs, 1982).

SUICIDAL INMATES

Current standards of care that have developed as a part of inmates' rights require that inmates be provided sufficient care to prevent harm while in custody. Punishment for failing to protect an inmate from committing suicide comes under civil action. That is, jail administrators, sheriffs, correctional officers, and other officials can be sued and held responsible for damages if an inmate commits suicide. Stating the responsibility in legal terminology, if the members of a jail staff "knew or should have known" that an inmate had suicidal tendencies and the staff "failed to protect" the inmate from committing suicide, the jail staff, including the administrative staff, may be found responsible, or legally "liable," for the "wrongful death" of the inmate. The logic of making jails and lockups responsible for the prevention of inmate suicide is spelled out clearly in the following court decisions:

> When government imprisons people, it deprives them of freedom to look after their own health and safety. In the free community, the man may run from his assailant. In the jail, flight is not possible. In the free community a man may see a doctor. In the jail, he must see the jail physician under the rules prescribed by the institution. In the free community he is not exposed to the hardships of the confinement which may bring out suicidal tendencies. Since the prisoner is very much at the mercy of his jailers, no one should be surprised that the common law requires the duty on the part of the jailer to confined persons reasonable protection against assault, suicide, and preventable illness. (*Wayne County Jail Inmates* v. *Board of Commissioners of Wayne County*, Wayne County, Michigan, Circuit Court Opinion, May 17, 1971, p. 32)

Based upon numbers alone, inmate suicides in jails and lockups do not seem to be a problem: 419 suicides are documented as having occurred in 1979 (Hayes, 1981). For 1978, the National Jail Census reported that 158,339 inmates populated the nation's jails. However, many of these suicides certainly could have been prevented. In addition, the dollar cost to local taxpayers as a result of civil litigation stemming from inmate suicides is growing and is a needless expense. Finally, most suicides can be prevented through

reasonable efforts, and most symptoms of suicide on the part of inmates can be picked up by correctional officers who come into direct contact with them.

Studies have shown a pattern among suicidal inmates. A profile of the inmate who commits suicide shows the inmate to be white male, 22 years of age, single, arrested for public intoxication and therefore under the influence of alcohol. The person does not have a significant arrest record, has been placed in jail immediately after arrest, and placed in isolation for his protection. This person would have been found dead approximately 3 hours after being placed in isolation. The method of suicide typically is by hanging with articles of clothing or bedding (Hayes, 1981). Other studies have developed similar profiles (Danto, 1979; Nielson, 1980; Rideau and Sinclair, 1982). Evidence indicates that jail inmate suicides are proportionately higher than for prison inmates and ten times higher than for the normal population (Esparza, 1973).

The suicide profile is based upon averages. Therefore, one may not assume that only 22-year-old white males commit suicide while in jail. However, such studies tell us that younger, less experienced inmates who are under the influence of drugs or alcohol are likely to attempt suicide. The use of drugs or alcohol is significant in suicide attempts. Drug or alcohol abusers are potential candidates for suicide. The jail environment itself can contribute to the potential for suicide, especially for an individual who has never experienced the trauma of being incarcerated. Being isolated in a drab jail facility where one is treated with clinical indifference can increase feelings of anxiety and depression. In addition, there are many stressors related to being locked up, such as possible loss of family, employment, and so on that can lead to psychological breakdown (Gibbs, 1982).

A potentially suicidal inmate will usually exhibit a series of behavioral clues that can be recognized by correctional officers after a period of training. With reasonable care, most jail suicides can be prevented. Once again, an old practice of isolating "drunks" must be replaced with a procedure that requires constant supervision and observation over the intoxicated inmate. Isolation itself can cause depression and precipitate a suicide attempt, especially for someone who must go through withdrawal from drugs or alcohol.

INMATE SOCIAL SYSTEMS

The chapter in this text on the inmate social system in prisons is rich in surprise for the reader unfamiliar with prison society. Little research has been done on the social and contraband system of jails, however. Rottman and Kimberly (1985) studied social relationships in a jail setting. Recently, Garafolo and Clark (1985) completed some preliminary research on the existence of an inmate social system in the jail environment. The research suggests that to the extent an inmate subculture exists in the jail environment, the basis of such a system lies with the repeat offenders who are accustomed to group norms from past experience or with inmates who expect to spend a long time in jail. Because of the rapid turnover of jail inmates, there may be little need or opportunity for most inmates to form patterns of group behavior within the jail.

Compared to our knowledge of inmate social systems in our prisons, we have a great deal to learn about jail inmate behaviors. There are four major areas in which we need to increase our knowledge of the inmate culture in jail systems (Stojkovic, 1986). First, we need to examine some of the basic elements that describe inmate subcultural relationships—violence, contraband exchange, race relations, power relations. Second, we need to understand the origins of the prison subculture. That is, is it a function of the jail environment, or is it based upon the kind of inmates who are kept in custody for longer periods of time? Third, we know very little about the unique or slang language used by jail inmates. Sykes (1958) was the first social scientist to investigate prisoner language. He attempted to relate it to the inmate social system and hierarchy, which he referred to as "argot roles." Finally, we need to understand if the size of the

Cramped police lockup cells are a scandal in Great Britain as well as in the United States. Here, a prisoner in London's Albany Street police station peers out at reporters investigating overcrowding. (© Topham/The Image Works)

jail has any effect on the existence of an inmate social system. For example, there may be a difference in the ways inmates relate to one another in a jail with 800 inmates than in a small jail with 20 inmates.

LOCKUPS

To this point, our discussion has focused on local jails, not on the short-term detention facilities referred to as lockups. There are approximately 15,000 lockups across the United States (National Institute of Corrections, 1986) compared to 3,338 local jails. Lockups are similar to jails, as they house pretrial offenders. However, there are several major differences between jails and lockups. First, lockups are used to jail offenders temporarily, usually for no more than 48 hours. Lockups are an arm of city or township police rather than being under the control of a county sheriff. In that context, they are under the political jurisdictions of cities or townships rather than county governments. Lockups detain only pretrial offenders, while jails house pretrial detainees as well as offenders who are sentenced by the local courts of punishment. Offenders detained in lockups who do not post bond within 48 hours will be transported to the local county jail for continued detention.

Like jails, lockups vary in size. In large urban counties, lockups may house large numbers of inmates. Smaller lockups may contain only one or two cells. Not every city or township has a lockup. In rural areas, small cities and townships depend on the county jail for all arrests. Most urban counties have a number of municipalities that are large enough to justify the expense of building a lockup. In the urban counties, offenders will be detained in the city or township lockups immediately following arrest. If they fail to effect release on bond within 48 hours, they will be transported to the county jail.

There are advantages for city and township police authorities and the offender in having a lockup. For the police, it allows an initial point of detention for offenders where they may be easily found for interrogation. It also eliminates the necessity after every arrest to transport an individual to a county jail which may be a considerable distance away from the city or township. Inmates can be transported to the county jail after several have accumulated at the lockup.

It is also much more efficient to transport pretrial offenders from local lockups to local courts rather than transporting offenders several miles from the county jail to a local city or township court. It is not unusual to find city police departments, lockups, and city courts housed in one building. This facilitates interactions among the three units and makes inmate transportation to and from court relatively easy.

There are also advantages for the person being arrested if he or she is a resident of that city or township. Contacting relatives, an attorney, or arranging bond may be easier in one's home town rather than in the town where the county jail is located.

Lockups are held to the same standards of care for inmates that we have ascribed to local jails. They must have comprehensive booking and intake procedures to identify inmates who are in need of medical treatment or who are potentially suicidal. As we have noted, the first few hours after an arrest are critical. This is the time in which an inmate may be suicidal or develop other psychological problems as a result of incarceration. In lockups, all offenders are facing that crucial first few hours and therefore all inmates need to be supervised closely and skillfully.

However, lockups are often poorly managed and receive less attention and resources than local jails. It is common for lockups to be run by police officers who are rotated into them on a short-term basis. Since inmates are in lockups for short time periods, little concern is given to services or programs. It is usually argued that little training is needed for people to work in a lockup because offenders are held there for so short a time. Great emphasis is placed upon custody in lockups, but almost none upon inmate services. Currently, the body of research on jails is growing. However, no attention has been given to the phenomenon of city and township lockups.

SUMMARY

1. Jails were built of concrete and steel at the turn of the century. The jail design of that period is still used. Jails built today using the traditional design are eighty-year-old institutions built with new concrete and steel.

2. Jails hold both convicted offenders and pretrial detainees. Approximately 60 percent of the inmates are convicted and 40 percent are awaiting trial. For jails across the nation, approximately 93 percent of the inmates are males, 58 percent are white, and 40 percent fall into the 18- to 24-year-old age group.

3. Historically, the function of jails was to keep inmates from escaping or rioting and to deliver pretrial detainees to local courts for judicial hearings. These roles are still basic to jails; however, contemporary jails must also place substantial emphasis upon inmates' health and general well-being while they are incarcerated.

4. Pretrial detainees pose a special problem for jail security as they must be taken from the jail to local courts to appear at appropriate hearings. In addition, the administrator and the staff is expected to secure the inmate during the court hearing even though the inmate must be temporarily free from physical restraints such as handcuffs and other security devices.

5. Approximately 60 percent of inmates are serving time in the local jail as punishment for their offenses. Usually misdemeanants are sentenced to local jails, and usually the sentence cannot exceed one year. In some states, convicted felons can also be sentenced to the local jail for periods of one to two years.

6. Comprehensive inmate programs make jails more secure and easier to manage. Programs provide activities for inmates that can help them adjust to the jail environment and allow jail personnel to structure the inmates' time and behavior.

7. In most states, jails are under the jurisdiction of the county sheriff, who is an elected official, and are funded by the county government. In six states, however, the state has taken complete control over the administration and fiscal responsibilities of their local jails. The federal system has five jail facilities under its jurisdiction.

8. Jails are currently held to much higher standards of care than they were traditionally. That is, jails must protect the health and well-being of the inmates entrusted to them, and shield inmates from physical and psychological harm that may result from incarceration. These high standards are called the new rules. However, most jails function under traditional philosophies, policies and attitudes toward inmates, called old rituals, that limit the ability of jail personnel to manage inmates in accordance with current standards.

9. The majority of our nation's jails have suffered intermittent overcrowding during the last decade. There are many issues involved in understanding the phenomenon of overcrowding, including how one defines an overcrowded facility. Courts often put population caps on jails, reasoning that placing inmates in overcrowded jails is tantamount to cruel and unusual punishment.

10. Jail personnel must give special and intensive care to mentally ill and suicidal inmates. This standard of care includes the duty to identify inmates with such problems. However, jail personnel are not usually trained to work with this clientele, and mental health workers are rarely a part of the staff of a jail.

11. Few studies have been completed on jail inmate social systems. However, it appears that the basis of any social system lies with repeat offenders who are accustomed to group norms in a custody setting.

12. Lockups house only pretrial offenders for 48 hours or less, and are usually found in large urban counties with several police agencies. They are typically in far more deplorable condition than local county jails and managed with a great deal of indifference by city and township governments.

KEY WORDS

CONSTITUTIONAL JAIL. A jail that follows the rules for inmate management and treatment developed from civil litigation based upon constitutional law.

PER DIEM. The cost per day, here the daily cost of housing inmates.

PODULAR DIRECT. A process of inmate supervision that requires correctional officers to be in direct contact with inmates who are not confined to their cells.

PODULAR INDIRECT. A process of supervision wherein inmates are not confined to their cells and correctional officers can observe inmates but are physically separated from them.

TRANSPORTATION OFFICERS. Officers who are in charge of transporting inmates to other correctional institutions, usually to the state prison system after sentencing.

PROJECTS AND QUESTIONS

1. Devise a program for the transfer of inmates from the jails to the courts. When creating the program, be sure to include the duties of the administrative staff as well as the correctional officers in charge of transfer. Consider the problem created by removing restraining devices from inmates while they are in the courtroom. What other contingencies must be considered in developing sound procedures to transfer inmates from the jail to the local courts?

2. Is the local jail in your hometown overcrowded? What sources could you consider using to learn more about your jail? Does your source indicate any suggestions or programs to remedy the overcrowding? If so, what are they? Consider any additional ideas or programs you may have. Include what you feel would minimize the problem, such as building more facilities, assigning more security personnel, developing community alternatives, or redefining the problem of overcrowding.

3. Consult the U.S. Department of Justice, Bureau of Justice Statistics, *The Jail Census*, and summarize the data available that were not covered in this chapter. Which data or information in *The Jail Census* is most interesting to you, and why?

4. Contact your local community mental health clinic and learn the extent to which it provides services to the local jail. Include the type of services it provides and how cooperative the local jail is. If it does not provide services, ask why not.

ADDITIONAL READING

John Irwin. *The Jail: Managing the Underclass in American Society*. Berkeley, CA: University of California Press, 1985. A recent and highly readable analysis of the social function of the jail in America. Irwin proposes that the jail is a mechanism for processing and controlling the marginal people, those who do not fit and are not needed by the postindustrial economy.

Dave Kalinich and John Klofas. *Sneaking Inmates Down the Alley: Problems and Prospects of Jail Management*. Springfield, IL: Charles Thomas, 1986. This is a reader containing 14 articles covering current issues and problems about local jails. General solutions for some of the problems faced by local jails are addressed in the final section.

Standards for Adult Local Detention Facilities. College Park, MD: The American Correctional Association, 1985. This publication is a summary of standards for management of inmates in local jails, as well as general management and administrative procedures. These are ideal standards that this correctional organization has developed for the management of local jails.

INSTITUTIONS FOR ADULT MALE FELONS: HISTORY AND CURRENT CONDITIONS

QUESTIONS

1. What are the two major theories of prison development?

2. Why has the penitentiary been called an American invention?

3. How has prison design influenced the use of prisons?

4. How have prisons become specialized?

5. Why is it difficult to make judgments about prison crowding?

6. According to the 1978 Abt survey, are American prisons overcrowded? Is this a new situation?

PRISONS IN TWO STATES

When Phil first set foot in a Jefferson prison, he had no standards by which to judge what he saw. As he toured the state, various administrators, correctional officers, and inmates complained of certain practices and conditions, and he noticed other problems on his own. But he had no way of knowing whether correctional institutions in Jefferson were good or bad, as prisons go. Several years later, he did some consulting in another state. His duties there required visits to each of the prisons. The differences in the prisons of the two states were rather surprising.

Both states were relatively small and had

similar correctional populations and about the same number of institutions. Both also had a number of administrators who seemed quite dedicated and competent. But those were about the only similarities Phil could find. The two largest prisons in each state provided a remarkable contrast in prison life and work. Both Mulwan, in Jefferson, and the prison we will call Midway, in the other state, housed about 1,200 men. Mulwan was rated as a maximum security unit, while Midway was called "medium," although there were few operational differences. Both were surrounded by a high double cyclone fence, counts were taken frequently, and attention to perimeter security was rather high. Midway was considered medium security because the state had another prison that provided even greater security, and a higher wall.

Mulwan was only twelve years old when Phil first saw it. Its central corridor was so long he could not see from one end to the other. Off this quarter-mile tunnel ran a number of crossing buildings for particular uses. None of the buildings was more than two stories high. The architecture was boring and inexpensive, but very functional. The building was kept in immaculate condition. The cafeteria was large and shining, and while the chairs and tables were bolted to the floor, the designers had used a great deal of color to create a sense of variety and diversion. The gymnasium was fully equipped and in constant use. Basketball and weightlifting were the favorite sports.

Midway was eighty years old and looked as if it had never been repaired. The buildings were built in a circle around a large courtyard, with a guard tower in the middle. Guards refused to staff the inside tower, however, because they would be trapped in a riot. The yard had no grass whatsoever, as thousands of footsteps over eighty years permitted nothing to grow. The original circular design had been compromised by the need for some additional buildings. These now stood here and there within the outer circle, providing ample hiding places and making internal security almost nonexistent. Two cellblocks had deteriorated so badly that they had been condemned and stood like bombed-out buildings in a war zone. While inmates were ordered to clean, and while repairs were made from time to time, there was really nothing that could be done with Midway. Rats roamed the grounds freely, especially in the abandoned cellblocks. In the other housing units, water pipes leaked so badly that the constant hissing and dripping was heard above everything. Paint would not stay on the constantly damp walls. All the

buildings were the color of the dirt courtyard. When lunch was served, Phil did not want to eat. There was little for the inmates to do but stand in the yard and talk.

When Phil left Midway and returned home, he was struck by how different a one-year sentence in the two institutions would be. One year in Midway would have been 365 days of physical suffering. One year in Mulwan would be unpleasant at best, but one would be guaranteed safe, clean shelter. When Phil had first seen Mulwan, he had had no appreciation of that. When he returned, he realized that, as prisons go, safety and cleanliness are themselves achievements.

THE DEVELOPMENT OF PRISONS

According to Gordon Hawkins (1976), histories of prison development can be misused. As we have seen in Chapter 3, disagreements about prison history are not so much arguments about facts as debates about the significance of connections among facts. Historians with different perspectives on the use of prisons often seek to peel back the layers of time in an effort to discover in the historical record the "true" reasons for the use of prisons (1976:3). These searches generally emphasize the motivations behind the prison movement, as if the discovery of previous motivations will help us know what to do with them now.

There are several difficulties with this approach, not the least of which is the hazardous and ultimately unresolvable problem of how to determine the motivations of anyone, living or dead. More important, argued Hawkins, is that our understanding of historical development should not blind us to the important questions about prison use facing us now. No historical rendering of why prisons became the preferred punishment option helps us very much to face the question of what to do with them now.

While there are many specific theories of

prison development, there appear to be two major theoretical threads. One stresses the impact of ideas within the political culture of a time, and relies heavily on such evidence as the explicit goal statements of policy leaders. The other stresses the impact of economic forces and relies heavily on such evidence as changes in the dominant production forces of a society. Neither interpretation, however, necessarily indicates that we have much choice in the matter of prison development. The evolution of public policy is not always determined by culture or economy.

Hawkins has also engaged in an important and influential historical analysis (Sherman and Hawkins, 1981). The major thesis of that analysis is to stress that policy choices within the strong influences of current economic and cultural context can be made, and that those choices have a significant impact on the shape of prisons in the years ahead. Specifically, that analysis sought to understand why use of imprisonment went through a number of dramatic reversals in Great Britain while showing a slow and steady increase in the United States. Sherman and Hawkins succeed in demonstrating that imprisonment changes are not an inevitable outgrowth of changes in crime rate, but their ability to show us the power of political choice in the matter is more ambiguous. They conclude that confidence in prison fluctuated in England while remaining strong in the United States because the American policy was heavily influenced by religious faith in reformation. The more secular, economic view in England was more liable to fluctuate with arguments that there were punishment technologies less expensive than prison (1981:57). Whether this analysis is cause for optimism about our chances of changing prison policy is difficult to say.

IMPRISONMENT PRIOR TO 1780

Fifteen years ago, one of the more widely accepted statements about prisons was that they were invented in the United States shortly after the Revolution. While in many respects that statement is still true, the American penitentiary was not an invention so much as a policy application of a social control instrument that had existed for thousands of years.

For example, in Israel in 2000 B.C., six "cities of refuge" provided safety for persons escaping crimes subject to settlement by blood feud (Murton, 1976:2). The refugees were safe as long as they remained in the city. This concept of prison as refuge carried over to the early Church. Persons seeking to escape the consequences of state law sought sanctuary on Church property. In these cases, voluntary imprisonment was an attractive alternative to punishment. Murton claims that the first recorded use of imprisonment as a punishment following conviction occurred in England in the thirteenth century. A statute permitted imprisonment of two years for the crime of rape (1976:6). Imprisonment as punishment for felonies was not a preferred option for many years, however; the death penalty and corporal punishments were much more common. Prisons were frequently used for detention pending trial and for some minor crimes. Jails were sufficiently populated that rudimentary efforts at prisoner classification were evident by the sixteenth century. Inmates were distributed to separate housing on the basis of age, sex, and reason for detention (National Advisory Commission on Criminal Justice Standards and Goals [NAC], 1973:198).

Throughout the mercantile era, many of the European powers relied upon deportation to their colonies as a form of punishment. Portugal had penal colonies as early as 1414. Transportation from England to the American colonies began in 1597. In colonial America, the deported felon had the status of slave to the colonial government (Murton, 1976:3). When the War of Independence cut off transportation to the American colonies, English jails rapidly became overcrowded. In 1778, a bill before Parliament proposed two penitentiary houses. Parliament was reluctant to allocate the money. Prisons of a sort were established in convict hulks—ships anchored in the Thames (Sherman and Hawkins, 1981:53). In addition, penal colonies were established in Aus-

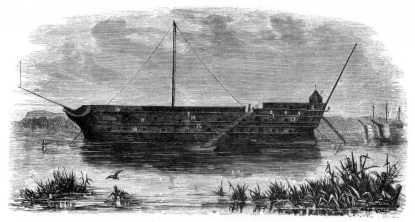

THE "OLD JERSEY" PRISON-SHIP.

While the English Parliament was debating the wisdom of prison construction in the early nineteenth century, convicts were incarcerated in old hulks on the Thames. (Culver Pictures)

tralia in 1787 and Tasmania in 1803 (Murton, 1976:3). As a consequence, construction of a penitentiary in England was delayed. In the interim a number of prisons were built, but by counties rather than the national government. Most of these were small. Finally, the General Penitentiary of Millbank of London, containing 1,200 separate cells, was built in 1812. The penitentiary encountered immediate problems with riots and epidemics, and had to be closed temporarily on two separate occasions (Sherman and Hawkins, 1981:53).

This evidence suggests that imprisonment as the preferred option for punishment actually preceded its adoption as explicit policy. Jails were increasingly used for the punishment of misdemeanors, and their use for detention of felons gradually spilled over to postconviction use while the government waited to locate additional space. Moreover, the penal colony, while not a prison as we know it today, certainly served the same purpose of isolation from society and exploitation of prisoner labor.

In colonial America, jails were used for detention, but most punishments took place in the community, or by banishment from the community. A number of punitive options were used rather creatively, according to Rothman (1971: 45–52). Colonial villages frequently "warned out"

(banished) undesirables and troublemakers and the poor in order to avoid a drain on the town coffers. A number of normative punishments, such as shaming a neighbor, or corporal punishments, such as stocks and pillory or the whip, were used independently or in combination. Villages clearly paid attention to the social situation and background of minor offenders when determining punishment. Punishments that relied upon the offender's commitment to local values were reserved for community members who had roots in the group; banishment was preferred for strangers. Recidivism drew harsh responses, usually the death penalty.

According to Rothman, the colonial jail was not designed for long-term incarceration. Jails were usually built on the model of almshouses, and lacked perimeter security and internal discipline. Their physical and social structure were not seen as providing sufficient deprivation to function as punishment (1971:52–56).

EMERGENCE OF THE PENITENTIARY

Perhaps the English reformer John Howard deserves the most credit for anticipating the penitentiary system (Barnes, 1972:122–123). He inspected many prisons and jails in Europe during the eighteenth century and exposed the sordid conditions he found. But he was impressed with the workhouses as an institution for housing young people. The workhouse movement had begun in the sixteenth century in England and on the Continent (McKelvey, 1972:3–5). One of the first workhouses was the Bridewill in London. The facility held a range of persons considered unruly or menacing. Two eighteenth-century European facilities appeared to have had more influence on the penitentiary concept, however. One, the Hospice of San Michele for delinquent boys, was erected in Rome by Pope Clement XI in 1704. The other, the Maison de Force, was established in Flanders in 1773.

The Hospice of San Michele was built as a retreat for "wayward" boys. Discipline and reformation were based on solitude and labor. The boys worked in a central hall during the day and observed a strict rule of silence. At night they were locked in their cells. They were forced to listen to readings of religious tracts and were flogged for violation of institutional rules. In nearby Florence, a home for vagrants operated by Father Filippo Franci also utilized measures to control communication. The inmates wore hoods over their faces to prevent mutual recognition. The disciplinary regimes in these two institutions were copied in the American penitentiaries a century later.

The Maison de Force was a workhouse reserved primarily for beggars and vagrants. The institution stressed the work ethic. A rudimentary classification system was practiced, with felons separated from misdemeanants and vagrants. Separate quarters were given to women and children. The sleeping quarters were individual cells, and medical care was provided.

John Howard recommended the basic workhouse design and discipline in his 1777 classic *The State of the Prisons*. Along with the writings of Bentham, Beccaria, Voltaire, Paine, Montesquieu, and Hume, Howard's treatise influenced reformers in Philadelphia who were not satisfied with the harsh Pennsylvania Penal Code of 1718. One of the leaders of this Philadelphia group was Dr. Benjamin Rush, a physician and surgeon who

was opposed to both capital and corporal punishment (McKelvey, 1972:5). Rush advocated the classification of prisoners, individual treatment based on need, and a system of prison labor. On May 8, 1787, this reform group, called the Philadelphia Society for Alleviating the Miseries of Public Prisons (now the Pennsylvania Prison Society), met in Philadelphia to draft proposals for penal reform (Barnes and Teeters, 1951:391). While the new penal code of 1786 had substituted work gangs for capital punishment for most crimes, these reformers apparently found the chain gangs trooping around the city abhorrent (Sherman and Hawkins, 1981:50–51).

Three years later, on April 5, 1790, the proposals led to the construction of a cellblock on the grounds of the Walnut Street Jail. The new cells were to be used for solitary confinement of hardened criminals. The new cellblock was supervised by Caleb Lownes, a member of the society. For a few years, he and his colleagues took great pride in showing the new cells to interested visitors. However, the high visibility of the cellblock apparently attracted increased judicial use. Lownes resigned in disgust in 1804, complaining about the overcrowding due to a rise in commitments (Sherman and Hawkins, 1981: 50–51).

Other prisons quickly followed. A cellular prison, designed by Thomas Jefferson, was constructed in Richmond, Virginia, between 1796 and 1800. The State of New York passed prison legislation in 1796 and opened the Newgate prison in Greenwich Village on November 28, 1797. New Jersey completed a prison in 1799, and Massachusetts built a maximum security prison in 1805 at Charlestown.

THE PENITENTIARY MOVEMENT

These new prisons used a number of different designs, and some seemed to have been given little forethought whatsoever. The New Jersey prison did not segregate by sex, age, or mental state. The Newgate prison also employed congregate confinement, was small, and became rapidly overcrowded. Connecticut used an abandoned mine shaft as a prison and required only a guard at the entrance to prevent escapes. Between 1800 and 1830, improving the design of prisons became a major social preoccupation, a full-blown **penitentiary movement.** Two models, called the Pennsylvania and the Auburn systems, dominated the debate.

The **Pennsylvania system** borrowed heavily from the European workhouse and the religiously based recommendations of John Howard. The Eastern State Penitentiary at Cherry Hill in Philadelphia, which was still used by the Bureau of Corrections in the 1970s, was designed by the English architect Haviland based on the workhouse of San Michele (Hawkins, 1976:4). Its construction encountered great expense and delays, and it finally opened in 1829, three years after the opening of Western Penitentiary in Pittsburgh.

The Cherry Hill prison was built for solitary and silent confinement. The building was surrounded by a huge wall. The prison itself was built in a **radial design,** with lines of cells emanating from a central hub. Each cell was designed to hold one prisoner and contained a small exercise yard and workspace. Prisoners entered the prison blindfolded and were led to the cell,

where they remained at all times. Their routine consisted of one hour of exercise in the yard, craft labor that could be accomplished alone in the cell, and worship (Barnes and Teeters, 1951:406). Prison sentences tended to be longer than in European countries, with the explicit purpose of allowing time for penitence.

The prison at Auburn, New York, was quite different. Called the **congregate and silent system** of prison discipline, Auburn brought prisoners together during the day for group labor, and housed them at night in individual cells. Since the cells were intended only for sleeping, they were considerably smaller than those at Cherry Hill. Some of them measured only 7 feet long, 7 feet high, and 3½ feet wide (1955:407). Instead of a radial, single-level design, with spokes of outside cells, Auburn living quarters were a **block design.** The cells were stacked back to back in tiers, some five rows high (1955:407). Between the cells and the small barred windows, narrow corridors ran the length of the building.

Auburn was the country's first major factory prison (Miller, 1980:37). It was designed from the beginning to get maximal work from the inmates. When congregate work led to disciplinary problems, the warden, Elam Lynd, invented a

The Auburn prison was one of the two most famous prisons at the start of the penitentiary movement. The Auburn block design and congregate work system won out over the Pennsylvania system of isolation. (Culver Pictures)

The lock step was invented by Elam Lynds in New York. Here prisoners are in lockstep formation in the Sing Sing yard. (Bettmann Archive)

series of measures to keep inmates from communicating despite their physical proximity. These included strict rule of silence enforced with the whip, and the lock step formation. The lock step was a close-order shuffle, with men moving in unison, single file, with faces downcast and facing right. The formation was designed to retard communication and make attempts at it easy to spot. Inmates were dressed in stripes and their heads were shaved, more to degrade them than to hamper escapes. Lynd believed that discipline was achieved by breaking a man's spirit, and when necessary, the body. He was no champion of reform: He wrote to the governor that the best that could be expected from prisons was deterrence through suffering (Rothman, 1971).

EARLY PROBLEMS IN THE PENITENTIARY

The Pennsylvania system, borrowing heavily from European models, was in turn influential in later prison construction in Europe. The congregate but silent system of Auburn became the standard for most prison construction in the United States. But both penitentiaries had immediate problems. Like the Walnut Street cellblock before it, the Eastern State Penitentiary rapidly became overcrowded. The solitary design was abandoned, and two or more persons were placed in each cell. Even before the overcrowding, however, prisoners devised ingenious methods of communicating by tapping out coded messages on water pipes. Silence was impossible to enforce in either type of penitentiary.

The Pennsylvania system was also prohibitively expensive. The state refused to allocate sufficient funds to maintain the solitary design in new prisons. Moreover, the solitary design prohibited mass labor.

One of the primary objectives of the Auburn prison was economy. Auburn was proposed by John Beach, who lobbied in the legislature and in his town for construction of the prison, which began in 1816. Beach saw the economy of Auburn swelling after the construction of the Erie Canal in 1815, and urged Auburn businessmen to become industrialists using prison labor. Convict labor was even attempted in the construction of the canal, but it proved unsuccessful (Miller, 1980:38). According to Miller, the original plan for Auburn was adopted from the congregate plan at Newgate. The single cells and the silence were unintended, but discipline and security were problems from the start. Flogging as a prison discipline was legalized in 1818. The tiered cells were constructed in 1819 after complaints from townspeople about corruption and escapes. The silent system was instituted by 1820 as a means of punishing inmates and maintaining discipline (1980:38). Miller reported that the hope of profit from prison labor was usually unmet (1980:40).

THE NORFOLK ISLAND PENAL COLONY

While most attention at the time was directed at these events in the United States, changes were also occurring in the English penal colonies. The most significant of these reforms, at Norfolk Island (Tasmania), was in many ways far more advanced than the Auburn and Philadelphia prisons. Alexander Maconochie (1787–1860), a British naval officer, began writing about prisons and their proper administration in the 1830s. In 1839 he asserted (Murton, 1976:194):

> The first object of prison discipline should be to reform prisoners and thus to prepare them to separate (from the prison) with advantage both to themselves and to society after their discharge.

Shortly thereafter, Maconochie was appointed the new head of the Norfolk Island colony. He arrived in 1840 and immediately instituted a number of changes in discipline consistent with his theories of reform. He established a **mark system,** or point system, by which inmates could earn better quarters and privileges. He used minimum security camps for trustees, and relied on

peer pressure from other inmates to enforce conformity with prison rules. According to data which Maconochie kept, less than 3 percent of the first 1,450 persons released from his regime returned to prison. Despite these accomplishments, recognized by both the governor of the island and the Crown, Maconochie was dismissed after three years. His mark system, with graduated reduction in custody, reappeared in the Irish prison system under Sir William Crofton, and became the forerunner of parole as well as a model for American reforms after the Civil War (see Chapter 17).

INTERPRETATIONS OF MOTIVATIONS FOR REFORM

Most accounts of the early penitentiaries agree that implemenation was a problem from the start. Disagreement surrounds the interpretations of motives for the movement. For years, the dominant explanation was focused on the goals enunciated by interest groups such as the Philadelphia Prison Society. These goals centered on (1) the need for some intermediate punishment between the community punishments and execution employed by the colonies, (2) the need to introduce order and discipline in the prison, as it began to replace corporal and capital punishment, and (3) the desire that prisoners would be reformed by the experience (see, for example, Rothman, 1971). The histories that focus on these expressed intentions tend to stress the role of penological theory in the development of prisons and imply that the quick failures of implementation led to despair or cynicism among administrators and the adoption of scaled down goals, such as retribution or deterrence.

More recent histories take issue with that order of events. For example, Miller could find no major role for reformation in prisons until the construction of Elmira Reformatory in 1877. He claimed that reformative rhetoric was adopted after the prison movement was under way as a means of justifying the economic exploitation of prisoners (1980:41). Unemployment and crime were exceedingly high in the United States following the War of 1812. During the war, an embargo on European goods had guaranteed the fledgling U.S. economy domestic markets. When the embargo was lifted, a number of businesses failed. Miller reported that many of the early prisoners in Auburn were shoemakers who were arrested for job actions when they protested the industrialization of their craft (1980:39–40). While prison labor rarely paid off directly, industrialists on the outside pointed to it as an excuse for low wages outside (1980:40). The increasingly harsh treatment of prisoners was adopted to reinforce their scapegoating for the problems of the early industrial economy (1980:39).

While the economic explanation of penitentiary development appears important, it too tries to explain too much. For example, the French visitors Beaumont and de Toqueville recognized tremendous variation from prison to prison and state to state, even in 1830. They commented very unfavorably about the harsh regime of Lynd at Auburn and later at Sing Sing, and reported that the prison at Wethersfield in Connecticut was not only far more profitable but far more humane, operating without corporal discipline. (See Insert 11.1 for the original Wethersfield prison rules, which Beaumont and de Toqueville took back to France as models). Moreover, while economic motivations appeared quite attractive to some policymakers, such as John Beach, they do not appear to have been the conscious objectives of persons such as Dr. Rush, or Maconochie.

Comments from the day indicate considerable pride in the invention of the penitentiary, and an awakening to the importance of correctional administration as a measure of the quality of a government. The translator for Beaumont and de Toqueville's work, Francis Leiber, wrote in 1833 of European government (1964:5):

> . . . in none of its branches has this progress, which alone affords the standard by which we can judge of the civil development of a society, been more retarded than in the organization and discipline of its prisons. . .

He blamed the state of European prisons on the fact that there were no interest groups to represent prisoners and no competition among such groups to work toward improvement. The rude treatment of Maconochie would support such a view. Turning his eye toward the handful of new penitentiaries in the United States, Leiber continued (1964:6):

> The American penitentiary system must be regarded as a new victory of mind over matter—the great and constant task of man.

While Leiber was quite optimistic about the new prisons, several of his comments indicate that even those favorable to the system saw problems with it. He found it poor planning that so much energy was put into the prisons and so little into the jails—which, he pointed out, touched more people than the prisons. He argued that more attention to the prevention of crime than to the penitentiary would have been sensible (1964:7). He also indicated that women offenders had been neglected (1964:12), and that many groups in society resisted the penitentiary because they did not perceive incarceration to be punishment (1964:13–14). Finally, he complained that Maryland, Pennsylvania, New York, and Connecticut were remiss in their recordkeeping. He pointed out that without routine collection and analysis of statistics, rational policies would be impossible. Other commentators, including Beaumont and de Toqueville, were suspicious of enforced treatment, and a number argued that prolonged incarceration was unnatural and could only damage human beings (Scull, 1977).

The penal reform movement of the early nineteenth century would appear very much like any wave of correctional reform today. Economic incentives, both recognized and hidden, obviously played an important role in the initial funding for the prisons, and in the decisions on whom to incarcerate. But the reformative ideology would seem occasionally to have predated rather than followed economic forces, and in some cases would appear to have worked. There is also evidence that rehabilitation did become a magic wand, waved in support of any prison practice that was in need of additional justification. In short, rather than learn in this history "why" prisons began, we learn that as they took shape, the same confused set of aspirations, ulterior motives, and uneven administration were already present.

POST-CIVIL WAR REFORM

Prison were built in many states before the Civil War. As prisons moved to the West, rehabilitative rhetoric was less evident, and the prisons in all states were rapidly populated (Rothman, 1971). The period from 1850 to 1880 saw extensive prison construction, as well as the growth of other portions of the criminal justice system. Police forces were formed, and criminal legislation was increasingly formalized. As prisons grew in number, the utilization of the poorhouses declined (Calhalan 1979:11). As prison construction continued, overcrowding quickly followed. The incarceration rate in the United States went from 29 in 1850 to 117 in 1880 (Sherman and Hawkins, 1981:52).

In England, reliance on transportation declined as free citizens in Australia began to complain, and the practice ceased in 1868. A major new penitentiary, Pentonville, was built in 1842, and the construction boom soon hit. Fifty-four prisons were built in the second half of the nineteenth century (Sherman and Hawkins, 1981:54–55). The rehabilitative objectives never seemed very influential in Great Britain, despite the penological theories of Howard and Bentham and the work of people such as Maconochie and Crofton.

By 1870 in the United States, the failures of the 1830 penitentiary were evident to any number of people. In England, leaders began to look for alternatives to institutions, but in the United States, people began to look for new modes of prison discipline. On October 12, 1870, a meeting was called by Enoch Wines, secretary of the New York Prison Association. The officials gathered at this Cincinnati Prison Congress to form the National Prison Association, now the American Correctional Association (American Correctional Association, 1966:11–12).

THE CINCINNATI PRISON CONGRESS

The congress adopted a set of principles, which, among other things, opposed the doctrine of punishment, advocated a classification system for prisoners, argued for the indeterminant sentence and parole, called for the promotion of inmate self-respect, and advocated programs of vocational and academic training (Barnes and Teeters, 1959:524–525). The congress also appealed for the gathering of penal statistics and for centralization of the management of all prisons in a state.

The immediate impact of these proposals was felt only in the innovation of corrections for young, first offenders. A number of states built separate institutions for these persons, with the first opening in the State of New York.

THE REFORMATORY MOVEMENT

The first **reformatory** was constructed in Elmira, New York, in 1876. The new correctional regime to be practiced at the reformatory was made possible by indeterminant sentencing legislation passed in 1868 and 1870, largely through the work of the New York Prison Association. Zebulon Brockway was appointed the first superintendent. The essential features of Elmira were based on the principles enunciated at Cincinnati, and closely modeled on the work of Maconochie and Crofton. Parole was determined by a prison board using the mark system to grade a prisoner's accomplishments. Prison programs included physical education, military discipline, basic education, and vocational training (McKelvey, 1972:69–91).

Compared to the early penitentiaries, the reformatory placed greater stress on rehabilitation and less emphasis on reform through expiation and penitence, or hard labor. Another major

Insert 11.1 RULES AND REGULATIONS FOR THE CONNECTICUT STATE PRISON

[Note: *the following passages are excerpted from Appendix B in Gustave de Beaumont and Alexis de Toqueville,* On the Penitentiary System in the United States and Its Application in France *(1833), from the 1964 edition published by the Southern Illinois University Press, Carbondale, Illinois. These French visitors to early American penitentiaries spoke with respect throughout their book for the well-managed and humane prison in Wethersfield, Connecticut. It should be noted that the prison warden in Connecticut reported to the prison directors.]*

DUTIES OF THE WARDEN

1. He shall reside at the prison, and shall visit every cell and apartment, and see every prisoner under his care, at least once a day.

2. He shall not absent himself from the prison for more than a night, without giving notice to one or more of the directors.

3. It shall be his duty to cause the books and accounts to be so kept as clearly to exhibit the state of the convicts, the number employed in each branch of business, and their earnings. . . .

4. It shall be the duty of the warden to make all contracts, purchases, and sales, for and on account of the prison. . . .

5. It shall be his duty to treat persons visiting the prison with uniform civility and politeness, and to see that they are so treated by the inferior officers.

6. As it is by law the duty of the directors to see personally to the condition and treatment of the prisoners, no regulation or order shall be made to prevent prisoners having ready access to the director who shall be present, nor shall any punishment be inflicted on them for speaking with a director. . . .

. . . .

DUTIES OF THE DEPUTY WARDEN

1. He shall be present at the opening and closing of the prison, during the performance of religious services, and also at all other prison hours.

2. He shall daily visit the hospital, cookery, cells, and see that every part of the institution is clean and in order.

. . . .

DUTIES OF THE OVERSEERS

1. There shall be an overseer of each shop, to be appointed by the warden.

2. . . . He shall see that all the property belonging to his department shall be carefully preserved, and that the work is well and faithfully done, and shall consult and promote the interest of the state, or the contractor who may employ the convicts. . . .

No conversation between the prisoners shall be allowed. Nor shall any overseer converse with a prisoner, except to direct him in his labor. . . .

. . . .

DUTIES OF THE WATCHMEN

1. It shall be the duty of the several watchmen to perform all such various duties and services, for the safety and security of the prison, as may be directed by the warden . . . ; to be vigilant and active while on post, and to maintain, while off from duty, and in the guard room, both towards each other and all other persons, a gentlemanly deportment. . . . No watchman shall be allowed to hold any conversation with a prisoner, except to direct him in his labor. Nor shall he receive from, or deliver to a prisoner, any article or thing,

change was the stress on education. The reformatory was limited to housing young offenders, usually between 18 and 25 years of age. The regimen for older offenders continued to follow the Auburn model for a number of years.

While the reformatory was considered a major change at the time, compared to prisons or reformatories today Elmira would be considered harsh, maximum security imprisonment. Indeed, today Elmira is used by the New York Department

without the knowledge of the warden or his deputy.

. . . .

DUTIES OF THE CONVICTS

1. Every convict shall be industrious, submissive, and obedient, and shall labor diligently and in silence.

2. No convict shall secret, hide, or carry about his person, any instrument or thing with the intent to make his escape.

3. No convict shall write or receive a letter to or from any person whatsoever, nor have intercourse with persons without the prison, except by leave of the warden.

4. No convict shall burn, waste, injure, or destroy any raw materials or articles of public property, nor deface or injure the prison building.

5. Convicts shall always conduct themselves toward the officers with deference and respect; and cleanliness in their persons, dress and bedding, is required. When they go to their meals and labor, they shall proceed in regular order and in silence, marching in the lock step.

6. No convict shall converse with another prisoner, or leave his work without permission of an officer. He shall not speak to, or look at visitors, nor leave the hospital when ordered there, nor shall he make any unnecessary noise in his labor, or do any thing either in the shops or cells, which is subversive of the good order of the institution.

. . . .

SOURCE: From Gustave de Beaumont and Alexis de Toqueville, *On the Penitentiary System in the United States and Its Application to France*, pp. 166–170, 173. Carbondale, IL: Southern Illinois University Press. Reprinted with permission.

of Correctional Services as a high-security facility for younger inmates. As reformatories aged, greater attention was paid to military discipline and less to education and vocational training. Again the rhetoric of individualized change was given short shrift or never taken seriously, depending on one's view.

THE INDUSTRIAL PRISON

With a few isolated exceptions, prisons stood still or regressed from 1900 to 1935 in the United States. The emphasis was on prison labor and obtaining economic advantage from the inmate. Little concern was shown for education, training, or counseling. In the South and the West many prisons were privately owned. The southern "prison" was more like the old penal colony or slave plantation. While the prisons in the newly emerging states of the West were more likely to copy the factory model of Auburn, exploitation and corruption were equally widespread. Conditions were deplorable. (These private prisons will be examined in more detail in Chapter 20.)

Conley's examination of the development of the Oklahoma State Prison in the period 1890 to 1920 provides one example (1981). The Oklahoma Territory boarded out its prisoners in the Kansas State Prison on per diem contracts. Interest in building a prison within the territory increased as Kansas continued to raise the daily inmate charge and as the Oklahoma incarceration rate went up (1981:248–251). Oklahoma became a state in 1907, and the first commissioner of charities and corrections made the boarding out in Kansas a political issue. She charged that conditions in the Kansas prison were cruel and that the administration of the contract was corrupt. A committee investigating these charges discovered that the Kansas prison was a money-making operation (1981:253–254). The new state was not impressed with the need to provide social services, and the Oklahoma counties resisted any state programs that would result in charges to them. The political culture stressed that the new state government was to stimulate economic development while protecting the small farmer (1981:255). The prison proposal remained dormant until the state found a way of tying a prison to the economic role. Prison construction began in 1920 when the governor pushed the image of an industrial prison that would make money and cooperate with Oklahoma businesses (1981:255–257).

While cheaply run prisons that make a profit through industry and agriculture have always been the rule in some states, the **industrial prison** ran into increasing difficulty in the first part of the twentieth century. Labor unions and businesses that did not benefit from prison connections objected to prison labor and the sale of prison goods on the open market (the impact of such objections is discussed in Chapter 14). The historical significance is that by the middle of the Great Depression in 1935, many prisons were shifting goals away from profit toward treatment.

In England, prison policy during this same period took a remarkably different turn. A number of laws were passed limiting prison terms and supporting community alternatives (including probation, which became a national program in 1907). While the American incarceration rate continued to climb, the English incarceration rate during this period began to fall dramatically. Many of the 55 prisons built from 1850 to 1900 were emptied, and some were demolished (Sherman and Hawkins, 1981:58–75). However, England adopted the new treatment approach at about the same time as it reappeared in the United States.

INNOVATION POCKETS IN THE INDUSTRIAL PERIOD

As was true in earlier periods, a few prisons and a few innovative, reform-oriented administrators deviated from the norm during this period. In particular, the inmate-government reforms of Thomas Matt Osborne and Howard B. Gill stood out. As was true of earlier innovations such as the reformatory, Osborne's and Gill's contributions can be traced to smaller innovations during earlier periods.

Although the trusty system now in effect in many jails and prisons cannot be called **inmate self-government,** its development did pave the way by demonstrating that inmates could be trusted with some degree of responsibility. The **trusty system** probably originated with Amos Pilsbury in 1835, at the Connecticut State Prison in Wethersfield. Pilsbury allowed certain inmates to go unguarded to nearby towns on errands. This practice was eventually expanded to the designation as trusties of inmates with good records (Barnes and Teeters, 1959:688).

Crude forms of self-government were found in the early houses of refuge for juveniles in New York City and Boston. Children were promoted to various status grades and were permitted to hold office and vote. In 1885, Warden Hiram Hatch of the Michigan Penitentiary at Jackson initiated a Mutual Aid League. Although his experiment was short-lived, it anticipated similar leagues established by Osborne in Auburn and Sing Sing.

Thomas Matt Osborne was a prominent citizen of Auburn, New York. He had been involved for years with George Junior Republic, a private program for delinquents that stressed citizenship, and had been chairman of the New York Prison Commission, a state advisory and visiting group overseeing prison administration. While serving on the commission he became a hero of Auburn inmates by engaging in unusual practices such as spending a night with the inmates in the cellblock. Osborne felt that if inmates were allowed to participate in the duties and responsibilities of citizenship while in prison, they would lead more responsible lives when released. He started the Mutual Welfare League at Auburn and established a similar league at Sing Sing, where he was warden briefly from 1915 to 1916, and at the naval prison in Portsmouth, New Hampshire.

Every inmate in the prison was eligible to join the league. Infractions of discipline were dealt with by a judicial board of five inmates elected by league delegates. Appeal from the board's decision went to all inmate members, without staff interference. Every aspect of prison life was supervised by standing league committees, whose members also performed many custodial roles. An employment bureau was set up by league members and outdoor recreation, lectures, and entertainment were provided. Osborne viewed league governance as self-imposed by the inmates, rather than imposed from without by officials.

Osborne's system did not last; other prison officials and the press called it a form of coddling. Instances of abuse and manipulation by inmates were exposed. While warden at Sing Sing, Osborne was investigated by the Westchester County prosecutor. Although no evidence of corruption was found, he resigned when he felt he had no support from the superintendent of prisons (Murton, 1976:200–206).

Another system of inmate self-government was established by Gill in Massachusetts in 1927. With no correctional experience, Gill was appointed superintendent by the governor because of his reputation as an innovative administrator. He established cooperative self-government as a mean of helping control escapes and contraband. He later extended the inmate powers to the nature of prison programs. Unlike Osborne's system, Gill's government included staff, with the exception of guards. Committees were charged with different aspects of prison life, and each committee had staff and inmate representatives. Like Osborne, Gill was attacked in the press and eventually forced to resign (Barnes and Teeters, 1959:695–698).

Osborne's and Gill's programs were resuscitated at Walla Walla in Washington in the 1970s, again with much public criticism and evidence of internal problems (Stastny and Tyrnauer, 1982). However, Gill's collaborative structure was recommended by the President's Commission on Law Enforcement and Administration of Justice (1967), and continues to be a model for inmate-staff cooperation (see Duffee, Steinert, and Dvorin, 1986). Such innovations tied the advances of Pilsbury, Maconochie, and Brockway to renewed efforts at rehabilitation in the 1930s.

THE EMERGENCE OF REHABILITATION

The transition to rehabilitation as the predominant justification for punishment and as the principle for prison administration emerged in the 1930s (Dession, 1938). Again, this was not an overnight change, but the gradual strengthening of one traditional thread in the cloth of correctional history. As was true of reformative rhetoric in the 1820s and 1870s, one can question the substance of the change.

Many overt efforts to transform prisons from workplaces to therapy units were little more than label switching. For example, in England, Alexander Paterson proposed to the Committee on Persistent Offenders that prisons should be abolished and replaced with "training centres" and "places of detention." His language was adopted in the British Criminal Justice Act of 1948, but little physical change in prisons followed the new nameplates. Similar instances of labeling can be found in the United States. Disciplinary committees became adjustment committees, convicts became inmates, wardens became superintendents, and guards became correctional officers.

Some real changes in management, structure, personnel, and prison conditions also took place. These cannot be dismissed as superficial name games, but they should not be interpreted as full-fledged revolution either. Some of the more important changes of this period may have been by-products rather than explicit goals. The evidence suggests that prison violence decreased and that the prison environment became more humane. Administrators gained greater control over inmate behavior, as we will see in detail in Chapter 15. Greater security accomplished in the name of effective treatment may have been the most significant result of the modern prison. Simultaneously, the emergence of treatment therapies grounded in behavioral science made correctional organizations responsible for correctional failures.

One of the major changes in prisons was a renewed and more sophisticated form of classification. Bolstered by the great enthusiasm for the new behavioral sciences, especially psychology, inmates were classified on the basis of diagnostic categories presumed to be relevant to treatment (NAC, 1973:198–199). In order to provide inmates with access to treatment programs, institutions began to specialize. They were graded according to security level and program emphases, and inmates were moved through prisons as their security ranking changed or as their treatment needs changed. While many of these classification systems were probably totally invalid, and while security grading probably dominated treatment variety in most state prison systems (see Chapter 14), the movement of inmates reduced the strength of the inmate subcultures and resistance to staff-controlled norms and values (see Chapter 15).

One of the best examples of the emergent treatment prison is the California Institute for Men at Chino. This facility was opened in 1941 by Kenyon Scudder with a busload of inmates he had selected from San Quentin. In place of concrete walls, Chino was surrounded by a 10-foot cyclone fence. There were gun towers, but they were not staffed, and there were no inside cellblocks. Along with the new physical plant there was an attempt to provide a number of treatment programs. Prisoners were permitted more freedom within the grounds than was true in maximum security prisons, and there was provision for more recreational programs.

As the larger states and the federal government began to open new prisons, pressures were exerted for centralized administration of the more complex systems (these management changes are discussed in detail in Chapter 18). The addition of central offices meant the birth of planning staffs and a new layer of bureaucracy between the state's chief executive and the prison administration. Planning for the coordination of prison facilities and movement of prisoners was nominally controlled by a new set of correctional professionals, those with advanced degrees in the social sciences. Perhaps the ethos of professional treatment was symbolized in the designation of special facilities for reception and classification (see Chapter 14). There were three diagnostic centers in 1947 and 22 by 1967 (Shover, 1974:348). While it is questionable how much control the new treatment staff actually wrested from custody administrators (or indeed, how much they

wanted), prison staffing patterns became considerably more complex, and more frequent inter-staff conflicts occurred. As power struggles ensued between the old and new regimes, prison disorder was not uncommon. A large wave of prison riots swept the country in the mid-1950s (see Chapter 15).

A number of commentators have suggested that the disorder during the transition from custody to treatment retarded or aborted the full transition. In any case, by the 1960s treatment was an accepted part, but not the dominant power, in prison administration. By the time of the President's Commission on Law Enforcement and Administration of Justice (1967), the correctional treatment model was being questioned, and particularly the effectiveness of rehabilitation in large and remote prisons.

PRISON DESIGN

PHYSICAL DESIGN

At the height of the penitentiary movement, prison architecture was considered a moral science. It was presumed that the physical design of the building was an important component in the control of behavior and the facilitation of penitence. Arguments raged about the comparative behavioral effects of the Pennsylvania and the Auburn designs.

Among the other early penologists to give careful thought to prison design was Bentham, the utilitarian philosopher. He spent a number of years planning the Panopticon, a circular prison with the cells in tiers on the circumference and a guard station in the middle of the circle. One staff observer could keep track of hundreds of inmates. Bentham lobbied for the adoption of his design for a number of years in England without success. In 1919, the State of Illinois copied the Panopticon at Stateville, a maximum security prison for 4,600 inmates. Panopticon designs can also be found in Spain, Holland, and Cuba (Nagel, 1973:37).

The most popular early penitentiary designs were the spoke or radial design of Eastern State Penitentiary and the block design of tiered internal cells at Auburn. Few new prisons have adopted either, but they proved so sturdy that many block prisons are still in use, including Auburn and Sing Sing (Nagel, 1973:36).

Perhaps the controlling issue in prison design is level of security. Security is a complex concept that includes behavioral control, classification, and prediction issues in addition to physical design concerns. The social side of security will be discussed in Chapters 14, 15, and 16. The physical design issues are not totally separable from these human behaviors, because the penitentiary designers were right to a certain extent: Environments can influence behavior.

Unfortunately, not all the physical environments designed to control prisoners have had the intended effects. Some physical designs intended to provide control over escapes or importation of contraband have actually increased control problems. Additionally, the social and physical aspects of security interact. For example, the prevention of escapes through internal intelligence reduces the need for security precautions. Reduction of prison violence and other types of internal disorder is a far different set of activities than making sure persons or things do not enter or exit without approval. Probably the greatest internal security measure is open and frequent interaction among all staff and inmates.

Nagel (1973:62) complains that in achieving security, prison architects have abdicated their responsibilities to hardware salesmen. In other words, security precautions have become the province of technology—for example, remote control cameras. Security has been depersonalized, with guards placed in more remote places with less interaction with inmates. Silas (1984) reported on the development of a robot guard that would patrol empty prison areas, such as cafeterias, at night (see Insert 11.2).

Security is achieved through a number of related features. Nagel categorizes these (1973:57):

1. The training of personnel in vigilance
2. Classification
3. The threat of punishment for misbehavior
4. Internal surveillance procedures
5. A level of perimeter security matched to the designated escape risk of the inmates

It is not easy to describe the security gradations in use in the United States. As Phil discovered in the opening case, security classifications have relatively local definitions. The most common designations for prison security levels are maximum, medium, and minimum. However, what passes for medium in one state may well be considered maximum in another. Similarly, what one state defines as minimum would serve as medium security space in another. Some prison systems, such as the Federal Bureau of Prisons, contain so many separate institutions that additional security gradations are possible. The federal system, for example, utilizes two different grades of maximum, medium, and minimum.

Nevertheless, the general principles for designated security levels remain fairly simple and are rather similar. Two chief concerns are how easily one can enter or exit the prison and how easily staff can watch and control behavior within the prison. Maximum security prisons generally have high walls or fences, vantage posts from which guards can easily command a view of anyone or anything approaching the perimeter from either side, and means of locking inmates up within living quarters. Minimum security designs, in contrast, are often built without any perimeter fence, often do not have guard towers, and usually offer inmates considerably freer movement about the grounds without constant physical surveillance and checkpoints. Minimum security units include rural camps, ranches, and farms and urban work release and halfway house facilities. Medium security facilities fall in between. Most of the early penitentiaries were maximum security designs. When most prison systems included only one prison, these were built to accommodate the worst possible behavior. As prison systems expanded and individual units be-

Insert 11.2 BEEP! JAILBREAK! Robot Builder Eyes Prison Use

An inmate who gets the urge to break out of prison may think twice if he risks running smack into a 350-pound guard clad in armor and wielding ultrasonic sensors. If a high-tech company and a manufacturer of prison security systems have their way, some of the prison guards of the future will be robots.

Denning Mobile Robotics of Woburn, Mass., has developed such a robot for Southern Steel Co. of San Antonio, the nation's largest manufacturer of prison security systems. The first robot will be tested this fall, and 1,000 have been ordered by Southern Steel. Company officials hope the robots will be used in correctional institutions by next year, said A. Steve Allison, president and general manager of Southern Steel. He would not, however, divulge the names of prisons that have expressed interest in the robot guards.

The prototype robot, called Denny, is designed to roam areas of prisons to detect the presence of humans, but it will not replace human guards, said Benjamin Wellington, a Denning vice president. "There are areas in prisons that must be patrolled at night even though no one may be present," Wellington said, such as cafeterias, recreational facilities and workshops. "The robots can patrol these areas and leave guards to patrol the cells where inmates are located."

Because of high construction and operating costs, many prisons have high prisoner-to-guard ratios, and this makes the potential for violence and escape greater, Wellington said. Robots can fill the gap, he added.

Denny glides along on three wheels and somewhat resembles R2-D2, one of the robot characters in "Star Wars." It can detect movement, human presence, smoke or other environmental abnormalities with its sensors, infrared detectors and ultrasonic range finders. When it senses something wrong an automatic circuit alerts security personnel.

"Robots are more efficient, and this can affect the bottom line," Wellington said. The robots will cost about $30,000 each.

SOURCE: Faye A. Silas, "Beep! Jailbreak! Robot Builder Eyes Prison Use," *ABA Journal*, Vol. 70, September 1984, p. 35. Reprinted with permission of the *ABA Journal, The Lawyer's Magazine,* published by The American Bar Association.

---

gan to take on specialized functions and populations, physical variety became more plentiful.

The most common maximum security prison of recent vintage is the **telephone pole design.** A number of prisons in the 1950s and 1960s were built this way. These prisons are likened to telephone poles because their dominant feature is a central corridor running the length of the building, with cross arms of shorter length providing the space for special uses, such as cell tiers, program space, work space, hospital, and cafeteria. The central crossing corridor structure is favored as a security device in maximum security units because the corridor provides an unobstructed view of all within-prison movement.

Nagel criticized this design because it hampers classification of prisoners into all but a few grades, provides no small spaces, and seems to be associated with internal disciplinary problems (1973:39–40). Nagel's consulting architects argued that the central corridor was so long and the total environment so monotonous that prison inhabitants literally lose a sense of time and place (1973:40).

The vertical version of the telephone pole is the high-rise prison. There are many high-rise urban jails, but few high-rise prisons. The high rise has produced the same behavioral control problems found in high-rise housing projects (1973:41–42).

A more popular recent design, particularly for medium and minimum security prisons, is the

courtyard prison. Buildings are arranged in a square or circle as the external perimeter of an internal courtyard. The Jefferson minimum security prison of Dunmore is an example of this kind of construction. Nagel argues that the courtyard design offers security without monotony, and without the constant crowding feeling of the telephone pole. People are constantly forced out of doors as they change activities (1973:42).

Another recent innovation is the **campus style prison.** The minimum security prison at Vienna, Illinois, is a prototype. At Vienna, a "town square" of office, recreation, food service, and other common-use buildings are surrounded by townhouse-style low-rise dormitories. The campus design provides the greatest on-grounds freedom of movement and variety. Nagel also pointed out that the campus design permits other uses if the prison is no longer needed (1973:43–44).

Table 11.1 presents data on the construction of recent prisons by security level and design type. The telephone pole design, despite its faults, is still the most popular high-security design. Minimum and medium security prisons are diversifying in shape, with the campus style the most popular.

PRISON LOCATION

Prisons continue to be located, by and large, in rural settings. Nagel indicated a number of reasons for this preference (1973:49):

- Rural legislators have lobbied heavily for prisons in their districts, especially if unemployment was high.
- Urban communities have often lobbied against prisons, often claiming a fear of increased crime.
- States already own rural land.
- Administrators with rural backgrounds prefer rural staff.
- Corrections personnel have continued to believe in the virtues of a bucolic setting.

TABLE 11.1   Basic Design Forms of 60 New Correctional Centers

TYPE	MAXIMUM SECURITY	MEDIUM SECURITY	OPEN	TOTAL
Radial	1	0	0	1
Panopticon	0	0	0	0
Telephone Pole	10	8	0	18
High-Rise	0	1	0	1
Courtyard	4	5	1	10
Campus	2	11	17	30
TOTAL	17	25	18	60

SOURCE: William Nagel, *The New Red Barn: A Critical Look at the Modern American Prison.* New York: Walker, 1973, p. 46. Reprinted with the permission of the American Foundation, Inc.

The continuing rural location, however, will continue to supply prisons with a number of logistical problems. Nagel observed (1973:48):

> They were far removed from universities, unable to be reached by public transportation, and seemingly designed to discourage citizen and community involvement.

Observing the relationships between the minimum security prison and the town of Vienna, Illinois, James B. Jacobs (1976) argued that there may also be some advantages to a rural location. He pointed out that a large correctional facility can play a significant role in the economic life of a small town, but a prison, no matter how large, cannot play a significant role in the economic life of a large city. For this and related reasons, mutual interdependence may develop in the rural setting, providing for townspeople active participation in and support for the prison.

Unfortunately, it also places inmates, who are most often urban and very often of minority race or ethnicity, hundreds of miles from home and in an area often devoid of potential minority staff. Favoring reintegration policy, the President's Commission on Law Enforcement and Administration of Justice urged the construction of smaller prisons, located closer to the places from which most inmates come. Most departments have ignored such advice. Table 11.2 provides data on the location of 23 new prisons visited by Nagel (1973). They averaged 172 miles from the state's largest city.

SIZE, DISTRIBUTION, SECURITY, AND AGE

In 1978, Abt Associates took a total census of United States prisons and jails for the United States Congress. Table 11.3 reproduces the Abt data on state and federal prisons by age, size, and gender of the inmate population, and security level of the institution. The same data were used in Figure 11.1 to demonstrate the distribution of inmates in the United States across prisons of different security level, size, and age. The average prison built prior to 1960 housed 1,100 prisoners, with the range from 250 to 4,800 at Jackson, Michigan. Since 1960, administrators have realized the hazards of large prisons and have scaled down somewhat. In Nagel's survey, the new prisons averaged 770 capacity (1973:55). Many of the prisons being constructed in the 1980s are smaller still; a capacity of 500 appears to be a favorite number.

As indicated in Table 11.3, there were 559 prisons in 1978, the vast majority of them for men. The most common state prison was rated as medium security. There were 174 minimum securitiy facilities and 140 maximum security facilities. In addition to these, the Federal Bureau of Prisons had 38 prisons, 17 graded as medium security, 13 as maximum, and 8 as minimum. Despite the fact that most prisoners are not classified as maximum security risks, there is more maximum security prison space than any other type. Maximum security prisons usually have the largest capacity. The endurance of the walled fortress prison is in large measure responsible for the poor condition of much of our prison space. Many of the original prisons in the country are still in use, although their design is no longer compatible with anyone's correctional objectives.

Prisons are unevenly distributed across the country. The South, which has the highest incar-

ceration rate, also has 43 percent of all the prisons (Mullen, 1980:54).

THE DESIGN OF PRISON SYSTEMS

Just as important as the design of individual prisons is the way in which prisons are related to each other. As was described in Chapter 5, correctional departments are generally incomplete systems because they do not include important components of correctional systems, such as sentencing decisions. Nevertheless, the centralization of prison administration, so that different activities could be coordinated, was advocated in the Cincinnati Prison Congress in 1870. The states and the federal government responded to such recommendations very slowly. The advent of more complicated classification and expanded treatment programs in the 1930s spurred the design of "systems of prisons." Since correctional departments were established after many prisons were built, they have inherited a large portion of their resources. Historical accident rather than planning has therefore shaped many departments. Nevertheless, central offices attempt to arrange prisons and manage the flow of prisoners through them in order to accomplish certain objectives.

In 1975, Steele and Jacobs attempted to isolate the potential underlying goals of prison systems. Classifying systems by the functional relationships among prisons, Steele and Jacobs identified three ideal types: the hierarchical system, the differentiated system, and the autonomous system (1975:150).

The hierarchical system is a system of prisons designed to achieve custodial and security objectives. Security level of the prisons and of the prisoners are the key management variables. All inmates are initially assigned to maximum security and are gradually moved through medium and minimum security settings based on behavior ratings. Privileges expand and living conditions improve with less security, and order in the less secure institutions is enforced through threat of

TABLE 11.2   Locations of 23 New Correctional Institutions for Men

	INSTITUTION	ROAD MILES TO STATE'S LARGEST CITY	POPULATION OF SUPPORTING COMMUNITY	PERCENT MINORITY INMATES	PERCENT MINORITY STAFF
EAST	Max security	125	3,000	55	1
	Max security	35	6,000	42	9
	Max/Med Security	70	2,500	49	11
	Max/Med Security	40	4,000	50	20
	Med security	140	2,500	54	4
	Med security	100	35,000	65	1
	Med security	30	3,200	2	0
SOUTH	Max security	450	1,300	51	2
	Max security	240	8,000	54	0
	Max security	65	2,500	55	11
	Med security	110	9,000	unknown	unknown
	Min security	100	2,500	50	20
MIDWEST	Med security	275	44,000	unknown	unknown
	Med security	236	6,000	52	25
	Med security	157	13,000	45	7
	Med security	90	2,500	24	6
	Min security	455	2,500	40	5
WEST	Max/Med Security	172	6,500	unknown	unknown
	Med security	435	15,000	20	1
	Med security	425	2,000	52	5
	Med security	120	9,000	31	2
	Med/Min Security	33	20,000	59	14
	Min security	60	27,000	49	17
	AVERAGE	172	9,900	45	8

SOURCE: William Nagel, *The New Red Barn: A Critical Look at the Modern American Prison*. New York: Walker, 1973, p. 48. Reprinted with the permission of the American Foundation, Inc.

transfer to the onerous "big house," which everyone has experienced.

In contrast to this arrangement is the differentiated system, a design that applies medical model assumptions. Treatment programs rather than security is the design principle, with the different institutions specializing in various forms of treatment. Inmates are moved from one institution to another based on diagnoses of needs and treatment progress.

Steele and Jacobs argue that the hierarchical system ignores inmate needs because security risk, not social or psychological problems, determines placement (1975:153). The differentiated system requires many prisons of equal and relatively high security level so that inmates can be moved about without regard to security risk (1975:157–158).

In contrast to both of these systems, they also identified an "autonomous system," or a system

TABLE 11.3 Number of Federal and State Facilities by Age of Facility, Size of Inmate Population, Security Classification, Sex Designation, Region, and State, 1978

REGION AND STATE	TOTAL NUMBER OF FACILITIES	FACILITY SECURITY CLASSIFICATION			SIZE OF INMATE POPULATION			AGE OF FACILITY					SEX DESIGNATION OF FACILITY	
		MAXIMUM	MEDIUM	MINIMUM	LESS THAN 500	500-999	1000 OR MORE	BEFORE 1875	1875-1924	1925-1949	1950-1969	1970-1978	FEMALE	CO-ED
United States	559	153	224	182	376	38	85	25	79	141	164	150	42	26
Federal Total	38	13	17	8	10	18	10	0	3	16	8	11	2	5
State Total	521	140	207	174	366	80	75	25	76	125	156	139	40	21
NORTHEAST	77	24	30	23	50	15	12	7	20	14	15	21	3	5
Maine	3	1	1	1	3	0	0	0	2	0	0	1	0	1
New Hampshire	1	1	0	0	1	0	0	0	1	0	0	1	0	0
Vermont	2	0	1	1	2	0	0	0	0	0	1	1	0	0
Massachusetts	13	5	2	6	11	2	0	0	3	1	3	6	0	1
Rhode Island	5	1	2	2	5	0	0	1	1	1	2	0	1	0
Connecticut	10	6	2	2	9	1	0	2	1	2	2	3	1	1
New York	27	6	13	8	15	5	7	3	5	6	4	9	1	1
New Jersey	8	2	5	1	2	4	2	1	3	2	1	1	0	1
Pennsylvania	8	2	4	2	2	3	3	0	4	2	2	0	0	1
NORTH CENTRAL	90	30	27	33	53	18	19	9	24	13	30	14	9	4
Ohio	11	2	6	3	3	1	7	1	3	3	3	1	1	0
Indiana	9	5	4	0	6	1	2	1	3	0	3	2	1	1
Illinois	10	5	4	1	4	2	4	2	3	2	3	2	1	0
Michigan	23	6	4	13	17	4	2	0	2	4	11	6	1	0
Wisconsin	8	2	3	3	5	2	1	1	3	0	3	1	1	0
Minnesota	5	2	0	3	3	2	0	0	3	0	2	0	1	0
Iowa	5	2	1	2	3	2	0	2	1	0	2	0	1	0
Missouri	8	2	2	4	5	0	2	1	0	3	3	1	0	1
North Dakota	2	1	0	1	2	0	0	0	1	1	0	1	0	1
South Dakota	1	0	1	0	0	1	0	0	1	0	0	0	0	1
Nebraska	2	0	2	0	1	0	1	0	2	0	0	0	1	0
Kansas	6	3	0	3	4	2	0	1	2	0	2	1	1	0

SOUTH	284	75	108	101	220	34	30	6	22	93	81	82	18	3
Delaware	5	0	4	1	4	1	0	0	0	1	0	4	1	0
Maryland	14	3	4	7	10	2	2	1	1	3	5	4	1	0
District of Columbia	5	1	3	1	4	0	1	0	0	2	2	1	0	0
Virginia	36	3	33	0	33	2	1	1	3	6	22	4	1	0
West Virginia	6	1	2	3	5	1	0	1	0	2	0	2	1	0
North Carolina	79	3	29	47	73	5	1	0	3	64	8	4	1	0
South Carolina	23	5	2	16	21	1	1	1	1	0	6	15	1	0
Georgia	17	14	3	0	13	1	3	0	0	1	9	7	1	0
Florida	35	19	13	3	22	7	6	0	1	3	16	15	2	1
Kentucky	11	1	2	8	9	0	2	0	1	2	1	7	1	0
Tennessee	7	2	5	0	4	2	1	1	0	1	1	4	1	0
Alabama	8	2	3	3	5	3	0	0	0	4	1	3	0	1
Mississippi	1	0	1	0	0	0	1	0	0	0	0	0	0	0
Arkansas	5	2	1	2	3	1	1	0	1	2	2	2	2	1
Louisiana	7	1	1	5	4	2	1	0	0	0	1	3	1	0
Oklahoma	10	4	1	5	9	0	1	0	2	2	2	6	2	1
Texas	15	14	1	0	1	6	8	1	8	1	4	1	2	0
WEST	70	11	42	17	43	13	14	3	10	5	30	22	10	9
Montana	2	0	1	1	1	1	0	0	0	0	1	1	0	0
Idaho	3	0	2	1	2	1	0	0	0	0	0	3	0	1
Wyoming	2	0	2	0	2	0	0	0	1	0	0	1	1	0
Colorado	8	1	3	4	5	3	0	1	0	0	5	1	1	0
New Mexico	4	0	1	3	3	0	1	0	1	1	2	0	1	1
Arizona	5	1	2	2	3	1	1	0	0	0	0	4	0	0
Utah	1	0	1	0	0	0	1	0	0	0	1	0	0	1
Nevada	5	1	4	0	4	1	0	1	0	0	2	2	1	0
Washington	9	3	2	4	6	2	1	0	2	0	3	4	1	0
Oregon	3	0	3	0	1	1	1	1	1	0	2	0	1	0
California	12	1	10	2	0	2	10	1	1	2	8	0	1	1
Alaska	9	3	5	1	9	0	0	0	0	1	5	3	1	4
Hawaii	7	1	6	0	7	0	0	0	2	1	1	3	1	1

SOURCE: Joan Mullen, *American Prisons and Jails. Vol. I: Summary Findings and Policy Implications of a National Survey.* Washington DC: United States Department of Justice, 1980, p. 55.

FIGURE 11.1 Percentage Distribution of Inmates* in Federal and State Facilities† by Security Classification, Size of Inmate Population on March 31, 1978, and Age of Facility

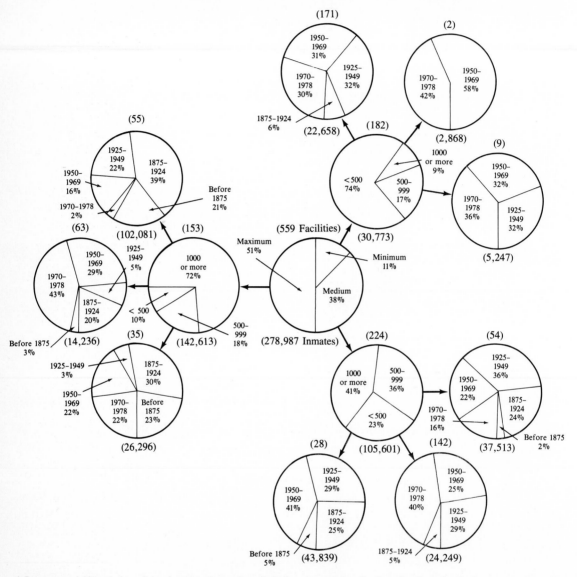

* Percentages within circles refer to inmates, the number of which are recorded at the foot of each circle. At the top of each circle, the number of relevant facilities is noted.

† Includes only facilities primarily holding inmates 24 hours per day.

SOURCE: Joan Mullen, *American Prisons and Jails*, Vol. 1: *Summary Findings and Policy Implications of a National Survey.* Washington, DC: United States Department of Justice, 1980, p. 57.

of benign neglect. In this system, inmates are assigned to one prison for the length of their stay. Behavior change, through treatment or security level, is not attempted. The prisons are conceived as separate warehouses, which seek to prevent escapes and to provide a modicum of comfort to each prisoner for the length of the sentence (1975:160).

Actual correctional departments never follow one of these organizing principles to the exclusion of the others, but the ideal types can help to identify the relative strength of various goals within a department. The Massachusetts Department of Correction has explicitly adopted a hierarchical model, moving inmates as often as possible through a graded series of prisons, with each successive move permitting greater contact with the community and less overt control. The Massachusetts Department defends its design on security grounds and also argues that the graduated custody reduction is important to reintegration (LeClair, 1978). The Federal Bureau of Prisons also operates on the hierarchical principle, starting inmates in close security and moving them toward minimum security as release approaches. Kentucky also uses a security hierarchy to make most movement decisions, but this department starts off most men in the medium security "reformatory," moving them up to maximum security for misbehavior or to the minimum security farm or the minimum security prison in Lexington for good behavior.

The California Department of Correction, at least prior to the 1976 sentencing change, was considered the best example of a differentiated system. Although security still played a significant part in prisoner movement, California did use a large number of moderate security institutions with special treatment programs.

Other organizing principles are found in practice. For example, the Pennsylvania Bureau of Correction for some time maintained a regionalized system. The state's various human services were organized into six human service regions, with attempts to provide all necessary services within a region and to permit some decentralized

policy decisions so that services could fit the needs of a region. The Bureau of Correction followed this master plan, with a major prison located in five of six regions of the state. As much as possible, the administrators attempted to keep prisoners in the region from which they were committed. Hence, there were classification centers, prerelease programs, and a variety of programs and security levels available in each region.

CONDITIONS IN PRISONS

LIVING QUARTERS

According to Nagel (1973), there are basically six kinds of living space in most prisons: (1) inside cells, usually in tiers, (2) outside cells or rooms, (3) segregation cells, (4) "squad rooms" or large cells with 4 to 8 beds, (5) open wards, and (6) cubicles. Traditionally, segregation cells have not been perceived as normal living conditions, but as temporary assignments. Segregation cells are often differentiated as **administrative** or **punitive.** Punitive segregation, often called "the hole," usually offers higher security and worse conditions than administrative segregation, because it functions as the prison within the prison. Punitive segregation is more common in maximum security prisons than in those with lesser security, since lower-security institutions often transfer disciplinary cases. However, most prisons offer some very secure space for holding, brief punishment, and "cooling out" distraught inmates. Administrative segregation supposedly is not punitive in nature, but isolates inmates from the general population for administrative or safety reasons. As violence has increased in recent years, many inmates have requested transfer to protective custody on a permanent basis. Unfortunately, most prisons never intended administrative segregation as permanent housing. Such cells usually entail a high degree of isolation from human company, little opportunity for activity or programming, and few comforts. The four other

Prisons are often built on a scale that is both monotonous and disorienting, according to William Nagel. Above is the interior of one of five cellblocks in the Graterford maximum security prison, outside of Philadelphia. (Pennsylvania Department of Corrections)

types of living space are commonly found across different types of prisons and are all intended for prisoners in the general population.

According to the Abt survey, 63 percent of measured state prison living space was cell space and 54 percent of federal prison living space was in cells. The remainder of the living space was in dormitories of varying sizes, including those that had been divided into cubicles. Almost all experts agree that while cell conditions are generally awful, dormitory space is even worse (Nagel, 1973:66). The American Correctional Association Commission on Accreditation adopted a standard precluding any further construction

of dormitories in mainline prisons (Mullen, 1980:60). The major objection is that dormitories offer no internal security whatsoever, even less privacy than cells, and are subject to even greater overcrowding, since there are no natural barriers in a large room to the continual addition of new bunks:

> In the quite typical 6 by 8 foot or 6 by 9 foot . . . cell, actual floor space must accommodate the usual wall-hung bed and some sort of open toilet and wash sink in combination or separately mounted. The bed reduces floor space by about 18 square feet, and the toilet facilities by an additional 4 square feet. Frequently one finds a chair, table, and shelves which reduce the square footage again by up to another 10 square feet. This leaves 16–22 square feet of net movement space—including space between the table and toilet and bed, or cell door and bed, all of which are normally inaccessible and therefore, constructively unusable. (Mullen, 1980:57)

In other words, living in the typical cell is much like living in the typical bathroom with the door open.

When most prisons were built, staff offices, including counseling offices, were placed in an exterior building to which inmates had little access. Prison administrators are trying to change this situation and incorporate the prison housing units into the organization of treatment (Nagel, 1973:79). Unfortunately, the design of much prison living space makes this a difficult task. Cellblocks are extremely noisy and crowded and offer no space for confidential and quiet discussion between staff and inmates. In some prisons, one or two bottom tier cells have been converted into counseling offices, but this is hardly satisfactory. Newer prisons, especially those in the Federal Bureau of Prisons, have been designed to integrate treatment staff into the housing units.

PRISON CROWDING

As prison commitments and prison populations have soared, administrators have complained that

Dormitory housing is very frequent in prisons in the United States. The dormitory unit above is typical of the modular "temporary" housing rented in some Pennsylvania prisons. (Pennsylvania Department of Corrections)

there is simply no more room. But attempts to clarify the amount of prison space or to define "overcrowding" have been difficult. Prison space is notoriously elastic:

> While overstatements (of available space) might occur in response to the threat of litigation, understatements were equally likely to be used as a means of dramatizing need for additional bedspace. (Mullen, 1980:52)

In its attempt to get around these changing notions of **rated capacity**—the capacity designated by the correctional administration—the Abt survey team sought to rely on standards for living quarters and to measure available prison space against these standards (Mullen, 1980:53). The standards used by Abt are presented in Table 11.4. The American Correctional Association, which would seem to be the most influential standard setter, recommended 60 square feet per inmate cell or dorms containing no more than 50 inmates with 10 cubic feet of airspace for each inmate. Comparing blueprints for each prison to the standards and the population counts, Mullen and colleagues examined four variables (1980:52):

- Comparisons between measured square footage and official rated capacity
- Occupancy, or the distribution of inmates to cells and dorms
- Density or the amount of square feet per inmate actually available
- Crowding, which was defined as the application of standards to occupancy and density.

Table 11.5 presents the Abt data on utilization of prison space by three different measures of capacity. The southern prisons appear the most overcrowded by the official capacity ratings, but as one moves to the more rigorous (or more liberal) definitions of capacity on the right side of the table, prisons in all regions appear equally overcrowded. Mullen found that: "70% of all celled inmates were accorded less than 60 square feet of floor space each" (1980:59). In addition, 69 percent of federal prisoners and 56 percent of state prisoners who were housed in dorms had less than standard amounts of living space. In the federal system 46 percent and in the states, 44 percent of the inmates lived in high-density multiple-living units, the most dangerous and unmanageable kind of space (1980:61). Mullen

TABLE 11.4   Comparison of Correctional Space Standards

ACA COMMISSION ON ACCREDITATION FOR CORRECTIONS		U.S. DEPARTMENT OF JUSTICE DRAFT
MANUAL OF STANDARDS FOR ADULT CORRECTIONAL INSTITUTIONS[a]	MANUAL OF STANDARDS FOR ADULT LOCAL DETENTION FACILITIES[b]	"FEDERAL STANDARDS FOR CORRECTIONS"[c]
4142 There is one inmate per room or cell, which has a floor area of at least 60 square feet, provided inmates spend no more than 10 hours per day locked in, exclusive of counts; when confinement exceeds 10 hours per day, there are at least 80 square feet of floor space. (Important) DISCUSSION: The institution should provide humane care. Single cells provide privacy and enable inmates to personalize living space. Less personal living space is required for inmates who have programs and activities available to them throughout the institution.	**5102** All cells and detention rooms designed for single occupancy house only one inmate. (Detention—Essential, Holding—Essential) DISCUSSION: Single-cell occupancy provides privacy and protection for the inmate, and should be provided based on the designed capacity of the facility. **5103** Single rooms or cells in *detention facilities* have at least 60 square feet of floor space, provided inmates spend no more than 10 hours per day locked in, exclusive of counts; when confinement exceeds 10 hours per day, there are at least 70 square feet of floor space. (Detention—Essential, Holding—Not Applicable) DISCUSSION: Rooms or cells of sufficient size enable inmates to personalize living space. Inmates who have access to programs and activities throughout the facility require less space in their rooms or cells because they do not spend as much time there. **5106** Multiple-occupancy cells are designed to house no more than 16 inmates, with a minimum of 50 square feet of floor space per inmate in the sleeping area. (Detention—Essential, Holding—Not Applicable) DISCUSSION: The facility classification committee should carefully evaluate each inmate, before assigning him/her to a multiple-occupancy cell, for the purpose of ensuring the protection of the individual being assigned as well as the protection of the other inmate(s) already assigned to the cell. Only minimum security inmates should be assigned to multiple-occupancy cells.	**002** All cells and detention rooms rated for single occupancy house only one inmate. **003** Single rooms or cells in *holding facilities* have, at a minimum, 50 square feet of floor space. **004** Single rooms or cells have at least 60 square feet of floor space. Where inmates spend more than 10 hours per day in the room or cell, there is at least 70 square feet of floor space in *detention facilities* and at least 80 square feet in *long-term institutions*. **005** Multiple-occupancy cells house no more than *16 inmates*, with a minimum of 60 square feet of floor space per inmate in the sleeping area (excluding activity spaces). DISCUSSION: The facility classification committee should carefully evaluate each inmate before assigning him/her to a multiple occupancy cell for the purpose of ensuring the protection of the individual being assigned as well as the protection of the other inmate(s) already assigned to the cell.

4414 Where used, dormitories house not more than 50 inmates each, and have:

At least 10 cubic feet of fresh or purified and recirculated air per minute for each person occupying the dormitory:

Access to hot and cold running water;

Adequate toilet and shower facilities;

Locker for each individual;

Lighting of at least 20 footcandles;

A minimum floor area of 60 square feet per inmate and a clear floor-to-ceiling height of eight feet;

Noise levels low enough so as not to interfere with normal human activities;

No double or triple bunking; and

Clear observation supervision lines of sight for staff. (important)

DISCUSSION: Where dormitory housing cannot be avoided, the number of inmates per dormitory should be kept low. Living conditions may be enhanced by placing partitions between beds or by increasing the space between beds as much as possible. Chairs and desks should be provided for reading and writing.

5107 Dormitory living units are designed for a capacity of no more than 50 inmates, with a minimum of 50 square feet of floor space per inmate in the sleeping area. (Detention—Essential, Holding—Not Applicable)

DISCUSSION: Dormitories are large multiple-occupancy rooms that can be used to house minimum security inmates who do not need to be segregated and who pose relatively little risk to the facility or other inmates. Living conditions may be enhanced by placing partitions between beds or by increasing the space between beds as much as possible.

5108 There is a separate day room for each cell block or detention room cluster. (Detention—Essential, Holding—Not Applicable)

DISCUSSION: Day rooms equivalent to a minimum of 35 square feet per inmate should be available to all inmates for reading, writing or table games. Tables should be provided, which may also be used for dining.

012 Dormitory living units house no more inmates than can be *safely and effectively supervised* in a dormitory setting with a minimum of 50 square feet of floor space per inmate (excluding activity spaces).

DISCUSSION: Dormitories are large multiple-occupancy rooms that can be used to house *minimum security inmates* who do not need to be segregated and who pose relatively little risk to the facility or to other inmates. Insofar as possible, living conditions should be enhanced by placing privacy partitions between beds or by increasing the spaces between beds as much as possible.

006 There is a separate day room for each cell block or detention room cluster.

a Commission on Accreditation for Corrections, *Manual of Standards for Adult Correctional Institutions* (Rockville, Md.: American Correctional Association, August 1977), pp. 27, 28.

b Commission on Accreditation for Corrections, *Manual of Standards for Adult Local Detention Facilities*, (Rockville, Md.: American Correctional Association, December, 1977), pp. 21, 22.

c United States Department of Justice draft, "Federal Standards for Corrections," June, 1978, pp. 10, 12.

NOTE:

Other standards address the minimum space necessary or desirable for persons incarcerated in prisons and jails. For example: the National Advisory Commission on Criminal Justice Standards and Goals, *Corrections* (Washington, D.C.: U.S. Government Printing Office, 1973), p. 358, established 80 square feet as the minimum standard. The National Sheriffs' Association, *A Handbook on Jail Architecture* (Washington, D.C.: National Sheriffs' Association, 1975), p. 63, recommended 70 square feet of floor space for jails. The American Public Health Association, *Health Standards for Correctional Institutions* (Washington, D.C.: American Public Health Association, 1976) recommended a minimum of 60 square feet of floor space. The ABA Rights of Prisoners draft recommends one inmate per unit of adequate size and dorms designed for maximum privacy consistent with prisoner safety. The National Clearinghouse for Criminal Justice Planning and Architecture has recommended 70 square feet per inmate. SOURCE: Joan Mullen, *American Prisons and Jails, Vol. I: Summary Findings and Policy Implications of a National Survey.* Washington, DC: United States Department of Justice, 1980, p. 53.

TABLE 11.5   Utilization of Federal and State Correctional Facilities Using Reported Capacity and Two Values of Measured Capacity by Region, 1978

	TOTAL NUMBER OF INMATES	REPORTED CAPACITY[a]	REPORTED UTILIZATION	MEASURED CAPACITY[b]	MEASURED UTILIZATION	PHYSICAL CAPACITY[c]	PHYSICAL UTILIZATION
Federal and state total	257,300	268,300	96%	224,000	115%	150,900	171%
Federal	28,100	24,800	113	23,800	118	18,700	150
State	229,200	243,500	94	200,200	114	132,200	173
Northeast	30,400	34,800	87	33,700	90	17,800	171
North Central	56,700	66,000	86	52,900	107	37,200	152
South	107,200	103,400	104	77,500	138	56,900	188
West	34,900	39,300	89	36,100	97	20,300	172

NOTE: Almost every state system had a few confinement units for which there were some missing values. Five of the states had over 500 inmates housed in confinement units not included in this table. Hence, the total measured capacity for state facilities provided in this table probably underestimates by 10,000 to 15,000 beds the figure that would have been obtained if there were no missing data.

Northeast:	Connecticut	850
	New York	5,000
South:	North Carolina	2,100
	Virginia	1,700
West:	California	750

[a] The capacity of individual confinement units as reported by the jurisdiction.

[b] Measured capacity defined as one inmate per room of any size or, for dormitories, the smaller of: (1) Number of square feet of floor space/60 or (2) The jurisdictionally reported capacity.

[c] Physical capacity defined as a minimum of 60 square feet of floor space per inmate.

SOURCE: Joan Mullen, *American Prisons and Jails, Vol. I: Summary Findings and Policy Implications of a National Survey*. Washington, DC: United States Department of Justice, 1980, p. 65.

found some correlation between a state's incarceration rate and overcrowding and an inverse relation between the amount spent per inmate and overcrowding (1980:66). But few states could claim to be providing safe and humane living conditions, by their own or ACA standards.

The situation has not gotten better since the Abt survey. As of 1983, in South Carolina 1,500 prisoners were living in less than 30 square feet per person (Gettinger, 1983). BJS reported that across the nation space per prisoner had decreased 11 percent between 1978 and 1984. On the average, an inmate was allotted 57 square feet and was confined in a cell eleven hours each day. Although additional guards have been added and prisoner homicides have recently fallen, suicides have gone up (Yost, 1986). One result has been a rash of prison condition litigation, which is discussed in Chapter 13. As of April 1985,

only Alaska, Minnesota, Montana, Nebraska, New York, New Jersey, North Dakota, and Vermont had not experienced court litigation due to overcrowding or other confinement conditions (BJS, 1985b:4). The major response at this time is construction. In the winter of 1984, 237 new state and federal facilities were under construction. One year later, the number had risen to 378 ("Cage Count," 1985).

While corrections is often saddled with far grander goals than providing adequate and safe housing for inmates, Gordon Hawkins reminded policymakers that humane care by itself would be more than we have yet achieved (1976:55):

The adoption of custodial methods and procedures which genuinely reflected the belief that prisoners share a humanity common with our own would alone constitute an immense step forward along the path from barbarism to civilization.

THE DESIGN OF PROGRAMS AND SERVICES

Food Services. Prison dining halls are often the most feared places for mass disturbances and are therefore usually built with security in mind. Often, dining halls are small relative to the prison population, so that not all the inmates can assemble at one time. Consequently, the cafeteria may be busy all day, as different groups are shuttled in and out. Dining hall furniture is fixed to the floor, not designed for comfort, and often makes sociability among small groups impossible (Nagel, 1973:87–88).

Religious Facilities. Prisoners have a constitutional right to the free exercise of religious beliefs (see Chapter 13). Most prisons have at least one interfaith chapel; many larger and newer prisons may have several different religious facilities. Nagel and his team were somewhat surprised at the expense that sometimes went into religious buildings when other parts of the same

prison were inadequate. He reported that separate and extravagant chapels were often wasted space six days a week and hypothesized that they were probably built to impress visitors (1973:93–95). (The important role played by prison chaplains is discussed in Chapter 14.)

Recreation Facilities. The author knows one maximum security prison which included a swimming pool when it was built. When neighbors complained about the lavish facilities for convicts, the pool was filled with sand and cemented over. In another nearby facility, inmates built a modest nine-hole miniature golf course during hobby time. A local newspaper published a photograph of the completed course and naturally called the prison a country club. Such reactions to adequate recreation facilities for prisoners are not uncommon. Nevertheless, a variety of adequately built and equipped recreation facilities would seem to be a necessity, not a frill, in a prison (Nagel, 1973:96–102). Some newer facilities have adequate athletic facilities and equipment, but most prisons lack satisfactory recreational alternatives for the nonathletic. In many institutions, the television set is the only outlet.

Facilities for visiting have always been poor. Here, visiting day at Sing Sing, 1869. (Culver Pictures)

Insert 11.3 MY HUSBAND IS IN PRISON

Over the years, I've become quite resourceful in offering half-truths to those who ask about my marriage. "It is a commuter marriage," I say. Or: "My husband is an artist, working on a government grant." Sometimes, particularly when I'm tired, I try to change the subject. When my spirits and energy are high, though, I say the simple truth: "He is in prison."

The truth requires stamina, as any prison wife will explain. There are pitying smiles, silent reproaches, numerous questions and shocked responses. I believe that few marriages come under such close scrutiny as those of inmates and their spouses. There are many reasons for the questions, usually founded on a lifetime of media images. But as with other marriages, there are no generalizations that hold true for all prison marriages. There are, however, experiences all prison wives share.

During the four years I have visited my husband in prison—he is serving a 20-year sentence with a 10-year mandatory minimum for bank robbery—I have discovered an incredible support system among inmate wives. Some of the women have jobs; others receive public assistance. Many of them are single-handedly raising their children. Often it is the first time they have been on their own. One 50-year-old woman waiting to visit her husband described to me the first time she changed a light bulb in her oven and completed her income-tax form. Another talked about taking the family cow to be slaughtered. Yet there is a camaraderie among us. We come from different ethnic backgrounds and economic classes, but we

understand each other. We understand that we have had to become strong.

Wives of prisoners must adjust to arbitrary treatment by prison guards and administrators who treat us as if we were criminals like our husbands. We are subjected to reprimands, searches and a multitude of bureaucratic requirements designed to discourage continued contact. One day, in the visiting room, I see a woman's hand slapped by a prison guard when she places it on her husband's knee. Another day, another woman is kept waiting for half of her three-hour visit as prison officials try to "find" her husband and bring him to the visiting room. By the time he arrives, she is so upset the rest of the visit is ruined.

In learning to cope with the oppressiveness of prison, we learn about our husbands' experiences. Just as women in the workplace study the behavior of their bosses in order to survive, we study the prison guards. We learn to use humor to vent our frustrations—and ways to channel our anger. Prison officials tend to discourage any type of networking among prisoners or their families. At the state penitentiary in Oregon there is a rule against "cross-visiting": one inmate's visitor can't visit with another inmate. When we ask if the rule can be changed in order to promote a positive "community" atmosphere, we are told that there is no community among prison families nor does the prison wish to facilitate one.

Yet over and over again, women who are total strangers assist each other with advice about transportation and child care—and the tech-

Facilities for Visiting. Nagel lists six visiting alternatives (1973:102):

1. Closed (noncontact) visits
2. Limited contact visits
3. Informal contact visits
4. Freedom of the grounds
5. Conjugal visits
6. Furloughs

Most prisons are not designed to provide frequent, comfortable, or private visits with prisoners. Facilities for family visits are particularly inadequate (see Insert 11.3). Adequacy of visit-

niques to fight bureaucratic battles. Our desire to keep our marriages and families intact is a taxing one. Coping with the incarceration of a loved one is difficult and can often result in financial burdens, health problems and social ostracism. Divorce is common; not all prisoners react positively when their wives begin to take control over their own lives. Some marriages break down when the prisoner is released and both parties have difficulty adjusting to the changes they have undergone.

There are only seven states that allow conjugal visits between prisoners and their wives. Therefore, prison wives must struggle with decisions about their sexual lives. Some base their decisions on individual moral and religious beliefs and remain celibate. Some work out detailed agreements with their husbands which may allow extramarital liaisons. Others base such decisions on the amount of time their husbands will be incarcerated. It is not sex with their husbands which most wives miss most of all; it is the intimacy and privacy. They long to be touched and held.

But until now, many wives have hidden the fact they love someone in prison. That is beginning to change; they are learning that they are not alone. Organizations of prison wives are forming across the country, resulting in pressure for family-support groups, improved visitation conditions—including special playrooms where fathers can see their children—and better transition programs for released inmates. Studies show that inmates who maintain close family ties are less likely to commit crimes again.

But becoming involved in prison reform can be especially difficult for us. We must plan our actions carefully because we are always aware that our husbands are under the control of prison officials. Many small injustices must be ignored because prison guards have the power to harass and punish. Still, I believe that change is possible. Some prison officials have begun to recognize that family members are often forgotten victims in the criminal-justice system and that we can assist in an inmate's rehabilitation. We know that prison is a destructive experience for those we care about, and we want to help lessen the negative impact. We also want to make sure they never return to prison.

I know the importance of love and trust in my relationship with my husband; of living in optimistic hope of a better future. I savor the time I spend in conversation with him, and I learn new ways of expressing intimacy in a crowded public area. I only hope that other prison wives will become proud of their special stamina. I hope that they, too, will cultivate connections with community leaders so they don't become isolated and that they will join to form the bridge from inside the prison walls to the outside world. For only we can help others understand that we are not crazy to love those who have made past mistakes. And we, who are strong enough to care, can really help keep our mates from going back to jail.

ing facilities is often determined by the age of the prison. In most prisons, except some minimum security facilities, any form of contact visit entails searches of the inmate before and after the visit, and searches of the visiting party. Few prisons provide the space or equipment for family visits. Mississippi, New York, and California provide secluded rooms where husbands and wives may visit in private and engage in sexual intercourse. Other states have considered the idea but dropped it as a political hot potato. Furloughs, which allow selected inmates to go home for one to three days, are the usual substitute, but they are not available to all inmates.

SUMMARY

1. Although prisons can be traced back to ancient times, the use of imprisonment as the preferred punishment for felons emerged in the late 1700s.
2. Major penitentiaries were built in the United States and in England in the first third of the nineteenth century. The most famous were the Eastern State Penitentiary in Philadelphia and Auburn (New York).
3. The early penitentiaries were plagued by the same ambivalence in purpose as is found today, and they were also rapidly overcrowded.
4. The reformatory movement, starting about 1870, rededicated American corrections to rehabilitation, but was also short-lived and poorly implemented.
5. The contemporary prison which includes treatment programs based on behavioral science emerged in the 1930s as the Great Depression brought an end to the industrial prison era.
6. Prison architecture was once considered a moral science. The early maximum security prison has endured long beyond its perceived utility; many prisoners are still housed in prisons built before 1900.
7. The most commonly found security grade of prisons in the United States is medium security, but the majority of prisoners are still housed in the larger-capacity maximum security units.
8. The Abt census of prisons and jails found that a majority of prisoners live in crowded conditions.

KEY WORDS

ADMINISTRATIVE SEGREGATION. Housing units in prison that isolate prisoners from the general population for nondisciplinary reasons.

BLOCK DESIGN. The prison design, used at Auburn and subsequently in a number of maximum security units, which provides for cells stacked in tiers or blocks within the center of a building.

CAMPUS STYLE PRISON. A relatively recent design used primarily in minimum security settings that provides separate living quarters (often dorms or rooms) dispersed around a central square of service and office buildings.

CONGREGATE SYSTEM. Now identified with the Auburn system, the original congregate prison, such as Newgate in New York City, provided for group living and work and little internal security. As modified at Auburn, the congregate system provided for silent group work during the day and sleeping in individual cells at night.

COURTYARD DESIGN. A recent prison design adaptable to a number of security levels. Buildings are arranged around the perimeter of an internal open space.

INDUSTRIAL PRISON. Any prison in which the principal activity is industrial labor by inmates, and also prisons in the period 1900 to 1930, when the principal focus of most prisons in the United States was the production of goods.

INMATE SELF-GOVERNMENT. Any prison management system that provides for formal inmate participation or control over some decisions regarding routine, discipline, and program; pioneered by Osborne and Gill.

MARK SYSTEM. A form of token economy designed by Alexander Maconochie at the Tasmanian penal colony in 1840. Provided for graduated increase in responsibility and freedom contingent on behavioral goals being met by inmates.

MAXIMUM SECURITY. A physical and social design that provides for high control over entrance and egress and strict control over physical movement of prisoners through the prison.

MEDIUM SECURITY. A physical and social design providing for moderate to high control over entrance and egress but somewhat more freedom within the prison grounds than maximum security.

MINIMUM SECURITY. Prisons (and often other correctional facilities) which provide little or no physical barrier to escape and little control of movement within the prison.

PENITENTIARY MOVEMENT. The period roughly from 1790 to 1830 in which political and social attention was focused on debates about the most effective penitentiary design, and when the first major prisons were built in the eastern states.

PENNSYLVANIA SYSTEM. The prison design associated with the Eastern State Penitentiary (1829), in which prisoners spent their entire sentence in solitary confinement. Quickly abandoned as impractical and expensive.

PUNITIVE SEGREGATION. High-security isolation cells utilized to discipline inmates. Length of placement and conditions in punitive segregation are restricted by regulations and constitutional limits.

RADIAL DESIGN. The physical design associated with the Pennsylvania system of housing units (usually untiered cells on outside walls) radiating from a central control hub.

RATED CAPACITY. The number of inmates determined by the prison administration as the upper limit for a particular facility. As a crowding measure, unreliable because administrators frequently alter the acceptable rate.

REFORMATORY. A type of facility, but more important a type of program, designed in the 1870s for youthful (generally age 16 to 25) inmates. Initiated at Elmira, New York, the program stressed vocational training, military discipline, and discretionary release during an indeterminant sentence. The term now refers to any facility (often maximum security) housing the youngest inmates in the adult correctional system.

TELEPHONE POLE DESIGN. Prison design that replaced the block design as the preferred design for maximum security units. A long corridor is crossed by several shorter living unit and program buildings.

TRUSTY SYSTEM. Perhaps initiated by Pilsbury at the Connecticut Wetherfield prison (1830), the practice of providing trusted inmates with considerable freedom and responsibility for a number of administrative and service duties in the prison.

PROJECTS AND QUESTIONS

1. Make arrangements to tour the nearest state or federal prison. What is the physical design? How old is it? Are its facilities adequate for its inmate population?
2. Divide the class into teams to design a prison. Assume the desired prison capacity is 500, that most of the inmates are from an urban area, that few of them are likely to require maximum security,

and that most are between 18 and 35 years old. What would your prison look like, and why? As you attempt the design, what other information do you find yourself wanting to know?
3. If you were a corrections department public information director, how would you respond to citizen queries about a new physical education complex to be built in a maximum security prison?

ADDITIONAL READING

James B. Jacobs. *Stateville, The Prison in Mass Society.* Chicago: University of Chicago Press, 1977. A history of an Illinois maximum security prison that examines the relationships between internal control and external social and political changes.

Blake McKelvey. *American Prisons: A Study of American Social History Prior to 1915.* Montclair, NJ: Patterson Smith, 1972. The classic history of prisons in nineteenth-century United States.

William Nagel. *The New Red Barn: A Critical Look at the Modern American Prison.* New York: Walker, 1973. A report of a tour of prisons constructed in the 1960s and 1970s in the United States.

12 INSTITUTIONS FOR WOMEN

QUESTIONS

1. Why have women's prisons and correctional institutions gone unnoticed over the years?

2. What are the differences between institutions for men and those for women?

3. Discuss the pros and cons of co-correctional institutions.

4. Would you say that the family groupings formed by women prisoners are based primarily upon their preprison experience or are responses to their prison experience?

5. What guidelines would you recommend for male correctional officers working in institutions for women? What guidelines would you recommend for female officers working in prisons for men? What are the advantages and limitations of having correctional staff members of both genders working in institutions?

WOMEN ARE TOUGHER TO MANAGE

Mansford was a tiny hamlet in the northern hill region of Jefferson. The town had grown up in the post-Civil War boom, as a country spa for the gentry from Adams. But the tourist trade had dwindled as railroads gave way to plane travel. The economy of Mansford gave way altogether, until a state senator won a bidding war for the new women's prison in the 1940s.

As was the case in many middle-sized and smaller states, the Mansford prison was the only state facility for women, with the exception of two small prerelease centers in Adams, and small detention wings in two of the state jails. As a result, Mansford held a rather bewildering array of prisoners. Although living quarters at Mansford were re-

This chapter was written by David Kalinich.

ferred to as "cottages," they were in fact two-story gray stone buildings in the style of college dormitories, except that sleeping rooms were bathroom-sized closets, locked from the outside each night. Each cottage served a single classification grouping of fifty inmates—when overcrowding was not a problem. Unlike the case in the men's prisons, there was one building for sentenced misdemeanants. Only unsentenced women and parole violators were housed in the Jefferson jails. All sentenced women, felons and short-termers, were bused to Mansford. Another building was set aside for honor residents. The doors in this building were not locked by the matrons, and the women held their own room keys. Two buildings housed women who had not yet earned honor status but were not considered security risks. Wolff Cottage, named after the first commissioner in the state, was a dual-function maximum security building. The northern wing housed administrative segregation and the southern wing held maximum security prisoners.

Except for the cyclone fence, which encircled the compound at a discrete distance from the buildings, and the guard at the front gate, a visitor's first impression upon negotiating the tree-lined drive was of a small liberal arts college tucked away in vacation country. However, most of the residents were city women in their twenties and early thirties, few of whom had earned high school diplomas, and most of whom complained loudly about the terrible isolation. The majority had been committed from the city of Adams, 125 miles south. Visits from family were difficult and expensive, and only in the warmer months, when the picnic area and playgrounds were habitable, could restless children be adequately accommodated while adult family members talked.

One winter day, this prison was the site of a conference on classification. The commissioner had asked for a systemwide re-

view and unification of classification procedures, but the women's prison always received exceptions to the general rules. Programs in the women's prison were always being criticized, usually from both sides at once. Some groups claimed that women inmates were routinely ignored when program innovations were proposed, and that the women's educational progam consisted of outdated home economics classes that degraded women and kept them out of the labor force. Others complained that the women needed more rather than fewer services devoted to parenting, budgeting, and housekeeping. Others complained that the per diem cost for women inmates was astronomically high, more than double the cost for men. Other critics pointed out that regardless of cost, the women had far fewer program choices available, especially for vocational training and prerelease. There were only sixteen prerelease beds for women in the entire state. But other observers pointed out that two of the fourteen prerelease facilities in the state were devoted to women.

The controversies were continual, and took their toll on the Mansford administration. Superintendents rarely lasted more than two years. The current occupants at Mansford were Barney Kelly, superintendent for the last six months, and Susan Rumford, the deputy for treatment. These two were currently being attacked by Susan's immediate subordinate, the director of treatment. The DOT was an elderly black woman who had returned to school when she was 55 to earn her MSW. She had publicly criticized Kelly and Rumford for running a racist program designed to keep black inmates from gaining economic self-sufficiency. The meeting got off to a bad start when the director of treatment refused to attend.

Phil paced impatiently for a few minutes, and then decided to begin without her. The other participants were tight-lipped and defensive. "The central issue for classification and program at Mansford may not be a program issue at all, but it certainly affects all efforts at this prison. And that question is why is Mansford so volatile?"

"You tell me," said Susan. "You're the consultant." A moment later, there was a loud rap on the door. A guard signaled to Susan, who went to the door for a whispered conference. She then excused herself to attend to a disturbance in Wolff Cottage. Phil was left with the Superintendent and four counselors, all but one male. Susan failed to return, and after an hour of ineffectual discussion the group broke for lunch.

The architect of Mansford had decided that the treatment milieu would be enhanced if staff and inmates ate in the same cafeteria. Phil and the superintendent were halfway through the food line when an altercation arose behind them. One woman attacked another with a metal tray. While an officer and two matrons rushed to break them apart, Phil watched in disbelief. He decided after lunch that the meeting should be canceled and rescheduled at an off-campus location.

As he reached the main gate on his way out, he recognized the guard on duty. It was Hennessey, who used to work at Dunmore. "Hiya, Doc," said the guard cheerfully. Bad day at Mansford, huh?"

Phil nodded. "What are you doing out here?"

"Put in for transfer three months ago."

"How do you like it?"

Hennessey grinned. "Actually, I do. There's not nearly as much tension here as at Dunmore. I can relax."

"Huh?" said Phil. "Maybe this is just a bad day, but. . ."

"Yeah, I know what you saw. I just came down from the Admin Building. But it's different here. The women are harder to manage, no doubt about that. You get a call at the max about an inmate fight, and nine times out of ten they'll break it up before we arrive, just so we can't tell what happened. Here, an angry woman sees there's staff around and they don't care. One of them kicked all of Ms. Rumford's teeth out last year."

"Well, then," said Phil. "In what ways do you find this relaxing?"

"One thing," Hennessey. "Most of these women aren't real cons. Here, staff and inmates have a real chance to—well, talk things through. None of that distance, and none of that tension. The women don't conform to rules like the men do, but they won't stick a knife in your back when you turn around either. It's just anger. Not that cops and robbers game. I burnt out on that."

TWO DIFFERENT SYSTEMS

The point of the case study is to show that there are differences between male and female correctional institutions. In the case study, we see through the eyes of the correctional officer that women inmates behave differently. The prison social system of female inmates is different from that of male inmates. In addition, female correctional institutions have typically been constructed differently from male institutions; they are smaller and often more attractive. The philosophy of correctional treatment and management of female institutions has historically differed from that of the male institution and has been based on our perceptions of gender roles. Treatment programs in female institutions have focused on domestic and family skills, while programs for male inmates typically focus upon industrial job skills such as welding and auto mechanics.

There are also far fewer institutions for women than for men, because women inmates make up a small percent of the prison population. According to the 1983 survey of inmates in federal and

Earlier women's prisons were often built to resemble "cottages" around a central square. The State Correctional Facility at Muncy, PA is fairly typical. (Pennsylvania Department of Corrections)

state institutions, only 4.4 percent were women. Of the 437,238 inmates in the nation's prisons in 1983, 19,154 were women. The number of women inmates has grown substantially since 1974, when 8,091 of the total 229,721 inmates were women (BJS, 1986b). The statistical survey shows that both male and female inmates have doubled since 1973. Table 12.1 shows annual increases in the nation's female inmate population.

In this chapter, we will cover some of the major differences between male and female correctional institutions and show that institutional corrections for women is in many ways a unique system. As we discuss the differences, we will show that the differential treatment of female offenders has not always been to their benefit and often has not considered their needs. We will also cover some of the current trends and programs in women's institutions. We begin by highlighting some of the major differences between male and female correctional institutional systems.

THE FEMALE INMATE PROFILE

A national survey of women's correctional programs developed a profile of incarcerated women (Glick and Neto, 1975:152). The following is a summary of that information:

- *Childhood:* Over half the women came from two-parent homes; 31 percent lived with their mother only.
- *Welfare:* Half received welfare as adults, and one-third as children.
- *Work:* Almost all of the women had worked at some time in their lives; 40 percent had worked for two months prior to their arrest.
- *Offense:* Convicted felons were serving one year or more, with 43 percent committing

TABLE 12.1 Women in State and Federal Institutions, 1974–1983

YEAR	NUMBER	PERCENT CHANGE	PERCENT OF PRISON POPULATION
1974	8,091		3.5
1975	9,667	19.5	3.8
1976	11,170	15.5	4.0
1977 (custody)	12,041	7.8	4.1
1977 (jurisdiction)	12,279	NA	4.1
1978	12,746	3.8	4.2
1979	12,995	2.0	4.3
1980	13,420	3.3	4.1
1981	15,537	15.8	4.2
1982	17,785	14.5	4.3
1983	19,154	7.7	4.4

NOTE: Before 1977, NPS reports were based on the custody population. Beginning in 1977, they were based on the jurisdiction population. Both figures are shown for 1977 to facilitate year-to-year comparison.
NA-Not applicable.
SOURCE: Bureau of Justice Statistics, *Prisoners in State and Federal Institutions on December 31, 1983*. Washington, DC: U.S. Department of Justice, June 1986.

violent crimes, 29 percent committing property crimes, and 22 percent committing drug-related offenses.

- *Offense history:* Nearly one-third had experienced their first arrest at the age of 17 or younger, and 49 percent had been arrested for the first time between the ages of 18 and 24. Almost one-third had served time in juvenile institutions.

DIFFERENCES BETWEEN MALE AND FEMALE INSTITUTIONS

Public Concern. Traditionally women's prisons have received little public attention. In addition, and as a result of less attention, women's prisons have been given low priority in the corrections systems. Female inmates have been aptly labeled the "forgotten offenders." According to Rita Simon (1979) there are three major reasons why female corrections has been effectively ignored. First, as we have pointed out, there are relatively

few women in prison. Presently, the federal system has 38 correctional institutions and 4 jail facilities for men, but only 4 correctional facilities for women, 3 of which are co-correctional. At the state level there are 509 male, 47 female, and 20 co-correctional institutions. The men's facilities thus require far more funds and become a major budgeting concern for federal and state government.

Second, the women's system does not have a history of riots, hostage taking and disruption. For example, the Attica and New Mexico prison riots brought a great deal of media attention to those institutions and to corrections in general. We can even argue that the Attica riot, in which both inmates and correctional officers were killed, held the media hostage. Following any prison riots, state governors typically appoint a commission to investigate the causes and recommend reforms for the prison system. Whether such events and commissions create real reform is debatable (Lurinskas, Kalinich, and Banas, 1985). However, public attention and indignation always follow a reported prison disturbance of any magnitude. Women inmates have not gained attention through any organized protests or riots. The media have rarely had an interest in informing the public of conditions in the female prison system.

The third reason for the lack of interest in women prisoners is that the crimes women commit are not considered as serious as those committed by men. Women, according to Simon, commit crimes that inconvenience society. The majority of women offenders have not been involved in organized crime, crimes that involve large amounts of property or have endangered the lives of numbers of people (Simon, 1979).

The lack of public concern for women' prisons has relegated female corrections to a subordinate position in the corrections system. Major concern for reform, progress, or even day-to-day management has been focused on the male system over the years. As a result of the feminist movement, more attention is being paid to female offenders and how they are treated by the criminal justice system and in the corrections process. The research literature on female prisons has been growing, and prescriptions for improved treatment programs that focus on economic independence for women offenders are currently popular.

Inmate Programs. An important issue that has been raised in the last several years is that women inmates have been short-changed in treatment programs in general, especially in the area of vocational training. The limited vocational training programs provided for women have deep historical roots and are based on traditional concepts of gender roles. That is, men need to earn a living, and women are charged with managing the household and raising a family. The treatment of women in prison has been to mold them into wife, mother, homemaker; however, most women in prison rarely meet this ideal (Feinman, 1984).

Seeing this as a problem in establishing sound programming for female offenders is not new. In 1870, penologists from across the country met in Cincinnati, Ohio, at the National Congress on Penitentiary and Reformatory Discipline to propose major changes in the country's prison system. A letter to the Congress written by Elizabeth B. Chance, active in prison reform in Rhode Island, argued that the limited training for female prisoners restricted their ability to reform. She states:

> . . . it seems to me that they [female prisoners] are too much confined to work that is to be done in families. . . . whereas, men are more generally taught trades, both useful and profitable, which they find little difficulty in practicing, when they are released, in shops, factories, and on the farm. (Wines, 1871)

Her ideas may have been ignored at the Congress. Thirty-eight papers covering an array of issues were presented, and 37 principles for prison and reformatory management were set forth. However, no emphasis was placed on reevaluating treatment programs for women prisoners. Again in 1973, the low priority given to women's

programs is recognized by the National Advisory Commission on Criminal Justice Standards and Goals (1973). In the section "Women in Major Institutions" (p. 378), it is argued that women are the forgotten inmates, considered to be in a separate system of corrections and provided with programs based on traditional gender role stereotypes that do not give them the opportunity to function independently upon release. The report states:

> Of primary concern in women's prisons is the almost total lack of meaningful programming. Work assignments serve institutional and systems wide needs.
> Women do laundry, sewing, and other "female tasks" for the correctional system. Such programming does not prepare a woman for employment and in fact greatly increases her dependency. (NAC, 1973:379).

A national study on women's correctional programs published in 1975 showed that vocational programs concentrated on traditional areas of cosmetology, clerical skills, and food services (Glick and Neto, 1975). It would seem that in 1975 little progress had been made in providing women inmates with the marketable skills recommended by Elizabeth Chance in 1870.

Currently, the issue of appropriate treatment for female inmates is being examined with some intensity. Assisting these offenders to become economically independent and providing them with programs that are not based on traditional gender roles is one proposal. One approach suggests that programming be based upon a continuum of economic independence, with the need for females to reach self-sufficiency as the determining factor in developing programs for them (DeConstanzo and Valente, 1984). Since institutional programs are limited, other suggestions focus on a gradual deinstitutionalization of female inmates, combined with appropriate training programs to make them self-sufficient in the community (Thomas, 1981). Programs have been developed to assist women in developing the necessary interpersonal skills to obtain employment and perform successfully after being placed. Such programs emphasize communications skills, assertiveness training, and development of self-esteem (Mazzotta, 1981).

Meaningful vocational training, job readiness, and self-sufficiency programs are as important for female inmates as they are for their male counterparts. Seventy-five percent of female inmates in one study were found to be self-supporting or the sole support of their families. The study also found that 50 percent of the female inmates studied had no job skills or prior experience (Sorensen, 1981).

Federal court intervention has required that female inmates be provided with similar treatment, educational, and vocational programs to those available to male inmates (*Glover v. Johnson*, 1979). Perhaps by the 1990s female inmates will receive the same range of programs their male counterparts now have available. On the pessimistic side, however, they may not have a major impact upon the ability of institutions for females to provide effective rehabilitation or self-sufficiency programs. The 1977 study on programs cited above also states that counseling and treatment programs for women were conspicuous by their absence (Glick and Neto, 1975). This is also true for male institutions. The similarity for both male and female prisons is that the primary goals are security and maintenance of order. Only a small percentage of expenditures for correctional institutions goes for programs for male or female inmates.

Physical Facilities. As we have seen, female inmates make up only a small percentage of the total population in our nation's prisons. Thus, the population of female inmates for each state is relatively small. According to the 1984 survey of prisoners in America, only 11 states had more than 500 female inmates, with California housing 2,310. Due to the low number in each state, most states house the female inmate population in one facility (Indiana, Florida, Michigan, Ohio, Oklahoma, and Texas have more than one facility for women inmates). While this may have economic advantages, it creates several management problems from the standpoint of accepted correctional procedures. This can be shown best by reviewing the structure of the prison system for men and the importance of multiple facilities within the system (for more details, see Chapter 14).

Historically, younger male adult offenders have been confined in the reformatory system and older offenders in the penitentiary system. This requires two separate facility systems. In addition, systems also classify inmates into maximum, medium, and minimum security groups. Each is placed in separate facilities. In most states, the prison and reformatory system for men is comprised of several physical plants scattered throughout the state. In addition, the system for men provides honor camps, farms, and other low-security institutions.

When only one physical plant is available, as is true for women inmates in most states, the two-tier reformatory and penitentiary system and the three security level classification system must take place under one roof. In addition, the women's prison system is typically denied an honor or farm system, which is an important mechanism for rewarding inmates who are not a problem. In other words, several institutions exist in one, and highly dangerous or mentally ill inmates must be kept in the same institution with the general inmate population. The National Advisory Commission recommended that state correctional systems with small numbers of women inmates that could not provide adequate programs should attempt to find community corrections alternatives for its female population or make contractual arrangements with states that can provide adequate programming (NAC, 1973).

In addition, having only one facility for female inmates in a state can make visitation difficult. Women from all parts of a state will be placed at one location, whereas male inmates will be housed in many locations throughout the state. The possibility of placing male inmates near home exists in a system with multiple facilities. However, for the women's system, no placement

The campus style of the women's prison hides some strong security measures. Above left the campus at Muncy is contrasted with above right, an inmate waiting to exit from one of the cottages. (Pennsylvania Department of Corrections)

options exist to facilitate visitation. For inmate, prison staff, and administrators, visitation is extremely important. Visits from friends and loved ones help inmates keep their links to their communities and reduce the sense of alienation. This in turn helps reduce tension in institutions and supports the order maintenance goal.

As a final comparison of physical facilities for men and women inmates, many argue that the physical environments of female institutions are superior to those of male institutions (Adriti, 1973). If you were to pass by the Mansfield Reformatory for Women in Mansfield, Ohio, you might think it was a beautiful campus for a small college. Although prisons for men are sometimes referred to as country clubs—always by people who have never been in a prison—it is difficult to find a male institution that looks like anything but an institution. The campus design consists of a series of cottages designed to house 10 to 20 inmates each. The administration building is

placed in the center of the cottages, and often homes for key employees are part of the layout. In addition, walls are not used to surround the cottages, so the institution does not appear like the typical maximum security fortress of the male system.

We must point out, however, that the **cottage system** was originally intended for women who were vagrants, prostitutes, and lesser offenders. The female offenders committing major felonies remained housed in congregate prisons, usually in more deplorable conditions than the male prisons (Rafter, 1985).

CONCERN FOR CHILDREN

Women traditionally have had primary responsibility for raising children. During a family breakup—divorce or separation—custody of the children has almost always been awarded to the mother. Our courts, reflecting our societal belief,

Many women prisoners are mothers and maintaining relationships with children is a central concern. Above is the highly regarded children's center in Bedford Hills. (New York State Department of Correctional Services)

felt that the mother was the most important figure in childraising. There is some truth to this, as a natural bonding takes place early between mother and child. When a woman is separated from her child due to imprisonment, a great deal of psychological trauma may be suffered by the woman and the child or children (Baunach, 1982).

Researchers have shown that a majority of women in prisons are mothers. Some give birth shortly after they are incarcerated, and being separated from their children is a major concern for them (Ward and Kasserbaum, 1965; Glick and Neto, 1975; Murton and Baunach, 1973; Stanton 1980; Baunach, 1982). Baunach has conducted extensive research in the area. She found that mothers in prison tend to be predominantly black, under 35 years of age, divorced or unmarried, and possessing inadequate educational and vocational skills. Most inmate mothers were found to have two or three children under the age of 13. Over half of the mothers lived with their children before being incarcerated, and the children were usually placed with relatives while the mother was serving her sentence. The local courts would often intervene, taking legal custody away

from inmate mothers in many cases, especially those with long sentences, and place the children in foster homes or welfare facilities against the wishes of the mother (Baunach, 1982).

Inmate mothers would often succumb to guilt or anxiety over the separation from their children. They would blame themselves for becoming caught up in the criminal activity that led to their incarceration and be concerned for the well-being and care of their children:

> For many mothers, the psychological repercussions may be analogous to those resulting from other forms of loss, such as death or divorce. The grief response emitted by inmate-mothers may be characterized by emptiness, helplessness, anger and bitterness, guilt, and fear of loss or rejection (Baunach, 1982, pp. 157, 158).

One pivotal point is that the mothers will be released from the institutions at some future date, and many will be reunited with their children. They will again have the responsibility of raising and caring for their children. To the extent that the separation breaks down normal parent-child relationships and "excon" mothers continue to suffer psychological guilt over the separation, their task will be made difficult.

To deal with this problem, as well as to help inmate mothers overcome their initial feelings of guilt and shame for having deserted their children, programs to allow mothers continuous contact with their children have been developed. Presently, California, Kentucky, Minnesota, Nebraska, New York, Tennessee, Washington, and Massachusetts have programs that allow mothers to have overnight visits with their children. In addition to overnight visits, contact visits between mothers and children have become the rule; visiting areas have been altered to create a more normal and less prisonlike environment for the mother-child interactions (Neto and Bainer, 1980). These programs are less than perfect, as they take place in the prison setting and concerns for security and the prison setting itself may have negative impacts on the effectiveness of the program.

An alternative to bringing children to the institution is to allow the inmate mothers to spend time with their children outside (Baunach, 1982; McCarthy, 1980). In addition, it is recommended that inmate mothers be prepared for their eventual reunion with their children by providing them with instructions on child growth and development to improve their parenting skills (McCarthy, 1980). While this has promise, having only one correctional institution in a state places many inmates a great distance from their homes, making community visits for inmate mothers a logistical burden most correctional systems might be reluctant to bear.

Finally, there are those in the business of corrections who claim that the majority of inmate mothers do not really care about their children, and they will return to a life of crime upon release. That is, inmate mothers, like all inmates, will make claims to good intentions when they are released; but the good intentions will be forgotten once they are out. In a study completed in Michigan, 65.5 percent of female parolees lived with their children upon their parole release. More important, 83 percent of those who participated in a contact program with their children returned to live with them after being released upon parole (Hunter, 1983). Such studies do not tell us about the long-term effects of inmate mother-child contact programs. The fact remains, however, that the mothers will eventually be released from prison and, in many cases, their children will be returned to them. Such programs seem justified upon those very practical grounds.

THE SOCIAL SYSTEM IN A WOMEN'S PRISON

As Chapter 15 will show, inmates in the male institutions have an intricate social system that includes a status hierarchy, norms and rules of behavior for personal interactions, power arrangements and leadership roles among inmates, and a contraband market system in which inmates may purchase drugs, food items, and so on. This all should have come as a rich surprise to the person who assumed that prisons were run in a rigid or even totalitarian manner, with inmates having little freedom to make choices. Prisons for women are also run within a context of rules and regulations that give the appearance the inmates are under the total control of the prison guards and administrators. But women inmates, like men, are deprived of their freedom, of normal goods and services, of heterosexual contact, and of their psychological safety. Women also form an intricate social system in their prison society that serves as a means to help soften the pain of imprisonment.

Some theorists of the male inmate social system argue that a significant part of the culture is imported to the prison (Irwin and Cressey, 1962). That is, inmates bring street skills and behaviors to the prison with them and rely upon these to function in the institutional setting. Research on women's prisons has shown that a significant part of the female inmate's culture is also imported (Giallombardo, 1966). However, the social system that evolves in female prisons is very different from that of male inmates. The social system of male prisons has been studied extensively over the last two decades. While the studies on women prisoner subcultures have lagged behind, some extremely valuable research has been produced in that area.

Prisons are harsh places, even the women's prisons that resemble college campuses. They can create a sense of hopelessness, despair, and powerlessness among the inmates. Women focus on adjusting to doing their time and take on a sense of alienation from the outside world while they are there (Mahan, 1984). The social roles acted out by the female prisoners, their alliances, and the reactions to staff are greatly influenced by the prison experience, or the pain of imprisonment (Giallombardo, 1966). Studies show, for example, that the majority of women inmates are opposed to staff expectations, rules and regulations, and so on. But unlike their male counterparts, women inmates do not solidly subscribe to a general inmate code or set of ethics (Kruttschnitt, 1981; Ward and Kasserbaum, 1965).

In an earlier work on social systems in women's prisons by Ward and Kasserbaum (1965), it was found that inmates initially felt uncertainty and a sense of normlessness about their situation. Like male inmates, the women experienced deprivations of liberty, material goods, heterosexual relationships, autonomy, and security. In reaction to such deprivations, a social system developed to provide interpersonal and normative support and material goods. Interestingly, the inmate code required a "silence" system—don't give information to the guards—but it was violated liberally, without sanctions. The overriding need of the majority of the female prisoners was to establish an emotional and sexual relationship with a partner. The relationship served to provide love, support, and social status while in prison. Inmates introduced to homosexuality for the first time while in prison were referred to in the inmate jargon as **jailhouse turnouts** (Ward and Kasserbaum, 1965).

In a major work on the female inmate social structure, *Society of Women*, by Rose Giallom-

bardo (1966), it was pointed out the inmate social structure was, in part, imported from their outside world. In imitating their former world, inmates formed families with husbands who protect the family, mothers who nurture, and so on. The family group meets the internalized needs and expectations of the traditional female family role. Prison marriages and homosexual relationships were utilized to make the time go more smoothly. Compared to male institutions where males taking on female roles were looked down upon, homosexuality in the women's prison was seen as an important aspect of forming families and linkages that helped smooth inmate relationships. While homosexual relationships appeared to be the most important form of inmate interaction, those who were not bonded by such a tie could become part of the family through kinship ties. That is, they could be part of a family group, sharing in the communal experience, without sexual contact or the degree of emotional contact needed in a marriage.

Giallombardo describes an argot, or inmate language. **Snitchers** were informants, **jive bitches** were troublemakers, **connects** were inmates who had institutional assignments that allowed them to acquire scarce information or resources, **squares** were inmates without a criminal orientation. In addition, a contraband system helped soften the material deprivations of the inmates. The female inmate culture was seen as more communal than individualistic male inmate culture.

Later research on the women's prison subculture by Ester Heffernan (1972) sheds further light on the way female inmates organize their social system. Here it was found that no single subsystem existed. Rather, there were multiple subsystems with goals, codes of acceptable behavior, and means of mutual support. This finding was repeated in more current research (Kruttschnitt, 1981). The subsystems were formed upon different reactions to imprisonment and perceptions of what an easy life in prison would be. The differing beliefs had their bases in the preprison socialization of each inmate. Three subsystems were found to exist: the square, the cool, and the life. The **square** are the noncriminal types, or situational offenders. They have accepted conventional values, but committed a crime due to an emotional impulse or other circumstances. The **cool** are the professional criminals. They see crime as their skill for making a living. The **life** have little identification with conventional norms. The majority of this group have spent a great deal of their lives in institutions.

Each group behaves differently in coping with imprisonment. The square does not rebel against staff, has solid outside contacts with relatives, and obtains goods and services through legitimate means. The cool does not rebel either, considering imprisonment an occupational hazard. She participates in both legitimate and illegitimate means to obtain goods and services, and maintains ongoing outside contacts. The life group has no outside support and will actively involve themselves in the contraband system to obtain goods and services.

As touched upon in Giallombardo's work, developing families was found to be a normal social process. However, the square typically avoided joining a family. About 22 percent of the cool participated in family groupings, and 57 percent of the life group became involved in familying (Heffernan, 1972).

The homosexuality prevalent in women's prisons is probably no more prevalent than in male institutions. Research suggests that fewer than 20 percent of the female population in the institutions studied was actively involved in homosexuality. Preprison homosexuality on the part of the women was seen as a good indicator of their likely involvement in prison homosexuality. Interestingly, the research found that homosexual experiences which began in prison—jail house turnouts—often continued after the women were released (Propper, 1981).

Patterns of female leadership were studied in one Alabama prison for women. That is, the researchers were attempting to determine which inmates had a strong influence over the behaviors of others. In the male prisons, inmates who could

manipulate the correctional officer staff and be highly successful in dealing contraband have a great deal of influence. In this study, it was found that female inmates who committed crimes such as armed robbery tended to assume leadership roles. Inmates who were actively involved in homosexuality and those with higher education also tended to be cast in leadership roles (van Wormer and Bates, 1979). The women identified most frequently as leaders "were most often young black women serving sentences for narcotics and property offenses" (Moyer, 1980: 233). Many had felony and lengthy prison records. The leaders "were women involved in homosexual relationships" (Moyer, 1980: 240). The leadership status allowed the women more freedom to establish these personal, homosexual relationships. Participation in the institutional programs provided the women with the opportunity to become leaders of the inmate social structure. Leaders seem to be given greater freedom from supervision by staff, which provided them with more privacy. These women leaders were the outspoken women who were able to defend themselves physically and who played a dominant male role in homosexual relationships. This suggests these leaders were not playing the traditional feminine roles expected of women in society.

There are several differences between the female social system and the social system in male institutions. While both prison cultures support homosexuality as a substitute for the deprivation of heterosexual contact, the women's culture promotes love, affection, and even pseudofamily structures as an important link with sexuality. The male inmates, however, do not typically express love or create families around their homosexuality. Homosexuality is frequently coerced in male institutions through physical rape or intimidation of the victim. This is rare in female prisons. Victimization rates other than rape also occur with greater frequency in male institutions. Both social systems promote opposition to prison staff members and support a subrosa or contraband market system. However, the market system in the female correctional institutions does not seem to be as extensive or elaborate as the system in male prisons (Bowker, 1981).

CO-CORRECTIONAL INSTITUTIONS

Co-correctional facilities can be defined as:

> . . . an adult institution the major purpose of which is the custody of sentenced felons, under a single institutional administration, having one or more areas in which male and female inmates are present and in interaction (Ross et al., 1978, p. 27).

Prior to the turn of the century, female offenders were housed within or contiguous to male institutions. During the earlier periods of banishment and early prison systems, women were housed with male inmates. The reform movement at the turn of the century separated the women from the male prison system for the general good of the women (Barnes and Teeters, 1959). The segregated system still dominates our correctional system. However, interesting experiments at co-corrections for adult offenders have taken place during the last decade. There are 20 state run co-correctional facilities and five federal co-correctional institutions for adult offenders (U.S. Department of Justice, 1982). Only a small fraction of the nation's inmates have been involved in co-correctional programs.

There are several reasons to implement co-correctional programs. Integrating genders in one institution is one approach to providing equity in resources. In addition, it is thought that a mixed gender staff would help prepare inmates for the return to heterosexual society, as well as reduce the homosexuality, tension, and violence that are prevalent in a same-sex prison. It also allows overcrowded systems to move a number of male inmates into predominantly female institutions (Smykla, 1980).

There are also some potential problems in co-correctional institutions. The major concern on the part of correctional administrators is the like-lihood of heterosexual activity between male and female inmates. Obviously, the possibility of prison pregnancies is of great concern. Beyond that, however, it might seem strange that while homosexuality is so common in same-sex prisons that it is an accepted part of the environment, we would be overly concerned with inmates becoming actively involved in "normal" sexuality. In addition, the possibility of love triangles, competition for affection, and so on may create rather than reduce tension. The evidence thus far does not justify these concerns. Instead, the studies that have been done on co-correctional facilities have been positive.

In one intensive study, it was determined that the positive aspect of co-correctional prisons far outweighed the problems (Smykla, 1980). This study reported that the tension level seemed low, violent homosexuality between males was nonexistent, and female homosexuality was infrequent (Smykla, 1980). Other studies similarly found that homosexuality was almost nonexistent (Heffernan, 1972), and institutional violence was reduced, which helped improve the prison atmosphere (Ross et al., 1978). Prison administrators, however, tended to overmanage the inmates, being highly concerned with sexual involvement between inmates (Ross et al., 1978; Ruback, 1975).

A study conducted in 1984 found that the inmates at a co-correctional facility had strong positive feeling about doing time in their institution. Inmates felt they were safe from violence in the setting. One inmate commented she felt safer in the prison than she did in her own neighborhood. Inmates felt positive about being able to interact routinely with both men and women. They felt it broke up the monotony of prison life, helped both genders relate to each other as friends, and helped create a "normal" atmosphere within the prison environment. In spite of overmanagement, some heterosexual activity did take place. Sexuality ranged from sexual touching to emotionally involved sexual relations. The study also found that traditional male-female relationships tended to evolve. Males tended to dominate programs and females tended to play subordinate roles with prison "boyfriends" rather than addressing their own needs for developing independence. Homosexuality, however, diminished; and violence was reduced (Mahan, 1984).

While many of the findings seem positive, a word of caution is needed. Correctional administrators approach new programs with a great deal of caution, fearing public criticism for failures or even unacceptable innovation. Thus, only the most tractable inmates will be placed in programs that might come under public scrutiny. That is, inmates who are unstable, violent, sex deviants, or even with a discernible record of being uncooperative with staff would probably not be placed in a co-correctional setting. The positive results of the co-correctional program may stem in part from the placement of cooperative inmates in such programs.

DOING TIME WITH THE GIRLS

"Doing Time With the Boys" is the title of an article which reports on women correctional officers working in a men's institution (Peterson, 1982). Presently, there are men working as correctional officers in women's institutions in at least five states (Kentucky, Michigan, New York, Pennsylvania, and Wisconsin) and in the federal system. Research on male correctional officers working in female prisons is limited. However, the topic is worthy of at least a brief discussion. Historically, women have not been eligible to work as guards in male prisons for a number of reasons. Women officers were given positions in low-risk areas in prisons and in areas where inmate privacy would not be invaded. Courts have ruled, however, that inmates had no inherent right to privacy and correctional officers cannot be denied an assignment due to gender.

Research has been done on the impact and problems of female officers working in a male prison. It seems that the major problem women faced was from some of the male staff rather than from inmates (Peterson, 1982). Most inmates have not expressed feelings of loss of privacy with part of the guard staff comprised of women; instead, they felt that the presence of women helped to reduce the level of tension in the prison setting (Kissel and Catsampes, 1980; Peterson, 1982). Inmates did suggest, however, that the presence of females, even as correctional officers, increased their sense of sexual frustration.

Concerns about male correctional officers working in female prisons include privacy issues, but also focus upon the potential sexual exploitation of inmates by officers. Preliminary research has been conducted by this writer on the impact of male correctional officers in an adult female prison. The initial interviews with inmates indicate that the "boys" have been favorably received. Privacy did not seem to be a concern for the inmates interviewed. From the inmates' perspective, sexual exploitation was thought of as inmates using sex to exploit correctional officers. They felt that the presence of male correctional officers helped create a more natural environment and reduced the tension level. In addition, they felt it was easier to talk to the men on some issues than it was to talk to the women guards. However, these findings are limited. The effectiveness and problems of male officers in a female institution will be discovered over time. It seems that as more women are added to the staff in male institutions, the number of male officers in female prisons will increase. In Michigan and New York, for example, no distinction is made between male and female officers. Officers are assigned to institutions as positions become open, without regard to gender.

ARE WOMEN INMATES MORE DIFFICULT TO HANDLE?

We began this chapter with a case study that portrayed women inmates as being more difficult to handle than male inmates. There is a sense among correctional staff that female offenders are somehow harder to work with than male offenders. Correctional officers feel they must be sensitive toward female imates' potential for emotional outbursts, as it is believed that female inmates readily display emotions from love to anger toward those around them. The belief that female inmates are more emotional than men and readily express their emotions does affect the way correctional officers manage them (Pollack, 1984). In addition, women probationers in one study were found to accumulate substantially more technical rule violations than male probationers (Norland and Mann, 1984). Managing an unpredictable clientele in a coercive environment is difficult. In our case study, Officer Hennessey made two distinct statements: women, unlike men, would act out without regard to the presence of staff; but they could be trusted. They did not play games like "cops and robbers." It may be more accurate to say that women need to be managed differently than male inmates rather than saying they are "harder to handle." However, with such a clientele, means can be developed to allow inmates to vent emotions through acceptable channels.

SUMMARY

1. There are three basic differences between male and female institutions. There are far fewer facilities for women than for men, a lower incidence of violence in female facilities, and a much lower level of public concern for female institutions.

2. Historically, treatment programs for women emphasized domestic skills. Programs in contemporary facilities also emphasize domestic skills as they relate to the traditional feminine role. Future proposals for programs are focusing upon the economic needs of women today. The programs are designed to provide marketable job skills, self-sufficiency, and interpersonal skills.

3. Female inmates represent a small number of incarcerated offenders. As a result, most states have only one facility for the entire female inmate population. This makes visitation difficult for inmates with families. Often, the facilities are configured as a cottage system, with the total facility taking on the appearance of a small college campus.

4. As opposed to males, females have a greater concern for their children. Society reinforces the traditional role of the mother by granting them custody of their children in almost all domestic relations disputes. The loss of a child for an incarcerated mother produces detrimental effects. Feelings of guilt, shame, and remorse are frequent and they worsen the effects of incarceration upon the women.

5. Female inmates form an intricate social system that helps them deal with the deprivations common to prison life. Women inmates feel a strong sense of alienation from the outside world. In an attempt to cope, they form emotional and homosexual relationships with other inmates. In addition, they often form family groups, with members playing out the roles of father, mother, and other family members. Unlike the social system of men's prisons, homosexuality in women's prisons is an accepted form of coping with the prison environment.

6. Co-correctional institutions are a rare and experimental phenomenon. There are several advantages to co-correctional prisons. The tension level seems to be lower, as is the incidence of homosexuality. They also help to promote social heterosexual relationships in the institutions and ease the inmates' reintegration into society. The disadvantages seem to focus around the potential for sexual relations between male and female inmates and the corollary problems, such as prison pregnancies. Love triangles may create security problems, and the public may perceive such institutions as being "country clubs" rather than prisons.

7. Historically, males worked only in male prisons and women were used as correctional officers only in female institutions. Currently, however, women are working as correctional officers in male prisons, and vice versa. The research looking at women correctional officers in male institutions suggests their presence has provided many operational and environmental benefits. Recently, male correctional officers have been assigned to female prisons. There is little research on this phenomenon. However, limited experience suggests that no sig-

nificant problems have been created with this personnel assignment. More research and experience will be required to evaluate this approach.

8. While there is some research to support the notion that women are difficult, for now, this remains a matter of perspective. Certainly, the behaviors and norms of female inmates differ from those of their male counterparts. If a correctional officer were to be transferred from a male prison to a female institution, the initial period of work experience would require an adjustment to and acceptance of the different social system being encountered.

KEY WORDS

CO-CORRECTIONAL INSTITUTIONS. Prisons that house both male and female inmates under a single administration.

CONNECTS. Inmates whose prison assignments allow them to acquire scarce information and resources that can be used for personal gain.

THE COOL. Professional criminals who see crime as their skill for making a living. This group readily takes on the norms of the inmate system.

COTTAGE SYSTEM. The design of many prisons for women that are built with a series of cottage-like facilities that surround the administration and other general use buildings. This design was developed at the turn of the century to provide women inmates with a home-like atmosphere that would preserve or create a family orientation.

JAIL HOUSE TURNOUTS. Inmates who are introduced to homosexuality while in prison.

JIVE BITCHES. Inmates who tend to be manipulative and unstable, causing problems for other inmates and staff.

THE LIFE. The majority of this group have spent a great deal of time in institutions and do not conform to conventional norms but take on and, to some extent, establish the norms of the prison social system.

SNITCHERS. Inmates who inform on other inmates.

THE SQUARE. Inmates who are noncriminal types and considered situational offenders. This group does not conform to the prison social system.

QUESTIONS AND PROJECTS

1. Find out where the female facility(s) are located in your state. How many women does it house, and for what types of offenses? Find out what treatment programs are available for the inmates. Do the programs cater to traditional values, or are they concerned with providing the inmates with eventual economic independence?
2. Develop an "ideal" visitation program for female inmates that takes into account their need to form mock families while in custody. Consider the needs or rights of inmate mothers and their children.

Think about the logistics involved in visitation—travel and housing for visitors living far from the institution, need for a wholesome environment, as well as security needs of the prison.
3. Conduct an informal survey with your friends and family regarding co-correctional institutions. Tell them about the concept and ask them what they think the advantages and disadvantages are. Obtain their overall point of view. Carefully summarize your results, and see if you predicted them accurately.

ADDITIONAL READING

Rose Giallombardo. *Society of Women.* New York: Wiley, 1966. Although this book was written over twenty years ago, in many respects it is a classic and is the first comprehensive attempt to apply both an organizational and a behavioral analysis to a female prison. The work examines the administrative and staff functions and goals, as well as the social system of the inmates. The reader is provided with comparison of female and male prisons systems, as well as a description of female social system studies.

Ester Heffernan. *Making It in Prison: The Square, the Cool, and the Life.* New York: Wiley-Interscience, 1972. This book provides a general study of the social system of the Columbia Women's Reformatory at Occoquan, Virginia. The study describes the adaptive modes of female inmates including adaptive types, formation of families, and other pertinent means of dealing with the prison environment that create the norms of the prison society there.

Nicole Rafter. *Partial Justice, Women in Prison, 1800–1935.* Boston: Northeastern University Press, 1985. This book examines the history and evolution of female corrections across the nation and provides insights into the current state of the art of corrections for women.

PRISONERS' RIGHTS AND THEIR IMPLEMENTATION

QUESTIONS

1. In what historical context did the prisoners' rights movement develop?

2. Have correctional adminstrators always lagged behind the judiciary in the provision and protection of inmate rights?

3. Which constitutional amendments are most important in prison litigation?

4. What is a Section 1983 suit?

5. What are institutional orders? Consent decrees?

"THE COURT JUST HANDED ME AN OFFICER"

Phil was having dinner with Lieutenant Pierce when Superintendent Smythe wandered in. "Evening, gents!"

Pierce looked at him suspiciously. "You have that grin, again, chief. What's the good news this time?"

"The district court just handed us another day shift officer, lieutenant. The lunch schedule won't be such a hassle anymore."

"No more mail to read, huh?"

"Nope. Decision came down this morning. I just got the phone call from the attorney general's office."

Phil was lost in this conversation. "I don't understand."

Smythe grinned. "The state just lost its case on mail censorship. For years, all

across this state, we've devoted one officer on every day shift in every prison to read inmate mail. Can't do it anymore. The A.G.'s office wanted to know if we wanted to appeal. I said that's the last thing we want to do."

The lieutenant looked around the room. "Better not shout that too loudly, chief. I wouldn't want Kravitz to hear this."

Smythe nodded and lowered his voice. He explained to Phil: "Kravitz is our mail officer. He's had a desk job for sixteen years now and he won't be too happy with the change. But we need the manpower. Sometimes the court comes in handy. He'll put up with the change now, and can grumble about inmate rights. It's a lot easier that way than if I have to take on the change myself."

Phil frowned. "You mean, you haven't

really wanted to censor the mail all these years?"

Smythe shrugged. "That's complicated. When I came to Jefferson straight out of the army, all the wardens insisted on the importance of reading the mail. You know—all the normal reasons. Find escape attempts, stop contraband. Those weren't usually the most important reasons, though. We can still search for contraband. And if someone was stupid enough to write about an escape attempt, he couldn't pull it off anyway. No, the real reasons were more subtle. Sometimes we had the inmate in mind. Kravitz got to be a genius at spotting bad news. A Dear John letter. News about a sick parent or a sick child. He'd relay that information to the day captain, and the captain could tell the officers to lay off the inmate. Or, if we knew an inmate was going to be depressed for a while, we could watch him, talk to him. Do what it took to calm him down. It was useful—and it wasn't censorship anyway. But that practice is a little outmoded. We started that back when inmates and officers didn't talk to each other much. We have all sorts of ways of knowing what inmates are doing and feeling now that we didn't have then. Lots of times, an inmate who gets bad news from home will come to an officer first to talk it over anyway. And in addition, with the furlough program, most of them can go home for a couple of days if something really important comes up.

"The more frequent use was censorship—to make sure inmates didn't send out any complaints about what happened in here. We didn't let complaints go out about me or the guards, or policy. Tended to overlook complaints about food. Everyone complains about the food. And we wanted to make sure nothing juicy came in. No love letters that got out of hand. No subscriptions to the wrong magazines. But all of that's changed. We can't protect ourselves

by shutting inmates up or shutting things out. The world's just changed." The lieutenant nodded in agreement.

"But," said Phil, "if that's the case, why not just change the prison policy. Why wait for a court decision?"

The superintendent and his lieutenant exchanged knowing glances. How do we tell someone who doesn't already know? Smythe started in a roundabout way. "I'm not one for avoiding conflict, as you know. I'm willing to tick an officer off, and to have them bawl me out, under appropriate conditions. But I guess you want to pick your shots when you're a manager. This decision doesn't affect just the one guy at the desk who now has to alter his job routine. It will affect all officers to some degree, especially the twenty-year men that I depend on the most. Some of them won't care; but some of them will take this as another symbol of giving in to the inmates. I can't fight those perceptions overnight; it takes time. So I'd rather have this decision come from the courts. If I'd changed the rules internally, they'd have done what I said. But my bank account would be a little smaller. When I needed their trust for something really important, I might not have it. So, yes, I avoided the decision. This way it looks like the court beat me."

THE EVOLUTION OF PRISONERS' RIGHTS

Formal social control systems such as the criminal law present disadvantages along with blessings. Delegation of the responsibility for punishment to public agents isolates the act of punishment from general knowledge and scrutiny and places it in the hands of experts. To some extent, society becomes dependent upon their expertise and their good faith. Yet the history of public organizations is full of examples of the experts' failures to adhere to specified purposes and to achieve purposes even when plans were followed. Thus we are faced with two related problems: whether there are some basic principles that limit the nature of punishment, and how to find out whether the actions taken by the punishment agents adhere reasonably well to the limits placed on the punitive act.

It has become common to think of courts imposing restrictions on unwilling correctional administrators, but historically this view would be inaccurate. The elaboration of rights for the punished has involved a sporadic negotiation among the courts, administrators, and legislatures. The leading and resistant parties have changed over time.

THE AMERICAN PRISON ASSOCIATION'S PRINCIPLES OF 1870

In 1870, the American Prison Association at its inaugural meeting in Cincinnati adopted a Declaration of Principles. These principles were both far-reaching and honored more in their breach than in their observance. Nevertheless, their spirit indicated a period in which professional administrators probably led the way toward the humane treatment of the punished, while the courts were unconcerned. Among the principles most relevant to restrictions on punishment were the following:

V. The prisoner's destiny should be placed measurably in his own hands; he must be put into circumstances where he will be able, through his own exertions, to continually better his own condition. . . .

VI. A system of prison discipline, to be truly reformatory, must gain the will of the prisoner. He is to be amended; but how is this possible with his mind in a state of hostility?

XIV. The prisoner's self respect should be cultivated to the utmost, and every effort made to give back to him his manhood. There is no greater mistake in the whole compass of discipline, than its studied imposition of degradation as part of punishment. . . .

Nearly one hundred years later, the successor to the American Prison Association had the same intent (American Correctional Association, 1966: 266):

The administrator should always be certain that he is not acting capriciously or unreasonably but that the established procedures are reasonable and not calculated to infringe on the legal rights of prisoners.

When prisoners began to demand rights in the 1960s, some administrators fought each suit almost as a knee-jerk reaction to being challenged (Singer, 1980). However, other administrators have often led the courts. For example, the Connecticut Department of Correction provides inmates with rights concerning prison transfers and body-cavity searches that the Supreme Court of the United States has decided are not constitutional requirements (Jacobs, 1980).

THE HANDS-OFF DOCTRINE

While administrators' policy statements have generally recognized the need for consistency, fairness, and reasonableness in the implementation of punishment, the courts have been slower to arrive at the position that punishments should be guided by rules and administrators held accountable for their observance. For example, one year after the American Prison Association drafted its Declaration of Principles, a Virginia judge concluded that prisoners had no more rights than slaves (*Ruffin* v. *Commonwealth*, 1871). The Eighth Amendment to the United States Constitution, forbidding cruel and unusual punishment, was not applied to prisons until 1892 (*Logan* v. *United States*). Even then, the Eighth Amendment was interpreted very narrowly to prohibit torture, mutilation, or other extreme physical abuse, and did not apply to the states until 1962 (*Robinson* v. *California*).

The courts were reluctant to interfere with legislative decisions about the nature of punishment or with administrative decisions about the nature of discipline in punitive settings. This reluctance was justified on the basis of two fundamental principles of American government, federalism and the separation of powers. First, the federal courts were loath to interfere with a governmental process that was seen as states' rights. While the United States Constitution was the supreme law of the land, for years the courts were reticent to test that supremacy in a correctional confrontation. Second, federal and state courts wished to observe the principle of separation of powers, essential to nontotalitarian governments. This principle implied that no one branch of government would have power over all governmental functions. The courts saw the administration of prisons as outside their province and expertise.

For years, judicial respect for federalism and separation of powers meant that judges would not review correctional issues. About the only complaints from prisoners that reached the courts at all were **writs of habeus corpus** challenging the legality of confinement. Judges took the position that if a conviction was legal and the sentence handed down was within statutory limits, then prisoners had no complaints. The refusal to hear legal challenges about prison conditions or prison administration became known as the **hands-off doctrine** (Note, 1963; Singer, 1980; Jacobs, 1980).

THE PRISONERS' RIGHTS MOVEMENT

The prisoners' rights movement did not emerge in a vacuum. The movement, while not inevitable, was a logical extension of the broader movement to democratize the United States after World War II (Jacobs, 1980). As the door to prison litigation opened slowly between 1964 and 1969, the broader rights movement was already well under way. Civil rights, welfare rights, juvenile justice rights, student rights all preceded the development of prisoners' rights. Rights for the mentally ill and the mentally retarded began at about the same time (Cohen, 1969). The radicalization of the American middle class during the

Vietnam era brought civil rights workers in touch with the prison, often for the first time (Jacobs, 1980). Many were appalled at what they found. As civil rights victories were achieved, a number of attorneys were recruited to prisoners' rights projects and organizations (Jacobs, 1980). Prisoners, and especially black prisoners, began to identify themselves with other victimized minorities. Spokesmen such as George Jackson and Eldridge Cleaver were recognized by many as civil rights leaders rather than as inmates.

Among the inmate groups to reach out toward their nonprison links, the Black Muslims were perhaps the most influential in initiating successful litigation. The first modern prisoners' rights case to reach the Supreme Court of the United States, *Cooper* v. *Pate* (1964), involved Black Muslims arguing for religious freedom in prison. The Supreme Court agreed that prisoners had the right to sue in federal court for abridgment of their civil rights. With this decision, the hands off doctrine began to crumble.

IMPACTS OF THE RIGHTS MOVEMENT

While many commentators agree that the significance of the prisoners' rights movement goes far beyond the specific court decisions, they also agree that the broader impacts are difficult to assess. Jacobs (1980) argued that the social significance of prisoners' rights cases is found in the symbolic effects of prisoners being vindicated in court and, through that vindication, of gaining status vis-à-vis staff.

Singer (1980) suggested that the rights movement had both positive and negative effects. On the positive side have been the involvement of other groups (such as the American Medical Association) in prison reform, the development of grievance mechanisms and prisoner councils, changes in mail regulations and visitation practices, the widespread disappearance of strip cells, and increased accountability of prison staff. On the negative side, Singer identified the increasing polarization of staff and inmates, the growth of prisoner guard unions, the blaming of lawyers for increased violence in prisons. Jacobs' proposed list of impacts include these:

1. The bureaucratization of the prison
2. The emergence of a whole new cadre of prison administrators
3. Expanded procedural protections for inmates
4. Increased public awareness of prison conditions
5. Politicalization of prisoners and a heightening of prisoner expectations
6. Demoralization of prison staff
7. Greater difficulty in maintaining control over prisoners
8. The move to nationalize prison standards

The prisoner's rights movement began to slow in the mid- to late 1970s. A reduction in funding for prisoners' rights attorneys put the brakes on, and several Supreme Court decisions, such as *Meachum* v. *Fano* (1976) and *Bell* v. *Wolfish* (1979), began to echo earlier hands off language. Nevertheless, as the 1980s closes, there is evidence that the prisoners' rights movement will continue to advance, although perhaps at a slower pace and perhaps in different ways. Even if the current conservative Court should refuse to break any new ground, active federal district courts can spend many years applying the rights that have already been enunciated (Singer, 1980; Jacobs, 1980; Collins, 1986).

Previous court decisions have changed administrative approaches to prisoners' rights. Prison improvements may now come from prisoner grievance mechanisms put in place as a means of avoiding court battles. Finally, the newer prison administrators may take a different view than some of their older colleagues about the relationship of the courts to prison administration. As Collins (1986) has pointed out, some administrators have discovered that "losing" a suit on prisoners' rights may mean that the prison budget increases and prison conditions improve.

Concerning judicial review of mental health facilities, Judge David Bazelon wrote (*Covington* v. *Harris*, 1969):

> Not only the principle of judicial review, but the whole scheme of American government, reflects an institutionalized mistrust of any unchecked and unbalanced power over essential liberties. . . . Judicial review is only a safety catch against the fallibility of the best men: and not the least of its services is to spur them to double-check their own performance and provide them with a check list by which they may readily do so.

One important impact of the prisoners' rights movement may be that more administrators see themselves as working with rather than against the courts.

SOME GENERAL PRINCIPLES

A major problem for prisoners who attempt to claim rights is overcoming their status as nonpersons: either "slaves of the state" or "civilly dead" and enjoying no civil rights (Cohen, 1969). There is no doubt that prisoners' claims to rights are severely limited both by the fact that they have committed wrongs against others and by the fact that the administration of prisons requires severe restriction on behavior. However, prisoners are not totally at the mercy of their punishers; several fundamental values may give rise to more specific rights. For example, most scholars find the notion of equity inherent in retribution. The punishment must fit the crime. The concept of just deserts clearly places some limits on the extent and type of punishment. Additionally,

> Having custody of another person invariably creates a legal duty to care for that person, although the nature of the custody determines the particular care required. (Cohen, 1985:36)

At minimum, argued Cohen, the state's duty to provide care must translate into prisoners' rights to maintain life and health (1985:36). In an earlier paper, Cohen (1969) suggested that the notion of fundamental fairness embedded in the Four-teenth Amendment also found its way into prison in some rudimentary fashion, because without it the right to life and health would be difficult to implement. In other words, we would want our prison administrators to adopt a process of prison governance that would ensure reliability in de-cision-making. Minimum levels of due process may be required in terms of notice, provision of hearings, and establishment and maintenance of records that permit administrators to process facts and make reliable judgments about them.

These rudimentary notions of humane care and orderly procedure suggest that even incar-cerated criminals have some rights and some means of redress if those rights are violated. An important question, however, is through what principles and rules to enforce those basic values. Two broad principles appear to compete in guid-ing administrators and courts in this area. On the liberal end is a principle enunciated in *Coffin* v. *Reichard* (1944) that argues prisoners have all rights of free citizens which are not expressly or by necessary implication withdrawn as a condi-tion of the punishment. The American Bar As-sociation phrased the Coffin principles as its Prin-ciple 1.1 in its *Standards Relating to the Legal Status of Prisoners* (1977):

> Prisoners retain all the rights of free citizens except those on which restriction is necessary to assure the orderly confinement or to provide reasonable protection for the rights and physical safety of all members of the prison society.

On the conservative side would be the reverse principle, that prisoners have lost all civil rights expect those expressly conferred upon them, or rights necessarily implied in those which are con-ferred. While the Coffin rule is still expressed, the conservative rule would seem to be the one more usually practiced (Cohen, 1985:40).

To these competing principles about how pris-oners' rights are conferred, Cohen adds two other general principles. The first is the rule that the greater the potential harm, the greater the claim to a right or protection:

> [T]he greater the impact on the conditions of pres-ent or prospective liberty, or the physical and psychic integrity of the prisoner, the greater (or more plausible) the claim to substantive and pro-cedural safeguards. (Cohen, 1969:78)

The other is a principle most courts appear to use when making determinations about the extent of prisoners' rights in particular prisons:

> A glaringly deficient prison system invited some federal judges to require programs and penal ob-jectives they would not likely impose if the partic-ular claim (rehabilitation, for instance) was made in isolation or if the overall prison conditions were minimally acceptable. (Cohen, 1985:37)

In other words, some judges appear to operate on the principle that "worst requires more"—that the greater the faults of the prison system (and per-haps the more its administrators have defended horrendous conditions), the more is demanded by way of repair (see also Collins, 1986).

Beneath these general principles, a number of specific prisoner rights have been elaborated. Most of these rights have their roots in just a few constitutional amendments. The National Advi-sory Commission on Criminal Justice Standards and Goals divided prisoners' rights into four broad categories (1973:22):

1. The right to seek protection of the law and access to the courts
2. Rights related to the conditions of con-finement
3. Rights related to the discretionary power of prison officials
4. The First Amendment rights

Cohen's more recent list is somewhat longer, but similar (1985:40–43):

1. Diluted First Amendment rights concern-ing religion and regulation of censorship (but no right to association)
2. Eighth Amendment rights
3. Access to the courts, and ancillary rights necessary to protect that access

4. Some very minimal Fourth Amendment protection regarding privacy
5. Some Fifth/Fourteenth Amendment protections in custodial interrogations about new criminal charges
6. Some minimum due process protections in prison disciplinary matters

ACCESS TO THE COURTS

While the courts have been slow to grant rights to prisoners, one of the first granted is reasonable access to the courts (*ex parte Hull*, 1941). Although the principle has not been seriously challenged since it was enunciated in *Hull*, it was not until some years after that the courts seriously considered the implementation of access. Important fueling of the prisoners' rights movement was the series of cases that made access to the courts meaningful (Cohen, 1969; Jacobs, 1980). Among the most important was *Johnson* v. *Avery* (1969), in which the Supreme Court held that lacking other viable forms of assistance, prison administrators could not prevent inmates from helping one another to prepare legal materials. While this case did not suggest that administrators had to be active in linking inmates with assistance of counsel, it did provide some protection for jailhouse lawyering, an activity prison officials had traditionally sought to frustrate.

Currently, the key court access case is *Bounds* v. *Smith* (1977) which has required "adequate law libraries or adequate assistance from persons trained in the law." In contrast with *Johnson* v. *Avery*, *Bounds* insists that administrators have an affirmative duty to provide access to the courts. The distinction is critical, since prison staff may now be sued for failing to assist inmates in reaching the courts (Collins, 1986:32). The right to access therefore gained teeth as implementation was addressed. Administrators must now have a plan for providing access, must monitor the implementation of that plan, and must make special provisions for those inmates with restricted access (such as those in segregation) or those with lim-

ited abilities (such as illiterates or the retarded) (1986:24–31).

FIRST AMENDMENT RIGHTS

The First Amendment to the United States Constitution protects some of the most cherished freedoms in this country:

> Congress shall make no law respecting an establishment of religion, or prohibiting the free exercise thereof; or abridging the freedom of speech, or of the press; or the right of the people peaceably to assemble, and to petition the Government for a redress of grievances.

Nevertheless, there are clear limits on the free exercise of religion, freedom of speech, and freedom of peaceful assembly in the prison context. These limits are justified on the basis of counterbalancing administrative claims, such as those of maintaining order or safety. Generally, the courts have required greater proof of the conflicting administrative need and have used stricter balancing tests for limiting the First Amendment freedoms than are used in the protection of some other rights.

FREEDOM OF RELIGION

A very basic but important question in the prison context is, What constitutes a religion? Courts still disagree on the appropriate test. Some courts use an "objective standard," such as the existence of fundamental beliefs and a resulting code of conduct. Other courts have relied upon a "subjective standard," saying that the beliefs held by an inmate function like a religion for that person (Collins, 1986:47–48). Inmate claims for protection of a particular religion may be rejected if the prison officials can show that the beliefs in question are frivolous or not sincerely held (*Theriault* v. *Carlson*, 1977).

A more common problem is the one of how strictly prison administrators can limit the practice of a recognized religious belief. In nonprison situations, the courts have generally required the government to meet a very strict test in order to justify restrictions of religious practice. This test requires demonstration of (1) **compelling state interest** and (2) adoption of the **least restrictive alternative.** The government would need to show an objective at least as important as the religious freedoms being restricted and also show that the restrictions enforced were the least intrusive of the available alternatives.

While some courts have applied this test in prison settings, less demanding balancing tests seem to prevail in many cases. The least rigorous test is showing the "necessity" of the state's interest and a "reasonable link" between a specific restriction and that interest. In between is one test that asks for an "important state goal," a showing of a relationship between the restrictions and the goal, and a demonstration that no alternatives "reasonably accommodate" the inmate interest (Collins, 1986:50–52). As Collins points out, the selection of the test by which the court will judge the imposition of restrictions often determines the outcome of the case. Administrators can almost always meet the least restrictive test, but are often hard put to justify their restrictions under the compelling interest/least restrictive alternative test.

A final religious issue involves the combination of the First Amendment freedom with the guarantee of equal protection of the laws in the Fifth and Fourteenth Amendments. This is the case in which administrators do not challenge the sincerity of a religion, but argue that so few inmates hold it that observance of certain practices is too cumbersome. The inmates' claim in this case is that their religious group is being unfairly discriminated against. The leading case, *Cruz* v. *Beto* (1972) involved equal protection for Buddhists in the Texas system.

OTHER FIRST AMENDMENT RIGHTS

Inmates have fared less well in some other First Amendment claims. For example, claims that a prisoners' union was protected by rights to asso-

Blanket censorship of prisoners' mail is no longer permitted. (New York State Department of Correctional Services)

ciation were not upheld (*Jones* v. *North Carolina Prisoners' Labor Union*, 1977). A number of attempts for open access to the press for press conferences have also been quashed. However, blanket censorship of prisoner mail was rejected by the Supreme Court, which argued that only those mail restrictions necessary to prison safety were permissible (*Procunier* v. *Martinez*, 1974).

Bronstein (1980) and Singer (1980) have both observed that the more rigorous tests for restrictions on fundamental rights, such as the First Amendment freedoms, have recently been attacked by the Supreme Court, particularly in the federal pretrial detainee case of *Bell* v. *Wolfish* (1979). Although some of the Wolfish complaints were First Amendment issues, the Court explicitly rejected the compelling interest/least restrictive alternative test that had been adopted by the lower federal courts. Justice Rehnquist, writing for the Court, asked only that the government show a valid purpose (other than punishment) for the restrictions on the detainees and a reasonable link between that purpose and the restrictions on mail. Bronstein and Singer arued that Rehnquist was thereby reissuing the hands off doctrine, since the minimal test relied heavily on the expertise of administrators. They needed only to assert (rather than demonstrate) that the restrictions they had imposed were linked to the valid purpose of institutional order.

Despite this charge, a state lawyer who has defended many prison administrators warns that failure to take First Amendment freedoms seriously may still be asking for trouble. Courts, he warned, are far more likely to accept policies that regulate the exercise of these freedoms than they are to accept policies that place absolute bans on inmate First Amendment rights (Collins, 1986:53–55).

THE FOURTH AMENDMENT

The Fourth Amendment guarantees:

> The right of the people to be secure in their persons, houses, papers, and effects against unreasonable searches and seizures, shall not be violated. . . .

Little of this protection survives the passage into jail or prison. The leading Supreme Court cases have left little doubt that staff can search prison cells at will and seize any material found there. The probable cause required to justify searches in a free society are not required in prison, where the practice of general shakedowns and confiscations has been upheld on security grounds (*Hudson* v. *Palmer*, 1985). The Supreme Court added that property loses suffered by prisoners in such shakedowns do not usually substantiate a constitutional claim.

Body cavity searches are more intrusive than cell searches and therefore might require somewhat stronger justifications. However, the courts have upheld strip and body cavity searches conducted as part of institutional security policy (Collins, 1986). It is possible that a court might listen to an inmate's complaint about such searches if it could be shown that the search was conducted specifically to humiliate or degrade— a difficult case to make.

There is one Fourth Amendment privacy complaint to which the courts have listened: It involves the privacy of prisoners from guards of the opposite sex during bathing, strip searches, or use of the toilet. On this issue, the courts are faced with a constitutional dilemma: the right of the prisoners to a minimum amount of privacy versus the right of women (or men, in women's prisons) to equal employment. Lower courts have split on how to handle this issue, and it has yet to reach the Supreme Court. A knowledgeable state's attorney proposed that the courts will be more favorably disposed to female prisoners' concerns for privacy against male guards than for male prisoners' complaints about female officers because male guards have greater opportunities for employment in other prisons than female officers (Collins, 1986). (This issue is discussed in greater detail in Chapter 16.)

DUE PROCESS RIGHTS

The due process clause of the Fourteenth Amendment prohibits any state from depriving "any person of life, liberty, or property, without due process of law. . . ." The same clause in the Fifth Amendment would govern the federal prisons. The due process clause provides for access to courts and to legal services. Because of their pivotal role in the emergence of the prisoners' rights movement, these rights were discussed above. Here we focus on the extent to which the due process clause protects prisoners from certain disciplinary procedures, or from certain modes of decision-making by officials.

Many persons have seen the introduction of due process requirements into the prison disciplinary process as the most intrusive move of the courts into correctional institutions. While procedural rights are not necessarily the greatest protection afforded inmates, they may be viewed as a direct challenge to staff discretion, long considered sacred in corrections.

The approach taken by the courts, and in particular the Supreme Court, has actually been quite conservative. Due process standards in the prison disciplinary process are considerably less rigorous than those applied in nonprison settings. In fact, the questions of whether and what due process rights applied in prison were framed in a different manner than due process questions concerning free citizens, including probationers and parolees. Understanding these differences is crucial to a full appreciation of just what procedural rights apply now or might be applied in the future.

In the welfare rights case of *Goldberg* v. *Kelly* (1970), the Supreme Court stated that all persons had due process protections from losses that might be suffered because of the arbitrary or erroneous decisions of officials. The stress in this case was upon the *harm* that was (or could be) done by officials. Due process protections such as notice of charges, a hearing with an opportunity to challenge the evidence and to mount a defense, assistance in defense, and a record of the hearing and the decision taken were imposed as means of protecting citizens from those harms. The question of whether due process rights of some sort should attach to a governmental deliberation was answered on the basis of what the citizen stood to lose in that situation. This was the approach to due process taken since the early 1960s, the beginning of the due process revolution. Courts framed the question of safeguards by examining the potential consequences. This traditional approach to the due process question was applied in both parole and probation revocation situations shortly after the Goldberg decision (see Chapter 8).

In 1974, a similar issue reached the Supreme Court regarding prison disciplinary hearings. A prisoner in the Nebraska prison system complained that as a punishment for alleged disci-

plinary infractions, prison officials had taken earned good time credits away from him, without affording him a hearing or other due process rights (*Wolff* v. *McDonnell*, 1974).

Many observers thought the Court would extend the same logic into the prison that it had used two years earlier in probation revocations. The Court did give eloquent support for some minimal due process rights: "There is no iron curtain drawn between the Constitution and the prisons of this country." But it did not take the "state-inflicted harm" or "grievous loss" approach as its justification for requiring some level of due process in Nebraska misconduct hearings. Instead:

> [T]he Court [required] that a liberty or property interest, as opposed to a state inflicted harm, be found before it [would] determine that any process [was] due. (Cohen, 1985:47)

Specifically, the majority opinion required 24-hour notice of a disciplinary hearing before an impartial body (not the staff member bringing the charges), opportunity to present witnesses and documents in defense, a statement of the evidence relied upon, and written reasons for the disciplinary action. The Court also ordered that inmates unable to present a defense themselves must be provided with assistance (not an attorney). And the Court left to the discretion of prison officials whether cross examination or presentation of witnesses should be limited on security grounds.

Many prison officials have interpreted *Wolff* to require these procedures whenever there is a case of "serious misconduct"—defined as cases in which the punishment may be placement in solitary confinement or loss of good time (Collins, 1986:45–46). This, however, is not exactly what the Supreme Court required, and some of its later decisions are uninterpretable without recognizing the difference. The Court argued that prisoners, unlike probationers and parolees, have had their Fourteenth Amendment liberty interest extinguished by incarceration. Under these conditions, due process applies only if the state provides its inmates with some rights. In *Wolff*, the Nebraska good time statute did limit withdrawal of good time to cases of misconduct. Consequently, said the Supreme Court, Nebraska could not take the good time away without following its own laws. The state had given the inmates a liberty interest (by ruling that loss of good time was not discretionary). Certainly, prison officials would have to prove the prison misconduct in an orderly and reliable manner in order to take it away (see Cohen, 1985; Collins, 1986).

Since *Wolff*, additional cases have filled in the gaps in the decision. Collins summarizes the implications of these cases (1986:40–46):

1. Staff should not rely on hearsay evidence from an unidentified informant; the reliability of the informant must be demonstrated.
2. Staff may deny inmates the right to call witnesses on the grounds that the testimony may endanger security.
3. The staff member who brought the misconduct charges need not be present at the hearing, but if the inmate calls this person as a witness, the request generally should be honored.
4. If assistance is to be provided to an inmate, staff must ascertain that the assistance is real.
5. Staff should not relax their attention to procedural regularities just because an inmate looks guilty.
6. Staff should be careful to preserve the disciplinary hearing record.
7. Above all, staff responsible for conducting hearings need training in the proper procedures.

Two years after *Wolff*, a decision about due process in transfer decisions demonstrated that the narrow interpretation of *Wolff* was the correct one. Inmates in the Massachusetts system were transferred from medium to maximum security following a series of fires in the institution in which the transferred inmates were implicated. They complained that the transfer to the far more onerous conditions of maximum security was a grievous loss and could not be undertaken without due process. The court disagreed (*Meachum* v. *Fano*, 1976), stating that without a state law or regulation to the contrary, prison administrators could move prisoners to any prison at their discretion.

More recent transfer cases have continued to insist on the state-created right before any process is due (*Howe* v. *Smith* 1981, permitting transfer from state to federal system without a hearing; *Olim* v. *Wakinekona*, 1981, permitting transfer from Hawaii to California). More recently, the court has applied the same logic to transfers within a prison from the general population to administrative segregation (*Hewitt* v. *Helms*, 1983).

These cases taken together indicate that the less the state elaborates its correctional decision process, the greater discretion its prison officials will have. It is unlikely that many states would want their prison administrators to make decisions by whim or accident, or by keeping no record of them, or to adhere to erroneous decisions when evidence to the contrary exists. Consequently, state governments and state courts may begin to demand more of administrators than has the Supreme Court in recent years.

EQUAL PROTECTION

The equal protection clause of the Fourteenth Amendment says that no state shall "deny to any person within its jurisdiction the equal protection of the laws." The equal protection clause has not been interpreted to prohibit discrimination, but it does prohibit discrimination without strong justification. The balancing test that would be used to justify discrimination against (or in favor of) some group would be a strict test, often requiring compelling state interest and adoption of the least restrictive alternative. As is the case with other rights, the courts may allow the balance to be achieved more easily in prison than in nonprison settings. There have been relatively few equal protection cases of significance in prison. A number of scholars have indicated that the equal protection case promising greatest change in prison administration is still ahead of us.

Equal protection balancing tests are strictest when the government uses "suspect classifications," such as racial, ethnic, or religious groupings, as the basis for distributing different treatments or resources. The Court's stance is that any unequal treatment of people grouped by these classifications is automatically suspect, and only the most compelling reasons would justify its continuance. In this fashion, the courts have rejected racial segregation in prison, except in temporary situations of racial unrest (*Washington* v. *Lee*, 1968), and unequal opportunities to practice a valid religion (*Cruz* v. *Beto*, 1972).

Equal protection challenges to other types of groupings has not fared as well. For example, a federal inmate once argued that he had a right to treatment as an addict rather than to punishment for his conviction and that the Narcotic Rehabilitation Act of 1966 unfairly discriminated against addicts with records of prior offenses. The Supreme Court disagreed (*Marshall* v. *U.S.*, 1974), and required of the government only "rational" rather than compelling reasons for refusing to divert addicts with prior records.

Collins (1986) and Singer (1980) indicate that the looming equal protection argument involves women prisoners. Almost all prison experts in the country agree that rights and programs for women prisoners lag far behind those for men. To date, the most sweeping decision on this issue comes from Michigan, where the federal district court required that programs for women had to be "substantially similar to men's in substance if not in form" (*Glover* v. *Johnson*, 1979).

Collins (1986:75–81) characterizes parity for women prisoners as a "ticking judicial time bomb." He admits that women have fewer educational and work programs, less medical care, and less access to trusty status or to minimum security programs. Significantly, the reasons that

prisoner administrators usually call upon to justify reduction of rights (such as security) simply do not apply to this issue. The only reasons women prisoners are more poorly treated are economic, and it is unlikely that any court will bend the Constitution simply to save money.

EIGHTH AMENDMENT RIGHTS

The Eighth Amendment to the constitution is surprisingly short:

> Excessive bail shall not be required, nor excessive fines imposed, nor cruel and unusual punishments inflicted.

The Eighth Amendment places a number of constraints on the punishment of convicted prisoners. At least since the Wolfish decision, detainees in jail are not protected by the cruel and unusual punishment clause, since they are not being punished (see Insert 1.1). However, most of the protections afforded convicted prisoners through the Eighth Amendment have been applied in detention situations through the due process clause.

The Eighth Amendment has been used in at least six different ways that have direct consequences for prison administration (Cohen, 1985):

1. To govern the use of force
2. To govern the use of isolation or segregation cells
3. To govern the availability of medical care
4. To govern the use of certain intrusive rehabilitation or treatment techniques
5. To govern the conditions of confinement
6. To control the length of confinement, the proportionality of the punishment to the crime, or the lack of purpose in punishment.

The three most common tests for violations of the ban on cruel and unusual punishment are (Bronstein, 1980:27)

. . . whether the punishment shocks the general conscience of a civilized society; whether the punishment is unnecessarily cruel; and whether the punishment goes beyond legitimate penal aims.

USE OF FORCE

The protection afforded against the infliction of pain is rather limited. In 1977, the Supreme Court observed that "brutality" was part of the total incarcerative experience (*Ingraham* v. *Wright*). The most recent standard used to determine if staff use of force violated the Eighth Amendment was that the force had to be wanton (officer intended the harm), unnecessary (the force was not reasonably related to a valid penal goal or objective), and caused severe pain or lasting injury (*Whitley* v. *Albers*, 1986).

ISOLATION CELLS

The use of isolation cells, and particularly strip cells, has been regulated by application of the Eighth Amendment. One of the earlier lower court cases detailed horrible conditions, including excrement smeared on walls, inability to flush the toilet (a hole in the ground), and severe cold and heat in a standard strip cell and declared that the practice shocked the conscience (*Jordan* v. *Fitzharris*, 1966). Other courts have followed suit. The leading Supreme Court decision (*Hutto* v. *Finney*, 1978) ruled out more than 30 days in the Arkansas segregation cells.

MEDICAL CARE

The courts have made major decisions about the right to medical care, including mental health treatment, in the last ten years. *Estelle* v. *Gamble* (1976) ruled that deliberate indifference to the medical needs of prisoners violated the ban on cruel and unusual punishment. While this is not a very proactive stance toward the provision of medical care, it is a standard sufficient to imply some rights for prisoners. For example, *Estelle* v. *Gamble* has been interpreted to require some min-

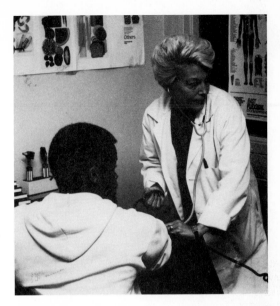

Inmates have a right to some health care. An important part of that care is an adequate examination upon reception. (New York State Department of Correctional Services)

imal level of classification as a means of separating the sick from the well and identifying those who need special care, and to require some level of recordkeeping to demonstrate the diagnosis and provide for continuity of care. *Bowring* v. *Godwin* (1977) applied *Estelle* v. *Gamble* to mental health care and has not been seriously challenged.

The right to mental health care has already wrought some significant change in some prison systems, but it is important to understand just what type of mental health services are required. A distinction between treatment and rehabilitation may help. Cohen (1985:37) distinguished between rehabilitation and treatment this way:

[Treatment] refers to efforts to provide short-term relief from acute psychic distress. Treatment in the sense of forward-looking, future-oriented improvement in, say, coping and relational skills [i.e. rehabilitation], is not the type of treatment we refer to here.

The level of care required by the Constitution would be low—"to provide minimally acceptable care in order to avoid death or needless suffering" (Cohen, 1985:33)—but some prison systems have agreed to far more elaborate treatment services, either on their own or in the context of a court order or consent decree.

INTRUSIVE TREATMENT TECHNIQUES

Prisoners have some right to refuse treatments, under certain conditions. Psychosurgery and castration, for example, have generally been ruled out. Some psychological programs have been halted. The most famous was a behavior modification program called Project START run by the Federal Bureau of Prisons. The court ordered that such programs in the future would have to provide participants with minimal amenities, regardless of their cooperativeness, and use rewards rather than punishments to shape behavior.

CONDITIONS OF CONFINEMENT

Among the most important of the Eighth Amendment cases are those which deal with the minimally acceptable conditions of confinement for the general population. How much money must a state put into its prison system? How many guards must it employ in order to run a constitutionally acceptable prison?

For a number of years, such broad questions about conditions were thought to be beyond the Eighth Amendment. For years, judges would consider only whether very specific conditions (such as the temperature in a strip cell) violated the Eighth Amendment. Prisons in extremely poor general condition, sadly understaffed and poorly managed, were safe from constitutional scrutiny unless a specific practice or condition by itself could be judged to shock the conscience. This approach started to change slowly in the 1960s. Eventually, the concept of **totality of conditions** was developed to deal with prisons in which the entire environment was substandard, but no single practice or condition stood out. The term was

pioneered by Judge Frank Johnson in *Pugh* v. *Locke* (1976) in the federal district court for the middle district of Alabama (see Johnson, 1986). The concept was also advanced in *Holt* v. *Sarver* (1970), the case declaring the Arkansas system unconstitutional for the violations exposed by Tom Murton (Murton and Hyams, 1969) and recently depicted in the film *Brubaker*.

Three guidelines for courts to consider when using the totality of conditions concept were proposed by the Supreme Court in *Hutto* v. *Finney* (1978):

1. Consider the totality of conditions of confinement.
2. Specify in the court order each factor that contributed to the Eighth Amendment violation and that must be changed to remove the violation.
3. Articulate, if necessary, minimum standards the prison must meet to satisfy constitutional standards.

The Finney opinion also cautioned judges, however, that they should not interfere in prison administration unless the conditions were "deplorable" or "sordid."

When many correctional officials now think of court intervention in prison systems, it is the specific corrective measures detailed in totality cases that they have in mind. These orders represent the most sweeping and proactive stance judges can take in prison administration, and it may involve the courts with the prisons for many years, as we shall see below. It is from these orders that Fred Cohen also derives the "worst get more" principle. Judges will often demand greater correction of conditions in response to this situation than if only a few glaring deficiencies exist.

The limits to Eighth Amendment protections have become visible in a number of other cases that sought relief for more specific conditions. *Rhodes* v. *Chapman* (1981) rejected overcrowding, in the form of double bunking, as unconstitutional, per se. *Atiyeh* v. *Capps* (1981) also rejected overcrowding per se as violative of the Eighth Amendment and went on to affirm retribution as a legitimate penal objective. The Eighth Amendment, said the Court, does not require pleasing housing.

A rather ironic situation has developed between conditions found acceptable in jails and those found acceptable in prisons. Although detainees have not been convicted, they may not enjoy rights to the same conditions as incarcerated felons. There are at least four cases in which prisoners have successfully challenged prison conditions that in other cases were found acceptable for detainees (Gill, 1981). This situation is a result of the Wolfish case, in which the Supreme Court made much of the fact that the detainees were not housed in the Metropolitan Correctional Center for long periods of time, or for long portions of the day. A number of judges have avoided the application of the Wolfish standard to prisons by pointing to the permanence or duration of the prison condition being challenged. Hence while the usual rule of thumb is that detainees have at least the rights enjoyed by prisoners, the shortness of jail detention may be used to justify poorer conditions in some situations.

PROPORTIONALITY

Finally, the Eighth Amendment may limit the length of prison sentence, in certain situations. For example, life without parole for issuing a bad check for $100 was deemed cruel and unusual punishment (*Solem* v. *Helm* (1983). However, mandatory life under a Texas recidivism statute was not found cruel and unusual, even though the third offense (which triggered the recidivism statute) was a conviction for obtaining $120 under false pretenses (*Rummel* v. *Estelle*, 1980).

REMEDIES

Rights without remedies for their violation are meaningless. As was the case with the right of access to the courts, the right gained meaning

only as subsequent court decisions provided for implementation. When inmates have complaints about the treatment they receive in prison, there are a number of possible remedies, depending upon the nature of the complaint and the orientation of the administration.

If inmates think their rights have been violated, perhaps the most common means of seeking redress is to go to court, and it is on the various types of litigation that this section will focus. However, there would also appear to be a growing number of alternatives to litigation which may also provide some remedies for violations of rights, and more important, may provide a means of communicating and resolving conflicts that are not constitutional issues.

ALTERNATIVES TO LITIGATION

An **ombudsman** is a public official, often an attorney, who has the authority to investigate complaints and recommend changes in public organizations. The ombudsman institution began in Sweden and has been adapted to a number of American situations, although most ombudsmen in this country appear to have less authority than those in Sweden. There are correctional ombudsmen in a number of states, although not all of them are independent of the correctional bureaucracy they are supposed to be investigating. For an ombudsman program to work, inmates must have easy access for filing complaints; the ombudsman must truly have sufficient access to prison staff, inmates, and records to investigate complaints thoroughly; and the ombudsman's recommendations must be respected by both inmates and staff. In states that employ them, ombudsmen may usually be considered as midway between internal dispute resolution and court litigation.

Mediation programs have sprung up in a number of settings, such as neighborhood dispute mediation centers, as a means of avoiding the court process. Mediation emphasizes face-to-face resolution of conflict. Mediators are trained professionals (although often not attorneys) who have skills in leading two disputing parties through a

Alternatives to prison litigation include prisoner grievance procedures. The Elmira grievance committee above includes three staff members and two inmates. (New York State Department of Correctional Services)

rational rather than emotional conflict. The mediator cannot impose an outcome; the parties must agree to one. Mediation has been tried in a few prisons, such as the federal prison at Danbury, Connecticut.

Grievance procedures are administrative means of resolving disputes within an organization. The federal Congress recently passed 42 U.S. Code Section 1997e, requiring exhaustion of state prison remedies before inmates can enter federal court with a suit (see McCoy, 1981). This statute will spur the development of certified grievance mechanisms in state prison systems, as state officials seek to avoid suits in federal court. Section 1997e requires that inmates exhaust administrative remedies before Civil Rights Act proceedings may begin, but requires the grievance process take no longer than 90 days. The attorney general of the United States is responsible for publishing standards for grievance procedures and for certifying prison systems that meet those standards.

Grievance procedures are a common organizational means of resolving conflicts between management and employees. This process is being adapted in prisons to grievances for both staff and inmates. A grievance procedure is a formal administrative procedure for resolving disputes. There is usually a first-level hearing committee, followed by at least one level of appeal. In the prison context, appeals from a grievance committee decision would usually go first to the warden or superintendent and then to the commissioner of the department.

Grievance procedures usually require that the parties to the dispute attempt a good faith effort to resolve the dispute informally before a formal grievance is filed. Many disputes are resolved in this fashion. If an informal resolution is not possible, the aggrieved party may file the appropriate papers, generally a memorandum stating the facts and the complaint, with a grievance officer to begin the formal process. If the claim is within its jurisdiction and not considered frivolous, the grievance committee will conduct an investigation and hold a hearing. The parties to the dispute have the right to a written report that sets forth the decision and the reasons for it.

A controversial issue in inmate grievance mechanisms is just how much influence inmates should have in the grievance process. The attorney general's standards require inmate participation in the grievance committee itself, or on a policy council that oversees the grievance program. Most prisons seeking certification of their program have chosen the policy route rather than have inmates participate directly in dispute hearings.

REMEDIES IN COURT

If alternatives to litigation are unsuccessful or unavailable, an inmate may file a complaint with an appropriate court. Inmates may sue for battery or negligence in state court under common tort law or appeal for protection of any relevant state statute or state constitutional provision. Inmates seem to prefer federal to state courts. The federal courts have been seen as more sympathetic to inmate complaints, although this view may change in the near future.

The oldest available legal challenge in incarceration situations is the writ of habeas corpus, which provides relief from unlawful restraint. Persons in lawful custody may seek a writ for total release or one placing limits on their incarceration. For example, habeas corpus may be effective for an involuntarily committed mental patient who does not receive the treatment promised by statute. Such relief is unlikely to apply to prisoners who have been duly convicted and sentenced to prison for a crime. However, it may be and has been used to seek relief from segregation in strip cells (e.g. *Jordan* v. *Fitzharris*).

SUITS UNDER THE CIVIL RIGHTS ACT

The most common inmate strategy is to claim that civil rights have been violated and to sue under 42 U.S. Code Section 1983, the **Federal Civil Rights Act.** Section 1983 was passed in 1871 as a means of implementing the Fourteenth Amendment to the Constitution, after the Civil War. It provides that

> Every person who, under color of any statute, ordinance, regulation, custom, or usage, of any State or Territory or District of Columbia, subjects, or causes to the subjected, any citizen of the United States or other person within the jurisdiction thereof

to the deprivation of any rights, privileges, or immunities secured by the Constitution and laws, shall be liable to the party injured in an action of law, suit in equity, or other proper proceeding for redress.

Cooper v. *Pate* (1964) determined that the Civil Rights Act protected prisoners, and opened the federal courts for suits about violations of constitutional rights in state prisons. The Civil Rights Act provides for the civil liability of the officials responsible for the rights violation. If they lose the suit, they may be required to pay compensatory damages, possibly punitive damages, as well as attorney's fees for the inmate bringing the suit. A significant change of interpretation occurred in 1979 when the Supreme Court decided that municipal corporations (which are legally considered individuals) were liable for damages under Section 1983 (*Monell* v. *Department of Social Services*, 1979). While this change does not affect states, it can have a major impact on jails run by municipalities. State officials can be sued as individuals, but if they can show that they operated in a truly official role, they do not have personal responsibility for damages (Collins, 1986:6–7).

Winning a Section 1983 suit for monetary damages is difficult. The inmate must successfully show that the official knew of the right and in denying the inmate's rights acted maliciously (Cohen, 1985: 42). Additionally, the Supreme Court has recently decided that money damages do not attach to rights violations per se. Financial compensation is available only if the plaintiff can demonstrate a real loss (*Memphis Community School District* v. *Stahura*, 1986). The effect of these limitations is that inmates may often be better off seeking an injunction (a court order for cessation of the offending practice) or court monitoring of the institution, rather than monetary damages (Collins, 1986:7; Cohen, 1985:42). McCoy (1981) calls these two alternatives for remedial action the monitoring model and the money model. The monitoring model provides direct judicial intervention in ongoing prison activities, while the money model provides for financial sanctions for past harms. Which type of relief may be more effective is debatable: Quite possibly several successful financial awards will be more effective control than years of court monitoring of conditions.

An important concept in 1983 suits is **qualified immunity.** Qualified immunity is a defense for public officials who were doing their job properly (as trained) and were not aware that their actions violated a right. This defense protects officials from financial damages awards when the law in question was ambiguous until the suit. This defense to 1983 damages will be less available as prisoners' rights are increasingly clarified (Collins, 11–12, 63).

Finally, supervisors can be sued under Section 1983 (or in state court for negligence) even if they were not involved in the incident. They would be liable if plaintiffs can show a positive link between the offending conduct of the subordinate officials and the management failure of supervisors. To determine if supervisors are liable, courts examine the circumstances of the incident, policies, training practices, and the pattern of staff discipline. The judge would be seeking evidence that the objectionable subordinate behavior was known to supervisors, and either condoned or encouraged.

JUDICIAL MANAGEMENT OF CORRECTIONAL ORGANIZATIONS

In the last two decades, a relatively new form of interorganizational relationship has sprung up that is making quick and massive alterations in correctional organizations. This new environmental force is the increasing activism of federal district courts in determining prison conditions. This emerging form of judicial action has been called **institutional orders** (Frug, 1978) or court decree cases (Note, 1977).

In the institutional order cases, the judge actively intervenes in the administration of the agency, specifying in great detail what the administration must do to bring an institution up to constitutional or statutory standards (Frug, 1978).

Gaes and McGuire (1985) report that at least 30 correctional departments were operating under court decrees to correct confinement conditions that violated rights.

This new form of correctional interaction with the courts presents new challenges to both the court and the correctional executives. In court decree cases

> [J]udges are placed in a new role: they become responsible for implementing broad reforms in complex administrative systems, without ordinarily having expertise in either public administration or the particular institutional field in question. (Note, 1977:428)

The institutional orders are initiated by an inmate complaining that prison practice or conditions violates rights. If the complaint is substantiated, the decision, rather than, or in addition to, awarding monetary damages, may involve a decree mandating the changes the judge believes are necessary to correct the problems. Prison decrees have included orders for extensive structural improvements, specifications for minimum square feet per prisoner, increases in custody personnel, limitations on the numbers to be confined in the facility, daily cleaning, funding for a bail project, improved hospital facilities, increased medical staff, hiring of nutritionists, specifications of recreation time and resources, changes in reading material, adding work, educational, and vocational training programs, and changing the classification system (Frug, 1978).

One special form of institutional order is the **consent decree.** The consent decree is a means of settling a lawsuit in which the defendants agree to make changes in practices or conditions but do not admit liability for past rights violations (Collins, 1986:111). The consent decree is a binding promise to meet the conditions set out in the order, and it applies to future as well as current administrators, unless there are provisions for terminating the order built into the decree. Because the consent decree is an agreement, rather than an order after losing a case, the conditions agreed to must be carried out even if constitutional interpretation changes. Other institutional orders have been modified when later constitutional decisions reduced the standards that applied.

Judicial insistence on specific changes alters the relationship of the three branches of government. The orders may involve legislative action to reallocate funds or raise new funds to pay for the changes, and the orders require the executive branch to implement particular programs (Frug, 1978). The decrees have resulted in ongoing, long-term collaboration between judges and executives because the judge retains jurisdiction over the case, and oversees the correctional organization, until the decree has been satisfied. Most decrees have not achieved full compliance and have meant years of court supervision (Note, 1977:431–432).

Opinions on the problems with court decree implementation vary. Some commentators point out that the cost of the decree can be massive—more than doubling expenditures for some systems (Frug, 1978:727). Others have noted that this cost increase does not always explain the problems of implementation. Often the correctional managers welcome the court decree as a means of pressuring the legislature for additional funds that they have been unable to obtain through normal requests (Gilhool, 1976; Johnson, 1986). When new funds have been necessary, they have usually been found. However, some systems have discovered that the new money cannot be spent appropriately (Note, 1977:454). For example, some decrees have ordered hiring of new officers, but neither the organization nor the court has been able to find sufficient qualified applicants to fill the positions.

The *Harvard Law Review* takes the position that the same new management techniques which apply to improving human relations in the correctional organization should be used in improving court decree implementation (these techniques are discussed further in Chapter 18). Specifically, the defendant managers in these cases should participate more actively in formulating the order and managing its implementation. In addition, it is recommended that the court involve other organizations in the correctional network that may be instrumental in implementing the decree (Note, 1977:457; and Collins, 1986:112–114).

The court decree has bred a new form of correctional manager, the **court master,** often appointed by the judge to oversee implementation of the order. Court masters have frequently been lawyers specializing in correctional law, but a number of court masters have been experienced correctional administrators. The master is delegated certain powers by the judge, and can back up his authority by requesting a judicial hearing and threatening contempt charges against noncompliant managers. However, both judges and masters are often aware that correctional managers named in the decree are not personally responsible for all implementation problems. Masters may be more effective if they are seen by the correctional staff as experienced correctional experts. But there is probably no substitute for active participation of all parties in formulating a feasible order that satisfies rights without damaging other legitimate correctional objectives.

SUMMARY

1. The courts have historically refused to hear prisoners' challenges to prison conditions. This judicial hands off doctrine was justified on the basis of federalism and separation of powers.

2. The courts did not truly begin to open up to prisoners' rights cases until *Cooper* v. *Pate* (1964) applied the Civil Rights Act to state and local prisoners.

3. Basic values underlying the justification of prisoners' rights include the proportionality inherent in retribution, the requirement that those in custody receive basic care, and the requirement that all people deserve fundamental fairness.

4. Four principles are important to the determination of prisoners' rights. The first two are conflicting approaches to the extent of prisoners' rights: either (a) prisoners have all rights not expressly or by necessary implication withdrawn, or (b) prisoners have only those rights expressly or by necessary implication conferred. In addition, would be the principle (c) that the greater the potential harm, the greater the plausibility of the argument for protection. Finally, many judges behave as if (d) the worse the prison conditions are, the more actions they can demand when correcting conditions.

5. Among the constitutional rights of prisoners are (a) reasonable access to the courts, and the materials and assistance necessary to reach the courts (Fifth/Fourteenth Amendment); (b) diluted First Amendment protections, especially to the practice of religion; (c) Eighth Amendment protections relative to use of force, intrusive treatments, medical care, isolation cells, conditions of confinement, and length of incarceration; (d) minimum Fifth/Fourteenth Amendment due process in disciplinary matters, provided the state has created some liberty interest; (e) equal protection of the laws, certainly from racial and religious discrimination, and perhaps from differential treatment by sex; (f) minimal Fourth Amendment protection regarding guarding by officers of the opposite sex.

6. When rights are violated, there are both judicial and less formal remedies. Prisons are beginning to experiment with mediation, ombudsman, and grievance procedures in order to avoid court litigation. Prisoners may have access to state or federal courts, but the favorite resort is federal district court under the Civil Rights Act. Civil rights suits may seek financial damages, but the case for an injunction or court monitoring may be more easily made in some circumstances.

7. The recent move toward institutional orders or court decrees as a means of correcting prisons after successful totality of conditions cases is both controversial and spreading quickly. More than thirty jurisdictions are currently under court order to correct unconstitutional conditions.

KEY WORDS

CIVIL RIGHTS ACT OF 1871. Federal legislation of 1871, 42 U.S. Code Section 1983, that makes public officials civilly liable for violating a person's civil rights. A means of implementing the Fourteenth Amendment after the Civil War.

COMPELLING STATE INTEREST. The strictest standard applied when a government seeks to limit a fundamental right. Often the test of conflicting interest in First Amendment and equal protection cases.

CONSENT DECREE. An agreement to correct conditions violative of rights, without an admission of liability for past violations.

COURT MASTER. An official appointed by a judge (typically from a federal district court) to oversee the implementation of an institutional order.

GRIEVANCE PROCEDURE. A formal administrative procedure to investigate and resolve disputes between management and lower employees, clients, or inmates.

HABEAS CORPUS. An extraordinary writ challenging the legality of confinement.

HANDS-OFF DOCTRINE. Judicial doctrine that legally confined inmates had no rights. Justified on the basis of federalism and separation of powers.

INSTITUTIONAL ORDERS. Also known as court decrees, the judicial orders applied to an institution to correct the conditions or practices that infringe on inmate rights.

LEAST RESTRICTIVE ALTERNATIVE. The only level of restriction the government is usually permitted to place on fundamental rights. The test is whether the government can achieve its legitimate competing purpose while placing fewer limits on the rights of the individual.

MEDIATION. Informal conflict resolution through the intervention of a trained mediator who seeks a mutually agreeable resolution between disputing parties.

OMBUDSMAN. Public official with authority to investigate complaints about government operations and to recommend changes.

QUALIFIED IMMUNITY. A defense to a Civil Rights Act suit that claims the right violated was not clearly enunciated and therefore the violation was unintentional and the official not liable for damages.

TOTALITY OF CONDITIONS. A concept developed in *Pugh* v. *Locke* to judge prisons in which the total weight of the environment, rather than single practices, was seen as violative of the Eighth Amendment ban on cruel and unusual punishment.

PROJECTS AND QUESTIONS

1. If there is a correctional officers' union in your state, contact it to find out if the union holds a position on prisoners' rights. What is it? What claims are made about how rights have affected supervision?
2. Find out if a prison or jail in your state has been or is under court order to correct conditions. What did the order entail? How is implementation of the order progressing?
3. Hold a debate on principles (a) and (b) in summary point 4 above.

ADDITIONAL READING

Tom Murton and Joe Hyams. *Accomplices to the Crime.* New York: Grove Press, 1970. Murton's account of the ugly and violent conditions he discovered at the Tucker Prison Farm in Arkansas. These conditions eventually led to the federal district court decision in *Holt* v. *Sarver* (1970).

Aric Press. "Inside America's Toughest Prison," *Newsweek* October 6, 1986:46–61. A recent account of conditions in a Texas prison before and after Judge Wayne Justice declared the entire system unconstitutional in *Ruiz* v. *Estelle*.

14 CLASSIFICATION AND PROGRAM

QUESTIONS

1. What are the major types of classification in current use?

2. What are the common problems with classification practice?

3. What are the characteristics of a good classification scheme?

4. What are some of the problems with prison industries?

5. How has prison treatment changed since correctional goals have shifted toward retribution and deterrence?

6. What roles do prison counselors usually perform?

7. What inmate groups often require special programs?

SEARCHING FOR A FEW GOOD MEN

One day when Phil was walking into Mulwan, he met the Madison prerelease center director, Doug Sims, walking out. Sims smiled and stopped for a chat.

"Well," said Phil. "Why are you here?"

"Looking for residents."

Phil was confused. "I thought the prison counselors did all the initial screening and sent the applications to you."

"Sometimes. That's the way the system is supposed to work. They refer, we accept. Simple. But it doesn't work. See, the counselors here have better things to do than find a few candidates for my prerelease center. They probably have caseloads of 150 each. They're so busy with program decisions and getting guys ready for the parole board that every once in a while they forget about us. So I come in here, rifle the files for likely candidates, and make my own referrals. Commissioner Rush wouldn't like it." Sims laughed, trying to imitate the Commissioner's favorite word. "I mean, you've heard him often enough—the whole system is a graduated release mechanism. All parts of it are working to get the inmate back on the street in an orderly, supervised progression." He trailed off. "Well enough of that. Rush might *hope* that the prison counselors move inmates into centers. But in the real world it just doesn't work that way. Don't get me wrong. It isn't that the counselors are uncooperative. If I have questions about a guy or want an interview, or want their opinion on whether this or that guy is a good bet for the center, they are more than helpful. But Rush doesn't see things the way a prison counselor does. These guys are pushing paper all the time. The most important paper comes first. Well, the most important paper is board paper, because that can't wait. The second most important paper is the new inmates. Listen, no matter what it says on paper, recommending a prerelease inmate for the centers is right on the bottom of the list.

First, it's complicated. You need signatures and you have to kiss the sentencing judge. And if the counselor sends me the wrong guy, somebody that doesn't fit in, I'll turn him down. So he's wasted his time, and on top of that, the inmate's mad at him now. Finally, if the counselor ignores the center, the guy will make parole anyway, right? He'll just get paroled from here instead of from the center. So big deal, as far as the counselor is concerned. Moreover, if he moves that guy over to us, he just gets another inmate. So he doesn't win anything."

Sims straightened up and took a long breath. "There. There's how the system really works. That's how it is that even with this place"—he jerked his thumb at the gray prison behind them—"full to the gills, my little center can have empty beds."

Phil laughed. "You seem to take it in good humor."

Sims turned and headed toward the electrified gate. "What can I do? You have to work with the system the way it is."

THE CLASSIFICATION OF INMATES

In most correctional institutions, the total inmate population is subdivided into a number of smaller groups. If **classification** is successful, the subdivision will produce groupings that are more homogeneous on one or more characteristics related to the achievement of the prison goals. For example, if lack of escapes is considered an important objective, then dividing inmates on the basis of escape potential will allow the administration to devote the most resources to the greatest escape risks. By permitting resources to be matched to relevant inmate characteristics, the organization increases its efficiency.

Classification is determined by purpose, and no classification system suits all purposes. Any system highlights some characteristics and ignores others. The characteristics to be highlighted and used for dividing and distributing the population must be related to the purposes of the organization. It does not improve efficiency or effectiveness to classify the inmates according to some treatment-related variables and then distribute them into programs and living quarters on the basis of security goals. Naturally, for classification to work, purposes must be clear, and the prison must have acquired and organized its resources on the basis of the same goals.

If purposes are clear and the classification scheme is related to purpose, accurate, and carried out effectively, then information is efficiently processed and decisions are made more quickly and effectively. If the purposes of an enterprise change, its classification practices should also change.

Unfortunately, correctional classification practice is not as cut and dried as classification in some other types of activities. As we already know, correctional goals are not very clear, and practices are not always directly related to goals. As we might suspect, hypothesizing which inmate characteristics are the best ones by which to subdivide the population are not very clear either.

One particular difficulty with inmate classification is that officials are often attempting to predict future behavior on the basis of the classification variables. Staff might use previous escape record as a means of predicting escape risk, or they might use history of violent crimes to predict risk of violent behavior in prison. Very often staff are using some indication of deficiency or need to predict which inmates will perform well in educational or treatment programs. In all these examples, staff are guessing at a relationship between outcome and some current information. Sometimes the "information" turns out to be inaccurate. For example, staff might administer to a new inmate a well-known psychological test. But because the newcomer is so frightened, the test results will be inaccurate. Sometimes the information is accurate, but the hypothetical relationship in fact does not exist. For example, many inmates with educational deficiencies do not become hungry students when placed in remedial educational programs. Sometimes the information is accurate and the relationship actually exists most of the time, but a particular inmate will be an exception. For example, an inmate accurately placed in low-security status may suddenly become violent for the first time.

Phil's conversation with Sims demonstrates a number of these issues and problems. Commissioner Rush had installed a particular classification system to move inmates through the facilities with gradual decrements in custody and gradual increments in responsibility and opportunity. This system was consistent with the goals of reintegration the commissioner espoused. He hoped that most persons leaving the prison system would do so through the prerelease centers. Prison counselors were responsible for making referrals to the centers in timely fashion, using a number of criteria predicting readiness for the community. But as the prisons became crowded and counselor caseloads escalated, these classification agents attended to higher priorities. The irony of the situation was that the maximum security prison was full, but the centers had space available. Director Sims short-circuited the breakdown by making his own referrals. Some-

times this informal procedure had advantages. Some of the information Sims liked to use in predicting an inmate's behavior in the center was not available in the prison, but only to Sims. Since he knew the personalities of the other center residents, he felt he could use that information in deciding how a new referral would adjust.

Good classification procedures are no panacea for correctional problems. At best, they allow staff and inmates a better start in the process of interacting on a daily basis. But a good classification process is important for that reason. It can be effective in reducing strain in the system because it matches inmate needs and requirements to resources (Toch, 1977:286–291). Recently, courts have placed new emphasis on classification. They have demanded that classifications not be capricious, irrational, or discriminatory (Wright, 1985:3). Correctional systems will have to invest increasing resources in the creation and implementation of rational classificatory devices. Megargee (1977) provides some guidelines for a good classification system:

- The system should be able to classify most offenders; there should be few inmates who cannot be accurately placed.
- The classification system should use clear categories that do not overlap.
- The system should be reliable; different persons using the same procedures should attain the same results.
- The system should be valid; inmates must actually possess the characteristics indicated by the classification or the predictions made about future behavior must be accurate.
- The system must allow for change.
- The system must have implications for the treatment or management of the inmates; a scheme without practice implications is useless.
- The system should be economical; it should require a modicum of information and a modicum of training to use it properly.

There are many specific classification schemes in use. Clements (1986) and Wright (1985) provide good reviews. Many of the specific systems, however, fall into three broad types which differ by purpose. The three purposes most commonly sought are classification for security, classification by personality attributes, and classification by need for particular prison settings.

CLASSIFICATION BY PERSONALITY ATTRIBUTES

Some classification systems seek to divide inmates into different groups on the basis of personality attributes. The origins of this type of system can be traced back to the positive school of criminology, which sought to reclaim or at least control offenders by examining those factors which determined their criminal behavior (Radzinowicz, 1971). Initial attempts by the positivists focused on physiological features which were thought to distinguish criminals from law abiders. Today these early classifications appear silly. However, the fundamental premises of the positivist school—that the behavior of individuals was determined by previous internal and external forces, and that behavior could therefore be predicted and controlled—were relatively sound. These are premises shared by all three classificatory systems currently in use.

Focus on personality as a fundamental concern for correctional classification arose as positivistic criminology and penology began to apply the findings of scientific psychology and psychiatry in the period from 1930 to 1960. During this period, the focus on personality attributes became associated with the **medical model** of correction. In an early attack on the medical model, Hakeem (1958) defined it as composed of two underlying assumptions: (1) the belief that crime is a symptom of mental illness, and (2) the belief that mental illness could be treated in exactly the same way as physical disease. Hakeem argued that many of the medical model classifications used in correction violated the principles of good classification schemes. Diagnostic categories often lacked reliability, and often the medical ex-

perts disagreed on the treatment implications for any particular category (1958:672–673).

Not all personality-based systems have shared these deficiencies. One of the better known systems is the Interpersonal Maturity Level (or I-Level) system first used by Grant and Grant (1959) in the Navy, and later applied by them to delinquents in the California Community Treatment Project discussed in Chapter 19. The I-Level system divided subjects into groups differing in stages of sociopsychological maturation. For each type or each I-level, there was a specific set of treatment prescriptions. Proponents of the system made the important point that not all treatments are equally effective with all types of offenders. Mismatching offender types and treatments can actually produce worse results than no treatment at all.

Under certain conditions, the I-Level system of classification has had very positive results (Palmer, 1978). When correctional systems can provide the clinicians to conduct the interviews for diagnosis, and can provide the training to treatment staff necessary to implement differential treatment, this personality-based system can be effective. Unfortunately, these requirements also indicate its weakness. It is expensive, complicated, and dependent on highly trained, rarely available specialists.

Other researchers have sought to devise personality-based systems that could operate at less cost. Among these, perhaps the most widely used currently was devised by Megargee. Megargee's system classifies inmates into ten groups by using scores from the Minnesota Multiphasic Personality Inventory (MMPI), a test many prison systems administer. The scoring scheme is computerized so the process does not require expensive clinical interviews. Megargee and his associates have recommended different prison treatment for each type in the classification.

CLASSIFICATION BY SECURITY

Perhaps the oldest objective of classification systems is that of security. However, between the ascendancy of the medical model in the 1920s and its demise in the 1970s, concerns for security in the classification process often operated underground. During the reign of the medical model, inmates were often classified in elaborate, professionally staffed reception centers on the basis of treatment-relevant criteria and then sent out to institutions where staff would either ignore or override the initial classification decisions on the basis of security. When the medical model began to crumble, this inefficient and hypocritical practice began to crumble as well.

In 1973, the National Advisory Commission on Criminal Justice Standards and Goals explicitly recognized the legitimacy of classification for "management purposes." The management purposes implied were basically those of running a smooth ship, by achieving two objectives long associated with security: (1) minimizing chances of escape, and (2) reducing risk of violence and disciplinary problems within the prison. These two objectives are not the same. The first objective, that of perimeter control, could be accomplished without a great deal of control within the prison. The second objective is far more difficult to achieve and is attractive to different groups for different reasons.

While the minimization of internal disruption, and especially violence, is obviously attractive to those seeking order and obedience, it is also sought by anyone concerned with the physical health and mental well-being of staff and inmates. Safety is a prime concern to many participants in the prison community, and minimal levels of safety are required by the Eighth Amendment ban on cruel and unusual punishment. Since the National Advisory Commission report, there has been a major shift in classification criteria away from differential diagnosis for treatment and toward security as the central issue (Wright, 1985:1–2).

According to Steele and Jacobs (1977:75), the hallmark of a prison system concerned primarily with control is the presence of prison settings that range from most secure and most distasteful to least secure and most attractive. The principal

means of control is classification of prisoners according to the risk they present and movement of prisoners through the range of settings from bad to good as a means of deterring disruptive behavior and rewarding good behavior. Desirable living conditions rather than access to rehabilitative programs is the principal resource of the system.

While there is a great deal of truth in these assertions, Steele and Jacobs oversimplify the means by which order in the prison is maintained. As we will see in the section on classification by need, defining "desirable" living conditions is not easily done. Inmates vary significantly in the kinds of living conditions they want or feel comfortable in. Thus, while the maintenance of a sequenced range of custody-graded settings is important for security classifications, it is not the whole issue.

Security Ranking of Facilities and People. In security classification systems, both inmates and facilities are graded, usually into the broad categories of maximum, medium, and minimum, although larger systems, such as the Federal Bureau of Prisons, make finer distinctions within these categories. The object of the process is to match as often as possible the security ranking of the inmate with the security ranking of the facility. However, in order to do this, the correctional system must have a mix of facilities proportionate to its mix of inmates. In the United States, this rarely occurs.

Most prison space in the United States is maximum security; minimum security space is rare. As of 1978, 51 percent of prisoners were housed in maximum security, 38 percent in medium, and 11 percent in minimum security facilities (Mullen, 1980:57). Few prison administrators would admit that this distribution is consistent with the security rating of the inmates. It is not unusual, therefore, to find minimum security inmates housed in maximum security prisons. To some extent, prison administrators try to accommodate this situation by creating more desirable subunits within an otherwise undesirable fortress-prison. However, this mismatch of resources and inmates can create all sorts of problems, both financial and, ironically, in security itself.

This mismatch contributes to a related problem, the **overclassification** of inmates, or classifying inmates as needing more secure settings than is indeed the case. The overclassification syndrome has many sources. One is the presumption of danger used in most correctional systems in the United States. That is, classifiers presume that inmates are dangerous unless they have strong evidence to the contrary. In many other countries, notably in Scandinavia, the reverse presumption guides classification: Inmates are presumed nondangerous unless there is strong evidence to the contrary. The conservative presumption and the oversupply of maximum security facilities feed each other in a vicious cycle. If classification is conservative, facility planning will also be conservative. And once the maximum security space is built, it has to be used, especially in periods of overcrowding. Feeding into that cycle is a breakdown in the security classification process. Instead of truly attempting to predict which inmates require high security, staff become cynical and automatically classify inmates on the basis of available space.

The New Security Models. Traditional security classification was typically done on the basis of hunches. Since all the classification professionals were busy with treatment-relevant classifications, the custodial staff was usually bereft of valid classification technology. While they probably relied upon offense, past escapes or attempts, and previous prison disciplinary records, no one had any means to validate these predictors, and no one had any means to control the use of totally irrelevant and discriminatory factors. In the last ten years, this situation has begun to change. The Federal Bureau of Prisons, the California Department of Correction, and the National Institute of Correction, among others, have developed statistically constructed security classification instruments.

Each model is driven primarily by current offense and past record. While some social variables are employed, Austin found that they had little effect on actual classification, since most inmates have very similar social backgrounds (1983:569). As an example of the differences between traditional committee-made classification decisions and the new models, Austin tested three new models on the records of 1,000 Nevada inmates. The quantitative systems divided the inmates into 2 to 8 percent maximum security, 35 to 40 percent medium security, and 50 percent minimum security. In comparing these results with the way the same inmates had actually been classified by the Nevada officials, Austin discovered that the committee routinely overclassified inmates to fit the large supply of medium security and low supply of minimum security space available in the Nevada system.

The development of the new models is not complete. Austin cautions that these schemes must be validated. He also points out that if the system does not have sufficient minimum security space, the models are not useful. Additionally, the statistical methods are hampered by missing data, and correctional records are notorious for missing data. Finally, if administrators override the statistically derived categories more than 10 to 20 percent of the time, the systems fail to work properly (1983:574–575).

The Problem of Validating Security Classifications. In order to turn the new quantitative guidelines into true security classifications, researchers must be able to demonstrate a valid relationship between variables used to make the inmate groupings and the likelihood that inmates will indeed cause security problems. Of major difficulty in this task is the unreliability of the indicators of security problems. One common indicator is the prison disciplinary infraction rate. Very little research has been conducted on the disciplinary process, and what exists suggests the information is incomplete and inaccurate (Poole and Regoli, 1980; Flanagan, 1982c).

A related problem is raised by Wallace (1966) in an ecological study of San Quentin. He reports that inmates in that maximum security institution were distributed primarily on the basis of security concerns into cellblocks that varied in living quality. But he argues that behavioral norms specific to each cellblock emerged over time as inmates learned what type of behavior was expected in particular zones of the prison. He observed that inmates adjusted their behavior to conform to these norms. Thus, concluded Wallace, inmate behavior was controlled by the norms of the area to which they were assigned, rather than assignment being controlled by the type of behavior exhibited by an inmate before the placement.

Wallace proposed that the classification process was a gigantic self-fulfilling prophecy rather than a true security measure. It created areas of peace and quiet, but simultaneously created areas of brutality and manipulation. The study suggests a major flaw with many security classifications: They are constructed on the assumption that the violent behavior is inherent in the inmate, when in fact the propensity for violence may be a product of the inmate adapting to the environment. This issue becomes central to the third classification type, which focuses on environmental adaptation.

CLASSIFICATION BY NEED

Some classification systems begin with the assumption that categorizing persons on the basis of preexisting knowledge misses an essential point about the way in which individuals and particular environments interact. If we are interested in how a person will behave in a specific environment, such as a prison cellblock, then we need to know not only about that person, but also about that particular cellblock. The behavior we are concerned about is the product of a transaction between that person and that particular setting. We cannot separate the classification of the person from the assignment to the setting.

In Toch's words (1977:284–285):

[T]he problem [with many classification systems] lies in the fact that what we know about job candidates, patients, and students predates their transactions with the environments to which we assign them and relates to personal traits (aptitudes, cognitive states, etc.) that may be overshadowed and neutralized by reactions to environmental presses. If we do not consider the individual's probable reactions to the attributes of an environment, we risk, *at best*, a fair amount of unhappiness or concrete problems of adjustment.

Two English researchers agree (Clarke and Martin, 1975:268):

Assessment requires measurement of the conditions which give rise to and maintain a person's behavior rather than the making of inferences about his attributes.

This approach to classification may be called a transactional approach, or an environmental approach. It can also be considered a "needs-based" classification, as long as "need" is understood as a particular interaction of the person and the setting. We could say, for example, that one person needs a prison environment that provides a great deal of structure and activity, while another person needs an environment which provides a great deal of privacy and quiet. The need is not directly evident, but we presume it is there because if there is a mismatch between the person and setting trouble arises, while if the match is right, the person is reasonably content.

A more complete account of Toch's research on the environmental concerns of inmates is given in Chapter 15; here we wish to focus on the ways in which those needs or concerns can become the basis for classification. Toch has measured the environmental concerns of inmates from a number of correctional systems using an instrument called the Personal Preference Inventory, or PPI (Toch, 1977). The PPI has eight dimensions, each measuring an inmate's desire for a particular environmental attribute. Across four prison systems, Toch found that the highest concern was for support (self-improvement programs), followed by emotional feedback and activity. Concerns for safety, social stimulation, and structure clustered as midlevel concerns, while the lowest-ranking concerns were for privacy and freedom (1977:241).

Individual preference profiles were often significantly different from these norms. An inmate's concerns varied with personal history and self-concept. For example, many blacks were more interested in environments with self-improvement programs, such as education, than were whites. Similarly, inmates with poor employment histories were more interested in such programs than inmates with good employment backgrounds (1977:250–257). Toch also found that preference profiles could vary from system to system (1977:236–237), probably because inmate demographics vary from state to state.

To use such information for classification, one must also have information about the resources to be matched to the expressed concerns or needs. Prison administrators would have to know what portions of their facilities presented what types of environmental characteristics. Toch observed that the front-line staff and inmates knew which cellblocks, programs, and jobs might provide the types of environmental presses that inmates were seeking. Since that research, Wright (1985) has been successful in constructing an instrument which measures prison environments on the same eight dimensions that appear in the PPI. Thus, while the two instruments have not been used together in actual classification, the technology is available to classify persons by need and to classify prison settings by environmental attributes and then proceed to match the two. (For more on this possibility, see Insert 14.1.)

Toch makes a distinction between two different levels of classification, although both involve matching persons and settings. (1) Routine matches involve placing normal inmates in common prison settings. The match is routine because there is a large supply of inmates with those preference profiles, and a large supply of prison settings that meet those concerns. While there may be some problems with fit, it is assumed that inmates with normal preference profiles are fairly

adaptable. Routine matching, says Toch, makes prison life "easier." (2) In contrast, special matches are the fitting of inmates with highly unusual PPI profiles into what are necessarily going to be harder to find settings. The special match, while much less frequent, in some ways may be much more important. For example, an inmate who has an overriding concern for safety may simply not be able to cope in the same environment most inmates consider sufficiently safe. Such an inmate can be consumed by fear, and fear can produce extremely damaging results, such as unpredicted aggression or attempted suicide (1977:290–292).

Two examples of groups who may benefit from special matches would be the small number of elderly inmates (Goetting, 1983) and the small number of ex-mental patients who are incarcerated in prison (Adams, 1983). Goetting proposed that the concerns of inmates over 55 years old may be sufficiently different from most inmates to require special attention. She found that only three states take special account of age in making classification decisions. Adams reported that ex-mental patients in the general population present significant difficulties. They differ from other inmates demographically, often have longer criminal records, and more frequently have records for assaultive behavior or weapons use. Within the prison, they have higher annual disciplinary infraction rates than other inmates. It is possible that such inmates are picked on by others or are treated differently by staff. In any case, it would appear that these persons may often merit the special matching described by Toch.

CLASSIFICATION PROCESS AND STRUCTURE

Classification is not a one-time event; decisions about where to place an offender and what resources he or she will have access to occur periodically during the inmate's stay. The earliest classification decisions typically rely upon information known about the inmate at reception; later

Insert 14.1 A MULTIDIMENSIONAL CLASSIFICATION STUDY

In a recent project for the National Institute of Justice, Wright (1985:129) proposed

> . . . that the value of classification information could be increased if something was known about how different groups react to different environmental settings. If we knew what types of individuals would adjust best to what types of prison conditions, placements could be made that would reduce the incidence of various behavioral problems among the population.

Wright used the Megargee MMPI classification, Toch's Personal Preference Inventory, a measure of prison settings, and a risk assessment instrument. Using these instruments separately and together, Wright attempted to predict disciplinary infractions, self-reported exploitation, incidence of self-abuse, and psychological deterioration.

He found that the risk assessment device was the best predictor of aggressive or assaultive in-fractions and frequency of sick call. The Megargee and Toch instruments were best in predicting inmate self reported adjustment problems. None of the instruments used alone was very powerful, however; none explained more than 5 to 19 percent of the variation in the outcome variables.

Wright then attempted to predict the same outcomes using all instruments at the same time. His ability to predict adjustment problems increased considerably; he could explain from 15 to 42 percent of the variation in adjustment outcomes.

This study confirms Toch's hypothesis that inmate behavior is a product of individual characteristics, organizational settings, and whether individuals are matched with congruent settings. Wright concluded that prison adjustment problems could be reduced if prison classification systems routinely used all three sources of information.

---

decisions rely more upon what the inmate has done or what others have done to him during his stay. Different correctional systems may vary considerably in the processes used to gather information and to make decisions with it. They may also vary significantly in the structure of classification: Decision-makers may be organized in different ways, and the decision-makers may have varying relationships with those who actually supervise inmates on a day-to-day basis.

INITIAL CLASSIFICATION

In most correctional departments, the process of categorizing has at least three distinct phases: initial classification, reclassification, and prerelease classification. **Initial classification** normally takes place in a **reception center,** a separate prison unit devoted to orientation and testing. The typical reception center process takes from 60 to 90 days to complete, although computerization and greater reliance on objective tests and questionnaires rather than interviews and observation may reduce this time period.

Initial classification concentrates on receiving, sorting, and reviewing previous records about the new inmate and often relies heavily on presentence investigations and police records. Staff must convert these other agency records into a form usable by the correctional agency. Additionally, staff must collect directly from the inmate information thought useful but not provided by the referring jurisdiction. Increasingly important parts of the initial classification process today are medical and mental health screening and assessment activities, as there are constitutional rights to health care.

Many experts agree that the typical reception process provides many threats to reliable and valid information. Particularly for first-time in-

An inmate is fingerprinted at the Downstate reception and classification center. (New York State Department of Correctional Services)

mates, the initial weeks of incarceration are probably the most traumatic. During this period the new inmate is often frightened, resentful, suspicious, and overwhelmed by rumors and expectations of what lies ahead. One would have difficulty inventing a less productive setting in which to question a person about his feelings, problems, and goals, or to make assessments about how he interacts with other inmates and staff, or to administer sensitive, complex psychological tests. Yet this is generally what happens.

Different systems vary in the degree to which they involve the inmate in initial classification information-gathering and decision-making.

Criminal justice information is poor enough that staff often have to rely upon the inmate for self-reports about drug and alcohol use, for example. Some systems rely upon the collection of short-answer and checklist information, while others place greater reliance on extended interviews. In some systems, inmates are told what will happen to them by a committee that makes decisions unilaterally. In other systems, the inmate is given an opportunity to express personal preferences about job assignments and program enrollment. Most systems attempt to provide some orientation to the prison experience, describing the types of resources available and the behavior expected of inmates. Very often, however, this orientation is cursory, amounting to little more than providing a rule book.

In some jurisdictions, the law allows the correctional authority to receive an unsentenced inmate for presentence assessment. In such cases, the reception center performs at least part of the task often assigned to probation officers. This infrequent option is used when the reception center has access to specialized diagnostic and testing procedures the judge believes are necessary in a special case.

RECLASSIFICATION

In most systems, the outcome of initial classification is the assignment of a security grade and placement in an institution, often maximum security, with recommendations about program participation. It will include notice of any special medical or mental health conditions, if they have been picked up. When the inmate is received at the institution, classification resumes. Actual assignment to sleeping quarters, job, and programs occur at the institution. Many reception center recommendations are overridden, often on the basis of local security considerations, and perhaps more often simply on the basis of available space.

Reclassification is not a one-time event, and is more interactive than initial classification. In the worst systems, inmates learn to manipulate assignment by causing the right kind of trouble. In a system insensitive to inmate concerns, for example, inmates who cannot cope with their living assignment may simply break rules repeatedly until they are moved. This is a destructive and inefficient means of matching needs to resources, but in many systems it is the only way in which inmates can influence the classification process. In systems where inmate concerns are more actively sought and considered, inmates may express preferences with positive results.

The reclassification process continues throughout an inmate's stay in the correctional system, but systems vary in (1) the formality with which reclassification takes place and (2) the frequency with which it takes place. In many systems, reassessments and reassignments take place only at times of trouble. Reclassification is initiated by the disciplinary process. In other systems, formal reclassification hearings occur on a regularly scheduled basis throughout the inmate's imprisonment. Reclassification may include changes in living quarters, changes in job, changes in program, or changes in institutions.

PRERELEASE CLASSIFICATION

The last classification phase is really only the continuation of the reclassification process, but it holds significant benefits for inmates in some departments and therefore receives special attention. **Prerelease classification** usually occurs within one year to three months of the expected release date. The most common form of release is parole, and a major portion of prerelease classification is the preparation of an inmate's file for consideration by the parole board. In addition, many states now have formal prerelease programs to which all or some inmates are assigned in preparation for parole or other release.

Some of these programs occur in an institution and require no special security clearance. However, most states now have a small number of openings that take the inmate out of the institution for part of the day, such as school release or work release, or altogether, such as prerelease

centers. Entrance to these programs is often authorized by special legislation that requires a formal reclassification process and the use of information not previously gathered. Since these programs reduce security, they are often prized by inmates. For the same reason, they are often politically controversial. For both reasons, prerelease classification may often receive greater attention than other classification decisions.

THE STRUCTURE OF CLASSIFICATION

Classification is an organizational behavior involving information processing and judgment. Its quality is often affected by the **classification structure** used to manage the process. Classification involves some degree of specialization of labor and more or less centralization of decision-making.

The typical division of labor in classification separates information feeders, information processors, and decision-makers. In both the initial and reclassification decisions, for example, many systems ask a selected officer, such as a cellblock officer, to report observations about an inmate's behavior. Other information feeders include persons administering and scoring tests, conducting interviews, or running programs in which the inmate has participated. Typically other persons, often called counselors, collate and distill the information in a manner desired by the decision-makers. The information processors are responsible for integrating and summarizing information from a variety of sources, but they inevitably interpret as well and may also be called upon for a recommendation. Finally, decision-makers usually rely on the completed file, although they may also interview the inmate briefly.

This specialized work structure has some advantages. The decision-makers generally possess more information about the inmate than anyone else, have a broad overview of available resources, familiarity with relevant laws and regulations, and a good deal of practice in making decisions. The disadvantages of this specialized structure are related. The quality of the information can break down at any number of points, and the decision-makers can end up with large doses of superficial information. This structure also routinizes decisions, often with bad results. Typical mistakes of this bureaucratic structure would include (Toch, 1981a:6).

- Labeling both aggressors and victims as high-risk offenders (because they both cause trouble)
- Isolating suicidal inmates (and thereby increasing depression)
- Placing inmates who hate school in educational programs (where they disrupt the program for any inmates who truly want to learn)
- Lumping inmates together on the basis of one or two superficial characteristics, with disregard for important differences.

Another structural dimension is the relationship between the classifiers and the front-line staff. The classifiers in many institutions are too distant from the results of their work. Feedback on the effects of the placement do not occur until the next regularly scheduled classification hearing. The centralization of classification in the hands of an elite committee often results in unilateral decisions.

One research project that focused on the structural relationships between prerelease classifiers and prerelease program staff found that the separation of the two groups was associated with differences in goals and philosophies, differences in the value placed on various types of information, and as a consequence of these, breakdowns in the transfer of inmates (Duffee, Briggs and Barnette, 1986). Toch points out that the structure must include means for decision-makers to get feedback quickly from inmates and front-line workers in order to improve decision-making and make it more realistic (1981a:7).

One alternative to this specialized, centralized structure is to push the decision-making down the hierarchy to those who have the information in the first place. This change entails recoupling of observation/reporting/processing and judgment tasks. It typically involves decisions by a team of persons closest to the inmate in question, and may involve the inmate working with the team. The advantages include higher-quality information and more considered, less routinized decisions. The disadvantages are again related. If more front-line people are involved in decision-making, administration must modify working assignments to get the group together. The group also needs to have access to experts or consultants who can help to interpret specialized information, such as aptitude tests. Finally, such a group can probably handle many fewer cases and decisions than the specialized committee; the structure is less efficient in the short run.

THE EFFECTS OF OVERCROWDING

As prisons have become overcrowded, many administrators admit that the classification process has broken down. When resources are stretched thin, there is less possibility of matching inmates and resources. Sheer numbers overwhelm the classification committee, information becomes less accurate, and decisions become more haphazard (Clements, 1982). An overtaxed classification system often becomes more conservative in its decisions, placing increasing proportions of inmates in maximum security first because there is typically more room there than elsewhere, and second because this placement presumably makes mistakes "safe." Overclassification and lack of programs, however, mean that inmates will not have the opportunity to earn their way out of maximum security. The movement of inmates grinds to a halt, and people remain in maximum security until release (1982:74–75).

Overcrowding is particularly harmful to prisoners who need "special" matches, since there are few programs available for special needs in the first place. In an overcrowded system, program staff in minimum security and prerelease facilities can raise the standards for admission to low-security placements. Since there are so many more inmates to choose from, why not have the best? This skimming phenomenon is common in any system that has more candidates than slots (1982:76–79).

While some administrators presume that such problems are inevitable in overcrowded conditions, Clements correctly points out that current classification practice is overly susceptible to these breakdowns and contributes to overcrowding in the first place. The solution is not to wait for overcrowding to go away, but to ease overcrowding by taking some of the kinks out of the process and some of the conflicts out of the structure.

PRISON PROGRAMS

Prison programs have diverse objectives. Some are ostensibly for the inmates' benefit. Some benefits are here-and-now, such as having a good time or earning some spending money. Some offer future benefits, such as a steady job. Some programs are clearly conducted to benefit the institution or the state, rather than the inmate. Usually programs have mixed objectives. Programs may keep inmates occupied and thereby reduce security problems. Programs may aid inmates financially, and perhaps increase their sense of self worth, and also produce profits for the state.

In the following sections, we review briefly some of the major types of prison programs: treatment programs, work programs, education programs, and inmate-run programs. Programs associated with release, such as prerelease and work release, are described in Chapter 17. There are other types, and there are too many variations within the types described, for us to be able to provide the full range here.

Programs represent some important resources which classifiers attempt to match to inmates. Most prison money, however, does not go into the programs described below, but into the boarding, feeding, and guarding of inmates. McDonald (1980), for example, points out that in fiscal year 1978, New York spent 10 percent of its correctional budget on programs and 87 percent on custody. In many states, the proportion given to custody is higher.

TREATMENT PROGRAMS

Treatment programs are designed for planned individual change. Sometimes the change is desired by the inmate, sometimes others desire it for him or her. Some treatment programs focus on feelings, attitudes, or psychological states. Others focus on interactions with other people. Some programs at least claim an interest in future behavior—they are advertised as attempts to alter how the inmate will be when released. Other programs have a much narrower focus—they help an inmate cope with one more day of confinement.

Both militant prisoner groups and reformers opposed to rehabilitation as a correctional goal have continued to support treatment programs (Stastny and Tyrnauer, 1982:209–210). Critics have argued that involuntary treatment is ineffective and vulnerable to corruption and abuse. But the same critics have observed that many treatment programs, while not clearly productive of changes in inmate behavior, were effective security measures. Programs provided variety, activity, social stimulation, and interest, whether or not they contributed to enduring change. The result was less idleness, disruption, and violence (Irwin, 1977).

When reformers called for "benign warehousing" (incarceration without deterioration of the persons being punished), a full supply of prison programs became a significant ingredient in keeping the warehouse benign. Programs which offer constructive use of time and perhaps some promise of self-improvement provide members of the prison community with some sense of meaning in daily routine. Maintaining that sense can be crucial to the well-being of both inmates and staff (Halleck and Witte, 1980). The negative evaluations of prison treatment programs, such as that of Lipton, Martinson, and Wilks (1975), do not focus on the immediate benefits of prison programs to inmates, but on the lack of impact on recidivism.

Toch (1981b) argues that recent attacks on

Some prison therapies include special housing units for program participants. Group therapy residents in the prison for women, Holloway, London, reside in a special wing of the prison. (Topham/ The Image Works)

prison treatment were often armed with an outmoded definition of treatment in the first place. The rehabilitative promises to which reformers objected most strenuously were the specialist-controlled, therapeutic endeavors of the medical model. Such rehabilitative technologies may be effective with certain persons, including some prisoners, under certain conditions. But most inmates do not suffer from the maladies with which therapy professionals usually deal. Nor do most prison systems have sufficient access to therapy specialists. The kind of individual change more likely to occur in prison, if it occurs at all, is not associated with a special program, but instead grows out of day-to-day interactions among inmates and between inmates and front-line staff:

The manifest content of desirable change for offenders has to do with their law-abiding citizenship, constructive interpersonal dealings and acquired work habits. Such content is communicable through a wide range of experiences, provided these include partnership in work, benevolent conflict resolutions, demonstrations of personal and work-related competence, and a model who is visibly content with a non-criminal lifestyle. (Toch, 1981b:332–333)

This type of positive personal change is more likely to occur as a by-product of relationships between an inmate and an understanding guard or a patient work supervisor than in the course of a therapy session. Prison administrators cannot make such change occur, but they can provide an environment in which opportunities for it arise. An environment conducive to such change includes (1981:330):

- The presence of some relevant work
- A peer group which legitimizes linkages between staff and inmates
- Insulation of staff and inmates from the more negative pressures of the larger prison
- The emergence within this staff-inmate work group of spontaneous, supportive interpersonal relationships

One place where these conditions emerge are in prison programs that have other objectives. Some of these programs, such as educational and vocational training, may hold out the possibility of individual self-betterment, but almost none of them aim directly at therapy.

Counseling in Prison. Prisons have long employed a cadre of staff called counselors or case-workers. While the first counselors were probably prison chaplains (see Smith, forthcoming, for an example), the infusion of psychological social work into corrections promoted the image of counselors as professional treaters operating under the medical model. Most prison systems could never attract many professionally trained caseworkers.

Through the demise of the medical model in 1974, the typical correctional counselor was still a preprofessional with a bachelors degree, often in a field irrelevant to therapy, who came to corrections as a switch in careers (Shover, 1974). Moreover, the most important duties of the correctional counselor were usually those of classification, not delivery of treatment services (1974:351). While some counselors have the time to run a group therapy session on the side, or to see a few inmates on an individual basis, most counselor-inmate contacts involve reclassification and permission-granting issues. These activities are extremely important, but they are managerial rather than therapeutic functions.

Glaser's landmark study of the Federal Bureau of Prisons (1964) included a question to previous prisoners about the prison staff who had had the most positive impact on their behavior. Many of the ex-prisoners mentioned shop supervisors, some mentioned guards and chaplains, but almost none mentioned counselors. These reports are consistent with Toch's position that treatment, in the sense of positive human relationships, is more often found in the midst of daily routine than in specialized relationships devoted to therapy.

Toch argues that the administrative roles of professional treaters should be recognized and cultivated. Professional treatment staff may help most when they are in position to generate positive relationships among inmates and other staff (1981b:338). Among the staff who are frequently in a better position to engage in change-inducing relationships are prison guards and prison chaplains. Correctional officers can be crucial because they can alter a prisoner's immediate environment and can often broker services. Moreover, a caring

and sympathetic officer can disconfirm an inmate's expectations that all authority figures are arbitrary and cruel (Toch, 1981b:335–336). Many correctional officers actively seek such a role (for more detail on the prison guard, see Chapter 16).

Prison chaplains can often play a strong role in treatment because they are confidential and neutral. Chaplains have rarely been studied systematically, but Toch (1981b:333–334) suspects they may be particularly helpful to inmates who feel lonely, abandoned by family and friends, or stifled by conflict. Additionally, chaplains, like prison guards, are often in a position to leverage for resources when they are especially needed. Not to be overlooked for their treatment potential are other inmates. Toch observed that older inmates, with the aid of a skilled staff consultant, could be effective in breaking down norms of toughness and helping a younger inmate explore reasons for unproductive behavior (Toch, 1981b:337).

Therapeutic Communities. (T-Cs) in prison are residential treatment units in which the individual change is promoted through communal processes, including norm-building, inmate participation in decisions, and group responsibility for member behavior. T-Cs may be used with alcoholics or drug abusers, or with inmates who share certain psychological problems. In such cases, the T-C is targeted at problems that predate the prison experience. The T-C can also be aimed at the problems of coping with prison life itself (Toch, 1980).

The T-C process is complex. The organizers must focus first on creating a viable group life for the inmate residents. This includes finding activities that make the daily routine significant. In some T-Cs, all inmate activity is contained in the unit. In others, T-C residents may participate in some general prison activities, such as education or work programs. The totally enclosed version provides more intense interaction. The open version permits a greater range of activities, but may dilute the power of the group process.

T-C organizers stress the development of

group identity and membership. This group commitment is then used to challenge inappropriate and antisocial behavior by group members. Group members must share in decision-making and take responsibility for the well-being of the group and the future of the program. These requirements must be balanced with the need to maintain a relationship with the larger prison. The sensitive staff roles in T-Cs necessitate continuous assignment to the program. If prison administrators are not committed to maintaining group cohesion, they can easily rip apart a project by changing staff or assigning unsympathetic custody staff (Studt, Messinger, and Wilson, 1968).

T-Cs can have powerful effects on residents, just like any other community. However, there is no reason to expect the changes occurring in the T-C to carry over once the inmate leaves. When the objective is humane survival in prison for residents who cannot cope with general population, carryover may not matter. But if the objective is permanent change, then the treaters must make provision for bridging the T-C support system to the subsequent placement of its residents (Fairweather et al., 1969). In most correctional systems, this rarely happens.

Drug and Alcohol Programs. Histories of substance abuse are frequent among prisoners. Tables 14.1 and 14.2 provide the results of self-reported drug and alcohol use among a randomized national sample of state prisoners. Considering the frequency of these problems among inmates, there is surprisingly little systematic treatment available. Clements' (1986) national survey of correctional classification practice indicates that most states do a poor job of identifying inmates with alcohol or drug abuse histories. Without any systematic means of identification, it is difficult for a correctional department to muster an effective argument for treatment services.

Probably the most widespread treatment for alcoholism is Alcoholics Anonymous. Many prisons have chapters of AA meeting regularly on the prison grounds. AA programs in prison typically include members from the community who help inmates run this self-help program. In recent years, administrative and custodial concern about inmate-run programs has apparently included some inconvenience or even harrassment of visiting AA volunteers (Fox, 1982).

A number of the larger prison systems often

TABLE 14.1 Drug Use Habits among State Inmates

CHARACTERISTIC	NUMBER	EVER USED	RECENT USE
Total	274,564	78%	56%
Sex:			
Male	263,484	78	56
Female	11,080	67	47
Age at admission:			
Under 18	6,412	82	66
18 to 25	139,251	87	67
26 to 34	81,533	79	53
35 and older	46,501	46	25
Race:			
White	136,296	78	57
Black	131,329	77	54
American Indian	5,440	75	50
Other	1,499	75	50

SOURCE: Adapted from Edmund F. McGarrell and Timothy J. Flanagan (eds.), *Sourcebook of Criminal Justice Statistics—1984.* Washington, DC: United States Department of Justice, Bureau of Justice Statistics, 1985, p. 658. The data are based on the 1979 Survey of Inmates in State Correctional Facilities. The survey consisted of personal interviews with a stratified random sample of 12,000 inmates.

TABLE 14.2   Drinking Habits of State Prison Inmates Just Prior to Current Offense

CHARACTERISTIC	NUMBER	LIGHT TO HEAVY	VERY HEAVY
Total	129,444	38%	62%
Hours spent drinking			
Less than 1	12,150	92	8
1 to 2	32,192	62	38
3 to 4	25,547	34	66
5 to 8	29,550	19	81
9 or more	27,330	11	89
Not available	2,675	52	48
Drinking setting			
Home	37,310	31	69
Friend's home	35,875	31	69
Bar	51,207	32	68
Car	36,889	28	72
Restaurant	2,566	32	68
Street	21,113	30	70
Workplace	0	0	0
Elsewhere	29	0	100
Current offense			
Violent	78,905	40	60
Property	39,774	32	68
Drugs	5,244	54	46
Public order	5,150	45	55

SOURCE: Adapted from Edmund F. McGarrell and Timothy J. Flanagan (eds.), *Sourcebook of Criminal Justice Statistics—1984.* Washington, DC: United States Department of Justice, 1985, p. 659. The data are based on the 1979 Survey of Inmates in State Correctional Facilities. The survey consisted of personal interviews with a stratified random sample of 12,000 inmates.

boast several different types of drug abuse programs, including T-Cs. However, far fewer such programs are available than there are inmates who need such services, and the programs are often dependent upon the presence of a staff member who just happens to have the interest and time to run a program.

A national survey of drug programs in local jails (Newman et al., 1976) found that many jails, particularly in urban centers, can provide drug counseling and other drug treatment through arrangement with local health organizations. Unfortunately, these interorganizational arrangements for state and federal prisons are probably less often available because of their more often rural location.

One difficulty with substance abuse programs in prison is that most inmates do not face the immediate problems of addiction or temptation while incarcerated. Contraband alcohol and drugs may be available (Kalinich, 1980), but not to the same extent as will be true when offenders are released. Prison treatments may have limited impact on behavior of released prisoners.

Programs for the Mentally Disabled. Within the last several years, increasing attention has been focused on the incidence of mental illness and mental retardation among jail and prison inmates, and upon appropriate screening and services. Some of this attention would appear to be fallout from deinstitutionalization of the mentally ill and mentally retarded. Critics of deinstitutionalization in those fields have complained that patients have been set loose on the streets without proper care and support and as a consequence, have ended up in trouble with the law. Correctional administrators have jumped on this bandwagon, claiming that perceived increases in jail and prison disturbances are due to increasing numbers of mentally ill, if not mentally retarded, inmates. The best current research indicates that there has been some increase in ex-mental patients in local jails (McCarty, 1984), but not in prison systems (Steadman et al., 1984).

Another reason for the increased attention is that mental illness has been included in court decisions about rights to health care. Consequently, many prison systems have rushed to improve mental health screening, diagnosis, and treatment services.

The new mental health services can be easily confused with traditional correctional rehabilitation, since very often the same professionals are involved, and often the programs may appear similar. Adams (1984:4–5) distinguishes the two on the basis of goals and service population:

. . . a distinction has been made between therapeutic services intended to achieve specific penological goals—the treatment of offenders so that they might become law-abiding citizens—and therapeutic services intended to achieve more general health care goals—the treatment of mentally disordered individuals so that they might function more effectively in social settings.

A national survey conducted of all correctional departments in 1983 sought a rough estimate of the number of mentally ill and retarded inmates identified in each system. The definitions used to make the identification, and the procedures used to screen inmates, varied considerably. Responses indicated that about 6 percent of the total inmate population was classified as mentally ill, and 2.5 percent as retarded (McCarthy, 1985). Most correctional departments did not receive persons who were labeled incompetent to stand trial, insane, guilty but mentally ill, or abnormal offenders; most such persons were diverted to mental health systems (McCarthy, 1985). Correctional departments do receive some

inmates who have previous histories of institutionalization for mental illness (Adams, 1985), and other inmates may develop conditions produced by the stress of confinement (Toch, 1977, Adams, 1984).

According to the 1983 survey, relatively complete screening and diagnostic procedures *at reception* existed in 33 states for mental illness and in 38 states for mental retardation. However, identification procedures for mental illness occurring later in an inmate's sentence appeared much less systematic. Many states indicated the importance of alert and concerned custodial staff to make such identifications (McCarthy, 1985). Program services have lagged behind identification procedures, particularly for the mentally retarded. Many systems responded that special programs for the retarded were not necessary. The majority of inmates with identified mental illness were reportedly in some form of treatment: About 25 percent were being seen by psychiatrists (see Insert 14.2). About 70 percent of the inmates with identified problems were housed in special prison units for the mentally disabled, although only about 20 percent were receiving in-patient rather than out-patient care (McCarthy, 1985).

The Unit Management Plan. One of the more ambitious treatment-related activities undertaken in corrections in recent years is the unit management plan of the Federal Bureau of Corrections. Unit management is more accurately defined as a total prison management plan than as a treatment program. However, the plan has implications for treatment, in the broad sense of providing opportunity for productive interactions among prison participants. Unit management rests on assumptions that small is easier and homogeneous is better.

The Federal Bureau has drawn the conclusion that large prisons are impossible to manage humanely. As a result, 26 of the 31 federal prisons have been internally subdivided to form small communities of no more than 100 inmates. These prisons receive high ratings from inmates and have lower disturbance rates than prisons which

Insert 14.2 A COMMUNITY MENTAL HEALTH CARE MODEL IN THE PRISON

One of the more sophisticated mental health care delivery systems for inmates was recently instituted in New York. By a new agreement between the Department of Mental Hygiene (DMH) and the Department of Correctional Services (DOCS), small mental health centers, staffed and run by DMH, are now located in all the major prisons of the state. The relationship between the mental health centers and the prisons is similar to the community mental health center model found in many communities in the United States. The mental health centers in DOCS facilities treat prisoners just as a center in the community would treat free patients. The units treat inmates when they request services, or upon referral by staff. The same laws that apply to involuntary mental health commitments in the community apply in the prison setting. The philosophy of this new system is that many inmates can cope with the stresses of imprisonment, if outpatient mental health services are available.

Research on the operation of these units in two prisons (Adams, 1984) indicated considerable promise for this new form of cooperation between two large state agencies. However, Adams discovered that the speed and effectiveness of the referral process depended on the structure of the prison, the work norms of the prison guards, and the specific resources available in the mental health units.

When correctional officers saw themselves as either professional human service workers or as prison troubleshooters, they became personally involved with inmates. Under these conditions, referrals to the mental health centers were quicker, more frequent, and often more accurate. When guards saw themselves as rule enforcers, they were often more distant from inmates. Under these conditions, referrals were slower, less frequent, and often less accurate. When guards were committed only to rules rather than to solving problems, they often turned to the prison disciplinary process instead of mental health referrals.

are not subdivided (Toch, 1981a). The unit plan overcomes a number of impediments to treatment in prison. Since every inmate in such prisons is grouped with similar inmates, the classification of inmates with special needs loses much of its stigma. The homogeneity produced within the small units provides better opportunity for meaningful interaction among inmates and staff, and special programs can be run within units without as much disruption as occurs in the undivided prison. Unit management, then, is a significant step in the organization of resources so that inmates and resources can be better matched.

WORK IN PRISON

Work and punishment have been intertwined for a long time. Toil in meaningless, endless work has long been a means of exacting retribution. When the United States outlawed slavery, enforced labor for convicts was excepted.

Work itself has had an ambivalent image through history. As the perception of work in the broader culture has changed, the association of work and punishment has also changed. The Protestant Reformation altered the image of work in Western culture. When Quakers in Philadelphia brought the Protestant work ethic to prison reform, they designed work programs to be restorative rather than retributive (Schaller, 1982). In the congregate plan, work was used to maintain security and order in the institution, and thereby reduce the chances that prisoners would corrupt each other. The early reformers hoped that the habit of industry, if retained upon release, would keep ex-prisoners from returning to crime.

Prison reformers were also willing to keep an

Work has always been part of prison. When slavery was declared unconstitutional, prisoners were excepted. Blacks, recently emancipated, were rapidly convicted and put to work for the state or private industry. (North Wind Picture Archive)

eye on the purse. One means of selling the penitentiary to new, poorly endowed state governments was promising that prisons could be self-supporting (Schaller, 1982:3; Conley, 1981).

Thus work by prisoners has been associated with at least four separate and, at times, incompatible goals:

1. Work has been used as a device to promote suffering and achieve retribution
2. Work has been used as a vehicle of rehabilitation
3. Work has been promoted to achieve order and security
4. Work by inmates has been a source of state income and a means of maintaining the institutions.

With increasing frequency, work in prison has also been viewed as a means of preparing prisoners for release (Lenihan, 1974).

Current work programs fall into at least four different types: prison industries, maintenance work, vocational training, and work release (which will be discussed in Chapter 17). All but

the maintenance work generally promises the inmate some postrelease utility, such as additional training or experience that might enhance a résumé. Inmates often have poor employment histories and few job skills (see Table 14.3). With those deficiencies, many inmates have a high demand for work and training programs (Toch, 1977).

PRISON INDUSTRIES

Prison industries are generally set up as separate corporations operating within the prison grounds. Industries almost always have more than one goal, but almost always include a profit motive. Industries are distinguishable from other types of prison work in several ways. Industry programs employ prisoners to make a product or provide a service marketed outside the prison itself. Selection of prisoners is based at least partially on skills or potential, and inmates are often rewarded, at least modestly, for their productivity.

In the United States, prison industry emerged from the Auburn model of the penitentiary (see

TABLE 14.3 Employment and Income of State Prisoners

Employment in month prior to current offense:	Number	Percent
Total	273,463	100.0
Employed full time	165,577	60.5
Employed part time	27,223	10.0
Not employed, seeking job	38,230	14.0
Not employed, not looking	42,433	15.5
Income in year prior to current offense:		
Total	128,011	100.0
None	2,218	1.9
Less than $3,000	35,503	27.7
$3,000 to 9,999	48,511	37.8
$10,000 and over	41,779	32.6

SOURCE: Adapted from Edmund F. McGarrell and Timothy J. Flanagan (eds.), *Sourcebook of Criminal Justice Statistics—1984.* Washington, DC: United States Department of Justice, 1985, p. 658. Survey questions on income were asked only to inmates admitted to prison after November 1977, in order to control for inflation.

Chapter 11). The earliest industries were run by private contractors who rented prison space, paid the state for a certain number of prisoners, furnished the raw material and equipment, and provided the training and supervision. This contract system was later modified after complaints about corruption. The prison administration became directly involved in production and sold the finished product to a private company which did the marketing (Schaller, 1982).

Both forms of prison industry came under wide attack by 1890. Competing companies claimed the prison contractors had an unfair advantage. Unionized labor complained about competition with prison labor. These attacks resulted in widespread restrictive legislation beginning in the early 1900s. These laws, often called state-use law, prohibited the sale of prisoner-made goods on the open market in many states. Some states, such as Texas, have never been restricted from within-state sale. However, federal legislation prohibited the transporting of prison-made goods across state lines.

These restrictions had a severe impact on prison industry. There was (1) lack of competition for prison-made products, which led to (2) reduction in economic incentives for quality and innovation, (3) deterioration of equipment, (4) outmoded management practices. Many prison industries turned from profit to vocational training as a rationale (Schaller, 1982). However, the same forces that reduced the business potential of prison industries also limited their training potential. No longer competitive, prison industry lost the capacity to train inmates in either the work skills or work habits associated with private enterprise (Weintraub, 1979).

In the 1970s, a confluence of factors sparked the reemergence of prison industries. Labor unions lost political clout. Efficiency in government became a buzzword. The inmate rights movement had some success in attacking restrictions on the employment of ex-convicts and inmates. Rehabilitation lost salience, while security and order became more important. Prison industries became valued as a security measure, as a means of providing inmates with gate money at release, and as a means of reducing the cost of incarceration (Schaller, 1982).

Part of the resurgence of prison industry was due to the free venture model. Instituted in the 1970s with aid from the U.S. Department of Labor, free venture programs provided inmates with a realistic work environment, including market wages, and placed successful inmate workers in exit jobs. From their salaries, inmates reimbursed the state for room and board and paid restitution to their victims. The programs demonstrated that the state could successfully employ business concepts within the prison (Schaller, 1982).

From this experience, it has been a short step to reinvolvement of private enterprise. Corrections has come full circle to private employers in prison industry. Privately run prison industry may have several advantages. It may be more efficient and effective than government-run business. Inmates may receive better wages and higher-quality instruction and so face better chances of reintegration (Schaller, 1982). In addition, in both

The machine shop at Attica is one of a number of prison industries in New York State. (New York State Department of Correctional Services)

the United States and Canada, many federal job training and employment programs include inmates as "special needs clients."

Private employers can take advantage of these programs, while the state department of correction cannot (Lightman, 1982). By 1982, over twenty states had passed new laws to permit private business to establish factories in prisons and to employ prisoners (Schaller, 1982:8). Similar change has occurred in Canada. Table 14.4 summarizes the kinds of prison industry in selected states, indicates the range of inmate wages, and whether the goods are sold to other than state agencies.

MAINTENANCE PROGRAMS

All prisons require a number of maintenance chores and services, and many of these are filled by inmates rather than paid staff. The assignments are made and supervised directly by the prison administration rather than by a separate prison industries staff. Many carry no compensation, and those that do usually carry a lower rate than available in prison industry.

Many of the jobs found in a small town are found within the prison community. While professional, skilled, and sensitive positions are usually filled by paid employees, most of these staff are assisted by one or more prisoners. Inmates perform clerical duties, building maintenance and repair tasks, janitorial work, kitchen duties, laundering, and even fire department and medical emergency services.

Within the complex inmate social system, the various prison assignments can take on special significance, either for their prestige or for the access they may provide to information or special resources. Inmate clerks may obtain information about administrative decisions and inmate movement. Kitchen hands, commissary clerks, and stockroom hands have access to goods recirculated as contraband. Firemen and farmhands may have the equipment to distill alcohol.

TABLE 14.4   Characteristics of Prison Industries In Eight Sample Jurisdictions, 1982

SYSTEM	TYPE OF PRODUCTS	SALE OUTSIDE INSTITUTIONS	INMATE PAY
Alabama	Auto tags, metal fabrication, printing, office furniture, construction, remodeling, frozen foods and canning, meat preparation, data processing, garment factory, catfish	Yes	$.10 to .25/hr
California	About 24 industries in 10 prisons, plus 3 dairies, 3 farms, 1 orchard. Products include wood and metal furniture, clothing	Yes	Average $.40/hr
Florida	Livestock, produce, food processing, plants, clothing, metal, wood, bricks, bookbinding, vehicle renovation, tire recapping, insecticides	Yes	No
Louisiana	Auto tags, mattresses, mops and brooms, pillows, signs, dentures and bridgework, clothing, soap, cleaners, meat processing	No	$.02 to .20/hr.
Maine	Print shop, upholstery shop, furniture refinishing, woodworking	Yes	Profit sharing
New Jersey	Auto tags, brushes/mops, beds and bedding, mattresses, sheet metal products, shelving, soap, janitorial supplies, clothing, signs, furniture, textiles	No	$.22 to .52/hr. + bonus
Texas	Soap and detergent, tire recapping, garments, signs, mops and brooms, dump truck beds, textiles, bus repair, dental lab, shoes, woodworking, boxes, auto tags, mattresses, validation stickers, records conversion, metal fabrication, furniture refinishing	Yes	No
Federal Bureau of Prisons	Data entry and computer programming, printing, signs, drafting, electronics, metal furniture, hardware, shelving, shoes and brushes, textiles, woods, plastics	Yes to other federal agencies	$.40– $1/hr.

SOURCE: Adapted from data supplied by Contact, Inc. *Corrections Compendium.* Lincoln, NE: Contact, Inc., 1982, as reported in Edmund F. McGarrell and Timothy J. Flanagan (eds.), *Sourcebook of Criminal Justice Statistics—1984.* Washington, DC: United States Department of Justice, 1985, pp. 114–117.

Work positions are also valued not for instrumental or symbolic gain, but because they provide ancillary benefits with special meaning to particular inmates. Assignment to the library, for example, can remove an inmate from the pressures of noise, competition, and danger. Assignment to a work supervisor with the right personality might be essential to an inmate who acts out around anyone else. Seymour (1980) calls these matches between inmate needs and environmental characteristics **niches.** They may be essential to survival in the prison, but their value is generally not recognized in the formal classification process. Inmates stumble upon them accidentally and often use great imagination to wrangle the assignment that works for them.

Inmate maintenance work is controversial in several ways. Reliance on inmate labor for essential prison jobs cuts down the cost of operations. Many southern prisons traditionally relied on inmates even to guard other inmates, a highly questionable practice that has been declared unconstitutional in many jurisdictions. The savings must be considered against safety, security, and humaneness. Even cost savings may be more apparent than real. Since many inmates see no personal reward in doing the job well, some states have contracted out work previously done by inmates. Since many maintenance positions require little skill and training, it is questionable whether they provide any lasting benefit to the inmate. Some states find this issue irrelevant, others make tortured justifications that changing lightbulbs provides a skill or mopping halls improves work habits.

On the other hand, there are few feasible alternatives to inmate maintenance jobs, and few inmates would prefer idleness. The most sensible approach would be to maximize the legitimate potential of maintenance work and reduce the chances for misuse and corruption.

PUBLIC WORKS

Midway between prison maintenance and prison industry lies the practice of assigning inmate work crews to public works projects, particularly to road maintenance. Table 14.5 lists states with inmate road crews. Inmate work crews have also been used for cleaning vacant lots and constructing public buildings. The practice came into vogue about the same time that prison industries were being severely restricted. It has been attacked as exploitation of inmates and as reduction in opportunity for free labor. At times, however, it has taken innovative twists. One warden received tuition waivers for inmate students in a local community college in exchange for a town cleanup. He also provided volunteer inmate consultants to local retailers seeking advice to reduce shoplifting.

VOCATIONAL TRAINING

While some training occurs in prison industry, many prison systems have a separate category of training and work experiences classified as **vocational training.** In contrast to general education, vocational training usually aims at providing an inmate with a specific marketable skill, such as data entry, refrigeration repair, and small engine repair.

TABLE 14.5   Inmate Road Crews within State Correctional Systems, 1984

STATE	NUMBER OF INMATES	INMATE PAY
Alabama	700	No
Arizona	20	No
Arkansas	80	No
California	100	Yes: to $3.76/day
Delaware	10	Yes: nominal
Florida	643	No
Georgia	500	No
Hawaii	30	Yes: $.30/hr.
Illinois	50	Yes: to $75/mo
Indiana	135	Yes: $.90/day
Kentucky	40	Yes: $1/day
Louisiana	124	Yes: to $.20/day
Maryland	220	Yes: $2.20/day
Mississippi	308	No
New Hampshire	6	Yes: $2.50/day
New Jersey	12	Yes: $1.55/day
New Mexico	20	Yes: $.35/hr.
North Carolina	2,000	Yes: $.70/day
Oklahoma	50	Yes: to $37.50/mo.
Oregon	15	Yes: to $3.00/day
Rhode Island	80	Yes: to $2.00/day
South Carolina	650	Yes: nominal
Tennessee	1,125	Yes
Utah	80	Yes: nominal
Vermont	60	Yes: $.40/hr.
Virginia	1,000	Yes: below $1/day

SOURCE: Data adapted from report by Contact, Inc., *Corrections Compendium.* Lincoln, NE: Contact Inc., February, 1984, as reported in Edmund F. McGarrell and Timothy J. Flanagan (eds.), *Sourcebook of Criminal Justice Statistics—1984.* Washington, DC: United States Department of Justice, 1985, p. 661.

In many states, vocational training programs are hamstrung by inferior, outmoded equipment, poor instruction, and legal restrictions on the types of jobs ex-inmates can apply for upon release. Often the vocational training curriculum has developed by accident, without regard for trends in the labor market. There is also evidence that vocational training in prison is hampered by poor classification procedures. Training placements are often not matched to measurements of inmate aptitude (Essler et al., 1976).

Any number of correctional practitioners and vocational rehabilitation experts have also observed that skill acquisition is not sufficient, if the aim is employment. Many inmates leave prison with inflated ideas about their market potential, with tremendous impatience for entry-level jobs, with no idea of how to be effective in a job interview or even of how to write a résumé. Thus some vocational rehabilitation should focus on job search, work habits, and career planning, rather than on skill acquisition.

EDUCATIONAL PROGRAMS

Educational programs are among the most widely sought by inmates, who typically suffer considerable educational deficits. One study reported that 90 percent of all Canadian inmates were school dropouts and that their educational achievement was retarded by three to five grade levels (Linden et al., 1984). Estimates based on the 1979 Survey of Inmates in State Correctional Facilities indicated that the education level of inmates in the United States was only slightly higher: 71.4 percent of all state inmates had not graduated from high school, while 18.3 percent had been graduated and 10.3 percent had some college before their current admission to prison (McGarrell and Flanagan, 1985:658).

Most correctional departments provide a number of educational programs, although enrollments vary considerably from state to state. Typical educational programs include:

- Literacy programs
- Adult basic education programs
- General educational development (GED) programs
- College programs

Adult basic education and GED courses reportedly have the heaviest enrollment (McGarrell and Flanagan, 1985:660). However, college programs are growing in numbers and enrollment. From 1976 to 1982, the numbers of postsecondary institutions offering courses in prisons increased from 224 to 347. In 1982, only Delaware, Rhode Island, and Vermont reported no such programs (McGarrell and Flanagan, 1985:133).

In 1983, Haber conducted an interesting study comparing college-enrolled and non-college-enrolled inmates of the District of Columbia prison system. The study revealed systematic differences in both the background and motivation of the two samples. College inmates more frequently came from two-parent homes, and their relatives more frequently had college education. The college inmates were more often employed prior to incarceration, were more frequently convicted of nonviolent offenses, and more frequently were first-time offenders. Psychological tests revealed that the college-enrolled inmates were more satisfied with themselves, more ambitious, and using more of their potential. In short, the college program appeared to attract low-risk inmates who saw their prison sentence as an opportunity to improve themselves.

Not many studies have investigated the effect of prison education upon the postrelease behavior of inmates. One recent study suggests that obtaining educational certificates in prison is associated with postrelease success for some inmate groups (Gottfredson, Mitchell-Herzfeld, and Flanagan, 1982). A Canadian report indicates mixed results for college education, one program showing the students did better than controls, and one study showing no difference (Linden et al., 1984).

One common problem with educational programs observed by correctional practitioners is lack of planning for transition. Linden et al. (1984), for example, complained that college courses were completed too long before release to retain their value. Other educational programs are sufficiently long that they are interrupted by institutional transfers or by release from prison. Some college programs have postrelease components but often do not provide sufficient support and supervision for the ex-inmate students on

There is no doubt that education is one of the most widely sought programs by inmates and one of the most important services that correctional systems can offer. Here, a GED program at the Hudson Correctional Facility. (New York State Department of Correctional Services)

campus. Study release programs are one attempt to deal with transition problems; they are discussed in Chapter 17.

INMATE-RUN PROGRAMS

Not all prison programs are organized and supervised by staff. Formally organized inmate groups are increasing in number and are being established for a number of different purposes. In 1980, the American Justice Institute conducted a national study of inmate organizations (Fox, 1982). The in-depth portion of the study focused on five maximum security prisons, and the researchers found that inmate involvement in formal organizations are widespread: 59 percent of the inmates in Stillwater (Minnesota), 49 percent of the inmates in Oregon State Penitentiary, 44 percent of the inmates in Bedford Hills (the New York maximum security prison for women), and 24 percent of the inmates in Rahway (New Jersey) were members of at least one inmate organization. In California, only 9 percent of the inmates were members of formal inmate groups, because the California Department of Correction had prohibited any groups organized along racial or ethnic lines (1982:141).

Fox reported that the inmate organizations could be classified into four broad categories. Across the five prisons, 18.5 percent were groups established expressly to advance ethnic or racial group interest, 13.8 percent were religious groups, 27.4 percent were self-help groups, and 40.3 percent were special interest groups, ranging from stock car clubs to chess clubs (1982:141). The membership in these groups was not random. Racial and ethnic minorities were more likely to join than whites, and the smaller the percentage of minorities in the prison population, the more likely were they to join an ethnic or racial organization. Older inmates were more likely to join than younger inmates. Prisoners serving long sentences were more involved than those serving short sentences (1982:141–144).

As we will see in Chapter 15, informal social cleavages along ethnic and racial lines have recently increased, along with intergroup violence.

Inmate organizations are an important part of prison resources and prison social structure. Here, inmates in Bedford Hills discuss plans for the children's center. (New York State Department of Correctional Services)

Fox reported that many prison administrators and security staff were concerned that the formal inmate organizations were often fronts for illicit activity, rather than vehicles for pursuing their chartered goals. This was particularly the case in California. The management teams of the five prisons were particularly cautious about changes within the prison that would give inmates more self-determination. As a result, the managers' stance toward inmate organizations was ambivalent. They gave overt support to groups with re-habilitative objectives (such as AA), but they also required all formal inmate groups to have staff sponsorship and to submit their membership lists. Fox claimed that the administrators often sought to control the inmates by controlling resources allocated to the formal inmate groups (1982:137). Occasionally, this tactic was seen as "divide and conquer" by the inmates and may have led to increased competition among the groups. This dynamic could lead to increased alienation and to increased violence (1982:138).

SUMMARY

1. Correctional classification subdivides the total inmate population into more homogeneous groups for more efficient distribution of resources. A classification scheme serves a particular purpose and is insensitive to alternate goals.
2. Good classification systems can classify most prisoners in clear, exclusive categories. The system is reliable: The same results will be obtained by different classifiers and at different times. The system is valid: The attributes ascribed to inmates actually exist, or the predictions made about them are accurate. In addition, the system allows for change, has clear program applications, and is economical.
3. Common classification types focus on personality attributes, security risk, and needs.
4. The classification process usually involves initial decisions in a reception center, periodic reclassification, and prerelease decisions. Many classification processes are managed through a centralized and specialized structure, but some systems utilize team classification that involves front-line staff and inmates.
5. Prison programs engage inmates in activities.

Programs have diverse objectives, including security, inmate self-improvement, and profit or cost reduction.

6. Treatment in prisons may involve special programs and professional staff but often occurs in the midst of other activity. Counseling staff often perform management and classification functions; other prison participants, including other inmates, may be effective in facilitating individual change under the right conditions.

7. Some treatment programs do not have goals of postrelease behavior change, but focus instead on helping inmates cope with confinement.

8. Work programs include prison industries, vocational training, and maintenance tasks. Many work programs are designed to reduce the cost of incarceration or to make a profit. Some are designed to increase inmate employability, but these are often severely deficient.

9. Education programs include literacy, basic adult education, general equivalency diplomas, and college courses. Many inmates have poor educational backgrounds.

10. The number of inmate-run programs is increasing. These include racial or ethnic organizations, religious groups, self-help groups, and special interest and recreation clubs.

KEY WORDS

CLASSIFICATION. The subdivision of inmates by characteristics relevant to goals, for the distribution of resources.

CLASSIFICATION STRUCTURE. The organization of persons and information to perform classification duties.

INITIAL CLASSIFICATION. The classification of newly received inmates, usually in a reception center, often with heavy reliance on past records and tests.

MEDICAL MODEL. The belief that crime is a symptom of mental illness and that this mental illness can be treated in a fashion similar to physical disease.

OVERCLASSIFICATION. The practice of invalidly rating inmates as high security risks.

PRERELEASE CLASSIFICATION. The final classification decisions prior to release for the purpose of allocating inmates to transition programs.

PRISON INDUSTRIES. Employment of prisoners in a business enterprise, often with market restrictions.

RECEPTION CENTER. A separate unit receiving inmates from the court for initial classification.

RECLASSIFICATION. Periodic reassessment of the inmate during incarceration.

THERAPEUTIC COMMUNITY. Residential treatment unit that promotes change through communal processes of norm-building, inmate participation in decisions, and group responsibility.

UNIT MANAGEMENT PLAN. The internal division of a large prison into smaller, separately administered units; devised by the Federal Bureau of Prisons.

VOCATIONAL TRAINING. Provision of a specific, marketable skill.

PROJECTS AND QUESTIONS

1. Invite a prison counselor to discuss the goals, process, and problems of classification in your state. What instruments or measures are used? What structure is employed? Has overcrowding affected the process?

2. Find out what restrictions on employment of ex-felons apply in your state. Do any of the exclusions appear irrational? Why might they have come about?

3. Debate the issue: Resolved that the state should not pay for the college education of prisoners. Besides inmates and correctional agencies, who are the interested parties in this issue?

4. Duffee and Ritti (1977) conducted a public opinion survey about a number of correctional issues. They discovered high support for rehabilitation programs in prison but very split opinion about programs such as work release, which releases inmates from prison during the day. Why might this be so?

ADDITIONAL READING

Carl B. Clements. *Offenders Needs Assessment*. College Park, MD: American Correctional Association, 1986. A recent and easily read overview of classification practices across the United States. Includes models for improvement and many examples of classification instruments.

Douglas Lipton, Robert Martinson, and Judith Wilkes. *The Effectiveness of Correctional Treatment: A Survey of Treatment Evaluation Studies*. New York: Praeger, 1975. This review of 231 correctional evaluations prior to 1967 led to the "nothing works" controversy.

New York State Department of Correctional Services. *Sourcebook on the Mentally Disabled Offender*. Washington, DC: National Institute of Correction, 1986. The results of a national survey of correctional departments concerning the incidence of and programs for mentally ill and retarded offenders. Includes reviews of legal and administrative standards for diagnosis and treatment.

Lee Sechrest, Susan O. White, and Elizabeth Brown. *The Rehabilitation of Offenders: Problems and Prospects*. Washington, DC: National Academy of Science, 1979. Another entry in the nothing works debate; a reassessment of the prospects.

CHAPTER 15 LIFE IN PRISON

QUESTIONS

1. What are the elements of a total institution?
2. What is prisonization?
3. What is the inmate culture?
4. How has the prison culture changed?
5. Do all prisons exhibit the same culture?
6. How has the high incarceration rate of minorities affected the prison?
7. What do we know about the effects of incarceration?

"BEHIND YOUR BACK"

Phil was entering his second year of work in the Jefferson Department of Correction. He was interviewing many of the staff and some inmates; then he would administer questionnaires to a random sample of all staff and inmates to measure issues that would be taken up in the staff development conferences later in the summer. This information-gathering was to take two weeks. Superintendent Smythe had invited Phil to stay at the Bachelor's Officers Quarters, known as the BOQ, a T-shaped cinder-block building down the hill from the prison. The officer who had met Phil at the airport and driven him out to the prison dropped him at the BOQ, and told him to call up to the prison for a ride after he had unpacked. "Cullen and Bradford will show you your room and the kitchen, and can answer most of your questions."

Two older inmates met him at the door. They didn't offer to take the luggage, but they seemed willing to help in other ways. "One of you must be Cullen and the other Bradford," said Phil.

"That's us. That is, he's Bradford, I'm Cullen," said the short one with a grin, pointing to the taller man with a large nose and gray hair. "You must be the doctor."

Bradford flung open a door with some pride. Phil examined his living quarters for the next two weeks. "There's clean linen in the bathroom. And you don't have to worry about making the bed; we'll do that. Why don't you unpack, and then we'll show you the rest of the facilities."

Phil nodded, and the two inmates left. He pulled open the curtains and was suddenly confronted with hundreds of black and white horned faces. The prison dairy herd was just outside his window.

The fourth night in the prison was a tough one. Superintendent Smythe had arranged for Phil to give questionnaires to inmates in groups of thirty at a time. The inmates were chosen randomly, so that the answers would be representative of the whole population. Consequently, the inmates were called to the classroom from a list and told they had no choice but to report. But when they entered the room and sat, among grumbles and wisecracks, Phil announced that any of them who did not want to participate were free to leave.

A tall, muscular young inmate picked up the questionnaire from his desk and waved at Phil. "You mean we don't have to do this?"

"Absolutely not. This is completely voluntary. I would appreciate your cooperation in order to design a training program for staff."

"What's that got do with us?"

"We'd like to have your opinion on a number of matters about how this prison is managed. We're asking you to help us to get an accurate view of how correctional officers and treatment staff behave on the job."

The inmate looked around the room. "I can tell you that in two words." Laughs. "Well, I don't think I need to do this."

When the inmate stood and strode toward the door, most of the others followed, as if they had been waiting to see what would happen. Phil was left looking at seven inmates, all older, sitting in the front row. One of them was Johnston, the editor of the newspaper. "We'll take your questionnaire, professor."

Two days later, Phil was in the kitchen at the BOQ during the late morning. He heard shuffling behind him and turned to find Cullen without Bradford. "Where's Hank?" Phil asked, having gotten on a first-name basis about two days ago.

"Caught a cold. He's up in the infirmary today. Probably be back tomorrow, unless someone drives him down this afternoon. Isn't prison such a waste of time?"

To Phil this question sounded profound, but he was cautious. "What do you mean?"

Cullen shook his head. "Well, all I mean is something simple. Look at this situation with Hank. So he wakes up with a bad cold, right? What's a cold? Life threatening? No. He just wants some decongestant and some aspirin. Reasonable request, right? Don't take all day, out there, does it? In here, he signs the slip in the morning to stay in from work. Then he signs the infirmary list to get there. Then he probably has to wait about two hours, because they take their own sweet time over there. Then he gets the medicine. Then what? He's stuck up there for a day, because it is irregular to take an inmate out to work later in the day. So he loses a whole day's work for a couple of aspirin. That's what I mean, waste of time."

Phil nodded in agreement. "So you have to clean the whole building by yourself?"

Cullen waved a hand and took a long drag on his cigarette. "Oh, that's nothing. That's more of the waste of time, really. One of us can do this building in half a day, except if something breaks. Two janitors down here is ridiculous, as far as work is concerned. But we get to keep each other company. There just isn't enough work to go around. So you always have two or three guys doing a job made for one. It's like the army."

Cullen was displaying interest in the questionnaires that were spread on the coffee table. "I would have taken one of these, you know." Phil smiled his appreciation and explained random sampling. Cullen shrugged. "So you're doin' the guards now?" Phil explained his next step. "I'll tell you," said Cullen. "Some of those guys are worse than the inmates." Phil shrugged. Cullen continued. "I mean take those lock boxes in there. They have to lock their own food up so they don't steal it from each other." Phil suggested college students in a dormitory could be just as bad. "I suppose," said Cullen. "But I'll tell you they sure talk behind your back."

Phil was caught off guard. "What do you mean?"

"Oh, one of them this morning was saying he'd be glad to see that young faggot get back to the university."

Phil turned beet red. Cullen noticed his distress. "Oh, don't take it personal. That's just prison term for a new young kid."

Phil's anger subsided slowly. He was shocked to find that he could be typified in a way that had nothing to do with his behavior. He thought it would be extremely difficult to face each officer individually, asking for cooperation, knowing what some of them thought of him. Then he began to wonder how he would feel if he were actually a new inmate, forced to live in a role that others had created for him.

PRISON CULTURE AND SOCIAL SYSTEMS

Phil's experience in the Dunmore prison was still two steps removed from the one impinging on its inmates, although he was close enough to suffer some of the pressures felt daily by the people who work and live in our prisons. Among the forces Phil felt all too strongly were (1) his separation from the unregulated world, and in particular, his narrowed range of choices, (2) his inability to escape from unpleasant associations, (3) the need to arrange his life to the schedule and constraints of the institution, (4) the difficulty of communicating with distrustful, alienated people, (5) and, in general, an inability to affect his

life, a reduction in his power to choose rather than be forced into roles.

In 1955, Erving Goffman (1961) spent a year in the St. Elizabeth mental hospital in Washington DC with the title of assistant athletic director. His real duties were simply those of observing the adaptations of hospital patients to the organization. Goffman asserted that the mental hospital, like prisons, concentration camps, monasteries, and the army, possessed characteristics which were relatively unusual for organizations in the twentieth century. They were organized, he said, to encompass totally the lives of their subordinate class. Mental patients and inmates worked, slept, and recreated together in undifferentiated masses. These institutions he called **total institutions** because they were organized for the total control of the lives of the people in them. Goffman argued that much of the deviant and bizarre behavior of inmates in total institutions did not have its source within them, but in their attempts to adapt to the environment.

The power of these forces in total institutions is substantial, although too easily underestimated by those who see prison only from a distance. Very often observers of prisons and other institutions that house deviant populations attribute all the behavioral problems found in them to the people who populate them. If only guards were not so cynical and insensitive and inmates so violent, the argument goes, prisons would not be such difficult places.

In one famous attempt to examine the proposition, Haney, Banks and Zimbardo (1973) simulated a prison in the basement of the Stanford University psychology building. Young men who had volunteered for the experiment were subject to an extensive battery of tests to determine that they were solidly normal individuals and were then randomly assigned to the roles of inmate and guard. The experiment was to have lasted two weeks, but after six days the impact on both "guards" and "inmates" had been so devastating that the experiment was curtailed. The experimenters argued that this role-playing exercise demonstrated that role and structure alone were sufficiently powerful to provoke deviant behavior and severe pathology. While the experiment has been criticized, the severe reactions from normal college students should make us very cautious about attributing prison problems solely to the deficiencies of the regular players.

CHARACTERISTICS OF INMATES

The regular players, to be sure, are not representative of the general population. In 1983, Nacci and Kane took a random sample of all prisoners in the Federal Bureau of Prisons. They found that 46 percent were black, 11 percent were Hispanic, and 40 percent were white, a racial distribution that is severely overrepresentative of minorities compared to the general population. The average number of arrests per inmate was eleven. The inmates averaged two felony convictions, had been placed in more than four different jails, and previously had been in three other prisons. The average age was 34, six years of which had been spent incarcerated. One-third of the inmates had been raised in broken homes by single women.

Around the country, people have complained that the prisoner population is changing significantly, perhaps as a result of changing sentencing practices. Guard unions have frequently cited the changing population as one of the reasons prisons are becoming more violent. While there are no national data by which to examine these claims, the New York Department of Correctional Services (DOCS) has conducted a study comparing the characteristics of inmates over the ten-year period from December 31, 1975, to December 31, 1984 (Chapman and Zausner, 1985). While New York is dissimilar to many states, the trends reported below probably reflect trends in other large urbanized states, which incarcerate many of our prisoners.

Perhaps the most shocking change in this ten-year period is the simple increase in the New York prison population from 16,074 in 1975 to 33,136 in 1984 (Chapman and Zausner, 1985:4). The researchers report that the increase appears to be due to changes in both the annual admissions rate and length of time served (1985:ii). In 1975, 21 percent had minimum sentences of 48 months or more. In 1984, 45 percent had minimum sentences of 48 months or more (1985:ii). Maximum terms and time served averages had also increased.

One of the apparent reasons for these increases was a precipitous increase in the percentage of inmates held for crimes designated as violent felonies. In 1975, 52 percent were convicted of these crimes; in 1984, 71 percent had been so charged (Chapman and Zausner, 1985:ii). Figure 15.1 depicts these changes graphically. Additionally, changes in prior criminal record would suggest that more serious offenders are being held. Figure 15.2 demonstrates a rapid drop in the percentage of inmates without a prior conviction. In 1984, 33 percent had had a prior prison commitment, and 27 percent had served a prior jail term.

During this period, some of the personal characteristics of inmates had also changed. Educational level had increased slightly to 9.9 grades completed from 9.6 in 1975. Additionally, there had been a large increase in the number who had completed high school. The percentage of inmates who had never been married increased from 52 percent to 58 percent. The average age had gone up slightly, to 29.7 years, by 1984.

Some characteristics had remained stable. The proportion of the inmate population which was male remained steady at 97 percent; however, the absolute number of women incarcerated had risen dramatically, from 428 to 1,015 (1985:iii). Racial distribution had also remained fairly stable over the ten years. The percentage who were Hispanic increased from 16 to 21 percent. Black inmates decreased slightly from 56 to 52 percent; while the white population remained stable at 27 percent. In general, we can say that over this ten-year period prison officials in New York faced a prison population that was increasingly older, somewhat better educated, less often married, more frequently convicted of violent felonies, and increasingly facing longer

FIGURE 15.1   Offense Type: Population under Custody, December 31, 1975–1984

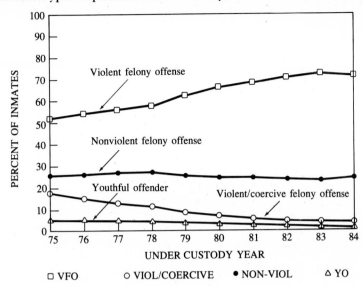

SOURCE: William R. Chapman and Stuart A. Zausner, *"Characteristics of Inmates under Custody: A Ten Year Trend Study."* Albany, NY: Department of Correctional Services, December 1985, p. 10.

prison terms. Many of these inmates had been habitually unemployed or had had experience only with manual labor in a worsening labor market.

PRISON CULTURE—EARLY VIEWS

The first observer to speak specifically of a prison culture was Hans Reimer in 1939. Shortly thereafter, Donald Clemmer entered the Menard Reformatory (Illinois) as a prison sociologist and conducted the first systematic investigation of the prison culture. His examination of life in prison has had a profound effect on all prison studies since. Clemmer approached his study using the dominant sociological concepts of the time: primary group and culture (Irwin, 1977:22). He coined the term **prisonization** to refer to

> . . . taking on, in greater or lesser degree the folkways, mores, customs, and general culture of the penitentiary. (Clemmer, 1940:270)

In 1981, the same term was defined as

> . . . the degree of assimilation into the inmate normative system and the adoption of the tenets of the inmate code. (Thomas, Petersen, and Cage, 1981:38)

A major part of Clemmer's effort was the study of the social relationships among inmates in the reformatory, focusing on the number who reported being members of primary groups and the numbers who accepted values and adopted roles that were seen as part of the inmate social system. Clemmer's conclusion was that the longer inmates were incarcerated, the stronger was their identification with inmate norms and values, and the more difficulty they would have readapting to life in the free community.

The early work of Reimer and Clemmer was developed by other sociologists, notably Sykes (1958), Sykes and Messinger (1960), and Cloward (1960). These researchers built Clemmer's

FIGURE 15.2   Prior Adult Criminal Record: Population under Custody, December 31, 1975–1983

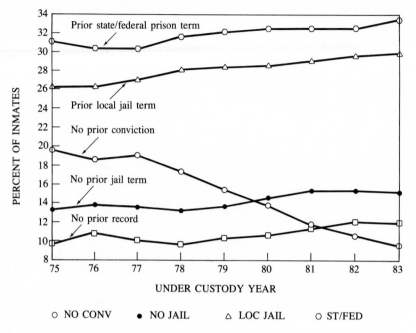

UNDER CUSTODY YEAR

○ NO CONV   ● NO JAIL   △ LOC JAIL   ○ ST/FED

SOURCE: William R. Chapman and Stuart A. Zausner, "Characteristics of Inmates under Custody: A Ten Year Trend Study." Albany, NY: Department of Correctional Services, December 1985, p. 29.

concepts into a full-blown social system, complete with values, roles, leadership positions, and a particular type of relationship between staff and inmates. The most commonly denoted inmate roles were the "right guy," the "politician," the "merchant," the "square john," the "outlaw," and the "ding." The most frequently heard prescriptions of the inmate code were "do your own time," "never rat on a con," and "never talk to a screw."

According to these students of the prison social system, the inmate culture was a essentially a means of accommodating the **pains of imprisonment** in a manner that allowed inmates to preserve some individuality and sense of dignity by rejecting the official norms of the prison while cooperating in under the table arrangements with staff as a means of preserving order in the prison (Irwin, 1977:22).

The best known of these studies was Gresham Sykes' *Society of Captives*, an observation of the maximum security prison in Trenton, New Jersey (1958). Sykes enumerated the pains of imprisonment as the deprivations of liberty, of goods and services, of heterosexual companionship, of autonomy, and of security. He proposed that because all inmates shared these deprivations, they naturally bound together to reduce the deprivations. These dynamics included adopting roles that redistributed both expressive and instrumental values. Inmate leaders, such as right guys, studiously personified the inmate code, refusing to buckle under to the desires of the staff. Other inmate leaders, such as politicians and merchants, played roles that put them in constant communication with staff but in ways that would allow them to redistribute information (in the case of politicians) or prison goods and contraband (in the case of merchants).

Sykes argued that the staff, and in particular the guard staff, were forced into compromising their authority in return for orderly behavior. Simultaneously, the inmate leaders enforced relatively peaceful and orderly inmate behavior as a means of maintaining their positions. In short, Sykes saw the ostensibly conflicting inmate and staff groups forming a functionally related system that preserved order in spite of, rather than through, the rules.

THE IMPORTATION HYPOTHESIS

Not long after the inmate culture and inmate social system had been fully elaborated, Irwin and Cressey (1962) issued an important critique of the predominant view. They argued that the **functional** approach to the prison social system downplayed the important contribution of values and roles imported into the prison from the street. Irwin and Cressey pointed out that many of the norms observed in prison were very similar to the lower-class "thief" subculture that existed outside the prison in the free community. In addition, they suggested that some roles and values were not indigenous to the current prison, but were adaptations of those they called "state-raised youth" who had spent virtually all their lives in some institution. Previous studies of prisons, they claimed, placed too much emphasis on the origination of prison culture in the shared deprivations of the current incarceration and too little emphasis on the shared experiences some inmates brought with them to prison.

One particularly well known prison study that capitalizes on and validates the **importation** hypothesis is James B. Jacobs' study of the Stateville Prison in Illinois. Jacobs traces the history of this major maximum security prison over fifty years. He notes that culture in the prison changed radically in the late 1960s when gangs from Chicago were imported wholesale into the prison. A summary of these observations about the impact of importation upon the Stateville prison are provided in Insert 15.2.

THE PRISON SOCIAL SYSTEM—MORE RECENT VIEWS

The debate about the relative power of indigenous and imported forces in shaping prison culture has continued since the early 1960s. Liberals frequently support the indigenous explanation of prison culture, while conservatives generally cite the evidence that prisoner attitudes and values are shaped before they get to prison. While the debate continues, there is growing evidence that either the deprivation or the importation theories alone are too simple to help us explain the social systems found in the modern prison (Irwin, 1977:22). Irwin has called for a new sociology of prisons because recent studies suggest

> . . . that currently there is more conflict among prisoners and among staff members and much less consensus or sense of purpose relative to philosophy and goals among prison administrators than existed in the past.

Attacks on the old conception of prison social systems have come from a number of directions. Poole, Regoli, and Thomas (1980) examined the reliability and validity of the instruments used to measure the classic inmate role types and concluded that the attitude measures did not achieve reliability and could not predict specific behaviors which should have correlated with the role measures. Marquart and Roebuck (1985) reported that the norms against snitching and ratting did not always apply. Ramirez (1984) concluded that staff and inmates are not necessarily opposed on many important prison issues. Such studies indicate that there may be some methodological problems with the previous examinations of inmate culture, but they also suggest that that culture, even if it did exist, is now changing.

The most significant change may be the redistribution of power in prisons (Stastny and Tyrnauer, 1982: Irwin, 1977). A number of observers have suggested that prison power originally belonged almost exclusively to the warden, was then shared with inmates, and is now shared with increasingly vocal guard unions, courts, and a number of other external groups that keep a watchful eye on our prisons. Irwin suggests that with this fragmentation of power, and the important increase in outside influence upon prison social systems, the prison culture is "interactive" rather than "imported" or "indigenous." Stastny and Tyrnauer view the pluralistic power bases as evidence that prisons are "detotalizing." (1982:35). They criticize the earlier explanations of prison culture as mistakenly taking a narrow view of the factors which influence what happens inside the walls:

> In reality, policies are made and budgets are allocated in a distant head office by an urban administrator or legislator. The decisions made in the head office are based on wider concerns that may be of regional, national, or even international importance. The life of an individual prisoner, like that of a coal miner in a company town, is affected by many of these forces—by the vagaries of state politics and Supreme Court personalities, and even international treaties on human rights, as well as by the attitudes of the guards and the policies of the warden. (Stastny and Tyrnauer, 1982:132)

Irwin argues that the major changes in prison society began in the 1960s. A full-blown prisoners' rights movement emerged from the black power, civil rights, and antiwar movements. Prisoners' rights spurred formal prisoner organizing (see Huff, 1977, for an example). Administrators had strong negative reactions to prisoner unions and sought to dismantle them by dispersing leaders and punishing members of the organizations. Huff reports that Ohio administrators successfully undermined the Ohio Prisoners Labor Union. Irwin (1977:29–35) concurs, but he also points out that official resistance to prisoner organizations often left the prisoner population without its traditional leaders. He suggests that the current prison is "an ordered segmenation" of small, mutually hostile cliques, held together by the contraband economy, but not by other values.

Simultaneously, the prison staff has become split into several distinct groups. There are rifts between subgroups in the guard force, and between administration and the guard force. Additionally, the death of the rehabilitative ideal took away from staff and administration their unifying ideology. Irwin believes that the new, interactive, fragmented prison is more violent and less stable than the older one, but he also projects that few changes in this situation are likely when the outside political climate is conservative and inmates are no longer organized politically.

VARIATIONS IN CULTURE ACROSS PRISONS

Another set of observations that complicates the explanation of prison social systems concerns the differential impact of different types of prisons. Many of the early studies of the inmate culture focused on large maximum security prisons. The characteristics of the inmate culture frequently reported in those institutions are less frequently observed in less secure institutions, or institutions with a heavy investment in treatment and self-improvement programming.

Some would argue that the evidence of organizational effects on prison culture would lend additional weight to the deprivation model of prison culture—the fewer the deprivations, the less the inmate culture appears. Others consider that the study of prison-specific effects has inadequately controlled for the different types of inmates routinely found in prisons with different security and program profiles. They suggest that the inmate culture is less apparent in minimum security situations because the inmates with whom the inmate culture is associated are rarely placed in such facilities.

While there is evidence to support both sides of this argument, it would appear again that the struggle for theoretical supremacy obscures more mundane but nonetheless important observations. First, as Jacobs (1976) and Steele and Jacobs (1975) point out, the various prisons of different types are connected by policy and transfer of prisoners. The greater staff-inmate cooperation, the less violence, and the fewer disciplinary problems of minimum security institutions are, in part, a product of threatening to transfer misbehaving inmates to more onerous surroundings. Second, as a number of researchers have demonstrated, both staff and inmates are influenced by their current social setting and by the formal policy of the administration (Cressey, 1958; Jacobs, 1976; Street, Vinter, and Perrow, 1966; McEwen, 1978). Such studies provide important evidence that prison administrators can have some impact upon the kinds of staff and inmate behaviors that are most common in prisons, and even if they cannot have a major impact on value and attitude change, they can at least modify how those are expressed. Consequently, managers or academicians who blame undesirable prison behaviors upon the nature of criminal confinement, or upon the nature and past experience of prisoners, propagate a pernicious cynicism that nothing can be done and that no one is responsible for prison problems.

COPING WITH LIFE IN PRISON

Different prisoners adapt to prison in different ways. Different prisons, and different parts of the same prison, may require different adaptations and coping strategies from the same individual. Parisi (1982:16) catalogues a number of factors that impinge on inmates and affect their prison behavior: the level and types of deprivations experienced, the particular concerns of management, inmate's concerns about life after release, the different characteristics of various staff and inmate groups, and the effects of coping styles used by other inmates. Some of these inmate adaptations are nonviolent. Some inmates may busy themselves with litigating their conviction or prison conditions, or may be active in filing formal grievances. Others may seek to withdraw as much as possible from the prison routine and from association with other inmates. Some inmates do quite the opposite; they seek to survive the prison experience by engaging in as many activities as possible. Some plan and engage in nonviolent collective actions, attempting to

change conditions thought political action. Others adopt violent coping strategies. Some may reserve their violence for staff by attempting to demonstrate individuality or maintain integrity through rebellious acts. Others may seek to survive by predatory acts against other inmates. Occasionally, large numbers of inmates engage in violent behavior simultaneously, and riots disrupt the fragile order of the prison (Parisi, 1982:16–24).

One of the more influential perspectives on coping with imprisonment is that of social psychologist Hans Toch (1969, 1977). Toch has studied prisoner adaptations as transactions between the needs of the individual and the stimuli of the prison environment. Particular adaptations cannot be predicted, he asserts, unless we have detailed information about both the person and the environment (1977:7).

One of Toch's largest studies of coping with imprisonment was based upon clinical interviews with a systematic sample of inmates in five maximum security prisons. Toch and his associates derived seven important environmental concerns of inmates from inductive coding of these interviews. Inmates are concerned, in varying degrees, with privacy, safety, structure (order and predictability), support (programs for self-improvement), emotional feedback (from other inmates and staff), social stimulation, activity, and freedom (particularly to preserve individual autonomy) (1977:16–17). The researchers found that the most salient concern was freedom; it was an issue in two-thirds of the interviews, and the predominant concern in 40 percent of the cases (1977:124).

The mix and strength of concerns, however, vary by prison (1977:136–137) and by a number of personal characteristics. For example, black inmates displayed more concern for freedom than white inmates, and were therefore generally more dissatisfied with their current placement (1977:128). Older inmates demonstrated a higher concern for structure than younger inmates, while younger inmates were more concerned about personal safety (1977:128). Married inmates were less concerned about freedom than other inmates,

Prison services and resources help to create smaller environments within the larger prison community. Different niches may appeal to different inmates and meet different needs. (New York State Department of Correctional Services)

but were more interested in receiving emotional feedback (1977:131). Long-term inmates were more concerned about structure than those serving short sentences, while short-termers were more concerned about access to self-improvement programs (support) (1977:132).

Toch's findings highlight the complexity of the interaction between an individual's needs and the natural variations in prison conditions. Probably no inmates want to be in prison, but the research indicates quite clearly that some suffer psychologically and physically much more than others. Some who have led marginal existences in the community fare well in prison. Others who seemed reasonably well adjusted prior to prison fall apart within the walls. It is clear that imprisonment has different effects on different prisoners. A significant minority do not find it an intolerable experience. The most satisfied prisoners, Toch discovered, were those who placed

a high value on intimate links with others (emotional feedback) and personal rehabilitation (support), had an interest in keeping busy (activity), and had limited resentment of authority (low concern for freedom) (1977:124). Some prisons cannot respond positively to such concerns. Those that can would be known for their rehabilitative orientation and for being well endowed with program resources.

PRISON VIOLENCE

One of the principal concerns of all participants in the prison community is violence. A number of observers suggest that prison violence is on the increase, although improvements in record-keeping and less reliance on informal adjustments make comparisons difficult between the prisons of today and those of several generations ago. Bowker (1983) indicates that while current violence levels are unacceptable, it is surprising that violent incidents are still not more frequent.

Lockwood (1982) argues that the threat of violence is probably more important than actual incidents in determining adaptation to prison. Some inmates react to imminent danger by staying in their cells; changing jobs, cellblocks, or prisons; or transferring to protection or a "weak company" that will receive special staff attention and isolation from other inmates. Others respond to the threat by becoming violent themselves, or by joining cliques that protect their members but may be violent toward nonmembers (1982:60). He finds that the most frequent reactions to the violent environment are passive ones, such as fear, anger, anxiety, and in a substantial number of cases, psychological crisis (1982:57). Toch (1977:181–182) finds that the men who feel most vulnerable in prison often seek "niches," special self-created settings in the prison which they see as more controllable and more congruent with their needs. Unfortunately, obtaining these niches of safety often means foregoing other needs.

The level of violence, and order more generally, is moderated by a number of informal and formal controls. Bowker lists antiviolence norms, the profit motive, fear of reprisal, legal and administrative sanctions, social acceptance needs, and concern for "housekeeping," or maintaining a routine, as all contributing to violence control (1983). Kalinich and Stojkovic (1985) argue that the formal controls are insufficient for maintaining order and that the contraband market creates informal leaders who seek order to maintain the market. Kalinich's study of the Jackson, Michigan, prison contraband system indicated that violence levels rose when administrators succeeded in temporarily closing down the flow of contraband, thereby inflating both the risk and the price (1980).

The Frequency of Violence. Estimating the extent of violence in prison is fraught with the same perils as the measurement of crime in the free world. Official reports are usually the only

readily available measure, but are known to undercount the number of incidents. Self-report studies are another means to estimate the level of violence, and disciplinary problems in general, but these are far more expensive to conduct and have their own methodological problems. One study in a federal prison sought to compare self-reports by both inmates and staff with official disciplinary actions (Hewitt, Poole, and Regoli, 1984). The researchers found that 391 inmates reported 2,265 infractions in a three-month period, while guards reported observing 1,879. However, only 66 reports were filed during the same period. The researchers did not find that the more serious infractions were more likely to be reported.

After the riot at Attica Prison in September 1971, the New York Department of Correctional Services set up a data keeping system that provides more systematic information on disciplinary problems than is typically available. DOCS hopes that by monitoring the level of "unusual incidents," it will be able to pick up signs of increased unrest and thereby to forestall, or at least to prepare for, mass violence.

DOCS reports 19 categories of unusual incidents, including inmate accidents, inmate altercations, assaults on staff, assaults on inmates, contraband, escapes and attempts, sodomy, suicides and attempts, thefts, and mass demonstrations (Zausner, 1985:12). In 1984 DOCS reported 3,812 unusual incidents involving 5,835 inmates. These incidents occurred at a rate of 318 per month, 12.5 percent higher than in the preceding year (1985:1). Especially alarming was a jump in inmate deaths to 109 in 1984 from 44 in 1983 (1985:11). Zausner reports that there has been a steady increase in incidents over the 1982–1984 period, as indicated in Figure 15.3.

The most common place for incidents to occur was in a cellblock (47.7 percent of all reported incidents), with the yard being a distant second (8.8 percent) (Zausner, 1985:8). The DOCS seems particularly careful in reporting staff response to these incidents. One thousand six hundred and twenty-five incidents resulted in use of

FIGURE 15.3   Number of Unusual Incidents, DOCS Facilities, 1982–1984

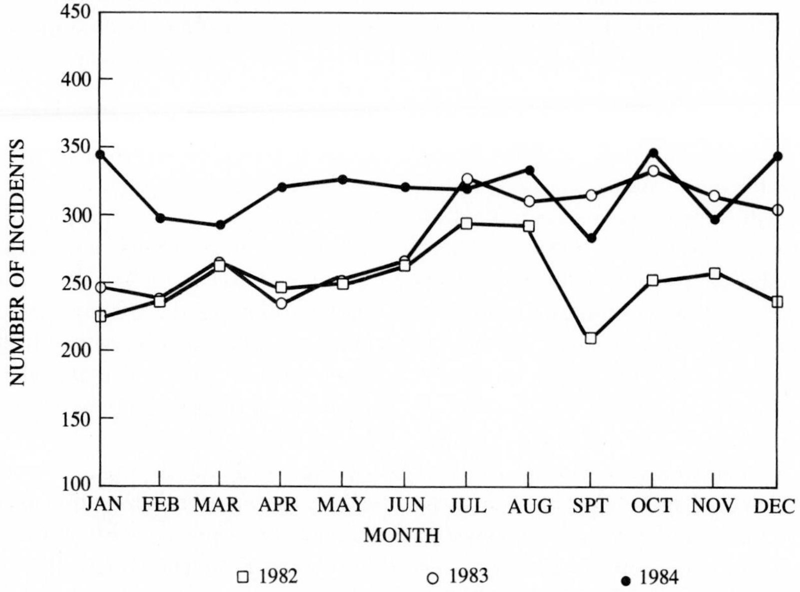

SOURCE: Stuart Zausner, "Unusual Incident Report, 1984 Calendar Year." Albany, NY: Department of Correctional Services, May 1985.

force by staff, with "holding" reported as the most common force exerted (1985:7).

The most frequent unusual incident was inmate assault on staff, accounting for 19.9 percent of all incidents reported. Assaults on inmates and inmate altercations were the next most common. Assaults of all types accounted for 34.5 percent of all reported incidents (1985:2). The vast majority (75.6 percent) of assaults on staff occurred in maximum security institutions, with one institution (Attica) accounting for nearly one-quarter of these. Maximum security was also the most frequent setting for assaults on inmates, although the distribution across prisons was more even (1985:3). Zausner reports that the most common assault on staff was throwing an object. Forty-six percent of assaults on staff resulted in no injury (1985:4).

The Correlates of Violence. Variables associated with violence have been studied on both the individual level of analysis (What are the characteristics of violent inmates?) and on the organizational level (What are the characteristics of the violent prison?) None of these studies should be interpreted as identifying the causes of violence, but awareness of these variables may allow prison officials to predict its occurrence and perhaps to control its consequences.

A number of studies have sought to examine the characteristics that distinguish the violent from the nonviolent inmate. The ultimate practical purpose of many of these studies is the prediction of violence during the prison classification process. This is a difficult undertaking. Although violence is more common in prison than in the general population, it is still rare. Many prisoners will be incorrectly classified during such attempts. A small study in New Zealand (Walkey and Gilmour, 1984) was able to classify correctly 71 percent of the subjects as fighting or not fighting in prison. The variables that proved helpful in the classification process were the inmate's score on a measure of interpersonal distance preference, age, height, violent history, evidence of alcohol before the offense, and marital status.

Another small study (Myers and Levy, 1978) sought to predict "intractability" among inmates. The variables that proved useful were proportion of adult life incarcerated, a measure of psychological depression and another of physical dexterity, use of aliases, extent of alcohol use, and number of police contacts as a juvenile. This study used the dubious methods of selecting inmates based on staff ratings as disciplinary and nondisciplinary. While alcohol use appears in both studies, it was associated with fighting in the New Zealand study, while nonabusers appeared more troublesome in the other study.

A much more exacting study was conducted by Flanagan (1983), who collected data on a representative sample of all prisoners released from a northeastern state between 1973 and 1976. His goal was to classify the ex-prisoners by personal characteristics so that prison officials would be able to predict which inmates upon entry would become disciplinary problems sometime during their careers in prison. It is important to underscore that Flanagan is not attempting to predict violence, but an inmate's disciplinary infraction rate. This is easier to predict, although not all inmates who present disciplinary problems are violent. Flanagan discovered that inmates averaged two disciplinary reports a year, but that as one might expect, there was wide variation. The group with the highest infraction rates were young, nonhomicide prisoners with drug problems. The group with the lowest infraction rate was older, homicide offenders who had no drug problems (1983:35) For more detail on Flanagan's study of long-term prisoners and their adaptations to prison, see Insert 15.1.

Some studies had sought to differentiate prisons rather than inmates on the basis of violence rates. The variables used in this type of study do not indicate which prisoners in the prison are being violent—they only serve to suggest how prisons with high rates of violence can be iden-

tified. Two of the larger and more sophisticated of these studies are Farrington and Nuttall's (1980) study of 55 British prisons, and Gaes and McGuire's (1985) study of 19 federal prisons in the United States. Contrary to widespread belief in the deleterious effects of prison size, the British study finds that official prison offense rates per 100 prisoners go down as size goes up, although this inverse relationship between size and infraction rate is weaker for assaults considered alone (1980:224–226). The researchers found that the most violent prisons were those that were most overcrowded, rather than the largest. However, they also pointed out that other variables, such as changes in inmate-staff ratios, or differences in types of inmates, might explain the finding (1980:226–227).

The study from the United States also singled out overcrowding as a problem variable. Gaes and McGuire studied four types of assaults, along with a number of possible explanatory variables, over a 33-month period. The level of crowding in the institution was found to be the strongest predictor of all assaults except those on an officer with a weapon.

HOMOSEXUALITY AND SEXUAL AGGRESSION

For a number of observers, the symbol of the ultimate personal degradation in prison is homosexual rape. The officially reported incidence of actual rape is very low (Zausner, 1985:2, reports four sodomies in New York prisons in 1984), and the rate indicated in self-reports is not much higher (Nacci and Kane, 1983; Toch, 1977:143–144). Yet the threat of sexual aggression in prisons is much higher and is a constant concern to both inmates and staff.

In a random sample of inmates in two New York prisons, Lockwood (1982:53) found that 25 percent of the inmates interviewed reported approaches by other inmates which they considered "sexually aggressive." The rate of victimization varied considerably among subgroups, with 65 percent of the young white males reporting that

Insert 15.1 FLANAGAN'S STUDY OF LONG-TERM PRISONERS

Early thinking about lifers and long-term inmates assumed that the effects of extended confinement were relatively predictable and profoundly negative. Extended incarceration was felt to be inexorably linked to deterioration of the personality, growing dependence upon the highly controlled regime of institutional life, and increasing levels of "prisonization" or commitment to the value system of the institution. (Flanagan, 1982a:116)

Flanagan set out to test these assumptions. His general conclusion is that the early views were inaccurate. While deterioration occurred in some cases, the most remarkable finding was the ability of long-term inmates to adapt to prison life and to adopt perspectives about prison that enhanced their ability to cope (1981:205).

Flanagan found that the three major concerns of inmates who had served at least five years in prison were (1) future time perspective, (2) maintaining external relationships, and (3) guarding against assaults on their integrity and self-esteem (1981:209–213). To deal with these problems, long-termers adopt behavioral responses of avoiding trouble and using their time profitably. Psychologically, they are far more concerned about deterioration than short-term inmates (1981:217).

Most long-termers found external problems, such as maintaining relationships, much more difficult than maintaining their mental health. Flanagan found the major problems to be

... the gradual slipping away of human resources, the ambivalence that they foster, and the fear that these losses will be irrevocable (1982a:119).

Relationships inside the prison also differed between long- and short-termers. Long-termers generally had a wider circle of acquaintances and friends in the prison, but also had to deal with losing them more often, compared to short-termers. In addition, the long-termer had a greater concern for saving face in all situations (1982a:120).

Misconduct patterns of long- and short-term inmates were considerably different. Short-termers committed almost twice as many infractions per year, and their infraction rates varied with the phase of sentence. Long-termers' infraction rates were low across all phases of their sentences. There was some tendency for the long-termers' infractions to be of a more serious nature (Flanagan, 1980b:360–363).

Flanagan argued that the worst problem for long-term inmates is that they are always at the end of the line for prison programs and alternatives because they had a long time to serve and usually had committed heinous offenses. Flanagan suggested a number of steps to ease the pressures on these inmates (1982b:86). He recommended that policymakers should consider (1) providing separate housing units for long-termers; (2) designing prison careers that would provide meaning and significance; (3) providing equal opportunities for programs and other prison resources; (4) taking steps to preserve family relationships; and (5) preparing long-termers for release.

---

they had been targets of sexual aggression. In a random sample of all prisoners in the Federal Bureau of Prisons, Nacci and Kane found similar figures. Twenty-nine percent of the prisoners reported that they had been propositioned in some prison. Nine percent reported being the target of actual attack in some prison, but only 2 percent

reported being the victim of violent sexual assault in a federal prison.

The targets of assaults were generally younger inmates who had been in prison only a short time (57 percent had been incarcerated for less than a month). The majority of those reporting attack also said that they did nothing official about the problem. Toch's survey of five maximum security prisons discovered that 28 percent of the inmates felt they were victims of sexual aggression, although the self-reported rate of actual physical attacks was much lower. Most of the aggressors were black inmates from New York City, while most of the victims were white, inexperienced prisoners from other parts of the state (1977:144–146). A number of the victims had a history of suicide attempts and mental health problems.

Toch proposes that sexually oriented aggression is much higher than actual rape because in many instances the aim of the aggression is to evoke visible signs of stress from the victim (1977:143–144). Lockwood's study of the victims indicated that the targets of sexual harrassment suffer severe psychological and physical consequences. He suggests that one of the more troubling aspects of sexual harrassment in prison is that the target is labeled by aggressors and becomes pushed into a deviant prison career, regardless of his own behavior and sexual orientation. The sudden entrapment in a deviant sexual identity that bears no resemblance to self-perceptions can be very stressful (1982:49). The most common reaction to such harrassment, according to Lockwood, is fear. This psychological reaction, he suggests, can be as damaging as the external aggression. Fear leads to anxiety and to crisis situations for about half of the targets. Suicide can result from the attempt to avoid what is perceived as unavoidable violence at the hands of others (1982:59). The aggressors in these situations neutralize guilt, according to Lockwood, by inventing myths that the victim is homosexual (1982:64–65), paralleling the rationales constructed by heterosexual rapists in the free world that the women they target are promiscuous and deserving or desirous of the aggression.

While not as troubling as homosexual rape and harrassment, administrators and researchers also display a good deal of concern about consensual homosexual acts in prison. This behavior is thought to lead to violence and disorder, and to be a natural outgrowth of the deprivation of heterosexual contact. Estimates of the scope of homosexual activity in prison settings vary widely, from 10 to 70 percent, depending on the prison and the reporting method. The more sophisticated surveys suggest that prison staff, and perhaps some inmates, overestimate the incidence of homosexual activity.

PRISON DISTURBANCES

Prison and jail disturbances have been recorded in this country since the late eighteenth century (Aziz, 1983:1). Prison disturbances are often broken into two broad categories, riots, or **collective violence,** and peaceful demonstrations, or **collective resistance.** Historical accounts and newspaper reports do not always distinguish between the two. It is probable that violent confrontations are more likely to be reported than nonviolent demonstrations such as work stoppages, sitdown strikes, or mass refusals to leave cells (Aziz, 1983:10).

We probably do not have an accurate idea of the frequency of either collective resistance or riots. For example, Aziz discovered that the New York Department of Correctional Services recorded 175 inmate disturbances in its eight maximum security prisons from 1974 to 1980, while his newspaper search turned up only 37 disturbances in all DOCS facilities from 1970 to 1980 (1983:8). Thus all types of collective actions by inmates are probably underreported, with nonviolent actions receiving even less attention.

Inmate disturbances do not appear to be evenly distributed across regions, institutions, or time. In his eleven-year survey of newspaper accounts, Aziz found that 51 percent of the 408 incidents uncovered occurred in just six states, with New York leading the way. (Although New York's dubious leadership in this instance may be related to the location of the *New York Times,* the source of most information about all prison disturbances.) Disturbances were most frequent in the Northeast, although the ratio of violent to nonviolent incidents was higher in the South. Disturbances also clustered in particular prisons.

The retaking of D yard, Attica prison, in 1971 by the New York State Police included the death of ten hostages and twenty-nine inmates shot by police gunfire. (AP/Wide World Photos)

Twenty-three prisons, of the 171 reporting any disturbance, accounted for 39 percent of the all disturbances. Disturbances also seem to bunch up in time; they are not evenly spread across the decade (1983:11–12).

While prison riots are both feared and fascinating, they have been subjected to little systematic scientific inquiry. Fox (1971) suggests that riots typically go through five stages: (1) the initial explosion, (2) organization, (3) confrontation of officials and inmates, (4) termination, and (5) reaction and explanation. Fox also distinguished between "predisposing" causes of riots by which he meant the underlying problems that give rise to unusual levels of frustration, anxiety, and anger, and the "precipitating" cause, by which he meant the triggering incident. Most observers agree that riots come in various shapes and sizes, but are rarely planned events. Collective resis-

tance, however, takes some planning, and thus does not begin with a precipitating cause.

All prison disturbances are of relatively short duration. In Aziz's survey of reported incidents between 1970 and 1980, the average length was 1 to 5 hours, and 76 percent of the events were resolved within 24 hours. Incidents of collective resistance generally lasted longer than collective violence. The longest reported incident was a twelve-week general strike at the Arizona State Prison (1983:16).

A particularly controversial issue in prison disturbances concerns the decision of how to terminate the incident. This question was hotly debated after the bloody retaking of New York's Attica prison in September 1971. Twenty-nine inmates and ten hostages died as state police stormed the institution with guns blazing, while only two inmates and one hostage had died at the hands of inmates prior to the retaking of the prison (New York State Special Commission on Attica, 1972:373). Garson (1972:420) found that use of force by officials in retaking the institution had resulted in the most deaths and injuries during the 98-year period of his study.

Most studies of riots and collective resistance mention a common set of predisposing causes. These include overcrowding, poor food, large, decaying physical structures, inadequate financial support, public indifference, substandard or ill-trained personnel, lack of professional leadership, inadequate programming, idleness, and political changes (Aziz, 1983:29). In a comparison of the two most famous recent riots, Mahan (1982:75) found a number of basic similarities in the institutions at Attica and at Santa Fe, New Mexico, which erupted in February 1980. She reports that in both cases the prisoners felt as if they were not treated as human beings, that the line officers were not trained or prepared to handle major disturbances, that the administration of the prisons had been inconsistent, that the two state legislatures were insensitive to penal problems, and that the public was equally unconcerned, except during dramatic events.

An old, but still one of the finest, case studies of a prison riot was conducted by McCleery (1969). He examined the Oahu prison in Hawaii from the appointment of a rehabilitation warden in 1946 through the transformation to statehood and a major riot in 1960. McCleery's main point is that there is never one cause of a riot, and that to understand how a riot erupts it is necessary to examine the historical, social, and political shifts in the prison. McCleery's account of the evolution of the Oahu prison suggests that the internal dynamics of the prison and the external political dynamics can be closely related.

The rehabilitation-oriented warden had transformed the prison from a traditional custodial institution into a treatment institution only with difficulty. The changes very nearly resulted in riot in 1953, but the prison stabilized by 1955, as the old inmate leaders were gradually replaced by inmates socialized into the new treatment

regime (1969:122–125). However, statehood changed the political position of the prison, and the warden and his new superior in a department of social services battled for both public and prison staff support. The warden lost. Consequently, the warden lost the legitimacy to lead the staff and the staff to control the inmates. McCleery argues that at least that riot was probably due to anomie and lack of authority—a search for order and definition of the situation (1969:132–135).

McCleery pointed out that over fifty riots swept major mainland prisons from 1950 to 1953, as post-World War II reform efforts were implemented. The riots very often had the effect of dampening the move toward rehabilitation. They were often interpreted politically to indicate that the treatment regimes did not offer enough control. A more accurate interpretation, according to McCleery, would have been that change in *any* direction can be disruptive to the hard-won and fragile social relationships in a prison.

To date, the most systematic comparative studies of prisons experiencing and not experiencing disturbances were conducted by the South Carolina Department of Correction (1973) and Ohlin and Wilsnack (reported in Wilsnack, 1976). Both studies used survey questionnaires in the attempt to find the correlates of disturbances. The Wilsnack study distinguishes peaceful from violent disturbances, while the South Carolina report does not. The South Carolina report found the following variables to be associated with disturbances: high security, larger planned capacity, age of the prison, less frequent contact between inmates and the warden, higher education among staff and inmates, lack of meaningful job assignments in medium and minimum security institutions, lack of recreation, and the presence of administrative or punitive segregation units in the prison (1973:32). Wilsnack's analysis found that violent actions were associated with inmate social system disintegration, administrative instability, external pressure, and publicity. Collective resistance was associated with rapid changes in the inmate population and the presence of inmate groups who are politically active and organized. Both types of incidents were associated with overcrowded and idle conditions in maximum security units.

RACE RELATIONS IN PRISON

Only twenty-six years after the abolition of slavery, blacks already comprised 40 percent of the state prison population (Owens, 1981:150.) Christianson argued that the penitentiary was created in part to control newly freed blacks. He pointed out that New York drafted its first prison legislation on the same day in 1796 that it emancipated its slaves (1982:75). Beaumont and Toqueville observed in 1833 that blacks comprised 25 percent of the inmate populations in New York and Connecticut, although only one-thirtieth of the state populations were black (1964). Other racial and ethnic minorities are also overrepresented in our correctional systems.

Despite a long history of incarceration of minorities, social scientists have generally ignored

race relations in prison (Jacobs, 1983a:63). Jacobs noted that between 1963 and 1974, the practice of maintaining segregated prison facilities was declared unconstitutional in seven jurisdictions (Jacobs, 1983a:64). Such court decisions indicate that racial segregation and discrimination in prison were widespread, although scarcely mentioned in the literature on life in prison (Jacobs, 1983a:63). In addition to segregation of inmates by race, many prison systems had virtually no minority staff members. At the time of the riot in 1971, Attica had only one black and one Puerto Rican employee. None of the guards were minority members (New York State Special Commission on Attica, 1972).

These conditions began to change in the late 1960s. Irwin (1970) noted in his study of California felons that black and Mexican inmates were supplanting criminal identities with racial/ethnic ones. He commented that the increased racial and ethnic awareness among minority inmates was increasing the distance and hostility among inmate groups.

Jacobs contends that a large measure of

The proportion of inmates who are black and Hispanic may reach 80 or 90 percent in some prisons, as is apparent in this picture of the audience of a live-entertainment program, Mid-Orange Correctional Facility, New York. (New York State Department of Correctional Services)

change in racial relationships in prison was wrought by Black Muslims. They challenged the caste system of the segregated prison, challenged the "do your own time" norm, and initiated litigation which resulted in court intervention against administrative policies of discrimination (1983a:66). Racial conflict has become a major preoccupation of inmate systems in some prisons, and a major administrative concern. Racial tension among highly organized inmate groups is perhaps worst in the California system (Jacobs, 1983a:70), but has been reported to be nearly as strong in Stateville (Illinois), where racially oriented gangs have brought their racial hostilities with them to prison (see Insert 15.2). Carroll's study (1974) of racial tension in the Rhode Island prison system documents inmate-imposed informal segregation despite prison administrators' attempts to integrate facilities.

Irwin (1977), Jacobs (1983a), and Fox (1982) agree that new racial tension and group dynamics based on racial friction have drastically altered the inmate social systems of the past. Increased racial tension has been accompanied by considerable violence, and a massive migration of threatened prisoners to protective custody (Jacobs, 1983a:78). Lockwood's (1982:47) and Toch's (1977:144–146) reports of sexual aggression in New York prisons found that the aggressors were often black and the targets often white (1982:47). Aziz's study of prison disturbances from 1970 to 1980 found racial tension mentioned as a cause by inmates or officials in 18 percent of the 218 incidents of collective violence (1983:39). The South Carolina Department of Corrections study (1973) cites race as a factor in eleven riots between 1969 and 1971. The New York State Special Commission on Attica (1972) viewed racial tension between white staff from the country and urban minority inmates as a prime factor in the building discontent in 1971.

What to do about racial conflict in prison is a difficult question. Jacobs reported that the federal courts have generally approached segregation in prison using the same principles that guided decisions in school desegregation cases

(Jacobs, 1983a:81). The only prison segregation case to reach the Supreme Court of the United States, *Washington* v. *Lee*, (1968), let stand a court of appeals order for the complete desegregation of the Alabama system. In Jacobs' view, it is unfortunate that this case does not define what "complete desegregation" might mean (1983a:84). Jacobs viewed prison segregation as substantially different from school segregation. He suggested that discrimination kept blacks in separate schools from substantial benefits, but that there are few benefits to distribute in prisons and that attempts to desegregate have escalated prison violence (1983a:81–98).

Walker (1982) strenuously objected both to the accuracy of Jacobs' perceptions and to his recommended limitations on prison integration. He pointed out that while prison itself is not a benefit, there are many benefits within prison, such as particular housing and work assignments (1982:488–489). He argued that Jacobs ignored the complexity of prison violence, especially the high frequency of intraracial violence, and let administrators off the hook in the search for positive solutions. Walker stated:

> The message is clearly communicated to all inmates that black prisoners are inherently too violent to be housed with white prisoners. This is but a contemporary version on the theme of blacks as savages. Such ideas cannot receive official notice and sanction. (1982:491)

Walker reminds us that the Nebraska prison system did not erupt in racial violence after the implementation of an integration order (1982:493).

Other commentators have also stressed that the wrong kinds of solutions to racial tensions in prison may be easy to concoct and difficult to remedy. Owens (1981) correctly insisted that members of minority groups should not necessarily be considered one group. There are many differences in individual needs within, as well as across, racial groups. Administrative policies and court decisions which treat all blacks, all His-

Insert 15.2 STREET GANGS ENTER STATEVILLE

James Jacobs (1977) conducted a longitudinal study of one maximum security prison, Stateville in Illinois. His general argument was that external changes in the environment of the prison altered the organization of control in the prison, which in turn altered social structure in the prison (1977:138). One portion of this study examined the entrance of Chicago street gangs into the prison and the resulting changes in the prison social structure.

During the late 1960s and early 1970s, many members of Chicago gangs, notably the Blackstone Rangers, the Vice Lords, and the Devil's Disciples, were arrested and sent to prison. The increase in arrests occurred after politicization of the gangs (see Fish 1974 for an account) led to a backlash by the police and the Chicago Democratic party machine.

Whether or not the gang arrests were truly politically motivated, the gang leaders interpreted their arrests that way. They entered prison with a sense of being political prisoners and with a strong sense that they could demand deference from correctional authorities (1977:146). Jacobs suggested that a recent change to a more professional administration in the prison, along with changes wrought by court orders, provided a context in which the new gang power could flourish (1977:138).

The old inmate system was stratified on offense (with murderers and armed robbers having the most prestige). The old system was challenged by the new gang norms. Gang inmates did not relate as individuals, but in groups based on gang affiliations. The old system left room for unaffiliated inmates to be left alone. The "balkanized" system of gang loyalties left loners vulnerable to attack and manipulation (1977:159).

Before the gang intrusion, inmate power depended on unspoken accommodations between staff and inmate leaders and on the distribution of prison jobs. The gangs placed the old con network in jeopardy (1977:159). Gangs took over the prison rackets; old inmate norms became less compelling than gang norms. Gang members had no qualms about stealing from unaffiliated inmates, and unlike the old cons, gang members looked after each other rather than "doing their own time" (1977:156–157).

Instead of the old balance between inmates and staff, violence in the new system was limited by delicate negotiations among gangs. Gang leaders believed the only winner in an all-out gang war would be the security force, which would crack down on illicit behavior.

Jacobs posited that the most important function gangs provided their members was psychological support. Gang members had a sense of belonging and an air of importance. New inmates who belonged to gangs were quickly identified and set up with prison amenities. Compared to unaffiliated new prisoners, reported Jacobs, gang members had no difficulty adjusting to the prison (1977:149). In addition to support, the gangs provided a ready-made network for distribution of contraband and an effective communication system, both of which rested on social organizations that evolved on the streets of Chicago rather than in the prison.

---

panics, or all Native Americans alike, either in the attempt to correct past segregation or in the attempt to avoid impending violence, may ignore the real needs of individuals and exacerbate racial tensions.

It is a positive sign that correctional commentators are no longer ignoring the problems of race relations in prison and the disproportionate incarceration rate of racial and ethnic minorities. Nevertheless, the problem in the United States is currently getting worse, not better. Figure 15.4 illustrates the incarceration rates for minorities and whites in the United States. Christianson (1982:66) pointed out that racially disproportion-

FIGURE 15.4   What Color Are America's Prisons? Incarceration Rates by Race/Ethnic Groups, 1980

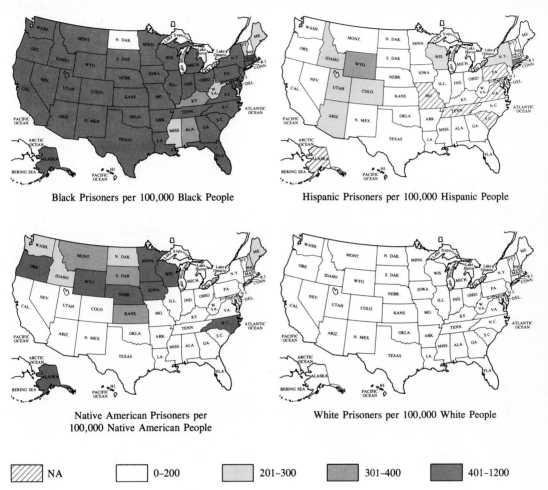

Black Prisoners per 100,000 Black People

Hispanic Prisoners per 100,000 Hispanic People

Native American Prisoners per
100,000 Native American People

White Prisoners per 100,000 White People

| | NA | | 0–200 | | 201–300 | | 301–400 | | 401–1200 |

SOURCE: *Jericho*, Newsletter of the National Moratorium on Prison Construction 32 (Summer 1983), p. 1, based on figures from United States Department of Justice, "Prisoners in State and Federal Institutions," December 31, 1980.

ate incarceration is increasing, not decreasing. For example, the gap between black and white rates increased from 321.7/100,000 in 1973 to 479/100,000 in 1979. This is a nationwide problem. In both 1973 and in 1979, only one of the ten states with the highest black rates were southern states. Immarigeon (1984) reported that the black incarceration rate was the highest in the

world. The rate in South Africa was 427.7, while in the United States it was 748.8. Green (1982) has observed that the high and increasing incarceration rate for blacks has a significant negative impact on black families.

Christianson (1982:70) complained that the rationales for the high black incarceration rate are becoming increasingly sophisticated and subtle. He argued that many writers have begun to excuse the high rate on the basis of differential involvement in crime (see the discussion in Chapter 6). This complaint may be unfair to some of these writers. For example, Blumstein (1982) was certainly not excusing the higher incarceration rate for blacks when he raised the differential involvement hypothesis. Instead, he was warning against the search for "quick fix" solutions, such as assuming that the differential imprisonment rate was evidence of mass discrimination by criminal justice officials. At the current time, the rising proportion of inmates who are racial and ethnic minorities in American prisons remains an unsolved problem. It is changing the nature of relationships among staff and inmates in the prison, and it is changing the image of the prison in American society.

THE EFFECTS OF INCARCERATION

Practitioners and researchers have traditionally been concerned with the effects of incarceration. Prison history suggests that prison reform emerged nearly simultaneously with prisons themselves. The invention of the American penitentiary in the early nineteenth century was seen in part as an attempt to alleviate the worst problems with the penal measures that preceded it. And the penitentiary movement included high if misplaced hopes for the positive effects of imprisonment on prisoners as well as on society (Beaumont and Toqueville, 1964; Rothman, 1971). However, even the early prisons were quickly attacked by other social critics who were doubtful about the positive impact of isolation, were concerned about prisoners becoming hardened and alienated in prison, or perceived difficulties in the reintegration process (Scull, 1977). Perhaps the common understanding has been that the lofty intentions of imprisonment have rarely been achieved, and that imprisonment generally has had negative effects upon its involuntary participants.

Observers would frequently use recidivism

rates as evidence that prisons damaged their inmates. However, without knowledge about how often the same offenders would have offended again without the experience of imprisonment, recidivism rates do not tell us whether incarceration has caused adjustment problems. By the time of the President's Commission on Law Enforcement and Administration of Justice (1967), the consequences of incarceration were certainly official doctrine. However, as with a number of other strongly held correctional beliefs, there was little systematic empirical evidence to substantiate the claims of personal and social damage (Hawkins, 1976:58–60).

In the last two decades, considerably more systematic knowledge has been gained. Not surprisingly, the evidence about the effects of incarceration is far more complex and considerably more ambiguous than many would have supposed. In 1980, Bukstel and Kilmann conducted a thorough review of empirical research to evaluate the effects of imprisonment. They conclude:

> Overall, the evidence suggests that an inmate's response to confinement is determined by a complex interaction of variables. Thus the findings do not unequivocally support the popular notion that correctional confinement is harmful to most individuals. (1980:487)

Nigel Walker, conducting a similar review in Great Britain, reviewed health, mental health, family, and criminalization effects. He concluded that we know very little about the negative effects of prison. He pointed out that we have found the positive effects to be short lived, and he posited that the negative effects might be equally likely to wear off after release. He proposed that the immediate environment is a more important determinant of behavior than past environment for most adults subject to imprisonment (1983). In a related study, Walker, Farrington and Tucker (1981) examined reconviction rates by types of sentence for 2,069 men who were followed for six years after completion of sentence. The researchers found that some types of offenders were less likely to reoffend after a prison sentence than after nonincarcerative sentences, while others fared better with community sentences.

Bukstel and Kilmann called for longitudinal research as probably the only means to resolve the ambiguity in the current studies about the effects of incarceration (1980:489). One of the few longitudinal studies conducted so far (Martin and Webster, 1971) provided tentative evidence that the impact of all punishments (including imprisonment) on the career of the offender was rather transitory. This English study, which followed a small sample of offenders in one court from arrest through completion of sentence, found that the punishment was less important than many other life situation factors in explaining what happened to individuals after punishment.

Such data do not deny that correctional experiences can have irrevocably damaging effects on some persons, and can turn the lives of others around for the better. But such data do indicate that the impact of incarceration on the postprison behavior of prisoners is impossible to predict without knowing more about the specific individual, the particular prison situation, and the release situation. These data would appear to refute Donald Clemmer's (1940) original hypothesis about the impact of prisonization. Clemmer had argued that the longer one was subject to prison, the more irrevocable the damage because the prisoner would be increasingly more committed to the inmate culture. As we will see below, the relationship is more complex.

Following Clemmer's lead that prisonization would affect attitudes and values which would be important after release, Stanton Wheeler (1961) examined the strength of adherence to the inmate code, controlling for the portion of the sentence they were serving. Wheeler proposed that it was not the absolute length of time which determined inmate values, but how far away from release they were. Wheeler described the now famous J (or U) curve: Inmates beginning their sentences held value positions most like those of staff; those in the middle portions of their sentences held values most in conflict with the staff; and inmates

nearing release returned to a value position closer to that of staff, although not quite as close as those just entering the prison. Wheeler interpreted these findings as signs that prisonization might not be lasting or stable. Signs of the inmate culture were strongest among inmates furthest from entry or release. As inmates neared release, argued Wheeler, anticipatory socialization occurred.

A number of studies have sought to replicate Wheeler's findings with mixed results. The J curve is not always found, and seems to be affected by type of prison and type of inmate (see Bukstel and Kilmann, 1980:483–484 for a review of these studies). However, studies of psychological effects of imprisonment have also found some evidence of a J or U curve in a number of dimensions. The length of time to release may have an impact on a number of variables besides value orientation (Bukstel and Kilmann, 1980: 477–480).

An intriguing study by Goodstein (1979) examined the impact on postrelease behavior of variations in adjustment to prison. Goodstein typed inmates by their release orientation and their satisfaction with prison. She hypothesized that inmates who were most satisfied with the institution and had a low release orientation, while model inmates, would fare poorly after release. She also proposed that "rebellious" inmates, who would not conform to prison rules or participate in prison programs in order to get release and who were dissatisfied with the prison, might do well.

These expectations were substantiated for the period immediately after release. At the start of parole, the institutionalized prisoners had the highest number of warnings and were the least likely to be employed. Rebellious inmates fared best on these measures, compared to the other three types. The release behavior differences disappeared by the third month, indicating again that the effects of adjustment to imprisonment may wear off relatively soon. Goodstein's study is particularly important for demonstrating that inmates who readily accept the prison routine and staff direction may not adjust easily to the free community, and that rebellious inmates, who display commitment to anti-staff norms in prison, may have an easier time adjusting after release.

Other researchers have asked whether length of sentence has an impact upon postrelease behavior. The National Council on Crime and Delinquency (Gottfredson et al., 1973:25) studied 100,000 prisoners after first release from prison. They concluded that when past record and current crime variables were controlled, the effects of time served were not great. There was some evidence that shorter time served was more effective than longer sentences, although the strength of the effect varied by type of crime. A number of studies have examined the impact of time served in conjunction with the practice of the split sentence, as discussed in Chapter 9. These studies routinely find that shorter jail or prison terms preceding a probationary sentence are just as effective in reducing new crimes.

Finally, a number of studies have sought to examine the impact of type of prison on release behavior. This is an increasingly difficult issue, since many prisoners in our state and federal systems are transferred from one facility to another during incarceration, so it becomes very difficult to measure the effects of one type of prison placement over the effects of the others experienced during the same sentence. An early study by Mannheim and Wilkins (1955) indicated that open institutions were more effective for juvenile males in England. More recently, Farrington and Nuttall (1980) reported that larger prisons did not have higher than expected recidivism rates, when overcrowding was controlled, but that there was a strong positive association between overcrowding and failure. Wright (1977), examining both halfway houses and prison living units, found suggestive, but not conclusive, evidence that units with strong group cohesion and group commitment may produce worse postrelease behavior than correctional units with a higher preparation for release orientation but less evidence of strong group cohesion.

SUMMARY

1. Adjustment to prison is a complex process involving the needs of the individual inmate, the social mix in the prison, the response of staff, administrative policies, and a number of situational factors.
2. Much policy debate has centered around the importation/deprivation controversy. Some have argued that the deprivations experienced in prison invariably lead to the emergence of an inmate culture which subverts attempts at rehabilitation and even routine cooperation between staff and inmates. Others have argued that the anti-staff norms found in prison are not unique to the prison setting, but are found in the social environments from which many prisoners come.
3. More recent research indicates that the explanation of behavior in and after prison must rely upon a combination of variables, some representing a prisoner's preprison experience, and others representing the current situation.

4. Evidence suggests that prison policy, staff, and particularly the custodial staff, can and do make a difference in the nature of the prison experience.
5. There is growing evidence that the prison as a social institution is no longer as isolated from the rest of the world as it once was. Organizational boundaries are more permeable, and changes in the free society do have impacts on the nature of social relations in prison. Perhaps most significant is the impact of this opening of the prison on the distribution of power within it. Clearly, prison management is now a much more complex task, as guards, inmates, the courts, and other groups exert influence upon the nature of life in prison.
6. One of the major changes in prison social systems has been increasing cleavages along lines of race and ethnicity. In addition, the increasing incarceration rates for blacks and other minorities is threatening the political legitimacy of the prison.

7. Almost all the empirical research on prison life and on the impact of imprisonment on its subjects indicate that long-held beliefs about the negative effects of the total institution, during and after the experience, have been overstated. Some inmates may be psychologically destroyed by the experience, others may be better adjusted to a particular prison environment than to their available environments on the outside. Most inmates fall within these extremes: Adjustments may be difficult but not debilitating, and the effects, either positive or negative, are probably not long-lasting in many cases.

KEY WORDS

COLLECTIVE RESISTANCE. Protests by groups of inmates without resort to violence.

COLLECTIVE VIOLENCE. Group actions by inmates that involve the use of violence.

FUNCTIONAL APPROACH TO PRISON CULTURE. Explanations of the prison culture that focus on shared experience within the prison, such as inmate responses to the pains of imprisonment.

IMPORTATION HYPOTHESIS. Explanations of the prison culture that focus on the background of inmates rather than current prison experience.

PAINS OF IMPRISONMENT. The deprivations associated with imprisonment, including loss of freedom, autonomy, goods and services, security, and heterosexual relationships.

PRISONIZATION. "Taking on, in greater or lesser degree, the folkways, mores, customs, and general culture of the penitentiary" (Clemmer, 1940:220).

TOTAL INSTITUTION. A term coined by Goffman (1961) to refer to organizations that controlled the work, play, and sleep of their lower participants.

U CURVE. Also known as the J curve; the graphed pattern of inmate value distance from staff as prison sentence progressed. Inmates first entering prison had values most similar to staff. Inmates in the middle of the sentence had values least like staff. Inmates preparing for release had values closer to staff, but not as similar as those just entering prison.

PROJECTS AND QUESTIONS

1. The simulated prison reported in this chapter is a very controversial experiment. Read the original report (Haney, Banks, and Zimbardo, 1973). How well do you think the researchers succeeded in simulating a prison? Did they use any procedures which may have undermined their attempt to see what normal people would do in a real prison setting?

2. Irwin and Cressey (1962) suggested that one set of values imported into the prison is the culture of "state raised youth" who have moved from one institutional placement to another and eventually ended up in prison. These inmates, argued Irwin and Cressey, have a difficult time on the street and are there for very short periods of time. They are very familiar with the roles and expectations of prison life. Would you agree that these values are imported into prison? Where did these values begin?

3. Search the major newspaper in your state for evidence of prison disturbances such as riots or demonstrations over the last ten years (several people can be assigned to each year of the search). How many incidents occurred? Did they bunch together, or were they evenly spread across time? Did they occur in the same institutions most of the time? What explanations were given for these events by officials? By the participating inmates?

ADDITIONAL READING

Malcolm Braly. *On the Yard*. Greenwich, CT: Fawcett, 1972. Braly was an accomplished novelist and ex-convict. This is his classic novel of life in a maximum security prison and is probably a richer account than social science methods can portray.

David Kalinich. *The Inmate Economy*. Prospect Heights, IL:Waveland Press, 1986. Kalinich provides an economic study of the inmate social system by examining the relationship between the underground economy and order in the prison.

Anthony Mannochio and Jimmy Dunn. *The Time Game*. New York: Dell, 1970. This is an enjoyable book written by a prison counselor and one of his inmates. Each chapter follows Dunn through his prison sentence, from both the counselor's and the inmate's perspective.

Hans Toch. *Men in Crisis*. Chicago: Aldine, 1975. Toch and his colleagues interviewed men who had experienced breakdowns in prison and examined the forces that lead to crisis. A richly detailed account of those who are damaged by the prison experience.

CHAPTER 16

THE CORRECTIONAL OFFICER: WORKING IN PRISON

QUESTIONS

1. Why has the correctional officer only recently received systematic attention?

2. How has correctional officer unionization affected prison social systems?

3. How have affirmative action and equal employment opportunity affected the guard force?

4. What do we know about prison guards' work attitudes?

5. Which group of correctional officers is typically more treatment oriented and more interested in performing human service roles?

6. Is there a correctional officer subculture?

"THE JOINT'S SECURE."

Phil was still in his first week of gathering information from inmates and officers at Dunmore. The interviews with officers had gone smoothly that day, but Phil felt stressed. He had talked with twelve officers of various ages and assignments. Some seemed very open; others were tight-lipped and suspicious. They would give one-word answers, no matter what the question.

Phil's favorite was a middle-aged officer who chain smoked, sighed heavily between each thoughtful sentence, and looked tired beyond his years.

"What do you see as your purpose in the prison?" Phil had asked.

"You mean the purpose of the guards?" Phil nodded.

"Damned if I know. You look around this place. You'll see the joint's secure. The formal job description says we're here for security, but we must be good for something else. Guarding isn't it. But we're not supposed to get too close to the inmates either. So I'm not sure what we're here for." When the interview was finished, the officer got up to go, then looked back at Phil. "The officers giving you a hard time?"

Phil knew that standard interview protocol did not recommend direct answers to such questions, but by this point Phil was eager to hear a sympathetic voice.

"Some," he said. "Can't get more than one word at a time out of some. And down at the BOQ it's a little worse."

The officer nodded. "Just remember it isn't you. It's anybody from out there. Some officers are distrustful about any kind of study. They've seen them before, they'll see them again. Each one starts with promises, but the officers don't see anything out of it."

Phil nodded. "So the officers think the inmates get most of the attention?"

"Sure they do. But they ought to. That's what prison is about, right? The guys who committed the crimes. Not us."

Phil frowned. "Well, not altogether. This isn't, for instance, a study about inmates. It is an attempt to examine work in prison and how it can be done more effectively. That should affect officers more than inmates. And if officers are not affected, then there's no way to change things for the inmates. I mean the officers will have more effect on the inmate than anyone else."

The officer lit another cigarette. "Well, some of us think so, but you don't get that message from the central office. I wish you luck. Don't get discouraged."

Phil thanked him. The next officer came into the interview room. "This where the test is?"

"No," said Phil, "it's not a test."

"Then I don't have to take it?"

One week later, on his last night, Phil was distributing his last questionnaire to the officer in B building. He found the man in the day room, idly straightening up chairs. To Phil's delight, he discovered it was the officer who had given him encouragement during the interviews the previous week.

"So," said Officer Walters, "How's the study going?"

"Okay," said Phil. "I have a questionnaire for you, if you don't mind."

"No, I don't mind. You been getting some flack from this?"

Phil frowned. "Well, just about everybody has filled them out, but I've heard rumors that some of the officers will be glad to see me go."

"Rumors," said Walters, "are no more accurate in here than anywhere else, although they might travel faster. Sure there's a few guys that can't see anything in this. You have to expect that. Look, some of them have been putting in eight hours for twenty years and have never seen anyone take any real interest in them. They haven't any reason to think this will be different. Some suspect this might just be the one— the one time the central office actually got something going that would affect how officers got along in here, rather than inmates. And when they stop to think about that, they think, hey, maybe that's not so good either. I mean, they don't like it the way it is, but then they know what it is. Change could be good or bad. If you want my opinion, most of these officers, if you gave them a real chance to do something different, something more rewarding, they'd jump at it. But they won't admit it when it might not happen. There have been promises before."

Phil nodded. "I guess I keep forgetting that the correctional officers are just as much in prison as the inmates."

Walters frowned. "Well, keep your perspective. These inmates can't leave until someone says go. We do our time in eight-hour installments. But it isn't really the same, and don't let anyone tell you it is. It is true that officers don't get much recognition. And that goes for the brass in here, not just the public. So you get pretty defensive after a while, or you become cynical, or you get into hobbies or a second job—something else to make life more rewarding.

There is a lot of conflict, but in a lot of ways the guards are a lot closer to the inmates on things than to any other group."

THE AMBIGUOUS CORRECTIONAL OFFICER ROLE

During Phil's two-week stay on the Dunmore prison grounds, three people in very different positions provided sufficient emotional support and friendship to help get him through a trying, lonely experience. One of these men was the superintendent, one was an inmate, and one was a prison guard. Through them, Phil learned a good deal about the forces that affect the people who live and work in prison. Perhaps his most valuable lesson was that the defensive, suspicious veneer that separates human beings in prison has not covered up all individuality, nor has it submerged in all its members their willingness to be helpful and concerned with the plight of others. Among this trio of manager, guard, and inmate, for Phil the most welcome surprise was Officer Walters, who said: ". . . the joint's secure. . . . we must be good for something else." This was an admission of some confusion; the officer role was not clear to Officer Walters. But it was also an expression of hope that his presence in the institution was not merely a means of keeping order or keeping the lid on, but provided him an opportunity to benefit others directly in his work.

As Phil reexamined his interviews and questionnaire findings upon his return to the university, he discovered that roughly half of the Dunmore officers held opinions similar to those expressed by Walters. If many correctional officers privately agreed with Walters, how was it that correctional officers were often criticized for their animosity toward inmates and their cynicism toward programs of self-improvement in prison? As we will see, the differences between the private and the public expressions of correctional officers on the nature of their jobs and the pur-

poses of imprisonment suggest some difficult conflicts built into the role of correctional officer and into the current personnel practices of many modern prisons.

CHANGING VIEWS OF THE PRISON GUARD

In *State of Prisons* (originally published in 1777), John Howard's recommendations for prison reform implied that employment in prison did not attract a high-quality staff (Howard, 1929). He stated that nothing could be more important to the efficient and humane administration of the prison than selection of a nongambling, nondrinking warden. He also recommended that the "turnkeys" should be salaried so that they would not have to extract fees from the inmates in order to make a living. The picture Howard painted of prison guards in the eighteenth century was an ugly one. It was a job designed to attract low-skilled, manipulative, and uncaring persons.

Beaumont and Toqueville's major tract on American prisons in 1833 provides evidence that conditions in the United States, prior to the penitentiary movement, were quite similar to those depicted by Howard in Europe. However, these French observers reported that between 1790 and 1830, the emphasis on the moral improvement of prisoners also changed the nature of prison work. Prison administration became a moral calling. While they admitted that the "inferior agents" did not match the caliber of the new penitentiary wardens, they did find that most guards were "intelligent and honest men." In addition, Beaumont and Toqueville provided evidence that even in the early penitentiary period, prison guards performed a more complex role than that of turnkey. These French visitors remarked that almost all guards they met had special technical knowledge in the areas in which the inmates worked and were often responsible for instruction as well as security.

Observations of penitentiaries in the nineteenth century also mention three phenomena still important today. The early prison reformers placed great importance on the role of the outside prison inspectors, whose duty it was to visit prisons and report to the public on conditions found there. The early reformers believed that such outside inspection was necessary because working in prison could be debilitating, and only constant exchange with outside public representatives would keep prison workers from loss of effectiveness and humaneness. Second, reports of the early penitentiary suggest that just as is true today, there were remarkable differences from prison to prison in the quality and management of the staff. Finally, historical accounts underscore the importance of public opinion in prison work. When prisons were high on the public agenda, public opinion uplifted prison work and improved the lot of prison workers. When the mood of the public swung away from reformation of prisoners toward retribution or deterrence, or when corrections dropped lower in public concern, then not only prisoners but also prison workers suffered more.

In the early penitentiary, there was not a great deal of concern about goal conflict among the prison staff. Staffing patterns were rather simple, and guards played a prominent role in both guarding and supervising work. When reformation was thought to occur through penitence and obedience, the role played by prison guards was an important means of securing those ends. This position of prison guards changed significantly between 1870 and 1930. In the second wave of correctional reform that swept the country in 1870, new divisions in the correctional labor force became visible, first in juvenile institutions, and then in adult institutions.

Beverly Smith (forthcoming) finds some evidence of conflict between the prison matrons and the prison chaplains responsible for the social and moral changes in girls in the New York Western House of Refuge in the 1870s. The matrons' attempts to enforce harsh order in the institution were not always congruent with the chaplains' attempts to place girls on parole or provide them with a proper education. By the 1930s, the split

in prison roles between security specialists and treatment specialists was complete (Dession, 1938). Inmate reformation was now to be accomplished through specialized social science techniques, in which the guards were not trained. Hence this era saw a significant change in the social position of the guard in prison. Guards lost power and respect. An entirely new line of authority was established alongside the security chain of command (Zald, 1962).

Despite the shift of the custody force from centrality to the periphery in relation to prison goals, the custodial force has always been the most numerous. While national statistics on the makeup of correctional staff do not frequently make distinctions among categories of staff, the National Manpower Survey of the Criminal Justice System (1978) found that in 1974, custodial staff comprised 73.2 percent of all workers in local adult corrections facilities, 62.9 percent in state facilities for adults, and 41 percent in facilities for juveniles. The National Manpower Survey observed that salaries for custodial staff varied considerably from state to state but were generally low, and that training for correctional officer positions was often brief, inadequate, and poorly implemented.

THE DISCOVERY OF THE PRISON GUARD

In the early 1970s the lowly position of prison guards in the prison hierarchy and in correctional research priorities began to shift again. This shift was probably related to two broad changes also occurring at the same time. First, this was the time when the rehabilitative ideal for correctional work began to crumble. As it was shown that treatment specialists were not making effective headway with the rehabilitative challenge, custodial workers began to take on new importance. For some, the custodial worker seemed central to the growing emphasis placed on retributive and deterrence goals. For others, the prison guard appeared more important than the tarnished treatment specialists—not as purveyors of pain and suffering, but as essential figures in the humane administration of punishment.

At about the same time, new interest in the United States and elsewhere arose in the plight of disgruntled, alienated blue collar workers (Special Task Force to the Secretary of Health, Education, and Welfare, 1973). A number of reports called for a new approach to the management of front-line workers, providing them with the opportunity to participate in formation of policy and the responsibility to control to a greater degree their own work conditions (Duffee, 1972). If worker discontent in a variety of settings was not reduced, it was predicted that workers would respond with reduced work quality and demands for increased benefits (Argyris, 1957). In corrections, this prediction proved accurate, as guards in many states organized either for the first time, or with increased zeal. By becoming an organized political force, guards sought, with some success, the attention and respect they had not previously been granted by the public or the system.

THE RISE OF THE GUARD UNIONS

According to Joan Potter (1981a:323), the first officer union to enter into formal negotiations with a government was the New York City Correction Officers Benevolent Association, in the late 1950s. However, most union action started a full decade later. The union representing the most prison guards in the United States is the American Federation of State, County, and Municipal Employees (AFSCME), representing over 50,000 officers in 15 states (1981a:322). At the present time, about half of the states operate under some type of formally negotiated agreement with an organized guard force, although the level and completeness of bargaining varies in accordance with state law. Some states make the unionization of public employees illegal. Some allow only for a rather informal "meet and confer" type of bargaining, in which the government still makes all major decisions unilaterally. Some states permit formal bargaining only on nonwage issues, while still other states permit comprehensive collective bargaining on wages as well as other work-related issues (1981a:324–325).

As collective bargaining has spread as a means by which prison guards can gain a say in the nature of their work, decision-making power in prisons has shifted on some important matters. Potter (1981a:325) reports that two primary issues for guard unions are permitting officers to bid on post assignments on the basis of seniority, and demanding that guards have some say in whether increases in inmate programming will be permitted. Correction officers view the bidding by seniority as a means of rewarding the most experienced officers with some power to control when they will work and at what position.

Correctional administrators have traditionally assigned officers to posts based on their view of which officers were best prepared for particular assignments. Administrators generally prefer to assign experienced officers to sensitive posts that require quick judgment and skill in relating to inmates or to the public. Where officers have gained a right to control their own assignments, some officers with greater experience have opted to leave posts with high inmate contact for less challenging and threatening posts, such as tower duty.

The second issue, approval of inmate programs, may be more important as a symbolic issue than a realistic concern in its own right. Officers have long felt ignored in decisions that affect their work. Their attempts to gain the right to veto particular inmate programs can be construed as an antirehabilitative stance. It is more likely, however, that officers want some say in decisions about where and when such programs will be offered. They claim that many inmate activities are scheduled without regard to the increased workload which falls to the security staff when such programs expand.

In 1979, a major guard strike in the New York prison system highlighted the salience of

During the correction officer strike of 1979, Governor Carey called in the National Guard to supervise the prisons. (New York State Department of Correctional Services)

these and other issues to an increasingly vocal correctional officer organization. On April 18, 1979, most of the officers in the Department of Correctional Services walked off the job. This was the largest guard strike in history, and Governor Carey called up 12,000 national guardsmen to keep the prisons operating during the walkout (Jacobs and Zimmer, 1983:142). Unlike strikes in other types of industry, the New York strike was instigated more by the officers' complaints about working conditions, and about their position in the department and society, than about money (Potter, 1981a:329). In fact, Jacobs and Zimmer claim that the underlying causes of the strike were not even negotiable contract issues. Instead, the guards were displeased by their perceived lack of control over inmates, by their perceived lack of status, and by intrastaff racial tension (1983:146). Such issues arise from political and structural dynamics that shape prisons in general. Since they cannot be ameliorated in a contract, the illegal strike may have had more symbolic than realistic objectives. Guards were

fed up and were committed to letting everyone know it.

In terms of concrete results, the guards gained little from the strike. The prisons ran smoothly in the guards' absence, as inmates cooperated with the national guardsmen (Jacobs and Zimmer, 1983:155). The court ordered a $2,550,000 fine against the union and jailed its director on contempt charges. The fine was later reduced to $150,000. The guards finally agreed to a contract that included a few face-saving concessions, but in general they were held to the line offered before the strike. The strike aftermath, which continues to haunt the New York prison system, includes considerable bitterness between the striking guards and employees who did not honor the picket lines. To some degree, the guards may have gained a limited political victory by publicizing their grievances and displaying considerable unanimity. But conditions in New York prisons have not changed a great deal since the strike, and guards still suffer the same dissatisfaction and voice the same complaints.

THE EMPLOYMENT OF DISADVANTAGED GROUPS

While a large proportion of convicted offenders belong to socially disadvantaged groups, particularly the poor and ethnic and racial minorities, socially disadvantaged groups are not well represented among correctional staff. There are any number of reasons for the inability and unwillingness of correctional agencies to hire minority staff, some of which will be discussed below. Some steps have been taken in recent years to improve recruitment and promotion of employees from social and economic groups underrepresented in the correctional workforce. Most of these efforts stem from the Title VII legislation of the 1964 Civil Rights Act (42 U.S. Code, section 2000). This legislation required equal employment opportunities for all groups. Employers were not to discriminate on the basis of sex, race, religion, or other personal characteristics unrelated to performance of the task.

In 1972, the Title VII legislation was amended to apply to state and local governments. Although the President's Commission on Law Enforcement and Administration of Justice (1967a)

and the Joint Commission on Correctional Manpower and Training (1969) both recommended that correctional agencies take special steps to recruit, retain, and advance women and racial minority personnel, it was not until the 1972 legislation that most correctional agencies began to respond (Nicolai, 1981)

There is one important distinction in agency response to discriminatory hiring practices, the difference between **equal employment opportunity (EEO)** and programs of **affirmative action (AAP)**. EEO, by itself, is a rather passive vehicle by which to address employment discrimination. Its basic principle is that in selecting candidates for employment or promotion, employers will not use discriminatory standards such as race and gender. All applicants of equal merit or ability are to have equal opportunity to compete for positions. EEO personnel policies forbid unfair discrimination among individuals, but do not require employers to take positive steps to correct imbalances in the work force that stem from previous discrimination.

Relying only on EEO, correctional agencies would never have any significant proportion of blacks, Hispanics, or women on staff, because

Affirmative Action and Equal Employment Opportunity programs have increased the proportion of minority and female correctional staff. This shows a training session for officers at the New York State Correctional Training Academy. (New York State Department of Correctional Services)

the few recently hired would always be at the lowest end of experience and seniority lists. EEO might correct some egregiously arbitrary practices in selections among individuals for a particular position, but it is unlikely that EEO alone could alter the proportions of disadvantaged categories employed in the agency. Consequently, affirmative action has become the accepted although still controversial means of implementing the spirit of EEO.

Affirmative Action Programs (AAP) operate on different principles. AAP provides, among other things, that among equally qualified candidates, persons from disadvantaged groups will receive preference, and that when a minority applicant is rejected in favor of someone else, a written justification for the decision must be given. Moreover, AAP policy pushes for aggressive recruitment of minority and women candidates for employment, to ensure that the agency has a fair pool from which to select. AAP policies also require agencies to establish and meet targets for the employment of minorities and women. AAP challenges to civil service tests have resulted in many agencies being required to devise new screening instruments that do not correlate with race or other prohibited selection characteristics.

While EEO and AAP have had some impact in corrections, their effects have been extremely uneven. It would appear—ironically, perhaps—that minority recruitment and promotion has advanced most in those correctional systems under court order to correct inmate rights violations. When courts have required the immediate hiring of more guards as a step in reducing prison violence, for example, more minority and women guards have been hired.

EMPLOYMENT OF RACIAL MINORITIES

One of the most controversial if unintended political symbols of many correctional systems is the urban, black, and Hispanic inmates guarded by rural whites. The New York Commission in-

vestigating the causes of the Attica riot perceived the racial differences of the captors and captives as one of the most significant contextual factors giving rise to the disturbance. Touring newly constructed correctional facilities for the American Foundation, William Nagel (1973:51) reported that many correctional administrators explicitly preferred white, rural guards to guards from racial or ethnic minorities. He suggested that this preference was not so much conscious discrimination, as a by-product of the historical location of prisons in rural areas. Over the years of recruiting in those settings, argued Nagel, entire administrative echelons in many systems have become dominated by white men with rural backgrounds.

Nagel points out that the continuing pressure to locate new prisons in rural areas continues to affect correctional agency hiring practices. Since in many states not only the most eligible blacks and Hispanics, but also the largest supply of treatment professionals, are urban, the rural location of prisons is detrimental to recruitment. Urban prisons, however, are difficult to establish. City dwellers, regardless of race, are more apt to object to prison construction than rural residents. Rural communities often want the employment opportunity, while urban people are fearful of crime. Additionally, many prison departments have simply built new prisons adjacent to the rural prisons already in operation, both to save land acquisition costs and to avoid neighborhood objections.

Nagel's hypothesis of ingrained racial problems in correctional administration is also advanced by Jacobs and Grear (1981). Interviewing 55 persons who had resigned or been dismissed from the Illinois prison system, they found that the most frequently cited reason for leaving among whites was problems with black inmates, while the most frequently cited reason for leaving among blacks was problems with white supervisors. Unfortunately, such a study is incomplete, because there is no information on the attitudes of guards from either race who stayed.

There are also some other factors that must be considered when exploring the employment of racial minorities in corrections work. Two of the most important are the age-seniority issue and the urban-rural issue. It is entirely possible that these two variables, separately or combined, explain much of the trouble attributed to race. Most black guards are among the newest workers in correctional systems. We know that the greatest dissatisfaction and the greatest difficulties with correctional work occur within the first five years of employment, regardless of race. Many minority employees may encounter problems because of inexperience that are attributed to race. This does not excuse administrators from making the incorrect attribution, but it could suggest that solutions based on race rather than training and socialization are misdirected.

A similar problem happens with the rural/urban distinction. A large body of literature suggests that urban blue collar workers are more alienated than rural blue collar workers. In systems where most minority recruits are urban, reliance on the racial rather than urban explanation for alienation from the organization is again misplaced. As we will see in the next section, Toch and Grant (1982) found that in an urban prison where most guards were black, there were indeed high levels of alienation. But *all* the guards, regardless of race, were alienated. Finally, against the often anecdotal and incomplete information about racial minorities being angry and alienated in correctional work, we also have contradictory evidence that minority correctional workers more often plan on corrections as a career and are more often satisfied with correctional work than white males (similar evidence is available concerning women).

Two other system problems must also be considered when dealing with the racial issue in correctional employment. First, to the extent that EEO and AAP are effective, racial minorities have greater opportunities in a number of occupational areas than previously. If minorities do not flock to correctional opportunities, one reason is that they simply have more attractive employment opportunities elsewhere. It may take correctional agencies longer to correct racial and

ethnic imbalances than some other kinds of organizations. Second, newly employed minority workers are often placed in an unfair and awkward position by both offenders and administrators. Some offenders are willing to attempt to manipulate any staff, however, that can be accomplished. Minority offenders may often complain that a minority guard has sold out. On the flip side, some correctional administrators probably harbor the irrational and racist expectation that hiring minority staff will somehow improve staff-inmate relationships. This is naive if nothing else, and certainly an unfair burden for minority staff. Inmates are still being punished, and they are still likely to be angry and alienated.

THE EMPLOYMENT OF WOMEN

Women have always been employed in correctional roles, but their employment has historically been limited to working with female offenders. There have usually been a greater proportion of women in the correctional work force than in the offender population, since the crime rates of women are so low. Consequently, women have never been recruited into corrections at rates representative of their frequency in the general population, where they are the majority, and they have never had equal access to managerial positions in corrections, since most of those occur in facilities or programs for men. The controversy over the employment of women in corrections is their deployment in the supervision of males, and particularly their use as guards in prisons for adult males.

The employment of women in the supervision of men met an apparently major setback in 1977, when the United States Supreme Court concluded that the Alabama prison system could legally exclude women from the maximum security prison. Relying on no empirical evidence whatsoever, the Court decided that in the violent, understaffed prison, female guards would be subject to attack from predatory sex offenders and could contribute to unrest in the prison (*Dothard* v. *Richardson*). However, that opinion has subsequently been in-

In a number of states, including New York, women have been hired as officers in prisons for men. (New York State Department of Correctional Services)

terpreted narrowly. Other courts have presumed that *Dothard* is controlling in undermanaged, maximum security prisons only and does not serve to exclude women from officer positions in most states or most prisons.

Significantly, the Court in *Dothard* avoided what many thought would have been the more legitimate argument for exclusion of female guards: the privacy rights of male prisoners. However, the courts have sought to avoid decisions on the privacy rights of prisoners in general. A U.S. district court in Iowa decided that the administrators' claim of privacy for its inmates could not support the refusal to hire women as officers. Instead, it directed the administration to create staffing and assignment patterns so that the deployment of women officers would not infringe on prisoners privacy (*Gunther* v. *Iowa*, 1979).

A survey of state correctional departments suggests that different states have taken remarkably different approaches to this issue. In 1978 women comprised 23 percent of the correctional work force, compared to 12 percent in 1969. In institutions for males, 6.6 percent of the guards were women, with the highest percentages occurring in the South and several western states (Ni-

colai, 1981:225). The hiring of women did appear to be inversely related to the percentage of prison space that was designated maximum security, and positively related to states that had been ordered to hire more officers quickly (1981:225).

THE WORK ATTITUDES OF PRISON GUARDS

Our information about who correctional officers are, their motivations for taking prison work, and how the job affects them is still sketchy, despite increasing attention to guards since 1974. The bitterly fought battles over working conditions, such as the 1979 New York strike, and statistics on guard turnover and absences suggest that something is wrong. For example, the New York Office of Employee Relations, while negotiating the 1979 contract, pointed out that in 1978 guards averaged 5.6 days per year of compensation time, compared to 1.7 days per year for other state workers. The office claimed that only one-third of these absences were due to inmate-related injuries and implied that guards were staying away from the job without appropriate reasons (Jacobs and Zimmer, 1983:149). Jacobs and Retsky (1975) reported that on any given shift at Stateville, Illinois, as many as 50 percent of the officers fail to show up for work, placing undue strain on other guards and administrators.

In Kentucky in 1978, the warden of the maximum security prison reported an annual turnover of more than half of his custody force, citing low commitment to the job, poor working conditions in a dilapidated facility, and an abundance of other jobs in the area which were more attractive financially. The National Manpower Survey (1978) found that the national turnover rate for correctional officers was 19.1 percent and that the daily absenteeism rate hovered around 15 percent. Such figures indicate that officers are too displeased with daily working conditions to show up for work or to consider custody as a career.

Naturally, working conditions and officer responses vary substantially from state to state and from prison to prison. However, even in prisons where salaries are relatively high and turnover low, resentment, alienation, and tension are generally observable by any prison visitor. At the same time, there is increasing evidence that many officers grow more interested in the provision of human services to inmates as they spend more time as guards. Moreover, there are accumulating accounts of officers going out of their way to take on special assignments, sometimes without additional pay, in order to improve conditions in prison (Duffee, 1986).

RELATIONS WITH INMATES

In sorting out the complex, contradictory information about the attitudes of guards, relationships with inmates would appear to be a useful place to start. Hepburn (1985) proposed that significant changes in prison administration and inmate demographics in the last ten years may have had an impact on how guards do their jobs:

> To gain compliance from prisoners on a routine basis, guards must have what Thibault and Kelly refer to as usable power; that is, guards must be able to mobilize a resource that is available, convenient, and practical to use. Since an organization's structure, values, and goals make particular resources more or less usable, . . . changes in an organization are likely to affect the bases of usable power. (1985:149)

Hepburn's findings do not paint a picture of guards as punitive, rule-minded, or inflexible keepers of order. Asking guards to rank various forms of power as important "to get inmates to do what you want them to do," Hepburn found that 52.2 percent of the guards ranked "legitimate power" and "expert power" as first or second. In other words, a majority of officers tended to rely upon an inmate's recognition of the power residing in their office and upon their skill in offering solutions which would be followed because of the effectiveness of the alternatives suggested (1985:154). "Referent power," or the ability to use one's personality to attract obedience and loyalty, was not common among guards, and most guards reported that the opportunity to use "reward power" to manipulate behavior was generally not available. Hepburn did find that officers who scored high on scales measuring custodial and punitive attitudes relied more on coercive power than other officers, but this group was not very large (1985:159).

In a related study, Heburn (1984) examined officer attitudes toward the various means by which inmates might protest their treatment by staff. On this issue there was considerably more similarity in guard attitude, with the vast majority of guards favoring only those protests, such as a letter to the warden or the filing of a grievance, that do not reach beyond the walls of the prison. Again, Hepburn found that officers who perceived themselves to be in greater control of the prison were less opposed to protest than those who felt less in control.

A four-prison survey by Klofas (1983) tended to substantiate Hepburn's findings that officers are not necessarily anti-inmate or overly concerned about maintaining distance. Among maximum security guards he found strong support for reducing social distance between inmates and guards. Sixty percent of the officers agreed with the statement "The way to get respect from inmates is to take an interest in them." Forty-one percent even agreed with the statement "You get to like the inmates you work with" (1983:110). Klofas reported that officers temper their approval of social interaction with inmates with their concern about corruption and about being conned or manipulated (1983:117). Nevertheless, this was not evidence of strong opposition to high interaction with inmates or to engaging in inmate interactions more complex than headcounts. While some officers harbored resentment toward inmates, believed they should be punished harshly, and believed officers should rely on coercive control to maintain order, these officers did not appear to represent most correctional officers in Klofas' sample.

ALIENATION OF CORRECTIONAL OFFICERS

In the 1980s stress has become a buzzword among organizational consultants, managers, and workers. Consultants mount programs to train workers to relax and manage the worst symptoms of stress. Managers seem proud of the fact that they run organizations that produce stress; it indicates a productive organization. Workers use stress as an excuse for aberrant behavior. By most measures, prison guard work should be among the most stressful jobs. Evidence of stress is available in the tense faces of prison guards, in higher than average incidences of alcoholism, mental illness, and shortened life spans (May, 1976).

In a 1980 address to correctional administrators, Hans Toch warned that signs of stress can be misinterpreted and manipulated to justify objectionable practices:

> Managers like stress, because it sounds like the God-given consequence of running an organization, and it is therefore less troubling than the idea that workers are acutely unhappy with their job conditions and your outdated management style. (1980c:4)

Toch suggested that officers were under stress and that within the last decade their morale had declined. But he also suggested that these morale problems were not due to changes in inmate characteristics or behavior, but instead were brought on by working conditions which are amenable to management action (1980c:5).

A key concept in understanding the stress and dissatisfaction brought on by working conditions is work alienation, a condition first noticed by Karl Marx, who thought that capitalism robbed workers of meaningful work and self-respect. More recent studies suggest that worker alienation is on the rise but appears in socialist economies and worker-owned organizations just as much as it does under capitalism (Blumberg, 1973; Zwerdling, 1978).

Alienation has been defined in a number of ways, although the most common definition is probably Melvin Seeman's (1959). Seeman identified five facets of work alienation: powerlessness, normlessness, meaninglessness, isolation, and self-estrangement. Several studies have used Seeman's concepts with prison guard populations. Poole and Regoli (1981), surveying 144 guards in one prison, found that relationships with peers, with superiors, and with inmates have varying effects on the five facets of alienation. For example, an officer's negative relationships with peers is related to an increased sense of self-estrangement, while a negative relationship with superiors increases a guard's sense of normlessness and powerlessness. Negative relationships with inmates also reduce a sense of power at work and are correlated with a heightened sense of meaninglessness.

The researchers cautioned that alienation is a complex phenomenon and that changes in one set of guard relationships are unlikely to have an impact on all its facets. They did indicate that highly alienated officers are unlikely to follow prison policy and are likely to devise idiosyncratic methods of surviving in work they do not like, regardless of whether these adaptations are congruent with organizational goals (1981:266). They did not, however, indicate the sources of the negative relationships.

In a study of guards in four Israeli prisons, Shamir and Drory (1982) searched for the correlates of "occupational tedium," a concept closely related to alienation. They found the same problems among Israeli guards as have been found among guards in the United States. The three most significant correlates of tedium, they discovered, were an officer's sense that he had too much to do (role overload), that he suffered a lack of management support, and that the public was not appreciative of his efforts (1982:90). In a recent New Zealand study, Long et al. (1986) related correctional officer stress to three elements of the guarding role: relationships with staff, relationships with inmates, and perception of low opportunities for promotion.

Klofas's study of prison guards in maximum security prisons indicates that alienation varies from prison to prison and affects some officers more than others, but is in general unacceptably high. However, he also discovered that work alienation affects some work attitudes more than others. For example, Klofas found no relationship between a guard's level of alienation and attitudes about social distance with inmates. Evidently, even alienated guards find that close interaction with inmates may solve more problems than aloofness. On the other hand, Klofas found that high alienation scores reduced an officer's interest in the human service aspects of the job and were associated with increased punitiveness. The alienation dimension that had the greatest impact on other job attitudes was meaninglessness.

It would appear from these and related studies that guard alienation is fairly frequent and has negative consequences for the officer's willingness to follow policy and interest in working with inmates. It thus becomes important to study how alienation is distributed across officers and whether there are any indications of how it might be reduced.

OFFICER ATTITUDES BY GENDER, RACE, AND EXPERIENCE

Most studies of guards have been limited to studies of male guards in prisons for male inmates. There is little information on whether attitudes of officers vary by gender, or on the effects of hiring female guards for work in prisons for male inmates. Owen (1985), reporting on observations in San Quentin, hypothesized that affirmative action hiring of both minorities and women has changed the social structure of the guard force, with divisions among guards based on sex and race. She believed that conflict between male and female guards was worse when affirmative action started than it is now. She suggested that attitudes of male and female guards toward their work are not very different, although female guards may use different tactics to get the job done. Owen's anecdotal evidence tentatively indicates that women guards may be more adept at defusing a problem situation through persuasion rather than force, a finding that mirrors some studies of women police officers.

A national survey of women in corrections and a much smaller but more in-depth study of one facility that had recently hired female officers yielded similar findings. In both surveys, the majority of male inmates and male officers were not opposed to the hiring of women. Both officers and inmates reported that the presence of women in the prison appeared to reduce tension and disorder, and men as well as women perceived that female officers were more skilled than men in deescalating potentially violent situations. The two issues that did appear to concern both men and women officers were (1) privacy for inmates and (2) the possibility that women would be less effective in a crisis if violence had already begun. Inmates appeared less concerned about privacy than staff. The predominant complaint of women in corrections jobs was that they had few avenues for promotion and poor access to management training (Nicolai, 1981:230–236).

One of the few comparative studies of male and female guards (Crouch and Alpert, 1982) examined recruits in the Texas Department of Correction. The study of new guards over their first six months of work reported that male and female guards entered the prison with similar attitudes, but that men became more punitive and aggressive over time while women became less so. Unfortunately, we cannot determine if these differential changes on the new job are related to gender or are the effects of the different prisons to which male and female guards are usually assigned. Similarly, a study of 14 Australian prisons found that guards, who are usually women, in prisons for women have a low concern for custody but a high concern for discipline, compared to guards in prisons for men. Again, one cannot isolate the effects of gender and the effects of assignment.

As affirmative action has successfully attracted minority guards, some prison observers have expected the racial change in the guard force to change inmate-guard relationships. Two studies, one from Illinois (Jacobs and Kraft, 1983) and one from New York (Klofas, 1983), have demonstrated that this is not the case. Klofas found that race of guard made no difference to the alienation and job enrichment issues he was studying (1983:177). While black guards frequently were alienated, most of them also worked in the one prison in an urban setting, where most guards, regardless of race, were alienated. Jacobs and Kraft surveyed Illinois guards and found that black guards were no more pro-inmate than white guards, although black guards had a greater tendency to chose high-contact job assignments than whites. Unfortunately, we cannot isolate in the Illinois survey the effects of race from those of seniority. Most black guards had been hired last, and thus had less experience than their white colleagues. Increased experience could change their attitudes.

Of the demographic and job-related factors studied so far, the most powerful variable appears to be experience on the job, or seniority. Hepburn (1985) found that the more experienced guards were those who ranked expert power as most important, and saw coercive power as least important. Klofas and Toch (1982) found that a guard's interest in the human service aspects of the job increased as guards aged on the job. They also found that alienation was related to seniority. The most alienated officers in their survey were those with five to nine years of experience; officers with less or more experience were less alienated. Only one study indicated that length of

service has no effect on work attitudes. Shamir and Drory (1982) found Israeli guards' sense of occupational tedium did not vary by seniority. They did discover, however, that the sources of tedium varied by length of service.

Toch and Klofas (1982:43) summarized the most important findings regarding officer seniority and work attitudes:

> The myth that "hardnosed older officers" will neutralize the liberality of "liberal young turks" with custodial war stories is clearly inapplicable; if anything the influence should be a softening, tolerance-inducing and liberalizing one.

Klofas observed that the most alienated officers are young and urban and that these officers are the least interested in the service side of their jobs. These findings are at once cause for hope and worry. Although contrary to some expectations, the findings are not surprising. They suggest that as officers gain experience, they find the work less frightening, less objectionable, and easier to do. As officers gain experience, they rely more on their expertise to work with and command obedience from inmates and less on the symbolism of the uniform or their access to coercive sanctions to get things done. They also become more interested in acting in a helping capacity and behaving in ways that reduce suffering. Such findings are cause for optimism because they imply that lengthy service in the prison world does not reduce a guard's compassion and search for competence. But these findings also warn us that younger guards may be improperly trained, assigned to the wrong first jobs, or simply do not have the same goals as their older colleagues.

THE EFFECT OF THE ORGANIZATION ON OFFICER ATTITUDES

A number of the studies cited above indicate that officer attitudes are also affected by the type of prison in which they work, a finding that suggests these attitudes are influenced by the specific work setting rather than by the guard role itself. The most complex survey of 284 correctional officers in 14 institutions of different types found that officer attitudes could be clustered by place of work. Officers were differentiated into three groups, those in maximum security settings, those in medium security or less, and those in women's prisons (Williams and Soutar, 1984). The researchers found two dominant factors by which to distinguish guards, concern for custody and concern for discipline. Officers in maximum security prisons were high on custody and medium in concern for discipline. In women's prisons there was high concern for discipline but low concern for custody, while in the medium and low security settings, officers were generally low on both dimensions. The researchers found that the prison security level alone, rather than the espoused goals of the institutions, differentiated officer attitudes.

Hepburn's study of officer attitudes about inmate protest found that security was not the distinguishing variable. Officers working in prisons where there was a high degree of perceived authority had greater respect for inmate protest (1984:588). Klofas and Toch (1982) also found that alienation varied considerably from one institution to another. Guards in the most urban prison were the most alienated. However, Klofas reported (1983:156) that the relationship between alienation and interest in helping roles by guards varied across prisons. In prisons where the average alienation level was low, the most alienated officers were least interested in helping roles. In the urban prison where alienation was widespread, there was no relationship between alienation and interest in helping roles.

Williams and Soutar, as well as Klofas and Toch, concluded that the observed differences by prison have important implications for the training and placement of new officers. Officers are more likely to develop negative attitudes about inmates and about treatment programs if they start their careers in high custody settings, surrounded by alienated guards. Younger guards are more likely to develop positive attitudes if they

can work first with older officers who have high interest in human service in institutions that are less security conscious.

THE CORRECTIONAL OFFICER SUBCULTURE

As attention to correctional officers has grown, it has become apparent that officers do not always subscribe to the goals and values promoted by the administration, and on certain issues even seem diametrically opposed. Borrowing from the literature on the inmate subculture, and from studies of police officers, some researchers have suggested that correctional officers might also share a subculture which separated them from the official norms of the organizations in which they work. For example, in a 1974 study of correctional officers in Connecticut, Duffee provided evidence that officers did not experience the same social environment as correctional administrators or inmates, and that the daily pressures on the job might push them to adopt value positions unique to their class. However, Duffee found no direct evidence that a subculture existed and suggested that officers in the interview sample were better characterized by alienation and normlessness rather than subcultural isolation. Since that research, a good deal of debate has begun on the issue of a correctional officer subculture. The issue is an important one, since if officers do subscribe to values that separate them from noncustodial staff, the task of unifying staff around one set of correctional goals would be difficult indeed.

To date, the bulk of the evidence suggests that officers are too isolated from each other, both on the job and off, and rely too heavily on idiosyncratic working styles, to be characterized as belonging to a subculture. Poole and Regoli (1984) commented that officers in their study of guard alienation did not share much with prison administration, but did not band together either. Lombardo's clinical interviews with guards in the Auburn prison suggested that guards do not form a cohesive group with tightly knit norms. They do not identify with their work or with each other, and carry out their work as isolated individuals rather than in groups (1981:163). If this situation is accurate, it is puzzling to observe the type of anti-inmate, antiprograming attitudes so loudly expressed in collective bargaining situations and guard strikes. If guards are not unified in opposition to work with inmates, why is it that guards often speak of themselves as a unified group, committed to particular changes in current prison administration?

Several researchers have suggested that this apparently paradoxical situation can be explained through the use of the concept of **pluralistic ignorance.** Pluralistic ignorance was first uncovered in a 1931 study of Syracuse college students who felt they were surrounded by a reactionary student majority that, in fact, did not exist (Katz and Allport, 1931). Since that study, pluralistic ignorance has become a useful concept in explaining a number of disparities between public expressions of solidarity and private views that diverge from the perceived consensus.

Two major studies of pluralistic ignorance have been conducted among prison guards. Studying prison guards in Connecticut, Kauffman (1981) sought to investigate "the relationship between officers' perceptions of the attitudes of other officers and the attitudes actually expressed by officers." She found strong evidence that officers routinely underestimate the proportion of their fellow officers who are sympathetic toward inmates and treatment programs (1981:285). She also found that the officers most likely to underestimate officers' sympathy for inmates and treatment were officers who themselves were most opposed (1981:289). Kauffman concluded that this situation can be described as widespread pluralistic ignorance. Officers hold values themselves which vary considerably from the values officers believe are held by other officers. The mistaken beliefs exaggerate the officers' opposition to inmates and treatment (1981:291).

Klofas and Toch's study of pluralistic ignorance in New York substantiated Kauffman's findings (1982:245):

The pluralistic ignorance index confirms that the most cynical respondents are the most inaccurate and yet the most likely to believe their views are supported. These officers believe strongly in an anti-inmate subculture that does not exist.

Klofas and Toch were able to estimate the proportions of officers who fell into four groups distinguished by their own values and their views of the values of other officers. They found not a single officer who personally subscribed to a cynical, anti-inmate set of beliefs who did not also believe his views to be widely shared. Seventeen percent of the officers, whom Klofas and Toch call "subcultural custodians," believed that their alienated, cynical views were held by most other officers. A group called "Lonely Braves," comprising 26.2 percent of the officers, personally were sympathetic to inmates and program efforts, but felt their views were in the minority. Finally, a group called the "Supported Majority," consisting of 34.7 percent of the officers, were personally sympathetic to inmates and human service efforts in prison and also correctly perceived that most officers agreed with them (1982:247).

According to these data, if there is a correctional officer subculture, it is a very small one, consisting of less than one-fifth of the guard force. However, it is also true that this small group of officers opposed to inmates and to human service roles for officers "play a disproportionate role in trying to influence others through their unrepresentative, self-appointed role as spokesmen" (1982:251). These subculture custodians generally had less than four years of service, and were concentrated on the night shift and swing shifts. The supported, but quiet, majority officers were concentrated on the day shift when most programing and inmate interaction takes place (1982:248). Unfortunately, the loud complainers who favored punitiveness and purely custodial roles for officers were the officers most likely to have first contact with new recruits. Klofas and Toch concluded that a correctional officer subculture does not exist, but that current assignment and training patterns will help to perpetuate pluralistic ignorance and the undue influence of the most cynical and alienated officers (1982:252–253).

THE CORRECTIONAL OFFICER AND HUMAN SERVICE WORK

The prison guards most disaffected with their work and those most antagonistic to inmates and treatment efforts are also the guards most committed to defining correctional officer work in strict custodial terms. These officers appear to be in the minority in most prisons, although they wield considerable influence and mask the desires of other officers who desire work that is more complex and more challenging. While many correctional officers are unhappy with their present working conditions, withdrawing from the challenges and frustrations of human interaction with inmates would not appear to be an effective adaptation. As we have seen above, one of the more damaging influences on correctional officers is the perception that work as a guard is meaningless. Meaningful work is one of the key ingredients in high job satisfaction (Hackman and Oldham, 1980). Infusing the correctional officer role with meaning and significance is likely to be accomplished by increasing the opportunities for complex and helpful interactions with the people they supervise.

A number of studies have shown that many officers find their work more meaningful and significant when they have more contact with inmates in situations that permit service and recognition for providing it. (New York State Department of Correctional Services)

> [H]uman services appears to account for much of the "real substance" of correction officer work in prison. Human services behavior appear to arise spontaneously from the interaction of individual officers with inmates and the institutional environment. (Lombardo, 1981:160)

Lombardo portrayed much guard work as fraught with danger, tension, and boredom, and often barren of significant extrinsic or intrinsic rewards. The few psychic rewards available generally arise as guards interact with inmates.

One way to enrich the correctional officer role, according to Toch and Klofas (1982), is to promote the officers' widespread but often unspoken desire to participate in treatment programs or other activities which promote the welfare of inmates. In the survey conducted by Klofas (1983), only 31.9 percent of officers in maximum security agreed with the statement "Rehabilitation programs should be left to mental health professionals" and only 25.4 percent agreed with the statement "Counseling is a job for counselors, not correctional officers" (Klofas, 1983:122).

Toch (1978) observed that many officers have self-designed human service roles for themselves, despite the fact that these roles are not well supported by the system. Johnson and Price (1981:345) concurred, proposing that when correctional officers approach their work as helpers rather than guards, they help to create "resilient prisons," or prisons which can accommodate the needs of their inmates. They asserted that many officers do not respond to the twin demands of guarding and helping as goal conflict, but instead perceive the provision of help within the guard role as "complexity, stimulation and challenge" (1981:346). Officers performing human service roles in prison

> . . . gear their work to a central feature of imprisonment as seen by the inmates themselves, namely, that imprisonment represents a painful challenge to one's ability to cope. (Johnson and Price, 1981:344)

Klofas (1983:215) supplied strong evidence that this orientation increases among guards as they gain experience. He noted that, contrary to reports from other human service settings, guards do not burn out, but seek to enrich their jobs by increasing the human service aspects of their work. His study of assignment patterns in New York prisons revealed that as officers gain sufficient seniority to bid on jobs, those with a human service interest elect jobs with high inmate contact (1983:197–213). Unfortunately this self-selecting system does not work efficiently. Guards need to accumulate about ten years on the job before they have sufficient seniority to match their interests with their post assignment. Many less senior officers with strong desires for human service positions are stuck with leftover assignments. Moreover, since many guards do not realize that the expression of human service goals is in fact supported by most guards, those who do not find their needs met in their work are often timid in expressing their real desires.

Johnson and Price argued that official departmental policies governing recruit training underscore the division between guarding and helping (1981:360). Lombardo contended that under these confusing conditions, even officers who seek to help inmates cope with imprisonment are likely to do so in a secretive, individualistic fashion, without regard to whether their efforts are congruent with management policy or treatment program efforts (1981:164).

Toch and Klofas (1982:43) admitted that many officers personally interested in enriched service-oriented roles are too alienated from correctional administrators to trust job changes suggested by the "brass." For these officers, efforts to reduce work alienation probably must precede efforts to have guards take on more active, helping roles with inmates. One small pilot program in Connecticut provided some support for this sequence of change (Duffee, Steinert, and Dvorin, 1986). In that program, a small group of experienced officers was given a chance to participate with management on decisions about administrative and program change in the prison. For the first several months of the program, officers were suspicious of management's intentions and concentrated on changes which they thought would benefit guards rather than inmates. As they gradually saw that management was accepting their suggestions for change, officers gained confidence in their ability and new status in the prison. Under these conditions, the officers began to design changes that would benefit inmates as well as officers and on occasion became strong advocates for inmates in protesting security practices which they came to believe were unfair and too stringent.

SUMMARY

1. The role of the prison guard has often been ignored in writings about prisons, and from those studies which exist, it appears that prison guards have traditionally been ignored by the system as well.
2. While guarding has usually been characterized as

the unskilled work in the prison, studies of prison guards at work make short shrift of such notions. Even in the early days of the penitentiary, it is clear that prison guards played an essential role in the running of the prison and in promoting the well-being of the prisoners. From the start of the nineteenth century, guards were often trade specialists as well as custodial officers and interacted with inmates on a number of dimensions at once.

3. It would seem that the rise of the behavioral sciences as a guide to rehabilitation is in large measure the source of the prison guard's loss of status and respect. As treatment staff came to be recognized by specialized training, the guard role became narrower.

4. By the 1970s, many guards felt ignored by the administration, less influential than inmates, and unappreciated by society. This disaffection with the job situation has led many correctional officer

unions to become more militant and more demanding in contract negotiations.

5. The correctional officer position has been recently affected by equal employment opportunity and affirmative action programs. Minorities and women have entered officer ranks in many places for the first time.

6. Almost all studies of correctional officers demonstrate that most officers are interested in providing human services to inmates. Prisons as currently structured and managed do not seem likely to tap this resource with any effectiveness, and correctional officers are likely to remain alienated for some time to come.

KEY WORDS

AFFIRMATIVE ACTION (AAP). A formal program to correct previous discriminatory hiring practices through aggressive recruitment and promotion of previously disadvantaged groups.

ALIENATION (from work). Disaffection with work and oneself, often defined in work research as having five facets: meaninglessness, powerlessness, estrangement from self, isolation (estrangement from others), and normlessness.

EQUAL EMPLOYMENT OPPORTUNITY (EEO). The policy of selection and advancement of personnel on the basis of merit, without regard to criteria such as race or gender. The EEO Act became federal law in Title VII of the 1964 Civil Rights Act.

PLURALISTIC IGNORANCE. A mistaken belief by an individual that values held by others in the group are significantly different from one's own values.

PROJECTS AND QUESTIONS

1. Although they examined very similar surveys of correction officer attitudes, James B. Jacobs and Hans Toch came to very different conclusions about the future of the correctional officer role. Jacobs has recommended that officer morale might be lifted if officers became true security specialists, receiving training in the use of electronic surveillance equipment, and in other ways becoming more surveillance-oriented. Toch, in contrast, has insisted that officer job attitudes will improve only if officers participate in activities that reduce the suffering of inmates. He believes officers should become human service professionals. In which direction do you think the officer role should evolve? Why?

2. Johnson and Price (1981) argued that the move away from rehabilitation and toward a "justice

model" of imprisonment is sheer hypocrisy unless the justice model can be implemented with humane results. Most prison experts agree that rehabilitation programs, while not perhaps effective in producing long-lasting change, did indeed temper the violence and aggression within prisons by modifying both inmate and staff behavior. As treatment goals decline in importance, what would you do to maintain among officers concerns for safety, compassion, and humaneness?

3. Find out if guards in your state are unionized and are allowed to engage in collective bargaining. If not, what are the arguments made by the state to prohibit such organization? Do you agree or disagree? If so, what were the most important issues in the last contract negotiation?

ADDITIONAL READING

Robert Ross. *Prison Guard/Correctional Officer.* Toronto: Butterworth, 1980. This is one of the few books in the correctional literature that focuses specifically on correctional officers.

Lucien X. Lombardo. *The Guard Imprisoned.* New York: Elsevier, 1981. Lombardo's dissertation was one of the first social science investigations to focus on the work of correctional officers. The report analyzes data from fifty lengthy interviews with guards in the famous Auburn (NY) prison.

CHAPTER 17 RELEASE FROM PRISON

QUESTIONS

1. What were some of the pressures that influenced the development of early release mechanisms? Were these pressures compatible?

2. How has reintegration policy been implemented?

3. What are the common elements of parole?

4. How has sentencing reform affected parole?

5. What is mandatory release?

6. What are the major problems with parole supervision?

BOARDING HOUSE OR GROUP THERAPY?

Phil and Ken were on the road, visiting each of the prerelease centers in Jefferson. They were surprised at the range of approaches to the task of preparing inmates for release. The starkest contrast involved the centers in the large city of Adams and the center in the grimy little industrial town of Wilton.

The Adams Fourth Street center had been in operation the longest of all the centers. While neighbors had demonstrated against its opening four years earlier, the director had discovered that much of the resistance was not directed at the concept of the center, but at what the neighbors had perceived as false promises by the city. The site initially chosen for the center had apparently been slated for demolition and conversion into a neighborhood park. After several meetings with neighborhood leaders, the director managed to find an alternative rental site down the block, with assistance from the neighbors. In return he promised that residents in the center would help build the park and followed through. The relationship in the largely black neighborhood had been generally supportive ever since.

Tom Watson used his connections to find neighbors, not just residents, jobs; and his residents and staff were active in community affairs. Banking on this mutual support, Watson's approach to administration was freewheeling. He was a frequent advocate for his residents, maintained a loose curfew and weekend furlough policy, and referred out almost all resident services to community social agencies, which were plentiful. Watson had been a vocal critic of Division Director George Jenison, and simply refused to implement a number of Jenison's policies, such as collection of rent from the residents and returning to prison residents who failed to find jobs. On their initial visit, Phil and Ken were surprised to find virtually no one in the center. After Phil and Ken had gained his trust, Watson admitted that he permitted many of his residents to live at home with their families and report in by phone, as long as they attended weekly house meetings.

"What do your counselors do, if the residents are rarely here, and get their services elsewhere?" asked Phil.

"My counselors are busy making sure things stay that way. Look, this is not a therapy house, this is a supportive boarding house. My job is to get these men back in the community. I don't want them hanging around the house. They had enough of that in prison. This is a chance to get on their feet, again or for the first time. If I keep them in the center, what's the point?"

Phil pressed on. "If I were to push your approach to the limit, I might conclude that a prerelease residence is unnecessary. This could be a drop-in center and provide the same services."

Watson squinted. "The answer is Yes and No. My residents stay here for three, four weeks. Then if they've shown they're straight with me, and they have a family, we start easing up. Some men don't have families, and they stay here longer—maybe until parole. For them, I try to keep this place as little like an institution as possible. They get their recreation out, they find their friends out, if they think they need counseling, that happens down at the community health cen-

ter. We're not in that business. So, we can't close down the residence, although we don't need it as much as it looks on paper. I could handle double my count, since most of the beds are empty half the time anyway. But I can't tell that to the Central Office."

"Okay, but in some sense, then, for a number of your residents, you're really running an early parole program."

"I'm running my center. All parole in this city cares about is keeping your nose clean. My counselors are the best job developers in the city. And my center isn't some parole dropin, where you go and read the want ads and play pingpong. This is a twenty-four-hour program, and we make contact with our people daily."

Across the state, Mike Workman ran a very different program in a very different city. Wilton was small, about 40,000 people, and deteriorating rapidly. Most of the citizens were children of immigrants who had been attracted to the Wilton steel mills a hundred years ago. When the Department of Correction had proposed a center in Wilton resistance had been strong, but civil. In a series of meetings with the city manager, parole, and George Jenison, the center had been permitted to open, provided that no residents who were not also Wilton natives would be permitted to stay in town when they were released to parole. Workman ran a tight ship. Curfew was enforced, and furloughs from the center were rare, awarded for good behavior only, and after six weeks in the center. Workman and his staff all had advanced degrees in clinical psychology, or other counseling fields, and they ran daily counseling sessions in the center. While they would occasionally refer a resident with a special problem to another agency, Workman reported that the agencies were not very receptive. Many agencies had told Workman that they considered center residents to be inmates, and the responsibility of the department until they were paroled.

In addition to counseling, Workman's major emphasis was that residents develop their parole plans as quickly as possible, in order to receive parole as soon as they were eligible. Residents and staff had a friendly, courteous relationship, but the residents complained to Phil and Ken that there were too many rules and regulations and that they did not like the counseling.

"Why does each resident receive group therapy?" Phil had asked.

Workman responded by pulling out Jenison's center policy manual. "It says right here, counselors will conduct group therapy."

"Does that mean every resident needs it?"

Workman thought before he answered. "These men have been in prison anywhere from two to ten years, in some cases. This program is a chance to decompress. Most of them come out with totally unrealistic expectations. They figure they'll get a good job, buy a fancy car, and take their beautiful dates to fancy restaurants. Well, it doesn't happen. They work in the car wash and eat at Burger Heaven. And they walk or ride the bus. Sure they need good jobs, but they also need training in most cases. And before any of that works, they need a change in attitude. Reality hits hard, and they need help in dealing with it, most of the time. There are exceptions, but there's no reason to keep those few out of group therapy. They can help the others. We stress commitment and cohesion in here. We want residents to help each other and to trust the staff. We stress that."

THE DEVELOPMENT OF GRADUATED RELEASE

These different approaches to running prerelease centers can help us understand many forms of release for prison, not just halfway houses. The same issues are debated concerning the supervision of persons on parole and the design of work release programs. By far the most important, and largest, form of gradual release from prison is through the discretionary parole decision and supervision by parole officers. But parole, work release, prerelease centers, mandatory release, and other transitional programs share a common heritage, a common set of problems, and common goal conflicts. In examining these programs, we will first trace the development of graduated release, or conditional release, in order to examine some of the roots of current practice. The focus of this theory is on the development of parole. However, the antecedents of parole and other current graduated release options are the same.

Travis and O'Leary asserted that the growth of parole as a means of release from prison prior to sentence expiration can be traced to two primary organizational objectives, the ability to control the size of the prison population and the ability to sanction obedience by prisoners (1984:108). Dawson (1981:80–81) agreed with them, concluding that the development of early release was primarily a matter of efficiency, not rehabilitation.

INDENTURING AND TRANSPORTATION

As a correctional practice, parole emerged in the 1840s but was preceded by some similar practices. The term **parole,** which means promise, comes from the French, who developed the practice of releasing military prisoners prior to the end of a war, on the prisoners' promise that they would not rejoin the fighting (Dawson, 1981:80). This release was used primarily to reduce the cost of caring for the captives. Released soldiers who did not keep the promise were subject to execution if captured again. This practice had several parole characteristics: release prior to the end of an issue, a promise to obey some conditions, and a desire to save some money.

Another contributor to the development was the English practice of transportation, discussed in Chapter 8. While transportation provided some precedent for the suspended sentence, it could also have been considered a conditional release from the death penalty. The prisoner escaped on condition of not returning to Great Britain (Travis and O'Leary, 1984:106).

Indenturing prisoners, or placing them out with families after they had served a portion of their sentence, was another harbinger. Indenturing apparently developed as a means of dealing with overcrowding in the early prisons. The families who received the prisoners were responsible for supervising their behavior (Dawson, 1981:80).

THE EMERGENCE OF GOOD TIME

Early release practices received early legal recognition. New York passed the first **good time** statute in 1817, in order to solve overcrowding at the Newgate prison in Greenwich Village (New York State Coalition for Criminal Justice, 1982, hereafter NYSCCJ). Prisoners who had worked hard and had earned at least $15 were permitted to return to the community before expiration of sentence. The statute permitted a sentence reduction of up to 25 percent for nonrepeaters. The revised good time law of 1862 repeated the prisoner behavior theme (NYSCCJ, 1982:51). The law permitted a prisoner 1 day off per month for the first six months of sentence and 2 days off per month thereafter:

> . . . if he shall diligently work the number of hours prescribed by the rules of the prison or penitentiary . . . and if he shall well obey the rules and quietly submit to the discipline of the prison.

EXECUTIVE PARDON

Another common means of reducing prison population in the new penitentiary was the rather frequent use of **executive pardon.** Francis Lieber, who translated Beaumont and Toqueville's treatise into English, had a number of observations of the pardon system in his 1833 introduction to the work. He argued that the pardon power could be easily misused if it resided in the hands of one person. He thought that a single person with power to cut sentences short would be subject to all sorts of undue pressures and that his behavior would be arbitrary, and interfere with reform of the prisoners (Lieber, 1964:28–29). Lieber recommended that the executive delegate his pardon power to a board.

Lieber's model for this was the *commission de recours* in Geneva, which heard petitions from Swiss prisoners. The commission consisted of nine officials and was empowered to release deserving prisoners after they had served two-thirds of their sentences (1964:30). Lieber recommended a similar body in the United States. The committees of pardon, he thought, should consist of 7 to 9 members, some of whom should be judges. They:

> . . . might convene twice a year to recommend for pardon those prisoners to the governor, who have been judged by them to be fit subjects of it, after hearing a deliberate report on each case by one of their members; because it would be improper to leave this important act dependent upon indefinite and vague feelings. (1964:30)

Lieber went further. He argued that inmates released on pardon should not travel from Auburn to New York City, but stay upstate where the pressures to return to crime were less severe. But he stressed that such decisions should not be made hastily. He scolded the state for not keeping better records so that placement decisions could be made on the basis of recommitment rates (1964:17–19). Lieber's suggestions for reform in the pardon system were seeds for the modern parole board. Unfortunately, many modern departments have not followed his advice about accurate records. Additionally, one could see in Lieber's approach an early concern for reform of the prisoner through supportive release environments, not just the easement of overcrowding, and a concern for decisions that did not diminish the justice of the sentence. This concern did not receive a sympathetic ear for years.

THE TICKET-OF-LEAVE

The English Penal Servitude Act of 1853 made it possible to grant a conditional release called a **ticket-of-leave** to those who had served a specified portion of their sentences. The ticket-of-leave permitted the prisoner license to be at large within specified areas. The conditions of release were written on the license, which the released prisoner was to carry at all times and present on demand. The conditions included avoiding any misconduct, refraining from association with bad characters and from a dissolute life, and maintaining a visible means of support. Violation of conditions could result in revocation of the license.

It was assumed by the general public that the conditions imposed were enforced. This was not the case, however. During the early stages of the program, no supervision was exercised. Prisoners on tickets-of-leave were blamed for a crime wave and citizens demanded abolition of the program or supervision of the men. It appears that the British Home Office had interpreted the leaves as indication that prisoners had completed their sentences for all practical purposes. After the supervision scandal, local police were used to supervise the released prisoners. Later, agents employed by prisoner aid societies provided supervision. These agents assisted prisoners in obtaining employment and finding shelter, provided a modicum of supervision, made visits to releasees having trouble, and explained the program to employers.

The Irish system of ticket-of-leave was put in use in 1855 after Sir William Crofton became head of the Irish prison system. This prison system became a model for the development of the reformatory in the United States. In the three-stage Irish system, prisoners in the second stage received marks for good conduct and participation in industry and education. Tickets-of-leave were awarded on the accumulation of marks. In rural areas, released prisoners were supervised by the police, but in Dublin they were supervised by the inspector of released prisoners. The released prisoners were required to report to the inspector at specified intervals, and field visits were made to homes and places of employment.

THE BIRTH OF THE INDETERMINANT SENTENCE

In the United States, these conditional release practices culminated with the passage of indeterminant sentence legislation in New York in 1868 and 1870. The New York Prison Association, whose members were instrumental in organizing the First Prison Congress in Cincinnati, pressed for a sentence tied to evidence of reform. The law called for imprisonment "until reformation, not exceeding five years," and was implemented in the new Elmira Reformatory in 1877 (Travis and O'Leary, 1984:106). Zebulon Brockway's administration at Elmira was the first early release practice that resembled modern parole. Prisoners were released after good conduct and active participation in prison programs and received supervision once released (Dawson, 1981). Release at Elmira was determined by a board of prison officials. Other states, copying the reformatory, vested release in an independent pardons board (Travis and O'Leary, 1984:107–108).

While the rhetoric of the indeterminant sentence was rehabilitative, there is ample evidence that efficiency still played a strong part in the growth of graduated release. For example, in 1902, the warden of the Iowa prison pleaded with the legislature to initiate parole as a means of reducing prison overcrowding (Wright, 1984).

THE SECOND WAVE OF SCANDAL

Just as lax administration had threatened the ticket-of-leave, a second major wave of scandal rocked parole in the United States in the 1930s. In a number of states there were complaints that the parole decision was corrupt or at least uninformed, and that supervision was nonexistent. Indeed, some states engaged in a practice called "sunset parole," releasing prisoners under the promise that they would leave the state by sunset.

As a result of increasing calls for parole abolition, President Franklin Roosevelt called the First National Parole Conference in 1939.

The flavor of the proceedings is evident in an opening speech by Robert Hutchins, president of the University of Chicago. He said: "The theory of parole in most of our states is completely defeated by sloppy, shiftless, political, stupid, corrupt, parsimonious, and vicious methods of administration" (Proceedings of the First National Parole Conference, 1939:10). Parole survived the scandals in essentially the same way that the ticket-of-leave had survived. Conditions of parole were made more rigorous, with greater attention to supervision. The decision to parole in many states was handed over to independent, full-time parole boards, who were to be less pressured by prison overcrowding or direct association with the prisoners (Travis and O'Leary, 1984:108). By 1945, all states had adopted parole, although frequency of use varied considerably. From 30 to 95 percent of prison releases were paroles, depending on the state.

REINTEGRATION AND PRERELEASE PROGRAMS

The prison systems of Crofton and Maconochie included graduated reduction in custody and inmate contact with the community prior to expiration of sentence. These were the forerunners of modern parole practice. But they were also the origins of prison policies that did not become popular until the 1960s. By that time, parole had become the normal means of release, and complaints had arisen that the transition to parole was not effective.

The President's Commission on Law Enforcement and the Administration of Justice (1967a) pointed to a major strategic fault as the source of the many specific difficulties offenders could face in the transition to parole. According to the commission, well before release prisoners should be engaging in activities (1) that focused on the development of skills which improved their chances of obtaining legitimate employment, and (2) that increased legitimate opportunities once they were released. Simultaneously, correctional staff should be (3) helping inmates to test new skills, and (4) developing the opportunities in the prison and in communities through advocacy and referral. This program strategy became known as reintegration (see Chapter 5 and O'Leary and Duffee, 1971a; Studt, 1973; Conrad, 1973).

Proponents of reintegration recognized that previous correctional programs had similar goals of reducing recidivism, and even provided some of the program elements recommended, such as graduated release. However, the reintegration strategists insisted that a system of graduated release was not sufficient. What happened during the reduction in custody was equally important. Incremental reduction in custody, by itself, could be a means of rewarding inmates for good behavior in prison, and therefore a security strategy rather than a means of influencing postrelease behavior. Other prison programs, said the reintegrationists, focused on change within the inmate rather than changes between the inmate and the social environment. Programs stressing attitude and motivation rather than skill and opportunity were misdirected because they ignored the practical realities of most prisoners' postrelease situations (Miller and Ohlin, 1985).

Like many other correctional policies before it, reintegration became a popular buzzword more often than a set of implemented programs. Probably the most frequently adopted aspect of reintegration policy has been more widespread use of graduated release. Probably the most frequently ignored aspect has been coupling skill development with increased opportunity for testing those skills under controlled conditions.

Many correctional departments seem to take the position that increasing the offender's contact with the community is itself the required change in opportunity. Such a position ignores the growing body of research findings in both corrections and mental health documenting the empty, unstructured, and resourceless lives of those deinstitutionalized without support (Scull, 1977;

Minnesota Governor's Commission on Crime Prevention and Control, 1976; Miller and Ohlin, 1985).

Very often, implementation of reintegration has been restricted to the tail end of an inmate's prison sentence, in the period known as prerelease programming. Many systems have introduced means of increasing an inmate's contact with community as he or she nears parole or expiration of sentence. Work release and educational release are two examples. Other programs often included in this group are prerelease programs occurring in the institutions, transfer to prerelease residences, and home furlough programs (LeClair, 1979).

HOME FURLOUGH

Many states have passed legislation permitting inmates to leave prison for short periods of time. **Furloughs** have been used for a variety of purposes, such as attending family functions, searching for postrelease employment, visiting a prerelease residential center, or making preparations for parole. For example, 1972 legislation in Massachusetts permits any prisoner leave for up to fourteen days per year, usually in one- to three-day intervals. Administrative regulations in Massachusetts limit the usual issuance of furloughs to inmates who have served at least 20 percent of their minimum sentence or three years, whichever is less (LeClair, 1978). Follow-up research indicated that furloughed inmates did better than expected and nonfurloughed inmates did about as well as expected one year after release from prison (LeClair, 1979).

IN-PRISON RELEASE PREPARATION

Prerelease programs in prison can take a variety of forms. Almost all prisons provide for some form of planning during this period, although this may amount to little more than a counselor preparing records for review by a parole board. Prerelease planning often includes attempts to increase the links between inmate and free world

or to forge new ones. These preparations often entail preparation of résumés, classes on job hunting, apartment hunting, establishing bank accounts, and keeping budgets. Preparations may also include group or individual sessions in which inmates explore their anxieties about release (Morgenbesser and Pollock, 1980). For details on one such program run by inmates, see Insert 17.1.

EDUCATIONAL RELEASE

Study release is one solution for some problems associated with prison educational programs. Inmates leave the institution during the day for education in the community (Smith, McKee, and Millan, 1979). Study release may have several advantages. First, it may increase the variety of educational programs available. Second, it may make higher-quality education available. Third, it may provide inmates who are continuing the program after prison with a gradual introduction to education in the free world. A 1974 survey found that 41 states, the Federal Bureau, and the District of Columbia systems offered one or more study release programs (Shichor and Allen, 1976). However, 1979 data suggested that study release, while widespread, did not involve many inmates. Only 938 prisoners in all 50 state systems were on study release at the time of that survey (Brown, Flanagan, and McLeod, 1984:577).

The 1974 survey indicated that college programs were the most common reason for study release, although some states reported its use for vocational education, adult basic education, and GED courses (Shichor and Allen, 1976). The correctional departments reported that the need for education was not the primary factor in making study release decisions. Custody grade, time served, and offense were given more weight. The majority of states limited study release to minimum security inmates, and many required that the sentence be near completion (Shichor and Allen, 1976).

Insert 17.1   A SELF-HELP PRERELEASE PROGRAM IN PRISON

One of the largest inmate-run organizations in the United States is a self-help prerelease program. Inmate-staffed prerelease centers operate in each major prison in the New York Department of Correctional Services (DOCS). The first of these was established in the Green Haven maximum security prison in 1971. The success of that effort led to similar centers in other prisons. In 1982, DOCS and the Division of Parole (DOP) drafted an interagency memorandum of agreement about the prerelease programs. The agreement established a standard set of prerelease services to be offered in each prison, and provided for joint staff supervision by both DOCS and DOP. Most of the work continues to be done by an inmate director and several inmate peer-counselors.

In each prison, the prerelease program is located in a separate room or set of rooms set aside by DOCS. Any inmates who are within four months of release may use the center during their free time, on a voluntary basis. The prerelease staff provide help in constructing résumés and writing letters to prospective employers, maintain a job bank, organize guest lectures on various aspects of community living, and provide some counseling on psychological preparation for release. The Green Haven center maintains a videocassette library of instructional material and publishes a regular newsletter on prerelease issues.

WORK RELEASE

Work release programs can probably trace their origins to the ticket-of-leave practices (see Chapter 11). Formal work release programs in the United States began in 1913, when the state of Wisconsin passed the first work release legislation, called the Huber Law, allowing counties to release selected inmates during working hours (Waldo, Chiricos, and Dobrin, 1973). In many states work release is much more recent, and the Federal Bureau of Prisons was not authorized to engage in work release until the Federal Prisoners Rehabilitation Act of 1965 (1973:348). According to the most recent available data, work release in state correctional departments is still an unusual occurrence. In 1979, only slightly over 4 percent, or 11,966 of all state inmates, were released every day to go to work or seek employment (Brown, Flanagan, and McLeod, 1983:577). The majority of these were housed in community prerelease facilities, while 3,371 were released from regular prisons.

Work release serves a number of purposes. It may ease the transition to the community by enabling offenders to be employed before parole or other release. It may help participants gain skill and experience. It may help offenders save money for postrelease expenses (MacDonald and Bala, 1985). In addition, work release inmates work for the prevailing wage in the community, rather than the lower prison rates. However, program requirements often reduce the achievement of some of these objectives. States often charge the working inmate for room and board, transportation, support of dependents on welfare, and perhaps restitution. These charges severely limit the amount that can be saved on programs that are usually of short duration. Moreover, the work release job may be far away from the parole destination, so that the work release job cannot be kept (Lenihan, 1974; Pooley, 1974; Ayer, 1970).

In addition to the economic objectives, positive attitude change has often been expected of work release inmates, on the presumption that participants have more contact with community members than other inmates and less contact with other prisoners (LeClair, 1979). One study of this possible benefit found the opposite. Work release participants, compared to controls, did not differ on perceived opportunity for legitimate activity, achievement motivation, legal self-concept, or self-esteem over the course of the program. The level of self-esteem for the participants actually dropped during the program (Waldo, Chiricos, and Dobrin, 1973:369). Some research suggests that negative attitude change during work release should be expected because of the conflicts experienced during the program. Many inmates in partial confinement programs indicate considerable stress because of the relative freedom during working hours followed by institutional restrictions at night (Kantola, 1977; Pooley, 1974).

A number of commentators have noted problems in selecting inmates for work release. Reviewing the large work release program in North Carolina, Knox and Humphrey (1981) observed that work release was generally reserved for inmates nearing release from prison, and often focused on those who had served long sentences and who had behaved well in prison. Elder and Cohen (1978) reported that statistical prediction of successful work release performance is possible, but that legislation often hampers the use of these predictor variables for classification. A study of work release selection in Virginia concurred that selection on the basis of risk could ·be made more accurate, but that administrators did not often use validated selection criteria (Brookhart, Ruark, and Scoven, 1976).

Evaluations of work release are relatively plentiful but often poorly done. The ambiguity of work release goals stand out in the findings. For example, Witte (1977) claimed success for the North Carolina program on economic grounds. But she also reported that participants did no better than nonparticipants after release. Jeffrey and Woolpert (1974) found that both participants and nonparticipants did poorly in a San Mateo County (California) program follow-up. However, the work release men did slightly better immediately after release from prison, and the higher-risk work release inmates did better than lower-risk inmates.

Perhaps the most exacting work release evaluation to date was a true field experiment in

Florida (Waldo and Chiricos, 1977). The experimenters found that the program participants did no better than the control group on 18 separate measures of outcome. In a major review article, Katz and Decker (1982) examined 40 different work release evaluations for economic benefit, recidivism, family adjustment, and personality changes. They could find little empirical support for work release on any of these dimensions and concluded that the programs must have provided benefits for the organization (such as greater control over prisoner behavior).

COMMUNITY PRERELEASE CENTERS

Community prerelease centers are separate residential units for offenders nearing release

The community prerelease center blends into the neighborhood and permits inmates a gradual transition to parole. (Pennsylvania Department of Corrections)

TABLE 17.1   Prerelease Facilities, Residents, and Rated and Measured Capacity

REGION AND STATE	FACILITIES				RESIDENTS		CAPACITY	
	TOTAL	STATE	PRIVATE	OTHER	SENTENCED	TOTAL	RATED	MEASURED
TOTAL	402	206	170	26	11,469	13,433	16,517	10,647
FEDERAL TOTAL	11	—	—	11	588	642	670	480
STATE TOTAL	391	206	—	15	10,881	12,791	15,847	10,167
NORTHEAST	64	35	25	4	1,445	1,776	2,234	1,461
Maine	5	2	0	3	58	58	69	49
New Hampshire	1	1	0	0	14	14	15	10
Vermont	4	4	0	0	266	308	344	163
Massachusetts	12	7	5	0	302	366	453	342
Rhode Island	2	1	1	0	35	39	65	48
Connecticut	11	0	11	0	79	246	380	205
New York	8	6	2	0	273	307	319	306
New Jersey	5	1	4	0	102	116	138	82
Pennsylvania	16	13	2	1	316	322	451	252
NORTH CENTRAL	110	52	52	6	2,243	3,003	3,786	2,666
Ohio	12	1	11	0	102	224	277	173
Indiana	12	4	8	0	238	313	480	299
Illinois	12	7	4	1	238	327	501	406
Michigan	23	17	5	1	695	919	994	873
Wisconsin	15	11	3	1	386	408	471	344
Minnesota	3	2	1	0	77	85	103	78
Iowa	9	4	2	3	127	166	273	131
Missouri	13	0	13	0	159	273	325	114
North Dakota	1	0	1	0	3	14	14	14
South Dakota	2	0	2	0	5	41	42	40
Nebraska	4	4	0	0	158	158	214	157
Kansas	4	2	2	0	55	75	92	37

from the prison authority. Some of these centers may be on prison grounds, but the typical prerelease center is a noninstitutional residence in an urban setting. Ideally, the resident can begin employment or a school program that can be continued upon parole. The capacity of these centers varies considerably. Average capacity in Oklahoma and Florida is about 48, while in Michigan, the Department of Correction contracts for single beds in small population centers. Across the country, the typical center holds about two dozen residents at a time (Mullen, 1980). In some jurisdictions, these centers are owned and operated by the corrections department and are legally classified as prisons. In other jurisdictions, the centers, whether run directly by the state or on a control basis, are a distinct class of facility. Such distinctions can be critical in determining whether absconders are charged with prison escape and whether residents who are being sent back to prison require a hearing (Duffee, Maher, and Lagoy, 1977).

Most of these centers were established in the 1970s, many relying heavily on the now defunct Law Enforcement Assistance Administration for startup funds. But despite the considerable rhetoric about reintegration, prerelease centers hold only about 4 percent of inmates in the United

TABLE 17.1 *(Continued)*

REGION AND STATE	FACILITIES				RESIDENTS		CAPACITY	
	TOTAL	STATE	PRIVATE	OTHER	SENTENCED	TOTAL	RATED	MEASURED
SOUTH	142	89	51	2	5,905	6,307	7,714	4,872
Delaware	1	1	0	0	62	62	59	18
Maryland	9	3	5	1	356	360	541	390
District of Columbia	6	1	5	0	162	181	199	94
Virginia	8	5	3	0	325	333	394	268
West Virginia	3	3	0	0	37	40	84	24
North Carolina	4	0	4	0	27	29	45	36
South Carolina	15	10	5	0	909	945	1,058	658
Georgia	7	6	1	0	354	362	445	333
Florida	35	31	4	0	1,877	1,988	2,316	1,208
Kentucky	4	0	3	1	37	46	75	44
Tennessee	12	6	6	0	564	579	721	533
Alabama	13	13	0	0	546	574	750	479
Arkansas	2	1	1	0	18	29	42	36
Louisiana	2	0	2	0	35	39	43	12
Oklahoma	10	9	1	0	467	481	605	499
Texas	11	0	11	0	129	259	337	240
WEST	75	30	42	3	1,288	1,705	2,113	1,168
Idaho	1	0	1	0	2	15	15	5
Wyoming	5	4	1	0	18	28	25	17
Colorado	10	3	6	1	193	281	425	315
Arizona	6	3	3	0	93	173	270	142
Utah	4	2	2	0	62	106	140	79
Washington	16	5	10	1	358	409	423	195
Oregon	11	9	2	0	231	236	251	125
California	19	2	16	1	303	422	533	284
Hawaii	3	2	1	0	28	35	31	6

SOURCE: Joan Mullen, *American Prisons and Jails, Vol. I: Summary Findings and Policy Implications of a National Survey.* Washington, DC: United States Department of Justice, 1980, p. 70.

States. Table 17.1 shows the number of prerelease centers in operation in 1978, whether these centers were publicly run or contracted, and number of inmates. Most states had a few centers and handled a small number of inmates at a time. Exceptions, such as Florida and Michigan, stand out. Some states, such as Connecticut and Missouri, have made a policy choice to contract with private agencies for prerelease services, while other states such as Florida and Texas have taken exactly the opposite route.

Analysis of four prerelease programs (Duffee, 1985; Wright and Duffee, 1986) demonstrated that these centers could have very different pro-

gram objectives and technologies. In Michigan and Massachusetts, for example, the object has been to release as many inmates as possible to parole through the prerelease centers. In Michigan this has meant short stays, high turnover, limited staff support, and a high rate of return to prison. The practice was justified as a means of testing which inmates were ready for parole and was used as a "screen" rather than as a change device (Johnson and Kime, 1975). In Pennsylvania, a very different program targeted inmates who had served rather lengthy sentences. The staff-inmate ratio was high, attention to treatment and referral intense, turnover low, and program failure rates low. Pennsylvania made the choice to run a change-oriented program rather than a screening program.

EFFECTS OF PRERELEASE AND REINTEGRATION

Whether prerelease makes a difference is not certain. The fact that in different jurisdictions these programs can have decidedly different objectives makes comparative research difficult. In Massachusetts, LeClair (1978, 1979, 1982, 1986) has conducted perhaps the most continuous research program on reintegration and prerelease effects. His results are tentative but promising. They show that Massachusetts inmates who have gone through any one component of the department's three-pronged strategy (graduated reduction in custody, home furlough, prerelease program) do better on one- and five-year follow-up after controls for prior risk are used. They also show that inmates who go through all portions of the program do best. The data indicate that after five years, recidivism differences between participants and nonparticipants are reduced, but do not disappear (LeClair, 1982, 1986).

CURRENT FORMS OF CONDITIONAL RELEASE

Although parole is still the primary means of conditional release, there are a growing number of other options, as states have moved to determinant sentencing or in other ways removed executive discretion in sentencing. **Conditional release** has two components: first, the selection process for release, or the time-setting function, and second, the means for enforcing the conditions of release.

The major distinction among the selection mechanisms is between those which are **discretionary,** like the parole board, and those that permit no discretion. The nondiscretionary release devices are often labeled **mandatory release,** implying that the prisoner must be released when some condition is met. The most common form of mandatory release is awarding good time.

GOOD TIME

Good time is the reduction in time served for adjustment to prison rules, work performance, program involvement, and in some states for other specific behaviors considered meritorious (New York State Coalition for Criminal Justice [NYSCCJ], 1982:1). Good time of one sort or another exists in all but five or six states, but good time also seems to be in rather constant flux. As we saw in Chapter 6, a number of the states that have abolished the parole decision have moved to increase the allotment of good time as an alternative means of controlling behavior in prison and the size of the prison population. As good time has increased in use, its award has also appeared to have become more discretionary. In some jurisdictions, it seems the abolition of parole in favor of determinant sentencing has not accomplished either determinancy or removal of discretion from the executive branch. In many instances, the executives in the prison system have gained discretion over release decisions because they control the awarding or taking away of good time. Consequently, while mandatory release implies that conditional release is determined by rule, the distinction between mandatory and discretionary has become extremely fuzzy.

The notion of good time as mandatory release arose in states that had parole. In those states, the parole board could release at its discretion prior to the maximum term. Good time was often subtracted from the maximum, reducing the period of the sentence over which the parole board could exercise discretion. If an inmate was turned down several times by the board but had conducted himself or herself in such a manner as to earn good time credit, that person would reach a point of mandatory release. In states without parole, almost all conditional release selections are good time selections. However, they are not necessarily automatic or nondiscretionary.

There are two major issues in the awarding of good time. One is the question of how it is credited to the sentence, the other is the question of how it is awarded. In states with indeterminant sentences, a policy decision must be made as to whether good time is subtracted from the minimum or the maximum term. In states where good time is subtracted from the minimum, it does not result in automatic release, but instead reduces the minimum term. The inmate who earns good time can be considered earlier by the parole board. In states where good time is taken off the maximum, award reduces the length of time to be served.

There are arguments in favor of both. One argument is that when taken off the maximum, the majority of prisoners get no benefit from good time, because they are paroled first (NYSCCJ, 1982:24). Another is that lowering the minimum is a more effective control over behavior, since the good behavior affects a longer portion of the potential sentence. The inmate is at risk of being turned down for parole for a longer period (The Correctional Association of New York, 1984). The argument for credit off the maximum is that it introduces more certainty for the inmate, who can to some extent control length of sentence. The more common form in indeterminate states is to take the time off the maximum term. In states that issue flat sentences, the point is obviously moot.

The second issue is how good time should actually be awarded in order to achieve the maximum effect. Some states start inmates off with no credit and award good time incrementally, based on periodic reviews. In other states, all potential good time is awarded when the sentence begins, and then taken away for misbehavior (NYSCCJ, 1982:17–18). The problem with adding good time is that it obviously increases the power of the prison officials who review behavior. Some would argue that this would also increase inmate conformity, but it can backfire if officials are seen as arbitrary. Clearly, it can coerce treatment or program participation. The usual problem with docking good time that has been initially awarded is that in practice this is rarely done. The maximum minus good time becomes the prison term in most cases.

In most states, those released via good time are held to conditions, and the most common condition enforcers are parole officers. Supervision of mandatory release inmates and paroled inmates does not differ in any significant way. In many states with indeterminate sentences, a mandatory releasee who violates release conditions also loses accumulated good time. When he or she returns to prison, he or she is facing the originally imposed maximum term (NYSCCJ, 1982:26).

OTHER FORMS OF DISCRETIONARY SELECTION

While the categorization of good time release as discretionary or nondiscretionary varies by the means of awarding it, a number of options other than parole are clearly discretionary. In those states where the split sentence includes a resentencing option, rather than pronouncing the probation and prison terms simultaneously, the judge has joined or replaced the parole board as the gatekeeper to discretionary release. In states where the resentencing period is relatively long, such as one year, the split sentence functions very much like parole. The supervision of the conditional release is simply transferred to probation officers.

Other forms of discretionary release have also popped up under control of prison officials. Some of these decisions are supported by statute; others appear to be informal expansions of prison authority. For example, when Indiana reformed its sentencing system and abolished parole, it included in the definition of "prison term" reporting to a prison official. In essence, prison officials were permitted to release certain offenders and keep track of them while they lived in the community.

EMERGENCY RELEASE STATUTES

Another type of release provision speeds conditional release with the sole aim of reducing the prison population—**emergency release.** The object of emergency release laws is to remove from the prisons before their regular departure date those who are considered good risks. Emergency release is triggered by the prison population. Statutes provide that when the population is over a certain limit (usually some percent over capacity), a state of emergency is declared and certain inmates can be released early. How selection for early release is accomplished depends on the sentencing structure. In states with parole, emergency release is used to accelerate the date of parole eligibility—in effect, it reduces the minimum sentence, often by 90 days. When the emergency is declared, the parole board can review a number of prisoners earlier than normal. The board attempts to select for release those it considers good risks, but it also attempts to select enough inmates to reduce the prison population and end the emergency (Gettinger, 1983). In states with flat sentences, emergency release provisions operate on good time awards. Additional good time is granted to inmates considered good risks who are within so many days of release (Austin, 1986:405).

Emergency release is now in widespread and frequent use. In 1984, a study of 14 states revealed that 17,365 inmates received early release in this fashion. The greatest use appeared to be in Georgia, Michigan, and Tennessee (Austin, 1986:406). Austin examined the practice in Illinois in detail for the National Council on Crime and Delinquency and found that between 1980 and 1983, 21,000 inmates, or approximately 60 percent of all releases, involved emergency sentence reductions. On the average, 105 additional days of good time were deducted, or about 12 percent of the inmates' expected prison term (1986:406). A study of the postrelease behavior of these inmates found that 42 percent were rearrested in the first year out, compared to 48 percent of those who had served the full term. These arrests contributed less than 1 percent of all arrests in Illinois during the release period. Thus, while arrest rates were relatively high, the effect on the state crime rate was minimal (1986:408). Austin estimated that the program resulted in a net savings to the state, even when costs to victims and costs of prosecution were included

(1986:409). But he concluded that emergency release is a poor substitute for

> . . . more permanent, rational, and cost-effective sentencing policy. It provides an excessive amount of discretion for correctional administrators, violates principles of equity and certainty in sentencing as assumed by the court, and increases the already low regard held for our criminal justice system by the public. (1986:409)

THE PAROLE RELEASE DECISION

Parole involves the discretionary selection of inmates by an executive body for release from incarceration followed by supervision of the paroled persons, who can be revoked if the conditions of that release are violated (Travis and O'Leary, 1984:105). The authority for selection typically is vested in a group of officials appointed by the governor, or other chief executive, and organized independently of the corrections department. The group is usually called the parole board, but in some states is called the board of prison terms, and in the federal system, the Federal Parole Commission. In six states (Maryland, Michigan, Minnesota, Nebraska, Ohio, and Wisconsin), the paroling authority is part of the institutional administration (McGarrell and Flanagan, 1985:131). Since the parole scandals of the 1930s, the trend has been toward full-time boards of professional personnel, such as lawyers, psychologists, and other behavioral scientists. However, appointments remain sensitive to political party affiliation, and members who symbolize "upstanding citizenry" are often included. Many boards are full time, but others consist of part-time board members with full-time support staff.

Traditionally, the parole board, following a regular schedule, would travel to the various institutions in a state and review files and interview the inmates being considered. A number of boards still perform in this way, but a number have changed the consideration process and the role of the board. The President's Commission on Law Enforcement and Administration of Justice and the National Advisory Commission on Criminal Justice Standards and Goals were both critical of the rushed and cursory procedures for parole selection. Some boards did not bother to provide the inmate with a hearing, and those that did often presented a sorry picture of justice at work. One board member would ask the applicant some ritualized questions for a few minutes, while other members busily reviewed files for other cases.

The NAC recommendations for improvement included changing the function of the parole board. Hearing examiners were to be employed to travel to the various institutions, review records, conduct interviews, and make recommendations. The full board was to remain in a central office and make decisions in a less hasty and more informed manner. The board would often accept the recommendation of the examiner in routine cases and save its full attention for unusual cases. This model turned the board into an appellate review panel and policymaking body, rather than the maker of case-level decisions. Following this model, the Federal Parole Board was reorganized as the Federal Parole Commission. It determines parole guidelines and considers exceptions to guideline decisions.

THE ATTACK ON THE PAROLE DECISION

Calls for the abolition of parole have had a cyclical history. The most recent wave in the attack did not raise many new issues, but was probably the most powerful assault. These attacks cannot be separated from the broader wave of sentencing reform. However, it is useful to highlight some of those reform arguments as they apply specifically to parole, and to examine the parole response.

The parole decision is often criticized because the discretion of parole boards can be used to pressure inmates into prison programs as a means of impressing the board members with the inmates' sincerity about self-improvement. The counterargument is that inmates often need to be able to feign disinterest about self-improvement to other inmates by making up stories about "impressing the Board," when in fact they sincerely desire the program service. (New York State Department of Correctional Services)

Since conditional release has two components, selection and supervision, it is important to keep the components separate when discussing reform. Some reform arguments, such as those of the American Friends Service Committee (1971), and the Citizen's Inquiry on Parole and Criminal Justice (*Report on New York Parole*, 1974), called for abolishing both components of conditional release (Travis and O'Leary, 1984:110). The more common attack has been on discretionary selection, while preserving supervision of persons released conditionally on mandatory release (Hussey and Lagoy, 1983). Between 1975 and 1982, 10 states abolished their parole boards (Bureau of Justice Statistics [BJS], 1983b:71). And as of January 1983, California, Colorado, Connecticut, Illinois, Indiana, Maine, Minnesota, New Mexico, and North Carolina no longer had discretionary parole release for new cases (McGarrell and Flanagan, 1985:145). In a number of these states, a board has been retained to review mandatory release revocations and to hear paroles for inmates who had been sentenced to indeterminant terms. Some states, such as Illinois, also permit the board to make a release decision on those who have been revoked (Travis and O'Leary, 1984:116).

The principal arguments against the parole decision have been (1) unbridled discretion, (2) the violation of just deserts by setting prison terms on the basis of predictions about future behavior, and (3) the inability to predict accurately (von Hirsch and Hanrahan, 1984:184). The unfairness of predictive parole decisions is no different from that in sentencing, and will not be reviewed again. The parole board's use of discretion merits special consideration, as does the issue of predictive accuracy.

DISPARITY IN PAROLE DECISIONS

For many years, one defense of the parole decision was that it corrected sentencing disparity. The crux of the argument was that a centralized decision-making group, such as a parole board, could provide more even-handed decisions than individual judges because the board reviewed all sentences in a state. Enjoying the broad perspective, boards supposedly could correct judicial excess or leniency. Inmates with excessively long minimum sentences could be released as soon as these expired, while inmates with unusually short minimums could be held beyond them. The board functioned as a sentencing review panel, it was argued, and as such would reduce sentencing variation.

An important test of this argument was conducted by Michael Gottfredson (1979a) using data on federal parole decisions prior to the change to parole guidelines. He discovered that the exercise of discretion by a centralized board did reduce sentence length. However, examination of the terms set by the board uncovered no reduction in "disparity," defined in this study as variations in time served that could not be explained by offender criminal record and seriousness of present conviction. Additionally, Gottfredson tested the argument that parole boards considered prison disciplinary records in setting release dates. When he controlled for prison disciplinary records, the amount of variation in inmate terms was not reduced (1979a). He concluded that centralization of the term-setting decision, by itself, did not ensure more consistent sentencing.

As is the case with judicial sentencing, parole boards have been criticized for racial discrimination. Unfortunately, we have much less information with which to assess these charges. Carroll and Mandrick (1976), studying parole in one eastern state, found that younger black inmates were more often required to participate in treatment programs than whites prior to parole, and consequently served more time. They also found that "nonthreatening" older blacks with multiple property convictions were not held to this requirement and were actually released earlier than similar whites. Carroll and Mandrick argued that the evidence suggested racial prejudice resulted in greater punitiveness against militant, younger blacks, while Uncle Tomism favored the older property offenders. Elion and Megargee (1979), reviewing parole outcomes for one federal institution for younger offenders, obtained rather ambivalent results. They discovered that blacks were less frequently paroled than whites or served a greater proportion of their sentences. However, the blacks on the average served less time, because they came in with shorter sentences.

PAROLE GUIDELINES

In states where parole has survived, the most important and effective response to claims of disparity has been to increase the board's attention to sentencing policy as a means of structuring discretion in individual decisions. Guidelines for parole decisions have been adopted in New York, Florida, Oregon, and the federal system (Travis and O'Leary, 1984:118). Two types of guidelines exist. In the matrix form, time served is determined on the basis of offense and criminal history. In nonmatrix guidelines, the rules indicate to board members what factors they should consider, but do not directly control time served (1984:118). Only the matrix should be expected to reduce disparity significantly.

Although von Hirsch has been one of the proponents of determinate sentencing, and in that role a contributor to the abolition of the parole decision, he and Hanrahan (1984) have indicated that parole may have some advantages. They observed that correctional systems have operated on "double time" (minimum and maximum terms) for so long that conversion to a single (flat) time standard can have a negative impact. If a commission or legislature, in converting sentencing to a flat mode, confuses the old maximum sentence with actual time served, then single-time sentencing can yield greater use of incarceration (1984:190). One way to avoid that problem is to retain a parole board to fix prison terms shortly after commitment. This, in fact, was Norval Morris's preference (1974), and the reform instituted in Oregon. In that state, the board sets the minimum term shortly after reception on the basis of desert-based guidelines (von Hirsch and Hanrahan, 1984). This alternative to legislative or judicial sentencing may be politically easier to ac-

complish. And Morris argued that this form of sentencing would result in more considered sentences, because the decisions were removed from the legislative arena and from the immediate heat of the conviction.

The pioneer in parole guidelines was the Federal Parole Board, whose initial guidelines are presented in Table 17.2. A study of federal term setting after guidelines implementation found that the guidelines had indeed reduced disparity. A greater proportion of board decisions could be explained on the basis of history and offense than was true of the judicial term (M. R. Gottfredson, 1979b). This important innovation has now been replaced with a sentencing commission, under the new Omnibus Crime Package.

PREDICTIVE ACCURACY

Norval Morris (1974:35) has argued that one reason to move term setting up in the process (to sentencing itself, or earlier in the prison stay, as in Oregon) was that behavior in prison was not predictive of behavior after prison. The indeterminate sentence at Elmira, New York, was built on the premise that officials observing prison behavior were in the best position to determine when an inmate was ready for release. The rejection of indeterminacy was based, in part, on the assertion that coerced rehabilitation was ineffectual. Believing that inmates manipulated appearances in order to impress the decision-makers, Morris and others argued that of course behavior in prison would not be predictive, because it would be invalid information.

This assumption was so widespread that it went untested for years. Finally, Gottfredson and Adams (1982) examined prison disciplinary information for federal inmates from 1970 and 1972 and discovered that parole boards and prison administrators had been right all along. While prison discipline was not as powerful a predictor as criminal history, adding it to that information would improve predictive accuracy (1982:386). Unfortunately, the researchers did not have program participation data available to test. How-

TABLE 17.2   Federal Parole Commission Guidelines (For Adults) [Guidelines for decisionmaking, customary total time served before release (including jail time)]

OFFENSE CHARACTERISTICS: SEVERITY OF OFFENSE BEHAVIOR (EXAMPLES)	OFFENDER CHARACTERISTICS: PAROLE PROGNOSIS (SALIENT FACTOR SCORE)			
	VERY GOOD (11 TO 9)	GOOD (8 TO 6)	FAIR (5 TO 4)	POOR (3 TO 0)
LOW Immigration law violations Minor theft (includes larceny and simple possession of stolen property less than $1,000). Walkaway	6 to 10 mo	8 to 12 mo	10 to 14 mo	12 to 16 mo
LOW MODERATE Alcohol law violations Counterfeit currency (passing/possession less than $1,000). Drugs: marihuana, simple possession (less than $500) Forgery/fraud (less than $1,000) Income tax evasion (less than $10,000) Selective Service Act violations Theft from mail (less than $1,000)	8 to 12 mo	12 to 16 mo	16 to 20 mo	20 to 25 mo

MODERATE
Bribery of public officials
Counterfeit currency (passing/possession $1,000 to $19,999)
Drugs:
  Marihuana, possession with intent to distribute/sale (less than $5,000).
  "Soft drugs", possession with intent to distribute/sale (less than to $5,000)
Embezzlement (less than $20,000)
Explosives, possession/transportation
Firearms Act, possession/purchase/sale (single weapon—not sawed-off shotgun or machine gun).
Income tax evasion ($10,000 to $50,000)
Interstate transportation or stolen/forged securities (less than $20,000).
Mailing threatening communications
Misprison of felony
Receiving stolen property with intent to resell (less than $20,000).
Smuggling/transporting of aliens
Theft/forgery/fraud ($1,000 to $19,999)
Theft of motor vehicle (not multiple theft or for resale).
	12 to 16 mo	16 to 20 mo	20 to 24 mo	24 to 30 mo

HIGH Burglary or larceny (other than embezzlement) from bank or post office.				

TABLE 17.2   *(Continued)*

OFFENSE CHARACTERISTICS: SEVERITY OF OFFENSE BEHAVIOR (EXAMPLES)	OFFENDER CHARACTERISTICS: PAROLE PROGNOSIS (SALIENT FACTOR SCORE)			
	VERY GOOD (11 TO 9)	GOOD (8 TO 6)	FAIR (5 TO 4)	POOR (3 TO 0)

Counterfeit currency (passing/possession $20,000-$100,000).
Counterfeiting (manufacturing)
Drugs:
  Marihuana, possession with intent to distribute/sale ($5,000 or more).
  "Soft drugs", possession with intent to distribute/sale ($500 to $5,000).
Embezzlement ($20,000 to $100,000)
Firearms Act, possession/purchase sale (sawed-off shotgun(s), machine gun(s), or multiple weapons).
Interstate transportation of stolen/forged securities ($20,000 to $100,000).
Mann Act (no force—commercial purposes)
Vehicle theft (for resale)
Receiving stolen property ($20,000 to $100,000)
Theft/forgery/fraud ($20,000 to $100,000)
	16 to 20 mo	20 to 26 mo	26 to 32 mo	32 to 38 mo

VERY HIGH
Robbery (weapon or threat)
Drugs:
  "Hard drugs" (possession with intent to distribute/sale) [no prior conviction for sale of "hard drugs"].
  "Soft drugs", possession with intent to distribute/sale (over $5,000).
Extortion
Mann Act (force)
Sexual act (force)
	26 to 36 mo	36 to 45 mo	45 to 55 mo	55 to 65 mo

GREATEST Aggravated felony (e.g., robbery, sexual act, aggravated assault)—weapon fired or personal injury. Aircraft hijacking Drugs: "Hard drugs" (possession with intent to distribute/sale) for profit (prior conviction(s) for sale of "hard drugs"). Espionage Explosives (detonation) Kidnapping Willful homicide	(Greater than above—however, specific ranges are not given due to the limited number of cases and the extreme variations in severity possible within the category.)			

NOTES: These guidelines are predicated upon good institutional conduct and program performance. If an offense behavior is not listed above, the proper category may be obtained by comparing the severity of the offense behavior with those of similar offense behaviors listed.

SOURCE: L. T. Wilkins et al. *Sentencing Guidelines: Structuring Judicial Discretion.* Washington, DC: United States Department of Justice, 1978, pp. 36–37.

ever, this study did suggest that inclusion of prison behavior in release decisions does have merit—if the prediction of future behavior is in fact relevant.

PAROLE BOARD RESPONSE TO OVERCROWDING

Another common justification for the retention of the parole decision is that parole boards are able to control prison population by serving as a safety valve. Whether boards *should* perform this function is just as controversial as whether judges should take prison population into account when making the initial sentence decision. Nevertheless, it has been commonly assumed that this control is often exercised.

The assumption ignores several characteristics of open systems. It implies, for example, that board members are less susceptible to the pressures for sentencing change than judges and legislatures. An alternative hypothesis would be that parole boards will become stricter and release less often at about the same times and for the same reasons that judges and legislatures increase sentence length. In other words, parole boards will contribute to, rather than decrease, the use of prisons by paroling less frequently and revoking more frequently.

National data from 1981 and 1982 indicate that this second dynamic appeared to be operating at least in those years. BJS reported (1983c) that the record prison growth in those years was due in part to decreased parole release. In Iowa, record prison growth in 1980–1981 was largely attributed to a get-tough parole board and resulted in the passage of an emergency release measure that bypassed the parole decision (Wright, 1984). The Correctional Association of New York (1984) directed the same indictment of the New York board. The association observed that parole was granted in 72 percent of eligible cases in 1972 but only 32 percent in 1982. Parole at the expiration of the minimum, which had been common, decreased to 50 percent in 1981 (NYSCCJ, 1982:22). Similarly, the increase in

federal prisoners in 1983 was greater than the state increases, apparently because of fewer paroles (BJS, 1983c).

Parole boards can make a number of responses to overcrowding. They can (1) increase the frequency of hearings, (2) revise the criteria for parole eligibility, (3) change the standards for revocation, and (4) find alternatives to reincarceration following revocation (Finn, 1984). In a recent survey of the states, Finn found that the most common of these was to alter revocation practice rather than change the granting of paroles. A number of states had instituted the use of stricter conditions, assignment to intensive supervision, or placement in a halfway house as the consequence of a revocation hearing. Other states reported that boards were simply ignoring more minor violations (1984:148). However, there is some evidence that boards have recently changed the frequency of granting parole as the pressure of overcrowding has intensified.

Parole went up considerably in 1983, and the ratio of prisoners to parolees dropped for the first time in five years. Texas and Michigan reported the largest gains in parole, reportedly as direct prison control devices (BJS, 1983c). Additionally, an Iowa case study suggested that parole boards have deviated from their "let's get tough, too" position precisely to avoid curtailment of their power. The Iowa emergency release statute has not been used because the parole board has always increased paroles as the prison population has approached the limit established in the legislation (Wright, 1984).

PAROLEE RIGHTS

THE GRANT OF PAROLE

The parole selection decision is one of the least scrutinized points in the criminal process and one least guided or constrained by legal requirements. Parole boards' traditional lack of concern for the appearance of justice was as damaging to their reputations as their lack of concern for substantive fairness. According to a 1972 survey of parole-granting procedures, many boards did not even bother to inform the inmate of the decision or the reasons for it; in thirty states counsel was prohibited; in thirty-four the prisoner was not permitted to present witnesses in his behalf; and in forty the boards did not even maintain a written record of the reasons for their decisions (Carroll and Mandrick, 1976:94–95).

The Supreme Court of the United States has not addressed due process standards for parole hearings. Several lower federal courts have denied that any due process protections apply, while others have required some minimal protections, such as providing the inmate with reasons for the decision (Travis and O'Leary, 1984:120). Since there is no constitutional right to parole, the few restrictions on discretion or requirements for an orderly process of decision-making have been self-imposed by forward-looking boards, or required by state law. There are some constitutional limitations on granting parole: Boards cannot refuse release in order to punish an offender for exercising his right to appeal. And boards cannot deny release on the basis of race, religion, or national origin (del Carmen, 1985:49). But demonstrating that such factors were at play in a particular case would be exceedingly difficult when the board need not even provide a hearing or written reasons for the decision (1985:50–51). In general, the federal courts will intervene in the parole granting process only if the inmate can show that the board had denied a right provided by state law or by board administrative rule.

Led by the Federal Parole Commission, a number of boards have instituted self-policing. Many of these changes occurred in the last fifteen years, after parole boards embraced the role of making explicit policy. Five states have implemented some form of contract parole: Florida, Maryland, Massachusetts, Michigan, and the federal system (Travis and O'Leary, 1984:119). Contract parole was developed under the concept of "mutual agreement programming" (MAP) pioneered by the American Correctional Association. MAP and other contract variations attempt to introduce greater certainty into the parole process and to give the inmate some control over release date by negotiating an agreement between the inmate, the prison authority, and the board about what the inmate must accomplish during the prison stay to be released early. The contract usually specifies that release will occur when all the steps have been accomplished.

As parole boards have moved away from asserting the importance of in-prison behavior and toward relying on guidelines that stress preincarceration behavior, a process contingent on program participation has become less important. The federal guidelines do allow the board some flexibility with which to reward program involvement, and parole dates set on the basis of crime and criminal history can still be pushed back if serious misconduct occurs. But the guideline process has increased the openness and accessibility of the parole board by making explicit to inmates the reasons for the decision. Twenty-seven states and the federal system have also instituted an appeals process, so that inmates dissatisfied with the initial decision can receive a review (Travis and O'Leary, 1984:119).

REVOCATION

Once parole has been granted, constitutional as well as specific state-created rights do apply. In effect, the Supreme Court has taken the position that parole can be granted or denied whimsically, but once it has been granted, its loss is protected from arbitrary action. But parole is far from unfettered freedom. The conditions of parole (see Insert 17.2 for an example) provide the parole officer and the board with rather broad control, and with authority for many specific interventions.

The specific procedural requirements imposed by the Constitution were discussed in Chapter 8, with probation revocation. It is instructive, though, to delve into the specific facts that gave rise to the *Morrissey* v. *Brewer* decision. While many states provided greater openness and formality to parolees than was true in the Morris-

Insert 17.2 SAMPLE PAROLE CONDITIONS

STATE OF CALIFORNIA
ADULT AUTHORITY

To: _____ No.: _____

THE ADULT AUTHORITY, having reviewed and considered your case, believes that you can and will successfully complete your term outside of an institution and hereby grants a parole to you effective on _____, 19__. This parole is granted to, and is accepted by you, subject to the following conditions and with the agreement that the Adult Authority has the power, at any time, in case of violation of the Conditions of Parole, to cause your detention and/or return to a State Prison. Whenever any problems arise or you do not understand what is expected of you, talk to your Parole Agent. It is his responsibility to help you understand the conditions of your parole. These conditions of your parole can only be changed by the Adult Authority.

AGREEMENT OF PAROLE

I do hereby waive extradition to the State of California from any State or Territory of the United States, or from the District of Columbia, and also agree that I will not contest any effort to return me to the State of California.

Whenever it is determined by the Adult Authority, based upon competent medical or psychiatric advice, that I am incapable of functioning in an acceptable manner, I agree to return to any facility of the Department of Corrections for necessary treatment.

Should I violate any condition of this parole and the Adult Authority suspends or revokes my parole and orders my return to prison, I understand that my term, or terms shall at that time be refixed at the maximum term pursuant to law and Adult Authority regulations.

I have read, or have had read to me, the following conditions of parole and the attached guidelines by which I have agreed to abide. I fully understand them and the penalties involved should I violate these conditions of parole.

CONDITIONS OF PAROLE

1. RELEASE REPORTING AND TRAVEL: I agree to report to my Parole Agent upon parole and to keep him continuously informed of my residence and employment locations. I will not leave the State of California without first having the written permission of my Parole Agent.

2. LAWS: I shall obey all Federal and State laws, and municipal and county ordinances.

3. WEAPONS: I will not own, possess, use, sell, or have under my control any firearms or other deadly weapons as defined in Section 3024 of the Penal Code.

4. PERSONAL CONDUCT: I will not engage in assaultive activities, violence, or threats of violence of any sort. I shall behave in a manner justifying the opportunity granted by parole.

5. NARCOTICS OR DRUGS: I will not illegally possess, use or traffic in any narcotic drugs, as defined by Division 10 of the Health and Safety Code, or dangerous or hypnotic drugs as defined by Section 4211 of the Business and Professions Code. I further agree to participate in anti-narcotic programs in accordance with instructions from my Parole Agent.

6. PAROLE AGENT INSTRUCTIONS: I agree to comply with or respond to verbal and written instructions which may be imposed by my Parole Agent from time to time as may be governed by the special requirements of my individual situation.

7. SPECIAL CONDITIONS: I agree to abide by the following special conditions of parole as stipulated below: _____
_____
_____
_____
_____
_____
_____

_____

Signature of Parolee

ATTEST & WITNESS:

_____   _____
Classification & Parole Representative   Date
or His Designated Alternate

_____

SOURCE: Elliot Studt, *Surveillance and Service in Parole*. Washington, DC: National Institute of Correction, 1973.

sey case, this revocation procedure was not atyp-ical of state's consideration for parolees.

Morrissey was arrested in Iowa as a parole violator and jailed in his home town. After a week of jail detention, and without ever interviewing Morrissey, the Iowa parole board revoked his pa-role status and returned him to prison, some 100 miles from his home. In deciding to revoke, the board relied strictly on the parole officer's written report, in which it was alleged that Morrissey had bought a car under an assumed name, had op-erated it without permission, had given false statements to the police after a minor accident, and had failed to report his residence to the parole officer. Morrissey's complaint was that he had never received a hearing.

It is apparent from reading the decision that the Court was particularly impressed with the power of the individual parole officer and with the ability of the board to transport the parolee many miles away from the alleged violations with-out ever checking the veracity of the claims or permitting the parolee to mount a defense. Based on these and related concerns, the Court required a two-stage hearing procedure. The parolee was not to be returned to the prison, and thus removed from his home community, without a review of the facts by an official other than the interested parole officer and without some opportunity for the parolee to challenge the case against him.

In arriving at this decision, the Court rejected Iowa's claim that parole was a privilege, not a right, and that therefore no particular procedures were required:

> It is hardly useful any longer to try to deal with this problem in terms of whether the parolee's lib-erty is a "right" or a "privilege." By whatever name the liberty is valuable and must be seen as within the protection of the Fourteenth Amendment. Its termination calls for some orderly process, however informal.

Many states have now gone further than the minimum process required by the Supreme Court. For example, the right to counsel and provision of counsel to the indigent are not uncommon. The National Advisory Commission, and a number of other standard-setting groups, along with parole experts such as Elliot Studt (1973), have argued strenuously for greater formality, and for greater participation of the parolee in this process as a means of stressing the parolee's adult status and responsibility for his actions.

PAROLE SUPERVISION

The parole population is the smallest of all those subject to correctional measures. BJS (1983c:6) estimated that the 10.5 percent of the total pop-ulation under correctional supervision was on pa-role. Influenced by the factors discussed above, the parole population jumped dramatically by 12.1 percent to just over 250,000 by year-end 1983. Unlike the probation and prison popula-tions, the parole population has grown rather slowly. Between 1979 and the end of 1983, the total growth was just 15 percent, with 80 percent of that increase occurring in 1983. This low growth rate, despite the large increases in prison population, is attributed to determinate and man-datory sentencing, as well as more conservative parole granting (1983c). As parole decisions have become less common, the mix of persons condi-tionally released to supervision has changed. Ta-ble 17.3 indicates admissions to parole supervi-sion by type of release in 1983. The percentage of persons supervised who entered through man-datory release is, as expected, particularly large in determinate sentencing states such as Minne-sota. But mandatory release is a rather high per-centage of all releases in some other states as well.

THE ADMINISTRATION OF SUPERVISION

There are arguments for and against the common administration of the parole selection decision and parole supervision. These arguments are very similar to the arguments for and against placing probation supervision in the judicial or the ex-

TABLE 17.3   Parole Entries by Type for Selected Jurisdictions, 1983

JURISDICTION	NUMBER ENTERING PAROLE	PERCENT OF ENTRIES DUE TO:		
		A DISCRETION— PAROLE BOARD DECISION	EARNED GOOD TIME OR DETER- MINATE SENTENCE RELEASE	ALL OTHER REASONS*
Federal	**9,381**	**62%**	**22%**	**16%**
Arizona	2,037	54	34	12
California	26,032	6	83	11
Colorado	1,756	14	83	3
Connecticut	1,151	92	0	8
Delaware	541	43	57	0
District of Columbia	1,722	75	2	23
Florida	6,874	64	0	35
Kansas	1,172	85	7	8
Kentucky	2,588	86	0	14
Louisiana	793	87	10	3
Illinois	8,231	4	96	0
Indiana	3,794	3	97	—
Maryland	4,061	44	56	0
Michigan	6,306	96	0	4
Minnesota	1,286	19	69	12
Mississippi	1,884	86	0	14
Montana	331	97	0	3
Nebraska	395	94	4	2
Nevada	582	99	0	1
New York	11,255	77	23	0
Ohio	8,909	86	0	14
Oregon	1,904	98	0	2
Pennsylvania	4,074	99	0	1
Rhode Island	378	98	0	2
South Dakota	371	87	0	13
Tennessee	3,881	68	17	15
Texas	16,362	53	47	—
Virginia	5,084	74	25	1
Wisconsin	2,217	57	43	0

* Includes reinstatement on parole or miscellaneous releases to parole.

SOURCE: Bureau of Justice Statistics, *Probation and Parole 1983*. Washington, DC: Bureau of Justice Statistics, September 1984, p. 4.

ecutive branches. Some argue that the parole board should oversee supervision policy, so that supervision is closely linked to granting and revoking. Others argue that supervision should be part of a unified correctional department, so that parole supervision is linked to prison services and programs. Additionally, some have argued that the board should not be burdened with administrative duties and should concentrate on the decisions. In most states, parole supervision is now a part of the same department that administers the institutions. Fifteen states and the federal system, however, have separate agencies for parole supervision (McGarrell and Flanagan,

1985:131). In some of these jurisdictions, such as New York and Pennsylvania, the parole board is also the supervision authority. In others, such as the federal system, the supervision agency (Federal Probation) is independent of both the Federal Parole Commission and the Federal Bureau of Prisons.

THE ACTIVITY OF SUPERVISION

Conditional release supervision does not differ significantly from probation supervision. The same conflicts between service and surveillance appear, and the same criticisms about lack of contact with clients. David Stanley (1976) concluded that parole officers were simply too inconsequential in the lives of parolees either to keep them in line or to provide them with assistance. Jester's in-depth study of eight probation and parole offices found that parole officers spent less time than probation officers in administrative work and somewhat more time in travel, but that in other respects the use of resources was very comparable. In her study, parole officers spent 29 percent of their time in direct contact with clients, and another 22 percent in contacts with community agencies; 28 percent was spent in administration, and 21 percent in travel (Jester, 1981:42). Within the direct contact category, parole officers appeared, on the average, to split time between activities that would be considered service and activities that would be considered enforcement: 15 percent in counseling and casework, referral and material assistance, compared to 14 percent in rule enforcement, risk assessment, and active surveillance.

PAROLE TECHNOLOGIES

According to Studt (1972:57), a technology determines

> (1) which problems will be attended to and which will be ignored, (2) how the problems to be addressed will be defined, e.g. do they arise because of inadequate persons or because of dysfunctional system arrangements, (3) what information is

needed to solve the problems, and how that information will be secured, (4) what methods may be used to solve problems, (5) what tools are required for problem solving work, and (6) what kinds of problem resolutions are possible.

Studt concluded that the surveillance technology was well developed but relatively ineffective, and that the helping technologies were poorly thought out and poorly supported by the organization. Jester (1981) found similar results ten years later. Jester described three possible supervision technologies: behavior control, mental health, and environmental manipulation. The control technology was dominant in five of eight offices and among most individual officers. One parole office stressed manipulation of the environment through the use of referrals, advocacy, employment assistance, and other means of changing the relationship between the parolee and the community.

The underdevelopment of service technologies, of any sort, are related to deeply rooted organizational practices. Studt (1972:191–192) found two organizational problems most troublesome: (1) The parole officer and more important the parole office maintained no systematic information about the tasks to be accomplished by the parolee and the problems faced; (2) the agents were in an inadequate position both in the agency and in the community to develop a helping technology. To improve this situation, Studt recommended that parole agencies maintain an ongoing needs census—from the point of view of the parolee, not the agency. She also recommended that the caseload model was totally inadequate for parole services and that parole administrators had to become more active in development and delivery of services. Finally, she thought that parole would not improve unless there were new roles for parolees. They should be seen as consumers of services, and their opinion sought on which were most helpful. They should be included on advisory boards to assist in policy development. They should be treated as co-workers with parole staff in developing and assisting community organizations. And they should be encouraged to organize their own resources. Studt's recommendations are just beginning to have some impact fifteen years later.

THE PAROLEE'S PERSPECTIVE

Irwin's study in San Francisco (1970) led to a threefold classification of the adjustment problems faced by parolees. Most immediately felt upon release from prison, according to Irwin, were the problems caused by the initial shock of reentry. These problems are common to any person going through a sudden and significant change in environment. Another set of problems was associated with "doing good." For most parolees, making it on the street included more than surviving. They wanted a good job, acceptable relationships with women, and a network of relationships and activities that provided a sense of meaningfulness (1970:142). Finally, according to Irwin, were the problems of dealing with the parole agency itself (1970:107).

Irwin reported that, contrary to many theoretical accounts of parole adjustment problems, stigma did not loom as a large barrier from the parolee's perspective. However, he pointed out that stigma was felt by "square johns" (persons who had never adopted a criminal life style), and by parolees who were trying to change their identity (1970:138). Duffee and Duffee (1981) found similar low reports of stigma from halfway house residents.

Irwin also cast some doubt on the typical ways in which parolee–parole agent relationships have been pictured. Irwin's criticisms have never been adequately addressed. Most accounts of the parole relationship stress the tension between the agent's service role and enforcement role. Irwin argued that parolees approach the relationship from a different perspective. They are concerned with how tolerant the agent is of deviant behavior or nonconformist lifestyles, how consistent and trustworthy (or "right") the agent is, and how intense the agent's intervention is into the parolee's life. While the treatment/control issue is of great importance to agents, especially in terms of

how they relate to superiors, that conflict was less salient to parolees (1970:165–166).

While Studt did not entirely agree with Irwin's view of the agent-client relationship, she did agree that one of parole's weakest elements is its lack of concern for the parolees' perspective. She catalogued the parolee's chief adjustment problems this way:

1. Economic support, money for maintenance and reestablishment
2. Status clearance (such as a driver's license)
3. Emergency service (the need for 24-hour availability)
4. Employment assistance and support
5. Advocacy with law enforcement agencies
6. Rights in decision-making
7. Reduction in surveillance emphasis
8. Restoration of civil rights

PAROLE OUTCOMES

As we have seen, parole emerged from a number of different forces, such as continual prison overcrowding, the search for ways to sanction good conduct in prison, and the desire to support released prisoners. The current justifications for parole still include these objectives. Consequently, evaluations of parole require measures on multiple dimensions. However, many of these parole objectives are more salient to the issue of the conditional release decision than they are to the issue of supervision. Control of prison population, reduction of prison expenses, and control of prisoner behavior are accomplished, if at all, through the selection process. Enforcement of conditions and support for released prisoners rests on a narrower range of objectives.

One could make a case for parole supervision on strict retributive rather than crime control or assistance grounds. The arguments for a retributive parole supervision period would be very similar to the arguments for the split sentence, or for probation under the justice model, as championed by McAnany and Harris in Chapter 8. Parole supervision would be structured as a punishment, with the length and level of intervention determined by the offense. However, this rationale for supervision has not been advanced.

One could also argue, with considerable historical support, that the merits of supervision are more closely related to maintaining political support for the selection decision than to its direct impact on the persons supervised. The cyclical scandals about early release have been sparked by discoveries that conditions were not enforced. While this argument for public protection is separable from arguments that focus on the merits of supervision per se, it would seem likely that it would be supported by the same data used in judging supervision effects—namely, some measure of recidivism.

The most widely accepted criterion for effectiveness of supervision is whether supervision on conditional release reduces the return to crime, compared to conditional release without supervision, or release without conditions at expiration of sentence. Unfortunately, while there have been many studies of parole recidivism, few have compared parole failure rates to the failure rates of comparable samples of ex-prisoners released in other ways.

Table 17.4 presents data from 1983 on exits from parole by completion of term and reincarceration. It is these data by which many administrators and interest groups either defend or damn supervision, depending on whether they believe such rates are high or low. However, there are no rational grounds for making that judgment based on such figures. The data do not report how long persons have been on supervision, nor do they indicate what the failure rates would be without supervision.

Greenfield (1985) has issued a grim report on the likelihood of recidivism among released offenders. This report was based on a national survey of inmates in state prisons during October and November 1979. Greenfield discovered that 61 percent of those admitted to prison in 1979 had been confined before. Of those, 46 percent would still have been in prison on the prior conviction if they had served the full term rather than being conditionally released (1985:4). By estimating future returns on the 1979 inmates' previous criminal history, Greenfield determined that nearly half of all persons who leave prison, by any means, will return within twenty years of release. Of those who will return, 60 percent will do so within three years of release (1985:1–2).

Table 17.5 indicates the legal status of the inmates at the time of their 1979 admissions to prison. Many were conditionally free—21.1 percent had been on probation and 20.5 percent had been on parole or mandatory release supervision (1985:6). Greenfield found that the return rates of releasees had not changed much in twenty-four years. A 1956 study of federal releases estimated that 47.4 percent would return within fifteen years. Greenfield's 1979 data suggested that 47.6 percent would return in fifteen years (1985:3).

The rates and reasons for return appear to vary for both type of release and type of offender. A New York Department of Correctional Services Report (Donnelly and Bala, 1986) examined over 7,000 inmates released in 1980. The total return rate after five years was 41.4 percent. Parolees were more often returned on parole violations (20.6 percent) than on new felony convictions (18.6 percent). Persons on mandatory release were more often returned on convictions (26.4 percent) than violations (20.5 percent). Of those who had been unconditionally released at the end of term, 39.8 percent were returned for new felony convictions. Return rates varied by race/ethnicity, with blacks and Hispanics returning more frequently (45.1 percent) than whites (33.2 percent). Those who had been released following burglary and robbery convictions returned at the fastest rate.

The data generally indicate that the first few years after release are the most hazardous. However, the data may be misleading. Minor and Courlander (1979) point out that several practices are likely to inflate the picture of early failure. The typical presentations of failure rates do not

TABLE 17.4   Parole Exits by Type for Selected Jurisdictions, 1983

JURISDICTION	NUMBER OF EXITS	PERCENT OF EXITS DISCHARGED FROM PAROLE DUE TO:		
		COMPLETION OF TERM	INCARCERATION ON CURRENT OR NEW CHARGES	ALL OTHER REASONS*
Total	119,472%	71,381	37,260	10,831
Percent	100%	60%	31%	9%
Northeast				
Connecticut	1,175	56	42	2
Maine	21	29	61	10
Massachusetts	2,995	78	15	6
New Hampshire	195	61	25	14
New Jersey	5,374	68	28	4
New York	8,828	69	29	2
Pennsylvania	3,330	58	39	3
Rhode Island	334	69	28	3
Vermont	148	68	30	2
North Central				
Illinois	8,541	66	27	7
Indiana	3,518	81	11	8
Iowa	834	52	17	31
Michigan	4,766	68	30	2
Minnesota	1,267	72	27	1
Missouri	1,040	61	38	1
Nebraska	340	84	16	0
North Dakota	196	72	18	10
Ohio	7,198	58	26	16
South Dakota	275	73	25	2
Wisconsin	1,976	71	26	1

subtract those who have already failed from the population before calculating the rate of later failures. This practice artificially lowers the failure rate of later returns. More important, they pointed out that parole offices routinely assign parolees to more intensive supervision for the first six months of release. Consequently, the risk of detection is higher.

While many failure studies have simply looked at rates and means of return and parolee characteristics, a few have sought to examine the levels of service received by parolees and whether those services have made any difference. The most commonly cited parolee problems are employment-related. Toborg et al. (1978) conducted a national evaluation of employment assistance programs, the characteristics of which are given in Table 17.6. Toborg regretfully concluded that she could come to no conclusions about the effectiveness of these services in reducing recidivism.

One of the largest field experiments ever con-

TABLE 17.4 *(Continued)*

JURISDICTION	NUMBER OF EXITS	PERCENT OF EXITS DISCHARGED FROM PAROLE DUE TO:		
		COMPLETION OF TERM	INCARCERATION ON CURRENT OR NEW CHARGES	ALL OTHER REASONS*
South				
District of Columbia	1,539	25	64	11
Florida	6,489	54	26	20
Georgia	5,202	72	28	0
Kentucky	2,518	49	32	19
Lousiana	791	69	29	2
Maryland	4,009	75	18	7
Mississippi	1,591	53	35	12
Oklahoma	802	77	21	2
South Carolina	1,217	65	27	8
Tennessee	3,621	76	18	6
Texas	10,505	53	45	2
Virginia	4,176	71	16	13
West Virginia	427	65	15	20
West				
Alaska	77	62	30	8
California	19,483	35	46	19
Colorado	1,438	77	23	0
Hawaii	73	86	14	0
Idaho	194	61	37	2
Montana	298	69	25	6
Nevada	565	64	35	1
Oregon	1,436	70	16	14
Utah	534	62	38	0
Wyoming	146	88	10	2

* Includes absconders, transfers to another parole jurisdiction, deaths, discharges to custody, detainer or warrant or other forms of discharge.

SOURCE: Bureau of Justice Statistics, *Probation and Parole, 1983*. Washington, DC: Bureau of Justice Statistics, September 1984, p. 5.

ducted casts some doubt on the utility of employment assistance and financial support as contributors to recidivism reduction. Rossi, Berk, and Lenihan (1980) reported that employment assistance did not increase employment, or reduce crime, and that a weekly stipend to released inmates increased the length of time for them to obtain employment and was associated with higher failure rates. Curtis and Schulman (1984), examining the same experiment from the perspective of the significant women in the lives of these parolees, reported that the financial payments usually had negative effects on family relationships. The impact appeared to have different effects on different types of relationships. Wives reported some positive family adjustments, while mothers and girlfriends more often reported that the parolees used the cash payments to buy their freedom from the relationship. Curtis and Schulman concluded that the needs of parolees and the situations that might cause problems have not been sufficiently studied or specified to en-

TABLE 17.5   Criminal Justice Status at Time of Entry to State Prison in 1979

	ADMISSION TYPES			
STATUS AT ADMISSION	NON-AVERTABLE RECIDIVISTS	AVERTABLE RECIDIVISTS	FIRST-TIMERS	TOTAL
Number of admissions	50,899	43,235	59,331	153,465
Percent of admissions on each type of supervision	100.0%	100.0%	100.0%	100.0%
No supervision	66.7	28.8	72.9	58.4
Probation	25.5	7.8	27.1	21.1
Parole/other conditional release*	7.8	63.4	—	20.5

* Includes persons admitted as escapees.
SOURCE: Lawrence Greenfeld, *Examining Recidivism*. Washington, DC: Bureau of Justice Statistics, February 1985, p. 6.

TABLE 17.6   Program Characteristics of Employment Assistance Programs
Summary of Program Characteristics (N = 257)

CHARACTERISTIC	PERCENTAGE OF PROGRAMS	CHARACTERISTIC	PERCENTAGE OF PROGRAMS
Length of Operation:		*Budget Size:*	
Less than one year	12%	Less than $50,000	22%
One to three years	37	$50,000 to $99,999	14
Four to six years	27	$100,000 to $299,999	24
More than six years	24	$300,000 to $499,999	7
No response	0	More than $500,000	18
		No Response	15
Clients Served, Past Year:			
Less than 100	17%	*Major Funding Source:*	
100 to 299	27	Federal government	51%
300 to 499	13	State government	21
500 to 999	13	Local government	5
More than 999	17	Private	9
No response	14	No response	14
Average Client Contact Length:		*Staff Size:*	
Less than one month	2%	0 to 10 persons	60%
One to six months	55	11 to 20 persons	19
Seven to twelve months	26	21 to 40 persons	9
More than twelve months	13	More than 40 persons	11
No response	4	No response	1
Frequency of Contact:		*Ex-Offenders on Staff:*	
Daily	29%	50% or more	12%
Several times a week	26	20 to 49%	18
Once a week	23	1 to 19%	29
Less than once a week	19	None	38
No response	4	No response	3

able effective support programs to be designed.

A few studies have been able to compare conditional release supervision to unconditional release while controlling for the characteristics of the different populations. This control is essential, since most inmates who remain in prison until expiration of term present higher risks than those conditionally released. Consequently, we should expect them to fail more often, even if supervision was irrelevant. Sacks and Logan (1980) provided a very thorough examination of a very small sample of minor felons released with and without a short period of parole supervision.

They found that the seven-month parole period pushed back the time to failure by about four and a half months, but did not prevent return to crime, compared to unconditional release. Waller's Canadian study indicated similar delaying effects. Parolees found jobs more quickly than those who had maxed out, but those released on termination usually displayed more satisfaction with the jobs they found. For that and related reasons, parole conditions may have retarded failure, but they did not reduce it (1979).

One of the more thorough and careful comparisons was conducted by Gottfredson, Mitchell-

TABLE 17.6   *(Continued)*

CHARACTERISTIC	PERCENTAGE OF PROGRAMS	CHARACTERISTIC	PERCENTAGE OF PROGRAMS
Major Client Ident. Method:		*Prison Releasees Served,*	
Referred by:		*Past Year:*	
Prison officials	18%	Less than 50	21%
Probation/parole officers	28	50 to 99	12
Family or friends	2	100 to 199	14
Other community agencies	4	200 to 299	8
Program outreach efforts	12	300 to 499	8
Other	14	More than 500	16
Multiple responses	13	No response	22
No response	9		

SERVICE	PROVIDED DIRECTLY	PROVIDED BY REFERRAL	NOT PROVIDED
Vocational testing	35%	56%	11%
Vocational counseling	80	31	3
Work orientation/adjustment training	56	41	8
Education	27	67	7
Skills training	25	71	8
On-the-job training	25	70	10
Transitional employment/supported work	30	43	21
Job development	82	28	4
Job placement	89	30	2
Follow-up counseling after employment	82	17	4
Other follow-up after employment	70	17	7
Other	50	20	0

SOURCE: Mary Toborg et al., *The Transition from Prison to Employment: An Assessment of Community Based Assistance Programs.* Washington, DC: National Institute of Law Enforcement and Criminal Justice, 1978, p. 4.

Herzfeld, and Flanagan (1982). They studied 5,312 cases released in 1972 and followed for five years. Releases were on parole, mandatory release, or no supervision. They employed three different definitions of failure in order to determine how the treatment of technical violations affected comparative failure rates. Since two-thirds of the parolees and one-half of the mandatory releasees were returned on technical violations, while none of those serving full term were subject to such violation, the conceptualization of technical violation is crucial to parole evaluation. Is a technical return a "success" because it avoids a new crime (and others are not subject to it), or a "failure" because it leads back to prison (1982:218–282)?

This large study concluded that parole is more effective than unconditional release only when technical violations are not counted as failures. They also discovered that supervised release was an advantage for some types of offenders and a disadvantage for others. Finally, they found that, even under definitions of failure that are favorable to parole, the effects of parole supervision are not great, providing a 5 to 15 percent decrease in failure, compared to unconditional release, when technical violations are excluded (1982:295–296).

SUMMARY

1. In the development of graduated release mechanisms, both efficiency and control of prisoners' behavior were probably more important than concerns for easing the transition to the community.

2. Origins of parole included indenturing and transportation, executive pardon, the use of good time, and the ticket-of-leave.

3. The modern version of parole required the passage of indeterminate sentence legislation, first accomplished in New York in 1868. In 1877, parole was implemented at the Elmira Reformatory.

4. By 1967, a number of correctional experts felt that parole by itself was insufficient support for the released prisoner. The policy of reintegration was promoted. It included arguments for preparing inmates for release earlier in their prison sentences, and avoiding incarceration where possible. However, the primary impact of reintegration was the growth of graduated release programs such as furlough, prerelease centers, study release, and work release.

5. There are currently two major forms of conditional release from prison. Discretionary release, most commonly parole, and mandatory release, in which early release is determined by good time statutes. In either type of release, supervision is usually provided by parole officers.

6. As prison populations have risen and the parole decision has been used less frequently, other mechanisms for early release have evolved. The most significant of these are emergency release statutes.

7. The parole release decision had been criticized for being arbitrary, for creating disparity, and for making inaccurate predictions. The response by a number of parole boards has been increased attention to explicit policymaking, such as the adoption of parole guidelines.

8. Inmates have few substantive or procedural rights in relation to the discretionary release decision. Minimal due process protections have been applied to the revocation decision.

9. In most states, parole supervision is administered by the same department in charge of prison administration. The technology of supervision has been criticized for being underdeveloped, for being overly concerned with surveillance, and for not accommodating the parolee's perspective.

10. There are few rigorous evaluations of parole outcomes, and the few that exist suggest that supervision may either delay return to crime or may actually make small reductions in likelihood of recidivism. The interpretation of technical violations is crucial to these evaluations.

KEY WORDS

COMMUNITY PRERELEASE CENTERS. Residential centers, usually off prison grounds, that permit inmates nearing release greater contact with community roles and responsibilities than is possible in most prison settings.

CONDITIONAL RELEASE. Release from prison prior to the expiration of a prison term, upon condition that the released prisoner will abide by the law and certain regulations.

DISCRETIONARY RELEASE. A conditional release decision in which the authority to release rests within the discretion of the release officials. The most common discretionary release is parole. Some good time statutes also provide for discretionary decision-making.

EMERGENCY RELEASE PROCEDURES. A legal means to reduce prison population when it reaches a certain size (usually defined as a percent of capacity). These procedures will permit earlier than normal consideration for parole, or earlier than specified mandatory release dates through award of additional good time.

EXECUTIVE PARDON. As a forerunner of parole, executive pardon often involved application to the chief executive of a jurisdiction for shortening of sentence. Pardon is still in use, and may be full or partial. Pardons in some states are used to reduce very long sentences so that an inmate may be considered for parole.

FURLOUGH. Where statute permits, temporary leaves that may be granted to inmates by prison officials,

usually for one or two days at a time. Also called home furlough, although used for purposes other than home visits.

GOOD TIME. Statutory provisions for reduction in sentence in return for good behavior in prison.

INDENTURING. A forerunner of parole; inmates were released to the custody of families or manufacturers prior to expiration of sentence.

MANDATORY (CONDITIONAL) RELEASE. Usually refers to conditional release of prisoners through accumulation of good time credits.

PAROLE. Conditional, discretionary release, usually at the determination of a board, followed by supervision to ascertain that conditions are adhered to.

PRERELEASE PROGRAMS IN PRISON. Programs within the institution designed to prepare the inmate for release; usually include assistance in applying for a job and a suitable residence.

STUDY RELEASE. Release from the prison grounds to pursue education in the community; may require return to the prison at night or residence in a prerelease center.

TICKET-OF-LEAVE. An early form of conditional release used in the English and Irish prison systems.

WORK RELEASE. Release from prison grounds to find or engage in employment in the community; may require return to the prison after work hours or residence in a prerelease or work release center.

PROJECTS AND QUESTIONS

1. If you were a parole board member, would you be sensitive to prison population when making individual parole decisions? Why or why not?
2. Consider Tom Watson's use of his home furlough authority in the case that opened this chapter. If you were a correctional administrator, would you take such risks with your own career? Why or why not?
3. Investigate the examples of reintegration policy in your state. How extensive are furlough, work and study release, or prerelease programs? Has the corrections department made any effort to maintain prisoners' contacts with their home community, or to reduce the use of incarceration? Are these programs coordinated in any way?
4. Have there been any recent debates in your state about the retention or abolition of parole? What were the arguments for and against the discretionary release decision?

ADDITIONAL READING

Richard McCleary. *Dangerous Men*. Beverly Hills, CA: Sage Publications, 1980. An observational study of parole supervision in Chicago; a detailed account of parole officers at work.

David Stanley. *The Prisoners Among Us*. Washington, DC: The Brookings Institution, 1976. Stanley's study is an interesting companion to McCleary's work. Stanley covers more states, but provides less in-depth coverage of any of them. He is concerned with the wisdom of retaining parole supervision.

Elliot Studt. *Surveillance and Service in Parole*. Washington DC: National Institute of Justice, 1978, or National Institute of Corrections, 1980. Various agencies have tried to keep this document in print. A study of parole supervision technology from the perspective of officers and parolees.

CHAPTER 18

CORRECTIONAL ORGANIZATION AND MANAGEMENT

QUESTIONS

1. What is a complex organization?
2. What are the different dimensions of organizational effectiveness?
3. What are some of the major differences between public and private organizations?
4. What are the basic functions of management?
5. How has correctional management changed over the years?
6. What is the common result of too much control?
7. How have human relations concerns changed correctional management?
8. Why are interorganizational relations important?

THE SUCCESS THAT FAILED

Phil and his graduate assistant John had spent the last ten months evaluating a "community related" center attached to the Chisolm Hill medium security prison. The CRC, as it was called, was the new pet project of Randy Tedesco, a senior counselor at Chisolm. Randy had a reputation as a little too "treatment" oriented to suit the new group that had come in with Commissioner Comstock. But he also had a reputation as a doer.

The CRC was a cross between a prerelease center and a work release program for the prison. It was located on the prison grounds and staffed by prison employees, but its residents never entered the prison; they slept and ate in the center. They spent most of the day in the city of Madison, just across the river. Most of them were employed, although two were attending community college full time. The center was a circle of five old trailers that had at one time been a forestry camp run by the prison. When Warden Macklin disbanded the camp, Tedesco got the bright idea of hauling the trailers out of the woods.

The project had several goals. Tedesco wanted to get inmates out of the cellblocks and into a more realistic setting prior to release to parole. He felt the more informal atmosphere in the CRC broke down the usual barriers between inmates and counselors and would allow counselors to do some real prerelease counseling. He also wanted the inmates out in the city looking for jobs, searching for an apartment, holding down a job, and whatever else was necessary before they met the parole board.

Today John and Phil were to deliver their final report on the project. As far as they were concerned, it was off to a great start. The project was meeting all proposed objectives. Phil was eager to reach the warden's office; he rarely had such good news to report.

In Macklin's office, the secretary waved and said the warden might be tied up for a little while. Before Phil and John could sit down, they heard shouting from behind the closed door of the inner office—it was Tedesco's voice. They couldn't hear Macklin, who evidently was not as excited as Tedesco. A few minutes later, Randy burst through, almost knocking down the secretary.

Macklin was standing at the inner door, lighting a cigar. "Professor," he beckoned. "I know you come bearing good news, but I'm afraid I have bad." He ushered them into the office.

Macklin accepted the evaluation report graciously, but waved off an oral presentation. "Look, I know you worked as hard as Randy, and maybe we can learn something for the next time. But I've just canceled the CRC." John was stunned. He had developed quite a commitment to the staff and the residents. He had been caught up in Randy's enthusiasm. "I have nothing against the project; I just needed the men. It takes six correctional officers to staff that center. For

twenty-two inmates. I just can't afford that these days. I can bring them back in here and they can guard four times that many. And with the population in here so high, that's exactly where I need them."

The ride home was quiet for some time. Phil was enjoying the irony of delivering a glowing report for a program canceled two minutes before he got there. Finally John opened his mouth.

"Boy, that's bureaucracy for you. I mean isn't that crazy? This department runs lots of programs that fail and then it turns around and dumps a success. I'll never understand."

Phil was not so worried. "Now, wait a minute. I know how you feel. We get committed; obviously Randy is committed. But I didn't hear anything crazy in that office." "No, that was a case of two rational men with different purposes. Both were valid, but one had to go. If Macklin made a mistake, it was in letting the thing get started, not in shutting it down."

"Good grief," said his student. "You're starting to sound like one of them."

"Macklin is putting pieces of a puzzle together. Constantly. Then the picture changes and he has to rearrange the pieces. Take it apart, put it back together again. Randy's committed to his project. He's committed to treatment. Other middle managers in there are committed to their specialties, and they're all trying to do them well. They expect to get rewarded when their jobs go right. But sometimes, that won't happen. Randy started up the right project at the wrong time."

John pondered that for a minute. "You don't mean that Macklin's more in favor of custody than treatment, do you?"

"Absolutely not. Macklin might be all in favor of treatment. But he's the warden. He has to weigh options and resources from all sides. If the CRC had started ten years ago, he might have gone totally the other way."

THE COMPLEX ORGANIZATION

A **complex organization** is a human system of interrelated roles which must be performed simultaneously for the achievement of goals. The method of organizing is not the prime concern of most organization members. But in any organization, there are roles set aside for people who do focus on organization. These people are managers. They are concerned with purpose and achievement, but they are not responsible for the front-line work that gives organizations their identity. They are concerned with designing, structuring, monitoring, and changing that work. Their task is steering the organization.

The management task is not always straightforward; in the case, Warden Macklin was faced with a difficult decision. Success to Macklin was something different from success to Tedesco. An important part of the management task is balancing and compromising among diverse organizational parts in order to get the best overall mix. The fact that the "parts" are people makes the balancing and compromising a sensitive art.

An appreciation of the managerial art requires knowledge of the basic organizational elements managers must work with. The people in organizations are arranged in particular ways. They play particular roles. And the roles are grouped together to achieve certain functions or consequences. A good manager shows understanding of and empathy for people, but also must have an appreciation of how they fit together, and how to change the fit to meet changing conditions. That knowledge is gained through the study of organizations.

FOUR MODELS OF ORGANIZATION

In some recent research, Quinn and associates (1981, 1985) asked a number of organizational experts what standards they would use for assessing organizational effectiveness. The experts gave wide-ranging answers. Some stressed good leadership; some stressed relations with other organizations; some emphasized goal setting and planning; some highlighted morale building and teamwork; others elected still other criteria. Beneath these opinions about organizational effectiveness, three underlying dimensions were evident.

These dimensions represent what Quinn and his colleagues call the competing values of organizational effectiveness. Each dimension poses crucial value choices for managers: (1) the structural dimension, (2) the focus dimension, and (3) the means-ends dimension. The structural dimension varies from organizational structures that impose control and predictability on behavior to structures that provide for flexibility and innovation. The focus dimension varies from attention to internal concerns, such as staff morale and recordkeeping, to attention to external concerns, such as obtaining resources and reaching production goals. The means-ends dimension varies from concern for short-range objectives to concern for long-range accomplishments.

Managers and organizational researchers have often focused on one or two of the choices posed on these dimensions, but rarely on all three at once. As management experts have focused on these choices, four "models" or perspectives on organizations have developed. Each model captures some important issues, while leaving others out. The **competing values approach** to organizational effectiveness attempts to take a more comprehensive view by using all four models. The purpose is not to make choices about which model is better, but to understand the importance of the competing values represented by all four. The competing values approach to organizations, including the three underlying dimensions and the four common organizational models, is depicted in Figure 18.1.

THE RATIONAL GOAL MODEL

When many people think of organizations, their first thoughts are of goals. What is the organizational purpose? Toward what end are the efforts of the participants directed? How can we be assured of efficiency and productivity? The **rational goal model of organization** has an ex-

FIGURE 18.1   A Summary of the Competing Value Sets and Effectiveness Models

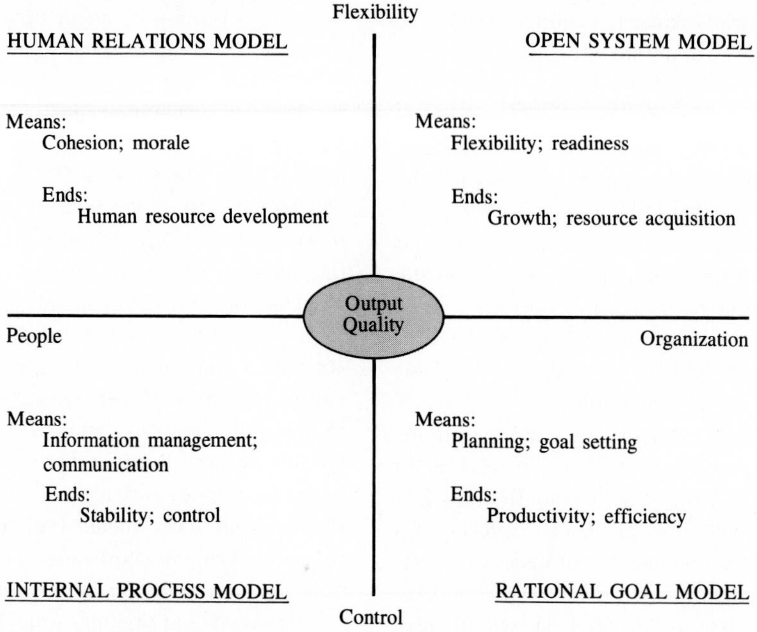

Flexibility

HUMAN RELATIONS MODEL   OPEN SYSTEM MODEL

Means:
   Cohesion; morale

Means:
   Flexibility; readiness

Ends:
   Human resource development

Ends:
   Growth; resource acquisition

People   Output Quality   Organization

Means:
   Information management;
   communication

Means:
   Planning; goal setting

Ends:
   Stability; control

Ends:
   Productivity; efficiency

INTERNAL PROCESS MODEL   RATIONAL GOAL MODEL

Control

SOURCE: John Rohrbaugh, "The Competing Values Approach: Innovation and Effectiveness in the Job Service." In Richard H. Hall and Robert E. Quinn (eds.), *Organizational Theory and Public Policy*, Newbury Park, CA: Sage, 1983, pp. 265–280. Copyright © 1983 by Sage Publications. Reprinted by permission of Sage Publications, Inc.

ternal focus and adopts structures that achieve control. The short-range issues in this model are processes for goal setting, planning, and evaluating. The long-range issues are productivity and efficiency.

Managers with these concerns follow the "better mouse trap" school of organization. There is a heavy interest in developing the best technology for solving a problem. Managers seem to assume that the best technical solution will appeal to every rational human being, because it is the most economical and effective in reaching a goal.

Early conceptions of organizations (Weber, 1947), and early conceptions of management (Taylor, 1967) focused almost entirely on the rational model. Weber wrote about bureaucracy as the most rational means of administering public agencies. Taylor invented time and motion studies and a whole class of middle managers to plan,

monitor, and evaluate the productivity of industrial workers. Both Weber's classic version of bureaucracy and Taylor's scientific management were models of how to control resources to get maximum output.

The rational model was predominant from the late nineteenth century through 1940. Slowly, research demonstrated some limitations. For example, it has been shown that some organizations can be orderly, or under high control, without clear definition of or agreement about goals (Weick, 1969:36). It was discovered that an apparently rational procedure could actually undermine goal accomplishment (March and Simon, 1958:36–47). Other research pointed out that hard-nosed pursuit of a goal did not mean that the goal itself was rational (Downs, 1967). The rational model insists that the organization of people is dependent on the needs of technology. But research demonstrated that there were often several different ways to organize people and material (Trist, 1981). Other research showed that despite agreement on goals, frequent conflicts could arise among team members because of inconsistency in implementation (Miner, 1984). Other research found that because workers in different parts of the organization had varying commitments, goal conflicts would be common (Simon, 1964).

The rational model of organizations ignores many of these unexpected findings, largely because the rational model ignores a good deal of organizational life. Other aspects of organization get in the way of rational theory and lead to inconsistency and conflict. The results can be disastrous. Most people have had experiences with the public bureau that has a procedure for everything but yields no public service. Others have experienced the manager who pushes so hard for production that workers revolt and nothing is produced. Such problems gave rise to other models of managing organizations.

THE INTERNAL PROCESS MODEL

Closely related to the rational goal model is the **internal process model.** It too opts for the control end of the structural dimension. The difference is that the rational model focuses outward on productivity, while the process model has an internal focus. The short-range interests in the process model are information management, communication, and decision-making. The long-range objective is achieving order and stability. This model places a premium on values such as predictability, security, and continuity.

Common issues within the internal process model are the coordination and supervision of work. Managers adopting this perspective tend to be concerned with the hierarchy and chain of command on the one hand and specialization and standardization on the other. There is a great deal of emphasis on formalizing relationships, on developing standard procedures, and on maintaining authority. Organizations managed from this perspective tend to have tall hierarchies, a large layer of middle managers, and a large number of specialized work units.

The strength of the internal process model is its ability to translate organizational goals into structured relationships among members. No organization can last without considerable attention to the principles of the internal process model. But its blind spots are twofold. The model tends to ignore the individual goals of its members and the group dynamics by which they relate to each other. It can also produce an unwieldy organization that simply cannot adapt to changing conditions.

One of the best examples of the strengths and weaknesses of the internal process model is a criminal justice example. For years, the dominant textbook on police administration was O. W. Wilson's adaptation of these principles to police administration (Wilson and McLaren, 1972). Wilson's model of policing was designed to cure the ills of police scandal in the first half of this century. Implementation of these principles was seen as one means of professionalizing the police and taking them out of politics. More accurately, Wilson's prescriptions standardized and bureaucratized the police (Langworthy, 1987). One result has been the inability of the bureaucratized police agency to handle changing city conditions and to deal with minority complaints of brutality and insensitivity.

THE HUMAN RELATIONS MODEL

The **human relations model** emerged as managers and researchers began to see the research evidence about the problems that occur when there is overemphasis on control. This model, like the internal process model, has an internal focus; but unlike either of the two earlier models, it values flexibility rather than control. It stresses group cohesion and morale as means to develop the organization's human resources.

The internal process and rational goal models tended to see the informal relationships among workers as detracting from the organization (Tay-

Staff relationships
have informal and
formal dimensions.
(New York State De-
partment of Correc-
tional Services)

lor, 1967) or as irrelevant to it (Fayol, 1949).
These views were first challenged in the Haw-
thorne plant of the Western Electric Company by
Mayo (1933), and Roethlessberger and Dickson
(1949). In one of their experiments, as a group
of workers became a cohesive group that felt
important to the company and made decisions
about their own work conditions, the productivity
of the group went up (see Blumberg, 1973). Later
studies within this tradition have found that managers of high-producing units violate the basic
assumptions of the internal process and rational
models by showing concern for the development
of workers and by letting workers make significant
decisions about methods and techniques (Likert,
1961; Blake and Mouton, 1964).

But the human relations model is also incomplete, and by itself can lead to major problems.
Likert (1961) demonstrated that some groups with
high cohesion were very low producers, because
the group norms were opposed to those of the
organization. Other research has shown that overemphasis on group process can reduce an organization's ability to deal with its environment.

The organization becomes too internally focused
and shuts out important resources (Freeman,
1973). Such organizations can have difficulty
dealing with growth because new members are
not included, delegation of authority does not
occur, and the formal communication patterns
necessary in larger organizations do not develop
(Quinn and Andersen, 1984).

THE OPEN SYSTEMS MODEL

The final model has an external focus and values
flexibility over control. It stresses the creation of
adaptable, changing relationships inside the organization as means of obtaining resources, external support, and growth. The **open systems
model** stresses the interactions of the members
with other groups and organizations to obtain personnel and material, to gain political support,
and to achieve goals. This view of organizations
emphasizes the importance of resources in understanding organizational behavior.

Like the rational goal model, the open systems model looks outward toward relationships

with the larger world. But it treats goals differently. The rational model stresses planning and technology to achieve goals; the open system model presents goals themselves as flexible, changing decisions made in order to obtain resources (Thompson and McEwen, 1958; Yuchtman and Seashore, 1967). Among the more commonly recognized resources are legitimacy and financial support (Benson, 1975; Warren, Rose, and Bergunder, 1974), although other common resources include information, personnel, and clients.

The open systems view has become more important as society has become more complex and more turbulent (Emery and Trist, 1965). As the environment changes in this way, managers of organizations must become more concerned with ideology, image, and joint projects, and less concerned with internal order and stability. Research has shown that organizations which are more heavily engaged in innovation and in interorganizational exchanges are more decentralized and flexible internally (Hage and Aiken, 1967).

One problem with the open systems approach is how to control the organization. Hackman (1984) describes the flexible, multifunctional teams that made up the structure of the airline People Express. The organization grew rapidly in a few years, and rather than dealing with internal issues of order and control, continued to increase services and acquisitions. In 1986, the corporation collapsed (Miller, 1986).

These four perspectives on the important issues in organizational behavior will be used throughout the rest of this chapter to examine correctional management. We will see that administrators have stressed the internal process model, and to a lesser extent the rational goal model, rather than the human relations model and the open systems model. But we will also see that this choice of values in correctional administration is changing. New internal and external forces have influenced administrators to deal with the concerns of human relations and open systems.

THE PUBLIC ORGANIZATION

Most correctional organizations are **public organizations.** Too much can be made of the differences between public and private administration; many problems faced by the two types of management are the same. But correctional managers hungry for new ways of solving problems can also jump too readily at innovations developed and tested only in private firms. Correctional managers need to be aware of the major differences between public and private organizations.

One frequently noted difference occurs on the external-internal dimension. While private corporations are somewhat limited by public law and regulation, and are increasingly exhorted to fulfill their social responsibilities, some still argue that the primary duty of the private firm is to provide a good return on investment to its stockholders or owners (Freidman, 1962). In democratic societies, the public organization serves a much broader constituency. The public organization serves, or at least claims to serve, the general public. There are sharp debates about how anyone can actually determine the public interest (Warren, 1978). But in practical terms, it is measured by votes and enunciated in legislation and executive policy.

The choice of public organization goals is quite different from goal choice in a private firm. The private corporation is relatively free in the selection and alteration of goals. If the private firm is unsuccessful in its pursuit of chosen goals, it fails. Its success is decided in marketplace competition with other corporations. The correctional agency, and other public organizations, are considerably more limited. A warden cannot turn the prison into a hotel if the prison does not work. But the flip side of the coin is that the warden does not have to. Even if a correctional agency does a terrible job, it rarely goes out of business (although this has recently become a possibility). One reason the public agency need not worry about failing has to do with the nature of its goals.

Public organizations are often engaged in providing those services or products deemed so central to a culture that they are to be available to everyone. They are "public goods," which cannot be distributed through marketplace competition and should be available to all. In a diverse and heterogeneous society, decisions about the nature of public goods can be controversial, and the actual level and quality of services offered to different groups can be extremely varied. However, the legitimacy of the organization, and of the government, depends in part on the image of serving all members of society equally. The public organization has little latitude in choice of goals, but lacking competition, wide latitude in measures of performance.

Describing this situation, as faced by the prison, Grosser had this to say (1960:131):

> The prison therefore need not . . . maintain competitive standards, adapt itself rapidly to technological progress, or respond to fluctuations in market conditions; nor is it as immediately dependent on the good will, benevolence, or loyalty of a group of sponsors or followers as are many other nonprofit organizations. The prison justifies its existence by fulfilling a legal mandate which, like most legal mandates, sets a floor below which achievement cannot fall but does not require the achievement of ever higher aims.

One consequence of this is that many public agencies adopt an internal focus. The correctional organization "succeeds" largely by maintaining itself, by focusing on procedures that keep it running. The push is toward the internal process model.

The tendency is strengthened by the public conflict about goals. Cohn has observed that many correctional managers "are effective because they are unwilling to commit themselves publicly to something which is very specific" (1982:20). This tendency toward secrecy about specifics arises from rifts in the electorate about the desirability of particular courses of action. (Duffee and Ritti, 1977, provide good examples of public cleavages about correctional policy.) Public managers gain or maintain support in part by expressing goals

on such an abstract level that most people can subscribe to them. They invoke goals such as public safety and justice without indicating how these values will be translated into programs or how the programs will lead to measurable achievements.

Some of the processes central to the rational goal model, such as planning, may be used. However, public organizations often lack the technology to deliver results anyway (Nokes, 1960). Saddled with controversial goals and uncertain means of achieving them, the application of the rational goal model is limited in many public organizations. Corrections is no exception. The result is increased reliance on hierarchical structure, standards for personnel, and formal procedures for communication, all hallmarks of the internal process model of organizations (Pugh, 1984).

THE EVOLUTION OF CORRECTIONAL ADMINISTRATION

THE PENITENTIARY PERIOD

Prior to 1860, the correctional organization was relatively simple, and the perspective of correctional management relatively narrow. The initial burst of reform is an excellent example of the rational goal model of organizations. Preoccupation with architecture and the engineering of social relationships between captives and captors are typical of economic rationality. The reformers had discovered a better instrument of social control and were convinced that the sheer logic of the plan would assure adoption and implementation.

The external focus predominated: The new institutions would not only reform individuals, but their example of orderly social relations was expected to reform society itself (Rothman, 1971). Attention to human relations issues was minimal. The orderly institution was not expected to generate its own social problems, but merely to strip from human beings the blemishes of habit and attitude developed in the evil, disorderly cities. The problems of control in the institution were attributed to the importation of deviance from the community. Personnel issues were principally matters of correct selection and recruitment.

Concerns of the open system model were almost nonexistent. The correctional organization was designed as a self-contained, closed system, not an open organization engaging in joint projects with other organizations or fighting politically to establish legitimacy. Many of the original managers were chosen from the military and instituted paramilitary regimes. One deputy and a number of guards comprised the staff. A private work overseer supervised industry, and chaplains provided special services such as reading lessons.

THE POST-CIVIL WAR PERIOD

The narrow concentration on the best technology for the achievement of goals did not last long. Inmates in the solitary system became mad rather than penitent. Inmates in the congregate system required continual discipline (Rothman, 1971). Internal order was difficult because of overcrowding. The promise of profit was often not kept, or manufactured through creative bookkeeping.

Reviewing these issues, Rothman concluded that by the end of the Civil War, American prison administrators had turned their focus inward. The goal of the prison, wrote the first warden of Sing Sing, was the maintenance of order and security, not social or individual reform. Management became preoccupied with discipline, rule enforcement, and rigid hierarchical control as means of achieving these ends.

THE REFORMS OF 1870–1920

While the internal process model probably continues to be the predominant managerial orientation even today, managers began to pay attention to human relations and open systems issues in the last third of the nineteenth century. The meeting of the American Prison Congress in Cin-

cinnati in 1870 is a milestone for the beginning of the new management tasks. The Declaration of Principles in 1870 indicated an emergent concern for the impact of prison itself upon its inhabitants. Management acknowledged the responsibility of staff to create humane settings in which change could take place. The focus remained internal, but a shift toward flexibility in structure occurred.

The open system concerns were also emergent. The formal introduction of parole at the Elmira Reformatory is evidence of some concern for managing a network of relationships. The idea of the self-contained correctional organization was modified. Managerial attention to external links developed even earlier in the juvenile corrections system; institutional managers there developed contacts for recruiting inmates and for placing them out (see Chapter 19).

New issues of coordination and control of staff emerged as the organization became more complex. Again, the change occurred first in the juvenile system. Professional "treaters" arrived in corrections as a consequence of positive criminology and the development of social work. Management faced new personnel specialties and greater division of labor.

THE GROWTH OF DEPARTMENTS: 1930–1960

As governments became larger and more complex, correctional management was affected. Correctional organizations were linked together. In some states, correctional departments were formed; in others, correctional institutions were placed with other social services. Departmentalization gave rise to specialized institutions, such as security-graded prisons and centers dedicated to reception and diagnosis. The professionalization of treatment continued. Correctional management acquired new tasks of coordinating staff, resolving conflicts, and meshing institutional and community services. Many of these tasks resided in new central offices, and a new component of correctional management, the staff responsible for planning, training, research, and budgeting, began to have influence. It was these new management roles that permitted the internal process model to blossom. Administrative directives, policy statements, training manuals, tables of organization, and the other accoutrements of internal process proliferated.

This period also brought a fuller appreciation of the prison as a social system. The society of captives was discovered (see Chapter 15), and new social relationships were sought to combat the inmate culture. This concern for group norms and group dynamics modified the high values placed on control with a new concern for flexibility. Not surprisingly, the tension between the older control-oriented management and the newer flexibility-oriented management was marked by a series of prison riots in the 1950s.

In addition, the individual facility manager lost considerable autonomy. Many changes inside a prison were the result of statewide politics and central office decisions (Galliher, 1972; McCleery, 1960; Jacobs, 1977).

UNIFICATION AND PROACTIVE MANAGEMENT: 1960–1975

In the 1960s, systems analysis was applied to a number of social problem areas, including corrections. This technological development had two major impacts on management. First, the focus shifted significantly from internal to external, and policymakers and top administrators became more concerned with flexibility and resource acquisition. Much management strategy was preoccupied with unification of the criminal justice system (Skoler, 1976). Fragmentation of the system, rather than conflict inside single organizations, was a major concern. On both the state and local government levels, this period included a great deal of restructuring of departments. The perspective of top management became broader and more abstract. It shuffled whole organizations into new patterns to increase effectiveness and efficiency. Combining prison departments and parole departments became popular. And state takeovers of local agencies increased.

Application of professional managerial techniques developed in private industry also occurred in this period. The best example is the work of the Joint Commission on Correctional Manpower and Training (1969). The Joint Commission volume on management (Nelson and Lovell, 1969) focused on the work of central office managers. The correctional administrator was redefined as a proactive problem-solver and strategist, and no longer as a reactive keeper of order. Managers were urged to seek the resources necessary for proper correctional services and to reshape staff and inmate social systems to develop cooperative, collaborative relationships. Human relations and open systems concerns predominated. The National Institute of Corrections was formed and placed a heavy emphasis on executive development.

THE REALITY SMASH: CURRENT PROBLEMS

The current management period, beginning roughly in 1975, is a continuation of the trend that began in 1960, but the optimism has disappeared. The older images of prison as factory and prison as hospital have given way to prison as warehouse. Doubts have arisen about the feasibility of proactive management. Along with other public administrators, correctional managers have entered the era of limits.

The change can be attributed partly to fallout from the information technology explosion of the preceding phase. Martinson's complaint of "nothing works" (1974) is one example. The correctional technologies that supposedly linked programs with social benefit were no longer credible.

Another significant factor was the realization that correctional management lacked a major power possessed by most professional, proactive management: Managers had little control over input and therefore of resources and limited ability to plan. Public and judicial sentiment about the purposes of sentencing overwhelmed correctional management. Some administrators have been inundated with inmates and left scurrying for cell space. Others who were touting the benefits of community corrections have been left to scurry for political support.

This period has included the first significant threat to the life of correctional organizations. Some parole boards and some parole supervision have been abolished. In other areas, probation and postprison supervision have been contracted out to private organizations. In the federal system and in some states, private corporations are running institutions (see Chapter 20). Thus, Grosser's 1960 characterization of correctional organization as immune to failure may finally be changing.

Managers of different correctional organizations will always be facing somewhat different problems. Managers in one system may be facing the need for more control, while in a neighboring state human relations issues are paramount. In this and the subsequent sections, we can only highlight some current management practices in each of the major areas.

CURRENT PRACTICE: CONCERN FOR GOALS AND TECHNOLOGY

One major legacy of the 1960s was a renewed emphasis on goals and on planning for the means of attaining them. The model of four correctional policies (O'Leary and Duffee, 1971a) discussed in Chapter Five (see Tables 5.1 and 5.2) has been used in an array of goal-planning activity. Several examples of applications are discussed below.

GOAL CLARIFICATION

One important step in planning is clarification of goals and exploration of the assumptions behind them. Executive training seminars facilitate this process by supplying a supportive, nonthreatening environment for self-exploration and sharing of ideas. Managers attending a seminar will fill out the Correctional Policy Inventory (O'Leary, 1970) as an aid in examining their own assumptions about corrections (O'Leary, 1967). After

scoring the CPI, a management trainer will lead a group discussion of the four policies. In these sessions, managers often come to grips with their assumptions about changing other people for the first time. They are able to compare their assumptions with those of peers from across the country. They are also able to consider whether specific programs in their organization are compatible with other programs and with their underlying philosophy. Because correctional administrators are often isolated and rarely have the opportunity to share problems and trade solutions, conferences such as those using the CPI can help reduce the intellectual isolation and clarify goals.

PLANNING FOR CHANGE

While the conceptual analysis done at training conferences has often been a positive experience for individual managers, training exercises are several steps removed from creating change in a working correctional system. Beginning in 1969, the CPI and the four policy models have also been used to create change in operating systems. For example, the first commissioner of a new department wanted his new central office staff and top institutional managers to meet to begin shaping the new department. One part of this process involved administering the CPI to all managers in the system, as well as to a set of inmates and officers. The results are given in Table 18.1.

These data provided the new management team with a picture of correctional policy in the system as they began planning. The data indicated that top managers preferred a reintegration policy, and that middle managers were more wedded to the older rehabilitation policy. Officers and inmates reported that reform and restraint were much more evident than either managerial preference. Data such as these provided managers with a firmer baseline from which to institute change. One question facing this group was how to manage the system differently so that their policy goals would be implemented.

A similar problem occurred in another sys-

The deputy commissioner and superintendents participate in a time management seminar. Departments have increased their investment in executive development. (New York State Department of Correctional Services)

tem. This department had decided in 1974 to reassess its entire classification system. It took inmates too long to be processed through initial classification, and prison staff complained that they rarely used the initial recommendations anyway. At the other end of the system, the prerelease staff complained that they could not communicate effectively with the prison counselors who were supposed to select inmates for prere-

lease programs. As part of the system review, the CPI was administered to all officials involved in classification.

The results relevant to the prerelease problems are given in Table 18.2. These data indicated that prerelease staff were strongly committed to reintegration, while prison classification staff were operating under a rehabilitation policy. High-level executives in this system had yet to

TABLE 18.1   Policy Means by Level in a Northeastern State*

LEVEL	POLICY			
	REINTEGRATION	REHABILITATION	REFORM	RESTRAINT
Top administration				
(N = 30)	*80.0*	76.8	57.7	48.2
Middle managers				
(N = 27)	69.8	*80.3*	66.0	56.2
Officers				
(N = 42)	55.2	68.4	*77.7*	61.5
Offenders				
(N = 88)	59.7	57.0	80.0	*90.9*

* Mean differences between groups are significant at the .01 level.

SOURCE: David Duffee, *Correctional Management Change and Control in Correctional Organizations*. Prospect Heights, IL: Waveland Press, 1986.

TABLE 18.2 Correctional Policy Scores for Four Classification Groups in One State*

	REINTEGRATION	REHABILITATION	REFORM	RESTRAINT
Top managers ($N = 34$)	66.4	53.6	55.0	36.6
Prison counselors ($N = 50$)	59.2	59.7	59.7	44.0
Center managers ($N = 8$)	80.0	58.0	60.0	44.0
Center counselors ($N = 36$)	74.0	66.0	47.0	35.1

* Correctional policy scores measured on the correctional policy inventory. Scores may range from 10 (low) to 100 (high).

make a clear choice among system objectives. An initial step was therefore to make a choice among policies. Then prerelease program staff and prison classification staff had to decide what information about an inmate was relevant to the prerelease goals chosen.

DEVELOPING A TECHNOLOGY CONSISTENT WITH GOALS

Goal clarification is essential to the rational administration. However, it is far from sufficient. Another major question is just what types of program interactions and services actually achieve those goals. This question is one of technology development. If the policy model or another goal statement provides a correctional system with desired objectives, what are the means for getting there?

One of the best examples of technology development is the evolution of objectives-based supervision in community corrections (see Chapter 9.) The focus on risks and needs began as a research project in California (Studt, 1972). One of the critical lessons of that project was that the helping technology was underdeveloped. Working with a number of departments, Clear and O'Leary (1983), Dell'Apa et al. (1976), and other management consultant groups began to focus on the technology of supervision. Since a **technology** is an arrangement of people and other resources to achieve goals, this process always begins with goal clarification. The managers then need to

decide what specific deployment of resources will have the desired results with specific groups of offenders. This process should be guided by theory when possible, but managers often have to depend initially on logic, experience, and trial and error (Clear and O'Leary, 1983; Beer, 1966). Gradually, as information is gathered and analyzed, technology development becomes more systematic (Gottfredson and Gottfredson, 1980).

This developmental process in prisons is not as far along as it is in community supervision. Some examples of recent attempts to develop a prison technology are described in Chapter 14. New classification models are being developed to reduce prison disturbances. If managers actually deploy the new systems and accurately record the results of placing inmates in settings that match with their needs, they may develop a technology for increasing institutional order and preserving inmates' mental health.

DEVELOPMENT OF RESEARCH

The rational pursuit of goals is impossible without a research capacity within the organization. In small organizations, research may be carried out by the same personnel who supervise staff and offenders. In larger and more complex organizations, the cost of gathering, storing, and analyzing information often makes a specialized unit more efficient (Downs, 1967).

The development of a separate research unit makes the organization even more complex, and new issues of coordination arise. How does the research group fit into the total organization? How much say should the research manager have over policy and program? How can the organization keep line managers from seeing the research staff as theorists with no correctional experience?

Research on the research process indicates that the solutions to these problems are not very different from the solutions to conflicts among other organizational units. Research is more likely to be useful and to be used if researchers and line managers operate as a team to solve problems jointly (Wilkins, 1981; Johnson, 1980). The success of this approach depends on the attitude of top management toward the research unit. If the researchers have easy and frequent access to top management, and if top management sets an example for other line managers of bridging research and practice, then an effective unit is more likely to develop.

Often, a major problem in the effective development of correctional research can be traced to the managers' fear that negative evaluations will undermine program support. Defensive managers push research units to justify programs rather than to provide useful evaluations. Under these conditions, the units can give no help to the practitioner and technology will not improve. This defensive posture, however, may backfire in the long run. For example, correctional rehabilitation became vulnerable to attack in part because correctional research was traditionally poorly funded, poorly staffed, and underutilized. Research staff can contribute to a more effective climate for research when they are careful in the framing of problems and in the phrasing of results. Most managers want useful suggestions. They don't want, and can't use, esoteric, highly technical reports that evaluate but offer no recommendations for change.

THE PLANNING PROCESS

Planning is actually a separate function from research, although it is hard to do good planning without good research. Planning in correctional

agencies is hampered by a number of facts of life. Correctional managers lack some control over resources flowing into the organization; they also lack some control over the work demands that will be made of the organization. A legislature can have a major impact on a correctional organization simply by changing the sentence values in a determinant sentencing scheme. It can have similar impact by becoming doubtful about the value of programs and cutting budget requests.

Many correctional managers respond passively to these limitations. Their style is reactive, on the assumption that they are merely responsible for implementing decisions made by political leaders. More active managers take a different approach. Their objective is to influence the external political decisions by making the strongest possible case for the goals they have chosen and the resources they believe are required to meet them (Nelson and Harlow, 1980). This approach assumes that a solid, empirically based argument can rationalize the political process and permit correctional managers to affect workload demands and choices of technology. For example, Chris Baird (1981) has developed a planning and budgeting process for the Bureau of Community Correction in Wisconsin that links personnel requests to the risk level presented by probationers and parolees. This is a far more effective argument than simply requesting so many staff to supervise so many offenders.

There are a number of different planning strategies in use in public and private organizations. Among the various types are comprehensive rational planning, disjointed incremental planning, and advocacy planning.

Comprehensive rational planning is typically done by experts who develop a long-range, step-by-step organizational road map for reaching predetermined objectives. This form of planning utilizes a number of quantitative techniques to assess inputs, measure resources, sequence action steps, and make forecasts. However, the comprehensive rational plan is often more applicable to a complex engineering feat, such as placing a man on the moon, than it is to a political endeavor such as punishing people. In corrections, the assumptions underlying a comprehensive plan often change before the plan can be implemented. However, correctional managers can use comprehensive planning techniques effectively for some purposes. For example, modeling and forecasting techniques can be used to test the economic implications of various sentencing options.

Because comprehensive planning is difficult to implement in a turbulent environment, a number of other techniques that require less time and provide greater flexibility have been proposed. Among the more controversial of these is the incremental planning strategy developed by Charles Lindblom (1958, 1984). Lindblom's position is that comprehensive planning is unrealistic in a complex political environment. He and Simon (1957), among others, have argued that public administrators simply do not have the time or the information to implement a comprehensive plan. There are always too many unknowns for managers to attempt optimal solutions. Lindblom's analysis of actual planning processes suggested that managers usually engage in an incremental process that does not require accurate knowledge of all the constraints or of all the available alternatives. Instead, from a small range of readily available options, they select the path that appears to be most consistent with their underlying assumptions and most feasible in the current political climate.

Critics have argued that incremental planning is really no planning at all, but simply flying by the seat of your pants. At best, suggest critics, incrementalism is a very conservative approach, because it relies upon what the agency has already done as a means of selecting the next step. Some supporters argue that incremental planning need not lead to trivial change or maintenance of the status quo. Stolz (1984) correctly points out that an incremental planning approach was used in Massachusetts to close down the juvenile training schools (see Chapter 19).

Lindblom has indicated a number of administrative techniques which can improve the incremental approach. He argues that managers must use conflict effectively within the organization if incremental planning is to have good results (1984). If the manager's advisors all have the same opinions and orientations, the manager will necessarily make conservative decisions. If managers value differences of opinion among staff and make sure that conflicting arguments are heard rather than stifled, incremental planning can be more flexible and more innovative.

A third strategy, advocacy planning, also utilizes conflict. Advocacy planning differs from other approaches not in the techniques used, but in the selection of the client of the effort. Advocacy planners assume that all political communities involve conflicting interests and that no planning expert can serve more than one interest at a time. These planners explicitly recognize the interests of the group engaging their services. Advocacy planning has not been used frequently in correctional settings, partly because of the long tradition against sharing power with front-line staff and offenders. However, advocacy planning will probably increase. For example, guard unions may hire their own planners to examine the implications of executive budgets or program recommendations. Formal inmate organizations may hire planners to analyze prison policy and resources from its perspective. Since the American criminal justice system has a long tradition of providing legal advocates to the indigent, the provision of planning advocates is not far-fetched. At the current time, the best example of advocacy planning is the use of court-appointed monitors to implement court orders in correctional organizations. (This important trend will be discussed later in the chapter.)

CURRENT PRACTICE: INTERNAL PROCESS CONCERNS

RESTRUCTURING ACTIVITIES

One of the most common internal process endeavors is the design of specialized work processes and means of coordinating the specialties. Part of this process flows from the planning of goals and the development of technology—but only part. Once goals are chosen and a technology developed, management still has many decisions to make about the arrangement of people in the organization.

These structuring decisions take place on two levels: One concerns the arrangement of organizational units, the other the arrangement of individuals. The problems that confront managers of classifications systems provide many examples of these issues. Should classification be done by a central committee or by a number of different teams? Should different prisons specialize by security grade, program options, or both? Unfortunately, new problems inevitably accompany specialization. Most important is the problem of coordinating the specialties.

Coordination of Work. Coordination problems are often solved through hierarchical arrangement of authority, so that the specialized units all eventually report to the same person. But there are many other coordination tools. Two examples are **standardization of work** processes and **standardization of personnel.** If work is planned in detail ahead of time, and every worker, regardless of unit, is guided by the same standards, then work is coordinated without the need for centralized authority. Most correctional departments have adopted this means of coordination, particularly for security, maintenance, and financial tasks. But standardization of work has limited applicability in a human service organization. Since human beings are self-starting, most tasks involving them, including security tasks, cannot be planned in advance.

Control of Personnel. Because the work is difficult to plan, correctional managers often depend on standardization of the work force rather than standardization of work. If they cannot predict work problems specifically, they can select and train workers so that they will respond appropriately. Emphasis on training has increased tremendously since 1968, when the Law Enforce-

ment Assistance Administration provided major impetus for the education and training of criminal justice employees. Since then, a number of commissions have developed selection and training standards and a number of organizations, including the National Institute of Correction and the National Council on Crime and Delinquency, have been involved in developing and delivering training.

Correctional managers have faced new personnel problems during the period in which training has increased. Unions have gained strength in the correctional field (see Chapter 16), and unions exert an independent force for the creation and exercise of personnel standards. Additionally, most correctional organizations now use civil service rather than political appointment methods for specifying job requirements and selecting applicants. While civil service can protect public organization personnel functions from some forms of interference, it can also create new ones. Civil service job descriptions often take all flexibility out of performance descriptions and push managers to quantify characteristics. A militant union can increase the pressure to take discretion out of job selection.

Many qualities sought in good correctional workers cannot be quantified. One increasingly relied upon standard, for example, is education level. Recent research indicates that the trend of requiring higher levels of education, especially for guard work, may lead to higher turnover levels and higher levels of dissatisfaction (Rogers, 1985). It may have little to do with the quality of work performed.

Correctional organizations seeking control of the personnel function may face a fundamental dilemma. Etzioni (1960) observed that there is often an inverse relationship between selectivity of recruitment and efforts at on-the-job socialization. Organizations that can attract highly skilled persons often do not need to spend a great deal of effort in training and orientation. Organizations that cannot be very selective spend more time socializing those who have already been hired. Correctional careers are rarely first choices (Geis and Cavanaugh, 1966; Harris,

In many correctional agencies, managers and unions have agreed to Employee Assistance Programs as part of the fringe benefit package available to employees. Among other services, EAP usually offers employees confidential counseling for drug abuse, alcoholism, stress, and other problems related to and/or affecting employees at work. Above, Commissioner Coughlin and union representatives sign the Employee Assistance Program Agreement at the Department of Correctional Services central office. (New York State Department of Correctional Services)

1968; National Manpower Survey, 1978), so organizations often have to depend on in-service training and informal socialization to prepare workers. However, many correctional tasks require judgment and human relations skills that are hard to develop. Management therefore needs to find new ways to identify, utilize, and reward persons with these skills, regardless of where they appear on a formal list of personnel roles. Using officers, work supervisors, and counselors in innovative ways, without violating union agreements or civil service regulations, will be a major challenge for correctional managers in the years to come.

SIZE AND DECENTRALIZATION

There are real limits on standardization and centralized authority for gaining control. One of those limits occurs with increasing size. The larger an

organization becomes, the more unwieldy and ineffective central controls become. Large organizations find they often must decentralize some operations and some decisions in order to solve day-to-day problems.

Correctional departments are no exception to this effect of size. Except in the smallest jurisdictions, the departments are geographically dispersed. Prisons, community centers, and probation and parole field offices located in different places will often face different problems. They often supervise offender populations with different offense histories and racial or ethnic mixes. Their personnel cadres typically have varying socioeconomic backgrounds. Local cultural, political, and law enforcement traditions differ. If correctional managers require each office to perform tasks in the same manner, these local variations cannot be accommodated.

Large geographically dispersed departments

face a major dilemma between balancing central office concerns for uniformity and predictability across suboffices against local office concerns for the autonomy to deal with local problems. Some departments try to deal with this problem by regionalizing facilities and policies. Others may seek to maintain central control over some practices, such as budgeting, while giving local offices more freedom over others, such as treatment programs (Duffee, 1985). Other departments fail to deal with the dilemma directly, and proceed to formulate uniform policies but then ignore them in practice (McCleary, 1978).

THE RESOLUTION OF CONFLICT

One important control task for correctional managers is balancing competing demands for resources by separate work units or work specialties. This need for conflict resolution skill arises because of the natural by-products of specialization. As division of labor breeds better work within a specialty, and pride and commitment to that work, it can also breed competition and conflict with other subdivisions. Kept under control, this competition is healthy. But subdivision of the organization also leads to a process called **suboptimization** (March and Simon, 1958). Organizational work units become committed to achievement of unit goals at the expense of organizational goals. This process can include familiar behaviors such as hoarding resources, misrepresenting achievements, and presenting breakdowns so blame falls on another unit. These problems are most likely to occur when top management is unwilling or unable to reward subunits for total system performance. When goals are ambiguous and achievement hard to measure, it may be difficult to indicate subunit contributions to global objectives. Subunits often become concerned only with behaviors that cast the unit in a favorable light.

The most widely known example of this problem in correctional organizations is the traditional conflict between treatment and custody. The guard force can be immensely effective in service

delivery (or, on the other hand, sabotage any treatment effort). It is also widely recognized that treatment staff and prison programs are essential to order. But correctional managers have often failed to reward specialized staffs for contributions to the other functions. When counselors are rewarded only for timely, if unusable, classification reports, or guards are rewarded only for enforcing rules, their joint responsibilities often remain unmeasured and unattended. This situation can place greater strain on management than necessary, since management rather than front-line staff then becomes responsible for making sure the separate functions mesh properly (Trist, 1981).

CURRENT PRACTICE; CONCERNS FOR HUMAN RELATIONS

In two influential books on industrial management, Rensis Likert (1961, 1967) proposed that managers had to invest the same care in the preservation of human resources that they spent in husbanding of financial resources. Failure to manage financial resources properly becomes apparent quickly in organizations. Likert argued that managers ignored human resources because failures in that area were less quickly visible. He proposed, however, that hard-driving, autocratic, control-oriented managers were using up their human resources "bank account." Eventually, the poor human systems in the organization would have negative consequences.

THE MANAGERIAL GRID

In the late 1960s, correctional executive training began to emulate techniques used in private organizations for the management of human relations. One conceptual device used in this training is the Managerial Grid (Blake and Mouton, 1964). The Managerial Grid provides executives with a means of examining their own management styles. Its two underlying dimensions are the manager's concerns for production and for people.

Blake and Mouton suggest that the two concerns can be treated as independent dimensions on a two-dimensional grid, and a manager's behavior can be charted by examining the emphasis placed on the two dimensions. The two axes of the grid are measured on 9 point scales, with 9 representing maximum concern and 1 representing minimal concern. Managers can actually display any combination of these two. But the variations in management style are best captured by examining "modal" styles in the four corners and the center of grid. These five common management approaches are described below (see Figure 18.2). Three styles treat the concern for production and the concern for people as mutually exclusive demands. Managers assume they can attend to one or the other, but not both.

9,1 Task Management. The task manager shows high concern for productivity and low concern for people. He behaves as if attention to morale, group cohesion, and other people issues would detract from the productivity of the organization. Such a manager focuses almost exclusively on production goals and seeks unyielding conformity from subordinates. He appears to assume that most workers are lazy, untrustworthy, and in need of constant supervision. The task manager tends to make decisions unilaterally and expects subordinates to carry out those decisions without question. Such a manager might inwardly feel that employees are important, and may like them as individuals. But he or she behaves as if there is no place in the management role for display of those concerns.

1,9 Country Club Management. Other managers behave in precisely the opposite fashion. They display high concern for the individual needs of their workers, and seek to facilitate positive group processes in the organization. Like the 9,1 manager, the 1,9 manager behaves as if people issues are incompatible with demands for production. This manager may quietly assume

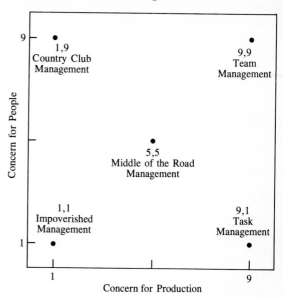

FIGURE 18.2   The Managerial Grid

SOURCE: David Duffee, *Correctional Management: Change and Control in Correctional Organizations.* Prospect Heights, IL: Waveland Press, 1986. Figure adapted from R. Blake and J. Mouton, *The Managerial Grid.* Houston: Gulf.

that happy and contented workers will produce, but makes only minimal direct demands for production.

1,1 Impoverished Management. Some managers behave as if they have been defeated by the conflict between concern for people and concern for production and make minimal efforts on both dimensions. Such managers often behave defensively. They ask workers to follow the rules and meet company expectations, but they show minimal personal commitment to the same objectives. Managers behaving in such a way are often rumored to be in early retirement or to be milking the job. However, research demonstrates that 1,1 behavior is often the product of 9,1 supervision. Many default managers may have been driven to that style by their superiors' domineering, autocratic style.

One of the modal styles attempts to compromise between equally important concerns. These managers seem to agree with the above three types that people and productivity issues conflict, but they are unwilling to sacrifice one or both altogether.

5,5, Middle of the Road Management. This tradeoff style shows moderate concern for production and moderate concern for people. The compromise can be achieved in a number of ways. A typical tradeoff approach permits workers to vent frustrations or air opinions, but then insists that workers conform to management demands for production. Another approach is a reliance on "side payments" (Argyris, 1957). This strategy seeks to build morale and good feeling in company-sponsored events and services that are separated from work itself. The side payment routine, for example, could include the provision of psychological services for employees to assist them in coping with the stresses of a work routine that remains demeaning or boring. The 5,5 manager does little to change the conditions of work itself.

The fifth modal style rejects the typical assumption that concerns for people and productivity are contradictory. This style seeks to integrate production and people issues by finding ways that the needs of workers can be met directly in the design of work itself.

9,9 Team Management. The team manager rejects the 9,1 assumption that most human beings are lazy and motivated only by close supervision. But this manager also rejects the 1,9 position that the social rewards of work must take precedence over task demands. The team manager assumes that psychological and social rewards of work can be built directly into the design of production (Trist, 1981). Such a manager relies upon workers' internal motivation rather than external supervision to attain production goals. This approach utilizes the capacity of motivated work groups to control their own behavior. Workers' ideas about the means of achieving organizational goals are sought, and workers make significant

decisions about how to organize in order to accomplish tasks. Such a manager does not give up authority or renounce responsibility for control. It is not a laissez-faire approach, but a more democratic one.

There are many other ways to conceptualize a manager's approach to subordinates. For example, Likert (1967), conceives of management strategies arrayed on a single continuum from autocratic or "close" supervision on the one hand to democratic or "open" supervision on the other. Any of these conceptual models oversimplifies the problem, but each captures important aspects of the need to balance human relations and productive concerns.

THE USE OF THE MANAGERIAL GRID IN CORRECTIONS

The Managerial Grid is especially important to correctional management because it was the method used to assess correctional management styles by the Joint Commission on Correctional Manpower and Training (Nelson and Lovell, 1969). A portion of the Joint Commission's work was a national survey of central office and top field managers in prison and community corrections. This survey indicated that many managers were too dependent on 9,1 and 5,5 styles for the types of correctional goals they espoused.

One example of potential conflicts between management style and correctional goals is provided in Table 18.3. These data show strong relationships between certain correctional policies and certain management styles. Managers espousing reform and restraint policies, for example, are frequently 9,1 managers. Rehabilitation policy is related to a 5,5 approach to workers, and reintegration is compatible with a 9,9 team orientation. Both Nelson and Lovell (1969) and O'Leary and Duffee (1971b) proposed that correctional managers could defeat their own purposes by managing in a style incompatible with their espoused correctional goals. Managers seeking to implement reintegrative programs for inmates may damage their own plan by managing

TABLE 18.3 Correlations of Management Style and Correctional Policy Scores for 56 Correctional Managers

POLICY	STYLE				
	9,9	5,5	9,1	1,9	1,1
Reintegration	.50*	.15	−.25	.18	−.13
Rehabilitation	.22	.46*	.13	.14	.23
Reform	.19	.25	.40*	−.04	.09
Restraint	.19	.09	.43*	.00	.19

* p = .01.

staff in a 9,1 fashion. Yet many correctional managers, particularly in security divisions, are deeply wedded to 9,1 assumptions about subordinates. Correctional workers who grumble that managers are more concerned about inmates than staff may have valid complaints. Workers who are supervised autocratically will have little sympathy for correctional goals that seek collaborative relationships with inmates.

Managers need not choose correctional policies of reintegration or rehabilitation to be concerned about the motivation and commitment of their workers. Toch and Grant (1982) and Adams (1984) provide strong evidence that correctional officers are less alienated and more likely to take creative and innovative approaches to goals of prison order when they perceive that managers value their ideas and seek their participation in decisions. Table 18.4 demonstrates the relationship between three levels of participation in organizational decisions by correctional staff and their perceptions of the quality of their work environment. The more open the management style reported by workers, the healthier their reported social climate.

Managers who are committed to improving work conditions for staff face a number of challenges in changing social relationships at work. Workers who are distrustful and alienated are not likely to accept sudden management overtures for participation. Initial reactions frequently involve anger, fear, and unreasonable demands. Staff who have developed ingrained defensive responses to

autocratic, rigid, or punitive treatment by superiors will view the first opportunities for taking greater responsibility and initiative as fraught with the danger of invoking old negative management reactions. There are, however, several tested methods of changing this situation.

ORGANIZATIONAL DEVELOPMENT

Organizational Development (or OD) was developed in the late 1950s (French and Bell, 1984). OD is an organizational change strategy that seeks to develop teamwork on every level of the organization. OD change projects often begin with the assumption that the culture of the organization must change before the organization can make significant improvements in goal achievement. OD change typically employs a behavioral science consultant to work with managers, and begins the change process at the top (Beckhard, 1969). Top managers must be sincerely committed to such changes, or they will scuttle attempts at participation by lower staff. And providing lower staff with greater participation only to take it away is probably more damaging than no change at all.

The Connecticut Department of Correction undertook an OD project in 1969 as a means of developing teamwork among central office staff and between the top field managers and the central office (O'Leary and Duffee, 1971a; Duffee, 1972). Eventually the project involved the development of two dozen work teams in one min-

TABLE 18.4 Social Climate Means for Three Management Profile Levels for Staff in Six Prisons

SOCIAL CLIMATE DIMENSION	MANAGEMENT PROFILE GROUP		
	LOW (CLOSED) $N = 51$	MEDIUM $N = 168$	HIGH (OPEN) $N = 52$
Spontaneity	3.65	4.36	4.69
Support	3.92	5.95	7.15
Practicality	4.18	6.37	7.60
Affiliation	4.94	6.80	7.75
Order	5.73	6.76	7.77
Insight	4.27	4.91	5.25
Involvement	2.75	4.48	5.83
Aggression	6.90	5.94	6.83
Variety	4.75	5.57	6.31
Clarity	3.45	5.27	7.29
Submission	6.63	6.58	6.15
Autonomy	2.84	3.74	4.63

imum security prison as a means of getting correctional officers to participate in solving organizational problems, of getting officers and treatment staff to work together toward common goals, and of advancing officer contributions to delivery of human services (Duffee, Steinert, and Dvorin, 1986). Clear and O'Leary (1983) used OD techniques to develop objectives based supervision in probation.

QUALITY OF WORK LIFE PROJECTS

A slightly newer form of change is **Quality of Work Life,** or **QWL.** QWL began as a means of improving the lives of workers at work, regardless of whether production was affected. Many proponents suggest that quantity of production may go down, but quality of work will improve. Many projects are union-guided efforts (Toch and Grant, 1982). They involve the creation of a QWL Steering Committee of managers, union officials, and front-line workers to consider any work improvements not covered in contract negotiations. The QWL Steering Committee receives proposals for change from a number of worker teams. If the Steering Committee finds the proposals valuable and feasible, it recommends implementation to top management.

In corrections, the best example of QWL to date is a project carried out in the New York prisons system by Toch and Grant (1982). In collaboration with the guard union and department executives, a number of guard QWL teams were formed to propose changes in working conditions and practices. The teams came up with a number of worthwhile projects, and some ideas were adopted immediately by individual prison wardens. However, proposals that required central office approval or new financial support did not fare as well. While both OD and QWL have had a number of successes in private corporations, their application in correctional settings is just beginning.

CURRENT PRACTICE: OPEN SYSTEMS CONCERNS

The greatest recent changes in correctional management have occurred in the last area of organizational effectiveness: correctional organizations have become increasingly interactive with forces outside the organization. In Chapter 15 we examined how some of these forces have had a major impact on the social systems of prisons. In Chapters 2 and 6 we examined effects associated with changes in sentencing. In Chapter 5, we examined systems analysis, with special attention to the problem of identifying the boundaries of political systems, and to changes in correctional networks. In Chapter 9, we examined a number of ways in which the boundaries between community and institutional corrections have blurred. In Chapter 13, we described the crucial connection to federal district courts in the management of institutional orders.

These and other changes in the relationship between correctional organizations and their environments make considerable demands on correctional management. In this chapter, we have space only to review two additional developments in this rapidly changing area. We will cover correctional managers' interactions with political interest groups and interactions in joint projects with other organizations.

CORRECTIONAL INTEREST GROUPS

Correctional organizations, and particularly the public ones, are political organizations. They are organized to carry out the public punishment function. It should come as no surprise, then, that correctional organizations, like other political endeavors, are surrounded and shaped by a number of interest groups that seek to promote their values over those of competing groups:

> The term *interest* is used to denote a line of current or future activity in which a person or group has invested its action resources and expectations. A group maintaining a certain interest becomes a **correctional interest group** when its activities conflict with, merge with, or otherwise engage the activities of a correctional agency in such a way as to focus the attention of both parties on the juncture of interests. (Ohlin, 1960:111)

Examples of correctional interest groups include private companies vying for contracts with prisons or community correctional units, labor unions arguing for restrictive laws on prison industries, a neighborhood improvement association objecting to the location of a halfway house,

and the NAACP Legal Defense Fund fighting for the abolition of the death penalty.

An effective correctional manager must be skillful in assessing the impact of his or her actions on various interests and predicting how interest groups will respond. In order to assess these groups skillfully, the manager should make judgments about several characteristics. No interest group is equally concerned with all aspects of correctional operations. A manager needs to be aware of which operational decisions are influenced by which groups; he or she needs to know how likely each group is to respond to changes in practice (Ohlin, 1960:114).

There are a number of ways in which interest groups gain information about correctional practice. Ohlin (1960:115) categorized the more common means. (1) Some groups have visible or secret liaison agents inside the organization. For example, a correctional officer union has frequent contact with members inside the prison. Other groups may have "moles"—hidden friends in the organization who are willing to leak information important to the interest group. (2) Some interest groups have a public relations unit which is responsible for routine contact with the correctional agency. During these routine contacts, the public relations officer will be on the watch for information of interest to the group. For example, a security equipment manufacturer may employ an agent to maintain business relations with a number of correctional managers. During sales visits, this agent will be seeking new information about proposed operations that are favorable or detrimental to that company.

(3) Some interest groups join together in a watchdog association or committee to keep tabs on correctional decisions. For example, the New York Coalition for Criminal Justice is a watchdog association of several groups that invest in the coalition to maintain their correctional interests. (4) Some interest groups guard their domain through memberships on advisory boards or commissions. Many correctional organizations have advisory boards of community representatives, in part so that the manager can inform community

members of the positions and needs of the organization. Advisory board members are frequently chosen for their expertise or interest in corrections. They may give advice or assistance to the correctional manager, but they will also bring back to their parent organizations information pertinent to those interests. For example, community corrections board members in Minnesota include representatives from the prosecutor's office, the trial court, ex-offenders, and neighborhood leaders. Each of these representatives assists in the creation of the county community corrections plan, but also guards the interests of other groups relative to that plan (Blackmore, 1978).

Interest groups vary in at least three important dimensions. Some are more alert than others, and any group will be more alert at some points than others (Miller, Ohlin and Coates, 1977). Research on correctional change in Massachusetts and Wisconsin suggests that interest groups are most alert just before they have gained their objectives, or just after they have lost them. Interest groups may be less alert and therefore less of a force in correctional administration when they feel that their interests are being promoted by current practice. One ticklish issue for any manager is whether change in routine will reawaken group influence.

Interest groups also vary in how much is at stake in the correctional organization (Ohlin, 1960:120). Some have only minor investments in corrections; others may be totally dependent on a particular practice. A criminal justice reform group may devote only 20 percent of its resources to corrections. It may find a correctional change undesirable but decide that fighting the issue would take more than that proportion of its resources. A certain neighborhood association, however, may make the location of a new prison its sole issue for months at a time.

Finally, interest groups vary in their potency, which ". . . lies in the group's readiness to mobilize as much power as it can, or as it needs, to realize [its] interests" (Ohlin, 1960:121). The potency of an interest group cannot be assessed

properly without consideration of all its connections to other groups and organizations. A particular interest group may itself be weak, compared to the correctional organization, but it may have more powerful allies who are willing to exert influence in certain circumstances.

Influence may be exerted in a number of ways (a good general review is Benson, 1975). Ohlin observed that common influence attempts by interest groups include control of a personnel system, stopping a program, and mounting a competing program (1960, 124–126). The more frequent influence attempts are relatively quiet. Issues do not become public concerns, in many cases, unless the normal sanctions at an interest group's disposal fail (see Warren, Rose, and Bergunder, 1974; Miller, Ohlin, and Coates, 1977). An interest becomes public when interest groups seek the opinion of other groups who are not normally interested in corrections. Going public may increase the influence a group can exert, but only if it can control the media effectively. In Massachusetts, Jerome Miller used the media skillfully in defeating conservative interest groups that wished to keep the training schools open. In the California tax revolt called Proposition 13, the conservative groups gained control of the media, and many public administrators, including probation chiefs, were on the defensive (Nelson and Harlow, 1980).

One lesson both managers and students should take away from the study of interest groups is that correctional activity is political by its very nature. Some managers complain that corrections should be left to the "professionals." But most often this is the complaint of a manager whose own interests in corrections are not being heeded. The professionalization of correctional staff is itself a political event—one of its aims is to give the professional group greater control over practice and to take influence away from some other group. Professionalism in corrections will not reduce the political nature of the organization. A professional correctional manager needs to be well versed in assessing interests and in predicting the process of influence.

MANAGING JOINT TASKS

Managers are often faced with the need to engage in cooperative ventures with other organizations. Joint ventures may be the only way to assure sufficient resources to achieve program goals (Levine and White, 1961; Litwak and Hylton, 1962); but may also be important to maintaining legitimacy (Warren, Rose and Bergunder, 1974). Since the goals of correctional systems are rarely products of single organizations, but instead are products of interorganizational networks (see Chapter 5), the need for coordination in the correctional field is particularly salient.

In the last twenty years, correctional policymakers and managers have considered a number of new interorganizational links as devices for increasing service delivery, reducing cost, or both. These links often stress new intergovernmental relationships. But the new cooperative arrangements also include connections with private organizations.

These new forms of cooperation may be understood better with the aid of a table. Table 18.5 depicts four possible arrangements for the delivery of correctional services as a product of two dimensions: (1) how closely linked is a particular service unit, such as a parole office, a prison, or a halfway house, to centralized policymakers and resources; and (2) how closely linked is the service unit to local policymaking and resources. Four common arrangements are described here.

Community-run Organizations. A number of correctional organizations are operated by local

governments. Goals are set by local actors, and resources are supplied through the local tax base. Common examples are county jails and county probation departments. Such organizations usually reflect the dominant political preferences of the local community, and may have close ties with other local groups and organizations. The nature and quality of services depends heavily on the wealth and political values of that local area, under certain minimal constraints set by state law, and state and federal constitutions.

Community-placed Organizations. A growing number of correctional organizations are in the opposite position. They are service delivery units of large, statewide departments. Consequently, they have strong ties to centralized policymakers and resources, and considerably weaker, less formal connections with other local service units. State prisons, state parole offices, statewide probation departments, and prerelease centers run directly by state departments are of this type.

Isolated Organizations. In the lower lefthand corner of Table 18.5 are a diminishing breed of correctional organizations which are relatively isolated, autonomous entities. Earlier in the history of correctional organizations, it was often considered a meritorious management goal to make organizations self-sufficient. Most policymakers and managers would reject this stance today. Isolated organizations may not differ in kind from community-run or community-placed. They may be units of county government or state

TABLE 18.5   The Community Linkage Patterns of Correctional Organizations

LINKS TO CENTRALIZED AUTHORITY FOR POLICY AND RESOURCES		Community Placed	Mixed Control
	Strong		
	Weak	Isolated	Community Run

Weak Strong

LINKS TO LOCAL AUTHORITY FOR POLICY AND RESOURCES

correctional departments. They can be differentiated on the quantity and quality of linkages they have with other organizations for goal setting and resource supply (see Steele and Jacobs, 1975). This category would also include some private organizations that have few direct connections with the public punishment process, but do serve correctional clients. For example, self-sufficient halfway houses run by ex-inmates may fall in this category (Yablonsky, 1965; Hampton-Turner, 1977).

Mixed-control Organizations. Finally, in the upper righthand corner of Table 18.5 are correctional units which have close, formal relations with both local and central sources of policymaking and resource supply. This type would include local public organizations that receive a large proportion of funding from state sources, and local service organizations that operate on a contract with a state correctional authority. Examples include misdemeanant probation in Florida, which is provided by the Salvation Army on a contract basis; the large number of private programs which on a contract basis provide juvenile correctional services in Massachusetts; and adult prerelease services in Connecticut. At the present time, the best example is the Minnesota Community Corrections Act programs in Minnesota (Blackmore, 1978). These programs are run by local boards, funded with state tax dollars in return for the reduction in commitments to the state prison system and monitored by the state Department of Correction.

Preference for the mixed-control type of organization appears to be increasing across the nation. Two major research projects concluded that the mixed control correctional organization offers more flexibility and cheaper per unit costs than community-placed organizations (Vinter, Downs, and Hall. 1975:42; Coates, Miller, and Ohlin, 1978:190). The mixed-control approach removes from the central government much of the initial startup risk and the complex problems of dealing with specific neighborhoods (Vinter, Downs, and Hall, 1975:70–72). The mixed-con-

trol program may also permit better quality administration than community-run organizations. Moreover, the mixed-control organization can utilize the power of its central linkages to urge a reluctant local community to provide services when it would not do so on its own (Coates, Miller and Ohlin, 1978).

The difficulty with the mixed-control type is that the complex combination of local and central decision-making and funding is hard to create and difficult to maintain. It asks of correctional administrators behaviors that they have not frequently needed in the past, such as designing service contracts, selecting service providers, and monitoring the quality of services provided by the contracting organizations. This complex network form of administration can backfire. For example, one of the earlier mixed-control efforts, the California Probation Subsidy, did not reduce costs to the state as anticipated, and may not have reduced the use of institutions (Lerman, 1975). More recent projects, such as the Minnesota Community Corrections Act, the Massachusetts community-based juvenile system, and the Polk County (Des Moines) Community Corrections Department, may have fared better.

The mixed-control organization may be particularly important if correctional policymakers are concerned about delivery of services to offenders in community settings. Table 18.6 provides data from twelve community prerelease centers on the types of client problems resolved during center residence and the means used to resolve those problems. Economic problems, such as finding a job, obtaining job skills, transportation, clothing, and emergency money, were by far the most common. The most frequent means of resolving an economic problem was referral from the correctional organization to another service agency in the community. The correctional unit by itself simply did not have the resources to solve these problems. Moreover, clients were less dependent on the correctional system if they could find help in the community. The researchers found that the centers which were most able to make successful service refer-

TABLE 18.6 Residents' Problems Solved During Halfway House Stay, by Means of Resolution

MEANS OF RESOLUTION	TYPE OF PROBLEM SOLVED			
	ECONOMIC	SOCIAL ADJUSTMENT	HOUSE RULES	TOTAL
Through referral	140 (61)	5 (11)	2 (6)	147 (47)
With internal resources	18 (8)	18 (39)	19 (56)	55 (18)
Using family or friends	73 (32)	23 (50)	13 (38)	109 (35)
Total	231 (100)	46 (100)	34 (100)	311 (100)

NOTE: Numbers in parentheses are column percentages.

rals were the centers with the most formal links to these other community agencies (Duffee and Warner, 1986). Correctional managers create these formal linkages by participating actively in joint policy decisions with other agencies, by joining community boards and commissions, and by sharing their resources with other agencies.

SUMMARY

1. Managers of complex organizations are responsible for steering the organization toward its goals. This process requires appropriate choices of whether to focus on internal or external issues, whether to adopt flexible or controlling structures, and whether to emphasize long-term or short-term outcomes.

2. Public organizations differ from private ones. They often have less latitude in goal selection, less exacting standards for goal achievement, and less competition. Public organizations often respond to ambiguous and controversial goals by focusing on internal processes.

3. Correctional administration since the early 1800s has shown varied interest in the competing values of organizational effectiveness. Early administration was heavily devoted to goals and technology development. Internal process concerns quickly took over. Human relations concerns have developed slowly throughout the twentieth century. Open systems issues have preoccupied managers only recently.

4. The management of goal planning and productivity involves clarification of correctional philosophy and assumptions, achieving agreement across units, and through planning and research, developing technologies that reach objectives.

5. Management of internal processes includes development of work specialties, personnel standards, appropriate division of authority, and conflict resolution strategies.

6. Managing human relations involves meeting the needs of employees. Organizational development and Quality of Work Life programs have been used to reduce alienation, increase worker satisfaction, and raise organizational effectiveness.

7. Managing the open system issues in a correctional organization includes effective interaction with interest groups, and formalizing relationships with service agencies in order to reach supervision goals.

KEY WORDS

COMMUNITY-PLACED ORGANIZATIONS. Correctional organizations with close links to centralized policy-making and resources, but weak links to local organizations.

COMMUNITY-RUN ORGANIZATION. A correctional organization with close links to local policymaking and resources, but weak links to centralized authority.

COMPETING VALUES APPROACH. A management approach which integrates the rational goal, the internal process, the human relations, and the open systems models of organizational effectiveness.

COMPLEX ORGANIZATION. A human system of interrelated roles that must be performed simultaneously for the achievement of goals.

CORRECTIONAL INTEREST GROUP. A group that interacts with a correctional organization to protect its investment in correctional activities.

HUMAN RELATIONS MODEL. A perspective on organizations which stresses the value of human resources and attempts to improve morale, group cohesion, and related variables in order to develop those resources.

INTERNAL PROCESS MODEL. A perspective on organizations which places high value on predictability and control and uses structures that make activities more predictable.

ISOLATED ORGANIZATIONS. Correctional organizations that have weak ties to both centralized and local sources of policy and resources.

MIXED-CONTROL ORGANIZATIONS. Correctional organizations in which policymaking and resource supply are shared by centralized and local sources.

OPEN SYSTEMS MODEL. A perspective on organizations which places high value on resource acquisition and growth through the use of flexible structures that can respond to opportunities.

ORGANIZATIONAL DEVELOPMENT (OD). An organizational change strategy that seeks to revitalize the culture of the organization by developing teamwork and sensitivity to workers' needs while improving organizational performance. Usually starts at the top of the organization and uses expert outside consultants to assist in the change process.

PUBLIC ORGANIZATION. An organization supported directly from public funds, responsible to the general constituency, carrying out the functions of government.

QUALITY OF WORK LIFE (QWL). Organizational change projects that seek to improve conditions of workers on the job through the use of joint management-labor committees.

RATIONAL GOAL MODEL. A perspective on organizations which places high values on productivity and efficiency and achieves these through goal planning, technological development, and evaluation.

STANDARDIZATION OF PERSONNEL. The selection and training of personnel to increase uniformity in knowledge, skill, or decisions.

STANDARDIZATION OF WORK. The planning of work routines and practices to increase uniformity of processes and outcomes.

SUBOPTIMIZATION. The practice by organizational subunits of valuing unit objectives over organizational objectives.

TECHNOLOGY. An arrangement of human and other resources to achieve the objectives of the organization.

PROJECTS AND QUESTIONS

1. In Fox's (1982) study of maximum security prisons, correctional managers ranked their most pressing problems as (1) racial tension, (2) overcrowding and scarce resources, (3) guard alienation, and (4) the formal organization of inmate subgroups. How would the four different effectiveness models discussed in this chapter approach these problems? Which approaches do you prefer? Why?

2. The rational goal model of organizations stresses the selection and achievement of goals. The correctional policy model is one means of assisting managers to select and clarify goals. However, it is often argued that correctional organizations must

achieve whatever goals are selected for them by the legislature and ultimately by the voting public. If you were a correctional manager, to what extent would you seek to be guided by public demand? How would you find out what that demand was?

3. What may be some of the reasons correctional managers have often paid less attention to the issue of the human relations model of organizations than managers in other types of organizations?

ADDITIONAL READING

Richard Cloward et al. *Theoretical Studies in Social Organization of the Prison.* New York: Social Science Research Council, 1960. One of the most influential works on prison organization; in many ways a key volume in directing correctional management toward human relations and open systems concerns.

Alden Miller, Lloyd Ohlin, and Robert Coates. *A Theory of Social Reform.* Cambridge, MA: Ballinger, 1978. This volume on the Massachusetts juvenile system focuses on interest group dynamics and their impact on correctional organization.

Gary Wamsley and Mayer Zald. *The Political Economy of Public Organizations.* Bloomington: University of Indiana Press, 1973. This book has had a major influence on the analysis of public organizations.

Hans Toch and J. Douglas Grant. *Reforming Human Services.* Beverly Hills, CA: Sage, 1982. This book reviews new approaches to the management of human resources in police and correctional agencies.

19 JUVENILE CORRECTIONS

QUESTIONS

1. How did the juvenile corrections system develop?

2. What is *parens patriae*?

3. What are the different types of programs for juveniles who have been adjudicated delinquent?

4. What is a status offense?

5. What is diversion?

6. What is deinstitutionalization?

7. What changes are currently taking place in correctional goals for juveniles?

A TRIP TO THE WOODS

In Phil's first summer working for the Department of Corrections, he had to drive around the state for two weeks while he conducted interviews. Someone got the bright idea of putting him up at the forestry camp. This was a juvenile facility run by a separate department, but the two departments cooperated frequently in minor ways.

When Phil finally negotiated the turns and pulled into a small compound of half a dozen buildings in the middle of the woods, it was midday and the place was very quiet. Three cars and a jeep were parked in the lot, and two boys, maybe 13 years old, were playing by a porch door.

Phil was met by an elderly gentleman who waggled a large cigar in constantly pursed lips as he stared through thick, wire-rimmed spectacles. He introduced himself as George Wopat, director of the camp. According to Phil's source in Corrections, Wopat was an ex-cop, ex-probation officer who had earned his Ph.D. in clinical psychology after fifteen years of night study. He was regarded as a sloppy administrator, but a wizard at keeping the delinquents sent to him from graduating to the reformatory. Phil liked him immediately, and could tell that the kids liked him too. Wopat waved to Phil: "I'll show you around. Ever seen a forestry camp before?"

The tour of the grounds took little time. The two dormitories, with individual, unlocked rooms, were clean and smelled like the pine forest that surrounded the compound. There was a small administrative office with separate rooms for the two counselors and a large group meeting room, empty at the moment, where the kids and the staff met once every day. A cafeteria/lecture hall, much larger than needed for the twenty residents, and a maintenance building completed the facility. Every few minutes Phil saw another boy going by without too much to do. Wopat explained that new residents spent about a week on the grounds before they were sent out with the work crews. Experienced residents left the grounds every morning after breakfast supervised by two forestry interns and the day shift counseling aid. They returned by 3:30 to wash up and relax for an hour before an early dinner and the group meeting. Evenings were fairly free, except for those who had individual appointments with counselors or with Wopat.

The two counselors were young. One had just been graduated from the social work program at State; the other was completing a masters degree in special education. They came on duty at noon, did their paperwork or had meetings with Wopat about individual boys until 3:30, and then spent their time with the kids. In the evening, the counselors were assisted by two aids who kept a watch on free time activity, organized games, and tried to carry out specific orders regarding individual boys. The forestry students didn't work for the department, but supervised the work in the woods during the day.

"In September, the whole schedule changes," explained Wopat. "All the kids, except a few of the older ones, are bussed out to local schools. The forestry work comes pretty much to a halt, except on weekends. I'm not sure what this forestry business is anyway, but it gets these kids out into fresh air, and I can use the experience out there sometimes in treatment. The kids have to cooperate in order to get the work done and not get hurt. They can't fool around with the food and water supply, because if they waste it it is just gone until they get back here. There are some elements of that experience we can concentrate on in group sessions. But that works only if the forestry supervisors or my aide keep their eyes open, and both are often too busy to pay attention to the dynamics among the boys.

Phil changed the subject. "Isn't it a long trip to send these kids out to school?"

"You bet. The school buses won't come in here; we have to truck the kids out to the main road. It can take two, two and a half hours sometimes just to get to school. But school out there is better than the alternative, until I can get the department to shut down this operation altogether. When I took over this place nine years ago, the kids were tutored—in a manner of speaking—right on the grounds. I had three special ed teachers on the payroll. It gave us some control over learning, and reading and math skills actually improved quicker then than now. But we'd release the kid right in the middle of the school year and he'd go right back to the same school where he'd had trouble in the first place. So I stopped that. At first the local school district wasn't too happy, but we've worked hard on that relationship, and now it works pretty well."

"You said you want the department to shut down the camp?"

Wopat looked at him with surprise. "You bet. You think inner city kids belong out here for six months just to get thrown back into the jungle? I want them to build me a day center downtown. Kids would stay in their own schools and sleep at home. They'd come to me after school and in the summer. We'd work with the teachers and the parents instead of with trees and rabbits."

"Do you think it will happen?" asked Phil.

"Not till the state needs this camp for something else. We inherited it from the National Guard, and we're stuck with it until—" Wopat smiled slightly "—maybe until they fill up that big prison at Mulwan. Then my camp will look valuable and I could get the kids out of here."

A SEPARATE SYSTEM FOR JUVENILES

Juvenile and adult corrections have long shared an uneasy relationship. Our legal tradition has always made some distinction between adults and juveniles. In the English common law, children under the age of 7 were not held responsible for what would have been criminal acts if they had been older. It was thought that children were not mature enough to harbor the criminal intent necessary for legal guilt. From that tradition, the law and correctional systems have struggled with the dividing line between childish and adult behavior, and between punitive and nonpunitive responses to that behavior.

ORIGINS OF JUVENILE CORRECTIONS

Juvenile and adult corrections systems are now legally and administratively separate systems, but that was not always the case. Prior to the penitentiary movement, adults and juveniles were often housed together in the same catchall jails. In the early nineteenth century, observers lamented the experience confronting young girls thrown into jail with hardened criminals (Beaumont and Toqueville, 1964). In this country, the beginnings of the separate system for juveniles began shortly thereafter. In 1824, the New York *House of Refuge* was established, based on an institution designed by the London Philanthropic Society in 1788. Similar Houses of Refuge soon followed in other eastern cities (Lerman, 1975:215; Carey and McAnany, 1984:56).

Children could be placed in the houses rather than punished with adults, but the laws of the time permitted referrals to the houses from any number of sources, and refuge managers were also likely to go out and recruit. Juveniles were, in effect, placed in involuntary servitude by the refuge managers. The children would work for a time in the house industries and would then be bound out to work, sometimes in other states. The subjects of this regime were often the children of immigrants attracted to the new cities in search of factory jobs. Neither the children nor their parents had much protection. Challenging the jurisdiction of the Philadelphia House of Refuge over his daughter, one father was told the following by the Pennsylvania Supreme Court:

The object of the charity is reformation, by training its inmates to industry, by imbuing their minds with principles of morality and religion; by furnishing them with means to earn a living; and above all, by separating them from the corrupting influences of improper associates. To this end, may not the natural parents, when unequal to the task of education, or unworthy of it, be superseded by the *parens patriae*, or common guardian of the community? (Ex Parte Crouse, 4 Wharton 9, 1838)

This statement, known as the **parens patriae doctrine,** became the foundation for the treatment of juveniles in the United States. The term was borrowed loosely from the practice of English chancery courts, where the kings stepped in to protect the property rights of juveniles upon the death of parents (Carey and McAnany, 1984). During the Industrial Revolution in the United States, the term came to mean that the state had jurisdiction over the welfare of all children, even if the exercise of that protection involved involuntary separation from family and forced servitude.

In the mid-nineteenth century, the refuge system gave way to the use of reform schools. This shift was led by Charles Loring Brace, founder of the Childrens Aid Society of New York. Brace, a champion of universal public education, saw

The House of Refuge in New York City was the first of a soon burgeoning supply of separate facilities for juveniles. (New-York Historical Society)

the reform school as a step in his fight for mandatory education enforced with truancy laws. While the Houses of Refuge were not houses as much as self-contained factories using child labor, the reform schools adopted a plan of smaller cottages surrounding a school. Cottage parents supervised the youth during the reform school stay. The practice of placing youth with families or businesses continued (Carey and McAnany, 1984).

THE RISE OF THE JUVENILE COURT

The reform school era lasted until roughly 1890, when a push emerged for a separate juvenile or family court, and the utilization of probation officers to determine what should happen to juveniles brought to court. The reform schools, like the houses of refuge, had operated fairly independently, with each schoolmaster drumming up business in entrepreneurial fashion. The Progressive Era at the turn of the twentieth century was characterized by a trust in the beneficial effects of nonpartisan, professional government. The fragmented juvenile correctional system was therefore pushed toward centralization under a new family court (Sutton, 1985).

The most widely known history of the juvenile court movement suggested that the new court form emerged from a combination of forces, such as the new profession of social work, the concern of the middle class over the behavior of immigrant children, and the perception of work with children as a legitimate occupation for newly independent, middle-class women (Platt, 1969). A more recent analysis (Sutton, 1985) indicated that the strongest factor in the diffusion of the juvenile court was degree of urbanization. Urbanized states, which had already invested a great deal of money in separate juvenile correctional facilities, were those quickest to adopt a separate court to oversee the juvenile system.

The first juvenile court in the United States was established in Chicago in 1899. The juvenile court had jurisdiction not only over cases of delinquency, but over cases of **dependency** and **neglect** as well. As juvenile or family court laws were adopted around the nation, *parens patriae* continued to be the distinguishing characteristic. Juveniles were not to be punished for their acts, but treated for their condition. Consequently, it made no sense to separate the delinquent from the dependent or neglected. Nor did it make sense to protect juveniles with the constitutional rights that protected adults in criminal court. The state intervened to protect, not punish, juveniles.

The emergence of the juvenile court changed to some extent how children reached correctional facilities, but did not really change what happened to them once they arrived. Institutional juvenile corrections remained fairly stable from 1900 until the 1960s (McGarrell, 1986). The bulwark of the system was the training school or reform school developed in the nineteenth century. However, the juvenile court era did increase the frequency of the use of probation, and increased the power of probation officers in determining the intake of juvenile court and decisions about placement.

DOUBTS ABOUT PARENS PATRIAE

In the early 1960s, the political independence of the juvenile corrections system began to weaken. In 1967, the President's Commission on Law Enforcement and the Administration of Justice voiced strong doubts about the efficacy of juvenile institutions and about the fairness of the juvenile court. These doubts were significantly influenced by the work of social scientists such as Cloward and Ohlin (1960) who caught the ear of the Kennedy administration in the early sixties. Opportunity theory suggested that some juvenile delinquency was the product of blocked opportunity, not improper emotional development. Labeling theory (Lemert, 1967) suggested that isolating juveniles could exacerbate deviant tendencies by stigmatizing people. Based on these and other new theories, the President's Commission recommended that more juveniles be diverted from the juvenile justice system, that delinquency treatment be deinstitutionalized, and that some behaviors be decriminalized altogether (see McGarrell, 1986; Carey and McAnany, 1984, for reviews).

THE LEGAL CHALLENGE TO PARENS PATRIAE

According to Carey and McAnany, juveniles lagged behind adults in asserting their rights and in litigating the conditions of confinement because (1) juveniles were less able to file without legal assistance; (2) juveniles typically stayed shorter periods of time in institutions; and (3)

attorneys were less interested in juvenile work (1984:303). Nevertheless, in the mid-sixties, legal challenges began to chip away at the autonomy provided by the *parens patriae* doctrine.

The first significant case was *Kent v. United States*, decided in 1966. Kent, age 16, was charged with housebreaking, robbery, and rape. The juvenile court for the District of Columbia determined that Kent should be tried as an adult for these crimes and waived him up to adult court. His lawyer objected, claiming that he had not had access to the social work records and probation report upon which the waiver decision was based, and that Kent had not received a hearing on the waiver decision and could not have had adequate defense of counsel. The Supreme Court of the United States, using very strong language, found in favor of Kent. The Court held that as a condition of a valid waiver, a juvenile was entitled to a full hearing, access to the records used in the decision, and a list of reasons for the decision. Although not a direct attack on the juvenile court, the Kent decision indicated that the Supreme Court was unconvinced that informal, unilateral decisions were always in the best interest of the child.

One year later, the Gault decision followed through with the threat apparent in Kent. Gerald Gault was arrested on a verbal complaint about an obscene phone call. Gerald's parents were not told that he had been arrested, and they were not given formal notice of a delinquency hearing. The woman making the complaint was not asked to appear at the hearing, at which Gerald was committed as a delinquent until he reached his twenty-first birthday. Had Gerald been an adult, the maximum punishment for his behavior would have been a $50 fine. The juvenile court had the authority to commit him for six years.

The Supreme Court of the United States objected to the behavior of these officials and handed down the decision that began to change the juvenile justice system. Specifically, the Court held that a juvenile has a right to notice of charges, to counsel, to confrontation and cross examination of witnesses, and to protection against self-incrimination. While the Gault decision is aimed at the juvenile court rather than juvenile correctional practice, the decision indicated that *parens patriae* was no longer a sufficient justification for arbitrary and unfair treatment. Some juvenile correctional officials felt that informality of procedure and lack of challenge to decisions were necessary. After *Gault*, these assumptions were finally on thin ice.

Since 1967, a number of other juvenile cases have expanded and refined the rights of juveniles in the court and in the correctional process. Although juveniles have never been accorded the same protections provided adults, significant limits have been placed on official discretion. Later decisions continued to alter the court process by providing for proof of guilt beyond reasonable doubt (*In re Winship*, 1970), to protection against double jeopardy (*Breed* v. *Jones*, 1975), but not to a jury trial (*McKeiver* v. *Pennsylvania*, 1971). State decisions have limited in-custody decisions, such as the length of solitary confinement (*Pena* v. *New York State Division for Youth*, 1976), and procedure for revoking parole status (*State ex rel R.R.* v. *Schmidt*, 1974).

While the juvenile corrections system has always been based on assumptions of rehabilitation rather than punishment, the Supreme Court of the United States has never ruled on the issue of whether juveniles have a right to treatment. A number of lower courts have ruled that the right to treatment exists within the statutory language of state juvenile law. Where this approach has been taken, officials have been forced to demonstrate that the correctional treatment of a youth has included attempts at rehabilitation. Warehousing of youth in custody institutions, in those instances, is not sufficient. Another possible argument for a right to treatment relies on an interpretation of due process as requiring treatment in juvenile and mental health cases. Since limitations on juvenile rights are justified on the grounds of the beneficent intent of state intervention, then fairness requires delivery of treatment services (see Carey and McAnany, 1984).

One could argue that despite significant legal changes in the last fifteen years, the juvenile correctional system is still stuck in the middle: It has always justified its actions on goals of treatment and care, but has always operated programs little different than those used to punish adults. Carey and McAnany argue that the entire juvenile justice system has always been correctional or remedial in nature (beginning with police apprehension), but the system has always been fatally flawed by the failure to define what the "best interest" of the child actually meant (1984:287). Lerman (1975) is considerably blunter: He argues that the societal reaction to juvenile deviance has always been predominantly one of restraint hiding behind the language of treatment.

THE JUVENILE INTAKE PROCESS

While the due process revolution in juvenile justice has pushed the system closer to procedures used in adult prosecutions, major differences remain. One of the more significant differences occurs in the front end of the juvenile court process, in a procedure known as intake. Juveniles can arrive at intake in a number of ways; any number of different parties can refer a juvenile, including police, family, and school officials. The decision of whether to accept a referral and file a delinquency petition in court is made by juvenile intake officers, who are usually probation officers.

Intake officers face several options. They can (1) send the juvenile home with no further action, (2) send the juvenile to a social agency (including the probation office), (3) petition the case to court, and (4) petition the case to court and detain the juvenile prior to trial (Bell and Lang, 1985). A number of other options also exist, but these four alternatives are by far the most common. In choosing among options, the intake officer will usually interview the referring person (most often a police officer), review arrest and social agency records, and interview the child and the parents.

In the last ten years, pressure from a number

of sources has increased the use of **informal probation,** or probation by consent decree. This option involves the child and parents agreeing that the juvenile will abide by certain probation conditions for a period of time, usually four to six months, without a formal finding of delinquency. The informal probation will typically begin with a probation officer conducting an investigation and filing a report which will summarize the difficulty and suggest what the child should do. Informal probation may, but often does not, include referral to other social agencies for services to the juvenile or the family. Informal probation is justified as a means of providing supervision while avoiding labeling the juvenile as delinquent. However, actual practice often means little more than filing a report and waiting for the next incident.

Not surprisingly, the factors that appear to have the most influence on the intake officers' decisions are not very different than those that would lead a prosecutor to seek conviction in an adult case. Research indicates that age and number of prior court appearances weigh heavily in the decision of whether to petition for an adjudicatory hearing. However, observers in a Los Angeles study discovered that the demeanor of the youth had some bearing on the decision, with cooperative and contrite youth receiving dismissals or informal settlements, and noncooperative youth being continued to court. Race was found to have a complex influence on intake outcomes, with whites more likely to receive informal probation than nonwhites, and nonwhites more likely to receive dismissals or petitions to court (Bell and Lang, 1985).

STATUS OFFENDERS

One result of the assault on the *parens patriae* doctrine has been the attempt to distinguish juveniles who have committed behaviors that would be crimes if they were adults from juveniles whose behavior is troublesome but not criminal. This latter group, called **status offenders,** may be truant, ungovernable, or runaways, but have

committed no crimes. Prior to the 1960s, few distinctions were made between delinquents and status offenders. One result of the major court cases was the discovery that many status offenders, particularly females, suffered more serious interventions than those who had committed serious crimes. For example, a national survey by the University of Michigan found that in 1973, 66 percent of the females incarcerated in juvenile facilities had committed only status offenses, compared to 25 percent of the males (Vinter, 1976:201). As the juvenile justice process began to approximate the adult criminal process, attempts were made to match the severity of intervention to the severity of the behavior—if not in the name of retribution, in the name of fairness.

One major impetus to the separation of status offenders from delinquents was the Juvenile Justice and Delinquency Prevention Act of 1974, and the Office of Juvenile Justice and Delinquency Prevention, established to implement portions of the legislation. Two major goals were separation of status offenders from delinquents, and separation of juveniles from adults during detention (McGarrell, 1986).

The Office of Juvenile Justice and Delinquency Prevention funded a number of demonstration projects to establish new programs for status offenders. The office also required states to separate status offenders from delinquents and juveniles from adults if the state was to continue to receive any federal funds. One result was a rash of new juvenile justice legislation, such as the 1977 law in Pennsylvania:

> Unless a child found to be dependent is found also to be delinquent, he shall not be committed to or confined in an institution or other facility designed or operated for the benefit of delinquent children. (Pa. Act 41, Section 24, 3b)

In all, 47 states agreed to changes that would keep status offenders out of institutions (Shichor, 1983). Unfortunately, this decision has been easier to legislate than to implement. One underlying weakness with the legislation at both the federal and state levels has been the assumption that status offenders are a separate group of persons, clearly distinguishable from delinquents (Klein, 1979:169). This has turned out not to be the case. For example, in one Arizona status offender program, it was discovered that only 8 percent of the juveniles referred to the program had committed only status offenses; 75 percent had committed status offenses, misdemeanors, and felonies (Klein, 1979:169).

A number of other difficulties became evident as status offender programs were implemented. In some states, officials began to label status offenders as delinquents in order to warrant pretrial detention, even though they knew there was not sufficient evidence to sustain a delinquency petition at a court hearing. Apparently, some officials assumed that some incarceration was better than none, even if only for a short time. In other states, officials played the relabeling game another way, committing status offenders to mental health facilities rather than seeking delinquency commitments (Jackson, 1979). Other jurisdictions have invented new types of facilities for the detention of status offenders. The new facilities, labeled "semi-secure," do not come under the prohibition against detention in the 1974 federal legislation. Other states have taken to upgrading status offenders into delinquents by relying on evidence of noncooperation in community programs as evidence of delinquency (Costello and Worthington, 1981).

Another faulty assumption of the new status offender programs is that status offenders, left to their own devices, will become worse, and "grow" into delinquents. Most recent research indicates that this belief is also faulty. Most juveniles do not graduate from truancy or ungovernability toward criminal behavior, but instead commit a variety of delinquent and criminal acts (Rankin and Wells, 1985).

DIVERSION

As is true of the adult system, the juvenile system has increasingly emphasized **diversion** from traditional, formal processing of cases. Definitions of juvenile diversion are diverse and contradictory. Some include as diversionary any decision to keep a juvenile out of court or in the community. The difficulty with such a broad definition, however, is that it includes a number of traditional practices, such as outright release of a juvenile by the police, and juvenile probation, both of which have existed for years. Malcolm Klein (1979) argues that the essence of diversion is handling in some alternative fashion youth who except for the program would have entered the postadjudicatory system or would have penetrated further into that system. He insists that the core of the diversion idea is the *turning away*. This definition excludes from diversion preadjudicatory but normal practices, such as informal police adjustment of minor cases, and postadjudicatory practices such as probation, which are not designed to turn youth away from more severe interventions such as institutionalization.

One major difficulty with the assessment of diversion programs is determining how many of the youth involved have indeed been turned away from the juvenile justice process. Many programs operate under a diversion label, but with no clear guidelines or constraints that limit their operations to juveniles who had truly been diverted. For example, the Turning Point Youth Services in Visalia, California, seeks to prevent delinquency through early intervention. Program elements include family therapy, individual group counseling, parenting classes, assistance to schools, and recreation programs. Most of the referrals to the program come through a "diversion" program (Clifford, 1985). However, if the program is true to its goals of preventing delinquency, diversion should not be occurring: intervention should be taking place before delinquency, and diversion, become necessary.

A number of diversion programs have been designed specifically for status offenders, albeit under the faulty assumptions described above. For example, in Pima County, Arizona, a Mobile Diversion Unit was established to handle all status offenders referrred to juvenile court. The object was that no status offenders were to be processed through the official justice system. An evaluation of the program (Rojek and Erickson, 1981) found that creation of the diversion program resulted in the processing of more youth rather than less as the new community treatment agencies vied with each other for clients. While the program may have resulted in fewer status offenders being adjudicated, they did end up in long, specialized treatment programs that may have been equally stigmatizing.

The evaluators could find no positive effects on attitude or on recidivism. An evaluation of the Illinois Status Offender Services Alternatives to Detention program found similarly disturbing results. Over the course of the project, fewer status offenders were detained, but more youth were classified as "detainable" and subject to alternative processing (Spergel et al., 1982). Once again, rather than divert persons who would have otherwise been adjudicated and subject to harsher treatment, the diversion program apparently widened the net over youth who previous to the program would not have been processed at all.

Summarizing a large number of diversion evaluations, Klein (1979) listed a number of common problems found in the implementation of diversion programs. (1) The goals and terms in the programs are not clearly defined, giving rise to ambiguities in target populations and types of services to be included. (2) The theories on which the diversion programs rely for their justification have never been fully explicated so that their practice implications are not clear. (3) No clear guidelines for selecting clients have been adopted, so that programs are usually free to accept any juveniles, rather than only those who are being "turned away." (4) Many programs upon close inspection involve very little in the way of remedial services. (5) Many programs have adopted services that are not clearly appropriate to the juveniles in the program; specifically, there has been an overreliance on counseling services, to the neglect of advocacy and skill-building programs. (6) In some cases, the professionals in the justice system have resisted the diversion efforts by upgrading status offenses to delinquency charges. (7) In some cases, diversion programs have been initiated in areas where most youth eligible for alternative programs have already been diverted.

Finally, Klein observed that few so-called diversion programs are actually totally separate from the juvenile justice system in the first place. Many are run under the auspices of probation departments or police departments. Moreover, few diversion programs have no strings attached. Most hold the threat over the juvenile that he will be processed in the traditional manner if the diversion effort does not succeed. It is questionable whether such programs should be considered alternatives to rather than additions to the juvenile justice system. Most of them would appear to be correctional programs that avoid the costs of adjudicatory hearings.

DETENTION

Juveniles who are not released to parents or programs at the intake decision may be detained until a court hearing. Juvenile **detention** in many respects is similar to the jailing of adults who cannot make bail prior to trial, although the justifications vary. Juveniles may be detained if the intake officer determines that the youth is a danger to himself or others. Preventive detention, which has doubtful status in the adult system, has been upheld in the juvenile system.

States very tremendously in the rates with which they lock up juveniles prior to a delinquency hearing. For example, in 1979, California had 28.9 percent of all admissions to detention in the United States, although it had only 10.5 percent of all age-eligible youth in the country. The state with the highest juvenile detention rate was Nevada, while South Carolina had the lowest. Eight of the ten highest detention states were in the West (Krisberg, Litsky and Schwartz, 1984). The length of time spent in detention also varied considerably, from a low of 3 days in Arkansas to a high of 33 days in South Carolina (1984:168).

One of the more controversial issues in juvenile corrections has been the detention of juveniles in adult jails. Despite major federal effort to stop this practice in the 1970s, several studies have found that it is still common. Reuterman and Hughes (1984) found that the frequency of the practice had not declined in the last ten years. Krisberg, Litsky, and Schwartz also found that locking juveniles in jails was still widespread, with South Dakota, Idaho, Mississippi, Arkansas, and Nebraska the most likely to use jails for juvenile detention.

The use of jails for detention purposes would appear particularly disturbing, since the rate of suicide by juveniles is about 3.5 times higher in jails than it is among the general juvenile population (Flaherty, 1983). In contrast, the suicide rate in facilities designed specifically for juvenile detention is lower than the rate in the general population (1983:89). Some states have made the detention of juveniles in adult facilities illegal. For example:

> After December 31, 1979, it shall be unlawful for any person in charge of or employed by a jail knowingly to receive for detention or to detain in such jail any person whom he has or should have reason to believe is a child. (Pa. Act 41 of 1977, Section 13 b1)

One would expect that the youth most likely to be detained pending a court hearing would be the juveniles involved in the most serious misconduct. This does not always seem to be the case. For example, Kramer and Steffensmeier (1978), examining detention practices in Pennsylvania, found little relationship between the seriousness of the misconduct and the likelihood of detention. They found that status offenders, and particularly females, were more likely to be detained than juvenile criminals. They also discovered that counties which had a juvenile detention facility nearby were far more likely to detain than counties without such a facility.

Given the tremendous attention to juvenile detention in the last ten years, one would expect that the practice would have changed a great deal. Reuterman and Hughes set out to test this assumption (1984). They found that average facility populations had dropped between 1970 and 1980, but they also found that yearly admissions had risen. They found no significant increase in programs or in use of volunteers over the ten-year period, and no reduction in the security level. They did, however, find that detention facility personnel were better trained and better educated in 1980 than in 1970.

ADJUDICATION AND DISPOSITION

Juveniles who are not released or diverted at intake face an **adjudicatory hearing** on the delinquency petition. These hearings are still more informal than adult criminal trials, although juveniles now have a right to counsel and the case against the youth is now presented by a prosecutor, rather than by the probation officer, as used to be the case. Recent research has indicated that plea bargaining, a hallmark of the adult system, has crept into the juvenile hearing (Sanborn, 1985). Nevertheless, the United States Supreme Court has not required jury trials, arguing that jury trials and the formal presentation of evidence as in adult court would diminish the concern for the youth's welfare. Some observers argue that defense and prosecution lawyers in the adjudicatory hearing do not play fully adversarial roles, but attempt to cooperate with each other and the judge in deciding what is best for the youth.

If upon hearing the facts of the case the judge determines that the juvenile is delinquent, the youth faces a number of options at **disposition.** The youth can be released with a warning, but no additional supervision. The youth can be placed on formal probation, the most common option. If the judge determines that more control is required than probation can provide, he or she can place the youth in foster care or in a group home. Finally, the judge can commit a youth to an institution, some of which are local and some of which are run by the state. If the juvenile is committed to the state corrections system, the judge may not have a choice of the specific institution in which the juvenile is placed. Additionally, some states have recently passed laws mandating secure incarceration for juveniles found guilty of certain crimes.

INSTITUTIONS FOR JUVENILES

The Michigan survey of juvenile corrections, still the most complete survey of the field, found that the rate of institutionalization of juveniles varied remarkably from state to state. For example, the rate was 41.3 juveniles committed per 1,000 in Wyoming, compared to 2.1 per 1,000 in New York (Vinter, Hall, and Downs, 1975:18). The researchers could find no relationship between the crime rate in the states and the use of institutionalization, a finding that others have verified with more recent data (Krisberg, Litsky and Schwartz, 1984:159–160). The Michigan survey team found that rural and poorer states were more likely to rely on institutions than urban and richer states. Krisberg, Litsky and Schwartz, in contrast, found that the single most powerful factor in explaining use of institutions was simply the number of training school beds available (1984:159–162).

Vinter, Downs, and Hall found that the average length of stay in institutions was 8.7 months for training schools and 6.6 months for less secure camps and ranches (1975:11). Krisberg and his colleagues found the average stay in 1979 to be about the same—7.5 months—but they found puzzling variation. The average stay in Rhode Island was only 30 days, while in Alaska commitments averaged over a year (1984:168). Vinter, Downs, and Hall found that in 1974, despite major efforts at deinstitutionalization, community residential programs were much less common than institutions. The Krisberg team reported that not much had changed by 1979.

Several researchers have sought to determine what characteristics of youth are related to the placement decision. Examining youth placed in day programs, group homes, and training schools, Sarri (1981) was not convinced that the placement paralleled severity of behavior. She reported that the youth in day programs had only slightly fewer previous correctional placements than those sent to group homes or institutions. But she also found that many juveniles in major institutions were clearly not serious offenders. In other words, the severity of the intervention did not seem to correlate with the severity of the delinquent behavior.

Sarri also found some interesting relationships with class and race. Whites were the majority in group homes, but nonwhites were more frequent in day programs and in training schools. Similarly, youth in day programs and institutions usually had unemployed or working-class parents, while youth in group homes often had middle-class parents. As was true in the Los Angeles study of detention decisions, there is some evidence that whites receive mid-range sanctions rather than the most or least severe. A more recent study in a southern state, however, could find no relationship between race and the placement decision, once other factors had been controlled. This study found that the decision to place in a group home or in an institution was best explained by age, criminal history, and behavior of the youth in the diagnostic center while the decision was being made (Kowalski and Rickicki, 1982).

The most recent survey of institutions for juveniles reports that many of the objectionable characteristics of the pre-Gault system still remain. For example, in 1984, 69 percent of all youthful inmates were still housed in secure facilities. Eighteen states reported that all their facilities for delinquents were secure, while only seven reported that all their training schools were nonsecure. There appeared to be no relationship between seriousness or violence of youth crime and level of security (Krisberg, Litsky, and Schwartz, 1984:173). In 47 percent of all training schools, the inmates were not permitted any contact with community or any community activities (1984:176).

The costs for training schools are generally higher than costs in the same state for state prisons. As with the rates of commitment, variations in costs across states are surprising. In Rhode Island, the average cost per youth per year in training school is $43,057; the cost in South Carolina is only $10,252. The average across the country is $17,219, and rising.

PROGRAM ORGANIZATION, TREATMENT, AND SOCIAL SYSTEMS

Until recently, almost all correctional programs for juveniles espoused treatment goals. Yet programs often have not attained their goals and have not even provided the rudiments of fair and humane custody. An important question is how this situation develops.

Programs for adjudicated delinquents come in many shapes and sizes. Indeed, there may be more variety in the juvenile correctional system than in the adult correctional system. The Michigan survey of juvenile corrections in the United States was able to uncover a number of patterns in the organization and delivery of services to juveniles. The survey discovered that three types of programs were the most common. In day programs, youths live at home and attend the program during the day or after school. In group homes, or halfway houses, youths are removed from the family setting to small (12- to 20-person) residential settings, often in their home communities. Training schools, or large congregate facilities, often secure, emphasize vocational training at sites often far removed from the home community.

In these programs, the following types of treatment objectives were the most frequent (Yarborough, 1976):

1. Skill development
2. Preparation for community transition
3. Enhancement of psychological states
4. Development/enhancement of problem-solving abilities
5. Behavioral change
6. Development of a conducive environment

The researchers found that type of treatment objective varied by type of program. In training schools, the most frequently sought objective was skill development. In day programs and group homes, the most frequently sought objective was behavioral change. He observed that by the time of the survey (1973), many practitioners in the juvenile system had given up the idea that training schools could change behavior. Too much evidence had accumulated that training schools did not accomplish that task. Why?

As long ago as the 1950s, a small number of juvenile correctional experts had observed that the organization of correctional services could reduce the likelihood that the goals of treatment would be reached. One of the more famous examples of a number of attempts to deal with that problem was the **Guided Group Interaction (GGI)** program. GGI was a particular application of group dynamics that involved using persons who shared a problem to help one another deal with the problem. Developed for treatment of veterans of World War II, GGI was first applied to juvenile delinquents in the Highfields program in New Jersey (Bixby and McCorkle, 1951; Weeks, 1958).

Highfields was a residential alternative to training school. The central component of the program was the frequent meeting of youth and staff in group sessions to discuss the behavior of program participants. During these discussions, the youths were systematically supported for socially desirable behaviors while the attractiveness of deviant behaviors was undermined. The group itself was given enormous power over its members, such as making decisions about which youth deserved home furloughs or were ready for release. But in addition, enormous peer pressure was placed upon each youth by holding the group responsible for the mistakes of its members. This was the type of program run by Wopat in the forestry camp when Phil made his visit.

The Highfields GGI program was replicated

in the Provo Experiment in Utah, with the exception that the Provo youth lived at home rather than in the program facility (Empey and Rabow, 1961). According to the program evaluators, the distinctive features of Provo, compared to traditional training school programs, were its attention to the testing of sociological theory in the implementation of the treatment program and the concentration on a program design that did not undermine the treatment goals of the program. To change delinquents, they proposed, the treatment program must work with, rather than ignore, the influence of the peer group. To do otherwise, they contended, led to two major problems found in many institutions for juveniles: (1) The ungoverned peer group would undo any advances made in individual therapy. (2) The peer group would rally against the staff, making youth inaccessible to staff influence.

To be sure, there are many difficulties with juvenile correctional programs other than those addressed by adherents of GGI. Moreover, there are many juveniles in trouble with the law who will not respond favorably to GGI interventions. However, the observations of the GGI proponents get at the heart of some major difficulties with correctional programs for juveniles. Many programs have been designed without any regard for a consistent and explicit theoretical framework in the first place. Consequently, many programs are simply odd collections of practice, without regard for whether the various elements fit together. One special aspect of this problem is the frequent lack of attention to how the program structure and environment affect the juveniles when "therapy" is not being conducted. Left to their own devices, the inmates in training schools will form informal social systems that reinforce commitment to delinquent norms and reduce the ability of staff to communicate with and control the youth who are ostensibly "being treated."

ORGANIZATIONAL STRUCTURE AND INMATE DYNAMICS

At this point, the classic study of this problem is still *Organization for Treatment* (Street, Vinter

and Perrow, 1966). This research examined six institutions that varied in program objectives. The institutions were arrayed on a treatment-custody continuum. Two institutions espoused obedience-conformity goals, two espoused goals of reformation-reeducation, and two had goals of treatment. The structure of each organization was related to the goals. The two custodial institutions employed large security staffs and small treatment staffs. The regime was harsh, and rules were strictly enforced. The youthful inmates were organized in paramilitary fashion, with emphasis upon enforced conformity. The two institutions with the middle-range goals of reeducation-reformation had fairly strict rules and regulations, but tempered these by sending the youth out to schools in the community and by stressing education rather than obedience. The staff were primarily teachers, interested in skill acquisition and in replicating a familylike environment. The treatment institutions had the most complex organizational structure, employing as many treatment experts as custodians, and expecting the treatment and custodial staff to cooperate in advancing the treatment plans for each youth. Emphasis was on understanding each inmate as an individual.

The researchers investigated the attitudes and behaviors of both staff and inmates in each type of institution. Predictably, they found that inmates in the obedience-conformity programs were most opposed to staff norms and values, least likely to trust or confide in staff, and most likely to adhere to antisocial inmate values. Youth in these programs valued toughness and shrewdness and victimized the weaker inmates. Inmates did not learn to obey, but to obey when watched, which was possible only sporadically. At the other extreme, youth in the treatment institutions were least likely to adopt antistaff norms, most likely to seek out and trust staff, and most concerned about working out their problems.

Staff attitudes and values paralleled those of the inmates in each case. Street, Vinter, and Perrow argued that while all the institutions claimed to act in the best interests of their wards, the way in which staff and services were organized had major effects on the probability that these interests could be reached. In a very real sense, *the way in which the program was organized was the treatment.*

Despite this early and provocative examination of the impact of adult organization on youthful attitude and behavior, most training schools in this country still approximate the custodial or obedience-conformity model in the delivery of services. This is the case even though the regimentation, deprivation, and harsh punishment may actually breed the very behavior the programs were mandated to change. According to Feld (1981), subcultures of violence emerge in juvenile institutions when the youth, borrowing on values from the street, seek to overcome the deprivations and stigma of harsh institutional regimes. Since there are usually more residents than staff, and always means for youth to hide from staff, the only way for staff to overcome this dynamic is for youth to trust the staff and inform on those who engage in violent behavior.

If the inmate subculture is strong, however, there will be strong and violent reprisals against any who are discovered confiding in or seeking the protection of staff. Traditional training school organization sets up a vicious cycle that staff simply cannot break. The more they try to control youth through sternness and manipulation of external rewards and punishments, the more alienated the youth become (Feld, 1981:358). Many staff do not recognize that it is their organization, rather than the nature of the youth, which has created this vicious cycle.

A number of studies support the basic propositions of the GGI experts, Street, Vinter, and Perrow, and Feld. For example, Ian Sinclair (1971, 1975) found that halfway houses for English youth had a major impact on their behavior. However, he found that whether that impact was positive or negative depended on the attitude of the staff. Both overly stern and overly permissive wardens were likely to produce high runaway and failure rates:

. . . it is difficult to combine warmth and willingness to discuss problems with strictness. . . . [A

program] must attempt to deal with the boys' underlying feelings and may, therefore, aim to encourage the expression of feelings. This is presumably easier in a permissive regime. On the other hand, a [program] must also try to satisfy the boys' need for security and limits. This may be more difficult in a permissive regime. (Sinclair, 1971:119)

Comparing inmate attitudes in day programs, group homes, and training schools, Yarborough (1976) found that the youth in group homes and day programs more frequently perceived the staff as working hard to implement treatment goals. In a related study, Vinter (1976) reported that even though most large training schools had the best educational facilities, compared to day programs and group homes, the youth in the secure training schools were universally the least satisfied with educational opportunities. Selo (1976) pointed out that the sterner control measures used in the larger training schools were associated with worse behavior than found in day programs and group homes.

Newcomb (1976) found that one reason large training schools often face the vicious cycle is that these larger institutions have larger proportions of youth facing longer stays and larger proportions of program "veterans." Long stays and concentrations of youth with long experience in programs are both associated with all youth in the institution reporting "hardened" antistaff, procriminal attitudes and behaviors. Bartollas and Sieverdes (1983) reported that sexual victims in youth institutions are not necessarily the smallest or weakest, but generally are those with long lengths of stay, records of running away, and poor, distrustful relationships with staff. In perhaps the most sophisticated analysis, Poole and Regoli (1983) reported that both pre-institution characteristics of youth and institution characteristics have some effect on the degree of violence in institutions. But they discovered that in the institutions with the most custodial orientation, many of the individual differences among inmates disappear as adherence to the inmate code becomes more widespread.

DEINSTITUTIONALIZATION

Like diversion, **deinstitutionalization** is a commonly used term with no commonly accepted definition. Klein's review (1979:150) insists on three related elements:

1. The removal of inmates from secure facilities at a greater rate than normal
2. Removal of inmates from secure detention at a greater than normal rate
3. Prevention of placement in such secure facilities of youths who traditionally would have been sent to them

Frequently, deinstitutionalization is used in a much broader and looser sense to refer to any programs of nonsecure care. The difficulty with this broad definition is that many community programs, such as probation, day programs, and aftercare supervision, do not reduce the use of institutions, but exist alongside them. Deinstitutionalization of juvenile offenders includes the use of these nonsecure community programs. But, as Klein correctly insists, officials cannot merely point to the existence of community programs as evidence that deinstitutionalization has taken place. The test is not the existence of nonsecure programs, but how frequently they are used, and for whom.

Based in large measure on evidence of the trouble with training schools, pressure for deinstitutionalization began in the late 1960s. Vinter, Downs, and Hall (1975) determined that the number of juveniles locked away in training schools did decline from 43,447 in 1969 to 28,001 in 1974. However, this drop did not convince them that deinstitutionalization was being given widespread or rapid adoption. For example, while the number incarcerated had gone down in 28 states, it had actually gone up in 22 (1975:13).

Another disquieting observation was that the decline in the incarceration of juveniles was uneven among types of facilities. Most of the drop occurred in publicly owned and run institutions. At the same time that state training schools were losing population, the population in private facilities was increasing at almost the same rate, "so it may be that juveniles are merely being recycled from public facilities to those under private auspice" (Sarri, 1981:35). A study of changes in institutionalization patterns in Minnesota suggests similar possibilities (Schwartz, Jackson-Beck, and Anderson, 1984). There, it was discovered that increasing numbers of youth are being incarcerated in mental health and chemical dependency institutions. The researchers suggested that reliance on traditional juvenile justice institutions may have been dropping, but that other institutions of social control were being utilized in their place.

Finally, Sarri argued that the distribution of youth to secure and nonsecure programs implied no consistent, theoretically guided policy of deinstitutionalization. Instead of reflecting the needs of youth, the relative emphasis on institutions and alternatives seemed to reflect political and organizational responses to environmental pressures (Sarri, 1981:36). The Michigan survey research team found that the factors best explaining deinstitutionalization rates were (1981:43):

- Level of political interest group activity in the state
- Social and economic heterogeneity of the state
- Degree of autonomy the juvenile corrections department had in making decisions
- Ideology and leadership of the agency director

In general

The more affluent and homogeneous a state's population, the more likely it was to retain and treat juvenile delinquents within their home communities. (1981:44)

CLOSING THE INSTITUTIONS IN MASSACHUSETTS

In 1968, the Commonwealth of Massachusetts had one of the oldest and most publicly criticized juvenile correctional systems in the country. The system handled 2,443 youths. More than 800 were locked in training schools, one of which was the oldest in the country. The remainder were out on parole. By 1974, the system handled 2,367 youths: 132 in secure facilities, 399 in group homes, 171 in foster homes, 724 in day programs, and 941 on parole. Massachusetts has succeeded in closing almost all its secure care beds and turning to many new forms of community programming, without widening the net and enlarging the capacity of the system (Coates, Miller, and Ohlin, 1978:30). The history of this rapid and massive transition is probably the best example of deinstitutionalization that we have.

Change began in 1969, when a series of scandals about the brutality and ineffectiveness of the training schools prompted the governor to reorganize the training schools into a new Department of Youth Services and seek an outsider to be its first commissioner. Neither the governor nor anyone in the legislature had a clear idea of what type of reform should take place. The situation had simply become so bad that both wanted a new commissioner to "do something" about the training schools.

The person selected for this post, Jerome Miller, was a relatively unknown professor of social work, who by his own admission had applied for the position on a whim. Miller had been very impressed with the work of psychiatrist Max Jones with therapeutic communities in mental hospitals. Miller's first attempt to do something with the training schools involved deregimentation, proscriptions against harsh punishments, and institution of therapeutic communities within the cottages of the training schools. In their first year, however, Miller and his new central office staff felt dissatisfied with the lack of progress. Miller eventually concluded that there was no lasting reform for the training schools because the political ties which maintained them and the staff and inmate behaviors (as described above) which made them violent and ineffective were simply too ingrained to be changed. Miller could make small improvements, but the basic vicious cycle of the training schools could not be broken through incremental, internal reforms.

During this frustrating attempt to improve the schools, another incident of brutality broke out at one of the worst of them. Riding a wave of public sentiment against such incidents, Miller and his staff decided to close the institution. They were surprised at how easily this was done and at how little opposition occurred. This accidental discovery, coupled with increased frustration at attempts to reform the institutions, led within a few months to a secret decision to close all the institutions.

Miller correctly perceived that any prolonged planning of this action would undermine it entirely. Instead, he moved swiftly while the legislature was out of session. As many youths as possible were paroled. The remaining youths were simply driven off to the University of Massachusetts campus in a cavalcade of cars. Over a semester break, the youths were each assigned to live with a volunteer college student until other arrangements could be made. The struggle to design and establish the community programs that would become the heart of the Massachusetts juvenile correctional system began *after* the institutions were emptied.

Many correctional experts would certainly have thought this was the wrong way to do anything. To be sure, Miller had and still has critics, who are quick to point out the havoc he caused for both staff and youth as a new system was developed. But it may not be backwards, if the goal is deinstitutionalization. Miller had become convinced that institutions were irredeemable and that they were inevitably damaging to kids. His staff were fond of saying that no matter what we do, we can't do worse (than the training schools). He was also convinced that the only way to deinstitutionalize (in Klein's sense of the term) was to do so quickly, forcing communities to adopt new programs in order to deal with the crisis of unsupervised youth.

Is Miller's approach a formula for closing training schools? It is highly unlikely that the strategy used in Massachusetts could be replicated. The events there have changed the rest of the country—no other state is likely to be caught off guard to the same degree. Moreover, it would be incorrect to say that Miller had a strategy. He had a set of commitments, particularly to youth, and an idiosyncratic operating style—but the closing of the institutions was not planned from the outset. The opportunity arose, and was consistent with Miller's goals (Stolz, 1984). The important point is that deinstitutionalization probably *does require* some set of actions equal in scope and spirit to those taken in Massachusetts.

What has happened since the initial closing in 1974? There have been a number of pressures since for reinstitutionalization, but so far these have been successfully resisted by the department (Calhoun and Wayne, 1981). Not all youths have left secure care. The Worcester Secure Treatment Program, a prison for youth, remains (Vogel and Thibault, 1981). However, the department has been able to keep the group in secure care limited to about 10 percent of youths in the system.

The Harvard evaluation team points out that not all the new programs provide a great deal of contact between their residents and the community. Many youths in the system live under conditions of relative isolation, although in programs smaller and less violent than the old training schools (Coates, Miller and Ohlin, 1978:176). While reductions in recidivism compared to the training school system are were expected, they did not occur statewide (1978:177). However, the region which was most successful in setting up a diverse set of community programs had the lowest recidivism rates.

DEINSTITUTIONALIZATION ELSEWHERE

Klein (1979:151) suggested that other than Massachusetts, the best examples of deinstitutionalization are the California **Community Treatment Project (CTP)** and the Deinstitutionalization of Status Offenders program funded in 1976 by the Office of Juvenile Justice and Delinquency Prevention. General difficulties with programs for status offenders have been discussed above. Problems with the California Community Treatment Program (CTP) were somewhat different.

CTP was technically an early parole program. Youth received at the California Youth Authority reception center were released to parole immediately after diagnosis and screening, without spending the usual nine months in training school first. The CTP program included classification of youth on the basis of interpersonal maturity level. Youths were assigned to parole officers, who were trained to interact differently with the youths, depending upon their maturity level classification. The CTP was highly regarded by the President's Commission on Law Enforcement and Administration of Justice, which held the program up as a prime example of innovative community programming. A later evaluation (Lerman, 1975) found that although youth in CTP were revoked less frequently than youth in control groups, the arrest rates for the two groups were the same.

Lerman claimed that the Youth Authority had changed the decisions made about youth rather than their behavior. He also suggested that the unplanned extension of the parole period for the CTP youth actually wiped out the planned financial savings from the reduced incarceration. Finally, Lerman argued that CTP parole officers relied very heavily upon frequent but short detention periods for misbehaving youth, rather than seeking revocations. He criticized this practice as arbitrary and dishonestly rationalized as part of the treatment regime.

Summarizing the problems with CTP and another California program, Lerman made the point that deinstitutionalization in Klein's sense is probably impossible if the program focuses on only one decision point in the system. If attention to restricting use of institutions is narrow, then discretionary decisions in the system will lead to increases in the use of institutions elsewhere (1975:209).

The conclusions of the Michigan research team would tend to support Lerman. Vinter, Downs, and Hall (1975) found that community programs generally supplemented rather than supplanted use of institutions. States with a large proportion of youth in community programs by and large still retained a significant number of youth in institutions. When states added new program elements, they tended to expand their client base, rather than use the new programs for the traditional clients.

THE VARIETY OF COMMUNITY PROGRAMS

Whether or not deinstitutionalization is actually taking place, the number and type of community programs have increased. Some of these programs operate in conjunction with probation, some operate after institutionalization, and some stand by themselves.

AFTERCARE

The juvenile justice equivalent of parole is typically called **aftercare,** a term borrowed from the language for medical care after hospitalization. The supervision strategies for juveniles on aftercare status are not very different than those used in adult parole, but there are legal and organi-

zational differences. Most release decisions in adult correctional systems are made by an autonomous parole board. Typically, this is not the case in juvenile systems. The decision of when to release a juvenile from training school is usually made by the school officials. Additionally, most juveniles serve indeterminant sentences without minimum terms (a situation that is now changing). Consequently, institutional officials often have vast discretion about when to release.

A second difference often found between adult parole and juvenile aftercare is that juveniles on aftercare are supervised by probation officers, rather than by a separate parole supervision agency. Several observers have criticized this practice on the grounds that there is a lack of continuity between the aftercare work and the institutional program, if only because the institutional workers are often within a state agency and the aftercare workers are often attached to the local family court (Carey and McAnany, 1984; McCord, 1974).

In some jurisdictions, attempts have been

The probation officer supervising juveniles spends a large amount of time communicating with others in the community about the children on her caseload. (David E. Duffee)

made in the last ten years to improve coordination between institutional and after care programs. For example, in New York, the State Division for Youth, which has responsibility for the institutions, devised Youth Service Teams that follow an individual from commitment through aftercare. Team members are supposed to work with institutional counselors and local probation departments to ensure that supervision is consistent. In Philadelphia Family Court, a special program was set up in 1973 which assigned a youth to a probation officer at the time of commitment to a state institution. The officer was responsible for maintaining some contact with the youth during the training school stay and then picking up supervision upon the release of the youth back to Philadelphia (McCord, 1974).

GROUP HOMES

Group homes for delinquents are similar in many respects to halfway houses for adults, although many group homes are used as alternatives to training school (halfway in) rather than as transition programs (halfway out). Group homes are not new. One of the more famous examples, the probation hostels in Great Britain, have roots in the London Police Court Mission programs that existed before 1907. In 1927, the hostels were established nationwide as an alternative for youth whose delinquency was diagnosed as stemming from environmental pressure rather than psychological problems (Sinclair, 1971).

Unlike many halfway houses for adults, many group homes for juveniles purposefully attempt to replicate a family atmosphere. The probation hostels in England and a number of the group homes in Massachusetts utilize live-in house parents and attempt to keep numbers small. Sinclair's research revealed that this family model has advantages and disadvantages. The youth and the house parents often do establish the same warm and intense ties that one would hope to find in families. But Sinclair found that house parents were often under prolonged stress, with too little support from other staff.

WILDERNESS PROGRAMS

One of the more recent additions to juvenile non-residential programming has been Outward Bound and similar wilderness experience programs. Outward Bound originated as a means of preparing English sailors in World War II for survival in the North Atlantic. Since then the program has been applied to a number of different groups, principally under the assumption that survival training will improve self-reliance and self-image. While Outward Bound has recently been touted as an effective alternative to institutions for juvenile delinquents, evaluations of its impact show quite ambiguous results. A recent review finds that about half the evaluations show positive results and about half show the opposite. In addition, most research shows that positive effects of a wilderness program diminish over time, and that none of the programs operate on a consistent theoretical model of which juveniles will benefit or how the benefit works (Winterdyk and Griffiths, 1984).

RESTITUTION

Restitution programs have also become extremely popular, and are often touted as deinstitutionalization programs. Most research suggests that in reality restitution programs are reserved for minor offenders. Restitution can operate as an add on to probation, or by itself. Some research indicates that restitution is most effective in reducing return to family court when it is the sole sanction (Schneider and Schneider, 1985; Schneider, Griffiths and Schneider, 1982).

Some important ethical and legal issues with juvenile restitution do not apply when restitution is ordered for adults. First, it is questionable whether juveniles under 16 can be ordered to make financial restitution, or ordered to work. Second, it is not known how often the parents of a youth ordered to pay restitution are actually the parties paying off the order. Third, youth are often far more limited in their financial resources and job opportunities than adults, making the level of restitution limited.

COMMUNITY SERVICE ORDERS

One common substitute for restitution is community service. Any number of communities have established community service programs for juveniles. Many of these are based on the Earn-It program in Quincy, Massachusetts. Like restitution, community service may be ordered as part of probation, or may be a sole sanction. Research in Canada and England suggests that community service is seen as a fair and appropriate sanction by youth, parents, and work supervisors. There is some evidence that community service works better with first offenders than repeat offenders (Doob and MacFarlane, 1984), a finding that would not recommend it as an alternative to training schools.

GETTING TOUGH

Beginning in the early 1980s, a number of states have moved toward more stringent measures to deal with juvenile offenders. The get tough trend sounds like the death knell for the *parens patriae/* rehabilitative era. Proponents of stiffer, more determinant sentences for youth are extolling the social benefits of retribution and deterrence rather than those of rehabilitation.

A number of factors have contributed to this trend. Oddly enough, many of them also contributed to efforts to reduce incarceration. For example, Singer (1985) lists eight contributory factors:

- Supreme Court rulings on procedural unfairness in the *parens patriae* justifications of juvenile corrections
- The backlog of cases facing the family court, and the lack of resources to deal with them
- The presumption that rehabilitation does not work
- The discovery that a few juveniles are responsible for many offenses
- The rise in the popularity of deterrence and

- the reduction in a concern for labeling effects
- The increase in the concern for retribution
- The increase in the fear of crime and concern for victims
- A reported increase in the severity and violence of crimes committed by juveniles

The National Advisory Committee on Juvenile Justice Standards and Goals (1976), the Juvenile Justice Standards project of the Institute of Judicial Administration-American Bar Association Joint Commission (1977), and the Twentieth Century Fund Task Force on Youth Crime (1978) all recommended consideration of the seriousness of the offense and the prior record of juveniles when judges were making disposition decisions.

The attempt to get tough with juvenile offenders has taken different forms. In the state of Washington, the entire juvenile code was revised. Family court jurisdiction over status offenders was dropped, and a determinant sentencing scheme was devised based on offense and prior record. The new code explicitly stated that the primary aim of the law was protection of the community through increased incarceration—not the welfare of the juvenile (McGarrell, 1986). New Jersey has taken a similar approach, increasing the severity of punishment and providing for more secure juvenile facilities (Singer, 1985). Illinois, like a number of other states, has provided for the automatic transfer to adult court of juveniles accused of serious felonies. Juveniles convicted of these crimes in adult criminal court will be housed in juvenile institutions until they reach adulthood (Illinois Revised Statutes Annotated, Chapter 37, Section 702–707, 16a, 1983).

In New York, both approaches have been taken, providing for one of the sternest approaches to juvenile crime in the country. In 1976 the Juvenile Reform Act mandated secure care placements for juveniles adjudicated of specified crimes, sending the Division for Youth scurrying to create more secure beds. Two years later, the Juvenile Offender Law required that juveniles accused of certain violent crimes would automatically be tried as adults. Prior to 1976, the maximum sentence for any juvenile was 18 months, renewable in additional 18-month periods until the youth reached age 21. Now juveniles convicted of murder, for example, may spend many years in prison. In the first six years of the Juvenile Offender Law, adult prosecutions of juveniles have been initiated sparingly. Evidence suggests that after an initial flurry of stiff sentences, the probability and length of incarceration has gone down, and that an increasing number of youths eligible for prosecution as adults are being waived down to family court (Singer, 1985).

In a lengthy article reviewing all aspects of juvenile justice in Minnesota, Barry Feld (1984) makes the argument that the entire juvenile justice process, not just sentencing, is becoming tougher. He argues that under recent Minnesota code revisions, juveniles are treated more stringently than adults. The state has adopted concerns for retribution and deterrence, but has retained juvenile system lack of procedural safeguards, which used to be justified on the basis of rehabilitative intent.

It is premature to assess the impacts of the get tough movement on juvenile corrections. One could hypothesize that this conservative trend will not go as far toward implementation of retribution and deterrence goals as its proponents would hope, just the way diversion and deinstitutionalization did not go as far in the other direction as its champions had desired. However, it would also appear that juveniles caught up in the correctional system continue to suffer the ambivalences always evident in systems for correction of juveniles—the tension between correctional action without concern for guilt and responsibility and punitive action concerned with just deserts and community protection.

SUMMARY

1. The juvenile correctional system began with the establishment of houses of refuge in 1824.
2. The legal justification for state intervention in the lives of juveniles was the *parens patriae* doctrine.
3. Reform schools or training schools were devised in the mid-nineteenth century and became the predominant placement for delinquents.
4. The family court, first established in Chicago in 1899, centralized all family and juvenile matters, in the hope that effectiveness and efficiency would increase. The rise of the family court included the ascendancy of professional probation work.
5. Attack on the *parens patriae* doctrine and on the rehabilitative ideal in family court began with the Kent and Gault decisions, providing greater due process in the adjudication of delinquency. Since then, the juvenile justice process has increasingly resembled the adult criminal process.
6. The juvenile court process has three major decision points: intake, adjudication, and disposition hearings.
7. In the 1970s, the federal government led a drive to separate status offenders from delinquents.

8. Diversion is a process of turning away from traditional processing. Much diversion has focused on status offenders, but it applies to delinquents as well. Diversion programs in practice have often led to widening the net of social control rather than reducing the number of persons in the normal process.
9. Juveniles may be detained pending adjudication if determined to be dangerous to themselves or others or predicted likely to flee rather than appear for adjudication. Many states have established separate detention facilities for youth.
10. Most programs for juveniles fall into three broad categories: training schools, group homes, and day programs. States vary tremendously in their preferences for secure rather than nonsecure care.
11. Much evidence supports the proposition that the more custodial the institution, the more violent the youth subculture and the less able the staff is to control the youth.
12. Deinstitutionalization is the process of reducing reliance on secure care. Massachusetts provides the best example of this process.

13. In recent years, many states have decided to make the juvenile system harsher, giving up rehabilitative intent for greater security and longer sentences. Getting tough is accomplished by tightening up juvenile disposition law and facilities for juveniles, by transferring the jurisdiction of violent juvenile offenders to adult court, or both.

KEY WORDS

ADJUDICATORY HEARING. The fact-finding hearing in juvenile court proceedings.

AFTERCARE. Supervision of juveniles after they have served a period in an institution, group home, or day program.

COMMUNITY TREATMENT PROJECT. Famous California Youth Authority program which released selected juveniles to aftercare immediately after reception. The project included use of classification by interpersonal maturity level and differential treatment based on classification.

DAY PROGRAMS. Any of a variety of programs entailing daily but nonresidential supervision of offenders.

DEINSTITUTIONALIZATION. Process of removing offenders from secure settings at quicker than normal rates and preventing new cases from being assigned to secure care.

DEPENDENCY. Status of a youth who has no parent or guardian or whose parent or guardian is unable to provide care and supervision.

DETENTION (of juveniles). The act of placing a juvenile in custody (usually secure care) pending adjudication.

DISPOSITION. Hearing in juvenile or family court following adjudication and concerned with placement of persons found to be delinquent or in need of supervision.

DIVERSION. Process of turning away offenders from the traditional correctional process.

GROUP HOMES. Halfway houses for juveniles.

GUIDED GROUP INTERACTION. Group dynamics based treatment used to change behavior by changing group commitments; used in Highfields and Provo experiments.

HOUSE OF REFUGE. Workhouses established in 1824 as a way of separating juveniles from adults in the correctional process.

INFORMAL PROBATION. Process of supervising a consenting offender on probation without adjudication or conviction.

NEGLECT. Status of juveniles whose parents or guardian have caused harm directly or have failed to provide supervision and care.

PARENS PATRIAE DOCTRINE. The legal doctrine providing the state with jurisdiction over the welfare of juveniles and other categories of people who presumably cannot care for themselves.

STATUS OFFENDERS. Juvenile offenders who have not broken the penal law, but have violated norms of control such as by running away or by being truant.

TRAINING SCHOOLS. Devised in the mid-nineteenth century, the most common form of institution for delinquents. Usually secure, and usually stressing skill training.

PROJECTS AND QUESTIONS

1. Juvenile corrections evolved rather slowly from 1824 through 1967, but has since then seen two major policy shifts in fifteen years. Why would such rapid, contradictory fluctuation occur now?
2. Find out if your state has recently imposed harsher sanctions on violent juvenile offenders or is considering doing so. What are the specific arguments for the change? What are the arguments against the change? What are the provisions in your state for waiving juveniles up to adult criminal court? Is such waiver available at all? If so, for what crimes?
3. Find out if there is a diversion program in use by the local family court. Invite a diversion program administrator to class to discuss the program. What procedures are used to determine who will be eligible for the program? What criteria are used to identify these people? Do the criteria ensure that program subjects are indeed being turned away from the traditional process?

ADDITIONAL READING

Robert Coates, Alden Miller, and Lloyd Ohlin. *Diversity in a Youth Correctional System*. Cambridge, MA: Ballinger, 1978. One of five books in the Harvard evaluation of the closing of institutions in Massachusetts, this book concentrates on the range of programs established after the change.

Charles Murray and Louis Cox. *Beyond Probation: Juvenile Corrections and the Chronic Delinquent*. Beverly Hills, CA: Sage Publications, 1979. This controversial study argues that more severe interventions, such as incarceration, are more effective than probation in reducing juvenile crime.

Robert Vinter (Ed.). *Time Out: A National Study of Juvenile Correctional Programs*. Ann Arbor, MI: School of Social Work, University of Michigan, 1976. This is the summary report of the national survey of juvenile corrections.

THREE RESOURCE ISSUES: COSTS, PRIVATIZATION, PERSONNEL

QUESTIONS

1. What are some of the problems encountered in determining correctional costs?

2. What has happened to correctional costs in the last ten years?

3. What are some of the proposals for reducing or controlling costs?

4. Is private involvement in corrections new?

5. Why is privatization controversial?

6. What types of correctional systems have the greatest private involvement?

7. What are the arguments for and against increased privatization?

8. Is the correctional work force expanding? What kinds of correctional jobs appear to be needed?

9. What are the problems with the employment of ex-offenders in correctional agencies?

10. What do we know about correctional volunteers?

THE COST TO WHOM?

Phil's team was completing the second year of the Jefferson prerelease center project. Standard contract procedure required the submission of a preliminary report to the Department of Correction. The department then had 90 days to respond to the findings. The departmental response had just come in the mail. One major focus of the research had been a cost-benefit analysis: The object was to weigh the relative advantage of transferring inmates to the centers rather than continuing their incarceration. Most of the department's objections focused on these findings.

"Their research guy argues that we seriously underestimated the cost of running the centers," said Irv. "I think it boils down to their not wanting the prisons to look so bad. They say the way we allocated costs is unfair."

"How can a cost be unfair?" asked Phil.

"Easy. It isn't the numbers that are unfair; it's the way we distributed the cost between centers and prison units. They want us to reallocate the central office overhead cost to make it look like the centers cost more and the prisons cost less."

"I don't understand," said Phil.

"Simple. The CO helps to manage both the prisons and the centers, right? And someone has to decide how to divide the central office cost up between prison operations and center operation. There's no right answer to that. It's a political argument, not a numbers game—unless we could stand behind each of the central office planners all day and count each minute of their work. We said the overhead cost should be allocated by the proportion of offenders in the parts of the system. Centers got 4 percent of the inmates, so charge them 4 percent of the overhead cost. This department guy is saying no—since the centers are new and have political problems, he wants to charge them 15 percent of the central office budget. Also, he wants to charge them 10 percent of every prison counselor salary because the counselors are involved in the center screening process. What he's trying to do is reduce the cost-benefit advantage of using the centers. He wants to say that in reality they are more expensive than the prisons."

"I see," said Phil. "In other words, he's trying to balance the lower recidivism rate at the centers with higher cost. That way he can say that the two types of facilities really give us equal benefit."

"That's it. For example, he's charging the cost of this evaluation contract to the centers, even though the Bureau didn't pay for it. But then he won't accept the taxes paid by the center residents as reduced cost, because that tax money doesn't come back to the department. Also, we said the room charges for the residents was a savings. He says that room money goes to the state general account, not the department."

"But those are costs savings to the state even if the department doesn't benefit. And if he charges this evaluation contract, then he has to add up all the contracts for prison research, doesn't he?"

"Sure, if he wants to be consistent. Moreover, look at this. The rent for each of the centers is considered a cost. Fair?" Phil nodded. "Well, I argued that to be really fair, you had to consider the opportunity cost for each of the prisons."

"The what?"

"Opportunity cost. What you give up to get something else. The state doesn't pay for the land the prisons are on. But you have to decide what it costs the state or the towns to devote that land to prisons. If the towns had industry on that land, they'd get taxes for it. So I figured the opportunity cost for each prison as the average tax value of the property. He won't buy that."

"It makes sense to me."

"Sure. But it isn't just cost that is involved here. It's cost to whom. I was calculating costs and benefits to society—since the reduction of recidivism is a benefit to society. He wants costs to the department, because that's all the department cares about *in this instance*. It depends on who they are trying to impress at the time. Right now the centers make the prisons look bad, so they want to manipulate the cost to make the prisons look good. Ten years from now, if the prisons are popular and the centers are in trouble, they'll grab at all sorts of costs going the other way."

THE COST OF CORRECTIONS*

Approximately 23.3 percent of all criminal justice and civil justice spending by government in 1981 was for corrections (BJS, 1983b:89). This may seem a relatively small amount when one considers that less than 3 percent of all government spending in 1981 was for civil and criminal justice (1983b:99). However, corrections expenditures in 1981 totaled over $7.9 billion (McGarrell and Flanagan, 1985:2).

The corrections field tends to be labor-intensive. Salaries constitute 71 percent of all corrections expenditures (BJS, 1983b:95). Corrections salaries are among the lowest in the field of criminal justice; police officers are often paid more.

In addition to salaries, costs include expenditures for the building and maintenance of facilities, medical care and treatment programs, food, guard and prisoner uniforms, and boarding out of some inmates (October 1983:95). Most of these costs are for the operation of jails, prisons, and other incarcerative facilities. Probation and parole do not involve many of these nonsalary

---

* The cost sections were co-authored by Shelley L. Kath.

---

costs. Table 20.1 demonstrates the relative costs of different types of correctional supervision in 1983. Incarceration in federal and state prisons is the most expensive type of punishment. Incarceration in community-based facilities and jails is the next most expensive, and supervision on probation and parole is the least expensive.

Since correctional systems are organized by level of government, it is useful to consider the proportions of total corrections expenditures for which federal, state, and local governments are responsible. In 1981, state governments spent nearly $5.2 billion on corrections, 66 percent of the nation's total corrections expenditure (McGarrell and Flanagan, 1985:2). Local governments accounted for 34 percent of spending. Slightly over $2 billion was spent by counties and about $602 million was spent by cities and towns (1985:2). The level of government responsible for the smallest proportion of all corrections expenditures was the federal government, which spent only $436 million, or about 0.5 percent of the total (1985:4). Corrections is more often than not a state responsibility.

As we will see, these national figures on expenditure are rather imcomplete. They reflect only direct expenditures for operations and cap-

---

TABLE 20.1   Comparisons of Average Annual Costs for One Adult Offender in Different Correctional Programs

SETTING	ANNUAL COST
Federal prison	$13,000
State prison	23,000–5,000[a]
State halfway house	12,000
Local residential facility	8,000
Local jail	8,000
Federal probation or parole	1,300
Nonfederal probation or parole	1,700–220[b]

[a] The cost of incarceration in a state prison varies tremendously due to a number of economic factors and the degree of urbanization (BJS, October 1983:97).

[b] The cost of probation and parole supervision varies widely, based on economic factors in the state, the level of government running the program, and the level of supervision or services provided.

SOURCE: Data excerpted from Bureau of Justice Statistics, *Report to the Nation on Crime and Justice: The Data.* Washington, DC: Bureau of Justice Statistics, October 1983, p. 92.

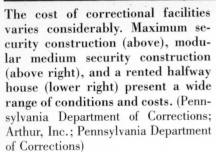

The cost of correctional facilities varies considerably. Maximum security construction (above), modular medium security construction (above right), and a rented halfway house (lower right) present a wide range of conditions and costs. (Pennsylvania Department of Corrections; Arthur, Inc.; Pennsylvania Department of Corrections)

ital outlays and "intergovernmental transfers," or payments from one level of government to another for fiscal assistance or services (McGarrell and Flanagan, 1985:718). By far the most common expenses are for direct operations. Other types of expenses for corrections will be considered in the section on accounting problems.

Data on the amount of expenditures for various types of punishment are relatively scarce. Spending information for 1979 showed that 74 percent of all state corrections monies went into construction, operation, and upkeep of facilities; 12 percent went to probation, parole, and pardon programs; and 14 percent went to other types of correctional facilities (BJS, October 1979:89). Data for 1981 showed that 80 percent of all direct expenditures by state was for correctional institutions, while noninstitutional activities accounted for the remainder (McGarrell and Flanagan, 1985:22). From either set of data, the allocation for different types of institutions cannot be determined. It has been reported that $2.7 billion was spent by all governments for jails in 1983 (BJS, 1984a:10). Operating costs for jails ($2.1 billion) far outweighed capital costs ($580 million). Expenditures for public and private ju-

TABLE 20.2 Direct Current Expenditures per Inmate in State Prisons by State, Fiscal 1977

RANK	STATE		RANK	STATE	
1	Texas	$2,241	26	West Virginia	$6,305
2	Georgia	2,467	27	Indiana	6,350
3	South Carolina	2,475	28	Wisconsin	6,366
4	Arkansas	3,088	29	Utah	6,990
5	Missouri	3,326	30	Wyoming	7,008
6	New Mexico	3,606	31	Delaware	7,221
7	South Dakota	3,609	32	Vermont	7,382
8	Alabama	3,649	33	Colorado	7,528
9	North Carolina	3,767	34	Maine	7,676
10	Oklahoma	3,772	35	New Jersey	7,943
11	Kentucky	3,818	36	California	8,173
12	Arizona	4,011	37	Iowa	8,305
13	Florida	4,205	38	Connecticut	8,962
14	Louisiana	4,270	39	North Dakota	9,032
15	Ohio	4,585	40	Pennsylvania	9,439
16	Oregon	4,953	41	New York	9,445
17	Michigan	4,990	42	Washington	10,030
18	Idaho	5,369	43	Montana	10,303
19	Virginia	5,434	44	Rhode Island	11,194
20	Nevada	5,651	45	Minnesota	11,852
21	Tennessee	5,815	46	Kansas	12,153
22	Illinois	5,841	47	Hawaii	13,943
23	Nebraska	5,869	48	Alaska	14,071
24	Mississippi	6,036	49	Massachusetts	14,442
25	Maryland	6,208	50	New Hampshire	15,946

SOURCE: Joan Mullen, *American Prisons and Jails, Vol. I: Summary and Policy Implications of a National Survey.* Washington, DC: United States Department of Justice, 1980, p. 67.

venile custody facilities in 1982 were $1.14 and $718 million, respectively (McGarrell and Flanagan, 1985:100, 103). The states vary considerably in their correctional investments. Table 20.2 shows the variation in cost per inmate, based on the 1978 census by Abt Associates.

COST TRENDS

If trends toward increased use of punishment continue, especially increased use of imprisonment, we would expect a rise in the cost of corrections. Because resources over any period of time are finite, absolute increases in spending on correc-

tions will make it necessary to allocate a greater proportion of our nation's fiscal resources to corrections. The dilemma might be summed up in the following question: If the number of people to be punished kept increasing, at what point would we decide that the costs of punishment were too high, given the need to use resources on other public goods? The need versus cost problem was already evident to some degree in the 1982 Gallup Poll about corrections policy. Of those polled, 57 percent answered Yes to the question of whether their state needed more prisons, while 30 perent said No and 13 percent said they did not know. But only 49 percent said they would be willing to pay more taxes to help build prisons, while 44 percent said No and 7 percent had no opinion (McGarrell and Flanagan, 1985:238–239).

The recently passed Omnibus Crime Package appears to provide for an increase in funds that will be needed to implement some "get tough" provsions, both at the federal and state levels. The package provides for the creation of a Bureau of Criminal Justice Facilities that will be able to extend federal grants to the states for the construction and modification of prisons (Bergman, 1985:1,12). Such an action seems to demonstrate a certain level of commitment by the federal government to the allocation of more resources for punishment.

Although the percentage of government expenditures we currently spend on corrections is low (0.7 percent), compared to other areas (16 percent for national defense, 14 percent for public education, 3 percent for hospitals, and 1.4 percent for health) (BJS, October 1983:99), it is clear that real tradeoffs are involved between correctional spending and spending on other government activities.

Such tradeoffs are not always considered. Mullen observed that debate on sentencing " . . . often proceeds as though incarceration was a free service or as though the only costs incurred

were those paid for by the state for room, board and custody" (1980:135). The Abt report strongly recommended viewing incarceration as an "exchangable commodity," so that the public would recognize the social costs involved (1980:125). The Abt researchers recommended that we develop ways of linking decisions about resource allocations to an "explicit public process" for determining how heavily crimes should be punished when both budget limitations and moral standards are considered (1980:125). We will come back to this issue when discussing possible controls on expenditures.

At the moment, it appears that corrections is a growth industry. Between 1960 and 1980, corrections costs rose 115 percent, compared to a 69 percent increase for police in the same period (BJS, October 1983:100). Table 20.3 shows the pattern of increase in direct expenditure for justice activities from 1976 to 1985. From 1979 to 1985, across all governments, correctional activity has shown the greatest increase.

Corrections has continued to be the fastest rising criminal justice expenditure. Correctional direct expenditure was up 15.1 percent in 1983 compared to 1982, the greatest increase in the three criminal justice areas. Between 1980 and

TABLE 20.3   Percent Change in Direct Expenditure for Justice Activity, by Activity and Level of Government, 1976–1985 and 1979–1985

LEVEL OF GOVERNMENT	TOTAL	POLICE PROTECTION	JUDICIAL (courts only)	PROSECUTION AND LEGAL SERVICES	PUBLIC DEFENSE	CORRECTIONS
All governments	132%	100%	138%	209%	219%	197%
Federal	132	85	288	295	231	176
State	182	90	263	212	297	227
Total local	110	108	73	155	175	157
All governments	75	58	71	96	77	116
Federal	68	45	131	122	43	100
State	98	62	77	79	136	129
Total local	66	62	55	74	81	97

SOURCE: Bureau of Justice Statistics, "Justice Expenditure and Employment, 1985." Washington, DC: United States Department of Justice, March 1987, p. 4.

1983 alone, direct costs for institutions and community corrections was up 50.9 percent (*New York Times*, July 14, 1986). State correctional direct expenditures for 1984 increased $1.2 billion over 1983, and an additional $1.2 billion in construction bonds were sold (BJS, April 1985:4)

Analysis in individual states indicates that these costs are rising faster than inmate population increases. Examining New York costs, for example, McDonald found that the state prison population increased 60 percent between 1971 and 1978, while the cost increase was 200 percent. In New York City alone, cost increased 106 percent in this period, while the city jail population actually declined (1980:3).

ACCOUNTING PROBLEMS

INCOMPLETE REPORTING

The usual reports of correctional costs are surprisingly incomplete. For example, McDonald discovered that the New York City Department of Correction report reflected only 64 percent of actual jail costs for the city in 1977–78, and that the state Department of Correctional Services annual report included only 77 percent of actual prison costs (1980:2). This incompleteness is not limited to New York reporting practices. The Minnesota Citizen's Council on Criminal Justice (1983:2) had similar complaints. The council found that when it recalculated the average daily cost per inmate on the basis of direct operating and construction cost, indirect cost, and financing charges, the final figure was twice that reported by the Department of Corrections! The council also complained that the advertised costs for new construction typically ignored the ultimate costs to taxpayers, since only principal charges were usually reported, not interest. Even the costs as recalculated by the council were underestimates, since cost of land acquisition, costs of lost taxes on land, welfare payments to the families of prisoners, loss of income tax from inmates, loss of the value of community service

and restitution, while *all* legitimately considered part of incarceration expense, are simply not available (1983:2).

THE COMPONENTS OF COST

Let us follow the Minnesota Citizen Council's recalculations as a means of understanding the complexity of correctional cost estimates. Figure 20.1 provides an overview.

Direct costs include salaries and fringe benefits, educational and vocational programs, supplies, health care, equipment and expenses, the cost of contracts, and any other costs for direct operations. **Indirect costs** include expenses for operating the central office, and costs incurred by other state departments for activities to support the prison system. Additional indirect costs in Minnesota included institutional improvements and repairs. The council's figures on expenses from other state agencies—expenses rarely reported in calculating the cost of punishment—are provided in Table 20.4. The addition of these items to the reported cost increased the annual cost from $2,853 to $4,917, a substantial jump. Finally, when the council estimated construction and financing costs for different size facilities, and calculated the annual inmate share of that expense, another $4,738 in annual costs appeared. Table 20.5 provides the original department cost report and the recalculation.

COST CONTROL

As is implied in the discussion of correctional cost accounting, many groups believe that one first step in cost containment is simply a more complete picture of costs in annual reports from various correctional departments (McDonald, 1980:9). Another accounting problem is the difficulty in obtaining a picture of **unit costs** (Culbertson, 1986; McDonald, 1980). That is, correctional departments rarely calculate the costs for specific services for a standard number of offenders. To understand the breakdown of var-

FIGURE 20.1   Cost Formula

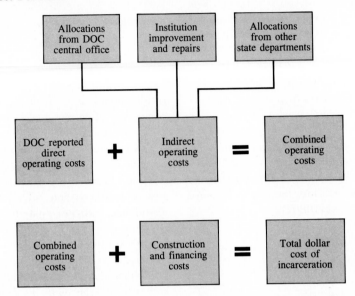

SOURCE: Minnesota Citizens Council on Crime and Justice, *Adult Incarceration: The Cost to Minnesota Taxpayers*. Minneapolis: Minnesota Citizens Council on Crime and Justice, 1983, p. 10. Reprinted with permission.

ious aspects of punishment, it could be useful to know the cost per presentence investigation versus the cost per 100 minimum-risk probationers supervised, or the cost of intensive supervision for one year per client versus the cost of one year of minimuum security incarceration. Cost can be controlled only if cost is known, and presented in comparable units.

Another problem with correctional cost control is that evaluation and accounting are made

TABLE 20.4   1982 Statewide Indirect Cost Billing, Minnesota Department of Corrections

Central mail	$ 1,839
Lease administration	10,305
Procurement	50,135
Telecommunications	71,065
Central payroll	55,358
Financial management	67,997
Statewide accounting	53,149
Personnel	147,768
Treasurer	2,997
Subtotal	460,612
ISB Credit	−11,843
Total	$448,769

SOURCE: Minnesota Citizens Council on Crime and Justice, *Adult Incarceration, The Cost to Minnesota Taxpayers*. Minneapolis: Minnesota Citizens Council on Crime and Justice, 1983, p. 9. Reprinted with permission.

TABLE 20.5   1982 Average Total Daily Annual Cost per Inmate at Minnesota State Adult Correctional Institutions

MINNESOTA CORRECTIONAL INSTITUTION AT	COMBINED OPERATING COST	CONSTRUCTION & FINANCING	TOTAL DAILY COST/INMATE	TOTAL ANNUAL COST/INMATE	*vs.* DOC REPORTED COST/INMATE
Lino Lakes	$78	$25	$103	$37,595	$22,783
Oak Park Heights	$94	$25	$119	$43,435	$26,539
St. Cloud	$57	$25	$ 82	$29,930	$16,819
Shakopee	$85	$41	$126	$45,990	$25,722
Stillwater	$45	$25	$ 70	$25,550	$12,735

SOURCE: Minnesota Citizens Council on Crime and Justice, *Adult Incarceration, the Cost to Minnesota Taxpayers*. Minneapolis: Minnesota Citizens Council on Crime and Justice, 1983, p. 7. Reprinted with permission.

difficult by the dispersion of cost across multiple agencies of government. For example, in his study of costs in New York, McDonald had to review expenditures from 3,000 public agencies supported by 1,600 separate government units (1980:2).

Even if all the figures were known, cost control in corrections is hampered by the structure of the correctional system. Prison administrators have little ability to control variable costs—the costs that fluctuate with size of population—because they have little control over sentencing and release decisions. Since many separate agencies make decisions about correctional input, and in many states an autonomous parole board still controls exits from prison, variable costs are exceedingly difficult to predict or control.

Because our democratic system does not permit centralization of these decisions, by what other means could the costs associated with the variable demand for punishment be controlled? The late Commissioner of Corrections in Connecticut, John Manson, proposed that prison space could be allocated to individual judges, in order to control their variable proclivity to use it. Judges should be given an allowance of prison space which they must budget over the course of the sentencing year. This procedure, thought Manson, could constrain those judges who use far more prison space than their colleagues.

The proposal was carried out in greater detail by Peter Nardulli (1983), using sentencing data from Illinois. Nardulli observed that corrections expenses went up 340 percent in Illinois from 1973 to 1982 (1983:1). He also noticed that there was tremendous variation in use of prison by the different counties (1983:3). Agreeing with Mullen that some judges approached prison as "free goods," he decided that the state, and taxpayers in other counties, were subsidizing the tendency of some counties to overincarcerate. Nardulli demonstrated that for serious violent felonies, all counties incarcerated at about the same rate. For less serious crimes, high-incarceration counties used up much more prison space than medium- and low-rate counties. Nardulli proposed that increased county fiscal responsibility for prison resources would reduce the intercounty disparity in sentencing and reduce correctional cost (1983:17–18).

Finally, some myth exploding might help. The Minnesota Citizen's Council on Criminal Justice blames part of the correctional cost inflation on public (and legislative) misperceptions about crime and criminals. The crime rate, and particularly the serious crime rate, is *not* rising, yet more people are being incarcerated. The council proposed that corrections was being financed on the false assumptions that criminals were on a rampage and that more prisons would control crime. Nardulli's conclusion (1983:16) is similar:

> Our findings suggest a somewhat different picture of the state's prison problem from the one usually presented. What emerges is not a picture of penal resources overwhelmed by a marked jump in the number of dangerous felons. Rather we see a system whose resources and capacity have outstripped increases in the crime rates.

Similarly, Wilkins (1981) concluded his history of sentencing guidelines with a plea for a more consumer-oriented approach to penal resources. The punishment-consuming (or paying) public should realize, Wilkins argued, that what we do with criminals and what we do about crime are two separate problems. What we do to punish the criminal will not affect the number of events called crimes, and if the public has bought punishment services with this use in mind, it has been misinformed.

CONSTRUCTION COST

Prisons have never been cheap. Beaumont and Toqueville observed in 1833 that one drawback of the new American penitentiary system was the expense of construction (1964:103–111). However, they also observed that construction cost was highly variable, depending, they thought, on the extravagance of design and the method of construction. Costs of the new penitentiaries ran from $1,624 per cell at Cherry Hill in Philadelphia to a mere $150.86 per cell at the Connecticut State Prison at Wethersfield. They reported that despite construction costs, the penitentiaries could show a profit within a few years if they were managed properly.

Cost has risen considerably since those early prisons, and few groups harbor hope for public profit. In 1986, various prison systems planned to spend $3 billion to construct 59,000 new bedspaces. The costs per cell ranged from $15,200 to $157,000, depending on security level and land cost ("1986 Prison Construction Tops $3

Billion," 1986:20). Of the 49 states and the federal system responding to the 1986 survey, 38 had new prisons in the works. California had the most extensive building plans; Ohio came second. The most commonly proposed new space was medium security (1986:20). The most common form of financing for the new prisons was direct government expenditure, but 19 states were issuing bonds to pay for the new construction (1986:20).

Public response to prison financing has not received a lot of attention. One ambiguous public referendum occurred in New York in the general election of 1981. The state legislature passed a **bond act** with the catchy title "Security Through the Development of Correctional Facilities Bond Act of 1981" (Jacobs and Berkowitz, 1983). The legislative action carried with virtually no opposition. The proposal called for $500 million in government bonds to be sold in order to finance the construction of three new prisons and 2,500 additional cells in existing prisons. The total cost to the taxpayer, as the bonds matured over 30 years, was estimated at $1,286,400,000 (1983:117).

The proposed bond had to be approved by the voters in November; it was defeated by 13,699 votes. An analysis of the voting indicated some interesting regional differences. The county variables which explained the greatest variation in the bond referendum were the percent nonwhite population in the county, and the county crime rate. Counties with a greater racial mix, and with a higher crime rate, were more likely to vote in favor of the financing plan. However, these relationships were much stronger in and around New York City than upstate (1983:123–130). Upstate counties, no matter what their crime rate or racial composition, were not swayed by this plan for paying for prison space.

During the election campaign, the loudest voice in favor of the bond was the Department of Correctional Services, which spent thousands of dollars on a "public education campaign." The DOCS argument for the bond was that (1) the prisons would be built with or without the bond money, and (2) without the bond, the construction money would come out of the general state budget, cutting into other social programs. A number of citizen and professional groups campaigned actively against the bond. They argued that the bond act was (1) too expensive, (2) that more prisons would not lower the crime rate, (3) that construction took too long to alleviate immediate overcrowding, (4) that there were less costly more effective alternatives, (5) that more prisons would mean reduction of other government services, and (6) that more prisons would perpetuate the injustices of racially disproportionate incarceration (1983:118–120).

Despite the heavy campaigning by both sides, the voters were generally unimpressed. Only 58 percent of the eligible voters went to the polls in that off-year election, and only 60 percent of the voters bothered to indicate a preference on the bond act (1983:123). After the narrow defeat, the victorious antiprison groups claimed that the election was a public referendum on prison construction. The Department of Correctional Services, and the legislature, disagreed. These groups interpreted the vote only as a rejection of the financing plan, not of the need for more prisons. In fact, DOCS had begun construction on the new prison before the election, and has continued the construction since, using bonds floated by the Urban Development Corporation (UDC), a move that required no vote. The UDC is a public benefit corporation, publicly financed but separately controlled, and not directly responsible to the electorate. While its functions are ostensibly to finance urban renewal projects, its involvement in New York prison construction is just one example of the newest controversy in correction: the privatization of correctional activity.

THE PUBLIC-PRIVATE DISTINCTION

Nongovernment organizations can sometimes engage in activities government organizations find impossible. Drawing on high levels of normative commitment from their members is one example.

Sustaining that type of commitment had much to do with the deinstitutionalization of juvenile corrections in Massachusetts. Some nongovernment organizations can also employ financing strategies unavailable to the government organization. For instance, the profit-making organization holds out to its investors the promise of a financial gain, above the value of their work. Now that corrections is a growth industry, investors are taking a hard look at the chances of profit from that growth. In turn, some governments have been attracted to the speed and flexibility apparently available through partnerships with profit-making firms.

The involvement of nongovernment organizations in corrections is not new. However, the vision of punishment for profit, especially the commercialization of the maximum security prison for men, is suddenly a controversial policy issue. The prison for profit, however, has to be discussed within the context of more general private involvement in corrections.

So far, we have used the term "government" and "nongovernment" organizations in this discussion. The more common terms are "public" and "private." Unfortunately, those terms can become ambiguous, especially when the private organization is involved in some public activity, like corrections.

Bayley (1985) has cautioned that the traditional distinctions between public and private can lead to inconsistent and confusing analyses, especially in relation to sanctioning authority. Punishment is a core government activity, which it undertakes in the pursuit of managing norms. Walzer (1985:130) argued that in the long run, governments cannot turn over the punishment function to nongovernment agencies. All that can legally be done is to "deputize" some nongovernment organizations to assist in carrying out the state responsibility. Whether we should call that deputization "privatization" is a complex legal and political question. Since it is the term in general use, we will use **privatization** to refer to the process of turning over some correctional activities to nongovernment organizations.

The literature generally distinguishes between two forms of "private" organization: the **non-profit** or **not-for-profit** agency, and the **profit-making firm.** In corrections, the not-for-profit organization is currently more common. The nonprofit organization can provide a service for a fee, but it cannot accumulate capital. It often runs on a small budget, since it often must provide the service before it is reimbursed. If through gifts, grants, or advances it manages to accumulate savings, by law these resources must be carefully managed and used only for the purposes for which the organization was established. Since many nonprofit organizations now operate with "public" money, it can be extremely difficult to maintain the public-private distinction in analyzing their operations. The profit-making firm obtains its resources under very different rules. Persons, groups, and organizations invest in them with the intention of obtaining a return greater than their investment—the profit. The profit-making firm intends, in the long run, to provide services or products for less cost than it receives in sales. The surplus may be turned back to investors, at their request. If the investors are optimistic, the surplus may be held and reinvested by the firm in any number of endeavors, with the objective of building even greater surplus.

THE DEVELOPMENT OF PRIVATE INVOLVEMENT

Since we have traced the involvement of "private" groups throughout this book, the specific events will not be repeated here. Instead, we will briefly emphasize a few patterns of private involvement in correctional activity.

From the beginning of the penitentiary movement, private organizations, particularly associations of volunteers, were engaged in conducting the work not done by the tax-supported agencies of punishment. In 1822, a group known as the Philadelphia Society for Alleviating the Misery of Public Prisons provided support and supervision for people released from the Pennsylvania prisons and jails (Cook and Scioli, 1976:74). A number of church groups were active in prison visiting, and following the work of Augustus, church groups continued to engage in probation work using paid staff and volunteers. In New York and elsewhere, Protestant ministers often functioned as parole officers or aftercare workers, especially in the juvenile system. Consequently, the energies of nonprofit philanthropic groups have always been evident in corrections, especially in the provision of care and services the public organizations either could not or would not provide.

The nonprofit involvement in corrections in the nineteenth century is difficult to separate from the involvement of volunteers. The difference during that period is not terribly important, but the distinction between volunteering and nonprofit agency work has become important in this century. Volunteers have a variety of motives, but they work without pay. They may work directly in or with public agencies, as John Augustus worked with the Boston courts, or they may engage in correctional work because of their commitment to a private organization, such as a church that has a mission of providing service. In the nineteenth century, many private service organizations were associations of prominent citizens, volunteering to do service work. However, it is clear that some of these private organizations were employing staff, such as ministers, to provide correctional service as part of their work for the private organization. Rarely was the private organization obtaining its service funds from the public correctional agencies. It is this situation that has changed. Today, nonprofit agencies not only employ staff to work in corrections rather than rely on volunteers, but these organizations also often specialize in correctional work and receive their funds from the public organizations for which they provide service.

The profit motive has been present in American corrections as long as the service motive. As we saw in Chapter 14, prison industries were run by private entrepreneurs attracted to cheap prison labor as a means of turning a profit. The town of Auburn was attracted to the idea of a prison as a means of invigorating the town economy (Miller, 1980). In the West, the attraction of profit from prison labor led to even greater private involvement. Prior to the Civil War, most prisons west of the Mississippi were privately owned and operated, although built with public money (Chaneles, 1986:1). After the Civil War, freed slaves were convicted, often on trumped-up charges, and turned over to private employers, a practice that continued through the 1930s (Sagarin and Maghan, 1986).

The treatment of prisoners in these profit-making prisons was so scandalous that the more visible forms of this public subsidy of private organizations were eventually curtailed. However, as Murton (Murton and Hyams, 1969), in his story of the Arkansas system, and Meyer (1976), in his analysis of pharmaceutical company drug experiments with prisoners, attested, a number of states have had a long, ongoing relationship with profit-making firms.

Logan and Rausch (1985:307) suggest that the first of the more recent profit-making ventures in prison administration occurred in 1975. The RCA corporation developed and operated the Intensive Treatment Unit, a 20-bed high-security facility on the grounds of a Pennsylvania training school. RCA became involved when a court order required the removal of troublesome delinquents from the Camp Hill prison run by the Pennsylvania Bureau of Correction. Flexibility and speed of development appeared to be the attraction for the state government in this case. RCA was able to develop a high-security program more quickly than the state itself.

Chaneles (1986:2–5) concluded that privatization could go in one of several directions. He argued the resurgence of the private prison is currently spurred by the desire of government and business to sidestep the reluctance of the public to foot the bill for construction cost. As such, it is a highly questionable practice. However, he points out that there are advantages of privatization from which the government could benefit. These incluude increased innovation through increased competition, and higher-quality service through the use of performance con-

tracts. Whether the new privatization trend mimics the negative excesses of previous eras or leads to more effective correctional activity, depends a great deal on the types of controls exerted by the government agencies as they continue to discharge their punishment function.

THE PRIVATE PRISON

In a recent survey of private involvement in public prisons, Camp and Camp discovered that 52 separate correctional agencies in 38 states and the District of Columbia had contracts with private organizations for the provision of a wide range of prison services (Logan and Rausch, 1985:310–311). Those systems reporting the use of private providers of security included California, Mississippi, Utah, Washington, and the Federal Bureau of Prisons (Flanagan and McGarrell, 1986:102–103). It is not a long step from providing contractual services for a public prison and contracting to run the entire prison.

The most privatized correctional system is the juvenile correctional system. About 65 percent of all juvenile facilities are private, and they house about 32,000 inmates (McGarrell and Flanagan, 1985:103). The private institutions employ far fewer staff than the public institutions, and yet the average operating costs are about equal (Flanagan and McGarrell, 1986:90,92). Since juvenile justice is not considered a punishment, private involvement in that system is far more common and less controversial.

By several counts, as of 1986 there were 24 privately owned and operated correctional facilities for adults (Logan, 1986; Walzer, 1985:128). The involvement of profit-making companies appears to be on the increase (Poole, 1985:124). Of the two dozen facilities, only one, a prison operated for the Federal Bureau of Prisons, incarcerated adult felons (Logan and Rausch, 1985:307).

A number of large, profit-making firms are now involved in incarceration. The Correctional Corporation of America, backed by the Hospital Corporation of America, owns and runs a 250-

bed medium security facility for Hamilton County, Tennessee. The CCA proposed to take over the entire state correctional system in Tennessee. The CCA vice-president for operations, Don Hutto, was recently elected president of the American Correctional Association. Behavioral Systems Southwest runs a number of detention centers for the Immigration and Naturalization Service (Logan and Rausch, 1985:307). Buckingham Security Limited has plans to open a 720-bed maximum security prison near Pittsburgh. The proposed prison is to specialize in providing protective custody for a number of state systems. (As we saw in Chapter 15, a number of prisoners have been rushing to protective custody to avoid prison violence. The protective custody population may be the fastest-growing classification group in many prisons, many of which lack sufficient space). The Pennsylvania legislature is currently fighting this commercial segregation unit. Table 20.6 provides an overview of current private prisons in the United States.

OTHER PRIVATE INVOLVEMENTS

Prisons are the most controversial but not the most frequent form of private correctional activity. As we noted in Chapter 6, private presentence reports are now available in some areas. In addition to the Center for Institutions and Alternatives in Washington, DC, the Psychiatry and Law Center in San Diego has been commissioned to provide presentence investigations in a number of states, and has also conducted prison classifications for use under mandatory sentencing (Rogers, Gitchoff, and Paur, 1984). In Oregon, Community Corrections Services, Inc., a for-profit firm, had a million-dollar contract in the early 1980s for provision of PSIs, job development, and enhanced probation services in nine counties (Cocks, 1982).

In California, Federal Probation for the Central District (Los Angeles) was involved in establishing two public benefit (nonprofit) corporations to provide job training to probationers and to develop and supervise community service place-

ments. Both organizations were established with the assistance of convicted white collar offenders who, as part of their own restitution orders, assisted the probation department with management and training expertise. The not-for-profit corporations were better able to develop the community services than the probation department (Cocks, 1982).

The involvement of private organizations in halfway houses is common. Since 1979, the Federal Bureau of Prisons has provided all of its prerelease center activities by way of contract (Poole, 1985). The State of Michigan uses both direct service and contracted services for prerelease centers as a means of expanding services to areas where there are few offenders at any one time. In the mid-1980s, private, not-for-profit halfway houses had a hard time. Governments began to cut back on contracts so they could reserve their funds for the overcrowded prisons (Taft, 1982, 1983). During this period, large, profit-making halfway house chains began to buy up the smaller operations. The larger organizations were better able to weather the dry periods.

THE ADVANTAGES OF PRIVATIZATION

The arguments in favor of privatization vary somewhat, depending on type of program. In general, however, the advantages appear to be flexibility, speed of development, greater diversity of program, and greater competition, leading in turn to higher quality at less cost (Logan and Rausch, 1985:313–316). In corrections for adults, the greatest attraction currently seems to be less cost. Whether private actually is cheaper remains to be seen. Studies of privatization of other public services (such as refuse collection) suggest that savings seem likely. The greatest area of savings is apparently in manpower cost. Government salaries for service positions are now higher than those in the private sector. But the greatest personnel-related savings is the lower retirement costs. Many private firms are nonunion, and provide small or no pensions for their employees (Logan and Rausch, 1985:310–313).

TABLE 20.6   **Summary of Privately Contracted Penal Facilities, 1984**

PUBLIC AGENCY	PRIVATE CONTRACTOR	FACILITY	COST
State of Pennsylvania	RCA	Heavy security training school for delinquents, Weaversville; 20 beds; 1975	$40,000/yr/inmate
State of Florida	Eckerd Foundation	Okeechobee School for Boys; secure; 425 beds; 1982	$14,588/yr/inmate (based on $6.2m/yr, total)
INS	Behavioral Systems Southwest	Detention centers for illegal aliens in AZ, CA, CO (proposed: NM); 350 beds; 1983	$5,110/yr/inmate (based on $14/day)
INS	Corrections Corporation of America	Detention center for illegal aliens, Houston; 350 beds; 1984	$8,670/yr/inmate (based on $24/day); covers construction ($5m) and operation
Hamilton Co., TN	Corrections Corporation of America	Medium security corrections facility; 250 beds; 1984	$7,665/yr/inmate (based on $21/day); incl $1m renovation
U.S. Bureau of Prisons	Palo Duro Private Detention Services	Medium security prison for convicted immigration offenders; 575 beds; 1984	$16,425/yr/inmate (based on $45/day)
Counties in WY, TX; CO?, NM?	Southwest Detention Facilities	Jails owned and run in TX, WY; negotiating same for CO, NM	$19,710/yr/inmate (based on $54/day)
U.S. Bureau of Prisons	Eclectic Communications, Inc.	Prison for youthful offenders, near San Francisco; 1983	—
INS	Corrections Corporation of America	(Contracted) alien detention facilities; 175+ beds; 1985	$10,585/yr/inmate (based on $29/day)
—	Buckingham Security Limited	(Planned) maximum security prison near Pittsburgh; 720 beds	$24,000/yr/inmate covers $15m construction

SOURCE: Charles Logan and Sharla Rausch, "Punish and Profit: The Emergence of Private Enterprise Prisons." *Justice Quarterly* 2 (1985): Table 1, p. 309. Reprinted with permission of the Academy of Criminal Justice Sciences.

The greatest attraction of the private prison is the perception that private firms can build faster, more cheaply, and pay off construction debts more quickly (Logan, 1986; Poole, 1985). Logan (1986) argued that another advantage of private construction is that it disperses among several organizations the risk for guessing about the numbers in the future offender population.

Reports of lower operation cost are still tentative. The Federal Bureau of Prisons has claimed that Eclectic Communications, Inc., runs a juvenile corrections facility for about half the cost required for a direct operation (Poole, 1985). The Connecticut Department of Correction, which has contracted out all of its adult halfway house activities for years, has reported that it saves about one third of state-run cost (1985).

Experience from Massachusetts and from the National Assessment of Juvenile Corrections suggests that state-contracted community-based facilities offered several advantages over state-run facilities:

> The diversity and flexibility of community based services, particularly those purchased through private vendors, seems to provide a situation that allows for individualized service, opportunity for innovation without changing the entire system, and creative management. (Coates, Miller and Ohlin, 1978:190)

Coates and colleagues observed that small and large private vendors offer different attractions and different hazards. Therefore, state policymakers would be wise to ensure that several different types of private organizations were supported. Small vendors could not always come up with the risk money to get started, and rarely could offer more than one type of service, but they were often innovative and sensitive to special needs. Large vendors often offered a complete range of services and had an easier time staying in business, but they often sought a monopoly over services in various regions of the state, and often attempted to dictate policy to the state (Coates, Miller, and Ohlin, 1978:194).

Logan has claimed that the kind of flexibility and speed which Coates, Miller, and Ohlin documented in Massachusetts juvenile corrections can and should be adapted to adult prisons. He proposed that the use of private prisons could actually increase the level of just deserts at sentencing, because the state would not have to fit its sentencing policy to its prison resource supply. If there were many serious offenders to be sent

to prison, another contract could be let. If there were fewer imprisonable offenders, contracts would just be cut. In other words, the private companies, not the state, would assume the risk for fluctuations in the supply of prisoners. Additionally, Logan argued that the generally poor conditions in our public prisons are explainable by the current public monopoly of the supply of prison space. If private vendors were competing for prisoners, conditions in prisons would be better (Logan, 1986).

THE DISADVANTAGES OF PRIVATIZATION

The claimed disadvantages of privatization tend to be longer-range concerns. Some of them focus on the predicted changes in the private corrections market. For example, Walzer (1985) has predicted that the advantages of competition will be short-lived. Eventually market competition will no longer control either the conditions within private prisons or the prices private vendors charge. He asserted that corrections is not the kind of market that will long permit competition because the initial investment is too great. Once the first several contracts are cut, the losers will leave the field to a few giants, who will then be in the position to charge the government whatever they want. The result will be similar to the defense industry monopoly.

That prediction has been supported by Sagarin and Maghan (1986). They have argued that private prison owners will have a vested interest in increased incarceration. They predict that these few rich companies will be able to bombard the public with advertisements for crime control through incarceration in order to protect their investments. Logan's response to that prediction is that the fear of lobbying is not unwarranted, just misplaced. He has pointed out that public employee unions already have strong lobbies for the use of prisons. Their lobbying efforts are directed at their own private interests, not the public good (1986).

Two separate observations suggest that privatization may already be causing some problems. Sagarin and Maghan (1986) reported that the Correction Corporation of America jail in Tennessee reported a $200,000 cost overrun in its first year of operation, and that the administration of the jail was poor. Within the first year, three separate administrators were appointed. Thomson (1987) reported that many public probation and parole officers resist the pressure to broker services rather than provide direct services. They fear that brokerage is just one small step from dismantling probation and parole and replacing them with private services. Such observations could imply that there may be considerable conflict during a transition from public to private service provision.

Finally, a number of observers have claimed that the profit motive is simply incompatible with the demands of distributing punishment and correctional services. Walzer (1985) complained that inmates housed in profit-making prisons will perceive themselves as exploited by both the government and their captors. Moreover, he insists that prison administration decisions made on the basis of what is profitable will conflict with criteria of humane care and fairness.

There is some evidence of conflict between profit-driven decisions and correctional objectives in the few studies of privately run prison industries. Schaller (1982) reported that private prison industry has several advantages. Private business may be more efficient and more effective than government-run business in production. And private business can take advantage of the several programs offering tax deductions for training "special needs clients." The private employer may therefore be more willing to offer inmates at least minimum wage (Lightman, 1982). For these and related reasons, over twenty states have passed new legislation allowing private employers into prisons (Schaller, 1982).

Preliminary evaluations of two private programs in Ontario prisons illustrated both the promise of private involvement and the conflict with the profit motive. Among other things, the evaluations suggested that private business will not rush in to just any prison situation. The at-

tractiveness of different prison work sites varies tremendously. One prison site was rented out very quickly, while another stood vacant for four years. Lightman concluded that the private business will always be seeking a government subsidy to set up shop inside a prison because it sees working with prisoners and government red tape as significant detractions. Business can seek two different types of subsidy: reduction in capital investment (such as reduced rates for rented prison space and equipment) or reduction in operating expenses (such as paying inmates lower wages). Although the Ontario government attempted to ensure that free world wages would be paid in both projects, the evidence suggested that in one site the inmates were paid less than market rates for equivalent work.

The employers also manipulated prison labor in other ways. For example, employers often reserved the best jobs for imported civilian employees and gave inmates the most mundane, least skilled tasks. From the employers' standpoint this division of work made sense, because they wanted to invest most heavily in workers who would remain on the job. But from a correctional standpoint, this meant that the private prison industry did not hold great promise for job training. In general, the experiments indicated that the same conflicts between employers and employees found in the free world occurred in the prison. However, theoretically the free laborer can organize in protest, or take his work elsewhere. The prisoner can do neither.

THE CORRECTIONAL WORK FORCE

There are about 1.3 million people employed in public criminal justice agencies in the United States. They earn about $2.3 billion a month (*New York Times*, July 14, 1986). As of 1983, nearly one-quarter of these people, or about 320,000, were employed in correction agencies, narrowly defined (the count does not include private corrections agencies, or the preconviction agencies, such as pretrial services, which do much correctional work). The corrections work force was the most rapidly expanding in criminal justice work. Between 1982 and 1983, full and part-time corrections employment increased 6.9 percent, compared to 1.3 percent for the police and 5.6 percent for the courts. State work grew at the fastest rate, and the states employed the majority of correctional workers (Flanagan and McGarrell, 1986).

Correctional staffing, not unexpectedly, has been increasing since 1971 (Duffee, 1981), and the proportional increase in guard positions has actually outstripped the proportional increase in the inmate population. Between 1979 and 1984, the states hired 35,000 new guards, bringing the total to 90,000. Despite the rapid growth in inmate populations, this hiring reduced the guard-inmate ratio from 1 to 4.6 to 1 to 4.1 (Yost, 1986). The ratio of correctional officers to inmates varies considerably from state to state.

Jail employees outnumber all but state prison employees: 70,515 jail workers were counted in the 1978 jail census, but only 64,650 appeared in the 1983 census. The decrease is probably related to the decrease in the number of jails (BJS, 1984a:5).

Probation employment figures are difficult to come by. A 1979 survey (National Council on Crime and Delinquency, 1981) reported 18,910 state and local probation workers supervising caseloads. This figure underestimated the number of probation personnel because it excluded officers who did not have caseloads, such as those specializing in PSIs or juvenile intake, and excluded supervisors, clerks, and training officers (1981:24). The survey also did not cover departments devoted to supervising juveniles. The Federal Probation Service employed a case supervision staff of 1,697 in 1979. These officers supervised all federal probationers, as well as persons released from the Federal Bureau of Prisons. Nationally, the probation caseload average was 66 clients per officer. This figure is rather midleading, however, since caseload size varies drastically; many urban officers supervise hundreds of clients.

State parole offices employed 6,927 officers in 1979. About 1,000 of these supervised only parolees or mandatory releasees. About 800 supervised only state probationers, while the others had mixed caseloads (Flanagan and McLeod, 1983:122). Employees of parole agencies also include 231 parole board members (McGarrell and Flanagan, 1985:131). Parole board sizes across the states ranged from 3 to 15 members in 1983, and many members were part-time.

After prisons and jails, the largest segment of the correctional work force is in juvenile systems. In 1982, the number of full- and part-time workers in public juvenile facilities was 58,654, while private juvenile facilities retained 37,411 that year (1985:100–103).

The attraction of correctional work is not in its financial compensation. In 1983, the average monthly earnings per correctional employee were $1,634, with the highs being $2,824 in Alaska and $2,008 in Connecticut and the low $1,034 in West Virginia (Flanagan and McGarrell, 1986). As we would expect, prison guards, who in many ways perform the most difficult correctional work, generally received the lowest pay in any department.

CORRECTIONAL ROLES

As we traced the history of correctional management in Chapter 18, it was evident that one continuing trend has been the elaboration of correctional work roles and the specialization of work. Through 1870, work roles in American corrections were very simple. Prison roles consisted of warden or superintendent, perhaps one underwarden, and a number of guards, called turnkeys. Inmate labor was overseen by private entrepreneurs. Most service work was conducted by clergy and volunteer visitors. Clearly, the reformative goals of the early penitentiary were not translated into work specialities. This began to change in the 1870s, and counseling specialists were employed in most prisons by the 1930s. The preferred professional degree for treatment workers was for many years the MSW, although most systems were usually unsuccessful in attracting personnel with graduate social work degrees. Probation and parole positions also gradually appeared in the same era, with professional staff replacing the clergy and volunteers in the provision of community supervision.

At each stage in the development of correctional employment, the work specialties of the earlier eras were retained. Since the beginning of the penitentiary, custodial work has always been the most plentiful. Security has always dominated in numbers if not in the rhetoric of corrections. The National Manpower Survey (NMS, 1979) calculated the percentages of institutional workers in custody, treatment, and administration for 1974, and the figures have not changed greatly since. In state prisons, 63 percent of the employees were designated as custody staff, 10.4 percent as treatment and education staff, and 26.6 as administrative, maintenance, and clerical. Jails, as one would expect, were more heavily custodial, with 73 percent of the workers in custody, only 7 percent in treatment positions, and 17 percent designated as "all other." A more even division of labor was evident in juvenile facilities, where 12 percent were in administration, 41 percent in child care (the custody equivalent), 31 percent in treatment and education, and 12 percent in other positions.

These broad categories, however, hide the increasing variety of task positions in corrections. As we noted in Chapters 8 and 17, specialties have developed within probation and parole officer positions. The numerous positions in pretrial programs (see Chapter 4) are generally not included in correctional manpower surveys. In institutions, there is an increasing array of special jobs. The Joint Commission on Correctional Manpower and Training (1969) listed 44 separate common personnel categories in institutions. Even this breakdown hides the possible variety within positions. Correctional officers in some departments are rewarded for special interests or expertise with either official special posts or informally recognized special assignments. Other systems do not recognize such specialties. Although it still oversimplifies the number of roles and skills in corrections, Table 20.7, from National Manpower Survey data, indicates correctional tasks which the Manpower Survey staff thought would be important in the 1980s.

THE EMPLOYMENT OF EX-OFFENDERS

One of the more ironic personnel issues in corrections is the employment of ex-offenders. While correctional staff and offenders routinely report employment as the most pressing problem for convicted persons, correctional organizations have been hesitant to hire offenders. In some states, statutes forbid their employment in correctional work.

The Joint Commission on Correctional Manpower and Training took a strong stance in favor of their employment (1968). And for a while, in the late 1960s and early 1970s, correctional careers for ex-offenders were spurred on by a broader movement called "new careers," an outgrowth of the Kennedy administration war on poverty (Pearl, 1965). The new careers movement pushed for the creation of new employment opportunities for the poor and unemployed in newly fashioned professional and paraprofessional human service positions. It was argued that those who had experienced a problem, such as unemployment, inmate status, or drug use, might have more success in working with others having that problem than professional staff with middle-class backgrounds. This hypothesis sprang from subcultural theory that sought to deal with the alienation and distrust between clients and helpers, and from therapeutic theory that dealt with the advantages of self-help.

Common difficulties with new careers programs include: (1) creating new positions for disadvantaged workers that do not, in fact, lead to careers but are dead-end positions; (2) expecting that any person who has experienced a social problem will automatically have rapport with others; (3) failing to develop effective training and support systems with which to help new careerists deal with being marginal in two worlds

TABLE 20.7   Correctional Roles and Skills Predicted to be Important by the National Manpower Survey of the Criminal Justice System (1978)

INSTITUTIONS FOR ADULTS

COUNSELOR SKILLS	CORRECTIONAL OFFICER SKILLS	OTHER
Crisis intervention	Team counseling	Planning specialists
Interpersonal relationships	Inmate supervision	Job development
Communications	Specialist positions	Evaluation
Ethnic customs	Work program development	
Alcohol and drug abuse counseling	Treatment program development	
Assessment	Staff-inmate interactions	
Intensive casework		

COMMUNITY SERVICES

Community resource development		Group counseling
Management and training of volunteers		Individual counseling
Interagency coordination		Crisis intervention
Planning and management		
Evaluation		
Surveillance		
Assessment and investigation		
Client advocacy		
Job development		

at once; and (4) having new careerists over-identify with the behavior of professional staff, thereby losing the presumed social benefit of the indigenous helper role (see Durham, 1974).

In corrections, the employment of offenders has been retarded by the deeply rooted response that two offenders in the same place is a conspiracy. Just as it has been presumed that parolees should not congregate together or associate with other offenders, it has been presumed that offenders in staff positions would be corrupted by their clients. In a 1974 survey of 20 states, only 203 ex-offender staff were identified (Allen and Gatz, 1976).

The best-known attempt to turn this situation around was the Ohio Parole Officer Aide Program (Scott, 1975; Allen and Gatz, 1976). In this program, 37 ex-parolees were hired over three years to supervise especially troublesome parolees. Although the ex-parolees were called "aides" and supervised by regular officers, they did carry caseloads of their own and had considerable dis-

cretion. However, they did not carry guns or have condition enforcement responsibility. A reasonably thorough evaluation of this program was conducted, particularly regarding the attitudes of other parole officers and the supervision behaviors of the aides. In general, the evaluators discovered that the aides were initially met with suspicion by many officers, but rather rapidly earned their trust and respect. Most staff thought the program was successful. Attempts to measure the outcomes, however, such as whether aides reduced recidivism, are hopelessly damaged by the differences between aide and officer duties. At least it can be said that both parolees and parole officers found the aides helpful.

VOLUNTEERS

As we have already seen, volunteers played an important role in the emergence of modern corrections, particularly in the delivery of community correctional services. This important role declined somewhat toward the beginning of this century, as the tasks previously done by volunteers were taken on directly by the growing public agencies. The role of volunteers became more important again in the 1960s, due in part to some highly publicized programs of probation volunteers (Cook and Scioli, 1976), and in part to the general trend of volunteering for social causes (such as the Peace Corps).

"Volunteerism" is a difficult term to define. At face value, the term implies an uneven exchange, or a nonexchange situation, in which one person works on behalf of others without reward. However, the attractions and rewards of volunteering are multifold, ambiguous, and understudied. Louis Harris and Associates, surveying volunteers for the Joint Commission on Correctional Manpower and Training, avoided the important but subtle complications and simply defined as a volunteer anyone "who offers his services to the correctional agency without payment, although he may be reimbursed for some out-of-pocket expenses" (1969:1). Harris found that the most commonly given reasons for volunteering were the search for interesting work, the desire to help others, and a desire to be with other people (1969:10).

The Harris survey found some interesting differences between correctional volunteers and staff. In general, volunteers were younger than staff, better educated, and had a higher than average income. Most volunteers had not been recruited by the correctional agency, but had heard of the opportunity through their membership in another organization, such as a church (1969:3). The majority of correctional volunteers in 1968 had been involved in corrections work for less than two years, although some had been involved steadily for as many as ten. Compared to the general public and to correctional staff, volunteers were considerably more liberal in their perceptions of the causes of crime. They were more likely to emphasize social conditions.

As one would expect from the demographic data, lower-class people and blacks were underrepresented among active volunteers. While 11 percent of the general population was black, only 4 percent of the volunteers were black (1969:6). However, Harris's survey of the general public had discovered that among persons who were not then volunteers, blacks were more willing than whites to volunteer if asked (1969:26). Hence, the data suggest that correctional agencies did not aggressively seek volunteers, but relied upon established community agencies to supply them. Blacks, while willing to volunteer, were less likely to be connected to those other organizations.

When asked about their reactions to their correctional tasks, the vast majority of volunteers were very satisfied. Most found the work very interesting, thought they had the right amount of work, and felt that their work was appreciated (1969:24). However, 50 percent of the volunteers also thought that they could have been used more effectively (1969:5).

A number of studies suggest that correctional agencies have a vast potential resource in volunteers, but that the agencies have failed to utilize it. Virtually no systematic devices exist to screen or place correctional volunteers (Kelley and Kennedy, 1982), and about two-thirds of correctional agencies have no volunteer program (Harris, 1969:1). Even agencies that use volunteers rarely engage in training or evaluation.

Volunteers perform a variety of correctional roles, including working in self-help programs, counseling, recreation, prison visitation and entertainment, teaching, job placement, and religious programs (1969:17). Probably the most frequent correctional volunteer works in probation. A 1972 survey found 200,000 volunteers in 2,000 court jurisdictions (Cook and Scioli, 1976).

A number of agencies claim that volunteers can perform some tasks more effectively than staff. For example, leaders of the San Mateo, California, program for victim and witness assistance claimed that use of volunteers kept the program from becoming bureaucratic and routine. They perceived volunteers to be more successful in linking people to community services than state officials could be (Helbush and Mandel,

Insert 20.1 AN INTERNSHIP IN A HALFWAY HOUSE   by Jennifer Silver

Note: The following paper was written by a senior undergraduate following an intensive internship involving approximately 25 hours per week for 15 weeks. The paper has been edited and is included with Ms. Silver's permission.

Working in a halfway house for a semester enabled me to acquire a different type of education than I received in the classroom. Through actually doing and observing (as opposed to reading), the internship supplemented what I learned in school, made it easier to understand many concepts that I had merely memorized before but couldn't truly visualize, and taught me some things I could never have learned in the classroom.

A halfway house is a community corrections program that helps bridge the gap from prison to community—it helps to integrate the offender into the community. That's all I remember about them from my community corrections course. It's difficult for the parole officer to play caseworker and supervisor. That's what I remember about the P.Os. Those issues were mere words to me, until the internship. What does it mean—what "gap" between the offender and the community? The "gap" encompasses much more than just reading the sentence. If someone were to ask me now what troubles an ex-inmate could possibly face, I could go on for hours, giving firsthand examples. Although I would be basing my answers on observations of only ten men in one program, I now know what I am talking about on a much different level than I achieved in a classroom. So the internship supplemented and expanded what I learned about corrections; it made it easier to understand the corrections process. When you learn something from a book, no matter how well you understand it, it's very different from actually seeing what is being described. For instance, I can now visualize a parole office, parole officers, and the conditions of parole as practiced. I can now explain parole, a halfway house, and an admission and classification process from experience, rather than relying on information that someone else is feeding me about something they may not have experienced either.

I also learned things that I do not think come across adequately in any criminal justice book. For example, readings about the management of a halfway house never portray its director as a human being, with human faults and strengths. When you learn about recidivism rates from a book, it is difficult to realize that the director's like or dislike for a client can affect whether or not he will complete the program. Similarly, when reading about support and assistance programs, I never considered the influence exerted by the clients. Call me idealistic, but I always thought that all the clients wanted to be helped and could be helped. After working in a program, I found that some of the men couldn't care less. Textbooks did not indicate that the men are quite street smart and that it takes a staff member with equal knowledge of survival tricks to run a halfway house. Someone with a master's degree in criminal justice but little street experience would not know about the tricks used to subvert drug testing. Since you are dealing with people, from top to bottom, conditions and situations keep changing—and different people need to be treated differently. Classroom learning does not illustrate this problem.

The internship also personalized corrections for me. What I mean by this is that when I learned about prison, rehabilitation, parole, etc., I thought of the "bad guy" who murdered or committed an armed robbery as almost inhuman. He was a "thing" who deserved to go to prison for ten years, or deserved the death penalty. Now I think of "the criminal" as a real person—a Mike who wasn't brought up well and may be learning disabled, a Miguel who is an alcoholic and commits crimes to support his disease. I don't know if this new view is good or bad, but I do know it has provided a more well-rounded understanding of persons convicted of crimes.

In addition to learning from observing, speaking with staff and clients, and actually doing things, I learned a good deal through thinking about what was going on, analyzing, and tying it together. The journal I kept was the best aid. Many times when I'd sit down to make an entry, I'd think I was only going to write a paragraph. Then I'd end up writing two or three pages. The more I wrote, the more I thought. I believe if I had not kept the journal, I would not have learned as much because I would not have realized how much I had actually experienced. Without it, I may not have thought twice about meeting with a parole official, or confronting one of the residents. A lot of what I learned was through my own thinking, rather than what someone else was telling me to think about. My professor's comments on the journal entries were quite helpful, in that they forced me to think more about certain topics, and brought my attention to points I would not otherwise have considered. This type of thinking was much more valuable than just spending additional hours at the halfway house.

The halfway house, parole, the residents—the knowledge about these is in my long-term memory. Although it may be biased, because it is only about one program for one period in time, I believe that I understand much more about community corrections now than I ever had before. This experience was not always pleasant, but it is irreplaceable. If I had the chance, I would do it again.

1977). Others have claimed that trained volunteer mediators are more effective than professionals in victim-offender reconciliation and restitution planning (Zehr and Umbreit, 1982). A number of similar claims have been made for volunteer probation counseling. Unfortunately, there are no data to sustain such claims. The research on volunteer effectiveness has not been given serious attention by either agencies or academics (Cook and Scioli, 1976).

Volunteering also can be abused. It is not uncommon for private correctional agencies to skirt minimum wage law by providing a "stipend" for expenses, knowing full well that the "volunteers" are in desperate need of employment and willing to work for the stipend. In some of these instances, the organization is clearly taking advantage of the volunteer. In other situations, the manipulation is much more ambiguous. One reason poor people do not volunteer is that they can't afford to. Federal labor, welfare, and tax laws do not permit a symbiotic "You scratch my back, I'll scratch yours" relationship between an impoverished private agency and its impoverished neighbors. In these cases the agencies and the volunteers are conniving against the government.

A number of students volunteer in correctional agencies in order to gain experience. A number of colleges also offer credit for internships. The dividing line between volunteering and interning is not very clear, nor is there a clear line between interning and doing field research. In any case, several months in a correctional agency can be a very different form of education, as Insert 20.1 attests.

CORRECTIONAL CAREERS

Correctional careers take some odd twists and turns. Correctional work has been described as one of the "dirty hands" jobs, required but undesirable work in most societies. But correctional work has also been described as a "calling," a moral undertaking, the attractions of which are difficult to describe but for some, once bitten, impossible to put down. In this last case of the book, let's take a broader view of the career paths of some of our several characters. These brief snapshots of correctional biographies are in many ways unfair to the actors. We have neither the time nor the information with which to delve into their motivations. However, if they'll forgive us, these brief synopses of months, or years, of work might serve as their farewell to us, or as their invitation to join them.

George Jenison. Remember George? Phil, Ken, and John bumped into him on many occasions in their evaluation of the Jefferson prerelease centers. George was a local hero on the Adams University football team. An injury pushed him toward graduate school rather than professional athletics. The Adams jail warden, an avid sports fan, was happy to hire George as the first counselor in the jail. Within two years, George had become head of jail services. When his boss replaced Commissioner Rush, George followed him to the Central Office in Madison and became Director of Prerelease Services. His management style quickly made him the enemy of many of the center directors, who nevertheless implemented many of his policies. Behind his back, they complained vociferously about his lack of concern for treatment and his lack of appreciation for the different problems faced by the different centers. His boss, Commissioner Comstock, was also considered autocratic. In fact, Phil suspected that Jenison was often following orders rather than establishing his own style. After a little more than a year as director, Jenison had a major falling out with Comstock. Some center directors gloated that George had gotten some of his own medicine. George, however, reported to Phil that he had resigned when the commissioner had ordered him to spy on another

administrator. Bitter about his correctional experience, he went back to Adams to work for his brother, a successful merchant.

Superintendent Smythe. Smythe must be one of our heroes. To many people, Phil included, Smythe embodied all the characteristics of those correctional workers who had taken up the calling. Smythe had enlisted in the Army during World War II, interrupting his education. When he returned, he married and reenrolled on the GI Bill. However, new family responsibilities cut short his academic intentions. He took his masters degree in psychology and went to work as a counselor in Mulwan. One promotion led to another, and he became the first superintendent at Dunmore when Rush decided to make it a full-fledged minimum security prison rather than an honor farm for Mulwan. Smythe had his problems. He reportedly had a quick temper, although Phil never saw it. Professor Masters suspected that somewhere deep down Smythe enjoyed the "hard-nosed, old school" approach to corrections. But Smythe also admitted his mistakes, and learned from them. At about the same time that Professor Masters and Phil entered Jefferson corrections for the first time, Smythe had decided, privately, that it was time for his prison to change. He used the university connection to create change, both in his own management style and in his subordinates. Phil would never forget his first welcome from Smythe. When Phil apologized for not knowing much about corrections, Smythe said, "You're just the kind of person we need."

Professor Masters. Masters got involved in corrections because, as he told it, he needed a new suit. Accepting what he thought was a summer job, he rose rapidly in parole administration in another state. He took delight in helping to create change and became widely sought as a correctional consultant. After serving on a number of important national commissions, he accepted his first academic appointment as a full professor. Professor Masters was not necessarily on the leading edge of correctional research; he was more often applying the ideas and developments of other fields to corrections. He had a keen eye for people's strengths and weaknesses. He could excite others to their best work. A key ingredient in this was his ability to get bureaucrats—subordinates and superiors alike—to work as a team on projects that became team property.

Marianne Shrievers. We met Senate staffer Marianne in Chapter 7 as she argued the merits of the death penalty with Morton Shafley. Marianne was not a correctional expert by training. She got involved in corrections because her boss controlled a good deal of correctional legislation in Jefferson. Shrievers was instrumental in facilitating Help House's first contract with the Jefferson Department of Correction. While Phil and other board members had been banging on the parole front door for years without an answer, Marianne simply called the parole director and threatened to embarrass him in the upcoming budget hearings unless he could come up with a good reason not to do business with Help House. The next day, Phil was called with a request that he prepare a contract. Several years later, Shrievers was instrumental in drafting Jefferson's first community corrections act, modeled on the successful program in Minnesota. A number of agency heads complained that "someone like that shouldn't have so much power," which, after all, she simply borrowed from her boss. But the citizen reform groups and private organizations, like Help House, saw her no-nonsense approach to the professionals in the executive branch as one of the necessary levers for change in the Jefferson correctional system. After a switch in party power in the state senate, Marianne left the legislature to return to school, and added a doctorate to her previous law de-

gree. She is now a professor in an Ivy League law school.

Doug Sims. Phil and his students met Sims for the first time in Chapter 3. Sims let Phil know in no uncertain terms that he did not care if his boss wanted control rather than treatment and did not care if the Department advertised prerelease as a crime reduction strategy rather than a service to its clients. Sims had been hired by the department when the prerelease centers were just opening. The first prerelease director had an ideologically driven hatred of prisons and refused to have any prison personnel considered for his centers. Instead, he went out to each community where a center was planned, and recruited human service experts who already knew that community. Sims had been working as a vocational rehabilitation specialist in a Madison social service agency. He didn't know anything about corrections, except that many of his boyhood friends had ended up in prison. Once he took on the Madison center he was hooked, although he always felt a conflict between his race and his role in the correctional system. He once told Phil: "You know blacks like me are getting locked up faster than we're being born. You walk down these streets for five minutes—or come listen to my residents—you realize this system is turning out a lot of really angry young men. They don't live in the same world you do—or that I do." After Commissioner Comstock was fired, Smythe retired. Smythe recommended Sims to the new commissioner as his replacement. Doug had a long discussion with his new boss about his misgivings. The commissioner said he wanted someone with those doubts running the prison. Sims accepted.

Phil. When we watched Phil walking through a prison door for the first time, he was so nervous he couldn't see the superintendent sign over Smythe's door. Like Masters, Phil was lured into corrections because

516 CORRECTIONS: PRACTICE AND POLICY

he needed a summer job. In one role or another, he's been there ever since. He has often wondered why and never found a satisfactory answer. The best justification he could come up with was a very personal one, although one he shared with most of the other people who have stayed. Very simply put, he, and they, enjoyed working with people. But of course that hardly explained the choice of corrections. "Do you enjoy punishing people?" his brother asked one day. "No," said Phil. "I don't know anyone that enjoys that. And to be fair, we're not doing the punishing. What I am hooked on, I guess, is working with people—the staff and the offenders—who are struggling to be human beings to each other, even in that situation."

SUMMARY

1. Correctional costs are rising faster than other criminal justice costs, but correctional costs as a proportion of all government spending are relatively small.
2. Correctional cost increases have recently outstripped population and inflationary increases.
3. A complete picture of correctional costs is difficult to come by, and most correctional departments underreport costs by a significant amount.
4. Corrections lacks important cost controls, including commonly accepted budgeting and accounting techniques, and control over the demand for services.
5. Much has recently been made of the privatization of corrections. Privatization is occurring in a number of government areas, not just corrections. Private involvement in corrections has always been significant, but often underestimated.
6. The major concern currently is with private, profit-making prisons for adult offenders. Arguments in favor include that private firms operate more quickly, more cheaply, and provide equal or better quality services. Arguments against are that private firms will lobby for incarceration, exploit inmates, and violate rights.
7. The most important correctional resource is its people, but human resources in corrections are undermanaged, often ineffectively utilized, and poorly compensated.
8. Ex-offenders are a potential resource, but ex-offenders have traditionally been mistrusted by correctional agencies. Correctional employment practices regarding ex-offenders do not serve an effective example for other employers.
9. Volunteers in corrections are interested and motivated but poorly recruited, ineffectively trained, and rarely evaluated.

KEY WORDS

BOND ACT. A common means of financing public construction with private funds by selling bonds to be paid back with moderate interest over a period of years. Bond financing drastically increases the cost of construction, but also removes construction cost from the yearly operating costs.

DIRECT COSTS. Operating expenses, such as salaries, fringe benefits, program services, equipment and contractual costs, plus capital costs.

INDIRECT COSTS. Costs that support operation, such as central office administration and expenses incurred by other departments in supporting corrections.

NONPROFIT ORGANIZATION. Any one of several types of organization that charge for services rendered only the equivalent of direct and indirect costs.

PRIVATIZATION. The process of contracting public functions to private organizations.

PROFIT-MAKING FIRM. An organization that charges greater than cost value for services rendered and returns the surplus value to its owners.

UNIT COST. The cost to provide services or products expressed in some standard measure, such as cost of probation supervision per probationer per year.

PROJECTS AND QUESTIONS

1. Find the most recent report of expenditures for corrections in your state. Compare it with expenditures for health, mental health, welfare, education, and other social services. Do you feel this is an appropriate distribution of resources? Why or why not?

2. Are there plans for prison expansion in your state? If so, what kind of construction is proposed? What are the cost estimates? How is the construction financed?

3. Invite to class an officer of a private organization that provides services to correctional agencies or to offenders. How are the services financed? What level of cooperation does this official see with public correctional agencies? How does he or she think relationships could be improved?

4. Interview several employees of correctional agencies. Try to reach persons from a mix of agencies and types of work. How did they become interested in corrections? Have they had experience in several agencies? If so, which organizations did they prefer, and why? What aspects of their work do they prefer most? Least?

ADDITIONAL READING

Paul Lerman. *Community Treatment and Social Control.* Chicago: University of Chicago Press, 1975. The chapter on the cost of the California Probation Subsidy is an excellent example of the complexities and dilemmas of correctional accounting and financing.

National Institute of Justice. *The Privatization of Corrections.* Washington, DC: United States Department of Justice, 1985. A review of the current trend toward privatization.

National Manpower Survey of Criminal Justice. Volume III. *Corrections.* Washington, DC: United States Government Printing Office, 1978. The most complete survey of correctional manpower. While its projections of needs and salary information are outdated, its identification of personnel issues is still pertinent.

Hans Toch and Douglas Grant. *Reforming Human Services.* Beverly Hills, CA: Sage Publications, 1982. A valuable overview of a number of work problems in the criminal justice field, and case studies of some measures for improvement.

GLOSSARY

ADJUDICATORY HEARING (Ch. 19) The fact-finding hearing or trial in juvenile court.

ADMINISTRATIVE SEGREGATION (Ch. 11) Housing units in prison that isolate prisoners from the general population for nondisciplinary reasons.

AFFIRMATIVE ACTION (Ch. 16) A formal program to correct previous discriminatory hiring practices through aggressive recruitment and promotion of previously disadvantaged groups.

AFTERCARE (Ch. 19) Supervision of juveniles after they have served a period in an institution, group home, or day program.

AGE COMPOSITION OF THE POPULATION (Ch. 2) The breakdown of an entire population into age-specific categories. In criminological and corrections research, an important variable in the prediction of crime rates or incarceration rates, since younger groups are at greater risk of crime, violent crime, and incarceration.

ALIENATION (from work) (Ch. 16) Disaffection with work and oneself, often defined in work research as having five facets: meaninglessness, powerlessness, estrangement from self, isolation (estrangement from others), and normlessness.

ANARCHIST IDEOLOGY OF PUNISHMENT (Ch. 3) Contains the beliefs that modern society is based on structured power relationships, that deviance is a product of fitting human relationships into hierarchical rules, and that the current punishment system preserves the power system while reducing human capacity for cooperation.

APPELLATE REVIEW OF SENTENCING (Ch. 6) The practice of reviewing sentences per se (rather than convictions) in appellate court.

BAIL SYSTEM (Ch. 4) The practice of releasing a defendant upon placing a financial guarantee with the court to ensure appearance. Usually the defendant may place the entire amount with the court or pay a bondsman a premium.

BENEFIT OF CLERGY (Ch. 8) An early form of clemency in England originally intended for clergy convicted in King's Courts but transferred to church jurisdiction for punishment. Eventually extended to many nonclerics who could read or who claimed to be able to read. Primarily an escape from the death penalty.

BLOCK DESIGN (Ch. 11) The prison design used at Auburn, New York, and subsequently at a number of maximum security units, which provides cells stacked in tiers or blocks within the center of a building.

BOND ACT (Ch. 20) A common means of financing public construction with private funds by selling bonds to be paid back at moderate interest over a number of years. Bond financing drastically increases costs of construction, but also removes construction costs from yearly operating costs.

BONDSMAN (Ch. 4) A person who provides a financial guarantee that a defendant will appear at subsequent hearings in return for a nonrefundable payment from the defendant.

CAMPUS-STYLE PRISON (Ch. 11) A relatively recent design, used primarily in minimum security settings, that provides separate living quarters (often dorms or rooms) dispersed around a central square of service and office buildings.

CAPITAL PUNISHMENT (Ch. 7) The imposition of the death penalty on an offender convicted of a capital offense.

CASE-LEVEL SENTENCING (Ch. 6) The sentencing of specific offenders.

CIVIL RIGHTS ACT OF 1871 (Ch. 13) Federal legislation of 1871, 42 U.S. Code Section 1983, that makes public officials liable for violations of a person's civil rights; a means of implementing the Fourteenth Amendment.

CLASSIFICATION (Ch. 14) The subdivision of inmates on characteristics relevant to goals, for the distribution of prison resources.

CLASSIFICATION STRUCTURE (Ch. 14) The organiza-

518

tion of persons and information to perform classification duties.

CLIENT-SPECIFIC PLANNING (Ch. 6) A new form of private presentence plan done on behalf of the defendant.

CO-CORRECTIONAL INSTITUTIONS (Ch. 12) Prisons that house both male and female inmates under a single administration.

COLLECTIVE RESISTANCE (Ch. 15) Protests by groups of inmates without resort to violence.

COLLECTIVE VIOLENCE (Ch. 15) Group actions by inmates that involve the use of violence.

COMMUNITY-PLACED ORGANIZATIONS (Ch. 18) Correctional organizations with close links to centralized policymaking and resources, but weak links to local organizations.

COMMUNITY PRERELEASE CENTERS (Ch. 17) Residential centers, usually off prison grounds, that permit inmates nearing release greater contact with community roles and responsibilities than is possible in most prison settings.

COMMUNITY-RUN ORGANIZATIONS (Ch. 18) Correctional organizations with close links to local policymaking and resources, but weak links to centralized authority.

COMMUNITY SERVICE (Ch. 1) A punishment that requires an offender to work a specified number of hours, usually in a public or nonprofit organization.

COMMUNITY TREATMENT PROJECT (Ch. 19) Famous California Youth Authority program that released selected juveniles to aftercare immediately after reception. The project included classification by interpersonal maturity level and attempted differential treatment based on classification.

COMPELLING INTEREST (Ch. 13) The strictest standard applied when a government seeks to limit a fundamental right. Usually the test of conflicting interest in First Amendment and equal protection cases.

COMPETING VALUES APPROACH (Ch. 18) A management approach that integrates the rational goal, the internal process, the human relations, and the open systems models of organizational effectiveness.

COMPLEX ORGANIZATION (Ch. 18) A human system of interrelated roles that must be performed simultaneously for the achievement of goals.

CONCURRENT SENTENCES (Ch. 6) The practice of ordering separate sentences for convictions on multiple charges to be served at the same time.

CONDITIONAL RELEASE (Ch. 17) Release from prison prior to the expiration of sentence, upon condition that the released prisoner will abide by the law and by certain regulations.

CONDITIONAL SENTENCE (Ch. 5) A sentence, such as probation, that can be revoked if certain supervision rules or conditions are not obeyed.

CONDITIONS OF PROBATION (Ch. 8) Rules to which a probationer must conform while on probation.

CONFLICTED SYSTEMS IDEOLOGY OF PUNISHMENT (Ch. 3) Contains the beliefs that modern society is composed of many diverse groups, that deviance is partly a product of formal control systems' inability to deal with social complexity, and that punishment organizations are more effective in maintaining their political support than in delivering effective social control.

CONGREGATE SYSTEM (Ch. 11) Now identified with the Auburn system, the original congregate prison, like Newgate in New York City, provided for group living and work and little internal security. As modified at Auburn, the congregate system provided for silent group work during the day and sleeping in individual cells at night.

CONNECTS (Ch. 12) Inmates whose prison assignments allow them to acquire scarce information and resources that can be used for personal gain.

CONSECUTIVE SENTENCES (Ch. 6) The practice of ordering separate sentences for convictions on multiple charges to be served in sequence.

CONSENT DECREE (Ch. 13) An agreement to correct conditions that violate rights, without an admission of liability for past violations.

CONSTITUTIONAL JAIL (Ch. 10) A jail that follows the rules for inmate management and treatment developed from civil litigation based upon constitutional law.

THE COOL (Ch. 12) Professional criminals who see crime as their skill for making a living. This group readily adopts the norms of the inmate system.

CORRECTIONAL INTEREST GROUP (Ch. 18) A group that interacts with a correctional organization to protect its investment in correctional activities.

CORRECTIONAL NETWORK (Ch. 5) That collection of agencies and decision-makers which funds, manages, and regulates the correctional process.

CORRECTIONAL PROCESS (Ch. 5) The sequence of decisions and activities through which convicted offenders are processed until the completion of sentence.

COTTAGE SYSTEM (Ch. 12) The design of many prisons

for women built with a series of cottagelike living facilities that surround the administration and other general-use buildings. This design developed at the turn of the century to provide women inmates with a homelike atmosphere that would preserve or create a family orientation.

COURT MASTER (Ch. 13) An official appointed by a judge to oversee the implementation of an institutional order.

COURTYARD DESIGN (Ch. 11) A recent prison design adaptable to a number of security settings. Buildings are arranged around the perimeter of an internal open space.

CRIMINAL PUNISHMENT (Ch. 1) "Persons who possess authority impose designedly unpleasant consequences upon, and express their condemnation of, other persons who are capable of choice and who have breached established standards of behavior" (Greenwalt, 1983:343–344).

CRITERION VARIABLE (Ch. 8) The outcome variable, the presence of which is predicted by using other variables thought to relate to it. In corrections research, the criterion variable being predicted is often some version of recidivism.

CRITICAL IDEOLOGIES (Ch. 3) Ideologies that challenge the dominant ideology, typically by analyzing social control systems as behaviors emerging from particular political and economic structures.

DAY PROGRAMS (Ch. 19) Any of a variety of programs entailing daily but nonresidential supervision of juvenile offenders.

DEATH ROW (Ch. 7) Cellblocks in prisons housing inmates convicted of capital crimes and sentenced to death.

DEINSTITUTIONALIZATION (Ch. 19) The process of removing juveniles from secure settings at quicker than normal rates and preventing new cases from being assigned to secure care.

DELEGATED SENTENCING POLICY (Ch. 6) The practice by the legislature of permitting or authorizing the construction of sentencing policy by a group other than itself.

DEPENDENCY (Ch. 19) The status of a youth who has no parent or guardian or whose parent or guardian is unable to provide care and supervision.

DESCRIPTIVE GUIDELINES (Ch. 6) Sentencing guidelines in which the sentence values are determined by studying the normal patterns for certain offenses and offender types. The sentence values in this case describe past practice.

DETENTION (OF JUVENILES) (Ch. 19) The act of placing a juvenile in custody (usually secure) pending an adjudicatory hearing.

DETERMINATE SENTENCE (Ch. 6) A flat sentence specified in advance of the specific conviction.

DETERRENCE (Ch. 1) Justification that seeks to use punishment to dissuade others from committing similar crimes.

DIFFERENTIAL INVOLVEMENT HYPOTHESIS (Ch. 6) The hypothesis that racially differential incarceration rates are caused by the different levels of involvement of different racial groups in specific types of crime.

DIRECT COSTS (Ch. 20) Operating expenses such as salary, fringe benefits, program services, equipment, and contractual costs, plus expenses and capital costs.

DIRECT SENTENCING POLICY (Ch. 6) The construction of sentencing policy directly by the legislature.

DISCLOSURE OF PSI REPORT (Ch. 6) The practice of sharing the PSI report with defendant and counsel.

DISCRETIONARY RELEASE (Ch. 17) A conditional release decision in which the authority to release rests within the discretion of release officials. The most common discretionary release is parole. Some good time statutes also provide for discretionary release decisions.

DISPOSITION (Ch. 19) Hearing in juvenile or family court following adjudication and concerned with the placement of persons found to be delinquent or in need of supervision.

DIVERSION (Ch. 19) The process of turning away offenders from the traditional correctional process.

DOMINANT IDEOLOGY OF PUNISHMENT (Ch. 3) The punishment ideology that is politically accepted. In the United States, the ideology that accepts punishment as a means of retribution, deterrence, incapacitation, and/or rehabilitation. Essential beliefs include (1) that society has a consensus of values; (2) that deviance from those values indicates individual, not system, malfunction; and (3) that punishment protects a fair system of social rewards.

EMERGENCY RELEASE PROCEDURES (Ch. 17) A legal means to reduce prison population when it reaches a certain size (usually defined as a percent of capacity). Those procedures will permit earlier than normal consideration for parole, or earlier than specified mandatory release dates through the award of additional good time.

EQUAL EMPLOYMENT OPPORTUNITY (Ch. 16) The policy of selection and advancement of personnel on the basis of merit, without regard to criteria such as race or gender. EEO became federal law in Title VII of the 1964 Civil Rights Act.

EXECUTIVE MODEL OF SENTENCING (Ch. 6) A sentencing structure that gives most discretion to the executive branch of government, usually to a parole board.

EXECUTIVE PARDON (Ch. 17) As a forerunner of parole, executive pardon often involved application to the chief of a jurisdiction for shortening of sentence. Pardon is still in use, and may be full or partial. Pardons in some states are used to reduce very long sentences so that an inmate may be considered for parole.

EXPLICIT SENTENCING POLICY (Ch. 6) A formal statement of goals, a codification of criminal penalties consistent with the goals, and an explicit structure and stated process for implementing sentencing goals.

FEEDBACK (Ch. 5) Output from a system or system component that loops back to become input to earlier components in the system.

FELONY (Ch. 1) A crime punishable by incarceration in a state or federal prison for at least a year.

FLAT TERM (Ch. 6) A specific, definite term for a conviction, not necessarily known in advance of sentencing.

FORMAL CONTROL (Ch. 1) A social control governed by written rules and usually employing formal organizations for implementation.

FUNCTIONAL APPROACH TO PRISON CULTURE (Ch. 15) Explanations of the prison culture that focus on shared experience within the prison, such as inmate responses to the pains of imprisonment.

FURLOUGH (Ch. 17) Where statute permits, temporary leaves that may be granted to inmates by prison officials, usually for one or two days at a time. Also called *home furlough*, although used for purposes other than home visits.

GOAL-DIRECTED SYSTEMS (Ch. 5) Managed systems or systems that effectively set, change, and reach objectives.

GOAL-ORIENTED SYSTEMS (Ch. 5) Systems lacking a management component.

GOOD TIME (Ch. 17) Statutory provisions for reduction in sentence in return for good behavior in prison.

GRIEVANCE PROCEDURE (Ch. 13) A formal administrative procedure to investigate and resolve disputes between management and employees, clients, or inmates.

GROUP HOMES (Ch. 19) Halfway houses for juveniles.

GUIDED GROUP INTERACTION (Ch. 19) A group dynamics treatment process stressing the use of a youth reference group and changes in group norms to change behavior; used in the Highfields and Provo experiments.

HABEAS CORPUS (Ch. 13) An extraordinary writ challenging the legality of confinement.

HANDS-OFF DOCTRINE (Ch. 13) Judicial doctrine that legally confined inmates had no rights. Justified on the basis of federalism and separation of powers.

HOUSE ARREST (Ch. 9) Also called home detention, a sentence or condition of sentence requiring an offender to be at home during specified periods of time. May also be a condition of release before trial.

HOUSE OF REFUGE (Ch. 19) Workhouses, the first of which was estalished in 1824 as a means of separating juveniles from the adult correctional process.

HUMAN RELATIONS MODEL (Ch. 18) A perspective on organizations that stresses the value of human resources and attempts to improve morale, group cohesion, and related variables, in order to develop those resources.

IDEOLOGY (Ch. 3) A tightly knit set of beliefs, often with political implications, that justify a particular action system.

IMPLICIT SENTENCING POLICY (Ch. 6) A legislative orientation to sentencing that must be inferred from its other actions.

IMPORTATION HYPOTHESIS (Ch. 15) Explanations of the prison culture that focus on the background of inmates rather than current prison experience as a source of values and attitudes.

INCAPACITATION (Ch. 1) Justification of punishment that seeks to reduce crime in society by preventing a convicted offender from committing new crimes.

INCARCERATION (Ch. 1) Confinement in a prison or jail as punishment for a crime.

INDENTURING (Ch. 17) A forerunner of parole. Inmates were released to the custody of families or manufacturers prior to expiration of sentence.

INDETERMINATE SENTENCE (Ch. 6) A sentence that permits discretionary release, sometimes based on factors unknown at sentencing, such as prison adjustment. Expressed in two figures, a minimum term (which may be zero) and a maximum term.

INDIRECT COSTS (Ch. 20) Costs to support an operation, such as central office administration and expenses incurred by other departments in supporting corrections.

INDUSTRIAL PRISON (Ch. 11) Any prison in which the principal activity is industrial labor by the inmates, and also prisons in the period 1900 to 1930, when the focus of most prisons in the United States was the production of goods.

INFORMAL PROBATION (Ch. 19) The process of supervising a consenting offender on probation without adjudication or conviction.

INITIAL CLASSIFICATION (Ch. 14) The classification of newly received inmates, usually in a reception center, often with heavy reliance on previous records and tests.

INMATE SELF-GOVERNMENT (Ch. 11) Any prison management system that provides formal inmate participation or control over some decisions regarding routine, discipline, and program; pioneered by Osborne and Gill.

INSTITUTIONAL ORDERS (Ch. 13) Also known as court decrees, the judicial orders applied to an institution to correct the conditions or practices that infringe on inmate rights.

INTENSIVE SUPERVISION (Ch. 8) The application in probation or parole of greater than normal supervision. There is no standard for intensive supervision, which varies from two contacts per month to daily contact. Most often applied to high-risk offenders.

INTERMITTENT CONFINEMENT (Ch. 9) The provision for specific periods of incarceration interspersed with periods of freedom in the community, often on probation.

INTERNAL PROCESS MODEL (Ch. 18) A perspective on organizations that places high value on predictability and control and uses structures which make activities more predictable.

ISOLATED ORGANIZATIONS (Ch. 18) Correctional organizations that have weak ties to both centralized and local sources of policy and resources.

JAIL CONFINEMENT RATE (Ch. 2) The number of persons confined in jails, both as detainees awaiting trial and as misdemeanants serving short sentences, per 100,000 people in the general civilian population.

JAIL HOUSE TURNOUTS (Ch. 12) Inmates who are introduced to homosexuality while in prison.

JIVE BITCHES (Ch. 12) Inmates who tend to be manipulative and unstable, causing problems for other inmates and staff.

JUDICIAL MODEL OF SENTENCING (Ch. 6) Sentencing structure that provides the judge with more discretion in fixing a term than either the legislature or the executive branch.

JUDICIAL REPRIEVE (Ch. 8) In England, originally the practice of temporarily suspending sentence to give a convicted person time to apply to the king for pardon; eventually coupled with deportation. It set the precedent for suspension of sentence.

JUDICIAL SENTENCING INSTITUTE (Ch. 6) An educational or training session for judges on issues relevant to sentencing.

LEAST RESTRICTIVE ALTERNATIVE (Ch. 13) The only level of restriction the government is usually permitted to place on fundamental rights. The test is whether the government can achieve its legitimate competing purpose while placing lesser limits on the rights of the individual.

LEGISLATIVE MODEL OF SENTENCING (Ch. 6) A sentencing structure in which the legislature retains most discretion, and does not permit a great deal of judicial or executive flexibility in fixing terms.

THE LIFE (Ch. 12) The inmate group that has spent a great deal of time in institutions and does not conform to conventional norms. This group takes on and to some extent establishes the norms of the prison social system.

MANDATORY (CONDITIONAL) RELEASE (Ch. 17) Usually refers to conditional release of prisoners through accumulation of good time credits.

MANDATORY SENTENCE (Ch. 6) A statutory requirement of a specific sentence or a proscription of certain sentencing options (such as probation).

MARK SYSTEM (Ch. 11) A form of token economy designed by Alexander Maconochie at the Tasmanian penal colony in 1840. Provided for graduated increase in responsibility and freedom contingent on behavioral goals being met by inmates.

MARXIAN IDEOLOGY OF PUNISHMENT (Ch. 3) Contains the beliefs that capitalist society has built-in conflicts between capital and labor, that deviance is a result of class structure, and that the punishment system protects the unequal distribution of resources.

MAXIMUM SECURITY (Ch. 11) A physical and social design that provides for high control over entrance and egress and strict control over physical movement of prisoners through the prison.

MEDIATION (Ch. 13) Informal conflict resolution through the intervention of a trained mediator who seeks a mutually agreeable resolution between disputing parties.

MEDICAL MODEL (Ch. 14) The beliefs that crime is a symptom of mental illness and that mental illness can be treated in a fashion similar to physical disease.

MEDIUM SECURITY (Ch. 11) A physical and social design providing for moderate to high control over entrance and egress but providing somewhat more freedom within the prison grounds than maximum security.

MINIMUM SECURITY (Ch. 11) A physical and social design that provides for little or no physical barriers and little overt control of movement within the prison.

MISDEMEANOR (Ch. 1) A crime punishable by incarceration for less than a year, usually in a local jail.

MIXED CONTROL ORGANIZATIONS (Ch. 18) A correctional organization in which policymaking and resource supply are shared by centralized and local resources.

NEEDS-BASED SUPERVISION (Ch. 9) A form of community supervision in which interventions by the correctional staff are designed to meet specific needs attributed to or claimed by the offender.

NEGLECT (Ch. 19) The status of juveniles whose parents or guardian have caused harm directly or indirectly or have failed to provide supervision and care.

NONPROFIT ORGANIZATION (Ch. 20) Any one of several different types of organization in which charges for services rendered equal direct and indirect costs.

OMBUDSMAN (Ch. 13) Public official with authority to investigate complaints about government operations and to recommend changes.

OPEN SYSTEMS MODEL (Ch. 18) A perspective on organizations that places high value on resource acquisition and growth through the use of flexible structures that can respond to opportunities.

ORGANIZATIONAL DEVELOPMENT (Ch. 18) An organizational change strategy that seeks to revitalize the culture of the organization by developing teamwork and sensitivity to workers' needs while improving organizational performance. Usually starts at the top of the organization and uses expert outside consultants to assist in the change process.

OVERCLASSIFICATION (Ch. 14) The practice of invalidly rating inmates as high security risks.

PAINS OF IMPRISONMENT (Ch. 15) The deprivations associated with imprisonment, including loss of freedom, autonomy, goods and services, security, and heterosexual relationships.

PARENS PATRIAE DOCTRINE (Ch. 19) The legal doctrine providing the state with jurisdiction over the welfare of juveniles and other categories of people who presumably cannot care for themselves.

PAROLE (Ch. 17) Conditional, discretionary release, usually at the determination of a board, followed by supervision to ascertain that conditions are adhered to.

PENETENTIARY MOVEMENT (Ch. 11) The period from 1790 to 1830 in which political and social attention was focused on debates about the most effective penitentiary design and when the first major prisons were built in the eastern United States.

PENNSYLVANIA SYSTEM (Ch. 11) The prison design associated with the Eastern State Penitentiary (1829), in which prisoners spent their entire sentence in solitary confinement. Quickly abandoned as impractical and expensive.

PER DIEM (Ch. 10) The cost per day, here the daily cost of housing inmates.

PLURALISTIC IGNORANCE (Ch. 16) A mistaken belief by an individual that values held by others in the group are significantly different from one's own.

PODULAR DIRECT (Ch. 10) A process of inmate supervision that requires correctional officers to be in direct contact with inmates who are not confined to cells.

PODULAR INDIRECT (Ch. 10) A process of supervision wherein inmates are not confined to cells and correctional officers can observe inmates but are physically separated from them.

POLICY-LEVEL SENTENCING DECISIONS (Ch. 6) Sentencing decisions by the legislature or its delegate about the goals and structure of sentencing.

PREDICTOR VARIABLES (Ch. 8) Variables used in prediction research to assess the likelihood of a particular outcome or criterion variable.

PRERELEASE CLASSIFICATION (Ch. 14) The final classification decisions prior to release for the purpose of allocating inmates to transition programs.

PRERELEASE PROGRAMS IN PRISON (Ch. 17) Programs within the institution that are designed to prepare the inmate for release. These usually include assistance in applying for a job and a suitable residence.

PRESCRIPTIVE GUIDELINES (Ch. 6) Sentencing guidelines in which the sentence values are determined on the basis of value judgments about appropriateness, rather than on the basis of past practice.

PRESENTENCE INVESTIGATION (PSI) (Ch. 6) An investigation by a probation officer prior to sentencing. The PSI report is one source of information used by the judge in determining sentence, especially in the decision to grant probation.

PRESUMPTIVE SENTENCE (Ch. 6) The sentence presumed to be appropriate by the sentencing policymaker, and that therefore must be selected by the judge unless there are compelling reasons to sentence otherwise.

PRETRIAL DETENTION (Ch. 4) The practice of detaining in jail a defendant who cannot make bail or obtain other release pending trial.

PRETRIAL DIVERSION (Ch. 4) Formal programs that provide community supervision of a defendant for a specified period of time, typically with the promise to drop prosecution if supervision is completed successfully.

PREVENTIVE DETENTION (Ch. 4) The practice of detaining a defendant prior to trial on the grounds that the defendant will commit a new crime if released.

PRISON INCARCERATION RATE (Ch. 2) The number of persons serving sentences in federal and state prisons per 100,000 people in the general population.

PRISON INDUSTRIES (Ch. 14) Employment of prisoners in a business enterprise, often with market restrictions.

PRISONIZATION (Ch. 15) "Taking on, in greater or lesser degree, the folkways, mores, customs, and general culture of the penitentiary." Clemmer, 1940:220.

PRIVATIZATION (Ch. 20) The process of contracting public functions to private organizations.

PROBATION (Ch. 1) Freedom granted by a judge to an offender under conditions supervised by an officer. In most states, legally defined as a suspension of sentence.

PROFIT-MAKING FIRM (Ch. 20) An organization that charges greater than cost for services rendered and returns the surplus value to its owners.

PUBLIC ORGANIZATION (Ch. 18) An organization supported directly from public funds, responsible to the general constituency, and carrying out functions of government.

PUNITIVE INTENT STANDARD (Ch. 1) A standard that distinguishes incarceration from other forms of confinement, such as detention, on the grounds of a demonstrable alternative purpose for the confinement, and reasonable relationships between the confinement practice and the alternate purpose.

PUNITIVE SEGREGATION (Ch. 11) High-security isolation cells used to discipline inmates. Length of placement and conditions in punitive segregation are restricted by regulations and constitutional limits.

QUALIFIED IMMUNITY (Ch. 13) A defense to a Civil Rights Act suit that claims the right violated was not clearly enunciated and therefore the violation was unintentional and the official not liable for damages.

QUALITY OF WORK LIFE (Ch. 18) Organizational change projects that seek to improve conditions of workers on the job through the use of joint management labor committees for decisions about the conditions or process of work.

RADIAL DESIGN (Ch. 11) The physical design associated with the Pennsylvania system of housing units (usually untiered cells) on outside walls radiating from a central control hub.

RATED CAPACITY (Ch. 11) The number of inmates determined by the prison administration as the upper limit for a particular facility. As a crowding measure, unreliable because administrators frequently alter the acceptable level.

RATIONAL GOAL MODEL (Ch. 18) A perspective on organizations that places high values on productivity and efficiency and achieves these through goal planning, technological development, and evaluation.

RECEPTION CENTER (Ch. 14) A separate unit receiving inmates from court for initial classification.

RECLASSIFICATION (Ch. 14) Periodic assessment of an inmate during the period of incarceration.

RECOGNIZANCE (Ch. 8) A forerunner of some current pretrial release practices (in this text referred to as ROR) and of modern probation. Recognizance was used in England and in the United States in the nineteenth century to release offenders on promise of good behavior.

REFORM POLICY (Ch. 5) In the correctional policy model, a correctional system with high concern for community, low concern for the individual offender, using compliance strategies to maintain conformity.

REFORMATORY (Ch. 11) A type of facility, but more important a type of program, designed in the 1870s for youthful (generally age 16 to 25) inmates. Initiated at Elmira, New York, the program stressed vocational training, military discipline, and discretionary release during an indeterminant sentence. The term now refers to any facility (often maximum security) housing the youngest inmates in the adult correctional system.

REHABILITATION (Ch. 1) A justification of punishment that seeks to reduce new crimes by a convicted offender by changing attitudes, values, beliefs, or behavior.

REHABILITATION POLICY (Ch. 5) In the correctional policy model, a correctional system with high concern for the individual offender and low concern for the community, using identification strategies to help the offender mature.

REINTEGRATION (Ch. 14) A broad correctional strategy stressing acquisition of legitimate skills by inmates and the creation of supervised opportunities for testing those skills, especially in community settings.

REINTEGRATION POLICY (Ch. 5) In the correctional policy model, a correctional system with high concern for the offender and the community, using internalization change strategies.

RELEASE ON RECOGNIZANCE (ROR) (Ch. 4) Release of a defendant without bail or other surety pending trial, upon his or her promise to reappear.

RESTITUTION (Ch. 1) Action by the offender to restore a victim to his or her condition prior to a crime.

RESTRAINT POLICY (Ch. 5) In the correctional policy model, a correctional system with low concern for the offender and the community, using no strategy to influence offender behavior; a holding strategy.

RETRIBUTION (Ch. 1) Justification for punishment on the grounds that it is a moral duty for society to punish wrongdoers; usually includes the notion of just desert—that the seriousness of punishment be commensurate with the seriousness of the offense.

SCOPE OF SENTENCING POLICY (Ch. 6) The breadth of sanctions covered by sentencing policy. The most important distinction is between broad policies that address probation as well as prison terms and narrow policies that address only length of incarceration, but not whether to incarcerate.

SENTENCING COMMISSION (Ch. 6) A group commissioned by the legislature to determine sentencing policy and usually to monitor implementation of that policy.

SENTENCING CONFERENCE (Ch. 6) An informal meeting prior to the sentencing hearing involving judge, prosecutor, defense attorney, and probation officer to discuss sentence recommendations.

SENTENCING COUNCIL (Ch. 6) The meeting of a panel of judges in a multijudge court to discuss sentencing of pending cases. Designed to temper individual decisions by comparison to group norms.

SENTENCING DISPARITY (Ch. 6) Differences in sentencing not attributable to differences in criminal history of offender or to differences in the current convictions.

SENTENCING GUIDELINES (Ch. 6) Determination of sentence based on decision rules that apply to all sentences. Typically the rules are based on severity of crime and length of criminal record.

SENTENCING STRUCTURE (Ch. 6) The division of decision authority at the individual case level of sentencing; provides the formal relationships by which to implement policy.

SHOCK PROBATION (Ch. 1) Judicial resentencing to probation after an initially imposed incarcerative sentence has begun.

SNITCHERS (Ch. 12) Inmates who inform on other inmates.

SOCIAL CONTROL (Ch. 1) Any measures or behaviors, formal or informal, that identify and attempt to control deviant behavior.

SPLIT SENTENCE (Ch. 1) Any sentence that includes an incarcerative term preceding a period of probation.

SQUARES (Ch. 12) Inmates who are noncriminal types and considered situational offenders. This type does not conform to the inmate code.

STABILITY OF PUNISHMENT HYPOTHESIS (Ch. 2) The hypothesis that the rate of punishment in a given society will remain stable, despite fluctuations in the crime rate.

STANDARDIZATION OF PERSONNEL (Ch. 18) The selection and training of personnel to increase uniformity in knowledge, skill, or decisions.

STANDARDIZATION OF WORK (Ch. 18) The planning of

work routines and practices to increase uniformity of processes and outcomes.

STATUS OFFENDERS (Ch. 19) Juvenile offenders who have not broken the penal law, but have violated norms of control, such as by running away or being truant.

STUDY RELEASE (Ch. 17) Release from prison grounds of inmates who pursue education in community programs. May involve return to prison at night, or residence in a prerelease center.

SUBOPTIMIZATION (Ch. 18) The practice by organizational subunits of valuing unit objectives over organizational objectives.

SUPERVISED PRETRIAL RELEASE (Ch. 4) The release of a defendant without bail but under supervision of a pretrial release agency or other supervising party.

SYSTEM (Ch. 5) "A set of parts coordinated to accomplish a set of goals" (Churchman, 1968:29).

SYSTEM BOUNDARIES (Ch. 5) The division between a system and its environment. In human systems, the boundary is often permeable and changing.

SYSTEM COMPONENTS (Ch. 5) The separate subroutines or activities that contribute to total system objectives.

SYSTEM MANAGEMENT COMPONENT (Ch. 5) The portion of a system that designs other components, distributes resources to them, coordinates activities, and evaluates system performance.

SYSTEM OBJECTIVES (Ch. 5) The measured performance of a total system, rather than of its parts; the joint products of system components.

SYSTEM RESOURCES (Ch. 5) Items a system can change and use to achieve objectives.

SYSTEMS APPROACH (Ch. 5) An analytical method that focuses on systemic properties and processes.

TECHNOLOGY (Ch. 18) An arrangement of human and other resources to achieve the objectives of the organization.

TELEPHONE POLE DESIGN (Ch. 11) Prison design that replaced the block design for maximum security units. A long central corridor is crossed by several shorter living unit and program buildings.

THERAPEUTIC COMMUNITY (Ch. 14) Residential treatment unit that promotes change through communal processes of norm building, inmate participation in decisions, and group responsibility.

TICKET-OF-LEAVE (Ch. 17) An early form of conditional release used in the English and Irish prison systems.

TOTAL INSTITUTIONS (Ch. 15) A term coined by Goffman (1961) to refer to organizations that controlled the work, play, and sleep of their lower participants.

TOTALITY OF CONDITIONS (Ch. 13) A concept developed in *Pugh* v. *Locke* to judge prisons in which the total weight of the environment, rather than single practices, was seen as violative of the Eighth Amendment ban on cruel and unusual punishment.

TRAINING SCHOOLS (Ch. 19) Devised in the middle of nineteenth century, the most common form of institution for juvenile delinquents. Usually secure and often stressing skill training.

TRANSPORTATION OFFICERS (Ch. 10) Officers in charge of transporting inmates to other correctional institutions, usually to the state prison system, after sentencing.

TRUSTY SYSTEM (Ch. 11) Perhaps initiated by Pilsbury at the Wethersfield prison in Connecticut (1830); the practice of providing trusted inmates with considerable freedom and responsibility for a number of administrative and service duties in the prison.

U CURVE (Ch. 15) Also known as the J curve; the graphed pattern of inmate value distance from staff values as prison sentence progresses. Inmates first entering prison have values most similar to those of staff; inmates in the middle of sentence have values least like those of staff; inmates preparing for release have values closer to staff, but not as similar as those just entering prison.

UNIT COST (Ch. 20) The cost to provide services or products expressed in some standard measure, such as cost of probation supervision per probationer per year.

UNIT MANAGEMENT PLAN (Ch. 14) The internal division of a large prison into smaller, separately administered units; devised by the Federal Bureau of Prisons.

UTILITARIAN JUSTIFICATIONS OF PUNISHMENT (Ch. 1) Justifications that promise an empirical benefit from the exercise of punishment, such as deterrence, incapacitation, and rehabilitation.

VOCATIONAL TRAINING (Ch. 14) Provision of a specific marketable skill.

WORK RELEASE (Ch. 17) Release from prison grounds to find or engage in employment in a community. May require return to prison after work hours, or residence in a prerelease or work release center.

BIBLIOGRAPHY

Abercrombie, N., Hill, S., and Turner, B. 1984. *The Dictionary of Sociology.* New York: Penguin.

Ackoff, Russell L., and Emery, Fred E. 1972. *On Purposeful Systems.* Chicago: Aldine Atherton.

Adams, Kenneth. 1983. Former mental patients in a prison and parole system: A study of socially disruptive behavior. *Criminal Justice and Behavior,* 10(3) September:358–394.

_____. 1984. Prison mental health services: An empirical study of the service delivery system in two New York State prisons. Ph.D. diss., School of Criminal Justice, State University of New York at Albany.

Adams, William P., Chandler, Paul M., and Neithercutt, M. C. 1971. The San Francisco Project: A critique. *Federal Probation,* 35:45–53.

Adriti, R. R. 1973. The sexual segregation of American prisons. *Yale Law Journal,* 82:1229–1273.

Allen, Francis A. 1964. *The Borderland of Criminal Justice.* Chicago: University of Chicago Press.

Allen, Harry, and Gatz, Nick. 1976. Exoffenders as parole officer aides: An outcome study. Paper prepared for annual meeting, American Society of Criminology, Tuscon, Arizona.

_____, Carlson, Eric C., and Parks, Evalyn C. 1979. *Critical Issues in Adult Probation.* Washington, DC: United States Department of Justice.

Allison, R. 1982. Overcrowding is now a national epidemic. *Corrections Magazine,* 7:18–34.

American Bar Association. 1970. Project on Standards for Criminal Justice: Standards Relating to Probation. (Approved Draft, August). Chicago: American Bar Association.

_____. 1985. America's 14,000 executions. *ABA Journal,* April: 71.

American Correctional Association. 1966. *Manual of Correctional Standards.* Washington, DC: American Correctional Association.

_____. 1981. *Standards for Adult Local Detention Facilities,* 2d ed. College Park, MD: American Correctional Association.

_____. 1984. *Standards for Adult Local Detention Facilities—Supplement.* College Park, MD: American Correctional Association.

_____. 1985. *Standards for Adult Local Detention Facilities,* 3d ed. College Park, MD: American Correctional Association.

American Friends Service Committee. 1971. *Struggle for Justice.* New York: Hill and Wang.

American Justice Institute. 1979. *Classification for Criminal Justice Decisions.* Vol. 2, *Probation and Parole Supervision.* Sacramento, CA: American Justice Institute.

Amnesty International Publications. 1985. *Amnesty International Report,* 1985. London.

Amnesty International Publications. 1986. *Amnesty International Newsletter,* March, 16(3).

Amnesty International Publications. 1987. USA The Death Penalty. Amnesty International Briefing, London.

Andeneas, Johannes. 1974. *Punishment and Deterrence.* Ann Arbor: University of Michigan Press.

Andrews, William. 1899. *Bygone Punishments.* London: Williams Andrews and Co. Pp. 1–50.

Archer, Dave, Gartner, Rosemary, and Beittel, March. 1983. Homicide and the death penalty: A cross-national test of a deterrence hypothesis. *Journal of Criminal Law and Criminology,* 74(3):991–1013.

Ares, Charles, Rankin, A., and Sturz, H. 1963. The Manhattan bail project: an interim report on the use of pretrial parole. *New York University Law Review,* 38:67–95.

Argyris, Chris. 1957. *Personality and Organization.* New York: Harper & Row.

Aristotle. 1946. *Politics,* Book III, Chapter II (The laws of Solon of Athens, 590 B.C.). Oxford: Clarendon Press.

Austin, James. 1983. Assessing the new generation of prison classification models. *Crime and Delinquency* 29(4):561–576.

_____. 1986. Using early release to relieve prison overcrowding: A dilemma in public policy. *Crime and Delinquency,* 32(4):404–502.

Austin, James, and Krisberg, Barry. 1981. Wider, stronger and different nets: The dialectics of criminal justice reform. *Journal of Research in Crime and Delinquency,* 18(1): 165–196.

Ayer, William A. 1970. Work release programs in the United States: Some difficulties encountered. *Federal Probation*, 34(1):53–54.

Aziz, David. 1983. The circumstances surrounding prison disturbances. Dissertation prospectus, State University of New York at Albany.

Bailey, William C. 1983. Disaggregation in deterrence and death penalty research: The case of murder in Chicago. *Journal of Criminal Law and Criminology*, 74(3):827–859.

Baird, Christopher. 1981. Probation and parole classification: The Wisconsin model. *Corrections Today*, 43(3) May–June:37–41.

Ball, Richard A., Huff, Ronald, and Lilly, J. Robert. 1988. *House Arrest and Correctional Policy*. Newbury Park, CA: Sage.

Bandura, Albert. 1969. *Principles of Behavior Modification*. New York: Holt, Rinehart and Winston.

Banks, J., et al. 1977. *Summary: Phase I Evaluation of Intensive Special Probation Projects*. Washington, D.C.: United States Government Printing Office.

Barnes, Harry Elmer. 1972. *The Story of Punishment*, 2d ed. Montclair, NJ: Patterson Smith Publishing Corp.

———, and Teeters, Negley T. 1951. *New Horizons in Criminology*, 2d ed. Englewood Cliffs, NJ: Prentice-Hall.

———, and ———. 1959. *New Horizons in Criminology*. 3d ed. Englewood Cliffs, NJ: Prentice-Hall.

Bartollas, Clemens, and Sieverdes, Christopher M. 1983. The sexual victim in a coeducational juvenile correctional institution. *The Prison Journal*, 63(1) Spring–Summer:80–90.

Baunach, P. J. 1982. You can't be a mother and be in prison . . . can you? Impacts of the mother-child separation. In B. R. Price and N. Sokoloff (eds.), *The Criminal Justice System and Women*. New York: Clark Boardman.

Bayley, David H. 1985. Social control and political change. Princeton, NJ: Princeton University Center of International Studies Research Monograph No. 49.

Beaumont, Gustave, and de Toqueville, Alexis. 1964. *On the Penitentiary System in the United States and Its Application in France*. Carbondale, IL: Southern Illinois University Press.

Beckard, Richard. 1969. *Organization Development: Strategies and Models*. Reading, MA: Addison Wesley.

Bedau, Hugo Adam, ed. 1982. *The Death Penalty in America*, 3d ed. New York: Oxford University Press.

Beer, Stafford. 1966. *Decision and Control*. New York: Wiley.

Bell, Duran, Jr., and Lang, Kevin. 1985. The intake dispositions of juvenile offenders. *Journal of Research in Crime and Delinquency*, 22(4) November:309–328.

Benson, J. Kenneth. 1975. The interorganizational network as a political economy. *Administrative Sciences Quarterly* 20 (June):229–249.

Bergman, Carol. 1985. Ominous legislation. *Jericho* 38, Winter:1,12.

Berk, Richard et al. 1981. A test of the stability of punishment hypothesis: the case of California, 1851–1870. *American Sociological Review*, 46:805–829.

Berry, Bonnie. 1985. Electronic jails: A new criminal justice concern. *Justice Quarterly*, 2(1):1–22.

Biles, D. 1983. Crime and imprisonment: A two-decade comparison between England and Wales and Australia. British Journal of Criminology, 23 (April):166–172.

Bing, Stephen R., and Rosenfeld, S. Stephen. 1970. *The Quality of Justice in the Lower Criminal Courts of Metropolitan Boston*. Boston: Governor's Committee on Law Enforcement and the Administration of Justice.

Bixby, F. Lovell, and McCorkle, Lloyd W. 1951. Guided group interaction and correctional work. *American Sociological Review*, 16 (August):455–459.

BJS. *See entries under* Bureau of Justice Statistics.

Black, Donald. 1976. *The Behavior of Law*. New York: Academic Press.

Blackmore, John. 1978. Minnesota community corrections act takes hold. *Corrections Magazine*, March:46–56.

———, and Welsh, J. 1983. Selective incapacitation: Sentencing according to risk. *Crime and Delinquency*, 29 (October):504–528.

Blake, Robert, and Mouton, Jane. 1964. *The Managerial Grid*. Houston: Grid Publishing.

Blumberg, Abraham. 1970. *Criminal Justice*. Chicago: Quadrangle Books.

Blumberg, Paul. 1973. *Industrial Democracy: The Sociology of Participation*. New York: Schocken.

Blumstein, Alfred. 1982. On the racial disproportionality of United States' prison populations. *Journal of Criminal Law and Criminology*, 73(3):1259–1281.

———. 1983. Selective incapacitation as a means of crime-control. *American Behavioral Scientist* 27(1):87–108.

———, and Cohen, J. 1973. A theory of the stability of punishment. *Journal of Criminal Law and Criminology*, 64:198–207.

————. 1979. Estimation of individual crime rates from arrest records. *Journal of Criminal Law and Criminology*, 70:581–585.

————, and Nagin, D. 1977. The dynamics of a homeostatic punishment process. *Journal of Criminal Law and Criminology*, 67: 317–334.

————, and Moitra, S. 1979. An analysis of the time series of the imprisonment rate in the states of the United States: a further test of the stability of punishment hypothesis. *Journal of Criminal Law and Criminology*, 70:376–390.

————. 1980. The identification of 'career criminals' from 'chronic offenders' in a cohort. *Law and Policy Quarterly*, 2:321–334.

————, Cohen, J., and Gooding, W. 1983. The influence of capacity on prison population—a critical review of some recent evidence. *Crime and Delinquency*, 29:1–51.

Boland, Barbara et al. 1983. *The Prosecution of Felony Arrests–1979*. Washington, DC: Bureau of Justice Statistics.

Boland, Barbara and Brady, Elizabeth. 1985. *The Prosecution of Felony Arrests—1980*. Washington DC: Bureau of Justice Statistics.

Bolduc, A. 1981. Jail overcrowding issues and analysis. *Annual Journal*, 4:122–136.

Bottoms, A. E., and McWilliams, William. 1984. A nontreatment paradigm for probation practice. In P. McAnany, D. Thomson, and D. Fogel, *Probation and Justice: Reconsideration of Mission*. Cambridge, MA: Oelgeschlager, Gunn, and Hain. Pp. 203–250.

Boudouris, James, and Turnbull, Bruce W. 1985. Shock probation in Iowa. *Journal of Offender Counseling, Services and Rehabilitation*, 9(4) Summer:53–67.

Bowers, William, and Pierce, Glenn. 1982. Racial discrimination and criminal homicide under post-Furman capital statutes. In Hugo A. Bedau. (ed.), *The Death Penalty in America*, 3d ed. New York: Oxford University Press.

Bowker, Lee H. 1981. Gender differences in prisoner subcultures. In L. Bowker (ed.), *Women and Crime in America*. New York: Macmillan.

————. 1983. An essay on prison violence. *The Prison Journal*, 63(1) March:24–31.

Box, S. and Hale, C. 1983. Economic crises and the rising prisoner population in England. Crime and Social Justice 17:20–32.

Bragg, Catherine. 1984. *Preventive Detention as a Means of Social Control*. Ph.D. diss., State University of New York at Albany.

Braithwaite, J. 1982. Comment on the criminal law as a threat system. *Journal of Criminal Law and Criminology*, 73(2):786–789.

Braly, Malcolm. 1972. *On the Yard*. Greenwich, CT: Fawcett.

Brennan, Thomas P., and Mason, Leonard. 1983. Community service: A developing concept. *Federal Probation*, 47(2) June:49–57.

Brewer, David, Beckett, Gerald E., and Holt, Norman. 1981. Determinate sentencing in California: The first year's experience. *Journal of Research in Crime and Delinquency*, 18(2):200–231.

Bronstein, Alvin J. 1980. Prisoners' rights: A history. In Geoffrey P. Alpert (ed.), *The Legal Rights of Prisoners*. Beverly Hills, CA: Sage.

Brookhart, Duane, Ruark, J. B., and Scoven, Douglas E. 1976. A strategy for the prediction of work release success. *Criminal Justice and Behavior*, 3(4) December:321–333.

Brown, Ed, Flanagan, Timothy, and McLeod, Maureen. 1984. *Sourcebook of Criminal Justice Statistics—1983*. Washington, DC: United States Department of Justice.

Buckley, Walter. 1967. *Sociology and Modern Systems Theory*. Englewood Cliffs, NJ: Prentice-Hall.

Bukstel, Lee H., and Kilmann, Peter R. 1980. Psychological effects of imprisonment on confined individuals. *Psychological Bulletin*, 88(2):469–493.

Bureau of Justice Statistics. 1982. *Prisoners 1925–1981*. Washington DC: United States Department of Justice, December.

————. 1983a. *Report to the Nation on Crime and Justice: The Data*. Washington, DC: United States Department of Justice.

————. 1983b. *Prisoners at Midyear 1983*. Washington, DC: United States Department of Justice, October.

————. 1983c. *Probation and Parole 1983*. Washington, DC: United States Department of Justice, September.

————. 1984a. *The 1983 Jail Census*. Washington, DC: United States Department of Justice, November.

————. 1984b. *The Prevalence of Guilty Pleas*. Washington, DC: United States Department of Justice, December.

————. 1985a. *Capital Punishment 1985*. Washington, DC: United States Department of Justice.

————. 1985b. *Prisoners in 1984*. Washington, DC: United States Department of Justice, April.

————. 1985c. *Felony Sentencing in 18 Local Jurisdictions*. Washington, DC: United States Department of Justice, May.

————. 1985d. *Jail Inmates 1983*. Washington, DC: United States Department of Justice, November.

————. 1986a. *Jail Inmates 1984*. Washington, DC: United States Department of Justice, May.

————. 1986b. *Prisoners in State and Federal Insti-*

tutions on December 31, 1983. Washington, DC: United States Department of Justice, June.

———. 1986c. *Capital Punishment—1985*. Washington DC: United States Department of Justice, October.

Cage Count. 1985. *Jericho* Winter:7.

Cahalan, Margaret. 1979. Trends in incarceration in the United States since 1880. *Crime and Delinquency*, 25:9–41.

Calhoun, John A., and Wayne, Susan. 1981. Can the Massachusetts juvenile system survive the eighties? *Crime and Delinquency*, 27(4):522–533.

Carey, James T., and McAnany, Patrick D. 1984. *Introduction to Juvenile Delinquency: Youth and the Law*. Englewood Cliffs, NJ: Prentice-Hall.

Carroll, Leo. 1974. *Hacks, Blacks and Cons Race Relations in a Maximum Security Prison*. Lexington, MA: Lexington Books.

———, and Doubet, Mary Beth. 1983. U.S. social structure and imprisonment: A comment. *Criminology*, 21:449–456.

———, and Mandrick, Margaret E. 1976. Racial bias in the decision to grant parole. *Law and Society Review*, 11(1):93–108.

Casper, Jonathan. 1972. *American Criminal Justice*. Englewood Cliffs, NJ: Prentice-Hall.

———, Brereton, David, and Neal, David. 1983. The California determinate sentence law. *Criminal Law Bulletin*, 19(5):405–433.

Cavender, Gray. 1984. Justice, sanctioning, and the justice model. *Criminology*, 22(2):203–213.

Chaiken, Jan and Chaiken, Marcia. 1982. *Varieties of Criminal Behavior: Summary and Policy Implications*. Santa Monica, CA: Rand Corp.

Champagne, A. 1983. Theory of limited judicial impact—Reforming the Dallas jail as a case study. In E. Fairchild, S. Nagel, and A. Champagne (eds.), *Political Science of Criminal Justice*. Springfield, IL: Charles Thomas.

Chaneles, Sol. 1986. Privatization of prisons: Which way the quantum leap. *Journal of Offender Counseling, Services and Rehabilitation*, 10(4) Spring:1–5.

Chapman, William, and Zausner, Stuart. 1985. Characteristics of inmates under custody: A ten year trend study. Albany: New York Department of Correctional Services, December.

Chen, Huey-Tsyh. 1981. Disposition of felony arrests: A sequential analysis of the judicial decision making process. Ann Arbor, MI: University Microfilm International (Dissertation, University of Massachusetts).

Cherniss, C. 1980. *Professional Burnout in Human Service Organizations*. New York: Praeger.

Christianson, Scott. 1982. Disproportionate imprisonment of blacks in the United States: Practice, impact, and change. Albany, NY: State University of New York at Albany, Center on Minorities and Criminal Justice.

Churchman, C. West. 1968. *The Systems Approach*. New York: Dell Publishing.

Chute, Charles. 1939. Forward. In National Probation and Parole Association, *John Augustus*. New York: National Probation and Parole Association.

———, and Bell, Marjorie. 1956. *Crimes, Courts, and Probation*. New York: Macmillan.

Citizens Crime Commission of Connecticut, Inc. 1984. *Connecticut Intensive Supervision Probation*. Hartford, CT: Citizens Crime Commission of Connecticut, Inc.

Clarke, R. V. G., and Martin, D. N. 1975. A study of absconding and its implications for the residential treatment of delinquents. In J. Tizard, I. Sinclair, and R. V. G. Clarke, *Varieties of Residential Experience*. London: Routledge and Kegan Paul. Pp. 249–274.

Clear, Todd. 1985. Managerial issues in community corrections. In Lawrence F. Travis, III, *Probation, Parole and Community Corrections: A Reader*. Prospect Heights, IL: Waveland Press.

———, and Barry, O. M. 1983. Some conceptual issues in incapacitating offenders. *Crime and Delinquency*, 29(4):524–545.

———, Hewitt, John, and Regoli, Robert. 1978. Discretion and the determinate sentence: Its distribution, control, and effect on time served. *Crime and Delinquency*, 24:428–445.

———, and Gallagher, Kenneth W. 1985. Probation and parole supervision: A review of current classification practices. *Crime and Delinquency*, 31(3) July:423–443.

———, and O'Leary, Vincent. 1983. *Controlling the Offender in the Community*. Lexington, MA: Lexington Books.

Clements, C. B. 1982. The relationship of offender classification to problems of prison overcrowding. *Crime and Delinquency*, 28(1):72–81.

———. 1986. *Offender Needs Assessment*. College Park, MD: American Correctional Association.

Clemmer, Donald. 1940. *The Prison Community*. New York: Holt, Rinehart and Winston.

Clifford, M. Amos. 1985. Turning tough points. *Corrections Today*, 47(1) February:14–16.

Cloward, Richard. 1960. Social control in the prison. In Richard Cloward et al., *Theoretical Studies in the Social Organization of the Prison*. New York: Social Science Research Council.

———, and Ohlin, Lloyd. 1960. *Delinquency and Opportunity*. New York: Free Press.

Coates, Robert B., Miller, Alden D., and Ohlin, Lloyd E. 1978. *Diversity in a Youth Correctional System*. Cambridge, MA: Ballinger.

Coch, Lester, and French, J.R.P. 1948. Overcoming resistance to change. *Human Relations,* 1:512–532.

Cocks, Jack. 1982. The use of 3rd sector organizations as vehicles for community service under a condition of probation. *Federal Probation,* 46(4):29–36.

Cohen, Fred. 1969. *The Legal Challenge to Corrections.* Washington, DC: Joint Commission on Correctional Manpower and Training.

———. 1980. *The Law of Deprivation of Liberty: A Study in Social Control.* St. Paul, MN: West.

———. 1985. Legal issues and the mentally disordered inmate. In New York State Department of Correctional Services, *Sourcebook on the Mentally Disordered Prisoner.* Washington, DC: National Institute of Correction. Pp. 32–95.

Cohen, Lawrence E., and Land, Kenneth C. 1984. Discrepancies between crime reports and crime surveys: Urban and structural determinants. *Criminology,* 22(4):499–530.

Cohn, Alvin W. 1982. Behavioral objectives in probation and parole: A new approach to staff accountability. *Federal Probation,* 46(4):19–28.

Collins, William C. 1986. *Correctional Law 1986.* College Park, MD: American Correctional Association.

Comment. 1983. The Supreme Court and pretrial detention of juveniles—a principled solution to a due process dilemma. *University of Pennsylvania Law Review,* 132:95–119.

Commentaries on the Laws of England, 1765–1769. 1900. Albany, NY: Banks and Co.

Conley, John A. 1981. Revising conceptions about the origins of prisons: The importance of economic considerations. *Social Science Quarterly,* June, 62(2):247–258.

Connecticut General Statutes sec. 54–76 p.

Conrad, John. 1973. Reintegration—practice in search of a theory. In *Reintegrating the Offender into the Community.* Washington, DC: National Institute of Law Enforcement and Criminal Justice.

———. 1984. The redefinition of probation: Drastic proposals to solve an urgent problem. In P. McAnany, D. Thomson, and D. Fogel, *Probation and Justice: Reconsideration of Mission.* Cambridge, MA: Oelgeschlager, Gunn, and Hain. Pp. 251–274.

Cook, Thomas J., and Scioli, Frank P., Jr. 1976. Volunteer program effectiveness: The reduction of recidivism. *Criminal Justice Review,* 1(2) Fall:73–80.

Corbett, Ronald P., Jr., and Fersch, Ellsworth A. L. 1985. Home as prison: The use of house arrest. *Federal Probation,* 49(1) March:13–17.

The Correctional Association of New York. 1984. *Leg-islation to Manage the Prison Crisis.* New York: The Correctional Association of New York.

Cost of justice system is put at $39.7 billion in U.S. study. *New York Times,* July 14, 1986.

Costello, J. C., and Worthington, N. L. 1981. Incarcerating status offenders: Attempts to circumvent the juvenile justice and delinquency prevention act. *Harvard Civil Rights–Civil Liberties Law Review,* 16(1):41–81.

Council of Europe. 1983. *Prison Information Bulletin No. 2.* Strasburg: Council of Europe.

Covington, Alice L. 1980. Parallel civil and criminal suits. *American Criminal Law Review,* 18(2):184–197.

Cressey, Donald R. 1958. Achievement of an unstated organizational goal: An observation on prisons. *Pacific Sociological Review* 1:43–49.

Cromwell, P. 1975. *Jails and Justice.* Springfield, IL: Charles Thomas.

Cross-Drew, Candice. 1984. *Project Jericho Evaluation Report: Final Report.* Sacramento, CA: Division of Program Research and Review, California Department of Youth Authority.

Crouch, Ben M., and Alpert, Geoffrey P. 1982. Sex and occupational specialization among prison guards: A longitudinal study. *Criminal Justice and Behavior,* 9(2):159–176.

Culbertson, Robert G. 1986. The escalating costs of justice: An economic analysis of correctional services in three midwestern states. *Journal of Offender Counseling, Services and Rehabilitation,* 10(4) Summer:27–41.

Cullen, Francis, and Gilbert, Karen E. 1982. *Reaffirming Rehabilitation.* Cincinnati: Anderson.

Curtis, Russell L., Jr., and Schulman, Sam. 1984. Ex-offenders, family relations, and economic supports: The 'significant' women study of the TARP project. *Crime and Delinquency,* 30(4) October:507–528.

Dale, J. 1980. *Strategies to Reduce Jail Overcrowding.* Washington, DC: National Institute of Justice.

Danto, B. L. 1979. Suicide prevention in jails and correctional facilities. In *National Conference on Medical Care and Health Services in Correctional Institutions, Proceedings.* Boulder, CO: National Institute of Corrections Jail Center.

Davies, Malcolm. 1985. Determinate sentencing reform in California and its impact on the penal system. *The British Journal of Criminology,* 25(1):1–30.

Davis, Michael. 1983. How to make the punishment fit the crime. *Ethics,* 93(1) July:726–752.

Dawson, Willa J. 1981. On the abolition of parole. In Roy Roberg and Vincent J. Webb, *Critical Issues in Corrections.* St. Paul, MN: West. Pp. 77–109.

DeCostanzo, E. T., and Valente, J. 1984. Designing

a corrections continuum for female offenders: One state's experience. *Prison Journal*, 64(1):120–128.

Dehais, Richard J. 1983. Racial disproportionality in prison and racial discrimination in the criminal justice process: Assessing the empirical evidence. Paper presented at annual meetings of American Society of Criminology, Denver.

del Carmen, Rolando V. 1985. Legal issues and liabilities in community corrections. In Lawrence F. Travis (ed.) *Probation, Parole and Community Corrections: A Reader.* Prospect Heights, IL: Waveland Press. Pp. 47–70.

Dell'Apa, Frank, et al. 1976. Advocacy, brokerage, community: The ABC's of probation and parole. *Federal Probation*, XXXX:37–44.

Dershowitz, Alan. 1976. *Fair and Certain Punishment.* New York: McGraw-Hill.

Dession, George. 1938. Psychiatry and the conditioning of criminal justice. *Yale Law Journal*, 47(3):319–340.

Differential use of jail confinement in California: A study of jail admissions in three counties—Final report. 1984. Washington, DC: U.S. Department of Justice, National Institute of Justice.

Doleschal, Eugene. 1977. Rate and length of imprisonment. How does the United States compare with the Netherlands, Denmark, and Sweden? *Crime and Delinquency*, 23:51–58.

Donnelly, Henry, and Bala, Gerald. 1986. 1980 releases: Five year post release follow-up. Albany, NY: New York Department of Correctional Services.

Doob, Anthony N., and MacFarlane, Dianne P. 1984. The community service order for youthful offenders: Perceptions and effects. Toronto: Centre for Criminology, University of Toronto.

Dore, Martha, M., Young, Thomas M., and Pappenfort, Donnell M. 1984. Comparison of basic data for the national survey of residential group care facilities: 1966–1982. *Child Welfare*, 63(6) November–December:485–495.

Downs, Anthony. 1967. *Inside Bureaucracy.* Boston: Little Brown.

Downes, David. 1982. The origins and consequences of Dutch penal policy since 1945. *The British Journal of Criminology*, 22:325–357.

Dubois, Philip. 1981. Disclosure of presentence reports in the United States district courts. *Federal Probation*, 45 (March):3–9

Duffee, David E. 1972. *The Use of Correctional Officers in Planning Change.* Washington, DC: National Technical Information Service.

———.1974. The correctional officer subculture and organizational change. *Journal of Research in Crime and Delinquency*, 11(2) July:155–162.

———. 1981. Careers in criminal justice: Correc-

tions. *Encyclopedia of Crime and Justice.* New York: Macmillan.

———. 1984. Limitations on citizen involvement in correctional programs. *The Prison Journal*, 64(2) Fall–Winter:56–67.

———. 1985. The interaction of organizational and political constraints on community prerelease program development. In Erika Fairchild and Vincent Webb, *The Politics of Crime and Criminal Justice.* Beverly Hills, CA: Sage. Pp. 99–119.

———. 1986. *Correctional Management: Change and Control in Correctional Organizations.* Prospect Heights, IL: Waveland.

———, Briggs, Joseph, and Barnette, J. Jackson. 1986. Organizational structure and decisions about offenders. In David E. Duffee, *Correctional Management: Change and Control in Correctional Organizations.* Prospect Heights, IL: Waveland.

———, and Clark, David. 1985. The frequency and classification of the needs of offenders in community settings. *Journal of Criminal Justice* 13:243–268.

———, and Duffee, Barbara W. 1981. Studying the needs of offenders in prerelease centers. *Journal of Research in Crime and Delinquency* 18:232–254.

———, Maher, Thomas R., and Lagoy, Stephen. 1977. Administrative due process in community preparole programs. *Criminal Law Bulletin* 13:383–400.

———, and Ritti, R. Richard. 1977. Correctional policy and public values. *Criminology*, 14(4) February:449–460.

———, Steinert, Richard, and Dvorin, Robert. 1986. Breaking the barriers to change: The reutilization of front line staff. In David E. Duffee, *Correctional Management: Change and Control in Correctional Organizations.* Prospect Heights, IL: Waveland.

———, and Warner, Barbara D. 1986. Interorganizational behavior and correctional programming. In David E. Duffee, *Correctional Management: Change and Control in Correctional Organizations.* Prospect Heights, IL: Waveland.

Durham, Earl L. 1974. St. Leonard's House: A model in the use of ex-offenders in the administration of correction. *Crime and Delinquency*, July:269–280.

Ehrlich, Isaac. 1975. The deterrent effect of capital punishment: A question of life or death. *American Economic Review*, 65:397–414.

Eisenstein, James, and Jacob, Herbert. 1976. *Felony Justice.* Boston: Little, Brown.

Elder, John, and Cohen, Stanley H. 1978. Prediction of work release success with youthful, nonviolent male offenders. *Criminal Justice and Behavior*, 5(2):181–191.

Elion, Victor H., and Megargee, Edwin I. 1979. Racial identity, length of incarceration and parole decision making. *Journal of Research in Crime and Delinquency*, 16(20) July:232–245.

Embert, Paul S. 1986. Correctional laws and jails. In David B. Kalinich and John Klofas, *Sneaking Inmates Down the Alley*. Springfield, IL: Charles C Thomas.

Emery, Fred, and Trist, Eric. 1965. The causal texture of organizational environments. *Human Relations*, 18:21–32.

Empey, Lamar T., and Rabow, Jerome. 1961. The Provo experiment in delinquency rehabilitation. *American Sociological Review*, 26 (October):479–695.

Erez, Edna. 1985. Random assignment, the least fair of them all: Prisoners' attitudes toward various criteria of selection. *Criminology*, 23(2) May:365–380.

Esparza, R. 1973. Attempted and committed suicide in county jails. In B. Danto, *Jail House Blues*. Orchard Lane, MI: Epic Publications.

Essler, Vic C., et al. 1976. Vocational potential: A comparison of inmates and free world workers via the Bookman method. Paper presented to American Society of Criminology Meeting, Tucson, November.

Etzioni, Amitai. 1960. *Complex Organizations*. New York: Free Press.

Fairweather, George, et al. 1969. *Community Life for the Mentally Ill*. Chicago: Aldine.

Fallen, David L., et al. 1981. Intensive parole supervision. Olympia, WA: Department of Social and Health Services, Analysis and Information Service Division, Office of Research.

Farrington, David P., and Nuttall, Christopher P. 1980. Prison size, overcrowding, prison violence and recidivism. *Journal of Criminal Justice*, 8:221–231.

Fattah, E. A. 1982. Making the punishment fit the crime—The case of imprisonment; the problems inherent in the use of imprisonment as a retributive sanction. *Canadian Journal of Criminology*, 24(1):1–12.

Fayol, Henri. 1949. *General Industrial Management*. New York: Pitman.

Federal Bail Reform Act of 1966. 18 United States Code, sec. 3146, 3150.

Feeley, Malcolm. 1973. Two models of the criminal justice system: An organizational perspective. *Law and Society Review*, 7(3) Spring:407–425.

———. 1979. *Process Is Punishment: Handling Cases in a Lower Criminal Court*. New York: Russell Sage Foundation.

Feinman, C. 1984. Sex role stereotypes and justice for women. *Crime and Delinquency*. January:86–94.

Feld, Barry C. 1981. A comparative analysis of organizational structure and inmate subcultures in institutions for juvenile offenders. *Crime and Delinquency*, 27(3):336–363.

———. 1984. Criminalizing juvenile justice: Rules of procedure for the juvenile court. *Minnesota Law Review*, 69(2) December:141–276.

Feld, J. S. 1979. Pretrial diversion—Problems of due process and weak cases. *Boston University Law Review*, 59(2):305–333.

Fielding, Nigel. 1984. *Probation Practice: Client Support Under Social Control*. Brookfield, VT: Gower.

Finn, Peter. 1984. Prison overcrowding: The response of probation and parole. *Crime and Delinquency*, 390(1) January:141–153.

Fitzgerald, Mike and Sim, Joe. 1979. *British Prisons*. Oxford: Blackwell.

Fitzmaurice, C. and Pease, K. 1982. Prison sentences and population: a comparison of some European countries. *Justice of the Peace*, September:575–579.

Flaherty, Michael G. 1983. The national incidence of juvenile suicide in adult jails and juvenile detention centers. *Suicide and Life-Threatening Behavior*, 13(2) Summer:85–94.

Flanagan, Timothy J. 1980a. The pains of long-term imprisonment. *British Journal of Criminology*, 20(2) April:148–156.

———. 1980b. Time served and institutional misconduct: Patterns of involvement in disciplinary infractions among long-term and short-term inmates. *Journal of Criminal Justice*, 8:359–367.

———. 1981. Dealing with long-term confinement adaptive strategies and perceptions among long-term prisoners. *Criminal Justice and Behavior*, 2 (June):201–222.

———. 1982a. Lifers and long-termers doing big time. In Robert Johnson and Hans Toch (eds.), *The Pains of Imprisonment*. Beverly Hills, CA: Sage. Pp. 115–128.

———. 1982b. Correctional policy and the long-term prisoner. *Crime and Delinquency*, January:82–95.

———. 1982c. Discretion in the prison justice system: A study of sentencing in institutional disciplinary proceedings. *Journal of Research in Crime and Delinquency*, 19(2) July:216–237.

———. 1983. Correlates of institutional misconduct among state prisoners. *Criminology*, 21(1) February:29–39.

———. 1984. Questioning the "other" parole: the effectiveness of community supervision of offenders. In L. F. Travis (ed.), *Probation, Parole, and Community Corrections*. Prospect Heights, IL: Waveland Press.

———, and Caulfield, Susan L. 1984. Public opinion

and prison policy: A review. *The Prison Journal*, 64(2) Fall–Winter:31–96.

———, and McGarrell, Edmund F. 1986. *Sourcebook of Criminal Justice Statistics—1985*. Washington, DC: United States Department of Justice.

———, and McLeod, Maureen. 1983. *Sourcebook of Criminal Justice Statistics—1982*. Washington, DC: United States Department of Justice.

Flemming, Roy B. 1982. *Punishment Before Trial*. New York: Pittman.

Flynn, Edith. 1973. Jails and criminal justice. In Lloyd E. Ohlin (ed.), *Prisoners in America*. Englewood Cliffs, NJ: Prentice-Hall.

Fogel, David. 1975. . . . *We Are the Living Proof*. Cincinnati: Anderson.

Foote, Caleb. 1954. Compelling appearance in court: administration of bail in Philadelphia. University of Pennsylvania Law Review 102:1031–1079.

———. 1965a. The coming constitutional crisis in bail: I. University of Pennsylvania Law Review, 113:959–999.

———. 1965b. The coming constitutional crisis in bail: II. University of Pennsylvania Law Review, 113: 1125–1185.

Forst, Brian, et al. 1982. *Targeting Federal Resources in Recidivists*. Washington, DC: INSLAW.

———. 1983. Selective incapacitation—An idea whose time has come. *Federal Probation*, 47(3):19–23.

Foucault, Michael. 1978. *Discipline and Punish*. Trans. Alan Sheridan. New York: Pantheon.

Foundation awards grant to court to initiate innovative home-sentencing program. 1983. *Corrections Digest*, 14(21) October:8–9.

Fox, James G. 1982. *Organizational and Racial Conflict in Maximum Security Prisons*. Lexington, MA: Lexington Books.

Fox, Vernon. 1971. Why prisoners riot. *Federal Probation*, March:9–14.

———. 1977. *Community-Based Corrections*. Englewood Cliffs, NJ: Prentice-Hall.

Frankel, Marvin. 1972. *Criminal Sentencing*. New York: Hill and Wang.

Franklin, T. M., and Peters, V. C. 1981. Standards for local detention facilities—An attempt at statewide management of Iowa county jails. *Iowa Law Review*, 66 (July):5.

Frederick, Bruce C., and Zimmerman, Sherwood E. 1983. Discrimination and the decision to incarcerate. Albany, NY: Division of Criminal Justice Services.

Freed, Dan. 1970. The non-system of criminal justice. In James S. Campbell, Joseph R. Sahid, and David Stang, *Law and Order Reconsidered*. New York: Bantam. Pp. 263–284.

Freeman, Jo. 1973. The tyranny of structurelessness. *M.S.*, July:76–89.

Freeman, R. B. 1983. Crime and unemployment. In J. Q. Wilson (ed.), *Crime and Public Policy*. San Francisco: Institute for Contemporary Studies.

French, Wendell, and Bell, Cecil. 1984. *Organization Development*, 3d ed. Englewood Cliffs, NJ: Prentice-Hall.

Freudenberger, H. 1974. Staff burn-out. *Journal of Social Issues*, 30(1):159–165.

Friedman, Lawrence M. 1979. Plea bargaining in historical perspective. Law and Society Review, 13:247–259.

Friedman, Milton. 1962. *Capitalism and Freedom*. Chicago: University of Chicago Press.

Frug, Gerald E. 1978. The judicial power of the purse. *University of Pennsylvania Law Review*, 126(4) April:715–794.

Gaes, Gerald G., and McGuire, William. 1985. Prison violence: The contribution of crowding versus other determinants of prison assault rates. *Journal of Research in Crime and Delinquency*, 22(1) February:41–65.

Galaway, Burt. 1983. Probation as a reparative sentence. *Federal Probation*, 46(3) September:9–19.

Galliher, John F. 1972. Change in a correctional institution: A case study of the tightening up process. *Crime and Delinquency*, 18(3) July:263–270.

Galster, George, and Scaturo, Laure A. 1985. The U.S. criminal justice system: unemployment and the severity of punishment. *Journal of Research in Crime and Delinquency*, 22:163–190.

Garofalo, J., and Clark R. 1985. The inmate subculture in jails. *Criminal Justice and Behavior*, 12(4) December:415–434.

Garofalo, James. 1983. *Measuring the Use of Confinement*. Washington, DC: National Institute of Justice.

Garrett, Carol J. 1985. Effects of residential treatment on adjudicated delinquents: A meta-analysis. *Journal of Research in Crime and Delinquency*, 22(4) November:287–308.

Garson, David. 1972. Force versus restraint in prison riots. *Crime and Delinquency*, 18(4) October:411–421.

Geis, Gilbert. 1972. Statistics concerning race and crime. In C. Reasons and C. Kuykenball, *Race, Crime and Justice*. Santa Monica, CA: Goodyear.

———, and Cavanaugh, Elvin. 1966. Recruitment and retention of correctional personnel. *Crime and Delinquency*, 12(3):232–239.

Gendreau, Paul, and Ross, Robert R. 1984. Correctional treatment: Some recommendations for effective intervention. *Juvenile and Family Court Journal*, 34 (Winter):31–39.

General Accounting Office, 1976. *State and County Probation: Systems in Crisis.* Washington, DC: United States Government Printing Office.

Gettinger, Stephen. 1983. Intensive supervision: Can it rehabilitate probation? *Corrections Magazine,* 9(2) April:6–17.

Giallombardo, R. 1966. *Society of Women: A Study of a Women's Prison.* New York: Wiley.

Gibbs, J. 1982. On demons and goals: A summary and review of investigations concerning the psychological problems of jail prisoners in mental health services in local jails: Report on a special national workshop. Rockville, MD: National Institute of Mental Health.

———. 1986. When donkeys fly: A Zen perspective on dealing with the problem of the mentally disturbed jail inmate. In David B. Kalinich and John Klofas, *Sneaking Inmates Down the Alley.* Springfield, IL: Charles C Thomas.

Gilhool, Thomas K. 1976. The uses of courts and of lawyers. In Robert B. Kugel, *Changing Patterns in Residential Services for the Mentally Retarded.* Washington, DC: President's Committee on Mental Retardation.

Gill, Joseph P. 1981. Confused concepts of due process for pretrial detainees—The disturbing legacy of *Bell* v. *Wolfish. American Criminal Law Review,* 18(3):469–491.

Glaser, Daniel. 1964. *The Effectiveness of a Prison and Parole System.* Indianapolis: Bobbs Merrill.

———. 1983. Supervising offenders outside of prison. In J. Q. Wilson, *Crime and Public Policy.* San Francisco: Institute for Contemporary Studies Press. Pp. 207–228.

Glazer, Nathan. 1979. The judiciary and social policy. In Theberge (ed.), *The Judiciary in a Democratic Society.* Lexington, MA: Lexington Books. Pp. 67–80.

Glick, R. M., and Neto, V. V. 1975. *National Study of Women's Correctional Programs.* Sacramento, CA: California Youth Authority.

Goetting, Ann. 1983. The elderly in prison: Issues and perspectives. *Journal of Research in Crime and Delinquency,* 20(2) July:291–309.

Goffman, Erving. 1961. *Asylums.* Garden City, NY: Doubleday.

Goldkamp, J. S. 1979. *Two Classes of Accused.* Cambridge, MA: Ballinger.

———. 1983. Questioning the practice of pretrial detention—Some empirical evidence from Philadelphia. *Journal of Criminal Law and Criminology,* 74(4):1556–1588.

Goodstein, Lynne. 1979. Inmate adjustment to prison and the transition to community life. *Journal of*

Research in Crime and Delinquency, 16(2) July:246–275.

———, Layton-MacKenzie, Doris, and Shotland, R. Lance. 1984. Personal control and inmate adjustment to prison. *Criminology,* 22(3) August:343–369.

——— et al. 1984. Determinate sentencing and the correctional process: A study of the implementation and impact of sentencing reform in three states—Executive summary. Washington, DC: United States Government Printing Office.

Gottfredson, Don, et al. 1973. *4,000 Lifetimes: A Study of Time Served and Parole Outcomes.* Davis, CA: National Council on Crime and Delinquency.

Gottfredson, Michael R. 1979a. Parole board decision making. *Journal of Criminal Law and Criminology,* 70(1):77–88.

———. 1979b. Parole guidelines and the reduction of sentencing disparity. *Journal of Research in Crime and Delinquency,* 16(2) July:218–231.

———. 1979c. Treatment destruction techniques. *Journal of Research in Crime and Delinquency,* 16:39–54.

———, and Adams, Kenneth. 1982. Prison behavior and release performance: Empirical reality and public policy. *Law and Policy Quarterly,* 4(3) July:373–391.

———, and Gottfredson, Don. 1980. *Decision Making and Criminal Justice.* Cambridge, MA: Ballinger.

———, and Hirschi, Travis. 1987. The methodological adequacy of longitudinal research on crime. *Criminology,* 25:581–614.

———, Mitchell-Herzfeld, Susan D., and Flanagan, Timothy J. 1982. Another look at the effectiveness of parole supervision. *Journal of Research in Crime and Delinquency,* 19(2) July:277–298.

Gottfredson, S. D., and Taylor, R. B. 1984. Public policy and prison population: Measuring opinions about reform. *Judicature,* 68(4–5):190–201.

Grabosky, P. N. 1980. Rates of imprisonment and psychiatric hospitalization in the United States. *Social Indicators Research,* 7:63–70.

Grant, Douglas. 1968. *Offenders as a Correctional Manpower Resource.* Washington, DC: Joint Commission on Correctional Manpower and Training.

———, and Grant, Marguerite Q. 1959. A group dynamics approach to the treatment of non-conformists in the Navy. *Annals of the American Academy of Political and Social Science,* 322:126–135.

Green, Alice. 1982. Case studies of the impact of separation due to incarceration on black families. Ph.D. diss., State University of New York at Albany.

Greenburg, D. F. 1977a. The dynamics of oscillatory punishment processes. *Journal of Criminal Law and Criminology*, 68:643–651.

———. 1977b. The correctional effects of corrections: a survey of evaluations. In D. F. Greenburg (ed.), *Corrections and Punishment*. Beverly Hills, CA: Sage.

Greenfield, Lawrence A. 1985. *Examining Recidivism, Bureau of Justice Services Special Report*. Washington, DC: U.S. Department of Justice, February.

Greenwalt, Kent. 1983. Punishment. *Journal of Criminal Law and Criminology*, 74 (Summer):343–362.

Greenwood, Peter W. 1982. *Selective Incapacitation*. Santa Monica, CA: Rand Corp.

Griffiths, John. 1970. Ideology in criminal procedure or a third model of the criminal process. *Yale Law Journal*, 79(3) January:359–417.

Grinnel, Frank. 1941. The common law history of probation. *Criminal Law*, 32:15–34.

Grosser, George H. 1960. External settings and internal relations of the prison. In R. Cloward et al., *Theoretical Studies in Social Organization of the Prison*. New York: Social Science Research Council. Pp. 130–144.

Groves, Walter B. 1982. Restructuring Criminological Theory: A Dissertation on Hegel, Marx, and Crime. Ph.D. diss., State University of New York at Albany.

Haber, Gilda Moss. 1983. The realization of potential by Lorton, D. C. Inmates with UDC college education compared to those without UDC education. *Journal of Offender Counseling, Services and Rehabilitation*, Spring/Summer, 7(3):37–55.

Hackman, J. Richard. 1984. The transition that hasn't happened. In J. R. Kimberly and R. E. Quinn, *Managing Organizational Transitions*. Homewood, IL: Irwin. Pp. 29–59.

———, and Oldham, Greg. 1980. *Work Redesign*. Reading, MA: Addison-Wesley.

Hagan, John. 1975. The social and legal construction of criminal justice: A study of the presentencing process. *Social Problems*, 22:620–637.

———, and Bumiller, Kristin. 1983. Making sense of sentencing: A review and critique of sentencing research. In Alfred Blumstein, Stanley Cohen, Sue Martin and Michael Tonry (eds.), *Research on Sentencing: The Search for Reform*, Vol. II. Washington, DC: National Academy Press. Pp. 1–54.

———, Hewitt, John D., Alwin, Duane F. 1979. Ceremonial justice: Crime and punishment in a loosely coupled system. *Social Forces*, 58(2) December:506–527.

Hage, Jerald, and Aiken, Michael A. 1967. Program change and organizational properties. *American Journal of Sociology*, 72 (March):503–518.

Hahn, Paul H. 1975. *Community Based Corrections and the Criminal Justice System*. Santa Cruz, CA: Davis.

Hakeem, Michael. 1958. A critique of the psychiatric approach to crime and correction. *Law and Contemporary Problems*, 23:650–682.

Halleck, Seymour. 1971. *The Politics of Therapy*. New York: Science House.

———, and Witte, Ann D. 1980. Is rehabilitation dead? In M. Schwartz, T. Clear, and L. Travis, *Corrections: An Issue Approach*. Cincinnati: Anderson. Pp. 183–193.

Hampton-Turner, Charles. 1977. *Sane Asylum: Inside the Delancey Street Foundation*. New York: William Morrow.

Haney, Craig. 1984a. Editor's introduction to a special issue on death qualifications. *Law and Human Behavior*, 8(1–2):1–6.

———. 1984b. On the selection of capital juries: The biasing effects of the death qualifications process. *Law and Human Behavior*, 8(1–2):121–132.

———, Banks, Curtis, and Zombardo, Philip. 1973. Interpersonal dynamics in a simulated prison. *International Journal of Criminology and Penology*, 1:69–97.

Harland, Alan T. 1982. An empirical examination of criminal restitution in law and practice. Ph.D. diss., State University of New York at Albany.

———. 1983. One hundred years of restitution: An international review and prospectus for research. *Victimology*, 8(1–2):190–203.

Harlow, Nora, and Nelson, E. Kim. 1982. *Management Strategies for Probation in an Era of Limits*. Los Angeles: University of Southern California School of Public Administration.

Harris, Louis, Associates. 1968. *The Public Looks at Crime and Corrections*. Washington, DC: Joint Commission on Correctional Manpower and Training, February.

———. 1969. *Volunteers Look at Corrections*. Washington, DC: Joint Commission on Correctional Manpower and Training.

Harris, M. Kay. 1980. *Community Service by Offenders*. Washington, DC: American Bar Association, Basics Program.

———. 1984. Rethinking probation in the context of a justice model. In P. McAnany, D. Thomson, and D. Fogel. *Probation and Justice Reconsideration of Mission*. Cambridge, MA: Oelgeschlager, Gunn and Hain. Pp. 15–38.

Hart, H. M., Jr. 1958. The aims of the criminal law. *Law and Contemporary Problems*, 44:401–411.

Hasenfeld, Yeheskel. 1972. People processing organizations: An exchange approach. *American Sociological Review*, 37 (June):256–263.

Hawkins, Gordon. 1976. *The Prison: Policy and Practice.* Chicago: University of Chicago Press.

Hayes, L. 1981. And darkness closes in . . . National study on jail suicides. Washington, DC: The National Center on Institutions and Alternatives. October.

Hedin, Tricia. 1986. My husband is in prison. *Newsweek,* December 15:14.

Heffernan, E. 1972. *Making It in Prison: The Square, the Cool, and the Life.* New York: Wiley-Interscience.

Helbush, Don, and Mandel, Dave. 1977. Aid to victims and witnesses. *Federal Probation,* 41(4) December:3–6.

Hepburn, J. R. 1984. The erosion of authority and the perceived legitimacy of inmate social protest—A study of prison guards. *Journal of Criminal Justice,* 12(6):579–590.

_____. 1985. The exercise of power in coercive organizations: A study of prison guards. *Criminology,* 23(1) February:145–164.

Heumann, Milton. 1978. *Plea Bargaining: The Experience of Prosecutors, Judges and Defense Attorneys.* Chicago: University of Chicago Press.

Hewitt, John, Poole, Eric D., and Regoli, Robert. 1984. Self-reported and observed rule-breaking in prison: A look at disciplinary response. *Justice Quarterly,* 1(3) September:435–447.

Hil, R. 1983. Conceptual images of social work and probation practice: A case study. *International Journal of Offender Therapy and Comparative Criminology,* 27(3):255–269.

Hindelang, Michael J. 1981. Variations in sex-race-age specific rates of offending. *American Sociological Review* 46:461–474.

Hirschi, Travis, and Gottfredson, Michael. 1983. Age and the explanation of crime. *American Journal of Sociology,* 89(3):552–584.

Hoffer, Frank William, House, Delbert, and Nelson, Floyd. 1933. *The Jails of Virginia.* New York: D. Appleton-Century Company, Inc.

Hogarth, John. 1971. *Sentencing as a Human Process.* Toronto: University of Toronto Press.

Home detention gaining support, 1983. *Criminal Justice Newsletter,* 14(23) November 21:3.

Howard, John. 1929. *State of Prisons.* New York: Dutton.

Hudson, J., and Galaway, B. 1980. *Victims, Offenders and Alternative Sanctions.* Lexington, MA: Lexington Books.

Huff, C. Ronald. 1977. Prisoner militancy and politicization: The Ohio prisoners' union movement. In D. Greenberg (ed.), *Corrections and Punishment.* Beverly Hills, CA: Sage. Pp. 247–264.

Hunnisett, R. F. 1972. Medieval crime and punishment. In *Purnell's History of the English Speaking People.* London: Purnell.

Hunter, Susan M. 1983. The relationship between offender mothers and their children. Ph.D. diss., Michigan State University, East Lansing.

Hussey, Frederick, and Duffee, David E. 1980. *Probation, Parole, and Community Field Services.* New York: Harper and Row.

_____, and Kramer, John H. 1978. Issues in the study of criminal code revision: An analysis of reform in Maine and California. In *Determinate Sentencing: Reform or Regression.* Washington, DC: United States Government Printing Office. Pp. 111–131.

_____, and Lagoy, Stephen P. 1981. The impact of determinate sentencing structures. *Criminal Law Bulletin,* 17(3):197–225.

_____, and _____. 1983. The determinate sentence and its impact on parole. *Criminal Law Bulletin,* 19(2):101–130.

Ignatieff, Michael. 1978. *A Just Measure of Pain: The Penitentiary in the Industrial Revolution, 1750–1850.* New York: Pantheon.

_____. 1981. State, civil society and total institutions: a critique of recent social histories of punishment. In M. Tonry and N. Morris (eds.), *Crime and Justice,* vol. 3. Chicago: University of Chicago Press.

Immarigeon, Russ. 1984. Race and imprisonment internationally. *Jericho,* 34(9) Winter.

The impact of imprisonment on black families. 1983. *Jericho,* 32 (Summer):9.

Inciardi, James A. 1984. *Criminal Justice.* New York: Academic Press.

Irwin, John. 1970. *The Felon.* Englewood Cliffs, NJ: Prentice-Hall.

_____. 1977. The changing social structure of the men's prison. In D. Greenberg, *Corrections and Punishment.* Beverly Hills, CA: Sage. Pp. 21–40.

_____. 1985. *The Jail: Managing the Underclass in American Society.* Berkeley, CA: University of California Press.

_____, and Cressey, D. 1962. Thieves, convicts, and the inmate culture. *Social Problems,* 10:142–155.

Jackson, Alphonso. 1979. Commitment of juveniles: A criticism of the use of consent decrees as a means of involuntary civil commitment by some juvenile courts. In Nicholas N. Kittrie and Jackwell Susman (eds.), *Legality, Morality, and Ethics in Criminal Justice.* New York: Praeger. Pp. 204–219.

Jacobs, James B. 1976. Town-prison relations as a determinant of reform. *Social Service Review,* 50:623–631.

————. 1977. *Stateville: The Prison in Mass Society*. Chicago: University of Chicago Press.

————. 1980. The prisoner's rights movement and its impacts. In N. Morris and M. Tonry (eds.), *Crime and Justice: An Annual Review of Research 2*. Chicago: University of Chicago Press.

————. 1983a. *New Perspectives on Prisons and Imprisonment*. Ithaca, NY: Cornell University Press.

————. 1983b. Female guards in men's prisons. In James Jacobs, *New Perspectives on Prisons and Imprisonment*. Ithaca, NY: Cornell University Press. Pp. 178–201.

————, and Berkowitz, Laura. 1983. Reflections on the defeat of New York state's prison board. In James Jacobs, *New Perspectives on Prisons and Imprisonment*. Ithaca, NY: Cornell University Press. Pp. 115–132.

————, and Grear, Mary P. Dropouts and rights: An analysis of the prison guard's revolving door. In R. Ross (ed.), *Prison Guard/Correctional Officer*. Toronto: Butterworths. Pp. 297–311.

————, and Kraft, Lawrence. 1983. Race relations and the guard's subculture. In James Jacobs, *New Perspectives on Prisons and Imprisonment*. Ithaca, NY: Cornell University Press. Pp. 160–177.

————, and Retsky, Harold. 1975. Prison guard. *Urban Life*. 4(1) April:5–29.

————, and Zimmer, Lynn. 1983. Collective bargaining and labor unrest. In James Jacobs, *New Perspectives on Prisons and Imprisonment*. Ithaca, NY: Cornell University Press. Pp. 142–159.

Jail of the future. 1982. *American Correctional Association Proceedings*, August 16–20:81–85.

Jankovic, I. 1977. Labour market and imprisonment. *Crime and Social Justice*, 8:17–31.

Jeffrey, Robert, and Woolpert, Stephen. 1974. Work furlough as an alternative to incarceration: An assessment of its effects on recidivism and social cost. *Journal of Criminal Law and Criminology*, 65(1):405–415.

Jenkins, W. O., et al. 1973. *A Longitudinal Follow-up Investigation of the Postrelease Behavior of Paroled or Released Offenders*. Elmore, AL: Rehabilitation Research Foundation.

Jensen, Gary F., and Erickson, Maynard L. 1978. The social meaning of sanctions. In M. D. Krohn and R. L. Akers, *Crime, Law, and Sanctions: Theoretical Perspectives*. Beverly Hills, CA: Sage. Pp. 119–136.

Jester, Jean. 1981. An analysis of the relationship between technology and organizational structure in community supervision agencies. Ph.D. diss., State University of New York at Albany.

Johnson, Frank M. 1986. The constitution and the federal district judge. In K. C. Haas and G. P. Alpert (eds.), *The Dilemmas of Punishment*. Prospect Heights, IL: Waveland Press. Pp. 211–223.

Johnson, Judith, McKeown, Keith, and James, Roberta. 1984. Removing the chronically mentally ill from jail: Case studies of collaboration between local criminal justice and mental health systems. Washington, DC: National Coalition for Jail Reform.

Johnson, Kirt. 1986. Overcrowding of jails in the city is said to affect drug sentencing. *New York Times*, August 9:1, 28.

Johnson, Knowlton W. 1980. Stimulating evaluation use by integrating academia and practice. *Knowledge: Creation, Diffusion, Utilization*, 2(2) December:237–262.

Johnson, Perry, and Kime, William. 1975. Performance screening—A new correctional synthesis. Lansing: Michigan Department of Corrections, mimeo.

Johnson, Robert. 1980. Warehousing for death: Observations on the human environment of death row. *Crime and Delinquency*, 26(4):545–562.

————, and Price, Shelley. 1981. The complete correctional officer: Human service and the human environment of prison. *Criminal Justice and Behavior*, 8(3) September:343–373.

Joubert, P. E., Picou, Steven J., and McIntosh, Alex W. 1981. U.S. social structure, crime and imprisonment. *Criminology*, 19(3):344–359.

Junger-Tas, Josine. 1984. The Dutch experiments with community service. The Hague, Netherlands: Research and Documentation Centre, Ministry of Justice.

Kahn, Robert. 1978. Burnout: prevention and remedies. *Public Welfare*, 16:61–63.

Kaiser, Gunther. 1984. *Prison Systems and Correctional Law*. Dobbs Ferry, NY: Transnational Publishers.

Kalinich, David. 1980. *The Inmate Economy*. Lexington, MA: Lexington Books.

————. 1986. New rules and old rituals: Dilemmas of contemporary jail management. In David B. Kalinich and John Klofas, *Sneaking Inmates Down the Alley*. Springfield, IL: Charles C Thomas.

————, and Postill, F. J. 1981. *Principles of County Jail Administration and Management*. Springfield, IL: Charles C Thomas.

————, and Stojkovic, Stan. 1985. Contraband: The basis for legitimate power in a prison social system. *Criminal Justice and Behavior*, 12(4):435–451.

Kant, Immanuel. 1973. The metaphysical elements of justice. In Jeffrie G. Murphy, *Punishment and Rehabilitation*. Belmont, CA: Wadsworth.

Kantola, S. J. 1977. Work release: A series of pilot

studies. *Australian and New Zealand Journal of Criminology*, 10 (March):41–51.

Kassoff, N. C. 1982. Jail management. In *Local Government Police Management*, 2d ed. Washington, DC: International City Managers Association.

Katz, D., and Allport, F. H. 1931. *Student Attitudes: A Report of the Syracuse University Research Study*. Syracuse, NY: Craftsman Press.

————, and Kahn, Robert. 1966. *The Social Psychology of Organizations*. New York: Wiley.

Katz, Jonathan, and Decker, Scott. 1982. An analysis of work release: The institutionalization of unsubstantial reforms. *Criminal Justice and Behavior*, 9(2):229–250.

Kauffman, Kelsey. 1981. Prison officers' attitudes and perceptions of attitudes: A case of pluralistic ignorance. *Journal of Research in Crime and Delinquency*, 18(2) July:272–294.

Kelley, Thomas M., and Kennedy, Daniel B. 1982. Assessing and predicting the competency of juvenile court volunteer probation officers. *Journal of Criminal Justice*, 10:123–130.

Kerle, K. 1985. Jail offenders pay and training—The Achilles heel of the sheriff's department. *National Sheriff*, 37(1) February–March:28, 30–32, 35–36.

Kerle, Kenneth E., and Ford, Francis R. 1982. The state of our nation's jails, Jail chapter. Washington, DC: National Sheriff's Association.

Keve, Paul. 1960. *The Probation Officer Investigates*. Minneapolis: University of Minnesota Press.

Kidder, Joel. 1975. Requital and criminal justice. *International Philosophical Quarterly*, 15:255–278.

Kissel, P., and Katsampes, P. 1980. Impact of women corrections officers on the functioning of institutions housing male inmates. *Journal of Offender Counseling Services and Rehabilitation*, 4:213–231.

Klein, Lawrence R., Fost, Brian, and Filatou, Victor. 1982. The deterrent effect of capital punishment: An assessment of the evidence. In Hugo A. Bedau (ed.), *The Death Penalty in America*. New York: Oxford University Press.

Klein, Malcolm W. 1979. Deinstitutionalization and diversion of juvenile offenders: A litany of impediments. In N. Morris and J. Tonry (eds.), *Crime and Justice: An Annual Review of Research*. Chicago: University of Chicago Press. Pp. 145–201.

Klein, Stuart M., and Ritti, R. Richard. 1980. *Understanding Organizational Behavior*. Boston: Kent.

Klockars, Carl. 1972. A theory of probation supervision. *Journal of Criminal Law, Criminology and Police Science*, 63(4):550–557.

Klofas, John. 1983. Enriching the role of the prison guard: An exploration of human service orientations among correctional officers. Ph.D. diss., State University of New York at Albany.

————. 1987. Patterns of jail use. *Journal of Criminal Justice*, 15:403–412.

————, and Toch, Hans. 1982. The guard subculture myth. *Journal of Research in Crime and Delinquency*, 19(2) July:238–254.

Knapp, Kay. 1984. What sentencing reform in Minnesota has and has not accomplished. *Judicature*, 68(4–5):181–189.

Knox, William E., and Humphrey, John A. 1981. The granting of work release. *Criminal Justice and Behavior*, 8(1):55–77.

Koestler, Arthur. 1957. *Reflections on Hanging*. New York: Macmillan.

Koppell, Herbert. 1984. *Time Served in Prison: Bureau of Justice Statistics Special Report*. Washington, DC: U.S. Department of Justice. June.

Kowalski, Gregory S., and Rickicki, John P. 1982. Determinants of juvenile postadjudication dispositions. *Journal of Research in Crime and Delinquency*, 19(1) January:66–83.

Krajick, Kevin. 1982. Community service: The work ethic approach to punishment. *Corrections Magazine*, 8(5) October:6–19.

Kramer, J. H., et al. 1978. Assessing the impact of determinate sentencing and parole abolition in Maine. University Park, PA: Pennsylvania State University, Institute for Human Development.

Kramer, John H., and Steffensmeier, Darrell J. 1978. The differential detention/tailing of juveniles: A comparison of detention and non-detention courts. *Pepperdine Law Review*, 5(3):795–807.

————, Litsky, Paul, and Schwartz, Ira. 1984. Youth in confinement: Justice by geography. *Journal of Research in Crime and Delinquency*, 21(2) May:153–181.

Krisberg, Barry, and Schwartz, Ira. 1983. Rethinking juvenile justice. *Crime and Delinquency*, 29(3): 333–364.

Kruttschnitt, C. 1981. Prison codes, inmate solidarity, and women: A reexamination. In M. Warren (ed.), *Comparing Female and Male Offenders*. Sage Research Progress Series in Criminology, Vol. 21. Beverly Hills, CA: Sage Publications.

Ku, Richard. 1980. *American Prisons and Jails. Volume IV: Supplemental Report Case Studies of New Legislation Governing Sentencing and Release*. Washington, DC: United States Department of Justice.

LaFave, Wayne R. 1965. Alternatives to the present bail system. *University of Illinois Law Forum* 8:8–19.

————, and Scott, A. W. 1980. Criminal law. In F.

Cohen, *Deprivation of Liberty*. St. Paul: West. Pp. 72–77.

Lagoy, Stephen, Hussey, Frederick A., and Kramer, John H. 1978. A comparative assessment of determinate sentencing in the four pioneer states. *Crime and Delinquency*, 24(4):385–400.

Langworthy, Robert. 1987. *The Structure of Police Organizations*. New York: Praeger.

Larkins, Norm. 1972. Presentence investigation report disclosure in Alberta. *Federal Probation*, December.

Launay, Gilles. 1985. Bringing victims and offenders together: A comparison of two models. *The Howard Journal*, 24(3) August:200–211.

LeClair, Daniel P. 1978. Home furlough program effects on rates of recidivism. *Criminal Justice and Behavior*, 5(3) September:249–258.

———. 1979. Community-based reintegration: Some theoretical implications of positive research findings. Paper prepared for annual meeting of the American Society of Criminology, Philadelphia.

———. 1982. Pre-release in Massachusetts. Boston: Department of Corrections, mimeo, June 23.

———. 1986. The effectiveness of community based corrections. Massachusetts experience. Paper presented at the annual meeting of the Academy of Criminal Justice Sciences, March 17, Orlando, Florida.

Legislative Audit Bureau, Wisconsin. 1985. An evaluation of restitution by adult probationers. Madison: Audit Bureau.

Leibrich, Julie. 1984. Criminal history and reconviction of two sentence groups: Community service and nonresidential periodic detention. In J. Leibrich, B. Galaway and Y. Underhill (eds.), *Community Service Orders in New Zealand*. Wellington, NZ: Planning and Development Division, Department of Justice. Pp. 161–204.

———, Galaway, Burt, and Underhill, Yvonne. 1984. Survey of people connected with the community service sentence. In J. Leibrich, B. Galaway, and Y. Underhill (eds.), *Community Service Orders in New Zealand*. Wellington, NZ: Planning and Development Division, Department of Justice. Pp. 29–156.

Lemert, Edwin. 1967. The juvenile court—Quest and realities. In *President's Commission on Law Enforcement and Administration of Justice, Task Force Report: Juvenile Delinquency and Youth Crime*. Washington, DC: United States Government Printing Office.

Lempert, Richard. 1983. Capital punishment in the 1980's: Reflections on the symposium. *Journal of Criminal Law and Criminology*, 74(3):1101–1104.

Lenihan, Kenneth. 1974. *The Financial Resources of Released Prisoners*. Washington, DC: Bureau of Social Science Research, Inc.

Lerman, Paul. 1975. *Community Treatment and Social Control*. Chicago: University of Chicago Press.

Levin, Martin A. 1976. Urban politics and policy outcomes: The criminal courts. In G. Cae (ed.), *Criminal Justice, Law and Politics*. Monterey, CA: Duxbury.

Levine, Sol, and White, Paul. 1961. Exchange as a conceptual framework for the study of interorganizational relationships. *Administrative Science Quarterly*, 5 (March):583–601.

Lichtman, Cary M., and Smock, S. M. 1981. The effects of social services on probationer recidivism: a field experiment. *Journal of Research in Crime and Delinquency*, 18:81–100.

Lieber, Francis. 1964 (1833). Translation preface to Gustave de Beaumont and Alexis de Tocqueville, *On the Penitentiary System in the United States and Its Application to France*. Carbondale, IL: Southern Illinois University Press. Pp. 3–33.

Lightman, E. S. 1982. The private employer and the prison industry. *The British Journal of Criminology*, 22(1):36–48.

Likert, Rensis. 1961. *New Patterns of Management*. New York: McGraw-Hill.

———. 1967. *The Human Organization*. New York: McGraw-Hill.

Lindblom, Charles. 1958. Policy analysis. *American Economic Review*, June:48.

———. 1984. The science of muddling through. In D. S. Pugh (ed.), *Organization Theory*. New York: Penguin. Pp. 238–255.

Linden, Rick, Perry, Linda, Ayers, Douglas, and Parlett, T. A. A. 1984. An evaluation of a prison education program. *Canadian Journal of Criminology*, 26(1):65–73.

Linnihan, Patricia A. 1977. Adolescent day treatment: A community alternative to institutionalization of the emotionally disturbed adolescent. *American Journal of Orthopsychiatry*, 47(4) October:679–681.

Lipton, Douglas, Martinson, Robert, and Wilks, Judith. 1975. *The Effectiveness of Correctional Treatment*. New York: Praeger.

Litwak, Eugene L., and Hylton, Lydia. 1962. Interorganizational analysis: A hypothesis on coordinating agencies. *Administrative Science Quarterly*, 6 (March):395–420.

Lockwood, Daniel. 1982. The contribution of sexual harrassment to stress and coping in confinement. In N. Parisi, *Coping with Imprisonment*. Beverly Hills, CA: Sage. Pp. 45–64.

Lodge, George Cabot. 1977. Ethics and the new ideology: Can business adjust? *Management Review,* 66 (July):10–19.

Logan, Charles H. 1986. Running prisons for profit: A viable alternative. *Albany Times Union,* January 19:E-1.

———, and Rausch, Sharla. 1985. The emergence of private enterprise prisons. *Justice Quarterly,* 2(3) September:303–318.

Lombardo, Lucien X. 1981. *Guards Imprisoned: Correctional Officers at Work.* New York: Elsevier.

———. 1986. Jail officer training: Goals, techniques and evaluation criteria. In David B. Kalinich and John Klofas, *Sneaking Inmates Down the Alley.* Springfield, IL: Charles C Thomas.

Long, Nigel, Shouksmith, George, Voges, Kevin, and Roache, Thannon. 1986. Stress in prison staff: An occupational study. *Criminology,* 24(2):331–345.

Lorinskas, Robert, Kalinich, David, and Banas, Dennis. 1985. Symbolism and rhetoric: The guardians of the status quo in the criminal justice system. *Criminal Justice Review,* 10:41–46.

MacDonald, Donald, and Bala, Gerald. 1985. Follow-up study sample of Edgecombe work release participants. Albany, NY: Division of Correctional Services.

MacKenzie, Doris Layton, and Goodstein, Lynne. 1985. Long-term incarceration of long-term offenders: An empirical analysis. *Criminal Justice and Behavior,* 12(4) December:395–414.

Mahan, Sue. 1982. An 'orgy of brutality' at Attica and the 'killing ground' at Santa Fe: A comparison of prison riots. In N. Parisi, *Coping with Imprisonment.* Beverly Hills, CA: Sage. Pp. 65–78.

———. 1984. Imposition of despair: An ethnography of women in prison. *Justice Quarterly,* 1(3) September, 357–384.

Maher, Thomas R. 1981. Accountability in a decentralized system: An organizational dilemma of the United States probation system. Masters essay, Pennsylvania State University.

Mannheim, Hermann. 1973. *Pioneers in Criminology,* 2d ed. Montclair, NJ: Patterson-Smith.

———, and Wilkins, Leslie T. 1955. *Prediction Methods in Relation to Borstal Training.* London: Her Majesty's Stationery Office.

March, James G., and Simon, Herbert. 1958. *Organizations.* New York: Wiley.

Marquart, James W., and Roebuck, Julian B. 1985. Prison guards and 'snitches': Deviance within a total institution. *British Journal of Criminology,* 25(3) July:217–233.

Martin, J. P., and Webster, D. 1971. *Social Consequences of Conviction.* New York: Humanities Press.

Martin, S. E. 1984. Interests and politics in sentencing reform: The development of sentencing guidelines in Minnesota and Pennsylvania. *Villanova Law Review,* 29(1):21–113.

———, Sechrest, L. B., and Redner, R. 1981. *New Directions in the Rehabilitation of Criminal Offenders.* Washington, DC: National Academy of Sciences.

Martinson, Robert. 1974. What works? Questions and answers about prison reform. *The Public Interest,* 35:22–54.

———, and Wilks, Judith. 1986. Save parole supervision. In Kenneth C. Haas and Geoffrey Alpert, *The Dilemmas of Punishment: Readings in Contemporary Corrections.* Prospect Heights, IL: Waveland Press. Pp. 404–411.

Maslach, Christine. 1982. *Burnout: The Cost of Caring.* Englewood Cliffs, NJ: Prentice-Hall.

May, Edgar. 1976. Prison guards in America—The inside story. *Corrections Magazine,* December:4–5, 12, 35–40, 44–48.

Mayo, Elton. 1933. *Human Problems of an Industrial Civilization.* New York: Macmillan.

Mays, G. Larry, and Thompson, Joel A. Forthcoming. Mayberry revisited: The characteristics and operations of America's small jails. *Journal of Criminal Justice.*

Mazzotta, C. 1981. Pilot program for women offenders: A job-readiness training manual. In *Wider Opportunities for Women.* Washington, DC: U.S. Department of Justice Law Enforcement Assistance Administration.

McAnany, Patrick, D. 1984. Mission and Justice: Clarifying probation's legal context. In P. McAnany, D. Thomson, and D. Fogel, *Probation and Justice: Reconsideration of Mission.* Cambridge, MA: Oelgeschlager, Gunn and Hain. Pp. 39–63.

McCarthy, Belinda Rogers. 1980. Inmate mothers: The problems of separation and reintegration. *Journal of Offender Counseling, Services and Rehabilitation,* 4(3) Spring, 199–212.

———, and McCarthy, Bernard J., Jr. 1984. *Community-Based Corrections.* Monterey, CA: Brooks/Cole.

McCarthy, Brian. 1985. Mentally ill and mentally retarded offenders in corrections: A report of a national survey. In *New York State Department of Correctional Services, Sourcebook on the Mentally Disordered Prisoner.* Washington, DC: National Institute of Corrections. Pp. 14–29.

McCarthy, David, and Wahl, J. 1965. The District of

Columbia bail project: illustration of experimentation and a brief for change. *The Georgetown Law Journal*, 55:218–250.

McCarthy, John D., and Zald, Mayer N. 1977. Resource mobilization and social movements: A partial theory. *American Journal of Sociology*, 82(6):1212–1241.

McCarty, Dennis. 1984. The scope and impact of mental health programming in local adult correctional facilities: Current practices and implications for the future. Ph.D. diss., School of Criminal Justice, State University of New York at Albany.

McCleary, Richard. 1978. *Dangerous Men*. Beverly Hills, CA: Sage.

_____, Nienstedt, Barbara C., and Erven, James M. 1982. Uniform crime reports as organizational outcomes: Three time series experiments. *Social Problems*, 29(4):361–372.

McCleery, Richard. 1960. Communication patterns as bases of systems of authority and power. In Richard Cloward et al., *Theoretical Studies in the Social Organization of the Prison*. New York: Social Science Research Council. Pp. 49–77.

_____. 1969. Correctional administration and political change. In Lawrence Hazelrigg, *Prison within Society*. Garden City, NY: Doubleday. Pp. 113–149.

McClintock, F. H., Walker, M. A., and Savill, N. C. 1961. *Attendance Centres*. London: Macmillan.

McCord, Joan. 1974. *An Evaluation of the Community-Related Institutional Probation*. Philadelphia: Philadelphia Crime Commission.

McCoy, Candace. 1981. The impact of section 1983 litigation on policy making in corrections. *Federal Probation*, 45(4) December:17–23.

McDonald, Douglas. 1980. *The Price of Punishment: Public Spending in New York. Executive Summary and Recommendations*. A Joint Report of the Correctional Association of New York and Citizens Inquiry on Parole and Criminal Justice, Inc.

McEwen, Craig. 1978. *Designing Correctional Organizations for Youths*. Cambridge, MA: Ballinger.

McFarland, Sam G. 1983. Is capital punishment a short-term deterrent to homicide? A study of the effects of four recent American executions. *Journal of Criminal Law and Criminology*, 74(3):1014–1032.

McGarrell, Edmund F. 1986. Change in New York's juvenile corrections system: A study of policy formation and system change. Ph.D. diss., State University of New York at Albany.

_____, and Flanagan, Timothy. 1985. *Sourcebook of Criminal Justice Statistics—1984*. Washington, DC: United States Department of Justice.

McGuire, W. J., and Sheehan, R. G. 1983. Relation-

ships between crime rates and incarceration rates—Further analysis. *Journal of Research in Crime and Delinquency*, 20(1):73–85.

McKelvey, Blake. 1972. *American Prisons: A Study of American Social History Prior to 1915*. Montclair, NJ: Patterson Smith.

McNally, R, and Florescu, R. 1974. *In Search of Dracula*. London: New English Library.

Megargee, E. I. 1977. The need for a new classification system. *Criminal Justice and Behavior*, 4:107–114.

Merritt, Frank S. 1984. Community restitution: An alternative disposition for corporate offenders. *Criminal Law Bulletin*, 20(4):355–360.

Meyer, Marshall. 1975. Organizational domains. *American Sociological Review*, 40 (October):599–615.

Meyer, Peter B. 1976. *Drug Experiments on Prisoners*. Lexington, MA: Lexington Books.

_____. 1986. The correctional services market. State College, PA: Pennsylvania State University, mimeo.

Miethe, Terance D., and Moore, Charles A. 1985. Socioeconomic disparities under determinate sentencing systems: A comparison of preguideline and postguideline practices in Minnesota. *Criminology*, 23(2) May:337–365.

Miller, Alden D., and Ohlin, Lloyd E. 1982. Baseline data on mobilization for day to day control affecting youth opportunities in two communities. Cambridge, MA: Center for Criminal Justice, Harvard Law School.

_____. 1985. *Delinquency and Community*. Newbury Park, CA: Sage.

_____, and Coates, Robert. 1977. *A Theory of Social Reform*. Cambridge, MA: Ballinger.

Miller, Armetta. 1986. The birth of an air empire. *Newsweek*, September 29:44.

Miller, Kent S. 1980. *Criminal Justice and Mental Health Systems: Conflict and Collusion*. Cambridge, MA: Oelgeschlager, Gunn, and Hain.

Miller, Martin B. 1980. Sinking gradually into the proletariat: The emergence of the penitentiary in the United States. *Crime and Social Justice*, Winter:37–43.

Mills, T. M. 1959. Equilibrium and the processes of deviance and control. *American Sociological Review*, XXIV:671–679.

Miner, Frederick C. 1984. Group versus individual decision making—an investigation of performance measures, decision strategies, and process losses and gains. *Organizational Behavior and Human Performance*, 33:112–124.

Minnesota Citizens Council on Crime and Justice. 1983. *Adult Incarceration: The Cost to the Min-*

nesota Taxpayers. Minneapolis: Minnesota Citizens Council on Crime and Justice.

Minnesota Governor's Commission on Crime Prevention and Control. 1976. Residential community corrections programs in Minnesota: An evaluation report. St. Paul: Minnesota Governor's Commission on Crime Prevention and Control.

Minnesota Sentencing Guidelines Commission. 1982. *Preliminary Report on the Development and Impact of the Minnesota Sentencing Guidelines*. St. Paul: July.

Minor, W. William, and Courlander, Michael. 1979. The postrelease trauma thesis: A reconsideration of the risk of the early parole failure. *Journal of Research in Crime and Delinquency*, 16(2) July:273–293.

Monkkonen, E. H. The organized response to crime in 19th century and 20th century America. *Journal of Interdisciplinary History*, 14(1):113–128.

Moos, Rudolph H. 1975. *Evaluating Correctional and Community Settings*. New York: Wiley.

Moran, T. Kenneth, and Lindner, Charles. 1985. Probation and the high technology revolution: Is a reconceptualization of the traditional probation officer role model inevitable? *Criminal Justice Review*, 10(1) Spring:25–32.

Morgan, C. 1982. Developing mental health services for local jails. *Criminal Justice and Behavior*, 8(3) September:259–273.

Morgenbesser, Leonard I., and Pollock, Joy. 1980. Evaluation research design for pre-release centers at facilities of New York State Department of Correctional Services. Albany: New York State Department of Correctional Services.

Morris, Norval. 1974. *The Future of Imprisonment*. Chicago: University of Chicago Press.

———. 1982. *Madness and the Criminal Law*. Chicago: University of Chicago Press.

Moyer, I. 1980. Leadership in a women's prison. *Journal of Criminal Justice*, 8:233.

Mullen, Joan. 1980. *American Prisons and Jails*, Volume I: *Summary and Policy Implications of a National Survey*. Washington, DC: United States Department of Justice.

Murphy, Jeffrie G. 1979. *Retribution, Justice and Therapy: Essays in the Philosophy of Law*. Boston: D. Reidel Publishing Company.

Murray, Charles A., and Cox, Louis A., Jr. 1979. *Beyond Probation: Juvenile Corrections and the Chronic Delinquent*. Beverly Hills, CA: Sage.

Murton, Thomas D. 1976. *The Dilemma of Prison Reform*. New York: Holt, Rinehart and Winston.

———, and Baunach, P. J. 1973. Women in prisons. *The Freeworld Times*, 2 (June–July).

———, and Hyams, Joe. 1969. *Accomplices to the Crime: The Arkansas Prison Scandal*. New York: Grove Press.

Myers, Louis B., and Levy, Girard W. 1978. Description and prediction of the intractable inmate. *Journal of Research in Crime and Delinquency*, 15(2) July:214–228.

NAACP Legal Defense and Educational Fund, Inc. 1986. *Death Row U.S.A.* New York, May 1.

———. 1987. *Death Row U.S.A.* March 1.

Nacci, Peter L., and Kane, Thomas R. 1983. The incidence of sex and sexual aggression in federal prisons. *Federal Probation*, 47(9) December:31–36.

———, and ———. 1984. Sex and sexual aggression in federal prisons: Inmate involvement and employee impact. *Federal Probation*, 48 (March):46–53.

Nagel, William G. 1973. *The New Red Barn: A Critical Look at the Modern American Prison*. New York: Walker.

Nakell, Barry. 1982. The cost of the death penalty. In Hugo Bedau (ed.), *The Death Penalty in America*, 3d ed. New York: Oxford University Press.

———. 1977. On behalf of a moratorium on prison construction. Crime and Delinquency, 23:154–172.

Nardulli, Peter F. 1979. The caseload controversy and the study of criminal courts. *The Journal of Criminal Law and Criminology*, 70(1):89–101.

———. 1983. *Prison, Dollars, and Crime*. Champagne–Urbana: University of Illinois Institute of Government and Public Affairs.

Nath, S. B., Clement, D. E., and Sistrunk, F. 1976. Parole and probation caseload size variation: The Florida intensive supervision project. *Criminal Justice Review*, 1:61–71.

National Advisory Commission on Criminal Justice Standards and Goals (NAC). 1973. *Corrections*. Washington, DC: United States Government Printing Office.

National Council on Crime and Delinquency. 1981. Probation in the United States—1979. San Francisco: National Council on Crime and Delinquency.

———. 1984. Differential use of jail; confinement in California: a study of jail admission in three counties. San Francisco: National Council on Crime and Delinquency.

National Institute of Corrections. No date. *N.I.C. Technical Assistance Report: Model Probation and Parole Management Program*. Washington, DC: National Institute of Corrections.

———. 1986. Telephone interview with the author.

National Institute of Justice. 1985. *The Privatization*

of Corrections. Washington, DC: United States Department of Justice.

National Manpower Survey of the Criminal Justice System. 1978. Volume 3: *Corrections*. Washington, DC: United States Government Printing Office.

National Sheriff's Association. 1974. Manual on Jail Programs. Alexandria, VA: National Sheriffs' Association.

Nelson, E. K., Cushman, Robert, and Harlow, Nora. 1980. *The Unification of Community Corrections*. Washington, DC: United States Government Printing Office.

————, and Harlow, Nora. 1980. *Responses to Diminishing Resources in Probation: The California Experience*. Los Angeles: University of Southern California, School of Public Administration, December.

————, and Lovell, Catherine. 1969. Developing correctional administrators: Research report of the Joint Commission on Correctional Manpower and Training. Washington, DC: Joint Commission on Correctional Manpower and Training.

————, Ohmart, Howard, and Harlow, Nora. 1984. Promising strategies for probation and parole. In Robert M. Carter, Daniel Glaser, and Leslie T. Wilkins (eds.), *Probation, Parole, and Community Corrections*, 3d ed. New York: Wiley. Pp. 403–412.

Nelson, W. Ray. 1986. Changing concepts in jail and management. In David B. Kalinich and John Klofas, *Sneaking Inmates Down the Alley*. Springfield, IL: Charles C Thomas.

Neto, V. V., and Bainer, L. M. 1980. Mother and wife locked up: A day with the family. *Prison Journal*, 5(63):125–141.

Newcomb, Theodore M. 1976. Youth to youth. In R. Vinter, *Time Out*. Ann Arbor: University of Michigan. Pp. 80–101.

Newman, Charles, et al. 1976. *Local Jails and Drug Treatment*. University Park, PA: College of Human Development, The Pennsylvania State University.

Newman, Donald J. 1966. *Conviction*. Boston: Little, Brown.

————.1978. *An Introduction to Criminal Justice*, 2d ed. New York:Random House.

Newman, Graeme. 1983. *Just and Painful: The Case for the Corporal Punishment of Criminals*. New York: Free Press/Harrow and Heston.

New York State Coalition for Criminal Justice. 1982. *Earned Good Time: A Concept Whose Time Has Returned*. Albany: New York State Coalition for Criminal Justice.

New York State Special Commission on Attica. 1972. *Attica*. New York: Bantam.

Nicolai, Sandra. 1981. The upward mobility of women in corrections. In Robert R. Ross, *Prison Guard/Correctional Officer*. Toronto: Butterworths. Pp. 223–238.

Nielsen, E. 1980. Suicidal behavior in jail—A preventative approach. *Crisis Intervention*, 11(1):19–27.

1986 prison construction tops $3 billion. *ACJS Today*, September:20.

Nokes, Peter. 1960. Purpose and efficiency in humane social institutions. *Human Relations*, 13:141–155.

No place like home. 1983. *Criminal Justice Newsletter*, 14(20):3.

Norland, S., and Mann, P. J. 1984. Being troublesome: Women on probation. *Criminal Justice and Behavior*, 11(1) March: 115–135.

North, Sunil B., Clement, David E., and Sistrunk, Frank. 1976. Parole and probation caseload size variation: The Florida intensive supervision project. *Criminal Justice Review*, 1(2) Fall:61–72.

Note. 1963. Beyond the ken of the courts: A critique of the judicial refusal to review complaints of convicts. *Yale Law Journal*, 72:506–558.

Note. 1977. Implementation problems in institutional reform litigation. *Harvard Law Review*, 91:428–463.

Ohlin, Lloyd E. 1960. Conflicting interests in correctional objectives. In Richard A. Cloward et al., *Theoretical Studies in Social Organization of the Prison*. New York: Social Science Research Council. Pp. 111–129.

O'Leary, Vincent. 1967. Correctional assumptions and their program implications. *Proceedings of the National Conference on Pre-Release*. Huntsville, TX: Institute for Contemporary Corrections and the Behavioral Sciences. November.

————. 1970. *The Correctional Policy Inventory*. Hackensack, NJ: National Council on Crime and Delinquency.

————, and Duffee, David. 1971a. Correctional policy—a classification of goals designed for change. *Crime and Delinquency*, 17:373–386.

————. 1971b. Managerial behavior and correctional policy. *Public Administration Review*, XXXI:603–615.

Owen, Barbara A. 1985. Race and gender relations among prison workers. *Crime and Delinquency*, 31(1):147–159.

Owen, David G. 1982. Civil punishment and the public good. *Southern California Law Review*, 56(1):103–122.

Owens, Charles E. 1981. Minority offenders: A new challenge in corrections. In Vincent J. Webb and Roy R. Roberg, *Critical Issues in Corrections*. St. Paul, MN: West. Pp. 150–170.

Packer, Herbert. 1968. *The Limits of the Criminal Sanction*. Stanford, CA: Stanford University Press.

Palmer, Ted. 1975. Martinson revisited. *Journal of*

Research in Crime and Delinquency, 12(2):133–152.

———. 1978. *Correctional Intervention and Research: Current Issues and Future Prospects.* Lexington, MA: Lexington Books.

Pappas, N. 1972. The Jail: Its Operation and Management. Washington, DC: Federal Bureau of Prisons.

Parisi, Nicolette. 1981. A taste of the bars? *Journal of Criminal Law and Criminology,* 72(3):1109–1123.

———. 1982a. The prisoner's pressures and responses. In N. Parisi, *Coping with Imprisonment.* Beverly Hills, CA: Sage. Pp. 9–26.

——— (ed.) 1982b. *Coping with Imprisonment.* Beverly Hills, CA: Sage.

———. 1984. Combining incarceration and probation. In Robert J. Carter, Daniel Glaser, and Leslie T. Wilkins (eds.). *Probation, Parole and Community Corrections,* 3d ed. New York: Wiley.

Pascussi, Raymond J., Strauss, Emanuel D., and Watchman, Gregory R. 1984. Capital punishment in 1984: Abandoning the pursuit of fairness and consistency. *Cornell Law Review,* 69(6):1132–1133.

Paternoster, Raymond. 1984. Prosecutorial discretion in requesting the death penalty: A case of victim-based racial discrimination. *Law and Society Review,* 18(3):437–478.

———, et al. 1982. Perceived risk and deterrence—Methodological artifacts in perceptual deterrence research. *Journal of Criminal Law and Criminology,* 73(3):1238–1258.

———, et al. 1983. Estimating perceptual stability and deterrent effects: The role of perceived legal punishment in the inhibition of criminal involvement. *Journal of Criminal Law and Criminology,* 74:270–297.

Paulus, P. B., and McCain, G. 1983. Crowding in jails. *Basic and Applied Social Psychology,* 4(2):890–907.

Pearl, Arthur. 1965. *New Careers for the Poor: The Non-Professional in the Human Services.* New York: Free Press.

Pearlman, E. Price, A., and Webber, C. 1983. Judicial discretion and jail overcrowding. *Justice Systems Journal,* 18:222–230.

Pease, K., et al. 1975. *Community Service Orders.* London: Her Majesty's Stationery Office, Home Office Research Report No. 29.

———. 1985. Community service orders. In Michael Tonry and Norval Morris (eds.), *Crime and Justice: An Annual Review of Research,* Chicago: University of Chicago Press.

———, Billingham, S., and Earnshaw, I. 1977. *Community Service Assessed in 1976.* London: Her Majesty's Stationery Office, Home Office Research Study No. 39.

Pennsylvania Commission on Crime and Delinquency. 1984. Preliminary assessment of the deterrent effects of mandatory sentencing: Robbery, aggravated assault and driving under the influence. Harrisburg: Bureau of Statistics and Policy Research.

Penrose, L. S. 1939. Mental disease and crime: Outline of a comparative study of European statistics. *British Journal of Medical Psychology,* 18:1–15.

Perrier, David C., and Pink, F. Steven. 1985. Community service: All things to all people. *Federal Probation,* 42(2) June:32–37.

Petersilia, Joan. 1983. *Racial Disparities in the Criminal Justice System.* Santa Monica, CA: RAND.

———. 1986. *Prison Versus Probation in California: Implications for Crime and Offender Recidivism.* Santa Monica, CA: RAND.

———, and Turner, Susan. 1985. *Guideline-Based Justice: The Implications for Racial Minorities.* Santa Monica, CA: RAND.

———, Turner, Susan, Kahan, James, and Peterson, Joyce. 1985. *Granting Felons Probation: Public Risks and Alternatives.* Santa Monica, CA: RAND.

Peterson, C. B. 1982. Doing time with boys: An analysis of women correctional officers in all-male facilities. In B. R. Price and N. Sokoloff, *The Criminal Justice System and Women.* New York: Clark Boardman.

Phillips, David. 1981. The deterrent effect of capital punishment: New evidence on an old controversy. *American Journal of Sociology,* 86.

Piliavin, Irving, and Gross, Alan E. 1977. The effects of separation of services and income maintenance on AFDC Recipients. *Social Service Review,* September: 389–406.

Platt, Anthony. 1969. The rise of the child-saving movement: A study in social policy and correctional reform. *Annals of the American Academy of Political and Social Science,* 381:21–38.

Pollock, F., and Maitland, F. 1952. *History of English Law.* Cambridge, England: University Press.

Pollock, J. M. 1984. Women will be women: Correctional officers' perceptions of the emotionality of women inmates. *Prison Journal,* 64(1) Spring–Summer:84–91.

Poole, Eric D., and Regoli, Robert M. 1980. Race, institutional rule breaking, and disciplinary response: A study of discretionary decision-making in prison. *Law and Society Review,* 14(4):931–946.

———, and ———. 1983. Violence in juvenile institutions. *Criminology,* 21(2) May:213–232.

———, and ———. 1981. Alienation in prison: An examination of the work relations of prison guards. *Criminology,* 19(2) August:251–270.

———, ———, and Thomas, Charles. 1980. The

measurement of inmate social role types: An assessment. *Journal of Criminal Law and Criminology,* 71(3) Fall:317–324.

Poole, Robert W., Jr. 1985. Privately operated prisons are economical. In Bonnie Szumski (ed.), *America's Prisons: Opposing Viewpoints.* St. Paul, MN: Greenhaven Press. Pp. 123–126.

Pooley, Richard. 1974. Work release programs and corrections: Goals and conflicts. *Criminal Justice and Behavior,* 1(1):62–72.

Potter, Joan. 1981a. Guard unions: The search for solidarity. In Robert R. Ross (ed.), *Prison Guard/ Correctional Officer.* Toronto: Butterworths. Pp. 321–336.

————. 1981b. The pitfalls of diversion. *Corrections Magazine,* 7(1):5–7, 10–11, 36.

Pound, Roscoe. 1906. The causes of popular dissatisfaction with the administration of justice. St. Paul, MN: American Bar Association Annual Meeting.

President's Commission on Law Enforcement and the Administration of Justice. 1967a. *Task Force Report: Corrections.* Washington, DC: United States Government Printing Office.

————. 1967b. *Challenge of Crime in a Free Society.* Washington, DC: United States Government Printing Office.

Press, Aric. 1986. Inside America's toughest prison. *Newsweek,* October 6:46–61.

Priae, Frank J. 1974. Con Ed treats alcoholism as medical problem. *New York Times,* August 10.

The Proceedings of the First National Parolee Conference. 1939. Washington, DC: United States Government Printing Office.

Propper, Alice M. 1981. *Prison Homosexuality.* Lexington, MA: Lexington Books.

Pryer, Donald E. 1982. *Practices of Pre-trial Diversion Programs: Review and Analysis of the Data.* Washington, DC: Pretrial Services Resource Center.

Pugh, D. S. 1984. The measurement of organization structures: Does context determine form? In D. Pugh (ed.), *Organization Theory.* New York: Penguin. Pp. 67–86.

QRC Research Corporation. 1982. *Study of Jails in West Virginia—Final Report.* Lexington, KY: QRC Research Corporation.

Quinn, Robert, and Andersen, David. 1984. Formalization as crisis: Transition planning for a young organization. In J. R. Kimberly and R. E. Quinn, *Managing Organizational Transitions.* Homewood, IL: Irwin. Pp. 11–28.

————, and McGrath, Michael. 1985. The transformation of organizational cultures: A competing values perspective. In Peter Frost, Larry F. Moore, Meryl Louis, Craig Landberg, and Joanne Martin (eds.), *Organizational Cultures and the Meaning of Life in the Workplace.* Beverly Hills, CA: Sage.

————, and Rohrbaugh, John. 1981. A spatial model of effectiveness criteria: Towards a competing values approach to organizational analysis. Albany: State University of New York at Albany, Institute for Government and Policy Studies.

Quinney, Richard. 1977. *Class, State, and Crime.* New York: McKay.

Radzinowicz, Leon. 1971. *Ideology and Crime.* New York: Columbia University Press.

Rafter, N. H. 1985. *Partial Justice: Women in State Prisons, 1800–1935.* Boston: Northeastern University Press.

Ramirez, John. 1984. Prisonization, staff and inmates; is it really about us versus them? *Criminal Justice and Behavior,* 11(4) December:423–460.

Rankin, Joseph H., and Wells, L. Edward. 1985. From status to delinquent offenses: escalation? *Journal of Criminal Justice,* 13(2):171–180.

Reiman, Jeffrey. 1979. *The Rich Get Richer and the Poor Get Prison.* New York: Wiley.

Reuterman, Nicholas A., and Hughes, Thomas R. 1984. Developments in juvenile justice during the decade of the 70s: Juvenile detention facilities. *Journal of Criminal Justice,* 12(4):325–333.

Rhodes, William M. 1980. Investment of prosecution resources in career criminal cases. *Journal of Criminal Law and Criminology,* 71:118–123.

Rideau, W., and Sinclair, B. 1982. Stranger in the jail. *Angolite,* 7(2) March–April:31–42.

Robinson, Louis N. 1922. *Penology in the United States.* Philadelphia: John C. Winston Company.

Roethlessberger, F. J., and Dickson, W. J. 1949. *Management and the Worker.* Cambridge, MA: Harvard University Press.

Rogers, Robert. 1985. The effects of education level on correctional officer job satisfaction. Unpublished Ph.D. dissertation, State University of New York at Albany.

Rogers, Thomas A., Gitchoff, G. Thomas, and Paur, Ivar O. 1984. The privately commissioned presentence report. In R. Carter, D. Glaser, and L. Wilkins, *Probation, Parole and Community Corrections,* 3rd ed. New York: Wiley. Pp. 31–36.

Rojeck, Dean G., and Erickson, Maynard L. 1981. Reforming the juvenile justice system: The diversion of status offenders. *Law and Society Review,* 16(2):241–264.

Ross, E. A. 1914. *Social Control: A Survey of the Foundations of Order.* New York: Macmillan.

Ross, J. G., et al. 1978. *Assessment of Coeducational Corrections.* Washington, DC: United States Department of Justice.

Ross, Robert R., and McKay, Bryan. 1981. The correctional officer: Selection through training. In R. Ross, *Prison Guard/Correctional Officer*. Toronto: Butterworths.

Rossi, Peter H., and Berk, Richard A. 1977. The politics of state corrections. In David F. Greenberg (ed.), *Corrections and Punishment*. Beverly Hills, CA: Sage.

――――, and Lenihan, Kenneth. 1980. *Money, Work, and Crime*. New York: Academic Press.

Rothman, David. 1971. *Discovery of the Asylum*. Boston: Little, Brown.

Rottman, D. B., and Kimberly, J. R. 1985. The social context of jails. In R. Carter, D. Glaser, and L. Wilkins (eds.), *Correctional Institutions*. New York: Harper & Row.

Roush, David W. 1986. Supervisors as trainers: Expanding the concept of training staff trainers. *Journal of Offender Counseling Services and Rehabilitation*, 10(4) Summer:61–70.

Rovner-Pieczenik, Roberta. 1976. *Pretrial Intervention Strategies: An Evaluation of Policy-Related Research and Policy-Maker Perceptions*. Lexington, MA: Lexington Books.

Ruback, R. 1975. The sexually integrated prison—a legal and policy evaluation. *American Journal of Criminal Law*, 3:310–330.

Rusche, George, and Kirchheimer, O. 1939. *Punishment and Social Structure*. New York: Columbia University Press.

Rutherford, Andrew. 1984. *Prisons and the Process of Justice: The Reductionist Challenge*. London: Heinemann.

Sacks, Howard, and Logan, Charles. 1980. *Parole—Crime Prevention or Crime Postponement*. Storrs: University of Connecticut School of Law Press.

Sagarin, Edward, and Maghan, Jess. 1986. Running prisons for profit: A pernicious proposal. *Albany Times Union*, January 19.

Sanborn, Joseph. 1985. Plea negotiation in the juvenile court. Ph.D. diss., State University of New York at Albany.

Sarri, Rosemary. 1981. The effectiveness paradox: Institutional vs. community placement of offenders. *Journal of Social Issues*, 37(3) Summer:34–50.

Schafer, Nancy. 1986. Jails and judicial review: Special problems for local facilities. In David B. Kalinich and John Klofas, *Sneaking Inmates Down the Alley*. Springfield, IL: Charles C Thomas.

Schaller, Jack. 1982. Work and imprisonment: The overview of the changing role of prison labor in American prisons. *The Prison Journal*, 62(2):3–11.

Schmolesky, John M., and Thorson, Timothy K. 1982. The importance of the presentence investigation *after* sentencing. *Criminal Law Bulletin*, 18(5):406–441.

Schneider, Anne L., and Schneider, Peter R. 1985. The impact of restitution on recidivism of juvenile offenders: An experiment in Clayton County, Georgia. *Criminal Justice Review*, 10(1) Spring:1–9.

Schneider, Peter, Griffiths, William R., and Schneider, Anne L. 1982. Juvenile restitution as a sole sanction or condition of probation: An empirical analysis. *Journal of Research in Crime and Delinquency*, 19(1) January:47–65.

Schwartz, Gary T. 1983. Deterrence and punishment in the common law of punitive damages—A comment. *Southern California Law Review*, 56(1):133–153.

Schwartz, I. M., Jackson-Beck, Marilyn, and Anderson, Roger. 1984. The 'hidden' system of juvenile control. *Crime and Delinquency*, 30 July:371–85.

Schwartz, Richard, and Miller, James C. 1965. Legal Evolution and Societal Complexity. *American Journal of Sociology*, LXX:159–169.

Schwarzchild, Henry. 1985. A social and moral atrocity. *ABA Journal*, 71 (April):38–42.

Schwitzgebel, Ralph K. 1972. Limitations on the coercive treatment of offenders. *Criminal Law Bulletin*, 8(4):267–320.

Scott, Joseph E. 1975. *Ex-Offenders as Parole Officers*. Lexington, MA: Lexington Books.

Scull, Andrew. 1977. *Decarceration, Community Treatment and the Deviant: A Radical View*. Englewood Cliffs, NJ: Prentice-Hall.

Sechrest, Dale. 1978. The legal basis for commission standards. *Proceedings of the American Correctional Association*. College Park, MD: American Correctional Association.

――――, White, S., and Brown, B. 1980. *The Rehabilitation of Criminal Offenders: Problems and Prospects*. Washington, DC: National Academy of Sciences.

Seeman, Melvin. 1959. On the meaning of alienation. *American Sociological Review*, 24:783–791.

Seligson, Tom. 1986. Are they too young to die? *Parade Magazine*, October 19:7–10.

Sellin, Thorsten. 1980. *The Penalty of Death*. Beverly Hills, CA: Sage.

Selo, Elaine. 1976. The control function. In R. D. Vinter (ed.), *Time Out*. Ann Arbor: University of Michigan. Pp. 102–124.

Seymour, John. 1980. Niches in prison: Adaptation and environment in correctional institutions. Ph.D. diss., School of Criminal Justice, State University of New York at Albany.

Shamir, Bouz, and Drory, Asmos. 1982. Occupational tedium among prison officers. *Criminal Justice and Behavior*, 9(1) March:79–99.

Sherman, Michael, and Hawkins, Gordon. 1981. *Imprisonment in America: Choosing the Future.* Chicago: University of Chicago Press.

Shichor, David. 1983. Historical and current trends in American juvenile justice. *Juvenile and Family Court Journal,* 34(3) August:61–75.

———, and Allen, Harry. 1976. Study-release: A correctional alternative. Paper prepared for annual meetings, American Society of Criminology, Tucson, Arizona. November.

Shover, Neal. 1974. 'Experts' and diagnosis in correctional agencies. *Crime and Delinquency,* October: 347–358.

Silas, Faye, A. 1984. Beep! Jailbreak! Robot builder eyes prison use. *ABA Journal,* 70:35.

———. 1985. The death penalty. *ABA Journal,* 71 (April):48–53.

Simon, Herbert. 1957. *Administrative Behavior,* 2d ed. New York: The Free Press.

———. 1964. On the concept of organizational goal. *Administrative Science Quarterly,* 9:1–22.

Simon, R. 1979. The forgotten offender: The women in prison. In F. Adler and J. Simon, *The Criminology of Deviant Women.* Boston: Houghton Mifflin.

Sinclair, Ian. 1971. *Hostels for Probationers.* Home Office Research Studies #6. London: Her Majesty's Stationery Office.

———. 1975. The influence of wardens and matrons on probation hostels: A study of a quasi-family institution. In J. Tizard, I. Sinclair, and R. Clarke, *Varieties of Residential Experience.* London: Routledge and Kegan Paul. Pp. 127–140.

———. 1980. The *Wolfish* case: Has the bell tolled for prisoner litigation in the federal courts? In G. Alpert, *The Legal Rights of Prisons.* Beverly Hills, CA: Sage. Pp. 67–111.

Singer, Simon I. 1985. Relocating juvenile crime: The shift from juvenile to criminal justice. Albany: Nelson A. Rockefeller Institute of Government, Special Report #7.

Single, Eric. 1972. The unconstitutional administration of bail: Bellamy v. the judges of New York City. *Criminal Law Bulletin,* 8:459–513.

Skoler, Daniel. 1976. Correctional unification: Rhetoric, reality and potential. *Federal Probation,* 40(1) March:14–20.

Skolnick, Jerome. 1966. *Justice Without Trial.* New York: Wiley.

Smith, Beverly. Forthcoming. Female admissions and paroles of the western house of refuge in the 1880's: An historical example of community corrections. *Journal of Research in Crime and Delinquency.*

Smith, Freddie V. 1984. Alabama prison option: Supervised intensive restitution program. *Federal Probation,* 48(1) March:32–35.

Smith, Robert R., McKee, John M., and Millan, Michael A. 1974. Study-release policies of American correctional agencies: A survey. *Journal of Criminal Justice,* 2:357–364.

Smykla, John Ortiz. 1980. *Co-ed Prison.* New York: Human Sciences Press.

———. 1984. *Probation and Parole: Crime Control in the Community.* New York: Macmillan.

Solomon, Hasim, 1976. *Community Corrections.* Boston: Holbrook Press.

Sorenson, V. 1981. Educational and vocational needs of women in prison. *Corrections Today,* 43(3) May–June:61–75.

South Carolina Department of Corrections. 1973. Collective violence in correctional institutions: A search for causes. Columbia, SC: Department of Corrections.

Special Task Force to the Secretary of Health, Education and Welfare. 1973. *Work in America.* Cambridge, MA: MIT Press.

Spergel, Irving A., Lynch, James P., Reamer, Frederic G., and Korbelik, John. 1982. Response of organization and community to a deinstitutionalization strategy. *Crime and Delinquency,* 28(3) July:426–449.

Stageberg, Paul. 1986. A re-examination of the impact of the Des Moines project on offender case processing and the justice system in Polk County, Iowa. Unpublished doctoral dissertation, State University of New York at Albany.

Stanley, David. 1976. *The Prisoners Among Us.* Washington, DC: Brookings Institution.

Stanley, Stephen, and Baginsky, Mary. 1984. *Alternatives to Prison: An Examination of Non-Custodial Sentencing of Offenders.* London: Peter Owen.

Stanton, A. 1980. *When Mothers Go to Jail.* Lexington, MA: D. C. Heath.

Stastny, Charles, and Tyrnauer, Gabrielle. 1982. *Who Rules the Joint?* Lexington, MA: Lexington Books.

Steadman, Henry J., et al. 1984. The impact of state mental hospital deinstitutionalization on United States prison populations 1968–1978. *Journal of Criminal Law and Criminology,* 75:474–490.

Steele, Eric H., and Jacobs, James B. 1975. A theory of prison systems. *Crime and Delinquency,* 21(2) April:149–162.

———, and ———. 1977. Untangling minimum security: Concepts, realities, and implications for correctional systems. *Journal of Research in Crime and Delinquency,* January:68–83.

Stojkovic, Stan. 1986. Jails versus prisons: Comparisons, problems, prescriptions on inmate subcultures. In David B. Kalinich, and John Klofas,

Sneaking Inmates Down the Alley. Springfield, IL: Charles C Thomas.

Stolz, Barbara Ann. 1984. Decarceration in Massachusetts: A study of disjointed incrementalism. *Criminal Justice Review,* 9(2) Fall:53–62.

Stone, A. A. 1975. *Mental Health and Law: A System in Transition.* Rockville, MD: National Institute for Mental Health.

Street, David, Vinter, Robert, and Perrow, Charles. 1966. *Organization for Treatment.* New York: Free Press.

Studt, Elliot. 1972. *Surveillance and Service in Parole.* Los Angeles: University of California at Los Angeles, Center for Public Affairs. Reprinted Washington, DC: National Institute of Justice, 1973, and National Institute of Correction, 1973 and 1979.

————. 1973. Reintegration from the parolee's perspective. In *Reintegrating the Offender into the Community.* Washington, DC: United States Government Printing Office.

————, Messinger, Sheldon, and Wilson, Thomas C. 1968. *C-Unit: The Search for Community in Prison.* New York: Russell Sage Foundation.

Sullivan, Dennis C. 1980. The Mask of Love. Port Washington, NY: Kennikat Press.

Sutton, John R. 1985. The juvenile court and social welfare: Dynamics of progressive reform. *Law and Society Review,* 19(1):107–145.

Sykes, Gresham. 1958. *Society of Captives.* Princeton, NJ: Princeton University Press.

————, and Messinger, Sheldon. 1960. The inmate social system. In Richard A. Cloward, et al., *Theoretical Studies on Social Organization of the Prison.* New York: Social Science Research Council.

Symposium: Punitive damages articles. 1982. *Southern California Law Review,* 56(1):1–206.

Taft, Philip B. 1979. Backed up in jails: county lockups overflow as courts clamp down on state prisons. *Corrections Magazine,* 2:26–33.

————. 1982. Private vendors, part I: The fiscal crisis in private corrections. *Corrections Magazine,* 8(6) December:27–32.

————. 1983. Private vendors, part II: Survival of the fittest. *Corrections Magazine,* 9(1) February:36–42.

Talty, Richard B. 1985. *Intensive Supervision Program: Report to the Advisory Committee.* Trenton: New Jersey Administrative Office of the Courts.

Taylor, Frederick W. 1967. *The Principles of Scientific Management.* New York: Norton.

Teplin, L. A. 1984. *Mental Health and Criminal Justice. Criminal Justice Annuals,* vol. 20. Newbury Park, CA: Sage.

Thomas, Charles W., Petersen, David M., and Cage, Robin J. 1981. A comparative organizational analysis of prisonization. *Criminal Justice Review,* 6(1):36–43.

Thomas, R. G. 1981. De-institutionalization: Managing independent living—An adult education program for incarcerated women. *Journal of Correctional Education,* 32(4) June:11–14.

Thomas, Wayne. 1976. *Bail Reform in America.* Berkeley, CA: University of California Press.

Thompson, James, and McEwen, William. 1958. Organizational goals and environment: Goal setting as an interaction process. *American Sociological Review,* 23:23–30.

Thomson, Doug. 1987. The changing face of probation in the USA. J. K. Harding (ed.), *Probation in the Community.* London: Tavistock. Pp. 100–125.

————, and Fogel, David. 1981. *Probation Work in Small Agencies: A National Study of Training Provision and Needs.* Chicago: Center for Research in Law and Justice, University of Illinois at Chicago.

Tifft, Larry, and Sullivan, Dennis C. 1980. The Struggle to Be Human: Crime, Criminology, and Anarchism. Orkney, UK: Cienfuegos Press.

Tittle, C. R. 1980. *Sanctions and Social Deviance— The Question of Deterrence.* New York: Praeger.

Toborg, Mary A., et al. 1978. *The Transition from Prison to Employment: An Assessment of Community-based Assistance Programs.* Washington, DC: National Institute of Law Enforcement and Criminal Justice.

Toch, Hans. 1969. *Dangerous Men.* Chicago: Aldine.

————. 1977. *Police, Prisons and the Problem of Violence.* Washington, DC: U.S. Department of Health, Education and Welfare, Public Health Service.

————. 1977. *Living in Prison: The Etiology of Survival.* New York: Free Press.

————. 1978. Is a 'correctional officer,' by any other name, a 'screw'? *Criminal Justice Review,* 3:19–35.

————. 1980a. The therapeutic community as community in Toch (ed.), *Therapeutic Communities in Corrections.* New York: Praeger.

————. 1980b. *Therapeutic Communities in Corrections.* New York: Praeger.

————. 1980c. Liberating prison guards. Paper presented to Sam Houston University 15th Annual Interagency Workshop, May.

————. 1981a. A revisionist view of prison reform. *Federal Probation,* June:3–9.

————. 1981b. Psychological treatment of imprisoned offenders. In J. Ray Hays and Kenneth S. Solway, *Violence and the Violent Individual.* New

York: S. P. Medical and Scientific Books. Pp. 325–342.

———, and Grant, Douglas. 1982. *Reforming Human Services*. Beverly Hills, CA: Sage Publications.

———, and Klofas, John. 1982. Alienation and desire for job enrichment among correctional officers. *Federal Probation*, March: 35–44.

Travis, Lawrence III, and O'Leary, Vincent. 1984. A history of parole. In R. Carter, D. Glaser, and L. Wilkins, *Probation, Parole and Community Corrections*, 3d ed. New York: Wiley. Pp. 105–121.

Trice, Harrison M., and Beyer, Janice M. 1984. Work-related outcomes of the constructive-confrontation strategy in a job-based alcoholism program. *Journal of Studies on Alcohol*, 45(5) September:393–404.

Trist, Eric. 1981. *Socio Technical Systems*. Toronto: Ontario Quality of Working Life Centre, Ministry of Labour.

Van Alstyne, David J., and Gottfredson, Michael R. 1978. A multidimensional contingency table analysis of parole outcome. *Journal of Research in Crime and Delinquency*, 15(2) July:172–193.

Van den Haag, Ernest. 1975. *On Punishing Criminals*. New York: Basic Books.

———. 1982a. Could successful rehabilitation reduce the crime rate? *Journal of Criminal Law and Criminology*, 73(3):1022–1035.

———. 1982b. The criminal law as a threat system. *Journal of Criminal Law and Criminology*, 73(2):769–785.

———. 1985. The death penalty vindicates the law. *ABA Journal*, 71 (April):38–42.

van Wormer, K. S., and Bates, F. L. 1979. A study of leadership roles in an Alabama prison for women. *Human Relations*, 32(9):793–801.

Vera Institute of Justice. 1981. *Felony Arrests: Their Prosecution and Disposition in New York City Courts*. Rev. ed. New York: Longman.

Vinter, Robert D. (ed.). 1976. *Time Out: A National Study of Juvenile Correctional Programs*. Ann Arbor: School of Social Work, University of Michigan.

———, Downs, George, and Hall, John. 1975. *Juvenile Corrections in the States: Residential Programs and Deinstitutionalization: A Preliminary Report*. Ann Arbor: University of Michigan School of Social Work.

Vito, Gennaro F. 1984. Developments in shock probation. *Federal Probation*, 48(2) June:22–27.

Vogel, Ronald E., and Thibault, Edward. 1981. Deinstitutionalization's throwaways—The development of a juvenile prison in Massachusetts. *Crime and Delinquency*, 27(4):468–476.

Von Hirsch, Andrew. 1976. *Doing Justice*. New York: Hill and Wang.

———. 1983. Commensurability and crime prevention: Evaluating formal sentencing structures and their rationale. *Journal of Criminal Law and Criminology*. 74:209–248.

———. 1984. The ethics of selective incapacitation—Observations on the contemporary debate. *Crime and Delinquency*, 39(2):175–194.

———, and Hanrahan, Kathleen. 1981. Determinate penalty systems in America: An overview. *Crime and Delinquency*, 27(3):289–316.

———, and ———. 1984. Abolish parole? In R. Carter, D. Glaser, and L. Wilkins, *Probation, Parole and Community Corrections*. New York: Wiley. Pp. 184–194.

———, and Julia M. Mueller. 1984. California's determinate sentencing law: An analysis of its structure. *New England Journal on Criminal and Civil Confinement*, 10(2):253–300.

Walakafra-Wills, D. V. 1983a. Innovative recreation in a county jail—Sacramento County main jail recreation program. Sacramento, CA: Sacramento County Sheriff's Department.

———. 1983b. Designing a responsive jail: religious education program for inmates. Sacramento, CA: Sacramento County Sheriff's Department.

Waldo, Gordon P., and Chiricos, Theodore G. 1977. Work release and recidivism: An empirical evaluation of a social policy. *Evaluation Quarterly*, 1(1):87–108.

———, ———, and Dobrin, Thomas. 1973. Community contact and inmate attitudes: An experimental assessment of work release. *Criminology*, 11(3) November:345–374.

Walker, Nigel. 1971. *On Crimes, Courts and Figures*. Baltimore: Penguin.

———. 1983. Side-effects of incarceration. *British Journal of Criminology*, 23(1) January:61–71.

———, Farrington, David P., and Tucker, Gillian. 1981. Reconviction rates of adult males after different sentences. *British Journal of Criminology*, 21(4):357–366.

Walker, Sam. 1982. The limits of segregation in prisons: A reply to Jacobs. *Criminal Law Bulletin*, 21(6) November–December:485–494.

Walkey, Frank H., and Gilmour, D. Ross. 1984. The relationships between interpersonal distance and violence in imprisoned offenders. *Criminal Justice and Behavior*, 11(3) September:331–340.

Wallace, Robert. 1966. Ecological implications of a custody institution. *Issues in Criminology*, 2(1):47–60.

Waller, Irvin. 1979. *Men Released From Prison*. Toronto: University of Toronto Press.

————, and Chan, J. 1974. Prison use: a Canadian and international comparison. *Criminal Law Quarterly*, 17:47–71.

Walzer, Michael. 1985. Privately operated prisons are unjust. In Bonnie Szumski (ed.), *America's Prisons: Opposing Viewpoints*, 4th ed. St. Paul, MN: Greenhaven Press. Pp. 127–130.

Ward, D., and Kasserbaum, G. 1965. *Women's Prison*. Chicago: Aldine.

Warren, Roland. 1978. *The Community in America*. Chicago: Rand McNally.

————, Rose, Stephen, and Bergunder, Ann. 1974. *The Structure of Urban Reform*. Lexington, MA: Lexington Books.

Wayne County Jail Inmates v. *Board of Commissioners of Wayne County*. 1971. Wayne County Michigan, Circuit Court Opinion of May 17, 1971, p. 32.

Webb, Sidney, and Webb, Beatrice. 1963. *English Prisons Under Local Government*. Hamden, CT: The Shoe String Press. P. 3.

Weber, Max. 1947. *The Theory of Social and Economic Organization*. Glencoe, IL: The Free Press.

Weeks, H. Ashley. 1958. *Youthful Offenders at Highfields*. Ann Arbor: University of Michigan Press.

Weick, Karl. 1969. *The Social Psychology of Organizing*. Reading, MA: Addison Wesley.

Weintraub, Michael. 1979. Prison industries: A comprehensive report. Master's essay, School of Criminal Justice, State University of New York at Albany.

What color are America's prisons? 1983. *Jericho*, 32(1) Summer:1.

Wheeler, Stanton. 1961. Socialization in correctional communities. *American Sociological Review*, 26:697–712.

Whitehead, John T. 1983. Burnout among probation and parole workers. Ph.D. diss., State University of New York at Albany.

Wice, Paul B. 1974. *Freedom for Sale: A National Study of Pretrial Release*. Lexington, MA: Lexington Books.

Wilkins, Leslie T. 1965. *Social Deviance*. Englewood Cliffs, NJ: Prentice-Hall.

————. 1981. *The Principles of Guidelines for Sentencing: Methodological and Philosophical Issues in Their Development*. Washington, DC: National Institute of Justice. March.

Williams, Trevor A., and Soutar, Geoffrey N. 1984. Levels of custody and attitude differences among prison officers: A comparative study. *Australian and New Zealand Journal of Criminology*, 17(2) June:87–94.

Willis, Andrew. 1983. The balance between care and control in probation. A research note. *British Journal of Social Work*, 13:339–346.

Wilsnack, Richard. 1976. Explaining collective violence in prisons: Problems and possibilities. In Albert Cohen, George Cole, and Robert Baily (eds.), *Prison Violence*. Lexington, MA: Lexington Books.

Wilson, O. W., and McLaren, Roy C. 1972. *Police Administration*, 3d ed. New York: McGraw-Hill.

Wines, E. C. (ed.). 1871. *Transactions of the National Congress on Penitentiary and Reformatory Discipline, Cincinnati, Ohio, 1870*. Albany: Weed, Parsons and Co., Printers.

Winterdyk, John, and Griffiths, Curt. 1984. Wilderness experience programs: Reforming delinquents or beating around the bush? *Juvenile and Family Court Journal*, Fall:35–44.

Witte, Ann. 1977. Work release in North Carolina—A program that works. *Law and Contemporary Problems*, 41(1):230–251.

Woestendiek, John. 1986. Suit contends death-row conditions cruel and unusual. *Centre Daily Times*, June 17:A-2.

Wolfgang, Marvin, and Riedel, March. 1982. Racial discrimination, rape, and the death penalty. In Hugo A. Bedau (ed.), *The Death Penalty in America*, 3d ed. New York: Oxford University Press.

Wolfson, Wendy Phillips. 1982. The deterrent effect of the death penalty upon prison murder. In Hugo A. Bedau (ed.), *The Death Penalty in America*, 3d ed. New York: Oxford University Press.

Wormith, J. Stephen. 1984. The controversy over the effects of long-term incarceration. *Canadian Journal of Criminology*, 26(4):423–437.

Wormith, J. C., and Goldstone, C. S. 1984. The clinical and statistical prediction of recidivism. *Criminal Law Bulletin*, 11(1):3–34.

Wright, Kevin N. 1977. Correctional effectiveness: A case for an organizational approach. Ph.D. diss., Pennsylvania State University.

————. 1985. Improving correctional classification through a study of the placement of inmates in environmental settings. Binghamton: State University of New York at Binghamton, Center for Social Analysis.

————, Clear, Todd R., and Dickson, Paul. 1985. A critique of the universal applicability of probation risk-assessment instruments. Binghamton: Center for Social Analysis, State University of New York at Binghamton.

————, and Duffee, David. 1986. Easing the transition: A policy analysis of post-release programs. Paper presented at the annual meetings of the Academy of Criminal Justice Services, Orlando, Florida. March.

Wright, R. Dean. 1984. Emergency prison release

policies: The Iowa experience. *The Prison Journal*, 64(2) Fall–Winter:88–96.

Wright, Ronald F. 1984. The civil and criminal methodologies of the 4th amendment. *Yale Law Journal*, 93(6):1127–1146.

Yablonsky, Lewis. 1965. *Synanon: The Tunnel Back*. New York: Macmillan.

Yarborough, James C. 1976. Rehabilitation in juvenile corrections: Objectives, means and resources. In R. D. Vinter, *Time Out*. Ann Arbor: University of Michigan.

Yeager, M. G. Unemployment and imprisonment. *Journal of Criminal Law and Criminology*, 70:586–588.

Yost, Pete. 1986. More guards being hired to quash prison violence. *Albany Times-Union*, A-3, December 15.

Young, Warren. 1979. *Community Service Orders*. London: Heinemann.

———. 1985. Cross-cultural prison rates. A comparative study of the use of custodial sanctions. Draft research proposal. United Nations, New York. Mimeo.

Yuctman, Ephriam, and Seashore, Stanley. 1967. A system resource approach to organizational effectiveness. *American Sociological Review*, 32:891–903.

Zald, Mayer. 1962. Power balance and staff conflict in correctional institutions. *Administrative Science Quarterly*, 6 (June):22–49.

Zalman, Marvin, et al. 1979. *Sentencing in Michigan: Report of the Michigan Felony Sentencing Project*. Lansing, MI: Michigan Office of Criminal Justice.

Zastrow, William G. 1971. Disclosure of the presentence investigation. *Federal Probation*, December:20–22.

Zatz, M. S. 1984. Race, ethnicity and determinate sentencing: A new dimension to an old controversy. *Criminology*, 22(2):147–171.

Zausner, Stuart. 1985. Unusual incident report 1984 calendar year. Albany: New York State Department of Correctional Services, May.

Zehr, Howard, and Umbreit, Mark. 1982. Victim offender reconciliation: An incarceration substitute? *Federal Probation*, December, 46(4):63–68.

Zeisel, Hans. 1981. The disposition of felony arrests. *American Bar Foundation*, (2):407–462.

Zupan, Linda L., Menke, Ben A., and Lovrich, Nicholas P. 1987. Implementing organizational change: From traditional to new generation jail operations. Paper presented at the annual meeting of the Academy of Criminal Justice Sciences, St. Louis, Missouri, March.

———, and Stohr-Gillmore, Mary K. 1987. Doing time in the new generation jail: Inmate perceptions of gains and losses. Paper presented at the annual meeting of the Academy of Criminal Justice Sciences, St. Louis, Missouri, March.

Zwerdling, Daniel. 1978. *Work Place Democracy*. New York: Harper & Row.

CASES CITED

Argersinger v. *Hamlin* 407 U.S. 25 (1972).

Atiyeh v. *Capps* 101 S.Ct. 829 (1981).

Bearden v. *Georgia* 33 CrL 3103 (1983).

Bell v. *Wolfish* 441 U.S. 520 (1979).

Block v. *Rutherford* 104 S.Ct. 3227 (1984).

Bounds v. *Smith* 430 U.S. 817 (1977).

Bowring v. *Godwin* 551 F.2d 44 (4th Cir. 1977).

Breed v. *Jones* 421 U.S. 519 (1975).

Christian v. *State* 298 SE2d 325 (Ga. 1982).

Coffin v. *Reichard* 142 F.2d 443 (6th Cir. 1944).

Coker v. *Georgia* 433 U.S. 485 (1977).

Cooper v. *Pate* 378 U.S. 546 (1964).

Covington v. *Harris* 419 F.2d 617 (D.C. Cir. 1969).

Cruz v. *Beto* 92 S.Ct. 1079 (1972).

Dothard v. *Richardson* 433 U.S. 321 (1977).

Eberhart v. *Georgia* 433 U.S. 977 (1977).

Estelle v. *Gamble* 429 U.S. 97 (1976).

Ex Parte Crouse 4 Wharton 9, 1838 Pa.

Ex Parte Hull 312 U.S. 546 (1941).

Furman v. *Georgia* 408 U.S. 238 (1972).

Gagnon v. *Scarpelli* 411 U.S. 778 (1973).

Gardner v. *Florida* 97 S.Ct. 1197 (1977).

Gideon v. *Wainwright* 372 U.S. 335 (1963).

Glover v. *Johnson* 478 F.Supp. 1075 (E.D. Mich. 1979).

Goldberg v. *Kelly* 398 U.S. 254 (1970).

Gregg v. *Georgia* 428 U.S. 152 (1976).

Gunther v. *Iowa* 462 F.Supp. 952 (1979).

Hewitt v. *Helms* 103 S.Ct. 864 (1983).

Holt v. *Sarver* 442 F.2d 308 (8th Cir. 1971).

Howe v. *Smith* 101 S.Ct. 2468 (1981).

Hudson v. *Palmer* 104 S.Ct. 3194 (1985).

Hutto v. *Finney* 98 S.Ct. 2565 (1978).

In re Gault 387 U.S. 1 (1967).

In re Kemmler 136 U.S. 436 (1890).

In re Winship 397 U.S. 358 (1970).

Ingraham v. *Wright* 430 U.S. 651 (1977).

Jackson v. *Hendrick* 446 A.2d 226 Pa. 1982.

Jenkins v. *State* 368 So.2d 329 (Ala. Crim. App. 1978).

Johnson v. *Avery* 393 U.S. 483 (1969).

Jones v. *North Carolina Prisoners' Labor Union* 433 U.S. 119 (1977).

Jones v. *Wittenburg* 509 F.Supp. 653 (N.D. Ohio 1980).

Jordan v. *Fitzharris* 257 F.Supp. 674 (N.D. Cal. 1966).

Kent v. *United States* 382 U.S. 541 (1966).

Lessard v. *Schmidt* 349 F.Supp. 1978 (E.D. Wis. 1972).

Logan v. *United States* 144 U.S. 263 (1892).

Marshall v. *United States* 414 U.S. 417 (1974).

Martin v. *Strasburg* 513 F.Supp. 691 (1981).

McClesky v. *Kemp* 753F 2d 877 (1985).

McKeiver v. *Pennsylvania* 403 U.S. 528 (1971).

Meachum v. *Fano* 427 U.S. 216 (1976).

Mempa v. *Rhay* 389 U.S. 128 (1967).

Memphis Community School District v. *Stahura* 106 S.Ct. 2537 (1986).

Monell v. *Department of Social Services* 436 U.S. 56 (1979).

Morrissey v. *Brewer* 408 U.S. 471 (1972).

O'Bryan v. *Saginaw County, Mich.* 437 F.Supp. 582 (E.D. Mich. 1977).

Olim v. *Wakinekona* 103 S.Ct. 1741 (1983).

Pena v. *New York State Division for Youth* 70 Civ. N. 4868 (S.D. N.Y. 1976).

People v. *Anderson* 6 Cal 3rd 628, 100 Ca. Rptr. 152 (1972).

Powell v. *Texas* 392 U.S. 514 (1967).

Procunier v. *Martinez* 416 U.S. 396 (1974).

Pugh v. *Locke* 406 F.Supp. 318 (M.D. Ala. 1976).

Ralph v. *Warden* 438 F2d 786 (C.C.A. 4th Cir. 1970).

Rhodes v. *Chapman* 452 U.S. 337 (1981).

Roberts v. *Louisiana* 431 U.S. 633 (1977).

Robinson v. *California* 370 U.S. 660 (1962).

Ruffin v. *Commonwealth* 62 Va. 790 (1871).

Rummel v. *Estelle* 100 S.Ct. 1133 (1980).

Santobello v. *N. Y.* 404 U.S. 257 (1971).

Schall v. *Martin* 104 S.Ct. 2403 (1984).

Solem v. *Helm* 103 S.Ct. 3001 (1983).

State Ex. Rel. R. R. v. *Schmidt* 216 N.W.2d 18 (Wisc. 1974).

Sullivan v. *Wainwright* 104 S.Ct. 450 (1983).

Theriault v. *Carlson* 495 F2d 390, cert. denied 419 U.S. 1003 (1975).

United States v. *Edwards* 430 A.2d 1321 (D.C. 1981).

United States v. *McDonald* 104 S.Ct. 567 (1984).

Wainwright v. *Witt* 83 L. Ed. 841 (1985).

Wayne County Jail Inmates v. *Board of Commissioners of Wayne County, Michigan* case #71-173-27 Wayne Co. Cir. Ct. (1971).

Washington v. *Lee* 390 U.S. 333 (1968).

Whitley v. *Albers* 106 S.Ct. 1078 (1986).

Wilkerson v. *Utah* 99 U.S. 130 (1878).

Williams v. *N. Y.* 337 U.S. 241 (1949).

Witherspoon v. *Illinois* 391 U.S. 510 (1968).

Wolff v. *McDonnell* 418 U.S. 539 (1974).

Woodson, et al. v. *North Carolina* 428 U.S. 280 (1976).

Zant v. *Stephens* 103 S.Ct. 2733 (1983).

NAME INDEX

SUBJECT INDEX

ABOUT THE AUTHOR

David E. Duffee is currently dean and professor of criminal justice in the School of Criminal Justice, University at Albany, State University of New York, where he received his Ph.D in 1973. He has also held faculty positions at the Pennsylvania State University and the State University of New York at Binghamton. His primary research and teaching interests are in the areas of community corrections, planned change, and public organizations. Among his other books are *Correctional Management, Change and Control in Correctional Organizations, Community Corrections, A Community Field Approach* (co-edited with Edmund McGarrell), and *Explaining Criminal Justice: Community Theory and Criminal Justice Reform*, which was given the book of the year award in 1982 by the Academy of Criminal Justice Sciences.